The People's Republic of China at 60

An International Assessment

The People's Republic of China at 60

An International Assessment

Edited by William C. Kirby

Published by the Harvard University Asia Center
for the Fairbank Center for Chinese Studies
Distributed by Harvard University Press
Cambridge (Massachusetts) and London 2011

Printed in the United States of America

The Harvard University Asia Center, in coordination with the Fairbank Center for Chinese Studies, the Korea Institute, the Reischauer Institute of Japanese Studies, and other faculties and institutes, administers research projects designed to further scholarly understanding of China, Japan, Vietnam, Korea, and other Asian countries. The Center also sponsors projects addressing multidisciplinary and regional issues in Asia.

The Fairbank Center for Chinese Studies, established in 1955, supports and promotes advanced research and training in all fields of Chinese studies. By bringing together leading researchers at Harvard with their counterparts from around the globe to share data, methods, approaches, and arguments, the Center aims to further analysis and understanding of the larger Chinese world in all its dimensions.

Library of Congress Cataloging-in-Publication Data

The People's Republic of China at 60: an international assessment (2009 : Harvard University)
The People's Republic of China at 60 : an international assessment / edited by William C. Kirby.
p. cm.
A collection of papers originally presented at "The People's Republic of China at 60: an international assessment," a conference held at Harvard University by the Fairbank Center for Chinese Studies during the Spring of 2009.
English and Chinese.
Includes bibliographical references.
ISBN 978-0-674-06064-7
1. China--Politics and government--2002---Congresses. 2. China--Social conditions--2000---Congresses. 3. China--Economic conditions--2000---Congresses. 4. China--History--1949---Congresses. I. Kirby, William C. II. Title.
DS779.36.P46 2009
951.06--dc22
2010053900

Book design by Kelly Maccioli
Copyediting by Nancy Hearst
Section page photographs by Alan Yeung
Cover photographs:
Mao Zedong: AFP/Getty Images
China goods: John Downing/Getty Images
Beijing National Stadium, rural street, and train platform: Alan Yeung

♾ Printed on acid-free paper

Last figure below indicates year of this printing
19 18 17 16 15 14 13 12 11

ACKNOWLEDGMENTS

This volume is the outgrowth of the Spring 2009 conference, "The People's Republic of China at Sixty: An International Assessment," held at the Fairbank Center for Chinese Studies at Harvard University. Neither the conference nor this book would have been possible without the efforts of many.

I am indebted to Lee Folger and to the Lee and Juliet Folger Fund for their generous support of the Fairbank Center and of this conference. Lydia Chen, associate director of the Fairbank Center, and a superb staff led by Linda Kluz and Wen-Hao Tien left nothing to chance. Colleagues from the Harvard University Asia Center and the Harvard China Fund offered much-needed assistance. Di Yin Lu and Song Chen provided expert translation. Bian He proofread the Chinese-language essays in this volume and provided the English-language abstracts.

Nancy Hearst, librarian of the Fairbank Center Collection in the Fung Library, worked closely with each author on the final version of the essays published here. The conference poster, book design, and book cover are the work of Kelly Maccioli. The Asia Center Publications Program provided technical and logistical support for this book, with Kristen Wanner overseeing the production of the printed volume. To these and other colleagues who assisted with the conference and this publication, I am most grateful.

No edited volume can quite capture the energy and rigor that distinguished this conference and its discussions. One can, however, thank the scholars from three continents who made this a memorable and truly international undertaking.

William C. Kirby
November 2010

TABLE OF CONTENTS

CONTRIBUTORS

Barry R. Bloom, Harvard School of Public Health
Timothy Cheek, University of British Columbia
Sheena Chestnut, Harvard University
Paul A. Cohen, Emeritus, Wellesley College
Mark C. Elliott, Harvard University
Feng Xiaocai (冯筱才), Fudan University
Merle Goldman, Emerita, Boston University
Chang-tai Hung, Hong Kong University of Science and Technology
Alastair Iain Johnston, Harvard University
William C. Kirby, Harvard University
Arthur Kleinman, Harvard University
Elisabeth Köll, Harvard University
Xiaoyuan Liu, Iowa State University
Yuanli Liu, Harvard University
Roderick MacFarquhar, Harvard University
Klaus Mühlhahn, Indiana University
Niu Dayong (牛大勇), Peking University
Jean Oi, Stanford University
Dwight H. Perkins, Harvard University
Elizabeth J. Perry, Harvard University
Robert S. Ross, Boston College
Peter G. Rowe, Harvard University
David Shambaugh, George Washington University
Shen Zhihua (沈志华), East China Normal University
Michael Szonyi, Harvard University
Xiaofei Tian, Harvard University
Alan M. Wachman, Tufts University
Andrew G. Walder, Stanford University
Susanne Weigelin-Schwiedrzik, University of Vienna
Martin King Whyte, Harvard University
Yang Kuisong (杨奎松), East China Normal University and Peking University

ABBREVIATIONS

BMA	Beijing Municipal Archives
CCP	Chinese Communist Party
CITIC	China International and Trust Corporation
FDI	foreign direct investment
FRUS	Foreign Relations of the United States
GAPP	General Administration of Press and Publications
GDP	Gross Domestic Product
GMRB	Guangming ribao
GZRB	Guangzhou ribao (Guangzhou Daily)
IRB	institutional review board
ISJP	International Social Justice Project
KGB	Committee for State Security
KMT	Guomindang
NKVD	People's Commissariat for Internal Affairs
PLA	People's Liberation Army
PLAN	People's Liberation Army Navy
PRC	People's Republic of China
RMRB	Renmin ribao (People's Daily)
SARS	severe acute respiratory syndrome
SASAC	State-owned Assets Supervision and Administration Commission
SEZ	special economic zone
SOE	state-owned enterprises
TFP	total factor productivity
TVE	township-village enterprise

The People's Republic of China at 60

An International Assessment

INTRODUCTION
MYTHS AND LESSONS OF CONTEMPORARY CHINESE HISTORY

WILLIAM C. KIRBY

On October 1, 2009, the People's Republic of China (PRC) commemorated its sixtieth anniversary. In anticipation of this event, the Fairbank Center for Chinese Studies at Harvard University convened a major conference, "The People's Republic of China at 60: An International Assessment." The conference brought together scholars and students of China from across Harvard, from China, and from around the world. The gathering witnessed an extraordinarily energetic exchange of views, and was followed later by meetings on similar themes in Hong Kong, Shanghai, and Beijing. The chapters in this volume represent the revised papers presented at the Harvard conference.

Participants at the conference were asked to deliver not scholarly papers but talks and essays for a general audience. And a very large general audience came to hear, to comment, and to question. Although the contributions in this volume have been edited and, in some cases, expanded for this book, they remain true to our original aspiration: to promote open, intelligent discussion of the past, present, and future of the People's Republic of China

This book seeks to assess where the PRC has been, where it is now, and where it may be going. The essays address four main themes: politics, or as we call it, *polities*—for there is an inescapably international dimension to Chinese politics; *social transformations*—of human communities, individual lives, spatial settings, and of governance; *wealth and well-being*, reflecting on the promise of socialism, the distribution of wealth and welfare, the revival of capitalism, and the prospects for future growth; and, finally, *culture, belief, and practice*, from the arts and humanities, to religious practice and ethnic identity. What did people believe in during this period? What did they stop believing in? How does "culture," broadly conceived, help to define patterns in contemporary China?

Sixty is an important birthday. As Confucius describes his maturation, in what Irene Bloom has called "the world's shortest autobiography":[1]

At fifteen, I had my heart set upon learning; at thirty, I stood firm; at forty I had no doubts; at fifty, I knew the decrees of Heaven; at sixty, my ear was an obedient organ for the reception of truth.

Or, as Bloom translates the last two lines: "At fifty I knew what was ordained by Heaven; at sixty, I obeyed" (五十而知天命，六十而耳順).[2]

At sixty, after all, one is to be mature and at ease, having concluded a full cycle of years. In China's traditional stem-branch cycle, the ten heavenly stems and twelve earthly branches mark the years of a sixty-year cycle. When one completes a *jiazi* (甲子) one has figuratively lived a full lifespan. If you live longer, you are blessed indeed—after all, the Master said: "At seventy I could follow what my heart desired, without transgressing what was right" (七十而從心所欲不踰矩).[3]

A central concern in this book, therefore, focuses on the health and longevity of a ruling system. Is the People's Republic of China, after its first three, and arguably its first four, decades of internal strife and turmoil, finally "at ease"? Is it here for the dynastic long-haul? This is a question lurking behind many of our chapters, and it is addressed also by the contributions of historians of earlier epochs.

Let us start from the point of view of modern and contemporary history. In the sixty years since Mao Zedong founded the "New China" of the PRC, the archives of Republican China have been opened. Historians have investigated the structural ills of "old China" that once seemed to explain the Communist rise to power. Yet the picture now emerging of pre-Communist China—be it in the realms of economic growth, state-building, or foreign relations—seems different from that understood by Mao and his comrades, or by foreign observers, at the time. Similarly, Communist answers to China's perceived problems in the 1950s have come under sharp historical scrutiny.

So to begin our inquiry we may ask: How do we now assess China's pre-revolutionary situation? How are we then to judge the record of "liberation" of the early People's Republic? And how does this compare with the record of the most recent thirty years of reform and opening? Let me discuss, briefly, several contemporary assumptions about China's pre-revolutionary conditions in three areas by which one may measure the performance of any government: economics, politics, and foreign relations. An examination of the founding assumptions, or perhaps myths, of the PRC may allow us to draw lessons about its first full cycle of life—its *jiazi*.

Economics

At mid-century, Chinese revolutionaries and many foreign scholars believed that China was in need of a revolution, perhaps above all for economic reasons. They saw a stagnant or even declining economy during China's Republican period, divided sharply between the internationally-oriented port cities and the unchanging, "feudal" interior, with its increasingly impoverished peasantry.

Without doubt, China was in a desperate economic condition in 1949. It had endured eight years of war with Japan, followed closely by another four years of civil war. But was it in need of an economic revolution?

The broad indictment of the pre-revolutionary economy is simply not sustainable today if we take seriously any of the solid economic history done by historians in China or the West in recent decades.[4] Rather, we have a picture of sustained, reasonably high economic growth during the 1910s, 1920s, and 1930s— up until the onset of the Sino-Japanese war in 1937. This was a growth fueled above all by private enterprise, urban and rural, in what we may now consider the *first* "golden age" of Chinese capitalism.[5] This new economic activity began and spread outward from China's centers of international trade and investment, particularly the lower Yangzi region and Manchuria. Growth was slowed significantly in the 1930s by the global depression and by the financial policies of the Nationalist government, and it would be stopped altogether by the onset of the Sino-Japanese and then civil war; but that did not mean it could not be revived in peacetime. With the total economic as well as political-military collapse of the Nationalist regime, the new PRC had a potentially wide range of economic policy options.

Its actual choices, however, were narrowed by the ideological conviction that China was in need of a fundamental economic restructuring. After a rather half-hearted attempt at a mixed economy under the slogan of "new democracy," early PRC leaders followed the road of high Stalinism.[6] They believed that land-owning farmers and entrepreneurial businessmen were not only reactionary in a political sense, but also part of the root cause of a combined economic stagnation and social backwardness that only socialism could cure. In the early and mid-1950s this would lead to the expropriation of the property or exile (to Hong Kong and overseas) of China's business classes; the political murder of hundreds of thousands (if not more) of small landlords, and the consequent destruction of entrepreneurial talent as well as opportunity. To this we must add the execution of between three to five million alleged "counter-revolutionaries" in the political-economic terror of the Korean War years.

Another lesson, born of simplistic class analysis, that the countryside was the proper place for peasants, the cities for workers, would lead to the system of nationwide household registration and internal passports known as *"hukou,"* which would consign rural communities, especially in China's poorest parts, to immiseration of a kind not known before, to stagnation *in situ,* without—as had been the case during the Republican era—the possibility of outmigration.[7] If the urban working class of the Republican period was constantly reconstituted by rural migrants, the Communist urban working class—particularly those in state industries—became a closed caste, an industrial elite with hereditary jobs, and with privileges and security far above that of their rural cousins. If anything, the gap between urban and rural identities became greater. And the difference between rural and urban—particularly during the Great Leap Forward, when at least 30 million perished—could become a matter of life and death.

One area of demonstrable economic success in the 1950s, the enormous growth of state enterprises, particularly in heavy industry, was the area of greatest continuity with the old Nationalist regime. In both strategy and detail, much of Communist China's first Five-Year Plan had been on Nationalist China's drawing boards.[8]

The result of all this was that as the rest of East Asia began to thrive in the postwar era, China was comparatively stagnant, or worse. The lessons of the catastrophe of Maoist economics were, however, learned by Mao's successors, whose economic counter-revolution dismantled his policies, returning to many aspects of pre-revolutionary China: allowing family farming; permitting again a form of mixed economy; welcoming international investment on a vast scale; and gradually limiting the state to the role of guiding, rather than running, the economy.

The results, though hardly without problems, have been simply stupendous, far exceeding the expectations of either Chinese or foreign observers when the reforms were announced three decades ago. One thinks only of what might have been, in the dark decades of the 1950s, 1960s, and 1970s, since many of the basic elements of Chinese economic growth, in fact, were there all along.

Politics

A second myth at mid-century was that the Republican era had been a political interregnum, without a functioning central government, an interregnum called to an end by the New China of the Chinese Communist Party.

China's central governments were indeed weak during the first half of the twentieth century. But the more we know of the pre-1949 decades, the more they emerge as a formidable period of state- and institution-building at the national, provincial, municipal, and local levels. The modern ministerial structures of a central government, the common features of provincial and municipal adminis-tration, a national system of higher education, and new sets of civil and criminal codes were all established during the reforms of the late Qing and Republican eras.[9] Much of this would be swept away, quickly and almost casually, by the new

Communist government. Later much of it would have to be reestablished, slowly and painfully, in the 1980s and 1990s.

Take the case of higher education. In the first half of the twentieth century, China developed one of the more dynamic systems of higher education in the world, with strong, state-run institutions (Peking University, Jiaotong University, National Central University, and at the apogee of research, the Academia Sinica), accompanied by a creative set of private colleges and universities (Yenching University, St. John's University, and Peking Union Medical College, to name but a few). All these, too, would be swept away in the late 1950s and 1960s, yet the traditions and memories of preeminence remained, and today's educational leaders have used these lessons to fuel the more recent, dramatic growth in scope and excellence of Chinese universities.[10]

The early PRC was widely believed to have provided a greater level of national unity and stability than its predecessors. Unity, perhaps: for only under a strongly unified political system could a policy such as the Great Leap Forward reach into every Chinese village with such lethal consequences. Stability? No. Each of the first four decades of the PRC was witness to major and destabilizing political upheavals.

Yet who among us would have predicted the comparative stability, accompanied by rapid economic growth, of the last two decades? The lessons drawn by China's post-Tiananmen leaders was to pursue vigorous, often audacious paths to economic growth, opening up also new realms of freedom in personal and professional lives, and new modes of communication (cell phones, the Web, the blogosphere) while maintaining, indeed enhancing and modernizing, the authoritarian state. How long this balance can be sustained is of course one of the questions in this book, but the apparent reality of the political stability of the last two decades is surely striking, compared to anything that came before it.

Foreign Relations

A third belief, common in and out of China in the 1950s, was that only under the People's Republic had China, in Mao's famous words, finally "stood up" to the outside world and successfully defended its long-impaired sovereignty. If there is one element of the sixtieth anniversary that many Chinese celebrated, it is this perception. Yet this too is a myth.

True, the Westerners were all exiled, and Westernized Chinese were placed under tight political wraps. But the PRC was heir to a state that was already sovereign, with internationally recognized borders that—as diplomatic historians have now shown—had been defended by its predecessor with remarkable success and skill, often from a position of great weakness. How else could the PRC have inherited almost all of the old Qing Empire intact? And unlike the Republic before it, the PRC was heir to a state unburdened by Western or Japanese "concessions" and settlements outside government control, not to mention the institution of extraterritoriality, which had immunized foreigners from Chinese law.[11] These were all done away with by its predecessors; it fell to the PRC to re-institute a form of extraterritoriality in the 1950s for its Soviet "elder brothers."

China certainly proved to be a great power in fighting the United States to a standstill in Korea. But did it need to prove that? It had already denied Japan victory in the second Sino-Japanese War from 1937 to 1945. In defending itself against Japanese aggression, China had shown that it was a major player in world affairs in the 1930s and 1940s, entering into alignments or alliances with three of the world's leading powers—Germany, the Soviet Union, and the United States— in order to fend off the fourth, Japan. Before that, it had been one of the leading citizens in the League of Nations and a most active participant in the influential international bodies of the day. By 1943 China was formally one of the "great powers" and would be a founder of the United Nations. With Japan prostrate, postwar China seemed assured of becoming the leading power in Asia, if only by default, and necessarily one of the leading actors in the global community.

That did not happen, and Chinese power was largely contained—in part self-contained—as China un-incorporated itself from both global communities: first from that of the West, and then a decade later from its Soviet and Eastern European allies. By the early 1960s a series of mutually reinforcing domestic and foreign policy decisions left China diplomatically quarantined, economically isolated, and in nearly a catastrophic military situation, if it were to face attack by either, or maybe even both, superpowers. In brief, China had "stood up" twice, only to find itself in the most dangerous strategic position of its modern history.

But again, after 1978 we see a different China, learning other lessons from its experience, taking once again a serious place on the global stage, and with little of the adventurism that would accompany Soviet and American foreign policy; participating in and helping to shape global organizations; and with a foreign policy voice that now matters on every issue of international consequence. By contrast with the Maoist decades, China has developed a mature foreign policy of consistent, and consistently limited, interests, with continuities back to Qing and Republican times. Perhaps it shows that if you are, in fact, a grown-up, you don't need to stand up.

*   *   *

I am drawn here, as have been so many, by the stark dichotomy between the first thirty years of the PRC and its last three decades. The former was a regime of a wasteful, and wasted—not to mention criminal—youth. Perhaps when Confucius talks of being thirty years old—"At thirty I stood firm" (三十而立)—we might translate it, in the case of the PRC in 1979: "I'm thirty and somehow still standing." Yet the People's Republic of China received something rare in history, a second chance, and it has made much of it.

The purpose of the chapters that follow is to look backward and forward: to contemplate the ideals and realities of the Maoist era, which look so different to us today than they did in the early decades of Communist rule; and to explore, from multiple perspectives, the flowering and restraining of Chinese life in an era of reform, entrepreneurialism, and internationalization. And as we look back, let us look ahead. Will the People's Republic of China be able to say a decade from now, as that first and most famous proponent of "harmonious society" once said of himself at 70: "I could follow what my heart desires, without transgressing what is right"?

ENDNOTES

1. Wm. Theodore de Bary and Irene Bloom, eds., *Sources of Chinese Tradition* (New York: Columbia University Press, 2nd ed., 1999), p. 46. The text of the translation is taken from James Legge, trans., *The Chinese Classics*, vol. 1, reprint ed. (Taipei: Southern Materials Center, Inc., 1985), pp. 146–147.

2. de Bary and Bloom, eds., *Sources of Chinese Tradition*, pp. 46–47.

3. Legge, trans., *The Chinese Classics*, vol. 1, p. 147.

4. See in particular the synthetic work of Thomas G. Rawski, *Economic Growth in Prewar China* (Berkeley: University of California Press, 1989).

5. See Marie-Claire Bergère, *The Golden Age of the Chinese Bourgeoisie, 1911–1937*, trans. by Janet Lloyd (Cambridge: Cambridge University Press, 1989).

6. For industry, see Deborah A. Kaple, *Dream of a Red Factory: The Legacy of High Stalinism in China* (Oxford: Oxford University Press, 1994).

7. Tiejun Cheng and Mark Selden, "The Construction of Spatial Hierarchies: China's *Hukou* and *Danwei* Systems," in Timothy Cheek and Tony Saich, eds., *New Perspectives on State Socialism in China* (Armonk, NY: M.E. Sharpe, 1997), pp. 23–50.

8. William C. Kirby, "Continuity and Change in Modern China: Chinese Economic Planning on the Mainland and on Taiwan, 1943–1958," *Australian Journal of Chinese Affairs*, no. 24 (July 1990): 121–141.

9. See Julia C. Strauss, *Strong Institutions in Weak Polities: State Building in Republican China, 1927–1940* (Oxford: Clarendon Press, 1998).

10. William C. Kirby, "On Chinese, European and American Universities," *Daedalus: Journal of the American Academy of Arts and Sciences*, 137, no. 3 (Summer 2008): 139–146.

11. William C. Kirby, "The Internationalization of China: Foreign Relations at Home and Abroad in the Republican Era," *The China Quarterly*, no. 150 (June 1997): 443–458.

KEYNOTE ADDRESS
THE PEOPLE'S REPUBLIC OF CHINA AT SIXTY

RODERICK MACFARQUHAR

As Mao famously remarked, "a revolution is not like inviting people to dinner ...,"[1] to which I would add that a keynote is not an after-dinner speech. Hence my desire to speak before dinner so that I can then enjoy the food and wine with you. I have found that speaking after dinner means that the speaker eats and drinks sparingly and then has to watch his audience glaze over when he rises to his feet. So please forgive me and I will try not to keep you too long from your food.

Our subject at this conference is sixty years of the PRC, which I wish to embed within a context of 170 years of China's interaction with the West. I will be emphasizing two elements: Chinese exceptionalism and national trauma. It is not surprising that after maintaining the Confucian-Legalist imperial system for two millennia—give or take a century or two of disunity from time to time—Chinese mandarins reacted to the onslaughts of Western imperialism with the conviction that they should do everything to restore their system to its full glory because then China would be impregnable. The reassertion of Chinese exceptionalism—the last stand of Chinese conservatism as historian Mary Wright termed it—had as its motto the well-known policy prescription: *Zhong xue wei ti, Xi xue wei yong* (Chinese learning as the core; Western learning for practical use). The problem was that it did not work. The imperialist powers continued to oppress China. And then Chinese exceptionalism was overtaken by national trauma: defeat by Japan in the war of 1894–95.

The mainly sea-borne barbarians who had hitherto imposed themselves upon the Chinese empire were too strange to be seen as anything more than a passing threat with some ingenious military hardware that the Chinese had to master. But the Japanese, who had been their younger brothers, had managed to emulate the West so effectively as to transform their country into a European-style nation-state, thus becoming an alien entity, an "other," within the Chinese cultural sphere. This transformation of a country that had been so dependent on

China for cultural borrowings over the centuries was deeply traumatic and sparked the abortive One Hundred Days Reform in 1898. The further humiliation of the Chinese empire in 1900 by a combined imperialist force, among which Japanese troops marched as of right, led inexorably to the dissolution of imperial Confucianism: the abandonment of the Confucian examination system in 1905 and then the abdication of the last emperor after the double-ten revolution of 1911.

By this time, patriotic Chinese intellectuals were searching the institutional and cultural warehouses of the West for keys to the restoration of China to wealth and power. Sun Yat-sen thought the strength of Western imperialism stemmed from its democratic systems, but the Chinese republic which he helped to found in the Western image soon became merely the creature of successive warlords. In the early 1920s, Sun turned to the Soviets to help him strengthen his Nationalist Party and build up his army. Other intellectuals and students were so inspired by the Bolshevik revolution and Lenin's anti-imperialism that they founded the Chinese Communist Party in 1921 under the aegis of the Comintern.[2] In this audience, I do not need to recite the tortuous history of the successive united fronts and civil wars between the Nationalists and the Communists. We all know the end of the story: the Communists won.

But I do want to underline the nature of the back-to-the-future system which the victors erected in 1949. Like the imperial system, it was leader-friendly, and Mao's personality cult and modern means of communication gave him a ubiquity never enjoyed by any emperor. Like their mandarin predecessors, the cadres of the CCP hastened to carry out the imperial Chairman's orders, and like them, justified their right to rule by their knowledge of the ideology which glued state and society together, replacing Confucianism with Marxism-Leninism-Mao Zedong Thought. The significant difference lay in the transformative aims of the Communist creed: the mandarins had been content to ensure that taxes reached the court and law and order was maintained, whereas the CCP was anti-status quo and the cadres were directed to change society and develop the economy. These CCP objectives induced traumas, both individual and national.

We can neatly divide the sixty years of the PRC into two thirty-year segments: the Maoist period ending with the sidelining of the Chairman's chosen successor, Hua Guofeng; and the Deng Xiaoping reform era beginning in December 1978. The first seven years under Mao were characterized by a series of often bloody campaigns in various branches of society: land reform, followed by collectivization in the countryside; the three-anti and five-anti campaigns in the cities, followed by state takeovers of industry and commerce; the thought reform campaign of non-Communist intellectuals, followed by the anti-Hu Feng campaign against Communist intellectuals who wanted greater freedom; two campaigns against counter-revolutionaries; and then the Hundred Flowers and rectification campaigns designed to open up society, followed by the Anti-Rightist movement to close it down again. By the end of 1957, China had been transformed into a nominally socialist society, and, despite the bloodshed,[3] without the massive disruption and high-level purges experienced in the Soviet Union.

Mao then turned his attention to economic transformation. He was dissatisfied with the rate of progress of the reasonably successful first Five-Year Plan (1953–57). Besides, I suspect he realized that running a Soviet-style command economy required a vast bureaucratic apparatus and considerable managerial skills, and he abhorred bureaucracy and lacked interest in and talent for management. If he were to retain of right his position at the head of the CCP, China's economic transformation would have to be achieved by means that played to his strengths: his vision for what China should become and his gift for inspiring CCP cadres. His solution was Chinese revolutionary exceptionalism, the Great Leap Forward during which the cadres mobilized the people for bootstraps economic development that Mao believed would enable China to overtake the Soviet Union and then the United States in steel output in just a few years.[4] Simultaneously, the cadres herded the recently collectivized peasantry into even more egalitarian and collectivist units, the People's Communes, aiming to produce a new multitasking, renaissance person: part farmer, part worker, part soldier, part educator. Again, everyone here knows the end of that story: disaster ensued, the greatest man-made famine in human history.[5]

The only benefit of this massive national trauma was that Mao abandoned his dreams of economic exceptionalism. But he did not discard his plans for ideological exceptionalism, nor his determination to keep setting the agenda for the CCP. His campaign against Soviet "revisionism" segued into the "Great Proletarian Cultural Revolution" which aimed to make Beijing the new Communist Mecca and again to try to transform China into a land peopled with revolutionary renaissance men and women. Society, in the form of the Red Guards, was unleashed against the state, both party and government.

There are no available figures on how many people were killed during the Cultural Revolution, but almost certainly it was some tens of millions less than the upper estimate of 43 million who died during the great famine. Yet, strange to say, the ten years of chaos unleashed by Mao during the Cultural Revolution were an even more traumatic experience for the Chinese leaders who survived. None of them had starved during the famine, but almost all of them were humiliated and driven from office during the Cultural Revolution. The famine had prompted Deng and some colleagues to propose economic and social adjustments, but within the socialist paradigm. The Cultural Revolution impelled Deng, at least, to think outside the box. During the thirty years of Maoist leftism, China's East Asian neighbors had transformed themselves economically. In the revolutionary dawn of 1949, China had been best placed for rapid economic development, but instead had torn itself apart. Deng put aside ideas of Chinese exceptionalism and instead geared up his countrymen to emulate the miracles of Japan, South Korea, Taiwan, Hong Kong, and Singapore. Reform and opening-up to the outside world were his watchwords; capitalist methods were acceptable in the interests of development. As he had said during the famine, it did not matter what color a cat was as long as it caught mice, and he encouraged Chinese with a truly revolutionary slogan "To get rich is glorious," a phrase which would never have been uttered by a Confucian mandarin or a Maoist cadre.

Once again, everyone here knows, and doubtless has witnessed, the results: thirty years of roughly 10 percent annual growth rate, a level of sustained economic development never before approximated by any nation in human history. Foreign direct investment has flowed in on a massive scale. Most Chinese have never been so prosperous and hundreds of millions of urban residents now lead comfortable middle-class lives. The transformation has been staggering and continues. On the occasion of the PRC's sixtieth anniversary on October 1, the celebrations will doubtless match the organization and display of the 2008 Beijing Olympics.

China may not be the revolutionary beacon Mao envisaged, but some academics believe it has become a model of "authoritarian resilience,"[6] and certainly China's success has been striking in the context of the collapse of communism in Europe. The Tiananmen events of 1989 shook and split the Chinese leadership, but Deng's decision to use military force against the students prevented the regime from collapsing as the Soviet satellites in Eastern Europe did later in the year. The demise of the Soviet Union in 1991 was an even greater shock for the Chinese leadership, even though the Chinese leaders had had no sympathy for Gorbachev's *glasnost*. Fortunately for them, the sudden disappearance of communism from its Soviet homeland was an external trauma. In its wake, Deng Xiaoping, supposedly retired, urged his successors to speed up economic growth to prevent a similar trauma occurring internally. The Chinese slogan of the 1950s, "the Soviet Union's today is our tomorrow," was retired once and for all.

But for all the resilience that the CCP has undoubtedly displayed in the two decades since the Soviet collapse, in my view the Chinese polity is fragile. The combination of Maoist utopianism and Dengist realism has undermined the party-state. By trashing the party machine during the Cultural Revolution and allowing its leaders and cadres to be denounced and beaten at mass rallies, Mao undermined its prestige and authority. Deng rehabilitated leaders, like Liu Shaoqi, who had died as a result of their mistreatment, and returned survivors to privilege and sometimes to power. But the cadres who returned in the 1980s were no longer the "Serve the people" cadres of the 1950s. They had taken to heart that to get rich is glorious; after their travails during the Cultural Revolution, why not them too? Despite repeated official campaigns, regulations, and exhortations, corruption on a colossal scale has infected all levels of state and society.[7] A typical scenario is that local officials are bribed by entrepreneurs to confiscate land for industrial purposes, leaving the peasants without land and often afflicted by deadly pollution. In response to such malpractices, there have been tens of thousands of demonstrations, clashes and riots in the countryside over the years, 87,000 officially admitted in 2005, and the number is rising. But so long as local leaders deliver taxes, promote development, and maintain law and order, the central leaders seem prepared to look the other way. Only if a particularly egregious case reaches the foreign press or enrages the domestic blogosphere is something likely to be done. But if the center were to attempt to replicate nation-wide anything like the anti-corruption campaign launched in Chongqing in 2009, the resultant purge would amount to a second cultural revolution.

Another factor in the collapse of cadre morality is the absence of any system of belief and ideals. Marxism-Leninism-Mao Zedong Thought is formally one of the party's "four cardinal principles," but in practice it is ignored. Deng's reform program is built on the principles of "seeking truth from facts" and, more importantly, a variation of the cat and mouse theme: "Practice is the sole criterion of truth"; i.e. if it works, we'll do it. The ideological glue that held state and society together during the Confucian centuries and again in Communist times has atrophied. China's leaders have put forward new ideas: "Deng Xiaoping theory"; Jiang Zemin's "three represents"; and Hu Jintao's "harmonious society." But these have been merely policy prescriptions, important in their way, but not overarching analyses of state and society.

Deng espoused "socialist spiritual civilization" but it did not catch on. He proclaimed that China was building "socialism with Chinese characteristics." But nobody who casts even a cursory eye over China's blend of state and private capitalism, market Leninism as it is sometimes called, can accept that definition. If one wants socialism with Chinese characteristics, one has to go to Singapore. For democracy with Chinese characteristics? Taiwan. Capitalism with Chinese characteristics? Hong Kong. And China? 1.3 billion people with Chinese characteristics. Ideologically, there is nothing there. In this vacuum, some leaders have been poking around in the Confucian storehouse for inspiration. But their subjects have sought solace and meaning in alternative ideologies: Christianity, Falungong, and local cults.

Mandarins in the nineteenth century were entirely sure of the nature of the Chinese "core" which they wished to revive and strengthen: imperial Confucianism and the "little tradition," the adulterated Confucianism which, blended with Daoism, Buddhism, and local cults, prevailed at the lower levels of society. Mao substituted Marxism-Leninism as the Chinese essence, though this too was adulterated by cults at the local level.[8] In current conditions, the only essence which CCP leaders can fall back on to connect with the people is nationalism. But the xenophobia of much of the blogosphere suggests that this is a two-edged weapon which could be turned against national leaders deemed insufficiently robust in their dealings with foreign countries.

Chinese "exceptionalism" today is historical rather than geographical. The PRC differs less from the outside world than it does from past Chinas, Confucian and Marxist-Leninist, in having no core, no essence. To reconnect with the populace, the CCP leaders would have to adopt some form of pluralism which would give people a sense of being a part of the governing system. This would require a massive transformation—rule of law, free elections, freedom of speech, and so forth—which Chinese leaders who comment on the issue emphatically reject.[9]

Looking back over the past 200 years of Chinese history, it can be seen that massive transformations have only occurred after national traumas: defeat by Japan led to the collapse of the 2,000-year-old imperial system; and Mao's Cultural Revolution led to substitution of the profit motive for egalitarianism. The Chinese people endured much during those two transformations. One can only hope that any future political transformation can be achieved without yet another national trauma.

ENDNOTES

1. In his "Report on the Peasant Movement in Hunan," as translated in Stuart Schram, ed., *Mao's Road to Power: Volume II, National Revolution and Social Revolution, December 1920-June 1927* (Armonk, NY: M.E. Sharpe, 1994), p. 434.

2. The Soviets promised in the 1919 Karakhan Declaration to restore to China territories and privileges seized by the Tsars; Allen S. Whiting, *Soviet Policies in China, 1917–1924* (Stanford, CA: Stanford University Press, 1968), passim. For the Comintern's role, see Tony Saich, ed., *The Rise to Power of the Chinese Communist Party: Documents and Analysis* (Armonk, NY: M.E. Sharpe, 1996).

3. In February 1957, Mao admitted that almost 800,000 people had been executed during the early 1950s; Roderick MacFarquhar, Timothy Cheek, and Eugene Wu, eds., *The Secret Speeches of Chairman Mao: From the Hundred Flowers to the Great Leap Forward* (Cambridge, MA: Council on East Asian Studies, Harvard University, 1989), p. 142. Some former Chinese officials believe the figure to be much higher.

4. Roderick MacFarquhar, *The Origins of the Cultural Revolution: 2 The Great Leap Forward 1958–60* (New York: Columbia University Press, 1983), p. 90.

5. Frank Dikötter, *Mao's Great Famine: The History of China's Most Devastating Catastrophe, 1958–62* (New York: Walker & Co., 2010).

6. See Andrew J. Nathan, "Authoritarian Resilience," *Journal of Democracy*, 14, no. 1 (2003): 6–17.

7. Xiaobo Lü, *Cadres and Corruption: The Organizational Involution of the Chinese Communist Party* (Stanford, CA: Stanford University Press, 2000), pp. 223–227.

8. Steve A. Smith, "Local Cadres Confront the Supernatural: The Politics of Holy Water (*Shenshui*) in the PRC, 1949–1966," *The China Quarterly*, no. 188 (December 2006): 999–1022.

9. "Wu Bangguo Says China Will Never Copy Western Political System," Xinhua, March 9, 2009.

POLITIES

1.

THE FOUNDATIONS OF COMMUNIST RULE IN CHINA:
THE COERCIVE DIMENSION

DAVID SHAMBAUGH

When one considers the early years of Chinese Communist Party (CCP) rule during the new People's Republic of China and the foundation upon which the CCP built its rule, there are, of course, numerous elements one must recall.[1] Many of these are very positive. These features include:

- The restoration of national pride and dignity;
- The restoration of territorial unity;
- The overthrow of the corrupt and incompetent *ancien regime*;
- The control of hyper inflation and financial stabilization;
- The replenishment of capital stock and infrastructure after years of devastating war;
- The improvements in public health and mortality rates;
- The control of public vices;
- The defense of China's Korean frontier in the face of threatened American attacks.

These and many other accomplishments are noteworthy during the early years (1949–53) of CCP rule. Collectively, they gave average Chinese much optimism about the future and they provided the new regime with a considerable amount of political legitimacy.

Not to neglect these positive elements, this chapter addresses one other key feature of the foundation of Communist rule during these early years (indeed throughout the Maoist era)—what I refer to as the "coercive dimension" and the building of the "coercive apparatus" that would constitute a central brick in the totalitarian edifice constructed by Mao and the CCP over the next three decades. Not only did the CCP's *accession* to power involve much violence, so too did the *consolidation* of power and the *exercise* of power. As Chairman Mao aptly put it: "Revolution is not a dinner party—it is a violent act in which one class overthrows another!" Mao and his colleagues understood this clearly—not the least of whom were the "returned Bolsheviks" who had been schooled by the People's Commissariat for Internal Affairs (NKVD), Committee for State Security (KGB), Comintern, and other Soviet organs of repression. The CCP did not have to start afresh, since it built on the foundations in intelligence services and coercive rule learned by the Nationalists from both Stalin and Hitler.

So the Chinese revolution culminating with the seizure of power and establishment of a new state in 1949 may have been many things—including positive social change in the cities and countryside—but it was also not a dinner party! It was a violent and coercive process on a number of levels. The hostile regional and international environment that the new PRC faced in 1950 certainly contributed to the "coercive impulse" of the new regime.

The use of coercion in the People's Republic took a variety of forms—some public and violent, some private and more subtle. Totalitarian systems function most "efficiently" when coercion and repression are hidden from public view, when society in effect polices itself, where self-control and self-censorship occur, and the "invisible hand" of the state penetrates society thoroughly and comprehensively. These systems are built on a combination of fear, intimidation, deterrence, and uncertainty, i.e., never knowing who can be trusted or who is going to report on you.

To establish such a system, the CCP set up an elaborate arrangement of coercion that involved a variety of local institutional control mechanisms: forcing everyone into *danwei* work-units, neighborhood residents committees (100–600 households), and residents groups (15–40 households), neighborhood monitors, and the *hukou* system. These control mechanisms guided various aspects of people's personal lives—their residences, physical mobility, jobs, marriages, birth control, health care, crime prevention, and so forth. In addition to these mechanisms that controlled people's physical lives, the CCP established an elaborate and extensive series of controls over the media, education, and people's minds.[2] Other more draconian instruments were also implemented: a large-scale prison and labor-camp system; a national public security system; a domestic intelligence and counter-intelligence apparatus; and various armed paramilitary and military forces.

Thus, any consideration of the foundations of Communist rule in China must take into account the coercive dimension.

To begin with, it is essential to view the CCP's victory not merely as a political victory and a social revolution, but as an *armed seizure of power* following protracted military campaigns in which one military defeated another on the battlefield. Not only did the five Communist "field armies" sweep from north to south in a series of epic campaigns from late 1947 through 1949, but these campaigns continued beyond 1949 as well. Large parts of China (Guangdong, Guangxi, Yunnan, Xizang, Qinghai, Gansu, Xinjiang, and Ningxia) were not fully "liberated" (i.e., invaded and conquered) until late 1951 (or, in the case of Tibet, 1952). Even then, large pockets of resistance remained in the mountains of Henan, Hubei, and Anhui, while the problems of what the CCP described as "localism" and "banditry" persisted through at least 1952 in Guangdong, Hainan, Hunan, Guizhou, Guangxi, Sichuan, and Yunnan. The same was true along the northwestern tier of Qinghai, Gansu, and Xinjiang where ethnic resistance proved stubborn. Tibet (Xizang) finally fell to 40,000 forces of the Second Field Army in 1951–52, and it required 30,000 troops of the Fifth Field Army to occupy and pacify Xinjiang in 1950–51. Large numbers of troops were committed to these campaigns to root out "bandits," and in many places Red Army units were seen as liberators in the latest of the century-long series of occupying forces. They were subject to random harassment and sabotage, and they had to ensure control through sheer physical presence, constant patrols, vigilant surveillance, mass arrests, and public executions in order to assert their rule over these regions. Throughout the 1949–54 period a series of "bandit extermination campaigns" (*qingjiao tufei yundong*) were carried out. Subsequently released PLA histories indicate that between 1949 and 1953 1.5 million troops were devoted to "bandit suppression," resulting in the "annihilation" (*jianmie*) of 2.65 million "bandits."[3]

Despite the claimed "success" in extinguishing "bandits," armed and organized opposition to the regime continued. Thereafter, a series of unremitting repressive "campaigns" (*yundong*) were unleashed by the regime.

The CCP undertook the "suppression of counterrevolutionaries" (*sufan*) campaign. Initiated in February 1951 and lasting into 1953 it ostensibly aimed at rooting out Guomindang "spies and collaborators," although this was a very vague category that was easily used to incarcerate or execute a range of "anti-socialist elements." A second wave of the campaign occurred in 1954–55. An estimated total of 1–2 million "counterrevolutionaries" were executed during these campaigns.

Then there was "land reform"—a process that predated the seizure of power in 1949, but deepened significantly from the summer of 1950 through 1952. There are many fine accounts of this process, especially the shift from so-called "soft" (persuasive) to "hard" (coercive) methods in the fall of 1950, particularly in the south.[4] No one knows for sure, but conservative estimates place the number of executions of landlords at about 2 million, although UK, U.S., and Taiwan intelligence sources estimate approximately 4–5 million executions. In addition to those killed, countless landlord families were terrorized, beaten, and lost all their possessions.

This was followed by the "Three-Anti, Five-Anti" (*san fan, wu fan*) campaign of 1952–53. Perhaps it was less violent, but it still was harsh. Several hundred thousand "capitalists" and "bourgeois elements" were attacked, humiliated, incarcerated, and stripped of their possessions. An estimated one million perished.

In 1955 the "Criticize Hu Feng" Campaign was launched—the first of many coercive campaigns targeted at intellectuals. Several hundred thousand writers and scholars were purged, imprisoned, or committed suicide. This was the forerunner to the 1958 Anti-Rightist movement, in which an estimated 300,000 were executed and several million intellectuals and civil servants were "capped" as "Rightists" and incarcerated for more than twenty years.

Other shorter and smaller campaigns targeted different sectors of society in the late 1950s and early 1960s. From 1958 to 1960 the entire nation was subjected to the coerced mass mobilization campaign of the Great Leap Forward. The result of this man-made (Mao-made) catastrophe was the death from starvation of at least 30 million in the famine, as well as countless others who died of physical exhaustion or suicide.[5]

Finally, came the mother of all political campaigns—the "Great Proletarian Cultural Revolution." There are many chilling first- and second-hand accounts of this ten-year national nightmare.[6] Hundreds of thousands, if not millions, of lives were lost or ruined as a result of Mao's attempt to attack his rivals in the CCP and cleanse the nation of "revisionism."

However, such coercive campaigns did not end with the Maoist era. The "Six Evils" Campaign of the mid-1980s (in which an estimated 25,000 were killed), the twin "Strike Hard" Campaigns of the mid-1990s (a total of 40,000–50,000 executed), the suppression of the Falun Gong spiritual movement from the late 1990s to the present, the 2008–9 crackdown in Tibet, and the 2009 suppression of riots in Xinjiang, are all reminders that the coercive dimension of CCP rule did not die with Mao. Many of the approximately 80,000 annual "public order disturbances" nationwide are dealt with forcefully (and sometimes lethally) by People's Armed Police and local Public Security forces.

Other instruments of repression transcended the Maoist era and new forms emerged. The extensive "reform through labor" gulag prison labor camps exist to this day,[7] as does substantial media and Internet censorship. The paramilitary People's Armed Police (now 1.5 million strong) and the Ministry of State Security are also substantial organs of coercion and repression. China's police forces (the Ministry of Public Security) have been expanded, are better equipped and trained, and continue to possess substantial coercive powers.[8] Some sources in China estimate the 2010 annual budget for internal security equal to the external military budget, approximately US$80 billion. The 2009–2010 unrest in Tibet and Xinjiang has given a strong boost to domestic security spending and recruitment. Taken together, the People's Armed Police, Ministry of State Security, and Ministry of Public Security employ as many as 12 million personnel. Furthermore, nationwide the people's militia (*minbing*) has been resurrected over the past decade, and the People's Liberation Army has transitioned from its former dual mission of internal and external security to a focus on the latter.

This is not a pretty picture—but it is an important part of PRC history (a dark part). The good news is that the worst excesses of this coercive totalitarian state ended during the past 30 years, some measure of rule of law has been instituted, and China's coercive practices are now more open to scrutiny, both domestically and internationally. Since the advent of the reform era, we have witnessed an improvement of standards of living and improved respect for human rights for all Chinese citizens. To be sure, China has a long way to go to meet international standards of human rights, but it must be recognized that there has been significant progress in recent years. Nonetheless, any full accounting of the history of the People's Republic of China, whether its early history or in more recent years, must take into account its coercive dimension.

ENDNOTES

1. Among the many accounts of these years, see A. Doak Barnett, *Communist China: The Early Years, 1949–55* (New York: Praeger, 1964); Kenneth Lieberthal, *Revolution and Tradition in Tientsin, 1949–1952* (Stanford, CA: Stanford University Press, 1980).

2. See Frederick T.C. Yu, *Mass Persuasion in Communist China* (New York: Praeger, 1964); Franz Schurmann, *Ideology and Organization in Communist China*, 2nd ed. (Berkeley: University of California Press, 1968); David Shambaugh, "China's Propaganda System: Institutions, Process and Efficacy," *The China Journal*, no. 57 (January 2007): 25–58.

3. See Deng Lifeng, ed., *Xin Zhongguo junshi huodong shi, 1949–1959* (A Compendium of New China's Military Activities, 1949–1959) (Beijing: Zhonggong dangshi ziliao chubanshe, 1989), p. 63; Deng Liqun, et al. eds., *Dangdai Zhongguo jundui de junshi gongzuo* (Contemporary China's Military Affairs' Work) (Beijing: Zhongguo shehui kexueyuan chubanshe, 1989), 1: 32, 276–379.

4. See, for example, Ezra Vogel, *Canton Under Communism: Program and Politics in a Provincial Capital 1949–1968* (Cambridge, MA: Harvard University Press, 1969).

5. The most recent and best scholarship on this human tragedy is Frank Dikötter, *Mao's Great Famine: The History of China's Most Devastating Catastrophe, 1958–1962*

(London: Bloomsbury, 2010). Also see Jasper Becker, *Hungry Ghosts: Mao's Secret Famine* (New York: Henry Holt, 1998).

6. See, in particular, the literature of the "wounded" (first-hand accounts) and the magisterial study by Roderick MacFarquhar and Michael Schoenhals, *Mao's Last Revolution* (Cambridge, MA: Belknap Press of Harvard University Press, 2006).

7. See James D. Seymour and Richard Anderson, *New Ghosts, Old Ghosts: Prisons and Labor Reform Camps in China* (Armonk, NY: M.E. Sharpe, 1998); Hongda Harry Wu, *Laogai: The Chinese Gulag* (Boulder, CO: Westview Press, 1992).

8. See Michael Dutton, *Policing Chinese Politics: A History* (Durham, NC: Duke University Press, 2005).

2.
毛泽东与整风反右运动的缘起
MAO ZEDONG AND THE ORIGINS OF THE ANTI-RIGHTIST RECTIFICATION CAMPAIGN

沈志华 SHEN ZHIHUA

Abstract

This chapter seeks to address a long-held puzzle about the Anti-Rightist Rectification Campaign: why, and exactly when, did the Rectification Campaign take its Anti-Rightist turn in 1957? In other words, when, and why, did Mao Zedong decide to "lure the snake away from its hole"? In order to separate the trajectory of Mao's own thinking from the sequence of events during the Rectification Campaign, the author carefully analyzes Mao's speeches, reports, and orders, as well as his published articles during and after 1957.

Whereas most researchers regard mid-May as the approximate date when Mao began to plot the Anti-Rightist Campaign, this chapter shows that the real turning point came later. First, there is no evidence to show that Mao had any significant sense of alarm prior to May 14–16. Even when the policy of "letting a hundred flowers bloom" elicited ever more fierce criticism and chaos, it was not until late May and early June that Mao finally decided to initiate a nationwide counterattack as a continuation of the class struggle against the Rightists. Although Mao later claimed that he had long foreseen and planned the scheme, in fact initially the Rectification Campaign was not a deliberate political trap.

毛泽东与整风反右运动的缘起

1956年波匈事件给毛泽东和中共领导人留下的最大教训是，即使消灭了国内的阶级敌人和反动势力，共产党的政权仍然有得而复失的可能，这种危险的根源就在共产党内——执政党的错误和弊病引起人民群众的不满和反抗，人民群众起来"闹事"，推翻执政党的统治。所以，毛泽东力主开展整风运动，并实行"大鸣大放"，邀请党外人士帮助整风。然而，整风开始不久，却突然转为全国的反右派运动，本来帮助共产党整风的民主党派和知识分子反过来成了斗争的对象。多年来，在有关1957年整风反右运动的研究中，最大悬念就是：整风运动为什么会转向反右运动？这个转变是什么时候发生的？哪些因素导致毛泽东改变了他以前的估计和判断？或者可以归结为一个人们常提的问题：毛泽东为什么和什么时候决定"引蛇出洞"的？

笔者的考察将沿着两条线索展开：一是整风事态发展的过程，一是毛泽东思想变化的过程。从1957年5月1日中共中央发出全党整风的指示，到6月8日《人民日报》发出反击右派的号令，全国各大城市、各个阶层、党内党外发生了太多的事情，且错综复杂。对这个过程不难考察，然而困难的是摸清毛泽东的思想脉络，他在这段时间及以后的讲话、报告、指示、文章虽然很多，但是真真假假，虚虚实实，有的文过饰非，有的强词夺理，令人眼花缭乱，需要仔细解读和认真领会。

开始警觉：毛泽东感到事情起了变化

毛泽东认为，广泛征求党外人士的意见，对这次整风能否取得成效关系甚大。因为阶级斗争基本结束以后，国家建设在很大程度上要依赖知识分子；知识分子多数不接受马克思主义，对他们必须长期改造，但只能说服，不能压服，因此需要百花齐放、百家争鸣，给他们一定的民主和自由；处理人民内部矛盾的主要任务是解决党内的官僚主义、主观主义和宗派主义问题，方法就是进行整风，也需要知识分子从党外加以推动。

在贯彻双百方针的氛围中，开门整风就此出现，其方式就是在会议上和报纸上"大鸣大放"，由原先"和风细雨"的"小民主"，变成了"急风暴雨"的"大民主"。

然而面对多数党内干部抵制整风的心理，毛泽东刻意动用宣传舆论工具，在党内进行吹风的同时，也对党外人士展开动员。5月

4日，在中共中央《关于请党外人士帮助整风的指示》中，毛泽东对开门整风的方式和效果大表肯定，"大多数的批评是说得中肯的，对于加强团结，改善工作，极为有益。即使是错误的批评，也暴露了一部分人的面貌，利于我们在将来帮助他们进行思想改造"。接着指出了整风正式开始以后的做法："中央已同各民主党派及无党派领导人士商好，他们暂时(至少几个月内)不要表示态度，不要在各民主党派内和社会上号召整风，而要继续展开对我党缺点错误的批判，以利于我党整风，否则对于我党整风是不利的(没有社会压力，整风不易收效)。他们同意此种做法。只要我党整风成功，我党就会取得完全的主动，那时就可以推动社会各界整风了(这里首先指知识界)"。

毛泽东5月4日的指示下达后，中央各部门为贯彻百花齐放、百家争鸣方针，纷纷召集各种座谈会，特别是非党人士座谈会，向党和政府的工作提意见。中央统战部长李维汉在一次研究高校里中共与民主党派、无党派人士关系问题的座谈会上说，各民主党派要求发挥更多的作用，在政治生活中，他们不仅要参与"设计"，还要参与"施工和检查"；要重视民主党派，在政治上信任他们，在思想、学术上允许争论，摆脱条条框框；要克服党内的宗派主义，消除中共党员与民主党派成员之间的隔阂；扩大高校校务委员会的自主权。

这一阶段的鸣放言论，基本上是针对基层单位的，所批评的官僚主义、主观主义、教条主义、宗派主义，也都是具体工作中的表现，而且完全没有超出毛泽东历次讲话指出的范围。对于中共领导人来说，这些都是可以接受和容忍的。

林克在日记中记录了毛对这些言论的一些反映。针对社会上有关"百家争鸣是为了钓鱼"的说法，毛泽东解释说，"这看如何理解，百家争鸣是方法还是目的？为了认识真理，那么也可以说是钓鱼"。不过是钓两条鱼，"一条是马克思主义的鱼，一条是非马克思主义之鱼，不仅是钓鱼，而且是撒网"。毛的戏谑不外乎要在两种世界观之间明辨是非的问题，而不是政治运动的策略。所以，这里所说的"钓鱼"与后来的"引蛇出洞"完全不是一回事。对于教条主义者和知识分子在学术思想上的论证，毛泽东也没有任何担心。

从这段时间毛泽东对最高国务会议讲话稿的修改，也可以看出他的思想倾向。根据胡乔木的记录稿，毛泽东曾写下这样的文字，"民主自由都是相对的，不是绝对的"，"我们不应当片面地强调某一个侧面，而把另一个侧面给否定掉"；我国私营工商业改造"所以做得这样迅速和顺利，是跟我们把工人阶级同民族资产阶级的矛盾当作人民内部矛盾去处理，密切相关的"；肯定知识分子的绝大多数在最近几年中有了很大的进步，强调团结知识分子，改善同他们的关系，帮助他们进步；"无论是共产党，或者是民主党派，监督它们的首先是人民。再则，政党的党员又监督政党的领导者。现在我们加上一条，各个政党互相监督，这样岂不是更有益处吗？监督的方法，就是团结－批评－团结。这个方法是百花齐放、百花争鸣的方法，是长期共存、互相监督的方法，是解决一切人民内部矛盾的方法"；"所谓公民权，在政治方面，就是说有自由和民主的权利"，但民主和自由都是有限度的；"一个人或一个党，耳边如果没有不同的声音，那是很危险的。大家知道，主要监督我们的是劳动人民和我们自己，并不是民主党派。但是有了民主党派，对我们更为有益"。"共产党力量很大，怕的是没有人讲闲话，不怕天下大乱。这个天下是乱不了的"。从上述增加的内容看，对群众闹事、知识分子、民主党派、双百方针等问题的论述，与5月4日的指示精神都是一致的，而在言词上显得更加放得开。这说明毛泽东对整风运动开展一周前后的情况是满意的。

那么，毛泽东究竟是什么时候开始警觉的？到底哪些言论让他感到不安了？人们最常引用的是李维汉的回忆："民主党派和工商界"两个座谈会反映出来的意见，我都及时向中央常委汇报。5月中旬，汇报到第三次或第四次时，已经放出一些不好的东西，什么'轮流坐庄'、'海德公园'等谬论都出来了。毛泽东同志警觉性很高，……决定把放出来的言论在《人民日报》发表，并且指示，要硬着头皮听，不要反驳，让他们放。……及至听到座谈会的汇报和罗隆基说现在是马列主义的小知识分子领导小资产阶级的大知识分子，外行领导内行之后，就在5月15日写出了《事情正在起变化》的文章，发给党内高级干部阅读。……这篇文章，表明毛泽东同志已经下定反击右派的决心"。李维汉的这段记忆很不准确。关于毛泽东开始警觉的时间，一般研究者都认为是5月中旬。这个说法应该可以接受，但是过于笼统，因为就是在这几天当中，毛泽东的思想发生了很大变化，究竟怎么变的，决不是一个"5月中旬"可以解释的。况且，很多论著提出这种说法的依据是靠不住的。

李维汉所说的毛泽东5月15日"写出"的《事情正在起变化》一文，正是他和其他许多人判断毛泽东决定开始反右的时间的依据，有研究者甚至认为"这篇文章发出了反击右派的信号"。但是根据《建国以来毛泽东文稿》（第六册）的题注，这个文件最初起草是在5月中旬，但毛泽东6月11日才最后修改并定稿，而他有意把写作时间改为"5月15日"。所以人们看到的文字所反映的不是或主要不是毛泽东5月中旬的想法，而是6月11日，即反右运动开始以后的想法。笔者的考察结果认为，对于所要回答的问题而言，与其他相关的文献和史料比较，这篇文章的研究价值最低。原因在于，此文是毛泽东后来修改的，如果研究者不知道修改的内容和过程，那么此文所能反映的，充其量是毛泽东自知对知识分子估计过高、对局势判断失误后所表现出来的愤怒心情及文过饰非的手法。因此，这篇文章根本就不能作为判断5月中旬毛有何想法的依据，而作为发动反右的"信号"更是无稽之谈（文件是6月12日，即反右开始后发出的），唯一值得注意的是，毛泽东修改这篇文章时标明的日期——5月15日，这很可能反映了他思想转变的时间。

李维汉有一个说法很在理："中央当时发动这一场斗争，有一个酝酿和发动的过程"。笔者将能够找到的有关文献、史料按时间顺序排队进行分析，希望能看清毛泽东这段时间思想变化的轨迹。首先，据5月12日林克日记的记载：

"毛主席在同我谈话时说，目前全国已经争鸣和齐放起来，知识界争得最响。民主党派不那么响，工商界最先神气，章乃器、罗隆基、章伯钧、陈铭枢等人发言有取消党的领导的味道。资产阶级唯利是图、争名夺利的本质也有所暴露，像定息20年。自1956年算起可以说是一种典型。有敌视社会主义的情绪的某些人也有所表露。春天来到，各种蛇也开始动起来了。民主党派某些人及资产阶级某些人的鸣放，并不增加他们长期存在、共同监督的资本，相反某些言论会使它[他]们在群众中丧失威信，这样就不是长期共存而是短期共存了。张奚若谈得好，己不正焉[而]能正人者，未之有也。

毛主席还谈到教条主义与修正主义问题。他说，有一部分人有教条主义错误思想，但这些人大都是忠心耿耿为党为国的，就是看问题有左的片面性，他们克服了片面性会大进一步。他们所以宁左勿右，他们是要革命的。右倾机会主义的人则比较危险。

毛主席进一步谈到争鸣和齐放的限度是什么？限度就是不能火烧房子。批评应该：（1）有利于人民民主专政；（2）有利于发展社会主义建设；（3）有利于党的领导。而共产党的领导是有决定性的。

毛主席在谈到新闻自由问题时说：新闻就是要控制，新闻应该服从国家的经济的基础，不能像资本主义社会那样为无政府主义的经济服务。例如：1956年上半年农业合作化时，只能宣传发展合作化的方针，不能存在（宣传？）削减农业合作化的方针。党内存在两条方针就会为工作造成损失。……[此处几句字迹不清]更不允许煽动性报道。

目前有三方面情况不报道或加以控制：（1）肃反案件；（2）物价；（3）外交政策。

关于反社会主义言论，可以多登一些，这有利于我们"。

据此可以做出判断，毛泽东感到，鸣放中存在两个"危险"倾向："有取消党的领导的味道"，敌视社会主义的情绪"有所表露"。核查被点名的这几个人当时的言论，引起毛泽东注意的应该是章伯钧、章乃器关于改变机关党组制和要职要权的言论，陈铭枢和罗隆基改变学校党委制的言论，以及罗隆基要求给予民主党派"平等、独立、自由"的言论。于是，毛泽东提出了鸣放的三个"限度"，核心是党的领导。还有，毛泽东已经意识到"各种蛇"开始动了，又说"反社会主义言论，可以多登一些"，表明他这时就产生了"引蛇出洞"的念头。再有，对新闻报道提出三个禁区，说明毛泽东对局势的发展开始有些担心了。

不过，毛泽东此时还只是有些疑心，他并没有立即采取行动。从《人民日报》、《解放日报》的言论看，也尚未出现异常。陈云为中共中央起草了一份电报，其中指出：在经济建设和文化建设方面各种不合理的现象普遍存在，要求"各地各部门应在整风运动中发动群众予以揭露，组织力量，抓住重点，进行系统地检查、纠正"。这也丝毫没有脱离中共中央整风指示的框架。《人民日报》甚至指出："凡是闹事的地方，大都是官僚主义比较严重的地方；职工不能通过'团结-批评-团结'的正常方法去解决问题的时候，才被迫走闹事这条路"。从各方的文献材料看，至少到这时，毛泽东还没有做出新的决定。一直到13日，毛泽东也都没有召集过会议。

但是从5月14日起，事情开始有了变化。

5月10日的《解放日报》以刊登了上海22位中、小学教师座谈会的发言摘要。所载言论虽然数量很多（整整一版），但所提意见要温和得多，且没有涉及政治制度、干部人事制度、经济方针、历次运动遗留问题等。而毛泽东于5月14日要求刘少奇等几位领导人"过细"地阅读这张报纸，笔者认为，其用意还是在于说明发动整风的必要性，说明党内问题的严重性。或许毛泽东想以此证明发动整风运动的必要性，毛泽东在意识到危险倾向开始出现的同时，仍然认为执政党本身的官僚作风和腐败堕落也是危及政权的重要因素。

然而到了当晚，事情就起了一些变化。14日晚上9时至次日凌晨1时，毛泽东在中南海主持召开了中央政治局常委扩大会议，并通过了《关于报道党外人士对党政各方面工作的批评的指示》：

最近各地党外人士正在展开对于党、政各方面工作的批评，这是很好的现象，这不但会大大帮助我党的整风，消除同党外人士的隔阂，而且可以在群众中暴露右倾分子的面貌。我们党员对于党外人士的错误的批评，特别是对于右倾分子的言论，目前不要反驳，以便使他们畅所欲言。我们各地的报纸应该继续充分报导党外人士的言论，特别是对于右倾分子、反共分子的言论，必须原样地、不加粉饰地报导出来，使群众明了他们的面目，这对于教育群众、教育中间分子，有很大的好处。近来我们许多党报，对于一些反共的言论加以删节，是不妥当的，这实际上是帮助了右倾分子，并且使人感到是我们惧怕这些言论。这种现象，请你们立即加以纠正。

但是，在报导中，有三类言论必须加以领导和控制，即：（一）对于市场物价容易发生影响的消息和言论；（二）违背国家外交政策，易为帝国主义挑拨和利用的消息和言论，其中包括对苏联和人民民主国家的消息和言论；（三）涉及个别肃反案件具体事实的消息和言论。

从中可以看出，中共高层领导已经认识到，整风运动中暴露出一些"右倾分子"和"反共分子"，并认为应对这一现象的措施是让他们继续暴露，在报道时不作任何删节。这与毛泽东12日私下谈话的思路相同，"引"蛇出动的策略虽尚未形成，但呼之欲出；第三，区别使用"右倾分子"和"反共分子"这两个概念说明，在未来的斗争中，还是要区分两类不同性质的矛盾，前者属人民内部矛盾，后者属敌我矛盾；第四，对舆论的领导和控制还是限于毛泽东12日谈话指出的三个方面，只是顺序调整一下：物价、外交、肃反，显然是有些担心出现社会动乱。在5月16日召开的中共中央书记处会议上，邓小平进一步解释了中央的指示，他虽然使用了"右派"这个概念，但显然此时还是作为人民内部问题来处理的。

5月16日晚9时至次日凌晨1时20分，毛泽东再次召集政治局常委扩大会议。当天，毛泽东又起草了一个党内指示。文件分两个部分，第一部分仍然强调的是发动整风运动的宗旨，言语之间透出一种急迫的心情。毛泽东急于看到转变党内作风、密切党群关系、恢复党的威信的结果，以便按照原来的部署，在结束党内整风后，进行包括民主党派在内的其他各界整风。对于这一阶段的鸣放言论，毛泽东基本上是持肯定态度的，并有意保护大多数鸣放者的——他们毕竟是在毛的鼓动下站出来给党提意见的。

但是毛当时对哪些人属于"右倾分子"或"右派"是心中有数的——因为他们的言行超越了毛一贯坚持的政治界线。"最近一些天以来，社会上有少数带有反共情绪的人跃跃欲试，发表一些带有煽动性的言论，企图将正确处理解决人民内部矛盾、巩固人民民主专政、以利社会主义建设的正确方向，引导到错误方向去，此点请你们注意，放手让他们发表，并且暂时（几个星期内）不要批驳，使右翼分子在人民面前暴露其反动面目，过一个时期再研究反驳的问题"。与14日的指示相比，这段文字显得明确而严厉。说这些"右翼分子"或"右派"具有"反动面目"，"带有反共情绪"，又说他们"企图"把运动"引导到错误方向去"，表明毛泽东更加深了对问题严重性的认识。不仅"不要反驳"、"不加粉饰"、不要"删节"，而且还要"放手让他们发表"，表明运动进行到这时，中共高层开始酝酿反击"右派"了，"引蛇出洞"的策略也已露出端倪。

就在这一天，行动开始了。到5月16日，统战部召集的民主党派座谈会已经开了7次，按照原来的工作计划，应着手处理这些鸣放意见了。然而李维汉却突然宣布休会几天，成立一个小组，把与会者谈的问题加以排队，准备以后继续开会，理由是座谈会"对全国整风运动起了推动作用"。这一切反常举动表明，是民主党派座谈会的发言引起了毛泽东的警觉，时间应在12日。14日中央统一了思想并决定让右派继续暴露，从16日开始，"引蛇出洞"的策略正式实施——整风运动进入了第二阶段。

引蛇出洞：毛泽东亲自策划的"阳谋"

对于发动反右运动的策略，毛泽东后来公开讲："本报及一切党报，在5月8日至6月7日这个期间，执行了中共中央的指示。……让资产阶级及资产阶级知识分子发动这一场战争，报纸在一个期间内，不登或少登正面意见，对资产阶级反动右派的猖狂进攻不予回击，……使群众看得清清楚楚，什么人的批评是善意的，什么人的所谓批评是恶意的，从而聚集力量，等待时机成熟，实行反击。有人说，这是阴谋。我们说，这是阳谋。因为事先告诉了敌人：牛鬼蛇神只有让它们出笼，才好歼灭它们，毒草只有让他们出土，才便于锄掉"。

同前一次的做法一样，毛泽东在这里又改动了时间。中共中央的第一个指示明明是5月14日晚上做出的，毛却改成5月8日——民主党派座谈会就是这一天开始的。毛泽东这样说的目的，是要让人们以为中共中央（或他本人）早已料到民主党派座谈会上会有"右派言论"，是有意让他们这样鸣放的。如此，一方面把座谈会上令他感到不悦的人物说成是"牛鬼蛇神"，把那些"带有反共情绪"的发言定性为"毒草"就顺理成章了；另一方面，也可以表明这一切都是在他的预料之中的，以阻塞党内（特别是苏共）对他鼓动大鸣大放的"不慎行动"的质疑。至于说在提出双百方针时就已"安民告示"，更是强词夺理——只要把他一年来的讲话都翻出来看看，就一目了然了。毛泽东这样做，不仅可以避免被人指责为"言而无信"，更主要的是可以在苏共和中共干部面前掩盖他对中国社会情绪和局势发展的判断失误。正因为如此，他在5月中旬后才把全部精力投入到反右运动中，其热情和关注程度，比发动整风时有过之而无不及。

5月17日，《人民日报》发表评论，要求非党同志"大胆尖锐毫无保留地揭发我们各方面的缺点和错误，帮助党员进行整风"，形式主要是"邀请各方面的非党同志举行各种座谈会"。5月19日《人民日报》又发表了社论《继续争鸣，结合整风》："我们首先要充分地揭露人民内部的各种矛盾，这就应该让各个方面人们的各种不同的意见都讲出来，大家推心置腹，畅所欲言。这样才算真正地实现了'百家争鸣'，同时帮助了我们党的整风运动"。

5月17日晚，《人民日报》编辑部电话通知各地记者站："中央决定，从现在起，全国各省市都要开展鸣放，帮党整风。各民主党派，党内党外，什么话都可以讲，就是骂共产党的话也要让他们放出来，记者要按原话写。各记者站都要发整风鸣放稿件"。《人民日报》编辑部这个通知显然是按照中央的新精神传达的。5月18日晚，文化部也召集紧急会议，传达中共中央的新指示，而且，对于整风运动将要转向，省部级领导人已经心知肚明了。于是，各种"引蛇"和"钓鱼"的行动便大规模展开了。各单位都纷纷邀请民主党派和无党派民主人士举行座谈。目的就是要鼓动非党知识分子站出来讲话，给共产党"提意见"。

与此同时，毛泽东对鸣放运动的指示更加具体、严格。5月20日中共中央发出的《关于加强对当前运动的领导的指示》为各地党报的报道方针做出规定："右翼分子的反动言论"应以"那些能够充分暴露他们的反动面目的言论（越反动的越好）"为主；逐步增加中间分子和左翼分子有关批评右翼分子的持论公允的言论；各地党员要"立即着手分类研究右翼的反动言论和其他资产阶级论点"，"准备在适当时机"予以反驳和批判。所以，整风运动中被引出的"蛇"和被钓上的"鱼"，基本上就是5月16日中共中央确定了新方针到6月8日宣布全面反击右派期间冒出的人物和言论。

实际上，真正的大鸣大放也确实出现在整风运动的第二阶段。这一时期针对共产党的批评意见和言论，不仅数量猛然增加，范围迅速扩大，而且情绪日益激昂，言词愈加刺激。毛泽东后来对这时的情形有一个概括：少数右派和反动分子一时间闹得"天昏地暗，日月无光"，"民盟、农工最坏。章伯钧、罗隆基拼命做颠覆活动，野心很大，党要扩大，政要平权，积极夺取教育权，说半年或一年，天下就将大乱。毛泽东混不下去了，所以想辞职。共产党内部分裂，不久将被推翻。他们的野心极大。完全是资本主义路线，承认社会主义是假的"。又说："民盟在百家争鸣过程整风过程中所起的作用特别恶劣。有组织，有计划，有纲领，有路线，都是自外于人民的，是反党反社会主义的。还有农工民主党，一模一样。这两个党在这次惊涛骇浪中特别突出。风浪就是章罗同盟造起来的"。这些资产阶级右派人物"呼风唤雨，推涛作浪，或策划于密室，或点火于基层，上下串连，八方呼应，以天下大乱、取而代之、逐步实行、终成大业为时局估计和最终目的"。

现在看来，毛泽东的这些看法无疑是过于偏激和敏感了。不过，"引蛇出洞"的结果，确实造成了混乱的局面。这主要表现为民主党派和知识界的鸣放言论，从北京大学开始并引向全国的学生民主运动，共产党组织的战斗力和影响力骤然下降。在知识界和大学生轰轰烈烈地进行大鸣大放时，中国的城市和农村也呈现出一种动荡的局面。中国最大的工业城市上海甚至出现工人闹事的情况，这说明"无产阶级"的不满情绪已经十分严重，更加危险的是，这种情绪正在与知识界和学生界的鸣放走向合流。党内的状况也很令人担忧。大部分党员干部对鸣放存在不同程度的抵触和不满情绪，有的公开抵制鸣放，有的态度消极、情绪低落，也有少数人甚至同"右派"站在一起。党员思想混乱、精神苦闷，党的组织严重涣散、威信扫地。这两种情况都是毛泽东不愿看到的，因为这反映了同一个问题——党的号召力和战斗力受到严重损害。这几种严重形势和倾向的交错汇合，已经构成了对共产党统治和社会安定的严重威胁，从而引起了毛泽东极大的注意和担忧，对推动他下决心反击右派起了重要作用。

决心反击：毛泽东再次诉诸阶级斗争

5月中旬毛泽东发现民主党派的言论有"危险企图"和"错误倾向"后，对于阶级斗争和思想动向的敏锐感受和观察，促使他下决心继续鼓励鸣放，直至"引蛇出洞"。那时毛泽东还没有放弃整风的打算，对于将要开展的反击右派运动，也还没有上升到阶级斗争的高度，他还想再观察一段时间。他要向党内和社会主义阵营内的怀疑论者证明"百花齐放、百家争鸣"方针的英明正确。然而，"引蛇出洞"后二十多天的风云变幻令他十分失望，由失望转而愤怒，毛泽东决心结束党内整风，而开展以阶级斗争为纲的反右运动。

毛泽东是什么时候下定决心的？种种迹象说明，至少到5月18日，毛泽东和中共领导人感到，当时的社会乱象还不至于打断国家机器和社会生活的正常运转，毛泽东还没有决定要采取任何重大措施或举动。同时毛泽东等人认为，现在虽然"右翼分子的言论颇为猖狂，但有些人的反动面目还没有暴露或者暴露得不够"，为了"好好掌握形势，设法团结多数中间力量，逐渐孤立右派，争取胜利"，需要"继续登载右翼分子的反动言论"，"暂时不宜过多"反驳，"党员仍以暂不发言为好"，并要求"不要到处点火"，并要求结合5月14日和16日两电"一并研究执行"。这就说明，5月20日指示不过是对此前的14日和16日两次电报的补充和强调，而没有做出新的决定。报纸的宣传方针，也主要是团结中间派，暴露和孤立右派，还没有提出反击右派的问题。在同秘书林克谈话时，毛泽东也说："什么拥护人民民主专政，拥护人民政府，拥护共产党和拥护共产党的领导，都是骗人的，一切都不要相信。他们违背了愿意接受共产党领导的诺言，他们意图摆脱共产党的领导"。显然，对民主党派违背诺言、向共产党争权的意图，毛泽东耿耿于怀，本来他邀请民主党派帮助共产党整风的前提，在很大程度上就是相信他们愿意接受共产党的领导，到头来"上当受骗"。毛泽东对此深感愤怒，决心对"右派人物"予以反击。但到目前为止，毛泽东还没有把这个问题看得很严重。

5月23日刘少奇主持召开的中共中央政治局扩大会议，关于整风运动的工作部署仍然没有超出中央5月中旬指示的框架。彭真向北京市传达政治局扩大会议精神时，在报告中继续强调整风，特别是开门整风的必要性和重要性，肯定绝大多数鸣放意见是正确的，"有些人的批评是从右的观点出发的，是从资产阶级观点出发的，但是右的方面的意见也可以起积极的作用，毒草也可以作肥料，起好的作用，事物总是在矛盾的斗争中发展的"。"对于一切意见，应该耐心地、冷静地倾听，不管是正确的还是错误的，不管是好的坏的……就是对于错误的、甚至反动的意见，目前也还不要忙着进行批驳，以免阻塞言路"。应该说，彭真所说的，大体是5月14日到23日期间中共中央的基本立场和方针。

到此，可以对"引蛇出洞"策略实施后的整风方针进行一下总结了。这里包含了两层意思：第一，鸣放中出现了错误甚至是严重错误的言论和意见，并且对多数中间派产生了巨大影响，因此必须坚决回击和批判这些右派言论。由于这些人物和言论有很大影响，且其反动性暴露得还不彻底，因此应该采取欲擒故纵的策略，让他们走到极端，走到反面，才利于分化瓦解。但是，第二，这个斗争还是在人民内部，还是属于思想领域，就是说仍然在整风运动的范围内，只是从党内跨到了党外——这是毛泽东原打算在党内整风结束后进行的工作。因此，整风的基本原则和内容都没有改变，改变的暂时只是策略。然而，在5月底的这几天，一切都改变了。

笔者注意到，毛泽东没有参加这两天的政治局会议（这也可以说明会议没有新内容），他正在关心的无疑就是北京大学出现的新情况，特别是学生运动可能导致的后果。那几天，毛泽东不断派他的秘书陈伯达、胡乔木和林克去北大了解情况，每天向他汇报。据林克回忆，当时"毛的心情是沉重的，甚至是忧虑的。他关心的是国家政权的稳定，而不是个人地位的安危。有一次他对我说：你看我们的政权能不能稳得住，会不会乱？"毛泽东的确对局势做出了相当严重的估计，他认为清华大学的党组织已经垮掉了，"几十个支部瓦解了"，而且几乎每一个大一些的学校和工厂的"知识分子中间都有右派"，他们"就是纳吉的群众，是小纳吉"。他甚至设想了最坏的情况——打算再上延安。毛泽东想出的应对办法，就是一方面继续共产党整风，一方面开展一场反击右派的运动。

　　在注意整风鸣放的新动向同时，毛泽东继续修改他在国务会议上的讲话稿，并于5月24日改出第二稿。其中重要修改和补充有：增加了关于知识分子必须完成世界观上的根本转变的一大段论述；关于阶级斗争的论述改为："在我国，虽然社会主义改造已经基本结束，大规模的群众性的阶级斗争已经基本结束，但是资产阶级还存在，小资产阶级刚刚在改造。无产阶级和资产阶级思想之间的斗争，还是尖锐的，长期的，有时甚至是很激烈的"。总之，强调思想斗争的尖锐性，强调阶级斗争的复杂性和长期性，强调批判修正主义的重要性，是这次最主要的修改。

　　就在25日这一天，刘少奇主持的人大常委会七十次会议讨论，决定将人大四次会议从原定的6月3日推迟到20日召开，毛泽东和中共领导人这时的注意力已经被学生运动的发展势头所吸引。也是在25日这一天，毛泽东和中共主要领导人一起接见了出席青年团三大的全体代表。毛泽东发表了"一切离开社会主义的言论行动是完全错误的"的讲话，语气中流露出来的是警告和暗示。简短的几句话，几近捅破窗户纸，反击右派的意思昭然若揭。参加接见的薄一波后来说，这个讲话是"反击右派的公开动员令"。这样说也许不大确切——毕竟还没有宣布开始反右派运动，不过，一场反右派运动的风暴已经浓云密布、雷声隐隐了。

　　这些都说明，这时毛泽东已经感到了事情的严重性：共产党的执政地位受到了真正的威胁。这个感受，体现在他对最高国务会议讲话稿的修改中。5月25日，毛泽东改出了讲话第三稿，并在批语中特别注明："我对百花齐放部分有一些重要修改"。其中最重要的就是：讲到关于意识形态的阶级斗争问题时，增加了"阶级斗争还没有结束"，以及"在这一方面，社会主义与资本主义谁胜谁负的问题还没有解决"的说法；增加了辨别香花和毒草的六条政治标准，并说"各民主党派对共产党提意见，作批评，要看那些意见、批评是否合乎上述六个政治标准。如果不合，那就会丧失监督的资格"。可以看出，这些修改已经是在为新的战斗做舆论准备了。

　　5月26日晚毛泽东召集刘、周、朱、邓、陈等人开会，听取各省、市、自治区党委负责人汇报。从第二天召开的省市区书记会议上的发言可以看出，中共对国内局势的估计已经相当严重。邓小平的报告讲述了中共中央政治局的考虑和部署。邓说，整风运动开始的目的是搞党内的三大主义，因为问题很严重，最初用的是内外夹攻的办法。运动开展以后，绝大多数的意见是正确的，有益的，

90％对我们有帮助，"但很显然有部分右派跟我们争领导权。这个斗争不只是在思想领域，已经扩及政治范围。有人提出纲领很谨慎的，不是打倒共产党，而是要我们退出阵地。各地都看得出，以上海、北京为典型。因此中央不能不做斗争，他们已经（这样）做了"。因此，"党内外归结起来一个目的，加强党的领导"。接着说到运动的方法，邓指出：关键是能不能团结中间派。右派在争取中间势力，左派、我们也在争取中间势力。我们争取中间势力有两条：一是改正自己的错误，二是孤立右派。用右派教育中间派，使中间派知道需要同右派划清界限。邓说，现在"右派大体都出来了"，如章伯钧、章乃器、龙云等等。邓指出右派活动现在有两个倾向，一是"向基层发展（康生插话：《光明日报》昨天对北大的报道有动员性质）"，二是"暗地组织活动的迹象明显了"。根据这些情况，6月1日，毛泽东又对讲话稿作了一次较大改动，其中增加的新提法是："我们在批判教条主义的时候，必须同时注意对修正主义的批判"。"它比教条主义有更大的危险性"。而且指出，修正主义是资产阶级"向马克思主义进行斗争"的最好助手。

上述材料表明，到5月底6月初，毛泽东要进行反右运动的设想又进了一步：同右派的斗争已经不是整风的一部分，而是与共产党整风并行的一场"阶级斗争"；这场斗争已经不再局限于思想领域，而是有了政治斗争的内容；在理论上和口头上还没有放弃整风，但是修正主义的危险性已经提到首位，而这些恰恰不在整风的范围内。还可以看出，中共对国内事态发展的严重性也有了进一步认识，现在的问题不在于民主党派和知识界的言论——他们的话已大体说完，阵线已基本清楚，右派只是极少数；也不在于学生运动本身——那里不会发生大问题，因为右派也是少数。最危险的就是民主党派和知识界的煽动性言论，与波及全国的学运风潮汇合起来，再同时涌向社会，影响到工厂、农村和中小学，其结果将是"天下大乱"，将会真正危及共产党的领导。毛泽东这时开始担心：中国"有出匈牙利事件的某些危险"了。这就是毛决定提前反击的真正原因。开展一场反右斗争的基本方针已经确定，主攻方向也已经明确，余下的就是何时开始战斗，如何开始战斗了。

5月27日省市区书记会的召开标志着新方针的确定，此后就是审时度势进行落实的问题了。首先是继续在党政机关和民主党派中鼓励继续鸣放。虽然党内讨论时已经意识到危险的存在，但在表面上社会的鸣放浪潮还在继续。各地党报也在宣传继续"广开言路，继续贯彻大'放'大'鸣'的方针"，对中央"引蛇出洞"

的斗争策略加以有意无意的呼应。与此同时，反击右派的斗争已经在进行各种准备了。

按照中共中央的部署，从6月1日开始，《人民日报》刊登反驳右派的报道和文章的数量明显增加。除了舆论准备，基层单位党委也接到了任务。"市委负责同志"对清华、北大、师大和北农大四所重点大学的党委书记说："你们几所大学老教师多，反党反社会主义的、翘尾巴的专家、教授、民主党派成员多，有影响的人物多，要用各种办法，制造适当气氛，'引蛇出洞'，让他们把毒都吐出来，以便聚而歼之"。最后又交待说："时间不多了，很快就要发动全面反击，反击开始后就没有人'鸣放'了"。6月3日彭真向北京市基层干部传达中央新方针时指出：当前有两个斗争，一个是党内的思想整风，另一个就是阶级斗争，并强调"这一时期主要是"搞阶级斗争。彭真指出，问题的严重性就在于，右派正在煽动农民、工人和学生。在如此激烈的斗争面前，他呼吁工人不要再闹事，而应该"停止内战，一致对外"。

6月4日毛泽东在同林克谈话时又提出几种新说法：第一，关于右派的性质，"资产阶级和民主党派中的右派表现得最猖狂，带有一种最后挣扎的性质，他们和蒋介石与帝国主义有共同点"。第二，关于双百方针，"百花齐放、百家争鸣这个口号是无产阶级性的，如果这个口号执行的结果不能驳倒谬误，整倒右派，那么这个口号是为资产阶级服务的，这是反动的"。第三，"右派有些冲昏头脑，以为中间派是属于他们的，其实是做梦"。说右派是"最后挣扎"，与蒋介石"有共同点"，这显然就不是人民内部的问题，更不是思想领域的问题了。这种认识为后来的反右斗争采取"急风暴雨"的方式奠定了思想基础。对双百方针这种后退一步的说法，一方面是毛泽东为实行双百方针的"失败"寻找的一个台阶，另一方面也表明，他准备放弃或暂时收起这一方针了。对敌我双方力量对比做出左派已经占有优势的判断，则意味着全面进攻可以开始了。现在只是要寻找一个合适时机。

6月5日晚毛泽东召集周恩来、彭真和罗瑞卿谈整风问题。当天，毛泽东为中共中央起草了《关于加紧进行整风的指示》，第一次明确提出了反击右派的行动安排："这是一场大规模的思想战争和政治战争"，"必须注意争取中间派，团结左派，以便时机一成熟，即动员他们反击右派和反动分子"，"你们应争取主动，并准备适当应付"。按照毛泽东的这个设想，大约10天以后，也就是他反复修改的讲话稿发表之际，反右运动将全面展开。然而，两个突发事件导致战斗提前打响了。这就是著名的"六六六事件"和"卢郁文事件"。

6月6日上午，民盟副主席章伯钧、史良在南河沿文化俱乐部邀集曾昭伦、吴景超、黄药眠、费孝通、钱伟长、陶大镛等六位教授讨论时局。章伯钧和六教授在会上究竟说了什么话，目前没有文献证据，无从核实，但有两点是可以肯定的：第一，与会者都认为由于学生闹事，大字报上街，共产党面临危局；第二，民主党派此时应该站出来，承担起收拾局面、平息内乱的责任。毛泽东对此事的判断是："他们是反动的社会集团，利令智昏，把无产阶级的绝对优势，看成了绝对劣势。到处点火可以煽动工农，学生的大字报便于接管学校，大鸣大放，一触即发，天下顷刻大乱，共产党马上完蛋，这就是6月6日章伯钧向北京六教授所作目前形势的估计"。毛泽东早就认为在民主党派中民盟是"最坏的"。反右运动开始以后，这次聚会就被作为右派阴谋活动的典型案例受到批判。

恰在此时，发生了"卢郁文事件"。毛泽东喜出望外，对胡乔木和吴冷西说："这封匿名信好就好在它攻击的是党外人士，而且是民革成员；好就好在它是匿名的，不是某个有名有姓的人署名。过去几天我就一直考虑什么时候抓住什么机会发动反击。现在机会来了，马上抓住它，用《人民日报》社论的形式发动反击右派的斗争。社论的题目是《这是为什么？》在读者面前提出这样的问题，让大家来思考"。于是，反击右派运动的号令就这样产生了，一场波及全国、影响数十万人命运乃至共和国发展方向的反右派运动就这样开始了。

最后要说的是，毛泽东两次在文件或文章中修改时间，目的自然是证明自己有先见之明，但他没有想到的另一个后果是，后来的历史研究者也堕入迷雾，认为他发动反右是早有预谋的。历史开了一个玩笑。

3.
社会主义在中国的理想、尝试与异化
——基于唯物史观的一点考察
IDEAL, EFFORT, AND ALIENATION OF SOCIALISM IN CHINA: AN EXPLORATION FROM A MATERIALISTIC VIEW OF HISTORY

杨奎松 YANG KUISONG

Abstract

What is socialism? Can post-Maoist China still be considered a socialist state? Perhaps no easy answer exists for such questions today. This paper aims to address this problem by looking at socialism in China from a materialistic view of history and by examining the twists and turns in the development of socialism over time.

Based on a brief survey of the origins and variations in the European socialist ideal, it is important to recognize that despite differences in ideology, the social democratic and Communist parties in fact shared a common set of concerns, i.e., a correction to the economic and social inequalities under capitalism. As long as one accepts shared property, a planned economy, and the distribution of products according to work as effective means to combat the ills of capitalism, they should, in general, be considered part of the socialist movement.

Other than passively receiving Soviet indoctrination, most early members of the Chinese Communist Party did not systematically read Marxist traditional thought and many were especially attracted to the economic prosperity under the authoritarian Stalinist state. The latter, however, was achieved at the expense of sacrificing the most fundamental Marxist concerns—the freedom and liberation of the individual.

Similarly, Mao Zedong believed that although the socio-economic prerequisites for socialism hardly existed in China, he could nevertheless create them through the coercive power of the state. Stressing personal willpower, Mao overlooked the material reality of Chinese society and eventually concluded that universal equality could only be guaranteed via continuous class struggle. In so doing, however, Mao only succeeded in forcefully imposing an alienated notion of equality on the Chinese people.

The tragic consequences during the Great Leap Forward and other political movements exposed the serious institutional defects of Stalinist socialism: the extreme irresponsibility of cadres with respect to the disastrous policies and the lack of a means of self-correction due to the fervent personality worship, government control of the media, and corruption. Given similar precedents in history, intellectual debates and political practices in China today must continue to take into account both economic development and social equality.

社会主义在中国的理想、尝试与异化
——基于唯物史观的一点考察

什么是社会主义？今天，在我们这个仍旧自称是社会主义的国家里，大概已经没有什么人能够有一定说服力地给出关于这个问题的答案来了。因为，无论是按照马克思的共产主义初级阶段的设想，还是按照斯大林定的社会主义标准，今天的中国在各方面都和过去所说的那个社会主义沾不上边儿了。不仅如此，由于西方的，乃至世界各国的资本主义，早就被社会主义理念所改造，大都变得半资本主义、半社会主义化了，因此，许多外国人对当今中国的印象，多半可以一言以蔽之，叫做"比资本主义还资本主义"。换言之，当今中国，更像十九世纪末二十世纪初的欧洲国家，或是二十世纪中期那些处于大规模工业化过程中的东方资本主义国家，几乎看不出社会主义的样子了。

其实，从放弃毛泽东的那一套办法，开始实行改革开放之日起，这个问题就一直在困扰着中共领导人。人们一度赞同改变毛时代的许多做法，赞成改革开放，同时却又被毛时代通行的种种观念所束缚，放不开自己的手脚。直到继毛之后成为中共最高领导人的邓小平发了话，这种纠结困顿的局面才终于被打破。邓小平的态度干脆明了：第一，什么叫社会主义？我们过去对这个问题的认识是不完全清楚的；第二，现在不要争什么姓社、姓资，先干起来再说。

但是，问题仍然存在，并且不断地引起争论。中国这个明明不是社会主义的国家，却依旧坚称自己从事的是社会主义事业，怀念毛泽东时代的人则认定中国搞的是资本主义，而大多数资本主义国家的政府却拒绝承认中国与自己是同类，它们仍旧从意识形态上，甚至从政治制度上认为中国属于异类。显然，要解决这个混沌不堪的问题，首先应当要解决何为社会主义的问题，并应考察它在中国的命运和变化。本文即试图利用中共所信奉的唯物史观，对此稍做研究和考察。

一、社会主义是什么？

众所周知，社会主义并非是共产党人的专利，而且也不能把它简单地与马克思主义混为一谈。作为一种理想社会的代名词，社会主义式的幻想甚至可以追溯到两千年以前，从欧洲古希腊柏拉图的理想国，到中国春秋时期孔老夫子的大同说，古代思想家们早就设计过人类理想社会的各种蓝图。我们今天所理解的社会主义，固然直接起源于近代欧洲思想家对资本主义种种弊端的理性批判，但他们所设想的解决方案，实际上仍旧集中了人类过去对于未来理想国的一切幻想。比如反对阶级压迫，反对贫富悬殊，相信导致社会不平等的关键在于私有财产制度，主张建立公有制，组织劳动公社，有计划地安排生产，大家团结互助，每个人既从事脑力劳动，又从事体力劳动，各尽所能，按劳分配，甚至各尽所能，各取所需，等等。总之，近代欧洲社会主义者渴望的理想社会中，再没有剥削压迫，再没有高低贵贱，再没有尔虞我诈，"人人平等，人人自由，人人是兄弟"。[1]

马克思和恩格斯的社会主义区别于古代乌托邦理想和近代欧洲社会主义的关键，在于它发现了资本主义大工业所带来的生产力井喷式的发展趋势。在他们看来："社会分裂为剥削阶级和被剥削阶级、统治阶级和被压迫阶级，是以前生产不大发展的必然结果"。[2] 换言之，在他们看来，历史上人类之所以无法找到消除压迫和剥削的有效途径，根本上是受到生产力发展水平的局限，人类物质财富无法达到极大丰富，和用来满足一切人的需要。

而资本主义大工业的发展使人类一夜之间有了呼风唤雨的能力，资本主义生产过剩危机的接连出现更使他们相信：在现代生产力已经高度发展的情况下，"某一特殊的社会阶级对生产资料和产品的占有，从而对政治统治、教育垄断和精神领导的占有，不仅成为多余的，而且成为经济、政治和精神发展的障碍"了。"这个阶段现在已经达到了"。新的生产力的强劲发展趋势，"不仅可能保证一切社会成员有富足的和一天比一天充裕的物质生活，而且还可能保证他们的体力和智力获得充分的自由的发展和运用"。如此一来，它也就为人类实现生产资料的社会占有，进而消灭阶级，实现各尽所能，各取所需的共产主义社会，提供了最坚实的物质基础。[3]

马克思并非不了解资本主义的历史进步性。他非常清楚，资本主义的民主政治制度是推翻了中世纪封建等级制度的一种革命性的结果，它第一次创造了人生而平等的社会政治法律制度，给予了每个人应有的政治自由与平等权利。也正是这样一种制度，给资本主义社会条件下的人提供了自由发展的机遇和广大的发展空间，从而也极大地推动了人类生产力水平前所未有的增长。但是，资本主义的早期发展以其不受控制的弱肉强食、优胜劣汰的残酷竞争法则，也给了马克思等理想家们强烈的道德刺激。因为这种权利平等的获得，对那些没有任何资本不得不为糊口而每日奔波的劳苦大众来说，明显地不具有太多的意义。由蒸汽机催生的欧洲资本主义的生产力，到马克思提出其理论设想的时候，才不过四五十年的时间。在这四五十年的时间里，马克思看到的是大工业迅速兴起所带来的社会贫富严重分化的情况：大批中间阶级破产，产业工人数量猛增，劳资双方持续冲突，而大量过剩的产品即使被毁掉，也不会用来改善工人们极端贫困的生活……。因此，马克思、恩格斯等所有的社会主义理想家几乎都相信，最重要的还不是政治平等的问题，而是如何实现经济即分配平等的问题。要实现分配的平等，就必须要解决对经济资源占有的不平等问题，即非要以公有制来取代私有制不可。

按照马克思的唯物史观，这个时候的资本主义生产方式，理应还没有到灭亡的时候。第一，资本主义正在发展上升的初期，而"无论哪一个社会形态，在它们所能容纳的全部生产力发挥出来以前，是决不会灭亡的；而新的更高的生产关系，在它存在的物质条件在旧社会的胎胞里成熟以前，是决不会出现的"。[4] 第二，每一个特定社会发展阶段中的对立阶级，"自由民和奴隶、贵族和平民、领主和农奴、行会师傅和帮工，一句话，压迫者和被压迫者"，都注定会随着整个社会受到革命改造而"同归于尽"。[5] 代表着新的生产关系和新的生产力的阶级，注定将会从原有的对立阶级之外的第三种力量中产生出来。而在资本家阶级和产业工人阶级之外，显然还没有这样一个新生力量产生出来。

但是，马克思没有把他的唯物史观坚持到底。尽管资本主义工业化的进程才刚刚开始，尽管在资本家阶级和产业工人阶级这两大对立阶级以外的第三种力量，还远未产生出来，马克思却已经认定：（1）资本主义制度因为容纳不下生产力的进一步发展会很快崩溃；（2）现代"整个人类奴役制就包含在工人同生产的关系中"，因此，他相信，只要解放了产业工人阶级，人类最后的奴役制度也就将被彻底消灭了。

为什么欧洲这个时候文化程度很低的产业工人完全可以承担起创造新的生产力和新的更高级社会的历史责任？恩格斯的解释是，因为除了个别技术性的问题以外，在现代化大工业的条件下，并不需要特别复杂的管理和技术知识，普通工人足以应付各种生产和管理的工作，"没有其他'有教养的人'也是完全过得去的"。[6] 正是基于这样一种逻辑，马克思、恩格斯终其一生都在努力

"使现代无产阶级意识到自身的地位和需要，意识到自身解放的条件"，从而组织成为一个强大的革命力量，以推翻资本主义。[7]

不过，除了这一具体方法问题外，马克思及恩格斯对未来社会理想形态的设想，他们的基本认识与早期思想家们的构想，严格说来却并无任何实质性的区别。

马克思和恩格斯是如何具体描述他们的理想社会的呢？他们把无产阶级革命，夺取政权，改造社会，到最终实现共产主义社会，划分成了三个历史阶段，即：

（一）革命的转变时期。

马克思和恩格斯写道："在资本主义社会和共产主义社会之间，有一个从前者变为后者的革命转变时期。同这个时期相适应的也有一个政治上的过渡时期，这个时期的国家只能是无产阶级的革命专政"。"无产阶级将利用自己的政治统治，一步一步地夺取资产阶级的全部资本，把开发生产工具集中在国家即组织成为统治阶级的无产阶级手里，并且尽可能快地增加生产力的总量"。"这个专政不过是达到消灭一切阶级和进入无阶级社会的过渡"。实际上，这个时期将是短暂的，"国家真正作为整个社会的代表所采取的第一个行动，即以社会的名义占有生产资料，同时也是它作为国家所采取的最后一个独立行动"。也就是说，"它在消灭了这种（资本主义）生产关系的同时，也就消灭了阶级对立和阶级本身的存在条件，从而消灭了它自己这个阶级的统治"。"对人的统治将由对物的管理和对生产过程的领导所代替"。[8]

（二）共产主义社会第一阶段（即社会主义社会）。

马克思和恩格斯写道：这个阶段，人们将"通过有计划地利用和进一步发展现有的巨大生产力，在人人都必须劳动的条件下，生活资料、享受资料、发展和表现一切体力和智力所需的资料，都将同等地、愈益充分地交归社会全体成员支配"。但是，"我们这里所说的是这样的共产主义社会，它不是在它自身基础上已经发展了的，恰好相反，是刚刚从资本主义社会中产生出来的，因此它在各方面，在经济、道德和精神方面都还带着它脱胎出来的那个旧社会的痕迹"。所以，这时还只能实行形式上平等，实质上不平等的按劳分配的原则。[9]

（三）共产主义社会的高级阶段。

马克思和恩格斯写道：只有"在共产主义社会高级阶段上，在迫使人们奴隶般地服从分工的情形已经消失，从而脑力劳动和体力劳动的对立也随之消失之后；在劳动已经不仅仅是谋生的手段，而且本身成了生活的第一需要之后；在随着个人的全面发展生产力也增长起来，而集体财富的一切源泉都充分涌流之后，——只有在那个时候，才能完成超出资产阶级法权的狭隘眼界，社会才能在自己的旗帜上写上：各尽所能，按需分配！"那时，"任何人都没有特定的活动范围，每个人都可以在任何部门内发展，社会调节着整个生产，因而使我有可能随我自己的心愿今天干这事，明天干那事，上午打猎、下午捕鱼、傍晚从事畜牧，晚饭后从事批判，但并不因此就使我成为一个猎人、渔夫、牧人或批判者"。[10]

在这里，我们可以看出，马克思的社会主义，或共产主义理想，包含着三个核心的观点。

第一是生产力进化的观点，即是认定社会主义，特别是共产主义社会，一定是人类社会生产力发展的最高阶段。一切理想的人类憧憬，都只有在那样一种生产力的水平上，在社会物质财富无限丰富的条件下，才有实现的可能。因此，这样的社会理想在资本主义工业化出现之前只是一种空想，它必须建立在资本主义大工业生产力的基础之上，是资本主义生产关系再也容纳不下新的生产力发展的产物。就这一点而言，邓小平坚信只有富的社会主义，没有穷的社会主义，认定社会主义的关键标志就是生产力水平高于资本主义，因而非发展生产力，不能实现社会主义，与马克思主义在理论上并无不合。

第二是阶级斗争的观点，即是认定社会主义的实现，必须经过阶级斗争，而且必须由无产阶级来取得政权，经过一个阶段的革命专政时期，完成剥夺资产阶级和消灭私有制的过程，才能进入到共产主义的第一阶段，即社会主义阶段，并只有经过社会主义的发展过程，才能实现共产主义。就社会主义必须经过一个革命的过渡时期，即无产阶级专政时期这一点，邓小平强调无产阶级和劳动人民当家作主，也与马克思的说法有某种契合之处。

第三是人的解放的观点，即是认定人是因私有制的出现和阶级的产生，而失去了人之作为人理应拥有的自由，最终亦必将因私有制的废除和阶级的消亡，而将人从财产、宗教及种种政治和社会的束缚与异化中解放出来。对于这方面的问题，一心想着解放生产力的邓小平严格说来还没有认真考虑过。而这恰恰是马克思、恩格斯和后来落后国家共产党人之间在观念上存在的一个最为明显的分歧。

作为欧洲历代注重人性、人道与人权的进步思想家的继承者，马克思和恩格斯对资本主义社会的全部批判，和对人类未来理想社会的全部设想，都是以人的彻底解放为出发点的。他们以极大的热情关注于人的自由和社会发展的关系的研究，对阶级社会所造成的人性扭曲、劳动异化、阶级压迫等等，深恶痛绝。他们显然相信，原始社会作为"氏族的根本原则"的自由、平等、博爱，也必定会"在更高级形式上""复活"于共产主义社会。用恩格斯的话来说，就是："管理上的民主，社会中的博爱，权利的平等，普及的教育，将揭开社会的下一个更高的阶段，经验、理智和科学正在不断向这个阶段努力。这将是古代氏族的自由、平等和博爱的复活，但却是在更高级形式上的复活"。[11]

显而易见，如果我们不把马克思、恩格斯早年所强调的实现共产主义或社会主义理想社会的手段也当成是他们所憧憬的理想社会本身的话，他们谈论的共产主义或社会主义的美好之处，与欧洲古代和近代理想家的追求并无不同。而且，他们对理想社会本质的理解与认识，实际上也是对欧洲自中世纪以来进步思想家为人的解放所提出的奋斗目标的继承。

三、欧洲人当年怎么做？

在马克思、恩格斯相继去世后，欧洲的社会主义运动逐渐分化成了社会民主党和共产党两大派别。欧洲社会主义运动的公开分裂，表面上似乎是人们对第一次世界大战的态度和立场不同造成的，实际上却主要是双方在要不要用革命手段推翻本国资产阶级政权这一问题上观点迥异的结果。

对于要不要用革命手段，即用暴力和强权的办法，来改造社会的问题，之所以会形成如此大的意识形态上的分歧与对立，其实在相当程度上反映出了处于资本主义不同发展阶段上的人们对自由民主等观念认识的巨大差别。

列宁主义者通常会把这一分裂归因于资产阶级改良主义的影响，但是，稍微注意一下历史就会发觉，马克思、恩格斯写作《共产党宣言》时，欧洲改良主义的主张同样存在，却远不如《共产党宣言》的革命主张传播速度快和广。事实很清楚，社会改良主张在欧洲影响的强弱，是与这个社会的发达程度成正比的。资本主义越不发达，社会贫富分化和阶级对立越严重，它的影响力就越小。反之亦然。二十世纪初列宁和他领导的布尔什维克，所以能够在俄国成功推动和坚持暴力革命，也正是因为当时沙皇俄国正处在和1848年马克思、恩格斯写《共产党宣言》同样的时代——资本主义工业革命的时期，一样社会贫富悬殊，阶级分化和阶级对立现象严重。

与此相反，恩格斯晚年的欧洲，工会合法了，议会选举了，私人占有股份化了，工人生活及劳资关系改善了，第二国际的领导人，甚至连同恩格斯本人，也感受到欧洲大部分地区自由民主制度的生长所带来的政治压力，因而不能不开始考虑通过和平选举和议会斗争的方法，争取使旧社会"和平地长入新社会"去了。[12] 一方面是欧洲多数比较发达的资本主义国家出现了政治民主化和"工人贵族化"的趋向，一方面是沙皇俄国专制独裁、社会分化日趋严重，欧洲多数国家工人政党及其第二国际走上议会民主道路，俄国布尔什维克另立第三国际，必欲诉诸暴力革命，两者分道扬镳，实难避免。

比较二十世纪早期政治上公开对立的第二国际和第三国际或可看出，两者的根本区别在于如何看待资本主义制度所带来的权利平等和自由。由于资本主义制度的建立，中世纪封建社会等级制度被完全打破，人们已经初步得到了起点的平等，即人权天赋，政治民主，机会均等，权利平等。法律面前人人平等已成社会信条并溶入人们的日常生活，要破坏这一切，哪怕只是口头上主张重新将社会划分成治人者和被治者，一部分人有权剥夺另一部分人的自由，在许多资本主义较发达的国家，都是注定要被多数民众所唾弃的。所谓社会主义，对于第二国际的社会党人来说，既是起点的平等，也是结果的平等，没有前者，就没有后者，二者不可偏废。

与此相反，以苏联为首的落后国家的共产党人，因为处在资本主义工业化初期，从未真正经历过民主生活已日常化的较发达的资本主义，他们更多地感受到的还是旧式的专制压迫和资本主义工业早期的残酷竞争所带来的阶级对立与阶级冲突。因此，剥夺并压制压迫者，在他们看来是天经地义的。非如此，便不能实现分配的平等。故他们看重和追求的，只是结果的平等，而为了实现结果，即分配的平等，人和人的权利绝不能平等，因为必须要压制被推倒的统治阶层，使之不能反抗。也就是说，至少在相当长的时期里，阶级斗争和阶级专政还必须存在，对于不同的人群而言，权利必须是不平等的。

正是这种不同社会发展程度所决定的不同认识，导致了集合在两个国际组织下同样主张社会主义的政党，意见根本分歧。第二国际相信，必须在尊重每个人的人权与自由的基础上，通过民主的程序，逐步用社会主义取代资本主义；而第三国际却主张以暴易暴，相信唯有通过阶级革命和共产党的专政，才能打碎资产阶级的国家机器，创造新的社会制度，由被压迫者转而压迫过去的压迫者，才能实现经济和社会平等的目的。

但是，双方在实现未来理想社会的路径和手段问题上观点相左，却不意味着它们对未来理想的追求，和对社会主义理想社会的构想，也截然两样。至少在理论上，他们之间的分歧在相当长的一段时间里并不十分明显。

按照斯大林的说法，社会主义社会的基本特征至少包含四方面内容：一是实现了生产资料公有制（包括全民和集体两种形式）；二是劳动人民当家作主，再不存在人剥削人的情况；三是国家有计划地发展生产，没有经济危机；四是社会实行了按劳分配的分配原则，没有贫富悬殊的现象。[13]

而第二国际的后续者社会党国际也在其成立大会上发表声明宣称：社会主义的目的是要把人们从对占有或控制生产资料的少数人的依附中解放出来，建立一个没有阶级、种族和民族压迫，消灭剥削和贫困的社会保证人人享有完全的自由和民主的权利。故它的标志有三，一是要实现公有制，把经济权力交到全体人民手中，以建立一个自由人能以平等地位共同工作的社会，以消灭资本主义的剥削与社会贫富悬殊的现象；二是根据有关国家的本身结构，在相当程度上实现计划经济，以避免资本主义生产制度下固有的周期性经济危机；三是要保证个人有按照其努力取得报酬的权利。[14]

比较共产党与社会党的主张，我们不难看出，它们至少在很长时间里对社会主义理想的认识，并无根本性的分歧。列宁主义的共产党也好，第二国际的社会党也好，他们在理论上都同意，资本主义造就了庞大的不占有生产资料、靠工资生活的劳动阶级，而少数占有和控制生产资料，因而也居于统治地位的资产阶级，盲目追求资本增值，不仅造成了阶级剥削、贫富悬殊的情况，而且带来了资本主义周期性的经济危机和社会动荡。社会主义是取代资本主义，消灭剥削与压迫，根本消除经济危机，实现社会平等与稳定的理想形式。社会主义实现经济和社会平等的最主要方法，就在于通过以公有制取代或相当程度上取代私有制，以计划经济取代无序竞争，和以按劳取酬等公平的物质分配形式，来消除阶级剥削所造成的社会权利不平等的状况，根本解决资本主义体制所带来的种种弊病。

通过对近代以来欧洲两大主流社会主义思潮对社会主义理想基本内容的简单考察与比较，我们应该大致可以对以往各派社会主义的共同点做出如下归纳：

第一，都相信社会主义是解除资本主义弊病的唯一出路；

第二，都相信实行社会主义的主要目的在于实现经济平等与社会公平；

第三，都相信公有制、计划经济和按劳分配是实现经济平等与社会公平的基本要件。

换言之，如果我们不是把社会主义简单地看成一种意识形态，不是以达成目的的手段作为判定其真假的依据，而是把它看成是人类追求的一种实现社会公平与正义的理想社会形态，那么，至少在上百年的时间里，凡是否定或批判资本主义，相当程度上认定公有制、计划经济和按劳分配对实现经济平等与社会公平有益的努力，理应都可以被归入到社会主义的尝试之列。从这个意义上，欧洲各国的社会党也好，共产党也好，显然都用不同的方法进行过社会主义的实践。

这种实践，在列宁主义共产党的政权下，就创造出了斯大林式的苏联一国社会主义模式，其突出标志就是：一党专政下的国家所有制、计划经济和按劳分配制度。苏联利用国家高度集权的优势，集举国之力，只用了三个五年计划的时间，就把一个落后的俄国变成了一个拥有强大生产力的先进工业国，并因此赢得了国内劳动民众，尤其是多数工人的支持。据此，它战胜了法西斯德国的入侵，并在战后很快发展成为世界上仅次于美国的工业和科技最发达的超级大国。

这种实践，在各国社会党的共同努力下，也使欧洲各国资本主义社会发生了重大的改变。瑞典是欧洲社会民主党中最早通过选举取得执政权的，它也开启了欧洲资本主义国家所有制改造的大门。虽然这一次改造并不成功，但放弃了过快过急的所有制改造政策后，它第二次上台后成功执政44年之久，不仅把国内主要行业基本上公共化，而且把瑞典从一个欧洲经济最落后的国家，发展建设为世界上人均国内生产总值占第二位的经济发达国家，和世界上第一个名符其实的"福利国家"。社会党人类似的努力也在欧洲和世界绝大多数发达国家发生了效力，各国原始的资本主义制度都得到了改造，新型的税收、福利、分配制度，乃至所有制改造，极大地抑制了资本家的权力和财富，工会在政治上和管理上发挥了举足轻重的作用，劳动者的权益得到了充分的保障，生活水平大幅提升，而工作时间和劳动强度却大大缩短和降低了。
欧洲社会党人的尝试，既推动了经济平等与社会公平目标的实现，
也延续了生产力的强劲发展势头，同时则有效地保持了自由、民主
的政治环境。

四、中共早期的理想观

和中国近代思想家们总想在西方经验中"去其糟粕，取其精华"，
找到一条救国捷径一样，中国共产党人接受俄国式的马克思主义，
同样是在相信诸路皆难的情况下，发现了俄国革命具有"一劳永逸"
的终极性质。

比如，以陈独秀、李大钊为代表的一批五四时期的激进知识分
子，他们早期的政治出发点也不离救人和救国的目标。在他们看来，
救国，先要救人，即先要把人心改变过来。既然是人心变动，他
们自然会着眼于文化的改造，想要从在中国人心中植入"人权"
和"科学"的观念入手。这一切尝试和努力，在1918年夏秋以后，
都随着俄国式社会革命的冲击，很快就没有人听了。俄国人何以
能一举成就社会革命？注意到俄国革命中工人的作用，和苏俄政
府对劳动民众的推崇，他们也迅速开始把目光转向"劳动"，转向"劳
动阶级"，相信最有力量的就是这个阶级了。然而，俄国毕竟是资
本主义国家，俄国毕竟有许多大工业，环顾中国，他们还是看不
到希望。因此，直到1920年5月，俄共代表吴廷康等人来到中国来
联络中国的各派社会主义者时，他们甚至还不是真正的社会主义
者。他们仍旧"不情愿阶级争斗发生"，"渴望纯粹资本作用——
离开劳力的资本作用——渐渐消灭，不至于造成阶级争斗"；他们
并且在劝说中国的资本家实行什么"Cooperative-society底一部分制
度"，来承认工人得红利的权利，以使"工人都可以渐渐变到资本
家地位"；他们仍旧在主张"从自己个人起，要造成完全公正廉洁
的人格，再由自己个人延长渐渐造成公正廉洁的社会"，相信必须
由此才能达到打破阶级制度，"实行共同劳工"和"公有主义"。15

我们可以很清楚地看出的是，陈独秀等人是在吴廷康到达上海
后的两三个月时间里产生了巨大的思想飞跃的。在7月里，陈已经
成为吴廷康所信任的主持中国社会主义者同盟的革命局负责人了。
一个月后，陈公开发表文章宣布赞同俄国布尔什维克的暴力革命
和无产阶级专政的观点，称："若不经过阶级战争，若不经过
劳动阶级占领权力阶级地位底时代，德莫克拉西必然永远是资产

阶级底专有物，也就是资产阶级永远把持政权抵制劳动阶级底利器"。[16] 再过两个月后，陈独秀已经在吴廷康的帮助下创办了《共产党》月刊，正式宣布了共产党的组成。他已经认识到："资本主义在欧美已经由发达而倾于崩坏了，在中国才开始发达，而他的性质上必然的罪恶也照例扮演出来了。代他而起的自然是社会主义的生产方法，俄罗斯正是这种方法最大的最新的试验场"。"要想把我们的同胞从奴隶境遇中完全救出，非由生产劳动者全体结合起来，用革命的手段打倒本国外国一切资本阶级，跟着俄国的共产党一同试验新的生产方法不可"。[17]

就在《共产党》月刊发布的同时，中国共产党人在吴廷康的帮助下，形成了他们最早的一份描述他们理想的正式文件。它写道：

第一，"共产主义主张将生产工具——机器工厂、原料、土地、交通机关等——收归社会共有，社会共用。要是生产工具收归共有共用了，私有财产和赁银（按即资本）制度就自然跟着消灭。社会上个人剥夺个人的现状也会绝对没有，因为造成剥夺的根源的东西——剩余价值——再也没有地方可以取得了"。

第二，"共产主义者主张废除政权，如同现在所有的国家机关和政府，是当然不能存在的。因为政权、军队和法庭是保护少数人的利益，压迫多数劳动群众的，在生产工具为少数人私有的时候，这是很必要的。要是私有财产和赁银制度都废除了，政权、军队和法庭当然就用不着了"。

第三，"共产主义者要使社会上只有一个阶级（就是没有阶级）——就是劳动群众的阶级。私有财产是现社会中一切特殊势力的根源，要是没有人能够聚集他的财产了，那就没有特殊阶级了"。

第四，"共产主义者的目是要按照共产主义者的理想，创造一个新的社会，但是要使我们的理想社会有实现之可能，第一步就得铲除现在的资本制度"，并将"政权转移于革命的无产阶级之手"，实行无产阶级专政，"一面用继续用强力与资本主义的剩余势力作战，一面要用革命的办法造成许多共产主义的建设法"。"一直等到全世界的资本家的势力都消灭了，生产事业也根据共产主义的原则开始活动了，那时候的无产阶级专政还要造出一条到共产主义的道路"。[18]

简而言之，这个宣言就是旨在说明，他们完全赞同俄国共产党的主张，即通过消灭私有制以达到消灭剥削、消灭阶级，进而使国家消亡的共产主义目标。这是人类社会最高最美的理想了，如果说佛教和基督教劝诱人们追求的还只是来世或天国，跟着俄国共产党创造的却是现世福祉和人间天堂，还有什么是比这个更理想的奋斗目标吗？为此，无论实行怎样的阶级斗争和无产阶级专政，当然都是值得的。

至于一个还是农业国的落后中国，是否有资本制度，是否有强有力的产业工人，中国的劳动阶级是否有掌握政权的能力，没有人认真考虑和研究过。他们的回答再简单没有了，那就是："中国农工商矿一切生产分配交换方法是资本制度还是共产制度？""中国人底衣食住等各生产力是何人造成的？""中国劳农底知识人格比徐世昌、梁启超还低几何？"[19] "要问中国今日是否已具实行社会主义的经济条件，须先问世界今日是否已具实现社会主义的倾向的经济条件，因为中国的经济情形，实不能超出于世界经济势力之外。现在世界的经济组织，既已经资本主义以至社会主义，中国虽未经自行如欧、美、日本等国的资本主义的发展实业，而一般平民间接受资本主义经济组织的压迫，较各国直接受资本主义的劳动阶级尤其苦痛。中国国内的劳资阶级间虽未发生重大问题，中国人民在世界经济上的地位，已立在这劳工运动日盛一日的风潮中，想行保护资本家的制度，无论理所不可，抑且势所不能"。因此，他们理直气壮地宣称："人家已达壮年，我们尚在幼稚；人家已走远了几千万里，我们尚在初步。在这种势力之下，要想存立，适应这共同生活，恐非取兼程并力社会共营的组织不能有成"。[20]

可以肯定，在最初的中共成员中，能够具体区别欧洲两大社会主义派别不同的人不多。他们中相当多数都相信，虽然主张劳农专政的第三国际"可称是各国社会运动最新的趋势"，但各派社会主义"在社会改造的根本原则上，都是主张将生产机关归社会公有的，不过所采手段，各派各不相同"罢了。而这种不同，很可能是因为各国国情和国民性不同所致。具体到中国，究竟采用何种范畴的社会主义，"大概也是要按照国情和国民性决定的。未到实行的时候，我们也不能预先见到"。[21]

在这方面，最接近俄共代表的陈独秀，这时应该是最接近俄国的布尔什维克的主张的。他在1921年初就已经能够分辨社会主义和共产主义的区别，并且能够分辨社会民主党的社会主义如何不同于俄国布尔什维克的社会主义了。他并且明白宣布：对于欧洲这两种社会主义派别，中国必须站到布尔什维克一边来。只不过他的理由是：第二国际领导下的欧洲各国社会党，都带来太浓的国家主义色彩，不像第三国际领导下的共产党，是以世界革命为本位，是联合各国无产阶级一同革命的。"中国底改造与存在，大部分都要靠国际社会主义的运动帮忙"，自然不能学社会党那一套办法。[22]

不过，无论中共早期成员对马列著作的阅读受到语言和资料来源的限制有多大，至少生活在北京和上海的多数成员明显地是读过马克思的《哥达纲领批判》、恩格斯的《社会主义从空想到科学的发展》，及列宁的《国家与革命》等书的。他们自然也很清楚马克思关于社会主义和共产主义理想的基本观点，并且是因此而加入共产党的。他们基本准确地把马克思的共产主义理想归纳为三个历史阶段：

"1. 社会革命期　　这期底特质，就是无产阶级专政。这期最大工作：（一）把开发生产机关收归国有；（二）征服有产阶级并消灭一切阶级；（三）整理生产事业并发展生产力。这期工作，大部分都属于破坏"。

"2. 共产主义半熟期　　这一期就是刚从资本主义社会脱出来的新共产主义社会的时期，也就是经过了社会革命期后的时期。（在社会革命期中，是正与资本主义社会战争的时期，不能说是已经脱出资本主义社会）因为他去资本主义社会未远，所以无论在经济上、在道德上、在精神上、在一切关系上，都还遗留着旧社会底遗风；因之，强制力在这时期也还不能免除。这个时期，已没有了阶级的区别和生产机关底私有。无产阶级的国家也已消灭，全社会人都已变做生产劳动者。这时破坏已完，完全努力建设。因为生产机关已为全社会所有，生产事情已有统一的计划，所以生产力也就能充分发展起来。至于分配消费品，还仅能采用'各取所值'一条原则，做多少工才给多少报酬，所以在这时候，还有许多不公平的事情"。

"3. 共产主义完成期　　这个时期就是生产力已达了十分可惊的程度，完全能够做到'各尽所能，各取所需'的自由共产社会的时期。这就是恩格斯所说的'自由的王国'，马克思所谓'协同的社会'"。[23]

李大钊更具体形象地归纳出了社会主义和共产主义的三大好处：一是富裕，二是愉快，三是自由。用他的话来说，社会主义、共产主义，就是要创造更大的生产力，更多的财富，以便"使我们人人都能安逸幸福，过那一种很好的精神和物质的生活"。因此，"社会主义是要富的，不是要穷的"。社会主义，尤其是共产主义条件下，劳动不再是谋生的手段，而成了一种创造的过程，因此，在社会主义，特别是共产主义条件下劳动，自然也就成了一种愉快的享受。而在社会主义，尤其是共产主义条件下，再没有剥削压迫，人人平等，每个人都有按照自己意志生活和发展的条件，因而人也只有在社会主义，特别是共产主义实现以后，才能得到充分的自由。[24]

但是，在中国，特别是在党内普及社会主义、共产主义理想知识的工作很快就中断了。1922年，莫斯科否定了中共自成立以来一直坚持的观点，即中国革命必须以推翻资本家阶级的统治，消灭私有制为目标，它要求中共转而以联合资产阶级反对军阀和外国帝国主义压迫为己任。[25]这种情况显然极大地改变了中共成立之初的理想追求，关于社会主义、共产主义理论及理想的研究和学习，从此淡出了中共的各种宣传和政策性文件，甚至不再见于中国共产党的任何一部党章或党纲之中。直到1940年前后，即中共的延安时期，共产主义的奋斗目标才进入到党员的入党誓词当中。[26]绝大多数二三十年代加入共产党的人，都是穷苦出身，文化水平较低，入党是为了翻身或救国，很少对马克思主义的理论能有所了解。换言之，所谓"共产主义"或"共产党"，对于他们多半只是一种最革命的政治派别的身份证明，只具有一种工具性的意义。[27]

"三八式"老干部宗凤鸣的认识经历就颇具代表性。他上中学时因日本入侵，受到"宁作断头鬼，不当亡国奴"等标语口号激励，一步步加入了共产党的组织。他对共产党的了解，完全是在入党后在中共有组织的各种浅显通俗的思想灌输的结果。如他最初树立起对共产党的信仰，是读了一本叫做《共产党员》的小册子。里面讲到共产党代表新社会，代表未来，是要建立自由、民主、幸福的新中国的，必须终生为之奋斗，因而让他感到入党既神圣又光荣。从上级不断进行的形势教育报告中，他又逐渐了解了共产党在中国，以及中国在世界上的地位和前途问题。知道了世界上还存在着社会主义与资本主义、帝国主义与殖民地等种种矛盾对立，知道了资本主义已经腐朽没落，苏联社会主义是解放无产阶级、支持殖民地弱小民族独立的舵手，是人类解放、社会进步的旗帜。在以后读了《政治经济学通俗讲话》的小册子后，他又进一步了解到人类社会是进化的，并且是必定向着光明走的，社会主义、共产主义是人类社会发展的终极理想和最高阶段，共产党就是为了实现这一现世的理想目标组织起来的，这自然让他对党的事业更加充满了神圣感和使命感。但社会主义或共产主义的理想学说，到底是在怎样得来的，它们的历史和理论的前提具体如何，他所知只是一些形式逻辑的教条而已。[28]

很明显，中共多数党员和干部并没有系统地读过马克思主义的理论著作，基本上都只是被动地接受了共产主义意识形态的思想灌输和熏陶，因而成为其主张的忠实信徒的。甚至可以说，除了毛泽东和少数留苏归国的干部外，大多数中共中高层干部只是到了抗战中期，特别是延安整风结束后，才按照规定，比较系统地读了规定的五本书，从而多少有了一些关于社会主义、共产主义理想的系统知识。[29] 但也仅此而已。

五、斯大林的错误"榜样"

1917年俄国十月革命成功后，列宁很快就按照马克思关于无产阶级革命的观点，一方面全力推动世界革命，力图整个颠覆欧洲资本主义；一方面在俄国建立无产阶级专政，以剥夺资产阶级的观点，开始实行国有化。1913年占人口15％以上的俄国工厂主、商人、房产所有者、职员、地主、富农的财产被没收了，所有工业、金融、贸易、运输企业，连同所有的住宅和土地都被国有化了。地主和富农的地产被分给了农村中无地少地的农民，小商业和小手工业，在1920年也被国有化了。依照马克思所主张的，新政府普遍提升了工人的工资，使他们的生活收入水平与政府工作人员变得不相上下。与此同时，新政府也开始尝试实行农业集体化。甚至，为了使执政党真正无产阶级化，列宁还亲自主持了党的组织清洗，使350万党员几年时间骤减到只剩下200万党员，整整淘汰了150万党员。他并照马克思所主张的，努力推动由基层直接选举产生苏维埃政权代表，想要最大限度地把能干的工人提拔上来。列宁的目的，就是要严格按照马克思的设想，实现革命的过渡，并力争在此期能借助于政权的巨大力量，补上俄国资本主义发展不足这一课，以便进一步创造出一个符合马克思设想的具有高度现代文明程度的新社会。[30]

国有化、集体化和平均主义等等作法，与内外战争相结合，形成了一种军事共产主义的非常状态，导致了生产效率的下降和农业产量的大幅度减产。列宁最后不得不改行新经济政策，即停止集体化的尝试，将相当部分小工厂、小商业和小手工业重新私有化，以恢复市场经济，刺激经济的恢复与增长。新经济政策不久即取得了成功，但列宁去世后，继任的斯大林却重拾列宁一度中止了的尝试，下决心要用政权之力，单独把苏联从一个落后的工业国，变成一个先进的工业国。为此，他不惜压制党内各派势力，冲破马克思主义的理论束缚，确立了一国社会主义的理论观点。[31]

　　1928年，苏联开始在全面实行配给制的基础上推行第一个五年计划，新经济政策宣告结束，全面计划经济时代开启。而一国社会主义也便利了斯大林用共产主义和民族主义两种意识形态，来统合全党全国的思想。从马克思、列宁的世界革命和国际主义观点，转变到"苏维埃爱国主义"观点。斯大林的逻辑很简单：一国社会主义能否成功，取决于生产力的发展。"我们比先进国家落后了五十年至一百年。我们应当在十年内跑完这一段距离。或者我们做到这一点，或者我们被人打倒"。[32]

　　在建设社会主义祖国的号召下，苏联依靠强力开始了新一轮的剥夺有产者和社会改造的过程。1925年前后占到工业产值18.7%的私营企业，占到商业57.7%的私营零售业，到1931年基本上都被国有化或合作化了。[33]几乎所有农户统统都被强行并入集体农庄，而新产生出来的数以百万计的富农，在剥夺了他们的房屋和财产后，被集体迁往西伯利亚北部和远东地区。农民对集体化的反抗，[34]以及对富农的全面剥夺，不可避免地带来了农业歉收，和国家强行征购进一步促成的农村中的严重饥荒，夺去了几乎同样数量的农民的生命。[35]

　　把国家的所有力量和资源集中在重工业的发展上，产生出了极为明显的效果。苏联第一个，乃至第二、三个五年计划都取得了相当的成功，光是第一个五年计划期间，就建立了1500个大型企业，修成了数千公里铁路和运河，奠定了苏联随后现代化重工业和军事工业发展的基础。到1937年，苏联的工业总产值已跃居欧洲第一位，世界第二位，成为世界上最大的工业国之一。这对几年后苏联能够调动整个国家的工业技术力量，大规模地生产战争所需的高水平的武器装备，成功打败工业发展水平十分先进的德国的入侵，无疑是有重大作用的。

　　集权专制与生产力增长和民族强盛之间的联系是如此的紧密，以至于每一个一心向往着国家强大的俄国人，都不能不自觉地忍受自由和权利被剥夺的情况。而事实上，当权力结合整个国家的资源被集中起来之后，个人的生命和作用，哪怕他是革命功臣、技术专家，面对这一庞大国家机器时，也注定会变得无足轻重。要知道，第一个，特别是第二、三个五年计划的成就，都是在血腥"大清洗"的同时取得的。在这十年时期里，上至季诺维也夫、加米涅夫、布哈林等联共（布）党的著名领导人，下至莫斯科发电厂上千名普通职工，大批被逮捕、监禁和枪毙，1934年联共（布）十七大刚刚选举出来的中央委员中的70%均遭捕杀。这场血腥残酷的清洗行动还杀害、监禁了几千名苏联急需的优秀的科学家、发明家、设计师、厂长和工程师，乃至车间主任。[36] 集权专制对国家强盛的神奇效力，甚至还可以通过战争体现出来。因为，尽管斯大林刚刚杀害了3.5万名红军指挥员和全苏联80％的高级将领（5名元帅中的3人和几乎全部一级指挥员和一级、二级军政治委员，全部二级集团军军长和绝大部分集团军、师及旅政委，全部一级、二级海军最高指挥员和指挥员，几乎全部军团长和大部分师长，一半以上的旅长，和1/3团指挥员），[37] 他还是有效地组织了抵抗行动，并且依靠很少训练与大战经验的大批临时提拔上来的指挥员，完成了军事上的反攻，打败了欧洲最强大的侵略国家德国法西斯力量。

高度集权产生出来的高效率和政权的高度稳定，无疑让斯大林对这一制度的优越性充满了陶醉感。苏联几乎是转瞬之间的改变与强盛，也让绝大多数没有直接受到伤害的普通苏联人，包括中国在内的许多落后国家的革命者，对这种社会主义模式，尤其是对独裁的斯大林，不能不充满景仰，乃至奉若神明。

1936年底，就在苏联大规模清洗和屠杀全面启动之际，斯大林郑重向全苏联和全世界宣告：苏联建成了社会主义。12月5日颁布的苏联新宪法宣称：苏联已经实现了社会主义公有制（全民所有制和集体所有制），已全面实行了计划经济，和"不劳动者不得食"与按劳分配的原则，无产阶级政权空前巩固。斯大林在说明宪法草案的报告中则信誓旦旦地表示：在苏联，"人剥削人的现象已被铲除和消灭，生产工具和生产资料的社会主义所有制已经作为我们苏联社会不可动摇的基础而奠定了"。苏联不会有危机，不会有失业，不会有贫困和破产，公民们享有充分的自由与民主，有一切可能享受富裕的有文化的生活。因此，可以确定地说，"我们苏联社会已经做到在基本上实现了社会主义，建立了社会主义制度，即实现了马克思主义者又称为共产主义第一阶段或低级阶段的制度。这就是说，我们已经基本上实现了共产主义第一阶段，即社会主义"。[38]

斯大林模式社会主义的最突出特点，就是斯大林凌驾于党之上，党凌驾于国家之上，国家凌驾于整个社会之上，斯大林或极少数人垄断并控制着苏联的一切，整个国家事实上就成了党内少数利益集团操控下的一部机器。所谓"国有"，就是"党有"，也就是少数人所有。全民财富任由党内少数人支配，这些人因决策错误造成任何损失，都无人问津和负责。这些既是集权体制经济上成功的秘诀之一，却也是它终将走向失败的难以去除的内部腐蚀剂。

集权的特点在于层层控制，因而它必须要建立一套异常庞大的官僚机构，才能够实现这种金字塔式的严密控制体系。据1954年统计，苏联全国有650余万干部，平均每7名职工就有1名干部，而每三四名干部中还有1名是领导。光是这些干部行政开支一项所耗费的金钱，就占到上一年国家总收入的将近15％左右。到1980年代初，苏联中央一级的部委机关就有近百个，光是正副部长级干部就有800多人。一个黑色冶金工业部，就有19人之多。而层层叠叠地由上至下严格依照计划、命令来管理从政治，到经济，到文化，到社会的一切事务，不可避免地会造成体制严重僵化，长官意志盛行，干部近亲繁殖，上级滥用职权，人浮于事；下级阿臾奉承，弄虚作假等等弊端。

集权体制催生官僚体制，官僚体制则必然促成等级制度和特权阶级的产生。因为，按照官员等级分配特权，根本就是集权体制下一种重要的制度安排。[39] 法国著名作家罗曼·罗兰1936年访苏时就已清楚地注意到了这一点。他写道：党的领导人看上去工资收入不是很高，但是，"他们却在利用其他特权（住房、食物、交通工具等）代替金钱，这些特权确保他们过上舒适生活并享受特殊地位。更不用说影响，他们利用影响为自己和自己的亲属谋利益"。而在这些上层的达官显贵们享受着特权阶级的生活的同时，"人民却仍然不得不为了谋取面包和空气（我想说的是住房）而进行艰苦的斗争"。[40]

事实上，当这种等级和特权俨然成为一种生活方式后，它不可避免地与官僚们的荣誉和颜面联系了起来，从而也就不可避免地造成了党政干部带有贵族制特色的终身制和权力继承制度。因为这个特殊阶层越来越脱离社会上的其他人，"孤立地生活、治疗、休养"，也因此"形成了自己的家庭、氏族关系——须知这个阶层的子女们在一起度时光，互相认识，往往通婚"。进一步发展的结果，就是权力的近亲延续。这些经过特殊环境教育培养起来的特权阶级的子女，自然而然地便成为权力核心最信得过的"革命接班人"，公权私授，子承父业，不可避免。[41]

马克思式社会主义理想的一个重大的理论缺失，在列宁，特别是斯大林模式的社会主义实践中表现得淋漓尽致。这就是，马克思一方面坚信社会主义是资本主义生产力充分发展，已经失去继续发展可能之后的产物；一方面却又断言他所处的那个欧洲工业革命还只是刚刚开始起步的时期，资本主义已经走到命运的尽头，必须要靠产业无产阶级把它推翻，另建一套新的生产关系，人类的生产力才会继续得以发展。很显然，马克思错判了时代，因而也就为列宁在一个更落后的国家里进行社会主义革命，包括为斯大林用政权之力人为制造"社会主义"，提供了某种理论上的依据。

斯大林模式的社会主义，除了把工人的地位在社会上抬得较高这一点上似乎和马克思的观点合拍之外，它在本质上都必定是根本违背马克思主义和一切社会主义理想的。这是因为，我们这里所谈到的马克思主义和一切社会主义理想，都是建立在对人的生命、权利和自由关怀，即追求人的解放这一思想基础之上的。而所有这一切，都离不开传统的资产阶级革命和资本主义工业化，即现代化发展的历史阶段。资产阶级革命把人类现代性的终极关怀——"自由、平等、博爱"，鲜明地书写在自己的旗帜上。资本主义早期工业化的问题在于，它所带来的现代化进程仅仅保护了人们在政治权利上的平等与自由，而将经济上的平等与不分阶级、种族和敌我的博爱思想，丢到了九霄云外。马克思固然主张阶级斗争和阶级专政，但他的根本目的并不是想要用仇恨和一个阶级压迫另一个阶级的办法来建立一个巩固的阶级压迫的社会。恰恰相反，他不过是一厢情愿地希望，通过这样一种临产前的"阵痛"方式，可以最迅速地免除人类因贫富战争而造成的无休止的伤害，即通过很快消灭私有制，进而消灭阶级，转入到一个没有阶级、没有剥削、没有压迫，没有战争，因而也没有人与人之间的仇恨与敌对的真正可以全面实现"自由、平等、博爱"的新社会去。而我们在斯大林模式的社会主义里面，不仅看不到博爱与自由，甚至就连一般社会主义理想中最基本的平等的影子也很少能够看到。换言之，马克思的终极关怀，即人的自由和解放，根本就不在斯大林模式社会主义的关心范围之内。

六、毛泽东建国初的尝试

苏联是世界上第一个社会主义国家，同时也是中共模仿和学习的榜样，"苏联的今天就是我们的明天"，这一五十年代曾响彻中国大地的响亮口号，其实自中共成立之日起，就一直是鼓舞中国共产党人的一根精神支柱。斯大林总结苏联革命和建设经验的《联共（布）党史简明教程》，也早就成了毛泽东用来指导中国革命最为重要的一本参考书。斯大林的《苏联社会主义经济问题》和苏联理论家的《政治经济学》，更是建国后毛泽东反复阅读、学习和讨论的经典著作。

中国较俄国更为落后，对人的自由和权利的观念更为淡薄。因此，它当然最容易接受斯大林模式的社会主义。毛泽东从俄国革命那里学到的第一条就是革命暴力加阶级专政。但是，早年受到过佛教思想、康梁思想、胡适思想等影响的毛泽东还相信：这实在"是无可如何的山穷水尽诸路皆走不通了的一个变计"[42]。在死人堆里摸爬滚打多年之后，毛泽东显然早就不再看重人的生命与权利了。他深信不疑的是："要革命就会有牺牲"。

马上得天下者，也必定会马上治天下。靠革命的方法夺取政权，一定会用革命的思维逻辑来治理和建设国家。根据目前已经公开的大量中俄档案可以清楚地了解，自从中国共产党开始提出建国的设想之后，他们的一切努力就是模仿苏联，尽快实现社会主义。除了不断地向斯大林和苏共中央请示和学习如何建立政府各级组织机构，如何有效地组织经济生产，如何制定各项计划和政策外，[43] 他们深信苏联经验的真传，主要不外乎三条。一是一党制下的无产阶级专政；一是通过所有制改造达成社会主义；一是先过渡，再改造，循序渐进。而他们所追求的所谓社会主义，自然也不外乎是共产党领导，用阶级斗争和阶级专政的办法管理国家，将生产资料全部转变为国家和集体所有，将整个国民经济纳入到"有计划按比例发展"的计划经济的轨道，并实行"各尽所能，按劳分配"的分配制度。[44]

毛泽东是相当典型的近代中国过渡时期的知识分子，既上过传统私塾，也读过西式学堂。但由于从未出过国门，又没有受到高等教育，他不仅受传统民间文化影响深厚，且其早年田园式小农经济环境下的生活经历，与列强欺凌及资本主义早期发展的残酷性造成的强烈对比，使他像众多中国旧式小知识分子一样，对资本主义的进步与发达鲜有体认，更多看到的只是资本主义的罪恶。可想而知，自信从无到有，用小米加步枪打败了国民党飞机加大炮的他，比斯大林更加不了解马克思主义关于社会主义需要产生于资本主义、继承于资本主义的意义。他更多相信主观意志的作用，更多相信"决定的因素是人不是物"；相信"一张白纸，好写最新最美的文字，好画最新最美的图画"。说"在资本主义有了一定发展水平的条件下，经济愈落后，从资本主义过渡到社会主义是愈容易"。[45]

对于类似的说法，恩格斯曾经有过一段非常有针对性的批评意见。他指出："现代社会主义力图实现的变革，简言之就是无产阶级战胜资产阶级，以及通过消灭任何阶级差别来建立新的社会组织。为此不但需要有可能实现这个变革的无产阶级，而且还需要有使社会生产力发展到能够彻底消灭阶级差别的资产阶级……但是生产力只有在资产阶级手中才达到了这样的发展水平。……因此，谁竟然肯定说在一个虽然没有无产阶级，然而也没有资产阶级的国家里更容易进行这种革命，他就只不过证明，他需要再学一学社会主义初步知识"。[46]

　　毫无疑问，毛泽东也并非完全不了解马克思主义关于生产关系必须与生产力相适应的观点。读过列宁的《社会民主党在民主革命中的两个策略》一文的毛泽东，对中国的生产力发展水平过低，距离社会主义条件过远，也曾有过相当的认识。他在1940年，尤其是1945年抗日战争结束前后，就曾特别提出过未来中国的"新民主主义"的选项问题，还一度极力宣传中国应当"广泛地发展资本主义"，这些无疑都是受到了列宁的观点的影响。但是，他最看重，也是最能理解的，还是列宁关于落后国家完全可以先用革命手段创造经济增长的"政治前提"的观点，和斯大林关于落后发达的资本主义国家五十年到一百年的俄国，如果不能在最短时间赶上和超过它们，就注定会遭到失败的说法。[47]

　　依据苏联的经验，实行生产资料所有制的改造不过是一件运用政权之力即可实现的工作，因此毛泽东显然不认为这是一件多少困难的事情。在此之前，按照苏联1917年革命成功，12年之后，即1929年开始全面进行所有制改造，然后7年之后，即1936年宣布改造成功，社会主义建成的时间表，中共中央曾经考虑到中国比当年的俄国更加落后的情况，一度也制定了一个用15-20年完成恢复、巩固和向社会主义过渡，然后再花相当时间完成所有制改造的时间表。但是，建国不过三年，经济即已恢复，又在苏联的帮助下开始了苏联当年在1928年才开始的第一个五年计划的建设工作，毛泽东马上就改变了原来的时间表，提出了社会主义过渡时期总路线，全面推动了社会主义改造运动的兴起。然后只用了不过三年左右的时间，即到1956年初，中国就基本上达成了生产资料所有制改造的目标，宣告社会主义基本建成。

　　毛泽东急于创造列宁所说的那个政治前提，一个根本目的，就是要发展生产力。几乎和斯大林当年一样，他自夺得政权并迅速实现了经济恢复的目标之后，一心想的就是如何把一个贫穷落后的中国，一步变成世界强国。1955年秋天，毛泽东公开宣布说："我们的目标是要赶上美国，并且要超过美国。美国只有一亿多人口，我国有六亿多人口，我们应该赶上美国。……哪一天赶上美国，我们才吐一口气。现在我们不像样子嘛，要受人欺负"。"我们一定要争这一口气"。[48]

1956年在中共第八次全国代表大会上，毛泽东又进一步提出了赶超美国的问题。他极具鼓动性地告诫大会的代表们说："美国只有一亿七千万人口，我国人口比它多几倍，资源也丰富，气候条件跟它差不多……应不应该赶上呢？完全应该"。"你有那么多人，你有那么一块大地方，资源那么丰富，又听说搞了社会主义，据说是有优越性，结果你搞了五、六十年还不能超过美国，你像个什么样子呢？那就要从地球上开除你的球籍！"[49]

不难看出，相信社会主义制度已基本建成，使毛泽东受到极大的鼓舞。他相信："国内阶级矛盾已经基本解决"，社会制度和生产关系已经成为最先进的了，社会的主要矛盾无疑转变为先进的生产关系与落后的生产力之间的矛盾了。[50] 在这一年召开的中共第八次全国代表大会上，经过毛泽东的同意，这样的观点甚至被写进了大会的政治决议案。[51] 而中国有了如此先进的生产关系，还大大落后于资本主义国家，那还像什么样子呢？

让毛泽东深感振奋的，是中国第一个五年计划的顺利实现。苏联政府总共承接了156个中国建设现代化工业急需的援建项目，涉及冶金、机械、汽车、煤炭、石油、电力、电讯和化工等各个部门，包括7个钢铁联合企业、24个电站、27个煤井和洗煤厂、10个冶金企业、7个化学工厂和十几个机械制造工业，以及其它工业部门的工厂。第一个五年计划就在相当程度上奠定了新中国大规模工业化的建设基础。[52]

但是，急于求成的毛泽东对此仍不那样满意。三年打败国民党，三年实现经济恢复，三年基本建成社会主义，这种超速度使毛泽东更加不愿意被动地跟着苏联的步伐走了。他从1955年底到1956年春，连续几个月时间听取政府各个经济工作部门汇报，提出加快社会主义建设和社会主义改造的十大关系问题，说到底也是要像斯大林当年那样，"调动一切直接和间接的力量"，为把中国加速建设成一个强大的社会主义国家"而奋斗"。[53]

1957年底，毛泽东在莫斯科听说苏联准备15年赶上美国，他再也坐不住了，马上开始部署赶超英美。1958年1月，在南宁会议上，他以一种不屑的口吻对与会代表们说："我就不信，搞建设比打仗还难?!"[54]

要想在不长的时间里就赶上英美，按照苏联帮助制定的五年计划，按部就班地进行生产建设显然不行。按照大规模战役组织的办法，毛泽东雄心勃勃地发动了一个"大跃进"运动。仅仅几个月的时间，高度集权的庞大国家动员机制的高效率和高速度就以令人难以置信的程度显露出来了。夏粮的产量到处大放"卫星"，各地上报的粮食亩产几十倍上百倍地增长，受此鼓舞，毛泽东一声号令，全国上下9000万人轰轰烈烈地又掀起了大炼钢铁的运动，各地同样捷报频传，钢铁产量也是直线上升。[55]

眼看赶超英国已经不是问题，毛泽东马上开始把赶超的目标锁定在了美国身上。从1958年《人民日报》元旦社论宣布准备15年左右赶上英国，再用20到30年的时间赶上美国，[56] 到5月份召开中共八大二次会议时，毛泽东就已经在内部提出7年赶上英国，再加8年赶上美国的15年奋斗目标了。[57] 又过了一个月，他估计："超过英国，不是十五年，也不是七年，只需要两到三年，两年是有可能的"。[58] 主张除了造船、汽车、电力这几项外，明年就要超过英国。[59] 进入到9月初，他已经不再注意英国了。他直率地要求党的领导人，要有大手笔，要解放思想，鼓动他们："为五年接近美国，七年超过美国这个目标而奋斗吧！"[60]

显然，对于毛泽东来说，社会主义已然建成了，中国建成共产主义，不过是个时间问题。1958年夏天，粮食、钢铁产量屡放"卫星"，公共食堂全面推广，人民公社遍地开花，全国上下大谈共产主义早日实现，毛泽东也信心满满地告诉党内干部说：中国很快就要进入共产主义了。这种把共产主义等同于粮食、钢铁产量加集体生活的观念在中国的流行，足以看出中共当年对这一"人间天堂"的理解曾经何等的世俗化。

1958年的大跃进运动，充分暴露出了斯大林模式社会主义的严重制度缺陷。即在高度集权体制下，个人迷信、领袖专权，政治动员，结合以对人间天堂的持续宣传，往往会成为国家的一种政治生态。而领袖意志通过金字塔式的官僚体制，作为党控国家的形式层层下达，更使得任何一种"瞎指挥"都能够畅行无阻。在这种体制下，上有所好，下必甚焉，任何高层政策指导失误，无论是造成怎样的浪费与挥霍，上层都无须承担责任，即使造成了极其严重的全国范围的灾难性后果，也没有人会出来承担责任。大跃进运动持续了一年，就已经对国民经济的发展造成了严重的破坏，但因为中共中央内部意见分歧，导致1959年仍未能及时采取措施纠正这一严重的政策错误，结果是进一步恶化了经济形势，终于造成了和苏联集体化运动期间一样的全国性粮食歉收与大饥荒，造成了和苏联一样极其惨重的农民大量非正常死亡的现象。[61]

　　高度集权体制的另一项严重的弊端，就是舆论一律，新闻报纸被牢牢地控制在党和政府手里。不仅新闻没有自由，就连学术研究也鲜能获得自由，而各种虚假的和武断的宣传不仅愚弄了民众，也在很大程度上愚弄了党的最高领袖。由于毛泽东关于苏联社会主义改造和集体化进展的所有知识都来自于《联共（布）党史简明教程》，因此，他完全无从了解苏联这段历史中所发生的种种政策错误和人间悲剧，既不能总结斯大林模式社会主义体制的经验教训，也不能避免重蹈苏联的历史覆辙。毛泽东在这次严重挫败之后，自己也没有从中汲取到应有的教训，只是从此不再插手经济工作而已。但是，体制和制度不变，毛泽东权力地位依旧，新的问题也依旧会如影相随，甚至会愈演愈烈。

七、毛泽东为何"继续革命"？

1956年，在毛泽东兴高采烈地欢呼中国基本建成了社会主义的几乎同时，苏共召开了第二十次全国代表大会，中央书记赫鲁晓夫在内部报告中揭露了三年前去世的斯大林在1930年代大清洗运动中所犯下的严重罪行。赫鲁晓夫秘密报告内容很快外泄，立即在世界范围内引发巨大的政治冲击波，苏联社会主义的"伟光正"形象瞬间崩塌，各国共产党遭遇了大规模的退党潮。在东欧各国中，最为严重的是匈牙利事件，在眼看政权可能易手的情况下，苏联出兵进行了镇压。几年来听了太多溢美之词的毛泽东，为显示中国与东欧那些靠苏军坦克解放的国家不同，政权稳固，政府民主，一时兴起，力推"百花齐放，百家争鸣"的方针，并实行共产党开门整风。想不到一直在恭维赞美的民主人士和知识分子，突然间提出了大量尖锐批评意见。原本一直怕大家不敢讲真话，亲自在各地动员党外人士提意见的毛泽东，承受不住，顿时开始认为有人在乘机反对共产党的领导地位。于是，对党整风运动一夜之间变成了反右派运动，在全国一举整出几十万敢对党提意见的右派分子。这件事显然极大地刺激了毛泽东，他开始怀疑，马克思、列宁关于生产资料改造完成之后，阶级不复存在的说法是否准确；斯大林关于社会主义建成后，国内"敌对势力"多半是帝国主义干涉和渗透的结果的说法是否科学？

　　据此，在长期革命和战争中已经习惯于阶级斗争思维的毛泽东，对社会主义阶段问题的看法逐渐发生了变化。他很快开始批评得到中共八大肯定的关于先进的生产关系和落后的生产力之间的矛盾的说法，开始相信阶级斗争以及两条道路的斗争仍旧应当是社会主义社会的主要矛盾。[62]

按照马克思主义的观点，阶级的存在从来都是与私有制联系在一起的。既然生产资料所有制改造已经完成，阶级存在的基础就已经消失，那么社会主义条件下这种持续不断的阶级斗争又是如何产生的呢？对此，斯大林的做法是，把一切矛盾都归结为外部敌人的颠覆活动。而这在毛泽东看来显然是不够的。

相信社会主义社会依旧存在着无产阶级和资产阶级的矛盾，不可避免地要修正马克思和列宁的观点。因为，如前所述，马克思在《哥达纲领批判》中描述得很清楚，他所设想的通向人类理想社会最高阶段的道路，是要经过三个阶段，即革命转变时期，再进到社会主义，经过社会主义，再进到共产主义的。[63] 也就是说，依照马克思和列宁的观点，阶级斗争以及无产阶级专政只能存在于生产资料所有制改造完成之前，亦即存在于从资本主义到社会主义的过渡时期。一旦消灭了私有制，进入到社会主义社会之后，阶级存在的基础即消失了，阶级专政也应当归于消亡。虽然，国家的管理职能还可以长期保留下来，直到建成共产主义之后国家才会彻底消亡，但其原有的镇压职能在没有阶级对抗和没有阶级可以镇压的社会主义社会，却绝不可能存在了。

在这一点上，斯大林是严格地遵守了马克思、列宁的说法的。1936年社会主义改造基本完成之后，他就宣布社会主义在苏联已经基本建成，剥削阶级已经不复存在，苏联已经没有阶级斗争了。和马克思的观点有所不同的只是，因为他创造了"一国社会主义"，苏联成了整个资本主义汪洋大海中的一叶孤舟。为防止资本主义的颠覆阴谋，及其侵略战争，已经不存在阶级斗争和阶级专政需要的苏联，还必须保持具有强大暴力和镇压功能的国家机器。

马克思所设想的无产阶级革命、无产阶级专政的过渡时期，尤其是社会主义和共产主义时期，都是建立在资本主义作为一种社会制度和生产方式，在世界范围内将被彻底推翻为前提的。这也是从列宁，到托洛茨基等共产党人，在俄国革命成功后始终坚持要推进世界革命，不相信俄国革命可以单独胜利的一个根本原因。因为从唯物史观和进化论的角度，马克思明确认为：资本主义工业化的兴起，"使一切国家的生产和消费都成为世界性的了"，"它迫使一切民族……采用资产阶级的生产方式"，"它使未开化和半开化的国家从属于文明的国家，使农民的民族从属于资产阶级的民族，使东方从属于西方"。因此，资本主义把全世界拖入到以欧洲为中心的工业化浪潮之中，因而也使阶级分化加速向着资产阶级和无产阶级两大阶级对抗的方向发展。资本主义条件下的阶级斗争必定是世界性的，没有任何一个国家的无产阶级可以单独解放自己，也没有任何一个民族可以自立于资本主义的世界体系之外。也正是在这个意义上，马克思主义认为："工人没有祖国"。推翻资本主义的斗争，无论首先爆发于哪一国，必定会引起世界革命，而各发达国家的联合行动，尤其"是无产阶级获得解放的首要条件之一"。[64] 换言之，落后国家或许可以首先引发革命，但是，资本主义的灭亡和社会主义的胜利，只能是世界革命的结果。

斯大林的一国社会主义主张与实践，不仅根本改变了马克思主义关于社会主义和共产主义的整套理论逻辑，丢弃了马克思主义关于资本主义生产方式已经全球化的观点，而且在事实上也背离了马克思的唯物史观。因为从唯物史观的角度，社会主义和资本主义一样，同样是一种生产方式和生产关系，它们不仅只能是相互继承、替代的关系，而且只能是在全世界范围内发生的现象。相信在社会主义条件下依旧存在作为暴力镇压工具而存在的国家机器，无异于对人类的社会主义理想和马克思的社会主义理论进行阉割。

但是，斯大林的这一主张与实践，却在毫无世界革命希望的情况下，给包括中国在内的所有落后国家的共产党提供了一条生路。而越是落后国家，也就越是可以进一步突破马克思主义的理论禁忌了。比如，如果说斯大林还坚持共产党必须以产业工人为主的话，那么，在中国、越南、朝鲜以及东南亚的大多数国家，共产党几乎都不再理会这样的"教条"了。

在这种情况下，毛泽东自然也不会把马克思、列宁的所谓三阶段论看成是不可改变的。只是，直到1958年底1959年初，毛泽东还在设法从译文上寻找答案：会不会译者误解了马克思的意思？马克思所讲的"过渡时期"，也许不是单纯指从资本主义到社会主义这一个阶段，而是包含着从资本主义到共产主义最高阶段到来之前这整个历史时期？[65] 由于他把社会主义改造看成是一个用暴力或强制的办法可以轻易完成的政治任务，特别是他始终高度重视人的作用，尤其是人的意志和人的思想的作用，因此他无论如何看不出，在中国被剥夺和镇压的数千万剥削阶级或国民党敌对分子，包括不断涌现出来的坏分子和右派分子，如何能够改变他们的反动思想，停止他们散布反动影响，和进行反革命活动？也就是说，社会主义社会如何能够在没有阶级和阶级斗争，没有强大的阶级专政的条件下生存与发展？

1960年12月27日，毛泽东明确告诉各中央局领导人，不要给地富分子"摘帽子"。他说："过去规定摘地主帽子一般是三、五年，现在看来，恐怕要到三十到五十年"。刘少奇的解释是：因为苏联过去是把地富都驱逐了，而我们没有这样做，还和地富在一起，因此如果界线划不清会很危险。[66] 中共从此摆脱了社会主义条件下阶级问题的困扰，不再管张三李四有没有生产资料，有没有剥削，直截了当地把一个人的思想政治倾向和他的阶级定性联系在一起了。

1962年8月9日，毛泽东在北戴河会议上讲：社会主义条件下有没有阶级斗争的问题，过去认识不清，我1955年底曾在《中国农村的社会主义高潮》一书中讲资产阶级消灭了，只有资本主义思想残余的影响的话，"讲错了，要更正"。其实，资产阶级人还在，心不死；"资本主义思想，几十年，几百年都存在"。凡是为国际资本主义服务的，就是反革命。[67] 9月，中共中央召开八届十中全会，毛泽东在会上阐述了他对社会主义条件下阶级问题的长期思考结果。他声称："社会主义国家有没有阶级存在？有没有阶级斗争？现在可以肯定，社会主义国家有阶级存在，阶级斗争肯定是存在的……反动阶级可能复辟……我们从现在起，就必须年年讲、月月讲、天天讲……使我们对这个问题有一条比较清醒的马克思列宁主义的路线"。[68]

把社会主义社会视为阶级社会，在社会主义社会里实行阶级斗争，这多半是从斯大林到毛泽东在落后国家创建一国社会主义的必然结果。斯大林囿于马克思列宁主义的理论束缚，不敢公然背离马克思主义的阶级定义，宣布社会主义建成后，只能宣布剥削阶级已经不复存在。但是，恐惧于政权的不稳，斯大林用阶级斗争方式进行内部清洗、监禁、流放、杀戮几乎从未停止过。同样基于对政权不稳的担心，毛泽东就没有那么多顾忌，他公开宣布社会主义社会存在阶级斗争，并据此大搞各种政治运动，从"四清"运动，一直搞到无产阶级文化大革命，并且还想要永远"在无产阶级专政下继续革命"下去。

八、平等理想在中国的异化

什么是社会主义？其实，在中国众多百姓和知识精英的内心里，最简单直白的理解，就是"平等"两个字。

　　有学者举过一个例子，很形象。他写道：恩格斯在《社会主义从空想到科学的发展》一文中说："以往的全部历史，除原始状态外，都是阶级斗争的历史；这些互相斗争的社会阶级，在任何时候都是生产关系和交换关系的产物，一句话，都是自己时代的经济关系的产物"。而国人在1907年出版的《新世纪》杂志中，却将此段文字译为："各种过去之历史，舍去古史外，皆系人类竞争史，而所以竞争之因，皆缘于经济之不平等"。他总结说："显然，理论上的生产关系、经济关系范畴，在中国人脑子里反映出的却是实用性极强的'经济之不平等'。说白了，社会主义无非是'等贵贱，均贫富'的同义词。世界之初直到五四，人们就是带着这种潜在的思维框架去理解和宣传社会主义的"。[69]

　　毛泽东对社会主义的最初观感，也不出其右。事实上，在他还很少提到社会主义一词的时候，他就一直在关注这个平等问题了。1919年7月，他在《湘江评论》创刊号上，就力陈了对不平等现象的由衷反感，他对贵族、资本家因占教育、资本和武器之利，而使社会中人分成了智愚、贫富、强弱等不同的阶级，感到不满；他尖锐批评资本主义托拉斯的实行是"几个人享福，千万人要哭。产业愈发达，要哭的人愈多"。[70]今人所能见毛泽东第一次谈"社会主义"，也是强调它"既能解决工人痛苦，且可补救现代社会之缺陷"。[71]面对社会上的种种不平，毛泽东认为他和其他知识分子最大的不同，就是其他人仅仅是从旁观者，甚至是教育者的立场看问题，在一边指手画脚，自己却是站在那些小人物和穷人的立场上，觉得这些人"也是些像我自己家里人那样的普通人"。[72]早年最能反映毛泽东这种心态和特性的，就是他替长沙铅印活版工会写给长沙《大公报》记者的一封公开信。他对记者教训工人口吻和态度之反感，在信中反映得淋漓尽致。[73]

　　毛泽东对平等的执着，与他出身、成长和受到传统思想影响的经历有密切关系。因为他生长在湖南韶山冲的山沟里，在家里总被父亲训斥，读书较晚，又因岁数大、家庭条件差和是外乡学生，常受同学歧视。以后虽升至中学，入读了长沙第一师范，但学历也仅及中等，毕业后即去附小教书，与北京、上海等大城市里众多大学生，以及年纪相同却已功成名就或学成归国的大学教授们[74]相比，为了湖南的事情常在北京、上海间奔走的毛泽东，心态上时有不平之感，可想而知。毛泽东后来回忆过他五四期间在北京大学的一段经历，可以很清楚地反映出他当时内心的失落和不满。他说：自己曾在北京大学图书馆做守助理员，学生、教授来来往往，谁也不注意他。他看到很多名人，包括一些有名的学生，曾试图同他们交谈，他们却"没有时间听一个图书馆助理员讲南方土话"。他的感觉是，"由于我的职位低下，人们都不愿同我来往……都不把我当人看待"。[75]

和多数从乡下进城，然后一步步跻入上层社会，包括因革命成功取得高位的政治人物不同，毛泽东从来不曾因为身份地位的改变而刻意让自己变得绅士化和贵族化。恰恰相反，他在衣食住行及日常生活习惯上，始终保持着农民的本色，而且在思想观念上始终对小人物和穷人表示同情，对任何高高在上，看不起小人物或压迫穷人的人或事，尤其是对所谓"官僚主义"，都会由衷反感。然而，这方面的问题从中共进城之日起，就层出不穷了。用毛泽东的话来说，那些都是资产阶级的臭气，是蒋介石的阴魂作怪。每天"要剃头，刮胡子，学绅士派头，装资产味，实在没有味道。为什么要刮胡子呢？一年剃四次头，刮四次胡子不是很好吗？"[76]

按照斯大林的说法，毛泽东相信，社会主义不过是一种新型的生产关系，而生产关系主要就是"所有制、劳动生产中人与人之间的相互关系、分配形式三个方面"的关系。[77]无论从苏联的经验，还是从中国的经验，毛都很容易看出，在这三个关系当中，所有制关系不难解决，只要掌握了政权就行。实行按劳分配在生产资料所有制改造完成以后，也很容易办到。真正困难的，只有一个人们在劳动生产中平等关系的实现问题，因为这种关系"是不会自然出现的。资产阶级法权的存在，一定要从各方面妨碍这种平等关系的形成和发展"。[78]事实证明，革命成功了，改造完成了，按劳分配实现了，"闹级别、闹待遇"的现象，干部官僚主义，以及各种不平等的现象都比战争时期反而大大增多了。

对此，毛泽东一度百思不得其解，刚进城时多把这些情况类比资产阶级的"糖衣炮弹"和思想侵蚀。但多年之后，他已转而相信，除了资产阶级思想影响以外，更主要的是环境变了，地位变了，生活富了。1958年以后，他开始反复讲，还是穷好。说中国所以能革命，根本上是一个穷字。说：现在看，还是穷好，富不好，穷则思变，"穷，就要干，要革命，要搞社会主义"。[79]说"'穷是动力'这句话，讲得很对。因为穷就要革命，就要不断革命。富了，事情就不妙了"。说西方世界就是太富了，所以"资产阶级思想成堆"。[80]在他看来，干部思想的改变，一个重要原因就是放弃了战争时期的供给制，实行了等级制和工资制，把人在级别及其收入上分成了三六九等。直到晚年，他都反复在强调这个问题，即：

中国属于社会主义国家，所有制变更了，但是却和旧社会没有多少差别，仍旧实行八级工资制、按劳分配、货币交换，还有商品存在，在没有资产阶级的情况下，依旧必须实行"资产阶级法权"，平等依旧还只是形式上的，实际上还很不平等。[81]

一方面，毛泽东不希望拉大人与人之间的差别；一方面，他又相信马列的理论，相信建国初必须要向资产阶级法权让步，因此放弃过去的供给制，实行了等级工资制，说"要保留工资差别"。保留的结果，在分配制度方面，新中国自建国伊始就照搬了苏联的职务等级工资制，并且发扬了中国传统的官本位制。国家党政干部，被规定为享受国家最好待遇的脱产群体。一切其他相关职业人员的工资收入，均比照干部待遇标准制定相应标准，且其各级待遇标准，均不得超过同级干部待遇标准。干部工资、住房及其各种待遇，则严格按照干部等级予以提供。党政干部及其普通公职人员工资收入分级，多到30个级别；最高最低之差，一度达到30倍，以后陆续降到20多倍。而且，和苏联的情况相同，普通干部的工资收入与生活待遇，通常与工人的等级工资收入差距不大，全国上下大家看上去分配很平均。但是，一旦达到高级干部的程度，特别是被列入中央组织部管理的职级名单，享受的各种其他保健、疗养、差旅、警卫、秘书、保姆、车辆、住房以及特殊商品的供应等种种待遇，就和苏联特权阶层的待遇相差不多了，那远不是一般干部和民众所能企及的。中国的官本位体制，正是这样来的。同样，所有高级干部的子女，从教育，到生长环境，相互通婚，到最后被优先安排为"革命接班人"，随着中共执政时间的延长，也逐渐和苏联的情况没有太大差别了。

因此，在毛泽东时代的中国，干部身份，尤其是它的级别高低，和苏联一样，明显地成为这个新社会中人们地位优越与否的最重要的标志。各地和中央党政军的大批高级干部，事实上也和苏联的官僚阶层一样，客观上逐渐成了社会上具有特殊身份、地位、权势和影响的一个特殊阶层。

毛泽东并非完全不了解这方面的情况，他很早就想到要预防的问题，提出要"破除老爷态度，三风五气"，来避免干群关系出问题。[82] 建国不久，还在1951年底，他就已开始号召整风，要求党外人士和他一起反对党的干部的官僚主义了。一次还不够，1953年1月，1957年初，他又几度发动过反对官僚主义的斗争。1956年底，1958，1960年，毛泽东还三度带头降低过高级干部的工资收入。在他看来，既然接受了等级制，就要用这些办法抑制干部的特权思想和作风，而且要常抓不懈，过几年就要来一次。毛泽东提议取消军衔制，提出知识分子"皮毛论"，[83] 主张干部下放"五七"干校劳动，号召知识青年上山下乡，指派工宣队、军宣队进驻大、中、小学，乃至于发动"四清"运动整农村干部，发动文化大革命整一切当权派，都和他的这种担心密切相关。

问题是，既然搞了等级制，如毛泽东自己所说："等级森严，居高临下，脱离群众，不以平等待人，不是靠工作能力吃饭，而是靠资格、靠权力，干群之间、上下级之间的猫鼠关系和父子关系，这些东西……破了又会生"。因为这些人官做大了，有汽车，有好房子，薪水高，还有服务员，自以为了不起，比资本家还厉害，成了一个"既得利益集团"。这个问题的困扰，导致他开始相信："在社会主义社会里，地富反坏右，一部分干部，一部分想扩大资产阶级法权的人，想退回到资本主义去，多数人想干共产主义，因此，必不可免要有斗争，要有长期的斗争"。[84] 他最终所以会认定"资产阶级就在党内"，并下决心大打党内走资本主义道路的当权派，原因也在这里。

除了在干群或官民待遇收入差别问题上，新政府的政策从一开始就没有真正朝着毛泽东所希望的平等方向努力外，作为社会主义社会最主要特征的分配制度及其社会福利制度，毛泽东的社会主义距离马克思、恩格斯设想的社会平等也相差甚远。这是因为，按照马克思关于社会主义是资本主义发展最后产物的论断，社会主义在物质丰富程度和可以满足每一个社会成员需要的程度方面，也理应远远优越于资本主义。反观毛时代的社会主义，全国民众却仅仅保持在一种勤俭奋斗、节衣缩食，很多时候甚至还要勒紧裤腰带过日子的水平上。

不错，必须肯定，在毛泽东时代，亿万普通中国人过的是一种大致平均化的生活。他们中相当多数都得到了温饱，特别是城里人，多数像在欧文所设计的公社制度里和移民实验区里一样，充分享受到均平分配所带来的物质生活上的大体平均。生老病死及其子女教育，以至住房，多由国家的公费医疗、义务教育和福利住房政策一包到底。生活水平虽低，物质条件虽差，吃穿住行基本不愁，无须担心上不起学、看不起病、住不起房，更不用担心因灾病困顿而流落街头。全国人民虽然只能穿大体一样的衣服，吃一样的饭菜，从事一样不需要消耗金钱的运动，受一样的教育，看一样的图书和电影，接受一样的信息，进行整齐划一的思考等等，但相对于许多过去曾经经历过颠沛流离、饥寒交迫的许多普通民众来说，这种生活已足以让他们感到满足了。只是，这种连人们基本生活消费，如粮、棉、布、肉、蛋、瓜子、花生、豆腐等，全部都要凭票限量供应，更不存在任何多样性选择的平均主义生活，就是理想家们世代所期望的社会主义社会吗？

至少，马克思是坚决反对这种社会主义的。他曾极其愤怒地谴责过巴枯宁等所宣传的普遍贫穷，且靠暴力维系的共产主义，说它败坏了社会主义运动的声誉。他们尖锐地指责巴枯宁所宣传的这种社会理想是"兵营式共产主义"，表面上一切齐全："公共食堂和公共寝室，评判员和为教育、生产、消费，总之为全部社会活动规定了各种办法的办事处"。实质上却没有个人自由，没有民主选举，每个人都生活在他人的监视之下，并且被要求"多劳动少消费"。他们指出，这种表面上看起来"超级革命"的理想，实际上忽视人的自由和生命的"共产主义"，不仅不合乎共产主义所追求的人的解放的全部理想，而且破坏了人类最基本的道德伦理。[85]

归根结底，在马克思主义看来，平等也是一种生产关系，它也必定要受到生产力发展的局限。落后国家的社会主义所以只能是一国的，而不是国际的，是因为它们原本就没有完全纳入到世界资本主义的生产方式中去。斯大林和毛泽东的社会主义之所以只能是集权专制的，而不可能是民主自由的，也是因为中苏两国原本就没有经历过资本主义民主政治阶段，依靠强力夺取的政权，也只有依靠强权才能够巩固与维系。同样，毛泽东的社会主义之所以无法达成他所期望的平等，既是因为他的集权统治必须要依赖于官僚体制层层控制，因而客观上必须要通过等级制的办法形成一个围绕着他的权力中心的既得利益集团，同时也是因为中国当时的生产力还无法满足大多数人较高水平的生活所需。实际上，即使是上述低水平的全民福利，在毛泽东时代，真正能够享受其恩泽甘露者，六亿人口中也不过十分之一二。

相信凡是关注过中国城乡差别或城乡二元结构问题的读者都能了解，因为要确保城市居民生活的稳定和秩序，特别是为了全力推进国家工业化的进程，国家甚至还实行了极端不合理的农村户口制度，将建国后很快就失去了刚刚到手的土地支配权的大量农民，强制性地拴在农村，既不能享有和城市居民同等的社会福利待遇，还必须承担极为沉重的赋税和交粮负担。正是因为强行推行了这样一种严密控制的制度，1958年"大跃进"时才会出现全国范围的胡干蛮干和"浮夸"作假；正是因为农民的迁徙自由遭到禁止，灾难来临才会发生空前绝后的大批农民惨遭饿毙的历史惨剧。换言之，毛时代对众多社会底层民众最具吸引力的全民福利政策，其实也只能惠及城市中全民所有制单位和企业中的人员，对于占全国人口六分之五，包括大批曾经为共产党的革命起到过关键性作用的农民，国家也只能完全放手，听由农民集体经济自己解决。经济条件较好的公社，则解决较好；经济条件恶劣的公社，则或者仰赖国家临时性救济，或眼看农民在灾病中自生自灭。而这种情况，直到改革开放之初，享受着全民福利的城里人才吃惊地发现，原来几亿农民大多数还没有解决温饱问题，不少地方的农民仍在过着吃糠咽菜、挨饿受冻的日子！

毛时代贫困公社的农民究竟有多穷，生活有多惨呢？这里仅举1980年党的若干历史问题决议稿讨论会上两位与会者的发言以见一斑。

王国权（曾任建国初热河省委书记、驻德、波、澳等国大使、民政部常务副部长、人大常委会副主任）发言称：“我们搞了三十一年，人民群众的物质、文化生活搞成今天这个样子，尚有千千万万人民饱暖问题存在很大困难，实在对不起人民。我不久前，曾到辽宁的朝阳，河北的承德地区走了一趟。那里的群众在战争年代是同我们同甘共苦的，但现在许多公社的人民‘衣不遮体，房上无泥，炕上无席，没钱治病，一贫如洗’……建昌过去是原热东一带较富的地区，几十年没有大变化，而今仅有一百九十五户的娘娘庙公社孟松沟大队，全队二十五岁到五十岁的男社员九十二人，因为穷，娶不起媳妇。朝阳县大屯公社天屯大队大犁树沟生产队，共二十六户，有三十四个二十五岁以上的光棍，没有一个育龄妇女。……群众说：‘我们实在困难，就怕饿肚子’”。[86]

丁明发言称：“我们有一批记者，最近几个月重点调查了陕甘宁五个地区的情况，他们说：若非亲自目睹，其穷困落后的程度，是难以想象的。……从社员生活来说，不少社员的家庭长年处于缺吃少穿的状况，炕上只有一、两条破烂不堪的被褥，身上鹑衣百结，补丁加补丁。少数极困难的户，家中不但没有被褥，而且炕席也没有。……相当多的队甚至比合作社之前、比建国前的陕甘宁边区更加贫困了。我们党是怎样领导这件大事的？”[87]

除了农民多数没有得到平等地位和均平待遇外，毛时代由于奉行阶级政策，实行阶级斗争和阶级专政，因此，不同阶级成份、不同阶级家庭出身，乃至于有这样或那样历史疑点，有这样或那样海外关系的人，都可能处在极不平等的地位上，受到极不公正的待遇。

在这方面最典型的，就是对毛泽东所说的"地富反坏右"分子及其家属子女的政策。在农村者，或被发配到农村、农场去接受管制者自不必提，即使是在国家党政军及企事业各部门工作者，亦均得随时通过干部人事以及各种相关组织制度，进行严格政审，并将相关调查及交待材料记入档案。所有单位均得根据该人阶级出身、社会成份和个人历史情况，依照政治可靠标准等级安排工作和考虑接受其入党、入团或其他级别升降等问题。凡占有过生产资料者和被查出有过"政治历史问题"者，均会被列入清理打击对象，或会被划入另册，控制使用。由于当政者在城乡几乎所有有人的地方，都要严格编列户口或人事档案，进而依照三六九等对在政治上进行排队，划定亲疏等级，因而在人与人的关系上，明显地存在着严重不平等的情况。所谓"红五类"和"黑五类"的社会身份符号，甚至在这个最讲平等的"社会主义社会"中形成了"老子英雄儿好汉，老子反动儿混蛋"之类具有浓厚封建色彩的血统论观念的流行。所谓地、富、反、坏、右及其家属子女，事实上也就成了中国社会当中的低种姓人群，且永无翻身之日。而阶级斗争持续不断，运动一个接着一个，也就造成了一波又一波新的"地富反坏右"分子及其家属。由此带来的社会不公平、不平等的范围，自然也就越来越大。

不难看出，毛泽东时代的社会主义陷入了这样一种自我异化的怪圈：它反对阶级压迫，又主张阶级压迫；它厌恶穷，又恐惧富；它崇尚平等，又坚持不平等；它靠革命取得了创造平等的机会，又为了把这种制造平等的机会永远控制在自己的手中，坚信必须用新的不平等来造成平等……。

九、"社会主义"——国家资本主义化的历史必然

从十八世纪末巴贝夫的"大国民公社"，十九世纪初欧文的"新协和村"、傅立叶的"法伦斯泰尔"，和十九世纪中后期马克思、恩格斯推崇的"巴黎公社"开始，人类探索实现社会主义或共产主义理想的努力，已经持续了两个世纪之久了。然而，迄今为止，不仅共产主义遥遥无期，就是社会主义也全无成功的榜样。甚至，人们至今还无法就人类理想社会的基本标准或要件，达成比较一致的看法。对于什么是社会主义，更是众说纷纭。

一个最值得讨论的标准问题就是，究竟什么算是公有制？

无论过去，还是今天，相信凡是承认社会主义有其实践的价值者，大都同意社会主义的最重要标准之一，是生产资料应该收归公有，或者是国有。问题是，经过苏联的社会主义实践，经过中国的社会主义实践，我们能够认为，斯大林，或者毛泽东时代苏联或中国两国的社会主义所有制，是马克思、恩格斯或一切社会主义理想家们所设想的那样一种所有制吗？

按照马克思的唯物史观，任何一种所有制，无论是私有，还是公有，都注定只能是现实生产力发展和需要的结果。马克思和恩格斯再三讲，社会之所以存在着私人占有生产资料的情况，并据此划分为不同的阶级，是因为社会总劳动提供的产品除了满足社会全体成员最起码的生活需要外，只有少量剩余，劳动谋生占去了社会大多数成员的几乎全部时间。能够占有这少量剩余，脱离直接生产劳动的，只能是社会上的一少部分人。这是现实生产力发展的水平所决定的。要想由社会占有全部生产资料，"只有在实现它的物质条件已经具备的时候才能成为可能，才能成为历史的必然性"。[88]

如果上述逻辑成立，那么，斯大林时代的苏联，或毛泽东时代的中国，具备这样的物质条件吗？回答无疑是否定的。那么，在它们两国的物质条件还不完全具备生产出足以满足社会全体成员生活需要，还缺少大量剩余的条件的情况下，苏中两国党的领导人宣布实现了的那个"公有制"（"国家所有"和"集体所有"），能够是全社会占有吗？对于这种情况，恩格斯早在十八世纪末就明确讲过，在生产力还不足以制造出那样大量的社会产品的条件下，即使有人宣布把生产资料国有化了，也"没有消除生产力的资本属性"。说到底，这种作法不过把资本的所有者，从私人改换成了国家而已。[89]

因为，第一，它不可能给劳动者提供恩格斯所说的"充分的生活和享乐的资料"，无论苏联还是中国，都长期生活在物资严重匮乏的条件下，中国甚至还存在着众多缺吃少穿的人群；第二，它不可能改变普通劳动者在生产劳动中被动的和从属的地位，苏联和中国农民的境遇自不必提，即使是政治上被提得很高，生活条件比其他阶层不差的工人，也一样不能有自己的工会组织，不仅不能选举自己信得过的人出任领导职务，而且不能为自身的利益监督干预产品的生产和销售；第三，它更不可能如马克思、恩格斯所再三强调的那样，在取消私有制的同时，"就消灭了作为无产阶级的自身，消灭了一切阶级差别和阶级对立，也消灭了作为国家的国家"。[90] 而这一结果，才是人们主张建立生产资料公有制的初衷和目的。换言之，生产资料和社会财富"国有"，不等于消灭了"私有"，不等于生产资料和社会财富变成了"公有"，即"社会所有"。[91] 它充其量不过是把生产资料和社会财富，从私人手中，转移到了以国家的名义控制着国家的官僚集团手中去了。这也正是为什么，在毛泽东时代，国家财产事实上成了无主的财产，人人都想从公家那里各取所需，却很少人愿意为社会各尽所能。改行市场经济，人们又可以合法拥有和享用财富之后，理论上应该是公共所有的财产，轻而易举地被大大小小的掌权者，通过各种合法与非法的方式，近水楼台地假公济私，甚或化公为私了。它和马克思所设想的那个没有阶级、没有国家*的共产主义第一阶段——社会主义，完全是风马牛不相及。

同样的情况，即使加上计划经济和按劳分配，也一样不等于有了所谓社会主义。欧文、卡贝等许多空想社会主义者都进行过种种局部的社会实验，包括在部分人群中实行财产公有和按劳分配，生活在这些实验中的人们是不是享受到了某种平等，并感到了某种幸福呢？回答无疑是肯定的。但是，在整个社会大的经济环境之下，在外部的经济运行法则资本主义化的条件下，他们的这种实验充其量只是局部的，和不可能持久的。斯大林、毛泽东等共产党人后来所推行的，以一国为范围的更大规模的实验，不过是在重蹈众多空想社会主义或空想共产主义者的小规模的实验的覆辙罢了。

更为重要的是，计划经济也好，按劳分配也好，也并非共产党国家所特有，近百年来，资本主义各国几乎没有哪国不曾采取过相同的经济政策和分配方式，只是程度不同而已。尤其是1960年代众多按照斯大林模式社会主义的办法，宣布实行了计划经济、按劳分配，甚至是建立了公有制的非洲国家，更是往往在一夜之间就转变成"社会主义"的了。然而，除了它们自己以外，无论是苏联人，还是毛泽东，大概也没有哪个国家的共产党人真的认为这些国家是在实行社会主义的。为什么？因为他们的这种实验多半只是建立在刺刀尖上，通常只是更加强化了占统治地位的那个部落头领的威权和某个所谓的党对整个国家财富的支配力罢了。那里往往连多数人内部的分配平等都难以实现，甚至与马克思、恩格斯所强调的"资本主义社会本身的最后产物"，即高度工业化，都毫不沿边。[92]

　　相比较而言，毛时代中国社会主义的超阶段性实验，与非洲许多国家的社会主义超阶段实验，究竟有多大本质上的差别呢？毕竟，就像恩格斯说过的那样："每一种特定的经济形态都应当解决它自己的、从它本身产生的任务，如果要去解决另一种完全不同的经济形态所面临的问题，那是十分荒谬的"。[93] 以中国当时的生产力水平，虽然在某种程度上确实大大高于非洲部落经济的水平，但它仍旧远远落后于发达的资本主义国家。要想以中国前资本主义的，或仅及于欧洲工业化早期的生产力水平，来解决远高于资本主义生产力水平的社会主义经济形态所面临的各种问题，从马克思的唯物史观的角度来看问题，其最终的不成功，也是可想而知的。用恩格斯的话来说，"只要生产的规模还没有达到既可满足社会全体成员的需要，又有剩余产品去增加社会资本和进一步发展生产力，就总会有支配社会生产力的统治阶级和另外一个阶级，即贫穷和被压迫的阶级存在"。[94] 基于这样的观点来看毛时代中国社会主义条件下继续存在的阶级压迫的现象，是不是会给我们另外一种启发呢？

　　不难了解，按照马克思主义的社会主义理论，当今的任何一种社会主义实践都注定要陷入死胡同。因为一个最基本的事实就是，资本主义至今不仅依然保持着强劲的发展势头，而且还在不断地为适应新的形势而改造着它自身，它依旧是当今，甚至是今后世界数百年经济运行的制度基础。在这种情况下，要么我们不相信马克思关于社会主义是"资本主义社会本身的最后产物"这一唯物史观的基本论点，不打马克思主义的旗号，像欧文、卡贝等人那样，或不管马克思他们说什么，像斯大林、毛泽东那样，自创社会主义；要么我们就不要去想在资本主义全球化继续发展的条件下，有任何一种社会主义成功的可能性。

　　很显然，即使进入到后毛泽东时代，即使我们开始了改革开放，并且使中国今天的生产力水平大大超越了毛泽东时代，我们至多也只是距离当代资本主义的生产力水平更近了一步而已。中国今天的生产和交换方式，乃至于中国今天的经济生活和社会生活，都更加明显地变成了以资本为主义，距离人类理想中的社会主义，或马克思主义的社会主义，相去更远了。而处在资本经济强势发展过程中的中国，不可避免地正在重蹈各资本主义列强的老路，通过资本输出和各种正当和不正当的手法，在世界范围争夺资源和商品市场。至于资本主义早期工业化所出现过的贫富悬殊、官

商勾结、道德失范、环境污染、资源浪费等等令人瞠目结舌的丑
陋现象，就更是到处滋生，且愈演愈烈。

相对于共产党人曾经矢志追寻的社会主义理想，今天的这一切，
到底是历史的进步，还是历史的倒退，甚或干脆像网上一些人所说，
是历史的反动呢？

对此，我们似乎还可以回到马克思唯物史观的立场来看问题。
按照马克思的唯物史观，有什么样水平的生产力，就有什么样的
生产关系和社会关系，也自然会产生出与之相适应的思想观念与
社会状况。今天的中国之所以会出现西方资本主义早期工业化过
程中出现的种种弊病，不正是中国自改革开放以来，与国际资本
主义市场全面接轨，重启资本原始积累和急速走上工业现代化道
路的进程带来的吗？事实上，无论过去，还是现在，高度集权的
制度体制，无论叫什么主义和实行怎样的所有制，用前述恩格斯
的说法，都改变不了其资本的属性。只不过，这种严重压抑了人
的自由权利的集权体制，从历史发展的角度看问题，却很难用好
或坏来做评价。这是因为，相对于计划开始大规模工业建设的国
家来说，这种高度集权的体制通常正是最能够推动生产力发展的
一种手段。事实上，自十九世纪以来，德国、日本等许多当时落
后的资本主义国家，都曾这样做过。如第二次世界大战爆发前后
的德国，强行将所有军需工业，包括所有重工业及能源工业，全
部纳入政府的生产计划之中，结合以战时统制经济，即以一国之
力占领了几乎整个欧洲，而且坚持战争长达数年之久。

作为落后国家，要想以最快速度完成资本的原始积累，最简便
的办法就实行中央集权的政治经济体制，以国家资本主义的形式，
通过国有化运动，垂直计划，集中国力，强化民众动员，压缩消费，
甚或剥夺农民，强购统销，榨取农产品以换取外汇和进口机器设
备等等办法，来加速实现国家的工业化进程。二十世纪的苏联，
其实也是这样做的。毛时代和当今的中国，也不例外。中国后
三十年之经济腾飞，正是建立在中国前三十年工业猛进的基础之
上的；中国今日政治经济进展之局限，也一样是受着中国整体发
展程度之困扰。

一言以蔽之，落后国家由农业化而至工业化，因而转向现代化，
是一个不可避免的过程。而这个过程，无论是走民主道路，还是
走集权道路，无论是实行市场经济，还是实行计划经济，就其发
展的阶段性和实质而言，其实并无多少差别，即都处于资本主义
的生长期。只不过前者属于以私人资本为经济发展主要支柱的社

会，后者则是以社会（或国家）资本为经济发展主要支柱的社会。而凡是后起的发展中国家，尤其是较大、较落后的国家，要想早日赶上先进国家，又往往以集中全社会资本于国家（实为政党）手中，并通过剥夺农民和用计划经济方式发展经济为最捷径。

这也正是为什么，同斯大林时代几乎一样，毛泽东时代也是内斗不断，伤人无数，政策失误导致经济危机和政治破产造成经济严重停滞和下降，但是，自1952–1978年间，中国经济生产总值年平均仍为6.1％，远超过印度等发展中国家，甚至超过了苏联。中国的粮食产量，也得益于政社合一的动员体制长年持续大规模地集中劳力兴修水利，因而从1952年的164亿吨，增长到1978年的305亿吨，即使算上人口增长数，人均粮食也由285公斤增加到了317公斤。而整个中国经济，工业部门所创造的产值在整个GDP中所占的比重，也从1952年的21％，上升到了48％，成功地改变了中国以农业为主的国民经济结构，并使中国的工业部门可以摆脱农业的牵制，成为一个相对独立的产业部门了。

一方面因专制集权而不得不压制人权、自由，甚至制造严重不平等和种种伤害，一方面却强力推进工业化，在短短二十多年时间里，一举把一个农业国，变成了一个初步的工业国，为文革后邓小平的改革开放与经济腾飞，提供了不可或缺的政治制度保障和物质基础。换言之，即使是改革开放，实际上也得益于毛泽东式的政治独裁体制甚多，否则，要想打破"凡是"原则和平均主义民众基础，都难于想象。如果没有毛时代奠定下来的已经相当庞大的工业基础，连同农业水利建设与沿海农村小工业（小钢铁、小机械、小化肥、小水泥、小水电）的成绩，和既无内外债，又无通胀压力的经济形势，中国1978年以后要想顺利纳入世界贸易体系，向外大量借贷和引进海外加工业，迅速实现经济转轨并保持经济的持续增长，也注定难上加难。

历史之吊诡，莫此为甚。这也正是如今左右两派观点对立，互不相下之所在。但是，如果我们不是拘泥于社会主义的理想概念，而是从唯物史观的角度，按照有什么样的生产力，就有什么样的生产关系这一逻辑来看问题，我们就不难了解：国家的资源无法真正实现社会占有，只能集中在一党的掌控之下，恰恰是经济发展程度所决定的。资本国家化，即利用国家的名义掌握或运用资本，不过是不同历史阶段下部分落后国家加速发展资本主义生产力的一种特殊选择而已。

在这种问题上，人们的主观愿望会与客观现实相背离，是不可避免的。也即是说，共产党人中许多人确实想要建设和实现一个人人平等、分配均平的社会主义社会，然而，客观的社会现实与条件却使他们完全偏离了他们设想的目标，造成了南橘北枳的效果。比较而言，毛泽东和邓小平各自的实践，在社会主义这一点上，只是五十步和百步的区别而已。

十、国家资本主义的未来选择与出路

国家资本主义是一把双刃剑，用它来发展经济，最大的益处是国家的经济会迎来高速发展，国力会大幅提升；最大的弊端则是对人的权利的侵害和对自由的剥夺，长此以往，难免会导致社会的深刻分裂与冲突，最终造成人们本不愿看到的惨剧与灾难。

但是，经济成长带来金钱至上和物质主义泛滥的同时，其实也会带来人们对自身权利和自由的重视，从而一步步推动政治的变革。资本主义早期工业化残酷剥削和野蛮争夺的历史之成为过去，已经很明显地证明了这种情况。欧亚一些国家一度高度集权，用国家资本主义的方式，剥夺国民的权利与自由，强力推进国家强盛进程，最终也或以失败告终，或以转型结束，也都印证了这一发展的趋势不可避免。这是因为，任何一种经济的成长，最终都注定会促成人的生活水平和文化程度的提升，并因此启蒙或强化人对自身权利与自由的认识与追求。这就如同中国政府的少数民族政策一样，少数民族的文化程度越低，中央政府的统治就越牢固。反之，为少数民族培养的知识分子越多，各种分离主义的思想和势力也就越容易滋长。尤其是在实行市场经济的情况下，经济权利的多元化，势必会促成人们对政治利益多元化的要求与企盼。社会经济增长越迅速，人们生活水平越提高，其思想文化的多元化要求也就会越明显，越强烈。因此中国改革开放后，生产方式、生产关系，包括所有制形式、经济运行模式和分配方式的改变，固然带来了思维方式和生活方式的改变，同时也催生了这个社会多元化趋向的发展。30年来，中国社会的自由度和人与人之间的平等感，随着社会整体富裕程度的提升，在潜移默化中明显地得到了很大的提升。

相信所有从毛泽东那个时代的社会主义中走过来的人应该都能够感觉得到，过去那个人们几乎没有可能跨出国门，几乎不敢与海外亲友发生任何关系，就连收听短波收音机都可能被打成反革命的时代,一去不复返了。今天的中国人已经不再满足于收音机了,甚至已经不再单纯从政府控制的电视节目里面了解中国与世界了。人们不仅可以很容易地拥有电话、手机、电视、电脑,可以在国内和国外自由旅行,可以通过网络查找他所需要的绝大部分信息,而且还可以匿名在网上随心所欲地批评政府,批评除了最高领导集体以外的几乎任何官吏了。而以往那种将人在政治上分成三六九等,"红五类"压迫"黑五类"的情况,也已成为历史了。

同样是集权和官僚体制,当今的中国和毛时代的中国,国民的自由、平等为什么会有很大的不同和差别?这是因为:

第一,这和经济发展的现实需要有关。毛泽东重的是阶级斗争,因此主张"紧张"。划清阶级界限,随时斗争,是他的一种统治手法。但要全面发展经济,尤其是要实行市场经济、自由贸易,就非消除紧张,调动一切积极因素,还人人平等的地位不可。

第二,这和生产力发展水平有关系。比照各国资本主义发展史,自由的程度通常都是与生产力发达的程度有联系的。生产力发展水平越高,国民对自由的要求程度相对也就越高,实现自由的手段和途径也就会相应增多。

第三,这和开放程度和经济运行方式有密切关系。毛时代搞闭关锁国,自力更生,与世界经济基本上不接轨。改革开放后,我们靠的是融入世界资本主义经济体系,广吸财源,博采众长,自由贸易,廉价竞争。经济开放,政治上不能不受影响,政治控制的松动不可避免。

考察资本主义的发展史,我们不难发现,自由、平等的问题归根结底是与生产力以及经济发达程度相联系的。在欧洲十七、十八世纪,人们对平等的主要要求是政治上的,即强调所谓天赋人权,人生而平等,追求的是人人都应享有均等的权利与机会,因为这是发展资本主义自由贸易和市场经济所必需的社会政治基础。进入到十九世纪和二十世纪初,人们对平等的要求更多地转向了经济问题,许多人主张要节制资本,公平分配,甚至有了力主消灭私有制的革命的社会主义主张。之所以会有这种区别,是因为不同的时代欧洲所面临的主要社会问题不同。十七、十八世纪欧洲的主要问题是封建专制特权的无法无天,及封建等级制度对社会和人的严重束缚,因而才会产生以强调天赋人权思想为特色的自由主义思潮。进入到十九世纪和二十世纪初,欧洲各主要资本主义国家的问题更多地变成了贫富悬殊和两极分化,出现了严重的经济危机和阶级斗争,这才促成了以要求分配平等为特色的社会主义思潮的兴起。而所有这些的关键，都与资本主义工业化发展的进程有关，反映了不同生产力条件下不同社会矛盾所造成的不同的社会要求。

无论我们对人类现代化进程的原因和走向有怎样不同的解读，我们显然没有办法回避一个基本事实，那就是：不管哪一国、哪一族的人，对自由、平等的要求注定是会随着社会经济发展与时俱进的。而今，也许没有人能够准确预见未来社会可能是怎样的，共产主义的理想天国多半只是一种乌托邦，但是，历史却早已告诉我们，人是社会性动物，必须在理性的相互交往中达到共生共荣的目的，因此，人类必须超越一般动物仅止于满足纯粹肉体需要的自然本能，从弱肉强食的相互伤害中摆脱出来，不断地改造和创造适合于人类共同生存的社会环境。而这也正是人类几千年来不断追求自由、平等和博爱理想的一个重要原因。

资本主义社会的生长，就是与人的价值发现、人权自由的获得，密切相关的。资本主义存在和成功运行至今的重要基础，就是价值规律，而价值规律的前提即要承认等价交换的原则。这一原则必须假设，交易的双方及其双方的地位事实上是平等的，任何一方不得以任何名义占据特殊的权利地位，使另一方得不到公平交易的结果。因此，没有天赋人权和人生而平等的牢固信念，没有法律面前人人平等的制度保护，也就没有自由贸易和市场经济的顺利发展，自然也就没有资本主义。没有资本主义，也就很难造成后来的民主政治和民族国家，自然也就不可能真正成就人类的现代化。

当然，仅仅承认天赋人权，人人平等是不够的。人先天的强弱与后天生长环境等种种不同所造成的不平等是客观存在的。仅仅满足于人生而平等、人权自由，满足于法律面前人人平等，即满足于资本主义的现代化进程，注定了也只会对社会上一部分人有利，人与人之间的不平等依然会存在，而且还会因为经济的愈益发展而形成严重的贫富悬殊、社会分化和阶级斗争。人类不能满足于既有的自由、平等，而必须要进一步改造资本主义，也是势所必然。

注意到上述历史进程，我们应该不难了解社会主义对当今资本主义的意义所在了。也许，社会主义最终并不能根本取代资本主义。但是，社会主义者对资本主义的强烈批判，社会主义、共产主义者们对社会主义理想方案的种种设计，以及各国社会主义运动和工人运动此起彼伏的诉求与斗争，却在根本上推动了资本主义的自我改造，成为众多资本主义国家社会主义化的强大推动力和最好鉴镜。如果我们把人类的平等要求分解为起点（权利）平等和结果（分配）平等的话，那么，早期资本主义及其民主政治，充其量只是实现了起点的平等。只有当它吸收了社会主义的理念，通过税收、福利、所有制改造和工会监督法等种种政策措施，抑强扶弱，极大地推动了结果平等的实现，它才得以从几十年前的一次又一次严重危机和冲突中解脱了出来，并且有了近几十年的长足的发展。这也是多年来越来越多的人质疑现代化，而强调现代性，强调"自由、理性"或"自由、平等、博爱"之类普世价值的原因所在。

当然，所有这一切的实现，在笔者看来，都是要以相应的生产力水平和经济发达程度为基础的。离开了相当的生产力水平和社会物质财富的积累，指望通过限制分配形式，消除人与人之间高低上下贫富贵贱的差别，只能是一厢情愿。实际上，对于今天的中国来说，即使是资本主义早期工业发展阶段已经基本实现的起点的平等，也还遥未可及。权利尚不能平等，国人自身的自由权，甚至基本人权尚且不能得到有效保障，又如何能实际取得和有效行使监督权与选举权，以促成结果平等的真正实现呢？

现实没有给今天中国的思想家或政治家们留下循序渐进的路径选择的空间与可能。毛的均平社会主义与当今社会贫富悬殊的强烈对比，早已让部分民众忍无可忍；西方资本主义普遍社会主义化的自我改造与变革，更是让相当一部分内外知识分子和国际舆论，对中国政府反其道而行之的做法，充满了非议。经济发展、财富增多、社会中产阶层的队伍日趋壮大，人权、自由、平等的政治诉求与呼声，势必愈益高涨。同时，贫富悬殊、贪污腐化、权力寻租等等丑恶现象愈演愈烈，民众要求分配公平、社会公正、政治民主的压力也愈来愈大。回顾资本主义各国早期发展史，类似情景俯拾皆是，有多少国家逃过了大动乱的浩劫，走上了健康发展的道路，在今天真是很值得研究者们留意与总结一番的。

ENDNOTES

1. 参见《马布利选集》，北京：商务印书馆，1960年，第62–63页；《欧文选集》，上卷，北京：商务印书馆，1965年，第20页；《傅立叶选集》，第1卷，北京：商务印书馆，1959年，第26页，等。

2. 恩格斯：《社会主义从空想到科学的发展》，《马克思恩格斯选集》第3卷，北京：人民出版社，1966年，第487页。

3. 恩格斯：《反杜林论》，《马克思恩格斯选集》第3卷，第387页。

4. 马克思：《政治经济学批判序言》，《马克思恩格斯选集》第2卷，第195页。

5. 马克思、恩格斯：《共产党宣言》，《马克思恩格斯选集》第1卷，第239页。

6. 恩格斯甚至认为资产阶级的知识分子反而会制造出许多麻烦来，故他明确讲，工人阶级必须要把知识分子和大学生"控制在一定范围内"，以免除他们所带来的种种危害。为此，可以恩威并用地对付这些先生，即一面用赎买的办法来"收买这些人为自己服务"，一面对其中少数"给以应有的惩罚以儆效尤"，使他们懂得要为自己的利害着想。恩格斯：《致奥·伯尼克》，《马克思恩格斯全集》第37卷，第443-444页。

7. 恩格斯：《在马克思墓前的讲话》，《马克思恩格斯选集》第3卷，第124页。

8. 马克思：《哥达纲领批判》；恩格斯：《社会主义从空想到科学的发展》，《马克思恩格斯选集》第3卷，第99，385页。

9. 恩格斯：《卡·马克思＜雇佣劳动与资本＞导言》，《马克思恩格斯全集》第22卷，第243页；马克思：《哥达纲领批判》，《马克思恩格斯选集》第3卷，第99页。

10. 同上，第89-91页；马克思：《致约·魏德迈》，《马克思恩格斯选集》第4卷，第333页；马克思、恩格斯：《德意志意识形态——费尔巴哈》；马克思、恩格斯：《共产党宣言》，《马克思恩格斯选集》第1卷，第36，272-273页。

11. 参见恩格斯：《家庭、私有制与国家的起源》；恩格斯：《反杜林论》，《马克思恩格斯全集》第21卷，第203页；第20卷，第103页。

12. 恩格斯：《1891年社会民主党纲领草案批判》，《马克思恩格斯全集》第22卷第273页。

13. 见斯大林：《和第一个美国工人代表团的谈话》，《斯大林全集》第10卷，第117-118页；斯大林：《和美国斯克里浦斯——霍华德报系总经理罗伊·霍华德先生的谈话》，《斯大林文集》，第92页。并可参见苏联科学院经济研究所编，中共中央马克列斯著作编译局译：《政治经济学教科书》，北京：人民出版社，1955年，第407页。其表述社会主义生产关系的特征为（1）以国家所有制和合作集体农庄所有制这两种形式存在的生产资料公有制，占绝对统治地位；（2）劳动者不受剥削，建立了同志式的合作和社会主义互助的关系；（3）根据按劳分配的原则，实行有利于劳动者本身的产品分配。

14. 社会党国际第一次代表大会：《民主社会主义的目标与任务》（又称为《法兰克福声明》），1951年7月3日，社会党国际文件集编辑组编：《社会党国际文件集（1951-1987）》，哈尔滨：黑龙江人民出版社，1989年，第2-8页。

15. 陈独秀：《北京劳动界》，《晨报》1919年11月1日；李大钊：《由经济上解释中国近代思想变迁的原因》，《新青年》第7卷第2期，1920年1月1日；陈独秀《我的意见》，《新青年》第7卷第6期，1920年5月1日，等。

16. 陈独秀：《谈政治》，《新青年》第8卷第1期，1920年9月1日。

17.《短言》，《共产党》月刊，第1号，1920年11月7日。

18.《中国共产党宣言》，1920年11月，《中共中央文件选集》第1卷，北京：中共中央党校出版社，1989年，第547—551页。

19.《短言》，《共产党》月刊，第3号，1921年4月7日。

20. 李大钊：《中国的社会主义与世界的资本主义》，《评论之评论》第1期第2号，1921年3月20日。

21. 李达：《马克思派社会主义》，《新青年》第9卷第2号，1921年6月1日。

22. 陈独秀《社会主义批评》，1921年1月19日，《陈独秀文章选编》（中），北京，三联书店，1984年，第85-98页。

23. 施存统：《马克思底共产主义》，《新青年》第9卷第4号，1921年8月14日；重远：《共产主义与无政府主义》，《先驱》创刊号，1922年1月15日。

24. 李守常：《社会主义释疑》，《民国日报》副刊《觉悟》，1923年11月3日。

25. 中共一大：《中国共产党第一个纲领》，1921年7月；中共二大：《关于国际帝国主义与中国和中国共产党的决议案》；《关于民主的联合战线的议决案》，1922年7月，《中共中央文件选集》第1卷，第3，61-66页。

26. 中共早年无入党誓词，红军时期的入党誓词各地不一，但内容大致为："严守秘密，服从纪律，牺牲个人，阶级斗争，努力革命，永不叛党"。延安时期才统一改为："我志愿加入中国共产党，坚决执行党的决议，遵守党的纪律，不怕困难，不怕牺牲，为共产主义事业奋斗到底"。转见孟红：《中国共产党入党誓词的来龙去脉》，《党史纵横》2007年第10期。

27. 查数十位活到建国后并有回忆录留下来的二十年代入党的中共党政军高级干部的经历，可知他们中入党前读过《共产党宣言》或《共产主义ABC》等马列著作者，不足十分之一。参见萧心力编：《我的选择——六十三位中共高级干部自述》，北京：中共中央党校出版社，1998年，第1-574页；《邓小平文选》第3卷，第382页。

28. 宗凤鸣：《心灵之旅》，香港：开放出版社，2008年，第18-22页。

29. 延安整风运动初期毛泽东先后指定的学习材料主要包括如下几种：（一）《"左派"幼稚病》（二）艾思奇译《新哲学大纲》第八章"认识的过程"；（三）李译《辩证法唯物论教程》第六章"唯物辩证法与形式论理学"；（四）河上肇著《经济学大纲》的"序说"；（五）季米特洛夫在国际七次大会报告；（六）《季米特洛夫论干部教育》；（七）《六大以来》。1943年底整风运动基本结束后又规定高级干部要学习五本书，即《共产党宣言》，《社会主义从空想到科学的发展》，《共产主义运动中的"左派"幼稚病》，《社会民主党在民主革命中的两种策略》，《联共（布）党史简明教程》。逄先知主编《毛泽东年谱（1893-1949）》（中），北京：中央文献出版社，2005年，第329-330，351，366，484页。

30.《列宁选集》第4卷，第776-778页。

31. 相关论述见斯大林：《论列宁主义基础》，《斯大林全集》第8卷，第60-64页。

32. 斯大林《论经济工作人员的任务》，《斯大林全集》第13卷，第38页。

33. 鲍里斯·迈纳斯主编，上海国际问题资料编辑组译：《苏联的社会变革》，北京：三联书店，1977年，第18-19页。

34. 这种反抗最典型地表现在农民群起宰杀牲畜上，据统计，仅1930年2-3月集体化运动开始后这两个月时间里，苏联2500万农户中就宰杀了1400万头牛，和1/3的猪、1/4的羊。与1928年比，1933年苏联牛、马、猪、羊的数量都减少了大约一半。见罗·亚·麦德韦杰夫著，赵询译：《让历史来审判——斯大林主义的起源及其后果》，北京：人民出版社1981年，第149，153页。

35. 麦德维杰夫著，李援朝等译：《让历史来审判》（续篇），长春：吉林人民出版社，1983年，第85-86页。

36. 麦德韦杰夫：《让历史来审判》（上），第353-365页。

37. 麦德韦杰夫：《让历史来审判》（上），第337页；李宗禹：《斯大林模式研究》，北京：中央编译出版社，1999年，第293页。

38. 斯大林：《关于苏联宪法草案》，《斯大林文选》，北京：人民出版社，1962年，第84–91页。

39. 杨茂东：《特权阶层在苏联解体中的功与罪》，百家讲坛，http://www.baijiajiangtan.com.cn/HQLW/2010/04/15/1749_4.html。

40. 罗曼·罗兰著，夏伯铭译：《莫斯科日记》，上海：上海人民出版社，1998年，第116–117页。另据张丹《1920–1930年苏联领导干部住房问题研究》（《一个大国的崛起与崩溃——苏联历史专题研究（1917–1991）》（上），北京：社会科学文献出版社，2009年，第240–254页）一文可知，1930年代初期列宁格勒一般民众的住房十分拥挤，人均不足5平方米。

41. 格·阿·阿尔巴托夫著，徐葵等译：《苏联政治内幕：知情者的见证》，北京：新华出版社，1998年，第308–310页。

42. 参见《毛泽东给肖旭东蔡林彬并在法诸会友信》，1920年12月1日，《新民学会资料》，北京：人民出版社，1980年，第148页；毛泽东：《论人民民主专政》，1949年6月30日，《毛泽东选集》，合订本，北京：人民出版社，1964年，第1477–1478页。

43. 其中比较著名的有，刘少奇1949年7月4日代表中共中央给联共（布）中央斯大林的报告（见《建国以来刘少奇文稿》，第1卷，北京：中央文献出版社，1998年，第1–18页。）和1952年10月20日写给斯大林征询他对中国向社会主义过渡等问题的信（参见《建国以来毛泽东文稿》，第3卷，北京：中央文献出版社，1989年，第694–695页），等。

44. 参见范若愚、江流主编：《科学社会主义概论—中国社会主义基本问题》，江苏人民出版社、中共中央党校出版社，1983年，第160，162页。

45. 毛泽东：《介绍一个合作社》，1958年4月15日，《红旗》1958年第1期；《毛泽东读社会主义政治经济学批注和谈话》（上），北京：国史研究所，1998年，第145页。

46. 见《马克思恩格斯全集》第18卷，第610–611页。

47. 参见列宁：《论我国革命》，《列宁选集》第4卷，第691页；斯大林《论经济工作人员的任务》，《斯大林全集》第13卷，第38页。

48. 毛泽东：《在资本主义工商业社会主义改造问题座谈会上的讲话》，1955年10月29日，《毛泽东文集》第6卷，北京：中央文献出版社，1993年，第500页。

49. 毛泽东：《增强党的团结，继承党的传统》，1956年8月30日，《毛泽东选集》第五卷，北京：人民出版社，1977年，第296页。

50. 毛泽东：《在中共八届二中全会小组长会议上的发言》，1956年11月，《建国以来毛泽东文稿》第6册，北京：中央文献出版社，1992年，第245页；毛泽东：《关于正确处理人民内部矛盾的问题》，1956年2月27日（油印件）。

51. 《中国共产党第八次全国代表大会关于政治报告的决议》，《建国以来重要文献选编》第9卷，第93–94页。

52. 参见孟宪章主编：《中苏经济贸易史》，哈尔滨：黑龙江人民出版社，1992年，第381页。

53. 毛泽东：《论十大关系》，1956年4月25日，《建国以来毛泽东文稿》第6册，第82–83页。

54. 转见郑谦、韩钢著：《毛泽东之路·晚年岁月》，北京：中国青年出版社，1994年，第78页。

55. 据当时的资料，英国年产钢2000万吨左右，而由毛泽东主持的北戴河会议则提出，1958年的钢产量要达到1080–1150万吨左右，下一年度则要超过2000万吨。毛泽东《在第十五次最高国务会议上的讲话》，1958年9月5日，《建国以来毛泽东文稿》第7册，第380页。

56.《人民日报》（社论）1958年1月1日。

57. 参见《八大第二次会议各代表团活动情况》第十四号，1958年5月21日。

58. 毛泽东：《关于向军委会议印发〈两年超过英国〉报告的批语》，1958年6月22日，《建国以来毛泽东文稿》第七册，第278页。

59. 毛泽东：《在第十五次最高国务会议上的讲话》，《建国以来毛泽东文稿》第七册，第381页。

60. 毛泽东：《对北戴河会议工业类文件的意见》，1958年9月2日，《建国以来毛泽东文稿》第七册，第368页。

61. 迄今为止，由于当政者不开放档案资料，这场灾难中非正常死亡人数的确切数字仍不为人所知。学界和海内外学者研究的数字中，从上千万到数千万都有。

62.《毛泽东读社会主义政治经济学批注和谈话》（上），北京：中华人民共和国国史学会，1998年，第121页。

63. 马克思：《哥达纲领批判》，《马克思恩格斯选集》第3卷，第90-91，99页。

64. 马克思、恩格斯：《共产党宣言》，《马克思恩格斯选集》第1卷，第240-250，257页。

65.《毛泽东读社会主义政治经济学批注和谈话》（上），第77页。

66.《毛泽东、刘少奇在各中央局汇报时的插话》，1960年12月27日。

67.《毛泽东在北戴河会议上的讲话》，1962年8月9日，《毛泽东思想万岁》，第424页。

68.《毛泽东在八届十中全会上的讲话》，1962年9月24日，《毛泽东思想万岁》，第431页。

69. 萧延中：《巨人的诞生——"毛泽东现象"的意识起源及中国近代政治文化的发展》，北京：国际文化出版公司，1988年，第146页。

70. 泽东：《民众的大联合》；《不许实业专制》，《湘江评论》创刊号，1919年7月14日。

71.《湖南工团联合会代表毛润之等二十一人日昨向警厅长沙县署及政务厅请愿各节详情》，（长沙）《大公报》1922年12月14日，第六版。

72.《毛泽东自述》，北京：人民出版社1993年，第12页。

73.《铅印活版工会致大公报记者盾书》，（长沙）《大公报》1922年12月14日，第七版。

74. 毛泽东熟识的梁漱溟、胡适均与毛岁数相当，却都已是北京大学教授了。

75.《毛泽东自述》，第33页。

76.《毛泽东在北戴河政治局扩大会议上的讲话》，1958年8月21日上午。

77. 毛泽东《读斯大林〈社会主义经济问题〉谈话记录》，1958年11月9-10日，《毛泽东读社会主义政治经济学批注和谈话》（上），第67页。

78. 同上引注，第67页。

79.《毛泽东读社会主义政治经济学批注和谈话》，第45页。

80.《毛泽东在最高国务会议上的讲话》，1958年1月28日；《毛泽东读社会主义政治经济学批注和谈话》，第页。

81. 毛泽东：《关于理论问题的谈话要点》，1974年12月，《建国以来毛泽东文稿》第13册，第413页。

82.《毛泽东读社会主义政治经济学批注和谈话》，第49页。

83. 毛泽东评论知识分子的典型语言是：知识分子从来都是依附于某个阶级的。"现在，知识分子依附在什么皮上呢？是附在公有制的皮上，附在无产阶级身上。谁给他们饭吃？就是工人、农民"。毛泽东：《在扩大的中央工作会议上的讲话》，北京：人民出版社，1978年，第32页。

84. 《毛泽东读社会主义政治经济学批注和谈话》，第67，70页；毛泽东：《在扩大的中央工作会议上的讲话》，第67–68页。

85. 《马克思恩格斯全集》第18卷，第470页。

86. 见第二组第四号简报，1980年10月26日。

87. 见第七组第三十二号简报，1980年11月10日。

88. 《马克思恩格斯全集》第19卷，第22页。

89. 恩格斯：《社会主义从空想到科学的发展》，《马克思恩格斯选集》第3卷，第484页。

90. 恩格斯：《反杜林论》，《马克思恩格斯选集》第3卷，第384页。

91. 马克思、恩格斯关于消灭私有制后生产资料掌握在何者手中的问题，显然存在着概念使用和论述不严谨，经常混用"公有"、"国有"、"社会所有"、"社会公有"等概念的情况，引起歧义甚至多。但需要注意的是，他们在以下两种情况下谈到"国有"是正常的：一是在并非无产阶级革命的条件下，比如谈及当时仍具有资产阶级革命性质的德国革命之类；一是在无产阶级革命初发阶段，即革命还局限在一国范围内的情况时。需要了解的是，无论他们这一概念的使用如何不严谨，有一点在他们看来是明白无误的。那就是，人类社会进入到社会主义阶段之后，私有制没有了，阶级没有了，国家也不存在了，因而生产资料"国有"肯定是不可能的。

　*列宁在《国家与革命》一书中具体解释马克思的这一设想时，认为社会主义阶段国家作为阶级镇压工具的职能已经消亡，但保护资产阶级法权的职能尚须存在，故可称之为"半国家"。《列宁选集》第3卷，第185页。

92. 恩格斯：《论俄国的社会问题》，《马克思恩格斯全集》第22卷，第501页。

93. 同上引注，第502–503页

94. 《马克思恩格斯选集》第1卷，第218页。

4.

CHINA'S THREE RISES, REGIONAL POWER TRANSITIONS, AND EAST ASIAN SECURITY:
1949 TO THE TWENTY-FIRST CENTURY

ROBERT S. ROSS

Sixty years after the establishment of the People's Republic of China, the rise of China has become the most pressing global security issue. For the first half of the twenty-first century, not only the United States but the entire East Asia region will be preoccupied with the implications of the rise of China for security and regional stability. And given East Asia's prominence in international security and economic affairs, the rise of China elicits concern not only in East Asia but throughout the globe.

But power transitions are not new to either China or East Asia. On the contrary, during the 60 years since the establishment of the People's Republic of China there have been two rising Chinas and a third rise may well be currently underway. The post-World War II diplomatic history of the PRC and post-World War II East Asian international relations is a history of China's multiple rises and the uneven ability of both China and the other great powers to adjust peacefully to changing great-power relations. This succession of power transitions offers a critical perspective on the sources of the 60 turbulent years of Chinese diplomacy and on trends in regional politics.

All three Chinese power transitions conform to the classic understanding of the dynamics of power transitions and the sources of instability. Rising powers, through uneven rates of economic and political change, develop greater relative power compared to the other great powers. This greater power enables the rising power to demand a greater say in the regional political order and thus greater security commensurate with its new capabilities. The rising power's demands for change can include demands for strategic goods such as new or expanded spheres of influence, control over sea lanes, or secure access to states with natural resources. These demands are intrinsically destabilizing. They frequently encounter opposition from status-quo powers that resist making the costly strategic adjustments necessary to satisfy the demands of the rising powers, fearing the reduced security associated with the loss of allies and their greater vulnerability with respect to access to resources. Thus, power transitions may frequently result in a great-power war, as a rising power may use preventive war to achieve what the status-quo powers will not peacefully cede, or a status-quo power may use force to eliminate the potential challenge posed by the rising power in the early stages of the power transition.[1]

Each of China's three post-1949 rises has created great-power dynamics associated with power transitions. The great-power dynamics associated with power transitions provide a critical perspective on the early instability and conflict in PRC diplomacy, the subsequent period of diplomatic cooperation, and the prospects for great-power cooperation into the twenty-first century.

China's First Rise: 1949–1950

There are two sources of power transitions. Most often observers associate rising powers with long-term unequal rates of economic change. As countries develop their economies, additional resources enable them to develop greater military power. But power transitions frequently reflect relatively rapid domestic political change that enables expanded international power. This was the process that led to the rise of Germany from 1866 to 1870 when the unification of the Germanic states under Prussian leadership established in the center of Europe a new state with a large population and a large economy, requiring significant strategic adjustments by Europe's traditional great-powers. In a mere four years, Prussia had transformed the European great-power order, creating Europe's "German problem" and the diplomatic challenges associated with the adjustment to German power.[2]

In 1949 China experienced rapid political change similar to the earlier rapid unification of Germany, with similar implications for regional order. At the conclusion of the Chinese civil war in 1949-50, for the first time in over 100 years China had become a politically unified state free from both domestic instability and foreign occupation. The Chinese central government now benefited from the economic development associated with the peace-time recovery and from the unified central revenue stream. Government financial resources were greater than at any time since the middle of the nineteenth century. Moreover, the central government could now deploy China's large armed forces to promote national security rather than to wage civil war and quell domestic instability. In the short span of two years, fundamental domestic political change had transformed China into a major regional power capable of exerting considerable pressure to realize its national security objectives.

Although China had become a major East Asian power, in 1949–50 the East Asian security order reflected the prior colonial order, which was predicated on a weak China that was a subject of great-power politics. In 1949 the British, the French, and the Japanese no longer exercised independent great-power authority, but following World War II the United States assumed the role of the prior great powers and sustained the preexisting regional order. It replaced Japan as the dominant power on the Korean Peninsula, attempting in 1950 to occupy the entire peninsula and to bring U.S. forces up to the Chinese border. It also replaced Japan on Taiwan, bringing the island into its regional sphere of influence. In Indochina, the United States first supported France, its subordinate NATO ally, in its effort to restore its colonial presence on Chinese borders and after 1954 it gradually replaced the French presence throughout most of Indochina. In maritime East Asia the United States assumed the nineteenth-century role of both Great Britain and pre-World War II Japan. It established naval supremacy throughout the region and strategic dominance in the Philippines, Singapore, and Thailand. Finally, it occupied Japan and by 1950 it was rebuilding the Japanese military, which only five years earlier had occupied China.[3]

In 1949–50, as a rising power China had the capability to demand a revised regional order and greater security commensurate with its improved capabilities. It was a "revisionist power." Yet the East Asian security order remained predicated on a weak and occupied China. This was a power transition destined to cause great-power tensions. Either the United States would cede greater regional influence to China, or China would use its enhanced coercive power to compel regional change and develop greater security.

East Asian instability and China's frequent use of force from 1950 to 1989 reflected the great-power instability associated with the rise of China. The status-quo powers—first the United States and then the Soviet Union—resisted Chinese demands for a revised regional order that reflected Chinese capabilities and demands for security. Faced with intransigent great-power threats to its security, China responded with the only means that could affect regional change—use of force. China participated in numerous wars between 1950 and 1989 and it initiated multiple crises with the great powers. In each case, it used force to demand change that reflected China's security requirements.

China's wars and crises with the United States represented China's efforts to coerce the United States to remove its strategic presence from Chinese borders. China resisted direct involvement in the Korean War until U.S. forces crossed the 38th parallel and established a U.S. military presence near the Chinese border. It then entered the war and drove U.S. forces below the 38th parallel.[4] China's ability to fight the United States to a draw on the Korean Peninsula established the rise of China. In 1948 China would have been unable even to enter the war, to say nothing of effectively contending with U.S. forces. After the Geneva peace agreement in 1954, China offered minimal support for North Vietnamese use of force against South Vietnam until the United States established a military presence in Indochina in the early 1960s. China's frequent threats of use of force against Taiwan in the 1950s not only reflected its political objective of unification but also its security objective of compelling the United States to reconsider its security commitment to Taiwan and to remove its strategic presence from the Chinese coast.[5] In each case, China sought to use its restored strategic capabilities to reestablish the traditional role of a strong China in the East Asian security order.

China successfully used force against the United States and thus established the strategic foundation for the U.S.-China rapprochement in the early 1970s during the administration of Richard M. Nixon and for the normalization of diplomatic relations in January 1979. China had removed U.S. forces from North Korea, achieving tacit U.S. recognition of Chinese influence over North Korea. It then supported North Vietnam in its successful effort to oust U.S. forces from its strategic "backyard" in Indochina.[6] And China's contribution to the U.S. defeat in Vietnam contributed to America's global retrenchment in the 1970s and to the necessity for the United States to compromise on Taiwan and end its strategic presence on the island so as to reduce U.S.-China conflict and its defense burden in East Asia. The U.S. compromise on Taiwan was the prerequisite to the normalization of U.S.-China relations. The U.S. defeat in Vietnam also contributed to Bangkok's 1975 decision to oust U.S. bases from Thailand and to develop cooperative security ties with China. By 1979, twenty years after the establishment of the PRC and the restoration of China's great-power capabilities, Beijing had made major progress toward creating a new regional order commensurate with Chinese capabilities and interests and it had secured U.S.-China cooperation on Chinese terms.[7]

But just as China had compelled the United States to withdraw from its frontiers, the Soviet Union emerged as the U.S. successor state on China's perimeter. Following China's 1958–60 Great Leap Forward and its subsequent development of an independent security policy and resistance to Soviet leadership of the Communist bloc, Moscow aimed to coerce China to return to the bloc and to accept Soviet leadership over Chinese security policy. In the mid-1960s Moscow began a major defense buildup on the Chinese border and by the mid-1970s it was deploying a full array of its military equipment against China in the Soviet Far East, thus threatening China with war. In essence, from the 1960s until the end of the Cold War in 1989 the Soviet Union had adopted the role of nineteenth-century imperial Russia as the greatest threat to China's territorial security. In

April 1975 the North Vietnamese military unified North and South Vietnam, the Khmer Rouge defeated the pro-U.S. Lon Nol government in Cambodia, and the United States withdrew its remaining military forces from all of Indochina, thus restoring traditional Chinese border security. But in November 1978 the Soviet Union and Vietnam signed a treaty and the next month Vietnamese forces invaded Cambodia, establishing Soviet influence throughout Indochina. The Soviet Union thus followed France and the United States in establishing a military presence on China's southern borders.[8] Moreover, the Soviet Union cooperated with India in promoting an Indian strategic presence on the Chinese border and it competed with China for influence in North Korea.[9]

The Soviet strategic presence on China's borders was no more compatible with Chinese great-power capabilities and China's corresponding demand for security than had been America's prior strategic presence on Chinese borders. And just as the 1949–50 power transition had elicited Chinese use of force against the U.S.-dominated status quo and violent political change, the Soviet presence elicited Chinese use of force against Soviet policy to compel change and a regional order commensurate with Chinese capabilities.

China resisted Soviet coercive pressure to accept Soviet domination of Chinese security. Beginning in the 1960s under Chairman Mao's leadership, it engaged in a protracted and costly border conflict with the Soviet Union, in which each side prepared for war and deployed large numbers of ground troops. China's "counter-coercive" policy sought to compel the Soviet Union to respect Chinese capabilities, acknowledge Chinese independence, and cede Chinese security along the Sino-Soviet border. The 1969 Sino-Soviet border war reflected Chinese determination to resist Soviet coercion and compel the Soviet Union to end its threat to Chinese border security and its strategic relationship with Vietnam. This policy continued after Mao's death in 1976, as Deng Xiaoping sustained Mao's border policy throughout the 1980s.[10] In February 1979, under Deng Xiaoping's leadership China invaded Vietnam in retaliation against Soviet-Vietnamese cooperation and the Vietnamese attack against the Khmer Rouge and its subsequent occupation of Cambodia. For the next ten years, China deployed up to 300,000 troops on the Sino-Vietnamese border to threaten another invasion of Vietnam, thus compelling Vietnam to sever its security relationship with the Soviet Union, withdraw from Cambodia, and acknowledge dominant Chinese influence on China's southern borders.[11]

Once again China had successfully used force to compel change commensurate with its post-1949 capabilities. China's resistance to Soviet power contributed to Moscow's effort to end the Cold War and to seek a Sino-Soviet rapprochement. But China's terms for rapprochement were clear. The Soviet Union had to begin to remove its forces from Chinese borders and end its support for Vietnamese resistance to Chinese power. By early 1989 Gorbachev had acceded to these demands. In exchange Deng Xiaoping changed Chinese security policy and in May 1989 he welcomed Gorbachev to Beijing to normalize Sino-Soviet relations and establish a relationship premised on China's great-power capabilities and China's legitimate and effective demand for border security.

The collapse of Soviet power and the Russian retreat from China's borders was the final chapter in the 1949–50 rise of China. In East Asia, China, rather than the United States, won the Cold War and filled the "vacuum" created by the Soviet defeat. China soon established dominance over Sino-Russian border regions in Northeast Asia and emerged as North Korea's only great-power benefactor. In Central Asia it developed military superiority over the former Soviet republics on its border, and in Indochina, the demise of Soviet power and Sino-Russian rapprochement compelled Hanoi to withdraw from Cambodia and to become resigned (however reluctantly) to its inclusion in China's sphere of influence in Indochina.[12]

China's frequent use of force during the Cold War did not reflect Maoist radicalism or militant expansionism intrinsic to totalitarian states or Communist ideology. Mao certainly imbued Chinese diplomacy with his unique revolutionary belligerence, but China's militant security policy transcended the post-Mao succession in 1976, despite the fundamental reforms Deng Xiaoping initiated in Chinese domestic policy; stability came to China's great-power relationships and to East Asian international relations once the status-quo powers, first the United States and then the Soviet Union, acceded to Chinese security demands and to a revised regional security order that accurately reflected the post-1949 distribution of capabilities among the great powers, including China.

China's Second Rise: 1978–2008

China's second rise and the second post-Cold War East Asian power transition began in December 1978, when the Third Plenum of the Eleventh Central Committee of the Chinese Communist Party redirected Chinese domestic policy from pursuing permanent revolution and waging great-power conflict to developing the economy. For the next thirty years, China's economy grew at an annual rate of about 10 percent. The result was a second East Asian power transition and a transformed regional security order reflecting the long-term unequal rates of change and the associated gradual change in relative great-power capabilities. This is the type of power transition associated with Germany's pre-World War I second rise, which began in the 1890s. But unlike Germany's second rise, this Chinese power transition reflected China's "peaceful rise."[13]

China's peaceful rise, cooperative diplomacy, and interest in stability did not reflect Chinese leadership change or reordered national priorities. Rather, the post-Cold War regional stability associated with China's focus on economic development reflected the culmination of China's demand for security and the close of China's 1949–50 power transition. For the first time since the 1840s, China had security around its entire territorial perimeter. This was the precondition not only for China's development of great-power cooperation but also for the redirection of Chinese financial resources and workforce away from forced industrialization and costly international conflict and to the rapid expansion of the domestic infrastructure and market forces supportive of Chinese economic growth. When China was threatened by the great powers, economic development necessarily took a back seat to waging conflict, regardless of the leadership or ideology. After China achieved security commensurate with its resources, economic development and peaceful rise emerged as China's foremost priority.

China's second rise was the result of China's thirty years of economic growth after 1978. Economic and technological development yielded expanded Chinese economic and military power over many of its neighbors.[14] Economically, by 2006 China had replaced the United States as the largest export market and the most important target of direct foreign investment for South Korea, Taiwan, Singapore, and Japan. Thus, for economic stability and continued economic growth these countries depended more on cooperation with China than with the United States. Trends in China's economic relations with the other East Asian economies suggest that they too soon will depend more on China than the United States for their prosperity. China also implemented the China-ASEAN Free Trade Agreement, which will accelerate the rate of growth of Southeast Asian exports to China. By 2010 China had become the "engine of growth" for the East Asian economies and was emerging as the hub of an East Asian trade zone, thus challenging U.S. political influence in the region.

China's economic wealth also enabled it to expand its military power over the East Asian continent and to achieve its remaining strategic objectives on the East Asian mainland—influence over South Korea and Taiwan, both at the expense of U.S. influence. On the mainland of East Asia, China's expanded military power reflected the modernization of Chinese ground forces.[15] After 1978 China improved its ability to wage war against its neighbors around its entire perimeter; China's ground forces could now perform far better against Vietnamese forces than they did in February 1979. Thus China's neighbors all had to adjust their security policies to accommodate the interests of a rising China.

These economic and military trends especially influenced the security of South Korea. South Korean economic dependence on China and its increasing vulnerability to Chinese military power required Seoul to reevaluate the security benefits of its strategic alignment with the United States and to gradually accommodate Chinese security interests. South Korea requested the end of the U.S.-South Korean agreement calling for U.S. war-time command of South Korean forces. Seoul also refused to cooperate with the U.S. military in planning for non-peninsular military scenarios. Understanding that such scenarios would involve U.S.-China hostilities, it decided that South Korea would not support the United States in a war against China. Regarding North Korea, South Korea frequently undermined U.S. coercive diplomacy toward Pyongyang by pursuing bilateral economic and diplomatic cooperation with North Korea and it developed greater cooperation with Beijing than with Washington in opposing North Korea's nuclear weapons program. Thus, the rise of China resulted in South Korea's gradual strategic realignment toward China and a gradual attenuation of the U.S.-South Korean strategic partnership.[16]

China's peaceful rise also transformed Taiwan's security environment and its strategic alignment.[17] By 2009 Taiwan's economic integration into the Chinese economy was all but complete. China had the capability to "blockade" the Taiwan economy without using its armed forces. By simply suspending cross-strait trade and "nationalizing" select Taiwan industries on the mainland, Beijing could devastate Taiwan's economy. Thus, Taiwan could no longer depend on the United States for its economic security. China's military modernization also undermined the value of the United States to Taiwan's security. The United States could not defend Taiwan from Chinese increasing deployment of ballistic missiles across from Taiwan. Moreover, Taiwan could not compete with China's defense spending and military modernization. As a small island, it lacks the economic and demographic resources to contend with China's great-power military potential. Taiwan thus abandoned its effort to achieve sovereign independence from mainland China. In 2008 it elected Ma Ying-jeou as president, who had publicly opposed Taiwan's independence and had promoted greater cross-strait economic and political cooperation. The people in Taiwan may have wanted independence, but they also recognized that the rise of China made this a very costly and ultimately unrealistic objective. Taiwan was also reducing defense cooperation with the United States. Its defense budget was rapidly declining and it was increasingly disinterested in purchasing high-profile, high-technology expensive U.S. weaponry that not only cannot enhance Taiwan security, given the mainland's strategic and economic advantages, but could also provoke Chinese hostility and thus undermine Taiwan's security.

China's second rise gave Beijing the capability to peacefully transform the East Asian strategic order. By 2009 China was emerging as the dominant power over the entire East Asian mainland and the United States was relinquishing its remaining forward military and political presence on China's borders, in South Korea, and on Taiwan, where in the post-Cold War era it had continued the role of imperial Japan. But unlike its first power transition, this was a peaceful power transformation. China realized a peaceful rise for two reasons. First, because the first rise of China yielded Beijing's strategic "requirements"—secure territorial borders—China could then focus on economic development and cooperative diplomacy and patiently await the gradual transformation of the regional order and realization of its strategic "electives." Beijing has thus patiently promoted "peaceful unification" with Taiwan since the 1980s, and it normalized diplomatic relations and has pursued economic cooperation with South Korea since 1992.

The second reason for China's peaceful rise was the American response to China's expanded capabilities. Whereas from 1949 to the end of the Vietnam War in 1975 the United States countered the rise of China with military containment and use of force, since the U.S.-China rapprochement in the 1970s the United States has peacefully attempted to accommodate China's rise. U.S. ability to accommodate China's second rise is a reflection of its limited strategic interests on China's periphery. America's Cold War interests in both South Korea and Taiwan reflected U.S. interest in deterring Chinese use of force against U.S. allies and maintaining the credibility of its alliance commitments throughout East Asia, rather than the intrinsic strategic importance of either the Korean Peninsula or Taiwan island and their strategic alignment with the United States. This strategic reality enabled the United States since 1950 to promote "peaceful resolution" of the Taiwan and Korean conflicts, rather than to pursue an American conception of victory or to insist on maintenance of the status quo. Because Taiwan and South Korea's peaceful accommodation to the rise of China does not challenge U.S. credibility to resist the use of force, the United States can acquiesce to China's rise and accept a reduced U.S. strategic presence on China's periphery in mainland East Asia.[18]

China's second rise also reordered East Asia's strategic environment. By 2009 the region was becoming divided into two great-power spheres of influence.[19] China's sphere of influence encompassed mainland East Asia. The two rises of China since 1949 enabled it to reassert its traditional strategic role in East Asia. For the first time in the 170 years after the Opium War China as the "central state" was now surrounded by compliant smaller states that recognized Chinese authority. With the decline of the West in East Asia and the rise of China, small power compliance with Chinese power includes small power denial of access to their territory to potential Chinese strategic rivals.

Today the U.S. sphere of influence is increasingly confined to maritime East Asia. China's second rise extended Chinese influence to its territorial and maritime perimeters, but it did not contribute to the rise of Chinese maritime power or enable China to erode U.S. influence on the oceans. Despite thirty years of Chinese peaceful rise, the United States remains the irreplaceable strategic partner of Japan and the maritime Southeast Asian countries—Malaysia, Singapore, Indonesia, and the Philippines. And all these countries continue to expand strategic cooperation with the United States rather than accommodate the rise of China. In this respect, just as China is now recovering a traditional strategic role in East Asia, the United States is establishing its strategic presence in East Asia that it had first envisioned in the immediate post-World War II period. Between 1945 and June 1950 prior to the outbreak of the Korean War, the United States assigned secondary strategic importance to the Korean Peninsula and Taiwan. In January 1950 Secretary of State Dean Acheson confined America's "defense perimeter" to the countries of maritime East Asia.[20]

China's peaceful rise has transformed the East Asian security order. In so doing, it has contributed not only to Chinese security but also to U.S. security and to regional stability. The United States no longer must prepare for costly war over secondary security interests on China's periphery, where it is strategically disadvantaged. Rather, it now defends important traditional security interests in maritime East Asia, where it enjoys the strategic advantage of overwhelming naval superiority. Moreover, both the United States and the region benefit from the division of East Asia into continental and maritime spheres. Rather than experiencing the repetitive great-power crises associated with the Cold War, the strategic buffer between Chinese and U.S. interests provided by the ocean waters contributes to the stability of the post-Cold War era, despite the instability frequently associated with power transitions.

China's Third Rise: 2009 to . . .

Just as the history of post-1949 Chinese foreign relations reflects great-power adjustments to China's rise and to power transitions, Chinese foreign relations in the first half of the twenty-first century will also reflect the rise of China and its impact on great-power politics. China's expanded political influence over its immediate mainland periphery does not signal the end of China's rise. China's economy continues to grow and its relative military capabilities will thus grow as well. Gradual economic development and unequal rates of change among the great powers may well produce a third rise of China.

The defining characteristics of this potential third rise of Chinese power suggest that it will challenge key U.S. security interests and it will be less susceptible to U.S. accommodation and compromise, likely occurring during a period of heightened Chinese domestic instability, declining leadership legitimacy, and increased societal nationalism, thus potentially constraining China's ability to await peaceful change. Therefore, international security politics and Chinese domestic politics may well combine to make the third Chinese power transition a difficult process.

As the Taiwan issue recedes as a source of war, China is turning its attention to other national security issues.[21] China's growing involvement in global affairs and its increasing reliance on international trade and imports of natural resources have created growing nationwide interest in developing an ocean-going navy that will enable it to assume international leadership on maritime issues, including humanitarian relief operations and maintenance of the global order, and to protect its overseas economic interests. China's participation since late 2008 in anti-piracy operations near Somalia is thus part of a larger process of the Chinese navy developing the operational and logistical capacity to operate with increasing sophistication for prolonged periods in distant waters.

Coinciding with China expanding maritime interests is the combination of growing popular nationalism and increased reliance on the part of the leadership on this nationalism to maintain its popular legitimacy.[22] One aspect of the popular nationalism is widespread public support for Chinese construction of aircraft carriers as symbols of great-power status. Now that China has developed wealth and technology and has expanded its international influence, many citizens are demanding that the leadership develop military capabilities that are commensurate with Chinese wealth and power. For these citizens, a carrier-centered blue-water navy will be the foremost symbol of Chinese wealth and power.[23] Simultaneously, China's leadership is responding to domestic instability, including widespread discontent with unemployment, corruption, inequalities, and environmental degradation, with appeals to popular pride at China's national accomplishments, including the development of its space program, its hosting of the 2008 Olympics, its construction of the world's largest airport terminal, and its construction of a "jumbo jet." In military affairs, the Chinese media have boasted of China's contributions to anti-piracy operations in the Gulf of Aden and they gave extensive coverage to the 2009 naval procession in the East China Sea on the sixtieth anniversary of the PLA Navy. On the sixtieth anniversary of the People's Republic of China on October 1, 2009, China held its largest-ever military parade with extensive displays of advanced Chinese weaponry.

Unlike China's first and second rises and corresponding Chinese demands for a revised regional order in mainland East Asia, which challenged only peripheral U.S. geopolitical security interests, should China's emerging maritime ambitions create a third rise of China, it will pose a significant challenge to U.S.-China cooperation. First, China's third rise and the capability to demand a revised regional order will require development of a blue-water power-projection navy. But since World War II the United States has understood that its national security requires naval superiority over all other powers. During the 1980s the United States developed its "600 ship navy" and it was prepared to engage in a naval arms race with the Soviet Union in response to the limited development of Soviet maritime capabilities. China's development of maritime power will suggest trends in its defense policy that likely will elicit similar heightened U.S. concern about Chinese intentions and capabilities.

Second, since the 1930s the United States has identified a maritime East Asia independent from the region's continental power as critical to maintaining an East Asian distribution of power compatible with U.S. security. U.S.-Japanese conflict prior to World War II and U.S. engagement in East Asia during the Cold War reflected America's enduring interest in preventing a single power from dominating both continental and maritime East Asia. This strategic perspective is informed by Secretary of State Acheson's January 1950 definition of the U.S. "defense perimeter."[24] Acheson suggested that although China might become the dominant power on mainland East Asia, this would be acceptable to the United States as long as Washington dominated maritime East Asia. The United States will likely perceive the emergence of a third rise of China and ongoing Chinese development of expanded maritime capabilities as a challenge to vital U.S. security interests.

Third, just as for the Chinese people a large navy and an aircraft carrier are symbols of China's emerging great-power status, for the American people naval dominance is a symbol of U.S. great-power status. As China gradually develops its naval capabilities, it will likely challenge American views of U.S. interests and elicit American nationalism, thus contributing to a politicization of American defense policy. American naval nationalism would exacerbate the national security challenges to Washington's management of a third rise of China.

The contemporary foreign policy challenge for Chinese leaders is to manage the third rise of Chinese power. On the one hand, compared to the post-1949 two rises of China, China's rise in the early twenty-first century should be the easiest to manage. China has already achieved its most important security objective—border security around its entire perimeter. Chinese leaders should thus be able to take a long-term perspective and adopt peaceful measures to achieve its regional objectives. However, while China is experiencing its third rise, both domestic instability and Chinese nationalism are increasing. This is a potentially destabilizing occurrence. Just as China is growing stronger and increasingly able to expect change in the East Asian security order, Chinese domestic developments will challenge the government's ability to develop patient diplomacy and a moderate defense policy, and to eschew provocative diplomacy.

It is in the U.S. interest to encourage China's peaceful rise. Just as U.S. resistance to the revision of the regional order commensurate with Chinese post-1949 capabilities contributed to the violence associated with the first rise of China and its subsequent accommodation of China's legitimate interests contributed to China's post-Cold War peaceful rise, the United States can influence the course of China's third rise. This is the challenge of engagement. Although the United States must adopt diplomatic and defense policies necessary for U.S. security, the U.S. response to China's rise should avoid overreacting to Chinese nationalist diplomacy and unnecessary hostility that will exacerbate Chinese nationalism and contribute to Chinese impatience with the pace of regional change. Greater Chinese capabilities will determine the development of Chinese security interests, but U.S. policy can influence how and with what urgency China pursues its interests. Promoting peaceful and gradual change will require the United States to focus on Chinese capabilities rather than on Chinese nationalistic rhetoric and on imagined threats posed by new high-profile Chinese capabilities that do not challenge U.S. security.[25] It will require the United States to maintain cooperative diplomatic and economic policies toward China, even as the United States develops the defense capabilities and regional strategic relationships necessary to maintain an East Asian security order vital to U.S. security.

Conclusion: Power Transitions, Chinese Diplomacy, and U.S.-China Relations

Power transitions are intrinsically destabilizing processes. The combination of shifting great-power strategic fortunes with differences over the distribution of regional strategic assets is a recipe for heightened tensions; power transitions frequently result in great-power wars. Both the rising power and the status-quo power have responsibility for peaceful management of power transitions. The United States and China have a mixed record in managing China's first two rises. The threatening presence of superior great-power strategic capabilities on Chinese borders elicited China's demand for rapid change. China's reemergence as a great power and its impatience for regional change combined with U.S. and Soviet insistence on strict maintenance of the status quo to make East Asia the most unstable region in Cold War politics. But in the post-Cold War era Chinese patience with the pace of regional change and gradual U.S. accommodation of Chinese interests on the Korean Peninsula and across the Taiwan Strait contributed to China's peaceful rise and to regional stability. In contrast to the heightened East Asian instability throughout the Cold War, in the post-Cold War era East Asia has been the most stable and peaceful region in the world, and Sino-U.S. management of China's second rise made a critical contribution to this prolonged era of peace.

Should continued Chinese economic development and technological modernization create a third Chinese rise, U.S.-China strategic competition will necessarily increase. It will be difficult for the United States to accommodate Chinese expectations of strategic change in maritime East Asia. Nonetheless, strategic competition does not require war nor does it preclude diplomatic and economic cooperation. China and the United States will share responsibility for maintaining peaceful competition. China will have to restrain foreign policy nationalism and await peaceful change rather than threaten war and use of force. As Chinese maritime capabilities improve, regional stability will also require that the United States resist the temptation to treat China as an illegitimate power and as an adversarial nation; this will require that the United States pursue coopera-tion with China even as it actively competes with China for regional influence. There is no more important great-power responsibility than the management of strategic change and the avoidance of destructive war. This is the shared twenty-first century responsibility of both the United States and China.

ENDNOTES

1. On power transitions, the classic works remain Robert Gilpin, *War and Change in World Politics* (New York: Cambridge University Press, 1981); Robert Gilpin, "The Theory of Hegemonic War," *Journal of Interdisciplinary History,* 18, no. 4 (Spring 1988): 591–613; A.F. K. Organski, *World Politics,* 2nd ed. (New York: Alfred A. Knopf, 1968), pp. 338–76. Also see Jack Levy, "Power Transition Theory and the Rise of China," in Robert S. Ross and Zhu Feng, eds., *China's Ascent: Power, Security, and the Future of International Politics* (Ithaca, NY: Cornell University Press, 2008), pp. 11–33.

2. On the "German problem" and its impact on Europe, see A.J.P. Taylor, *The Struggle for Mastery in Europe: 1848–1918* (New York: Oxford University Press, 1980).

3. For a discussion of China's perspective on the U.S. presence in Asia in 1949–50, see Zhang Shuguang, "'Preparedness Eliminates Mishaps': The CCP's Security Concerns in 1949–1950 and the Origins of the Sino-American Confrontation," *Journal of American-East Asian Relations*, 1, no. 1 (Spring 1992): 42–72.

4. See, for example, Thomas Christensen, "Threats, Assurances, and the Last Chance for Peace: The Lessons of Mao's Korean War Telegrams," *International Security,* 17, no. 1 (Summer 1992): 122–54; Sergei N. Goncharov, John Lewis, and Xue Litai, *Uncertain Partners: Stalin, Mao, and the Korean War* (Stanford, CA: Stanford University Press, 1993); Chen Jian, *China's Road to the Korean War: The Making of the Sino-American Confrontation* (New York: Columbia University Press, 1994).

5. On the Taiwan Strait, see Niu Daiyong and Shen Zhihua, eds., *Lengzhan yu Zhongguo de zhoubian guanxi* (The Cold War and China's Relations with Its Neighbors) (Beijing: Shijie zhishi chubanshe, 2004); Gong Li, "Tension Across the Taiwan Strait in the 1950s: Chinese Strategy and Tactics," in Robert S. Ross and Jiang Changbin, eds., *Re-examining the Cold War: U.S.-China Diplomacy, 1954–1973* (Cambridge, MA: Asia Center, Harvard University, 2001), pp. 141–72.

6. On the Cold War history of Chinese involvement in the Vietnam War, see Yang Kuisong and Shen Zhihua, *Zhongguo yu Yinduzhina zhanzheng* (China and the Indochina War) (Hong Kong: Tiandi tushu youxian gongsi, 2000); Zhang Baijia and Niu Jun, eds., *Lengzhan yu Zhongguo* (The Cold War and China) (Beijing: Shijie zhishi chubanshe, 2002); Priscilla Roberts, ed., *Behind the Bamboo Curtain: China, Vietnam, and the World Beyond Asia* (Stanford, CA: Stanford University Press, 2006).

7. On the strategic context for the U.S.-China rapprochement and normalization of relations and of U.S. and Chinese policy making, see Gong Li, *Kuayue honggou: 1969–1979 nian Zhong-Mei guanxi de yanbian* (Across the Chasm: The Evolution of Sino-U.S. Relations, 1969–1979) (Henan: Henan renmin chubanshe, 1992); Robert S. Ross, *Negotiating Cooperation: The United States and China, 1969–1989* (Palo Alto, CA: Stanford University Press, 1995).

8. Robert S. Ross, *The Indochina Tangle: China's Vietnam Policy, 1975–1979* (New York: Columbia University Press, 1988).

9. On Sino-Indian relations, see John W. Garver, *Protracted Contest: Sino-Indian Rivalry in the Twentieth Century* (Seattle: University of Washington Press, 2001).

10. On Sino-Soviet relations, see Shen Zhihua, ed., *Zhong Su guanxi shigang, 1917–1991* (Historical Outline of Sino-Soviet Relations, 1917–1991) (Beijing: Xinhua chubanshe, 2007); Odd Arne Westad, *Brothers in Arms: The Rise and Fall of the Sino-Soviet Alliance, 1945–1963* (Stanford, CA: Stanford University Press, 1998); Yang Kuisong, "The Sino-Soviet Border Clash of 1969: From Zhenbao Island to Sino-American Rapprochement," *Cold War History*, 1, no. 1 (2000): 21–53; Vitaly Kozyrev, "Soviet Policy toward the United States and China, 1969–1979," in William C. Kirby, Robert S. Ross, and Gong Li, eds., *Normalization of U.S.-China Relations: An International History* (Cambridge, MA: Asia Center, Harvard University, 2005), pp. 252–86; Elizabeth Wishnick, *Mending Fences: The Evolution of Moscow's China Policy, from Brezhnev to Yeltsin* (Seattle: University of Washington Press, 2001).

11. See Robert S. Ross, "China and the Cambodian Peace Process: The Value of Coercive Diplomacy," *Asian Survey*, 31, no. 12 (December 1991) 1170–85.

12. Michael Leifer, "Vietnam's Foreign Policy in the Post-Soviet Era: Coping with Vulnerability," in Robert S. Ross, ed., *East Asia in Transition: Toward a New Regional Order* (Armonk, NY: M.E. Sharpe, 1995), pp. 267–92.

13. The literature on the post-Mao rise of China is extensive. See, for example, Robert G. Sutter, *China's Rise in Asia: Promises and Perils* (Lanham, MD: Rowman & Littlefield, 2005); Ross and Zhu, eds., *China's Ascent*; Zhu Feng and Robert S. Ross, eds., *Zhongguo jueqi: Lilun yu zhengce de shijiao* (China's Rise: Perspective on Theory and Policy) (Shanghai: Shanghai renmin chubanshe, 2008); Yan Xuetong, et al., *Zhongguo jueqi jiqi zhanlüe* (China's Rise and Strategy) (Beijing: Beijing daxue chubanshe, 2005); Men Honghua, ed., *Zhongguo: Daguo jueqi* (China: The Rise of a Great Nation) (Hangzhou: Zhejiang renmin

chubanshe, 2004); Hu Angang, *Zhongguo jueqi zhi lu* (The Road to China's Rise) (Beijing: Beijing daxue chubanshe, 2007); Huang Renwei, *Zhongguo jueqi de shijian he kongjian* (The Space and Experience of China's Rise) (Shanghai: Shanghai shehui kexue chubanshe, 2002); William W. Keller and Thomas G. Rawski, eds., *China's Rise and the Balance of Influence in Asia* (Pittsburgh, PA: University of Pittsburgh Press, 2007); Xia Liping and Jiang Xiyuan, *Zhongguo heping jueqi* (China's Peaceful Rise) (Beijing: Zhongguo shehui kexue chubanshe, 2004).

14. On China's growing influence in East Asia, see, for example, Evelyn Goh, "Meeting the China Challenge: The U.S. in Southeast Asian Regional Security Strategies," *Policy Studies*, no. 16 (Washington, DC: East-West Center, 2005); Robert S. Ross, "Balance of Power Politics and the Rise of China: Accommodation and Balancing in East Asia," *Security Studies*, 15, no. 3 (July–September 2006): 355–95.

15. For a comprehensive discussion of Chinese ground-force modernization, see Dennis J. Blasko, *The Chinese Army Today* (New York: Routledge, 2006); Susan M. Puska, "Rough but Ready Force Projection: An Assessment of Recent PLA Training," in Andrew J. Scobell and Larry M. Wortzel, eds., *China's Growing Military Power: Perspectives on Security, Ballistic Missiles, and Conventional Capabilities* (Carlisle Barracks, PA: Strategic Studies Institute, U.S. Army War College, 2002), ch. 8.

16. On South Korea's response to the rise of China, see Byung-Kook Kim, "Between Rising China, Hegemonic America, and North Korea: South Korea's Hedging," in Ross and Zhu, eds., *China's Ascent*; Eric V. Larson, et al., *Ambivalent Allies?: A Study of South Korean Attitudes Toward the U.S.* (Santa Monica, CA: Rand, 2004).

17. Robert S. Ross, "Taiwan's Fading Independence Movement," *Foreign Affairs*, 85, no. 2 (March–April 2006): 141–48.

18. On early U.S. assessments of the strategic importance of Taiwan island and the Korean Peninsula, see Memorandum of Conversation, by the Secretary of State," January 5, 1950, U.S. Department of State, *Foreign Relations of the United States* (*FRUS*), 1950, vol. 6 (Washington, DC: Government Printing Office, 1976), pp. 260–61; and "Memorandum of Conversation, by the Secretary of State," December 29, 1949, *FRUS*, 1949, vol. 9 (Washington, DC: Government Printing Office, 1974), p. 467.

19. See Robert S. Ross, "Bipolarity and Balancing in East Asia," in T.V. Paul, James J. Wurtz, and Michael Fortmann, eds., *Balance of Power: Theory and Practice in the 21st Century* (Stanford, CA: Stanford University Press, 2004).

20. On U.S. policy toward China and Northeast Asia during this period, see Tao Wenzhao, ed., *Zhong Mei guanxi shi: 1949–1972* (History of China-United States Relations: 1949–1972) (Shanghai: Shanghai renmin chubanshe, 1999); Zi Zhongyun, *Zhanhou Meiguo waijiao shi: Cong Dulumen dao Ligen* (History of Postwar U.S. Diplomacy: From Truman to Reagan) (Beijing: Shijie zhishi chubanshe, 1994); John Lewis Gaddis, *The Long Peace: Inquiries Into the History of the Cold War* (New York: Oxford University Press, 1987); Rosemary Foot, *The Practice of Power: U. S. Relations with China since 1949* (New York: Oxford University Press, 1995).

21. Roy Kamphausen, David Lai, and Andrew Scobell, eds., *Beyond the Strait: PLA Missions Other Than Taiwan* (Carlisle, PA: Strategic Studies Institute, U.S. Army War College, 2009).

22. See, for example, Zhao Suisheng, *A Nation-State by Construction: Dynamics of Modern Chinese Nationalism* (Stanford, CA: Stanford University Press, 2004); Peter Hays

Gries, *China's New Nationalism: Pride, Politics, and Diplomacy* (Berkeley: University of California Press, 2004); Susan L. Shirk, *China: Fragile Superpower* (New York: Oxford University Press, 2007). For recent Chinese nationalist writings, see, for example, Song Xiaojun, et al., *Zhongguo bu gaoxing: Da shidai, da mubiao ji women de nei you waihui* (Unhappy China: The Great Time, Grand Vision, and Our Challenges) (Nanjing: Jiangsu renmin chubanshe, 2009).

23. For a critique of China's interest in expanded naval power, see Tang Shiping, *Su zao Zhongguo de lixiang anquan huanjing* (Construct China's Ideal Security Environment) (Beijing: Zhongguo shehui kexue chubanshe, 2003); Ye Zicheng, *Luquan fazhan yu daguo xingshuai* (The Development of Land Power and the Rise and Fall of the Great Powers) (Beijing: Xinxing chubanshe, 2007). For a Chinese nationalist perspective on Chinese interests in expanded naval power, see, for example, Zhang Wenmu, *Lun Zhongguo haiquan* (On China's Naval Power) (Beijing: Haiyang chubanshe, 2009); Ni Leixiong, "Haiquan yu Zhongguo de fazhan" (Naval Power and China's Development), in Guo Shuyong, ed., *Zhanlüe yanjianglu* (A Record of Talks on Strategy) (Beijing: Beijing daxue chubanshe, 2006). Also see Robert S. Ross, "China's Naval Nationalism: Sources, Prospects, and the U.S. Response," *International Security*, 34, no. 2 (Fall 2009): 46–81.

24. On U.S. policy during this period and Acheson's preferences, see Gaddis, *The Long Peace;* Nancy Bernkopf Tucker, *Patterns in the Dust: Chinese-American Relations and the Recognition Controversy, 1949–1950* (New York: Columbia University Press, 1983).

25. For recent alarmist views, see, for example, the opening remarks by Senator Jim Webb at the Senate Foreign Relations Committee Hearing on Maritime and Sovereignty Disputes in Asia, July 15, 2009, at http://webb.senate.gov/newsroom/pressreleases/2009-07-15-01.cfm, (accessed February 8, 2010); Robert D. Kaplan, "Center Stage for the Twenty-first Century Power Plays in the Indian Ocean," *Foreign Affairs*, 88, no. 2 (March–April 2009): 16–32.

5.
THE PEOPLE'S REPUBLIC OF CHINA AT SIXTY: IS IT RISING?[1]

ALASTAIR IAIN JOHNSTON AND SHEENA CHESTNUT

One of the long-time goals of Chinese foreign policy has been to "catch up" with the great powers. Whether this desire came, or comes, from the historical memory of the century of humiliation (in which case humiliation will be extirpated when China has a "rich state and a strong army"), or from Mao Zedong's desire to catch up with and possibly surpass the industrialized states in terms of raw material power, or from the contemporary drive to revive (复兴) the Chinese people and nation through policies of "peaceful rise" or "peaceful development" (和平崛起 / 和平发展), closing the perceived gap in power between China and the most powerful states has long been a driver in Chinese foreign policy.

In American policy and pundit circles, this drive to catch up is often seen as a challenge to U.S. primacy. Although there are debates over the degree to which China's "rise" should be considered a threat to U.S. interests, the drive animates a great deal of the military planning in the U.S. Department of Defense and broader policy establishment. In the U.S. academic world, analysis of this drive is often framed in terms of a power transition, whereby the probability of instability increases as a revisionist rising state challenges the interests of the status quo hegemonic state.

The problem is that in all of this discourse about catching up, reviving, rising, or emerging (and there are many euphemisms used more or less interchangeably)—whether it comes from Chinese nationalists, Maoists, Dengists, post-Dengists, or the governments, media, or academy in other countries—there is no consensus on how one would know whether China is rising relative to the dominant state in the system, the United States.

As a result, there are no rigorously derived expectations or forecasts about when and in what arenas of power China will catch up with the United States. The absence of common measures and indicators makes it difficult to compare China's rise with that of other states in the past, and therefore difficult to assess the potential consequences.

The media, pundit, and scholarly literature on China is all over the place when it comes to explicit and implicit definitions of "rising." There are at least seven definitions that one can find in contemporary discourse:

1. Historical: Simply put, China is more powerful than it was in the past. This measure does not compare Chinese power with that of other states, but rather with itself.
2. Visibility: China or Chinese entities (often assumed to be directed in some fashion by the leadership) are present and/or more active in more issue areas and more places around the globe than in the past.
3. Influence: Chinese policy and/or Chinese entities are impacting the lives of more ordinary people and economic and political actors around the globe than in the past.
4. Threat to the hegemon's interests: China has an improved ability to interfere with and reduce U.S. military dominance in the Asia-Pacific region compared to in the past.[2]
5. Size (or amount of material power capabilities): China is narrowing the relative and/or absolute gap in power between it and the United States.
6. Threat to the hegemonic order: China presents an increased challenge to the dominant norms and institutions that govern international and transnational interactions.

We focus on definitions five and six because these are, perhaps, the most commonly used or implied notions of "rising." We find that depending on which definition one uses, one comes to different conclusions about whether or not China is rising, has risen, or will rise.

Take definition five, for instance: "size." This definition can be further subdivided into numerous indicators to measure change in the size of Chinese power vis-à-vis the United States. One indicator of rising power, often used in quantitative international relations studies, is a state's share of world power capabilities compared to that of the hegemon. If we use this metric and the Correlates of War data, however, the PRC already caught up with the United States in the early 1980s (see Figure 1). (This indicator, however, includes total population as an element of state power, leading, some contend, to over-estimations of Chinese power.)

Using instead the Correlates of War iron and steel production figures, we see that Chinese material power began to catch up with the United States in the 1960s, and surpassed it in the 1990s (see Figure 2).

Using another material indicator of the degree to which a hegemon's power is challenged by other states, however, returns a very different result. This

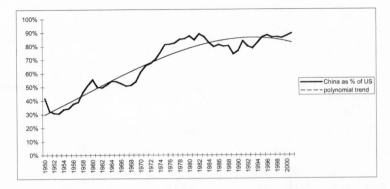

Figure 1:   China's Share of the World's National Capabilities as a Percentage of the U.S. Share

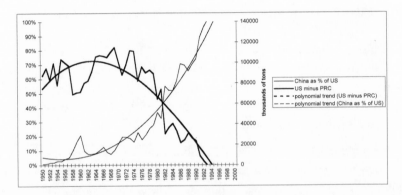

Figure 2:   China's Iron and Steel Production as a Percentage of U.S. Production, and the Absolute Difference between U.S. and Chinese Production

indicator, called the "largest drop-off rule," argues that a contending power is that state for which the difference between the hegemon's power and that state's power (here measured by GDP) is smaller than the difference between that state and the next-largest state's power (see Figure 3). Using this indicator, it appears that China has never been a contender to challenge the United States.

Another commonly used material indicator of power is relative size of GDP. Even though China's growth rate has been consistently around or above 10 percent for many years now, whereas the U.S. rate has been considerably lower, China began its economic growth at a much lower level of development. Thus, even as the size of its economy has grown as a percentage of the U.S. economy, the absolute difference in size of GDP between China and the United States continues to expand in favor of the United States (see Figure 4). Depending on the

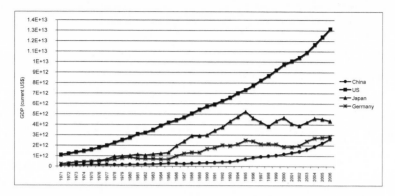

Figure 3:   Largest Drop-Off Rule and Contenders for Hegemony

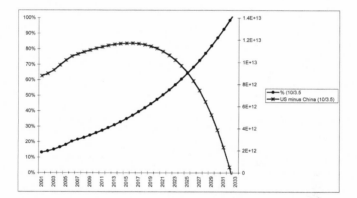

Figure 4:   Trends in Relative and Absolute Difference between U.S. and Chinese GDP

relative growth rates, there will come a time when this absolute gap begins to close and China will genuinely begin to "catch up" with the United States (see Figure 5). But we are not there yet. At this point in time, then, China is rising in relative terms (the size of its economy as a percentage of the size of that of the United States), but not in absolute terms (shrinking the gap in size).

This pattern essentially shows up not only in the economic data on China and the United States, but in U.S.-China comparative military spending as well (see Figure 6). China's spending as a percentage of U.S. spending is climbing, whereas the absolute gap between the two is still growing in favor of the United States. At very high numbers of military spending for both countries, this difference between relative and absolute power trends will not matter much.[3] But for the moment, the tens of billions of dollars more of military spending available to the United States each year does plausibly translate into military technical advantages for the United States.

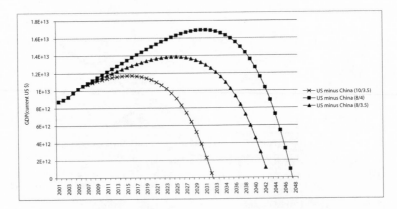

Figure 5:   Absolute Difference in the Size of U.S. and Chinese GDPs: Three Scenarios

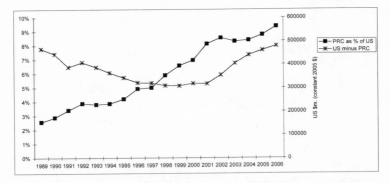

Figure 6:   Trends in the Relative and Absolute Difference between U.S. and Chinese Military Spending (Source: Stockholm International Peace Research Institute)

In short, as one goes through the various ways in which "rising" has been conceived, it turns out that there is no consistent answer about when China began to rise, how fast it is rising, and when (or even if) it will catch up to and surpass the United States.

What about the sixth definition whereby China could be considered to be rising if it were increasingly able to threaten or challenge the "international order" established by the United States after World War II? This is another common trope, especially in U.S. discussions of the intentions likely to govern China's rise. Even some Chinese analysts use this definition in their own internal discussions about whether China is satisfied or dissatisfied with the U.S.-dominated international system.

This definition leads, however, to the problem of defining the current international order. Some international institutions and international norms work at cross-purposes (e.g., sovereignty versus regulation of the global free-trade regime). So China might support some elements of this order while opposing or merely acquiescing to others. Developing a balance sheet of support and opposition with the aim of coming to an overall conclusion about the level of China's satisfaction depends on how much one weights the importance of different elements of this order to its overall robustness. For instance, it is probably more important for the longevity of the U.S.-dominated order that China is a member of all the major international economic institutions than the fact that it maintains good bilateral ties with Zimbabwe, Venezuela, or Cuba. There is room for debate, of course, but the point is that so far there has been no systematic effort to develop such a balance sheet. And even if there were, a dynamic, macro-historical perspective would surely indicate that since the end of the Maoist period, the PRC has become more, not less, supportive of the U.S.-determined order. The story of China's interactions with international institutions, for instance, is a story of a rather dramatic increase in China's engagement with institutions that regulate interstate relations, not a rejection of them (see Figure 7).

There is also the question of whether opposition to elements of the international order is the same as opposition to the hegemon's interests. The power transition literature generally assumes—as do many Americans—that U.S. behavior and the key norms of the international order are synonymous. Yet it is clear that some elements of this order have been opposed by U.S. policy and practice. In some cases, therefore, China has challenged U.S. interests while also upholding elements of international order (e.g., insisting that international efforts to resolve interstate disputes be sanctioned by the United Nations Security Council, rather

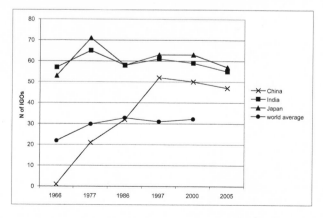

Figure 7:   Trends in China's Membership in International Governmental Organizations

than unilaterally by the United States or U.S.-dominated coalitions of the willing). In some cases, U.S. opposition to the dominant norms of the system has had Chinese support, as with joint U.S. and Chinese opposition to international efforts to control small arms trafficking, eliminate the death penalty, or set up an International Criminal Court.

In sum, different indicators of "rising" lead to different conclusions about China's ability to catch up with the dominant state in the system, the United States (see Table 1). By our rough "back of the envelope" calculation for the "historical," "visibility," and "influence" definitions, China can uncontroversially be said to be rising. As for the "threat to core interests" definition, it is unclear how much China's development of an anti-access or area denial capability fundamentally changes the U.S. ability to project power and defend its interests in Asia. As the Chinese note, for every sword there is a shield, and for every shield there is a sword. The most dramatic potential threat to U.S. military operations in the region—a fully deployed anti-ship ballistic missile capability—is still some time off, and the United States is not standing still in developing countermeasures.

As for the variants of the "size" definition, unpacked in previous sections, relative indicators generally suggest China is rising, whereas absolute difference indicators suggest "not yet." Finally, concerning the "threat to international order" definition, the above discussion demonstrates that it is unclear whether China's approach to the major norms and institutions of the post-World War II American-dominated international order (to the extent that it exists, and acknowledging the contradictions among many of these norms) constitutes a challenge, an acceptance, or something in between. Smart people have argued for each.

Despite the widespread disagreement on material definitions and indicators about how to define and measure China's "rise," there is one definition by which there is almost no controversy and for which the verdict is unanimous that China

Table 1:   Summary of Definitions of "Rising"

Definition of "rising"	Is China "rising"?
Historical	Yes
Visibility	Yes
Influence	Yes
Threat to the hegemon's core security interests	Unclear
Size	
as a proportion of the hegemon's power	Yes
closing the absolute gap in the hegemon's power advantage *– "catching up"*	No (not yet)
Threat to the hegemon's order	No?

is, in fact, rising: contemporary discourse. This leads us to a seventh definition: an inter-subjective definition. The vast majority of American, Chinese, and global commentary assumes without question that China is rising. As Figures 8 and 9 demonstrate, there has been a sharp rise in the number of references to "China rising" across both the English- and Chinese-language media discourse.

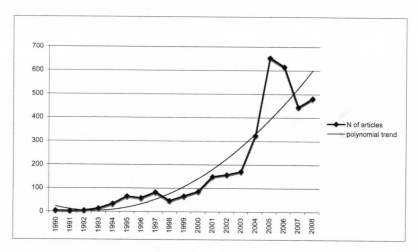

Figure 8:   Frequency of Articles Referencing "Rising China"
(Source: LexisNexis General News)

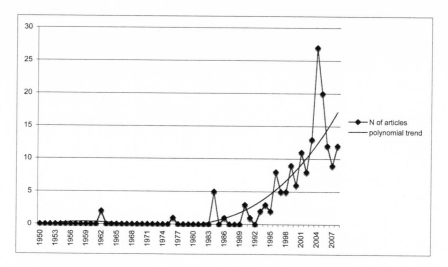

Figure 9:   Frequency of Articles Referencing "China's Rise" (中国的崛起) in the *People's Daily*

Why does this discourse matter? In the context of the inconclusiveness of the range of other indicators cited here, these figures suggest that there may be a disjunction between material indicators of rising and inter-subjective estimates. This suggests, in turn, that what matters most for predicting the future trajectory of U.S.-China relations is not the numbers on the balance sheet, but what leaders in the United States and China believe to be the case, because they will act according to these beliefs.

If this is the case, then analyzing the interaction of U.S. and Chinese perceptions of rising Chinese power is important for understanding the prospects for conflict and cooperation in the relationship. As a preliminary analytical exercise, one can conceive of a minimum of four logical outcomes in the interaction of U.S. and Chinese leadership perceptions of China's rise (see Table 2).

One possibility is that the two sides agree that China is indeed rising (regardless of whether it is or is not rising according to the definitions outlined earlier). This may give rise to an acute security dilemma, as the United States adopts diplomatic and military strategies designed to defend its hegemonic status, whereas China adopts what it believes are defensive strategies designed to prevent the United States from constraining or preventing China's rise. Security dilemma dynamics are difficult to dampen, but in principle they are amenable to credible information about the intentions of the two sides.

Another possibility is that the U.S. side believes China is rising, whereas Chinese leaders do not. This could lead to American responses intended by the United States to manage China's rise that Chinese leaders believe to be an overreaction to their vulnerable status. Perhaps even more than in a security dilemma, Chinese leaders are likely to interpret the stronger American side's aggressive response as an unjustifiable existential threat, aimed at suppressing China's future development and security.

A third possibility is that U.S. leaders do not perceive a dramatic rise in Chinese power, whereas Chinese leaders believe their power is indeed rising.

Table 2:   Interactions between American and Chinese Inter-subjective Understandings of China's Rise.

		Does the rising power think it is rising?	
		Yes	No
Does the hegemon think the rising power is rising?	Yes	*acute security dilemma dynamics*	*hegemon over-reacts; self-fulfilling prophecy*
	No	*status inconsistency drives rising power policy*	*satisfaction with status quo*

China might then perceive that the United States is denying—whether the United States is witting or not—China's desired status. If so, status inconsistency dynamics could then drive China's response, resulting in a renewed effort to use China's accretion of power to close the gap between its deserved and ascribed status. Chinese actions would be designed to "get the attention" of the United States, but could provoke a confrontation.

A final possibility is that neither side sees China's power as rising relative to the United States. For the United States, this would signal China's essential satisfaction with the uneven distribution of power. For China, this would signal U.S. acceptance of China's existence, its internal political system, and its external interests. This would, of course, be the most benign outcome.

The evidence about discourse on both sides suggests that the first possibility is more likely to capture the current U.S.-China relationship than the other three. This is not to suggest that security dilemma dynamics are unavoidable. Voices on both sides believe that these dynamics can be mitigated. Sometimes these arguments point to the constraining effect of economic interdependence, where mutual economic benefit trumps any and all of the conflict dynamics possible in the first three outcomes. Sometimes these arguments suggest that the environmental, social, and legitimacy problems currently faced by China, combined with post-9/11 and post-financial crisis limits on American hegemony, will essentially move the relationship closer to the last possibility. The empirical question is which of all these discourses is likely to dominate the decision-making processes in each country in the coming years.

ENDNOTES

1. For a fuller development of the arguments in this paper, see Sheena Chestnut and Alastair Iain Johnston, "Is China Rising?" in Eva Paus, Penelope Prime, and Jon Western, eds., *Global Giant: Is China Changing the Rules of the Game?* (New York: Palgrave MacMillan, 2009).

2. Some American analysts worry that China is beginning to develop technologies that could challenge U.S. technological and economic dominance, and that—linked to organizational innovation—may improve China's ability to exploit the next revolution in military affairs to the disadvantage of the United States. Some point, for example, to the potential for Chinese anti-ship ballistic missiles to neutralize U.S. aircraft carrier operations, which are at the heart of U.S. power projection in the Pacific.

3. We thank Alex Liebman for this point.

6.
WHY CHINA GETS A "RISE" OUT OF US:
RUMINATIONS ON PRC FOREIGN RELATIONS

ALAN M. WACHMAN

That China Rises

In 2009, it is commonplace to think of China as "rising" but less common to question what is implied by the term "China" and what is meant by "rise." The very phrase—"rise of China"—suggests an international phenomenon. So many observers gawk and point to this development because it affects relations between the People's Republic of China (PRC) and their own state, as well as between the PRC and the international system. Thus, in the context of the various reflections on the PRC's first sixty years presented in this volume, the following ruminations on foreign relations emphasize the international dimension of China's rise.

The term is enigmatic. What, precisely, is meant by the "rise of China"? One rarely encounters a reference to the "rise of the PRC." Is that because the PRC is now almost universally equated with China, obviating the distinction between the state established in 1949 and the civilization that has given rise to a multitude of long-lasting political entities, several of them coexisting in time and sharing a common geographic domain?

It makes a difference. China, considered a civilizational enterprise extending deeply into the past, has passed through periods of efflorescence, enfeeblement, and restoration. At each moment, the polity that was then considered "China" related to the people beyond its realm in ways that reflected their relative power and the structure of the international system in which they all were situated. China as the PRC, however, is a comparatively recent development. Located on the long arc of time, what is observed now as a "rise" may be less notable than if one emphasizes only the past sixty years. The expansion of wealth, power, and influence by the PRC has had extensive effects on Beijing's relations with other states and, perhaps, on the international system. If 1949 is the point of departure, the "rise" may be perceived as a recent, rapid, and novel transformation.

That said, it is worth observing that the PRC had a disproportionate influence on international affairs long before the onset of reform, opening, and brisk economic growth. During its first several decades, the PRC had an influence on international politics that was heftier than its economic or military prowess might otherwise have indicated. In that era, the PRC's sway was gauged in terms of the perceived potential of Beijing's ideological zealotry and military adventurism, not its economics or political throw-weight in international organizations.

From the grinding stalemate on the battlefields of Korea to the provocations Beijing directed against the United States, India, and the Soviet Union, to the apparent influence the PRC exercised over the Vietnamese Communists through-out the conflict between foreign forces and Vietnamese nationalists, the PRC's audacity and tenacity ensured that its preferences had to be taken into account by those concerned about geopolitical rivalries. Despite being comparatively poor, politically isolated, and perpetually at war with itself, the PRC's bellicose rhetoric and military activism on its periphery stoked the anxieties of its neighbors—small and great states alike.

In the past three decades, as the PRC has become more ideologically inert, politically stable, economically productive, and more confidently integrated into the international community, it has rather consciously eschewed bellicosity and adventurism. Yet, it continues to provoke trepidation in foreign capitals about what it will do with its swelling coffers, rapidly expanding military capabilities, and ever-increasing status at multinational rule-setting deliberations.

How much of the anxiety flows from an objective reading of Beijing's inten-tions and capabilities and how much results from unexpurgated prejudices is hard to know. What is evident, though, is that the prospect of lucrative commercial deals in the PRC and of beneficial investments by Beijing abroad has generated influence for the PRC, spilling over in the past decade from purely economic matters to other domains. Beijing's interests are given wide berth by many states that defer simply because of the hope of ensuring the PRC's favor and of profiting from interactions with it. One feature of the PRC's diplomacy is the credible projection of latent ruthlessness that leaves other states to conclude that it is unwise to cross Beijing. Beijing has deployed this credibility to great effect in commercial matters and, thereby, it has bought a high degree of political influence.

It would be inaccurate, though, to think of the PRC as having influence only since the 1990s, when its economic growth began to register in double-digits. The colossal state has played a colossal role in international affairs from its inception in 1949, although the nature of its role has changed significantly in the years since.

From one perspective, China has been "rising" since it fell during the final phase of dynastic collapse, at the end of the Qing in 1911. In the early twentieth century, the "awakening of China" captured the imagination of many, as if the Chinese people had been meekly slumbering and only aroused by the then recent depredations of imperialist avarice. Early in the twentieth century, nationalism and the remaking of a Chinese polity were the order of the day. Yet, when one encounters now the notion of China's "rise," the early post-Qing decades of "awakening" are hardly considered as part of the process.

After years of disunity and false-starts from 1912 to 1926, it might also be reasonable to date China's "rise" to the conclusion of the Northern Expedition and the founding of the government at Nanjing in 1928. Alternatively, one might peg the rise of China as a process that began with the establishment of the People's Republic of China in 1949.

Ordinarily, when the term "rise of China" is uttered, the early twentieth-century efforts at reform, reorganization, self-strengthening, rededication, and renewal are not accounted for, even though they may have been the runway from which China recently has taken off. It has been sixty years since the PRC was established. Has it been "rising" during all that time?

One senses that when the term "rise of China" is mouthed, it is not meant to encompass any of these earlier phases of China's post-Qing development. Rather, it is meant to characterize the implications of the economic and political reforms associated with Deng Xiaoping—policies undertaken in the late 1970s, a few years after the end of the Cultural Revolution.

At least to observers who hail from somewhere outside the former Communist bloc, that was the juncture when the PRC began to consider international politics from some vantage other than the convoluting lens of an ideological kaleidoscope. From then on, it seems, the PRC has been engaged in a massive transformative program that incrementally has brought it nearer to "us." In what first seemed rather tentative steps, the PRC crept from the isolation of abnormality toward the international community as "we" understood it. With each step, the PRC seemed to accept most of the rules and incentives by which "we" played. That made it appear ever more like "us," and, therefore, ever more likeable.

At some point in the past decade, observers found themselves marveling unexpectedly at how the most pressing international issues could no longer be addressed without Beijing's acquiescence. The PRC's speedy economic growth had bought it strategic, political, and commercial significance, all of which highlight its expanding relevance. Indeed, one way to understand the notion of the "rise of China" is as the PRC's increasing significance in the minds of people engaged in shaping policies and implementing practices that are the "stuff" of public, private, bilateral, and multilateral international interactions. If the notion of globalization has any merit as a description of the extensive intermingling of national and sub-national interests in a skein of transnational intercourse, then the PRC now certainly figures prominently as an influence on that process.

As the term "rise of China" is often employed, it seems to imply that this process of ever-more influence by Beijing over bilateral and global affairs is expected to continue. Indeed, the "rise of China" seems to connote a continuation of measurable growth by the PRC leading inexorably to Beijing's regional dominance and, perhaps, international hegemony. It is also associated with a belief that this will lead the PRC to challenge the military and political status of the United States.

Taking the PRC's current trajectory as leading to a certain conclusion seems analytically risky. Looking back, there have been other periods when Chinese had reason to hope for an end to division, internecine struggle, and national impotence, even though those hopeful moments were followed by disappointing relapses to turmoil. Precisely because the term "rise of China" is so annoyingly indefinable, it seems to mask more than it describes and is, therefore, of little value to those who aim to understand how the PRC's status and capabilities in the international context have evolved and will yet evolve in the future.

Many observers imagine the PRC is likely to emerge, in due course, as a world power—whatever is meant by that ill-defined term—or, in some of the more breathless accounts, as a superpower. Perhaps.

If the United States and the Soviet Union of the Cold War era offer the principal benchmarks for what constitutes a superpower, the PRC in 2009 is still far from having the attributes that would entitle it to that status. For one thing, in the first years of the twenty-first century it has only begun to exhibit a capacity to project military might far from its own shores. For another, its economy is less than one-third the size of that of the United States and also less than that of Japan—even allowing for the turmoil that financial crises have visited on all three. The PRC has also refrained from building a sphere of influence, military bloc, or network of formal military alliances—not that it would necessarily succeed in this endeavor if it were inclined to try. The point is that the PRC has grown substantially, but if by superpower one means what was meant when that term was applied to the United States and the Soviet Union, one may legitimately question whether the PRC should be considered a superpower.

Of course, the future may bring new measures for status as a superpower, or even new labels with which to describe states that enjoy a preponderance of influence. Still, one must acknowledge that it is not possible to know in what ways the PRC will continue to change. Indeed, observers of the PRC are sharply divided on this issue. Even after sixty years of analyzing the PRC's influence on world affairs, foreign observers are little better at discerning Beijing's intentions than analysts were in 1949, despite the proliferation of information emanating from the PRC. Indeed, the divisions among professional analysts cloud any effort to see with clarity what the PRC has become and what more it might be. These divisions may reflect as much about the preexisting analytical dispositions of the observers as about the PRC itself. Confronted with the same array of data, analysts of the PRC may invest their personal savings differently, vote differently, and pray to different gods. Why, then, should they see the PRC in exactly the same way?

Hence, the term "rise of China" may say as much about those who work to interpret China as about the PRC. This realization is underscored by the maddeningly imprecise meaning of "rise." It is used with wide latitude to mean a multitude of things that make it an infectious, but fundamentally meaningless, moniker. The term is used in a cavalier and indiscriminate way so that one is never entirely clear from what point the rise was meant to begin, on what measures the rise is observed, and whether rising is a welcome or menacing process.

Those who marvel at the many ways in which the PRC has changed in sixty years see in the changes reason for celebration. Similarly, those who find unsettling the prospect that the PRC may, with greater wealth and military might, become a bully beyond its borders—as many perceive it to be within its own boundaries—sense that the "rise of China" is far from salutary.

Reviewing the past sixty years, every decade brought with it essential alterations in the worldview embraced by leaders in Beijing and postures adopted in response that affected the PRC's foreign relations. Although the rhetoric at each moment may have implied a degree of constancy, the dominant impression of the PRC's apprehension of the international environment and the proper place for China in that context is one of perpetual change. At each moment, alterations within the PRC's domestic political arena had powerful consequences for its status in the international arena. The problem now, as in the past, is one cannot be certain how the current chapter will end and what will come next.

To be sure, there are plenty of Chinese commentators who fuel the idea that China is on the rise. Equally, Chinese analysts are wont to remind those outside the PRC who are fixated on the PRC's growth that China has a long way to go before it becomes what others have decided it already is. To date, the PRC seems rooted in two domains. In many real ways, it carries itself abroad as a major power—affecting relations among states in its region and having an influence in decisions made about global problems as a significant actor at the table. In other ways, the PRC still seems mired in its darker past and in the arduous processes of development and modernization. Chinese analysts persist in reminding those whose ears they can bend that the PRC remains beset by problems that were never properly worked out in the transition that began in the late 1970s. Also, the leadership in Beijing now confronts a cascade of new and potentially destabilizing controversies that are the unbidden byproducts of growth. Hence, the notion that China's rise signals its arrival as a superpower both overstates its capacities and underspecifies its fragilities.

In addition, the widespread presumption that the PRC's recent growth signals the inevitability of its future should be considered against the backdrop of the rather checkered record foreign analysts of China have established in anticipating with accuracy what lies just around the bend of time for the state about which they claim to have privileged insight. Some of the most consequential events that have undermined the PRC's stability and relationship to the rest of the world—the Great Leap Forward of 1958–60, the Cultural Revolution that occupied the decade from 1966–76, and the suppression of protests in 1989 to name only the most obvious—were cataclysmic disturbances arising from the PRC's domestic politics. These were not events that foreign observers saw coming, a realization that ought to give one pause as one contemplates expectations of the PRC that so many foreign observers now pronounce. Indeed, even the momentous adjustments to the PRC's ideology, economy, and foreign relations that emerged in the years after the Cultural Revolution came about rather more suddenly and have had more far-reaching effects than was generally understood at the time. Hence, much conventional wisdom about how the PRC will develop over the next decades should be understood as utterly speculative.

Beijing's Diplomacy

It appears as if each decade has brought with it a new approach by Beijing to foreign policy, articulated with new slogans and reflecting a newly established worldview. In one sense, this is unremarkable. Most states adjust their posture toward international relations in response to developments at home and perceptions of changing circumstances abroad. The early leaders of the PRC, though, cloaked their policies in ideological explanations that purported to derive from immutable laws of socio-economic progress. For mobilizational purposes alone, the PRC leadership may have projected a degree of constancy into its public pronouncements that stands at odds with its actual foreign policy preferences. One can surely find commonalities that link the impulses of the PRC over the past sixty years, but it is also rather easy to identify abrupt and meaningful change.

By and large, the foreign policy of the PRC has been reactive. Despite the oceans of ink that flowed from the pens of Chinese Communist Party (CCP) ideologues and PRC statesmen in emphatic statements about transformative revolution, communism has not mattered quite as much as the PRC's national interest as a guide to Beijing's foreign relations over the past six decades. Put differently, the nationalist inclinations of the CCP leadership seem to have overridden any devotion they expressed to transnational ideals, such as a worldwide Communist revolution. Indeed, looking back on sixty years of PRC foreign policy, one senses that Beijing has generally reacted to secure the PRC as a state in a world perceived as hostile and imposing—despite adherence to an ideology that was aimed at the eradication of the state.

Even during the period when the PRC was governed by an ideological zealous cadre of self-professed Communists, it was their perception of state interests that trumped their own stated ideals of creating conditions after which the state would wither away. Stripped of the mystifying and distracting verbiage of Marxism-Leninism-Mao Zedong Thought, the PRC's role in international politics falls within the expectations of conventional realists: a state that seeks security through "self-help" in an anarchic world by doing what it can to maximize power.

During the period of the Cultural Revolution, fierce ideological fury within China burned through the firewall that, to a considerable degree, divided domestic ideological struggles from determining the PRC's international posture. Yet, even in that radicalized phase, one may see evidence that rather conventional realist notions of state interest prevailed. The most evident illustration was the *volte face* on the Sino-Soviet alliance and the opening to Sino-U.S. normalization.

Throughout, then, one might conclude that formal ideology was a conceptual lens coupled to an evocative lexicon with which to perceive and describe international conditions. In and of itself, though, communism did not pervert the PRC's leadership from acting in ways that would otherwise be seen by realists as conforming to the conventional inclinations of a rational actor.

Moreover, the PRC does not appear to have been motivated in international interactions by any compelling, original, or enduring ideas. Nor has the PRC developed a particular perspective on international relations or made any novel contribution to the implicit rules by which states organize in the international arena. This, too, would be unremarkable, if not for the persistent intimations by PRC leaders that their foreign policies were, in some ways, exceptionally principled.

The Five Principles of Peaceful Coexistence (mutual respect for each other's territorial integrity and sovereignty, mutual non-aggression, mutual non-interference in each other's internal affairs, equality and mutual benefit, and peaceful coexistence) gained prominence in 1954 and have remained a rhetorical touchstone ever since. If adherence to these principles had been either consistent or infective, one might credit the PRC for having introduced a way of ordering international interactions that reflected some essentially transformative ideal. However, the PRC's own actions with other states have violated the five principles as often as they have reified them. Certainly there are states on the PRC's periphery that have not felt that Beijing disciplined itself in its interactions with them according to these lofty aims.

In its international relations, the PRC has been just as cynical and hypocritical as any other power. The rise of China, then, should not be seen as prompting in the PRC's foreign relations anything one might call Chinese exceptionalism. Much as Chinese patriots proclaim that the PRC is embarked on a foreign policy of peace and seeks only "win-win" solutions, offering assistance overseas without ideological or political strings attached, building friendships wherever there are partners prepared to deal with China as an equal, efforts to enfold PRC self-interest in the robes of exceptionalism are easily belied by careful inspection. The self-perceptions that emanate from the PRC are not matched by reciprocal perceptions abroad.

More often than not, the PRC acted toward smaller states as any larger state might be expected to act. Toward the United States and the Soviet Union, the PRC seemed perpetually on edge—challenging their prerogatives and vying with them for influence. Toward both, it seems, the PRC reacted from insecurity. Even as it becomes increasingly capable, its capabilities prompt an enlargement and redefinition of interests. That process leads Beijing to recognize that its greater capacities are not keeping pace with its expanding policy objectives, thus fueling continued insecurities.

To compensate for its material deficiencies, the PRC has proven itself highly skilled at creating and exploiting imagery—both of China and of its adversary-du-jour. It is quite adept at taking command of the conceptual framework in which its international interactions occur. One sees evidence of PRC successes in its efforts to use imagery to get much of what it wants from potential adversaries where Taiwan, Tibet, human rights, and the "China threat" are concerned.

This is not to say that it is uniformly successful in masking incapacity by imagery, but simply to acknowledge that where it lacks material resources to take what it wants, Beijing has employed imagery and rhetoric rather well to ensure it gets a good deal of what it seeks at as low a cost to itself as it can manage.

It appears the PRC has a well-stocked kit of foreign policy tools that it draws upon with considerable success. Among the tools it has used repeatedly is to play on the guilt of former imperialist states that once victimized China. Great Britain and Japan have been especially susceptible to this lever. Another is to play up the "peace-loving" nature of China—holding up the several voyages of the Ming admiral Zheng He as emblematic of a Chinese approach to expeditionary enterprise that seeks mutual benefit and does no harm.

Beijing is also quite adept at playing to the foreign fascination with China as the fount of an exotic culture. It gladly lays claim to "5,000 years of Chinese history"—an assertion that depends on widespread ignorance of the fact that Chinese historians themselves date recorded history to the Shang dynasty, a period that began about 4,000 years ago. The PRC is also shameless in only claiming moments of past Chinese glory, conveniently sweeping periods of decay, division, and despotism under the rug of collective memory.

Beyond the conceptual realm, the PRC has engineered an expansion of international influence by successfully identifying the interests of adversaries and using that as leverage to up-end potential opponents. In this, it has been aided by enviably meticulous control over its "message" and a generally credible display of sincerity about the "message" by disciplined diplomats and statesmen.

These diplomats and public spokespersons have peppered their statements with effective references to "interference in China's internal affairs"—a formulation that puts the other state on the defensive; assertions that China has "no choice but to" do something distasteful—a formulation that makes clear the bad thing about to happen is not really China's fault but is Beijing's only option in the face of some provocation; "some states . . ."—a formulation that China is about to scold another state for doing something, without actually mentioning the name of that state; some action contemplated by a given state that will or has "hurt the feelings of the Chinese people"—a formulation that is intended to evoke a sense of shame; the PRC interest in "win-win" solutions—a formulation that signals the intent of the PRC to avoid any appearance of big power chauvinism; and the claim that "China will never exercise hegemony"—a formulation that asks observers to put aside what they see and to believe only what Beijing wishes them to believe about its actions.

These tools have been especially apparent when the PRC has dealt with territorial matters. Thus, with a degree of bravado and masterful manipulation, the PRC projects a self-image of an aggrieved metropole combating foreign-inspired machinations to undermine its sovereignty. Who else but the PRC can dispatch diplomats to foreign capitals to read demarchés to sovereign leaders, demanding that they refrain from admitting the Dalai Lama or Rebiya Kadeer or the president of Taiwan to their own state, because to do so would "interfere in the internal affairs of China"?

These stratagems have worked so well in so many cases that the PRC has become insensitive to instances where the approach may backfire. These are, indeed, powerful tools. However, when they are applied inflexibly, they have become a source of fragility. The PRC has not entirely sorted out when diplomatic paternalism, duplicity, bullying, and shame-mongering work and when they do not. The fiasco of the 2008 Olympic torch relay is an illustration of how the approach can occasionally fail.

In sum, the PRC's rise has not come about because of a distinctive or useful new mode of thinking about international politics or the distribution of common international "goods." The PRC's increasing influence is an outgrowth of its newly developed economic clout and prospects for military power. The "rise of China" is much more a story of commercial opportunism by other states eager to profit from and to avoid being cut out of the development of the PRC's economy than it is a story about Beijing's contributions to institutions, regimes, or ideas that appeal to others as offering common goods.

Why China's Rise Gets a Rise Out of Us

Having noted that China's rise has been long in coming and faces a still uncertain future, and having suggested that its rise has been neither especially disruptive nor especially transformative, one is impelled to ask why it is that the expansion of the PRC's capabilities gets such a "rise" out of so many. Why does it seem to matter?

That the PRC's capacities are increasing is beyond dispute. That increase in capacities, though, has led to a widening scope of international operations and an expansion of ambitions. One only needs to look back ten or fifteen years and compare how the PRC was then involved in the international arena with how it is in 2011 to see what has changed. One now finds a Chinese state with massive investments in the exploitation of natural resources far afield, a prominent status at international organizational fora, the commitment of troops to international anti-piracy and peace-keeping missions abroad, active cultivation of relationships with states not only along its periphery but very far afield, and with a hand or finger or toe in almost every major international problem that now confronts the other major powers. These are significant adjustments in the role that the PRC now plays in international politics.

With the expansion of PRC ambitions to influence or ensure a correspondence of foreign behavior with its interests, one also notes the eroding persuasiveness of the mantra *"taoguang yanghui"*—that summation of foreign policy advice derived from classical texts, adapted by Deng Xiaoping, and encapsulated, simplistically, in the translation "bide your time, hide your capabilities" or "keep a low profile" in international affairs. The PRC has already pierced that veil. In 2009, it routinely showcased its capacities.

Not only has the PRC sent a small armada to the Gulf of Aden to participate in anti-piracy patrols, it also held a massive naval parade on the sixtieth anniversary of the PLA Navy and an even more spectacular parade of weapons systems on the October 1, 2009, National Day celebration. What kinds of symbols are these for the sixtieth anniversary of a state that otherwise proclaims that it threatens nobody and will never engage in hegemonic behavior? Surely a crack has now begun to spread in Beijing's reassuring rhetorical armor devised to counter perceptions of a "China threat." One can begin to see evidence of the PRC's newly emerging cockiness where foreign relations are concerned.

That is, with the end of the first decade of the twenty-first century, one now detects early indicators that the PRC has grown beyond the point at which biding its time and hiding its capacities is a credible characterization of Beijing's approach to international interaction. One detects a shift toward greater assertiveness and national self-confidence, veiled all the while in mild-sounding slogans and elaborate explanations by authoritative voices in Beijing that, of course, nothing has changed.

The PRC's domestic growth feeds its demand for resources and access both to markets and means of delivering goods, as well as confidence that the international regimes that enable the PRC to prosper will remain stable and resilient, rather than blunt further development.

All this contributes to ever-more complexity in the PRC's foreign relations. It has drawn PRC eyes farther afield, contributing to more compelling rationales for the PRC to acquire and develop capacities to project power and cultivate relations with states far from PRC shores in a growing array of functional domains in which Beijing had no prior involvement during simpler times. Beijing has also come to embrace the vital stake it has in confirming that international regimes and multilateral fora are swayed to ensure its own interests are better protected and its own values are more clearly projected. It has gradually emerged as an energetic participant, no longer a sullen or dismissive observer.

As the PRC's dynamic domestic development accelerates, it creates centrifugal forces propelling the PRC out of itself. The PRC's current trajectory appears to demand more interactions with more intensity than in the past. Indeed, the prosperity and security of the PRC now depend more than ever on its relations with the world well beyond its borders.

Yet, despite these considerable adjustments, the PRC clings to self-soothing rhetoric intended to appease others that its growth harms nobody, that it is a developing state whose growth should not be seen as a threat, and that it will never act in a hegemonic fashion.

In the United States, this condition "gets a rise out of us" because Americans understand some things about their own rise from marginality to centrality. It is easy to read through the PRC's bland statements of interest in harmony and mutual benefit and to see instrumentality. The notion of *taoguang yanghui* has been interpreted in some quarters as a deceptive means to an insidious end: supremacy. It is worth noting that Deng Xiaoping, as part of his exhortation to his successors, also expressed the view that while China was hiding its capacities, it should also "do something." After sixty years, the PRC is now embarked on doing a great deal in foreign relations. Its profile is no longer so low.

Emphasizing the interpretation of *taoguang*—literally to hide one's brightness—as "hiding capacities," some observers believe Beijing is effecting the strategic equivalent of the *zui quan*, or the "drunken master"-style of *gongfu*. Long before Jackie Chan's film performance as the drunken master, practitioners of *wushu* developed a style in which one feigns drunkenness to mislead one's adversary by seeing only the ill-coordinated flailing of an inebriated fool. Yet, when the adversary gets too close or too cocky, the apparently drunken master delivers devastating blows with sober force. Some foreign observers worry that the leadership of the PRC is emulating the drunken master in a calculated scheme to amass power for the purpose of achieving ultimate supremacy in the Asia-Pacific arena, if not beyond.

Americans are not the only foreign observers to see in China's apparently benign development of capabilities the foundation for use of those capabilities by future generations of Chinese leaders who will not feel bound by the anodyne assurances of the present leadership.

Much more likely is that the current leadership is as uncertain of the PRC's future as are the rest of us. They argue and struggle among themselves to determine what is in the PRC's best long-term interest. At sixty, the PRC is not much of a threat because, for the time being at least, its leaders are determined to continue developing the economy and the means of projecting power, but are equally determined to avoid provocations that will derail that fundamental enterprise. However, the PRC is also rapidly evolving into an international actor that will soon have capabilities that might be used by the leaders of the PRC at seventy-five, or at ninety, in ways that others find destabilizing. So one cannot know whether the "rise of China" is a destabilizing development akin to the emergence of Japan in the late nineteenth century and Germany in the early twentieth century, or whether the newly acquired capabilities of the PRC will one day be used, as Franklin Delano Roosevelt had imagined, as one of several pillars in a multi-polar system that sustains stability and contributes to an expanded sense of prosperity and security.

SOCIAL
TRANSFORMATIONS

⑤

7.

"SIXTY IS THE NEW FORTY" (OR IS IT?):
REFLECTIONS ON THE HEALTH OF THE CHINESE BODY POLITIC

ELIZABETH J. PERRY

For the title of this brief reflection on the condition of the Chinese body politic at age sixty, I have chosen the watchword of the American baby-boomer generation: "Sixty Is the New Forty." Culturally inappropriate though its application to China may be, the slogan captures some of the irony and ambiguity surrounding the health of the Chinese Communist political system. Just as there are debates in America about whether the apparent youthfulness of its sixty-something baby boomers is a reflection of genuinely good health acquired through a sound regimen of nutrition and exercise, or whether it is merely a cosmetic veneer artificially sustained by the generous injection of Botox, so too there is some question about whether the apparent resilience of the Chinese polity reflects genuinely effective governance or whether it is merely a temporary illusion artificially sustained by the generous infusion of foreign direct investment.[1] I will leave it to the medical professionals to deliver a prognosis on America's baby boomers, but I will try in this short chapter to indicate why the condition of the Chinese body politic may be less brittle than is sometimes suggested.

To put this matter in context, let us recall that observers have been fretting over the fragility of the Chinese Communist political system since the deaths of Chairman Mao Zedong and Premier Zhou Enlai more than thirty years ago. As Richard Baum wrote of that uncertain period, "The demise of China's two top leaders left the country rudderless and adrift ... ordinary Chinese openly questioned the benefits conferred on them by a rigid, aloof, and seemingly insensitive Communist Party."[2] Deng Xiaoping's post-Mao economic reforms breathed new life into the moribund polity, but the Tiananmen uprising of 1989 raised even more serious doubts about the durability of the regime.

The Puzzle: Authoritarian Resilience

Twenty years ago—approaching the fortieth anniversary of the PRC in 1989—it certainly did look as though the days of the Communist system were numbered.

Massive urban protests that spring, followed closely by the collapse of Communist regimes from Budapest to Bucharest, led many to expect a similar outcome in Beijing. The involvement of workers as well as students in China's 1989 protests prompted some to predict a Solidarity-like scenario of the sort that brought down the Polish regime that same year. And even though the PRC managed to outlast both East European and Soviet variants of communism, the predictions of its imminent demise did not disappear. In 1995, the sociologist Jack Goldstone in an often-quoted article in *Foreign Policy* entitled "The Coming Chinese Collapse," began with the question "Will China after the death of Deng Xiaoping avoid the fate of the Soviet Union?" and concluded that "China shows every sign of a country approaching crisis.... Deng's death will probably touch off popular protests, power struggles within the party, and the formation of provincial coalitions . . . proclaiming greater autonomy. . . . It is doubtful that the collapse of communism in China can be averted . . . we can expect a terminal crisis within the next 10 to 15 years."[3]

The fact that Deng's death did not usher in a terminal crisis did not silence the alarm bells. In the last several years we have seen a steady parade of books with titles such as *The Coming Collapse of China; China's Trapped Transition; China: Fragile Superpower*; or, more optimistically, *China's Democratic Future: How It Will Happen and Where It Will Lead.*[4] According to these various accounts, the vulnerability of the post-Tiananmen Chinese Communist system stems from a lethal combination of weak regime legitimacy (due to the discrediting of Marxist-Maoist ideology), on the one hand, and strong popular discontent (expressed in widespread protest), on the other. Roderick MacFarquhar sums up this perspective: "it is the interaction of diminished state authority and increased social volatility that makes for a fragile Chinese political system."[5] MacFarquhar continues to predict the collapse of China's Communist system within, as he puts it, "years rather than decades."[6]

With each passing decade, however, the case for the Chinese Communist system as exhausted and about to expire becomes a little more difficult to make. The regime—having weathered Mao's and Zhou's deaths in 1976, the Tiananmen uprising in 1989, Deng's death in 1997, and the Tibetan riots in 2008, appears over time to have become increasingly adept at managing the twin challenges of leadership succession and popular unrest. The Communist regime has also proven capable of surviving other serious unanticipated crises, from the SARS epidemic of 2003 to the Sichuan earthquake of 2008 and the Xinjiang violence of 2009. These challenges would surely have sounded the death knell of many a less hardy regime. As Andrew Nathan acknowledges in a recent discussion of China's unanticipated "authoritarian resilience": "After the Tiananmen

crisis . . . many China specialists and democracy theorists—myself among them—
expected the regime to fall to democratization's 'third wave.' Instead, the regime
has reconsolidated itself."[7]

Regardless of how far into the future the Chinese Communist system may
persist, an eventuality about which I hazard no prediction, it is surely worth
pondering the reasons behind its staying power *up to this point*. How has the
state managed to hold it together over these past several decades through a series
of potentially destabilizing top leadership changes (Mao Zedong to Hua Guofeng
to Deng Xiaoping to Jiang Zemin to Hu Jintao and Wen Jiabao), while at the same
time presiding over the fastest sustained economic transition in world history—a
transformation that has brought with it not only greater wealth and international
influence but also growing income and regional inequalities, a flood of migration,
and rampant popular protest?

Toward an Answer: Pragmatic Populism

The explanation for the regime's durability is of course complicated, but much of
the answer lies, I believe, in the Chinese state's uncanny ability—through an
unusual variety of *pragmatic populism*—to convert those very challenges that are
often seen as signs of its impending doom into powerful sources of regeneration
and renewal. Despite the Communist state's continued lip service to Marxism-
Leninism-Mao Zedong Thought (plus Deng Xiaoping theory), the secret to its
surprising success does not—and arguably never did—rest on ideological
legitimacy. On the contrary, from their revolutionary days to the present, the
Chinese Communists consistently demonstrated a ready willingness to dispense
with ideological orthodoxy in order to tackle intractable social problems.

Perhaps most noteworthy of these social challenges is popular protest.
Among the many surprises of the post-Mao era has been the remarkable upsurge
in protests that has accompanied the economic reforms. The Tiananmen uprising
of 1989 was the largest and most dramatic of these incidents, but it marked neither the beginning nor the end of widespread unrest during the reform period. In
the first decade of reform, China experienced a steady stream of collective protests, culminating in the massive demonstrations in Tiananmen Square (and
many other Chinese cities) in the spring of 1989.[8] Despite the brutal suppression
of the Tiananmen uprising, the frequency of protests has escalated in the years
since June 4. According to official Chinese statistics, public disturbances in China
increased tenfold during the period from 1993 to 2005, from 8,700 to 87,000.[9]
Most observers believe that the actual figures are considerably higher than
those suggested by these official statistics—which the Chinese government ceased
making public after 2005.

Mounting protest is often interpreted by outside observers as an indication of the instability and fragility of the Communist system. In a recent *New York Times* editorial entitled "Remembering Tiananmen," this familiar argument was again advanced. As the editorial concluded, "China's leaders prize stability. But . . . China's citizens are restive. Activists say there are 100,000 protests a year . . . [T]he yearning for freedom remains."[10]

In fact, however, few of these recent protests have much to do with a "yearning for freedom." Almost all of them concern concrete livelihood issues—from layoffs and withheld wages to land disputes and environmental pollution. Rather than calling for the overthrow of an oppressive state, protesters typically castigate lower-level officials for failing to implement central state laws and policies. Furthermore, it has become abundantly clear that the Communist state (like the imperial Chinese state before it) is remarkably skillful at managing and sometimes even benefiting from this widespread unrest. In an interesting paper entitled "Regularized Rioting," Peter Lorentzen has recently proposed that the central Chinese leadership strategically tolerates a surprisingly high level of protest as a means of garnering information and combating corruption at the grassroots level.[11]

Although the actual decision-making calculus of the top leadership in Zhongnanhai is far from transparent, at least to me, it *is* clear that in an authoritarian system where the ballot box does not provide an effective channel for articulating popular grievances or punishing unpopular officials, protests may perform these critical functions instead. So long as the central authorities respond sympathetically and sensibly to protesters' demands, the state can emerge strengthened rather than weakened by widespread contention. Take the case of tax resistance. Throughout the 1990s, the agricultural provinces of inner China seethed with tax riots.[12] Peasants railed against what they called "unfair burdens," or local taxes that exceeded the limits imposed by the central government. The result, however, was not rebellion or revolution, but rather a pragmatic populist decision by the central Chinese leadership to abolish China's 2,600-year-old agricultural tax.

A shared appreciation for pragmatic populism has long shaped the strategies of protesters and central state leaders alike. As is well known, China lays claim to one of the oldest and most influential traditions of popular protest of any nation on earth. Over the centuries, such contention occasionally escalated into large-scale rebellions aimed at seizing the imperial throne, but the vast majority of the incidents were directed at lower-level officials accused of petty corruption, the imposition of illegal taxes, and other types of malfeasance. Successful emperors kept close tabs on local unrest and were quick to discipline grassroots officials whose misbehavior generated popular unrest. A similar (albeit technologically modernized) pattern can be observed today.

To be sure, the protests that roil the contemporary Chinese landscape present significant challenges to the central leadership. Although most of the protests are directed in the first instance against grassroots officials, protesters often take their petitions to higher levels—including all the way to Beijing—if a local resolution is not forthcoming. Moreover, the protests can be highly disruptive of government operations as well as economic and social life when vociferous demonstrators surround government offices, march through city streets, stage sit-ins in public places, and block traffic on busy highways and railways.[13]

Yet, however visible and vocal (and sometimes violent) these protests may be, the protesters usually go to great lengths to demonstrate their loyalty to central policies and leaders. The breathless enthusiasm with which many journalists and some scholars have greeted the protests of recent years notwithstanding, contentious politics in post-Mao China continues to be highly circumscribed in its targets and stated ambitions. In these respects, today's protests perpetuate certain core features of both Mao-era and pre-Mao-era protests. Among these features is a pragmatic penchant on the part of the protesters to advance their claims within the "legitimate" boundaries authorized by the central state in order to signal that their actions do not challenge the ruling authority of the state. To be sure, these boundaries have shifted in significant ways over time—as a result of state initiative as well as societal innovation. But whether we are talking about the pre- or post-1989 reform-era period or for that matter about the Maoist era (or even the Republican or imperial periods) that preceded them, Chinese protesters have shown a pragmatic propensity to justify their actions in terms of the official discourse. Although the language of "revolution" articulated by "comrades" in the early years of the PRC has been supplanted by a language of "rights" proclaimed by "citizens" today, it is not readily apparent that protesters in the two periods differ fundamentally in either their mentality or their relationship to the authoritarian state. In today's China, where the government trumpets "rule by law" and where bookstores and television and radio broadcasts are replete with government-supplied legal information, protesters routinely invoke laws and regulations to justify their demands.[14] Rather than interpret such behavior as emblematic of a seditious "rights consciousness," in which nascent citizens assert their autonomous interests against the state, I see these protests as reflecting a seasoned "rules consciousness" that expressly acknowledges, and thereby serves to undergird more than to undermine, the ruling authority of the state.[15]

Strategic deployment of state-sanctioned rhetoric can sometimes win significant concessions from the authorities. For example, protesters against the high-speed Maglev train in Shanghai in 2008 humorously dubbed their demonstration a "harmonious stroll" (parroting President Hu Jintao's call for a harmonious society) in order to make clear that their action was not a challenge to state legitimacy. The result was a delay in the extension of the Maglev. Other recent outbursts of popular contention, mobilized through increasingly sophisticated communications technology (email, text messaging, computer blogs), have also wrung policy concessions from the Chinese authorities. The media controversy surrounding the tragic beating to death by police of the college-educated migrant, Sun Zhigang, led directly to the government's cancellation of discriminatory regulations concerning vagrants.[16] A similar pattern can be seen in a number of other highly publicized incidents (the Chongqing nail house, the Shanxi brick factory scandal, the Xiamen PX protests, and so on). All of these cases demonstrate that the authorities' careful monitoring of electronic communications media provides crucial intelligence on citizens' activities and attitudes—information that not only allows the state to anticipate and defuse protest, but also enables the state to improve its governance and enhance its legitimacy by crafting policies (new environmental protection laws, labor laws, property rights laws, and so forth) that speak directly to popular concerns. By responding swiftly and shrewdly to online chat-room complaints, the Communist state seems to have found in the Internet yet another powerful medium for prolonging its lifespan.[17]

Although the *technologies* of rule are new, the basic *techniques* are not. They have important precedents and parallels in earlier periods of Chinese history. I am increasingly convinced that the most fruitful framework for understanding the condition of the contemporary Chinese body politic is not comparative theories of regime transition or democratization, but rather China's own authoritarian heritage. This is not to suggest, à la Jackie Chan, that Chinese "need authoritarian control." It is rather to say that Chinese authoritarianism in its imperial as well as its various Communist incarnations, in contrast to many other non-democratic political systems, is notable for a set of unusually flexible governing principles and practices pragmatically invented and reinvented to evaluate, organize, influence, and accommodate popular concerns.

Pragmatic populism is a central element in classical Chinese political thought. Confucian (especially Mencian) ideas of the Mandate of Heaven highlighted the necessity of satisfying the basic livelihood of the populace as a condition of rule. Not royal blood, but an emperor's exercise of benevolence and justice—demonstrated above all in his ability to provide a decent livelihood for the ordinary people—was what earned him the right to rule.[18] Moreover, the imperial state's interest in assessing and addressing popular grievances went well beyond normative theories of benevolent governance. During China's earlier rise to wealth and power, numerous *concrete* institutions were established to mediate between the interests of state and society, institutions that served pragmatic as well as populist purposes and that changed over time to accommodate new realities. These late imperial institutions included the ever-normal granaries to provide famine relief, the imperial censorate to check bureaucratic corruption, the Ming and Qing legal codes and associated system of criminal confessions (which has left students of imperial-era rebellions such rich archival documentation), the civil service examinations for the recruitment of talented officials, the semi-official academies for providing examination preparation, the village lectures to communicate imperial edicts, the *baojia* and *lijia* systems of surveillance and taxation, the *tusi* system of native chieftaincy for controlling ethnic minorities, the rural militias for suppressing rebellion, and much, much more. These were dynamic forms of elite-mass linkages that served a variety of distinct purposes more or less effectively in different periods to be sure, but that in combination afforded the imperial state a substantial degree of information about and influence over society.

As the eminent historian of late imperial China, Hsiao Kung-ch'uan, wrote of the Chinese Communists back in 1960, "the methods of control they have adopted show a decided improvement over those used by the Ch'ing rulers, but the basic aim and underlying principle of control remain the same: to perpetuate the existing regime through ideological, economic, and administrative control. There is even some similarity between the imperial and Communist autocracies in the way they justify their political power: the former professed 'to benefit the people,' and the latter claims to do everything in the name of 'the people.'"[19]

Pragmatic populism both encourages and restrains social protest.[20] Whether or not Chinese protesters, in their heart of hearts, *believe* in the legitimacy of the state, they generally *behave* as if they do. (Even in the unusual case of the Falun Gong, where confrontation between the spiritual sect and state authorities escalated into an exceptionally bitter and protracted struggle, the protest began with submissive petitions seeking government recognition and registration.) Although overt adherence to official discourse obviously does not necessarily bespeak a deeply rooted belief in state legitimacy, popular compliance with state-sanctioned rules and rhetoric may nevertheless work to promote the stability of authoritarian regimes.[21] Moreover, in China where cultural norms have long valued "orthopraxy" (proper behavior) over "orthodoxy" (proper belief), public expressions of deference to political authority seem to play an especially powerful role in sustaining the system.[22]

Confucian conceptions of political legitimacy were infused with an appreciation of the advantages of pragmatic populism, from a need to provide for mass livelihood and welfare to a recognition that results were more important than royal blood in bestowing the right to rule, summed up in the well-known maxim, "He who wins becomes king or marquis; he who loses becomes an outlaw" (成者王侯; 败者贼). A pragmatic willingness to bestow the mantle of legitimacy upon successful challengers was an important ingredient in the longevity of the imperial system. The dynastic cycles for which Chinese history is famous demonstrated the capacity of the imperial authoritarian system to reconstitute and rejuvenate itself time and again over a period of two millennia.

Despite its remarkable longevity by comparison with other autocratic states, the imperial Chinese system of governance did of course eventually deteriorate and die. However, if as social scientists we focus only on the collapse, we miss the far bigger story—how the longest lived political system in world history managed to survive and change for centuries, presiding over a series of tremendous challenges from commercial transformation to territorial expansion. It would obviously be foolhardy to predict anywhere near as long a lifespan for the Communist authoritarian system as that enjoyed by imperial China—but it is perhaps equally misguided to speculate about the PRC's collapse at the expense of probing its actual mechanisms of rule and renewal.

Among these key mechanisms is a policy style (*zuofeng*) that displays a pronounced openness to experimentation and innovation.[23] The origins of this flexible approach to policy lie in the creative adaptation of central elements of China's political heritage, including its more recent revolutionary experience as well as its distant imperial past. Unlike Russia and Eastern Europe, the imposition of a national Communist regime in China required nearly three decades of revolutionary mobilization and struggle. In the course of that protracted process, which took the Communists out of the major cities into the rural hinterland and on a Long March from the southern to the northern regions of the country, invaluable lessons in adapting to a wide range of different environmental conditions and challenges were learned. During the resistance against Japan, the wartime base areas provided a particularly fertile source of policy variation and experimentation.[24] That these rich revolutionary experiences led directly to the dramatic successes—as well as the dismal failures—of Chairman Mao's signature programs during the initial years of the PRC is well recognized.[25] Less widely acknowledged, however, is the continued importance of this revolutionary heritage to the policies and practices of Mao's successors.[26] In the immediate post-Mao period we saw evidence of this decentralized experimentalism in the development of the household responsibility system that led to the rapid decollectivization of agriculture.[27] We see continuing evidence today in widespread grassroots experiments in medical insurance as China searches for a new system of public health in the wake of the demise of the communes.[28] China's long revolution generated a policy style capable of producing an impressive array of alternative solutions to unexpected challenges, a pragmatic populist framework that has proved highly effective when redirected to the economic and technological objectives of Mao's successors.

Conclusion: Is Sixty the New Forty?

Chinese history makes clear the advantages of pragmatic populism for regime survival and renewal. Confucian (and Mencian) norms of benevolent governance and mass livelihood helped give rise to a political culture that prizes practical results (and public rituals) over doctrinal purity (or devotional piety). A flexible and applied approach was also the bedrock of Mao Zedong's successful wartime revolutionary strategy. As Mao wrote in his famous essay *On Practice*, at the outset of the war with Japan: "The truth of any knowledge or theory is determined not by subjective feelings, but by objective results in social practice. Only social practice can be the criterion of truth. . . . Discover the truth through practice, and again through practice verify and develop the truth."[29]

If the "discovery of truth" comes only after extensive social practice, the age of sixty would seem to be an auspicious one for its attainment. Indeed, Confucius proclaimed that at age sixty he was able to discern the truth, a statement that should be comforting to sixty-something baby boomers and sixty-year-old polities alike—were it not for the disquieting fact that Confucius passed away just a decade later.[30] Be that as it may, the truth that the PRC leadership appears to have discerned, after sixty years of perpetual experimentation, is that the health of the Chinese body politic depends above all on adapting a kind of traditional—and revolutionary—populism to the pragmatic resolution of enduring and unexpected social challenges. It was that mindset that permitted the "reform and opening" of the post-Mao era and its escalation (including the massive infusion of foreign direct investment) following Deng Xiaoping's vaunted "southern tour" of 1992. This approach has been critical to China's rise to date and, barring unforeseen (yet always possible) calamities, appears likely to sustain the PRC's continuing rise in the years—perhaps even decades—to come.

In this post-Cold War era in which we live, pragmatic populism is surely a refreshing alternative to the dangers of strident ideology. The elderly Deng Xiaoping encapsulated this spirit in the iconic adage: "Black cat or white cat makes no difference. As long as it catches mice, it is a good cat." Happily, Chinese leaders are not alone in appreciating the advantages that pragmatic populism may offer for political rejuvenation. As the youthful American President Barack Obama put it in his inaugural address, ". . . the stale political arguments that have consumed us for so long no longer apply. The question we ask today is not whether our government is too big or too small, but whether it works, whether it helps families find jobs at a decent wage, care they can afford, a retirement that is dignified."[31] Or as that quintessential spokeswoman for the American baby-boomer generation, Secretary of State Hillary Clinton, replied when asked recently about the principles underlying U.S. foreign policy, "Let's put ideology aside; that is so yesterday."[32] Who knew: sixty may actually be *more* robust and resilient than forty!

ENDNOTES

1. For discussions of the effect of foreign direct investment on China's political economy, see Yasheng Huang, *Selling China: Foreign Direct Investment during the Reform Era* (New York: Cambridge University Press, 2003); and Mary E. Gallagher, *Contagious Capitalism: Globalization and the Politics of Labor in China* (Princeton, NJ: Princeton University Press, 2005).

2. Richard Baum, *Burying Mao: Chinese Politics in the Age of Deng Xiaoping* (Princeton, NJ: Princeton University Press, 1994), p. 3.

3. Jack A. Goldstone, "The Coming Chinese Collapse," *Foreign Policy*, no. 99 (Summer 1995): 35–52.

4. Gordon G. Chang, *The Coming Collapse of China* (New York: Random House, 2001); Minxin Pei, *China's Trapped Transition: The Limits of Developmental Autocracy* (Cambridge, MA: Harvard University Press, 2006); Susan L. Shirk, *China: Fragile Superpower* (Oxford: Oxford University Press, 2007); and Bruce Gilley, *China's Democratic Future: How It Will Happen and Where It Will Lead* (New York: Columbia University Press, 2004).

5. Roderick MacFarquhar, "Is Communist Party Rule Sustainable in China?" in *Reframing China Policy: The Carnegie Debates*, October 5, 2006, at http://www .carnegieendowment.org/events/?fa = eventDetail&id = 916 (accessed February 5, 2010).

6. Ibid.; see also Roderick MacFarquhar, "The Anatomy of Collapse," *New York Review of Books*, 38, no. 15 (September 26, 1991): 5–9.

7. Andrew J. Nathan, "Authoritarian Resilience," *Journal of Democracy*, 14, no. 1 (2003): 6.

8. For discussions of these early reform-period protests in the countryside, see Elizabeth J. Perry, "Rural Violence in Socialist China," *The China Quarterly*, no. 103 (September 1985): 414–40.

9. http://english.peopledaily.com.cn/200603/01/eng20060301_247056.html (accessed February 23, 2010).

10. "Remembering Tiananmen," *New York Times*, June 6, 2009, p. A20.

11. Peter L. Lorentzen, "Regularized Rioting: Strategic Toleration of Popular Protest in China," unpublished paper, June 2, 2008.

12. Thomas P. Bernstein and Xiaobo Lü, *Taxation without Representation in Contemporary Rural China* (New York: Cambridge University Press, 2003).

13. Yongshun Cai, "Disruptive Collective Action in the Reform Era," in Kevin J. O'Brien, ed., *Popular Protest in China* (Cambridge, MA: Harvard University Press, 2008), ch. 8.

14. See especially Ching Kwan Lee, *Against the Law: Labor Protests in China's Rustbelt and Sunbelt* (Berkeley: University of California Press, 2007).

15. Elizabeth J. Perry, "Popular Protest: Playing by the Rules," in Joseph Fewsmith, ed., *China Today, China Tomorrow: Domestic Politics, Economy and Society* (Lanham, MD: Rowman & Littlefield, 2010). For an argument about "rising rights consciousness" in contemporary China, see, for example, Merle Goldman, *Political Rights in Post-Mao China* (Ann Arbor, MI: Association for Asian Studies, 2007).

16. Benjamin L. Liebman, "Watchdogs or Demagogues? The Media in the Chinese Legal System," *Columbia Law Review*, 105, no. 1(January 2005): 1–157.

17. For another view, suggesting that online citizen activism in China is strengthening the hand of civil society at the expense of the state, see Guobin Yang, *The Power of the Internet in China: Citizen Activism Online* (New York: Columbia University Press, 2009).

18. See Elizabeth J. Perry, "Chinese Conceptions of 'Rights': From Mencius to Mao— and Now," *Perspectives on Politics*, 6, no. 1 (2006): 37–50.

19. Hsiao Kung-ch'uan, *Rural China: Imperial Control in the Nineteenth Century* (Seattle: University of Washington Press, 1960), p. 517.

20. An elaboration of this argument can be found in Elizabeth J. Perry, *Challenging the Mandate of Heaven: Social Protest and State Power in China* (Armonk, NY: M.E. Sharpe, 2002).

21. For a discussion of the contribution of "as if" politics to regime stability in another authoritarian setting, see Lisa Wedeen, *Ambiguities of Domination: Politics, Rhetoric, and Symbols in Contemporary Syria* (Chicago: University of Chicago Press, 1999).

22. James L. Watson, "Structure of Chinese Funerary Rites: Elementary Forms, Ritual Sequence, and the Primacy of Performance," in James L. Watson and Evelyn S. Rawski, eds., *Death Ritual in Late Imperial and Modern China* (Berkeley: University of California Press, 1988), pp. 3–19.

23. Sebastian Heilmann and Elizabeth J. Perry, "Embracing Uncertainty: 'Guerrilla Policy Style' and Adaptive Governance in China," in Sebastian Heilmann and Elizabeth J. Perry, eds., *Mao's Invisible Hand: The Political Foundations of Adaptive Governance in China* (Cambridge, MA: Harvard Contemporary China Series, Harvard University Asia Center, 2011).

24. Chen Yung-fa, *Making Revolution: The Communist Movement in Eastern and Central China, 1937–1945* (Berkeley: University of California Press, 1986).

25. Ping-ti Ho and Tsou Tang, eds., *China in Crisis* (Chicago: University of Chicago Press, 1968); Michel Oksenberg, ed., *China's Developmental Experience* (New York: Praeger, 1973).

26. Elizabeth J. Perry, "Studying Chinese Politics: Farewell to Revolution?" *The China Journal*, no. 59 (January 2007): 1–22.

27. Kathleen Hartford, "Socialist Agriculture Is Dead; Long Live Socialist Agriculture! Organizational Transformations in Rural China," in Elizabeth J. Perry and Christine Wong, eds., *The Political Economy of Reform in Post-Mao China* (Cambridge, MA: Council on East Asian Studies, Harvard University, 1985), pp. 31–61.

28. Wang Shaoguang, "Learning through Practice and Experimentation: The Case of China's Rural Healthcare Financing," paper presented at the conference on China's Adaptive Authoritarianism: China's Party-State Resilience in Historical Perspective," Harvard University, July 2008; Philip H. Brown, Alan de Brauw, and Yang Du, "Understanding Variation in the Design of China's New Co-operative Medical System," *The China Quarterly*, no. 198 (June 2009): 304–29.

29. Mao Tse-tung, *Selected Readings from the Works of Mao Tse-tung* (Beijing: Foreign Languages Press, 1967), pp. 68–69, 81.

30. H.G. Creel, *Confucius and the Chinese Way* (New York: Harper, 1960).

31. Barack Obama, "Inaugural Address," *New York Times*, January 20, 2009.

32. "Clinton Scores Points by Admitting Past U.S. Errors," *New York Times*, April 17, 2009, p. A4.

8.
POPULAR PROTEST AND PARTY RULE:
CHINA'S EVOLVING POLITY

ANDREW G. WALDER

It is common to remark on how much China has changed since the end of the Mao era thirty years ago. But we often overlook China's political transformation in the past twenty years, which in many ways is equally fundamental. In October 1989 China was in terrible shape. Martial law was still in force in Beijing, the reform coalition had collapsed, the country was internationally isolated and under fire for its gross abuse of human rights, and the economy was in the midst of a sharp downturn that would last for several years.

Although it is obvious that China's situation today is vastly different from mid-1989, the problems that year were simply the culmination of social and political circumstances that existed throughout the 1980s that contrast sharply with the present. In these pages I want to remind readers how fundamentally different 1980s China was from China today.

We can distill the key differences into four points.

- It is now clear that China's economic reforms have worked. It was far from clear in the 1980s that they had any possibility of succeeding, at least outside of agriculture.
- China's political trajectory now looks enviable when compared to many, if not most, post-Communist successor states around the world. The comparison with reforming socialist regimes during the 1980s was increasingly unfavorable to China as the decade progressed.
- China's youth and intellectuals today display a strong sense of national pride and, on occasion, a defensive patriotism. During the 1980s deep questioning of the Communist Party and the legitimacy of the system was far more common.
- China's party leadership today is fundamentally unified in its views about the direction the country should take. Throughout the 1980s, however, the leadership was deeply divided over both economic and political reform.

Let us take up each of these points in turn. First, China's economic reforms had not really proceeded very far by the late 1980s, and their successes were primarily in agriculture. Rural incomes went up rapidly, as did the supply of food to the cities, after the complete abandonment of collective agriculture in the early 1980s. At this point, China's reforms in agriculture were the most radical in the socialist world. Yet it was commonly observed at the time that this was the easy part, just a first step. The most difficult task of reform had yet to be addressed in any significant way—how to turn around a bloated and grossly inefficient state sector. It was evident that state-sector firms needed to be downsized, reorganized, and subjected to real competitive pressures, but this would involve a loss of state control over key parts of the modern economy. It would also risk unrest and political opposition due to layoffs and violations of the key tenets of socialism.

It was unclear during the 1980s whether the party leadership could even gather the political will to attempt such an unprecedented transformation, and if it seriously attempted it, it was unclear whether the party could survive the likely political consequences. There was also, finally, the equally contentious issue of price reform. The freeing of consumers' and producers' prices in an economy of shortage carried the real risk of rapid inflation, and the destabilizing impact of inflation was already evident in urban China in 1988 and early 1989. We need to remember that at this point in history no socialist regime had ever attempted a move to a market-oriented economy, and it was far from clear that this was even plausible, or that a ruling party could survive the transition.

Second, China's political trajectory by the late 1980s appeared to be lagging behind progressive change in the Soviet bloc. The party's backlash against liberalization in the wake of the student democracy movement of late 1986, and the subsequent purge of the liberal-minded Hu Yaobang, made China's leadership appear backward and reactionary. By 1988, the trend toward press freedom, democratization, and even multiparty rule was already well in evidence in Poland, Hungary, and especially the Soviet Union, and many in urban China, and even in the party and government, looked at these developments with envy. We should also recall that this was precisely the period when the neighboring East Asian regimes were emerging from long periods of dictatorship: the Philippines in 1986, South Korea in 1987, and Taiwan in 1988. To many in China, the country's political arrangements appeared increasingly anachronistic, dysfunctional, and reactionary—and incompatible with the rapid, market-oriented economic growth to which the party leadership apparently aspired.

Third, China's youths and intellectuals were deeply alienated during the 1980s. The decade began with a well-publicized "crisis of confidence" in both the party and socialism. Within the universities a liberal atmosphere of questioning and a curiosity about the democratic philosophies and institutions of Western civilization flourished. A generation of young adults in their twenties and thirties had emerged from interrupted educations, often spent as "sent-down youth" in the countryside, in a questioning and rebellious mood. Many liberal intellectuals participated in the general ferment as well. This was a society still recovering from the horrors of the Cultural Revolution, still trying to explain the root causes of this long national catastrophe. Many at the time dissented from the obviously self-serving party line—that these disasters were caused by a handful of evil leaders like the "Gang of Four." Many were convinced that the causes of the disaster were woven deeply into China's unitary political institutions and reigning ideology.

Finally, China's leadership was deeply divided about economic reform and political liberalization. Many leaders saw the economic reforms as a threat to the regime and a violation of fundamental socialist values. They could not understand why China did not simply return to an updated version of the Soviet-inspired planning practices that had worked relatively well during the 1950s. And attempts by reformers in the leadership to promote political liberalization and openness led to constant factional warfare within the top ranks of the party. The result of this constant jockeying was a pattern of abrupt policy change, as a move to liberalize and reform was followed by a period of backlash and retrenchment. Deng Xiaoping refereed the jockeying factions, moving first one way, then the other, hoping to steer the fractious leadership toward a middle course of economic reform and political continuity. These political differences were obvious to politically aware youths, intellectuals, and party members.

All four of these longstanding features of 1980s China came together in the spring of 1989 into a political crisis that can be likened to a "perfect storm." The alienated youth culture of the 1980s was on full display during the student protests of April and May. The students reacted to the death of the liberal-minded Hu Yaobang as an opportunity to show their dissatisfaction with the post-1986 reaction against student democracy protests, which culminated in Hu being fired from the top post. The students' rhetoric and symbolism showed a keen familiarity with Western models of democracy and an almost naïve faith in the efficacy of those models and their potency as an answer to China's problems. The students betrayed an awareness that China was lagging behind world democratic trends, that this was due to the reactionary views of a certain wing of the party leadership, and that they hoped to influence the political balance in the leadership in the direction of greater liberalization and democratization.

Intellectuals, reporters, editors, and even government functionaries eventually responded in a sympathetic way as the drama unfolded in Tiananmen Square. Many of them were frustrated with the retarded pace of political liberalization. They joined the protests calling for peaceful dialogue with the student leaders, and many made their own demands for press freedoms and other democratic rights. They were aware that press freedoms were quite extensive and competitive elections were already on the agenda in Poland, Hungary, and even the Soviet Union, and they thought it natural that China should be in step with these worldwide trends.

Ordinary citizens flooded into the streets to support the student protesters, a response that was especially consequential when they blocked the martial law troops from entering the city. This response reflected a widespread uneasiness with the impact of the economic reforms on urban livelihoods. The official inflation rate exceeded 25 percent in 1988 and early 1989, and there were episodes of panic-buying as rumors spread of the imminent freeing of all prices. There was also widespread anxiety created by the first tentative steps to lay off workers in overstaffed urban firms, and anger over the perceived rise in corruption and privilege-seeking by party and government officials. These concerns resonated deeply with the students' slogans calling for openness, dialogue, and an end to official corruption.

Finally, the pressures created by these events splintered the already-fractious political leadership and prevented it from formulating a coherent and consistent response. The leadership was paralyzed, and it seemed evident that there was a deadlock between two separate camps—one calling for dialogue, the other for repression. As a result, the official mass media began reporting extensively and even sympathetically on the unfolding protest movement, with many retired and lower-ranking officials speaking out in favor of moderation. The evident deadlock in the party leadership coupled with the official media coverage encouraged the protesters and the general population to think that there was a chance that their actions could succeed. The ultimate resolution of this crisis was the draconian military operation of June 3–4. As the streets of Beijing were engulfed in flames and gunfire in the dawn of June 4, Poland was holding its first multiparty national elections, which soon led to the end of Communist rule.

If we fast-forward twenty years to the present decade, we observe a very different country. The alienated youth culture is gone, and the political hangover of the Cultural Revolution is two generations in the past. Party membership is now in vogue among the young, especially among the highly educated and upwardly mobile. In a highly competitive environment, party membership is just another credential that opens doors to greater opportunity. If China's alienated 1980s generation was similar in many ways to America's "60s generation," China's current generation in many ways parallels our own 1980s "Reagan generation." Chinese youth today are pragmatic, career-oriented, and patriotic in ways that were rare in the 1980s. Over the past decade they have been politically active, but primarily in protests over Japanese textbooks, the NATO bombing of China's Belgrade embassy, rival claims over the tiny Diaoyu islands in the East China Sea, or criticism by foreign governments and media over China's handling of the Tibetan protests on the eve of the Beijing Olympics. This is a generation that feels China's rise and its accompanying national pride.

It is no longer as clear to China's intellectuals and other educated urbanites that the nation's political trajectory compares unfavorably to its former socialist brethren. In the late 1980s the socialist world appeared on the verge of a dramatic and promising democratic breakthrough, with China's hidebound leaders hesitating to take the plunge. Today a more sober realism is prompted by the history of these transitions over the past two decades. There are more than thirty regimes in the world today that were ruled by communist parties in the 1980s. Fewer than half of them are now reasonably stable multiparty democracies—and all of these success stories are small nations on the eastern flank of the European Union. The rest are a mixture of harsh dictatorships or deeply corrupted and illiberal regimes that attempted a transition to democracy that has largely fallen short. In some cases, the attempt to democratize led to the collapse of the nation-state: the Soviet Union and Yugoslavia are prime examples. In other cases, the transition touched off years of nationalist violence or civil war. And in virtually all the cases, the attempt to shift to a market economy ushered in a deep depression that lasted almost a decade. Many of these economies, including Russia's, only recently emerged from their years of hardship. By contrast, the two regimes in this group that have had by far the largest increases in per capita GDP, ironically, are both still ruled by their communist parties—China and Vietnam. The equation of political stability with economic and social progress is a far more appealing argument today than it was in the 1980s. The zeal for multiparty democracy as a panacea for China's problems is far in the past, replaced by a more sober awareness of the potential costs of a failed leap to a different type of political system.

China's record of rapid, inflation-free economic development since the early 1990s hardly needs comment. More important, however, is the fact that the aspect of the reform that was once viewed as the greatest single obstacle to China's gradual reform strategy is now largely a thing of the past. Since the mid-1990s China has systematically downsized and restructured its bloated state sector. Employing more than 110 million people at its height in 1997, the state sector now employs fewer than 60 million. In the course of this restructuring more than 40 million permanent employees were laid off or retired early. This did indeed touch off a wave of protest—about which I will have more to say below—but the downsizing has now been achieved. Not only has the regime been able to summon the political will to do what so many observers in the 1980s thought was highly unlikely, but it has weathered the consequences with relatively little political fallout.

Finally, the deep divisions in the national leadership so prominent in the 1980s are virtually nonexistent today. China's leaders are remarkably unified around a model of national development that combines single-party rule and limited political liberalization with a highly statist version of marketization, gradual privatization, and deep engagement with the international economy. The Tiananmen protests and the subsequent collapse of state socialist regimes worldwide reinforced this sense of unity. It is hard to find serious policy disagreements at the top, and the sharp policy reversals and abrupt start-and-stop pattern of the 1980s has not been observed for well over a decade. This is a more confident national leadership that is nonetheless still very cautious about ensuring political order.

To acknowledge these fundamental changes is not to assert that all is well in China and that the regime will last indefinitely in its present form. There are in fact extensive social forces at work in China today that portend future political change. But these are different forces than those at work in the 1980s and they have different implications. These can be seen in the large wave of popular protests that have been so widely reported, and so widely misinterpreted, in recent years.

China is in fact a much more contentious society in the current decade than it was in the 1980s, and the protests today are much more deeply rooted in the urban and rural populations. The protest movements of the 1980s were located in the major cities, involving students, educated youths, and to some extent intellectuals. Only in 1989 did they draw large segments of the urban population. And in virtually all cases their demands were aimed squarely at the national leadership and national policy—for political liberalization, a free press, and fairness in local elections.

The protest wave that has affected China over the past ten to fifteen years has been very different. It has been much less focused in the largest cities and students, educated youths, and intellectuals have been far less active. When these latter groups have been active, it has been largely to express nationalistic sentiments and anger at foreign powers. The wave of blue-collar protests that resulted from the downsizing of the state sector was not focused in China's major cities. Instead, it was scattered throughout the country, concentrated largely in the declining rust-belt—old Soviet plants from the 1950s, "third front" enterprises in the interior, or heavy industry in China's Northeast. Rural protest has been equally widespread, scattered across suburban villages as well as remote areas. These protests have been largely inspired by intensely local economic issues: the nonpayment of promised compensation or pensions to workers laid off during the restructuring or sale of state-owned firms; excessive fees or taxes levied on farmers by village governments; and unjust expropriations of land or homes from farmers or urban residents for commercial or industrial development projects.

These are all protests against local officials, and the protests invoke national law to charge local authorities with corruption or malfeasance. The protest leaders see the higher levels of government as the solution to their problems, and their protests are largely aimed at ensuring the even-handed enforcement of national laws that they claim are grossly violated locally. In these struggles, appeals to the higher authorities for help are common.

The upsurge of local protests—reportedly about 87,000 in 2005 according to official figures—is the result of profound changes in Chinese society and economy since the 1980s. Under collective agriculture village officials controlled the harvest, managed the land, and allocated incomes. With the shift to household farming, families controlled and farmed their own land, and rural officials had to extract fees and taxes from them in order to fund government activities. It was inevitable that this would breed conflict over extraction and land rights, especially in a country that was utterly without institutions designed to adjudicate such disputes fairly. Similarly, in the former planned economy, job rights and the associated pensions and benefits were guaranteed. When workers were stripped of these rights in the wave of downsizing, restructuring, and privatization that was poorly regulated and often benefited officials and managers in highly visible ways, conflict was also inevitable because China was largely without the union and government institutions that had evolved over generations to help regulate such conflict in mature market economies. China's development model has forced local officials throughout the country into a firm alliance with business interests, whether public or private, and this often makes them the targets of collective protests over these issues, accompanied by charges of corruption and collusion.

This is a very different socio-political landscape from the 1980s, which was utterly transformed by the sweeping changes of the 1990s. Farmers were still enjoying the rising incomes from household agriculture, and rural protest was rare. Urban workers were hard hit by inflation and feared future layoffs, but their job rights were still secure. During the 1980s, the protests were focused in the key cities and were directed at the central government. Today, the protests are dispersed across the landscape but are focused on local officials and enterprise managers. They create a real policy problem for the central government, but they are hardly the political challenge, or the political threat, that was presented by the sporadic urban democracy movements concentrated in Beijing and the large cities in the 1980s.

Some observers view the overall volume of protest as a harbinger of a future regime crisis, as if the sheer volume of protest activity gives protests an impact on a national scale. One sometimes reads speculation that the widespread dissatisfaction in the countryside bodes ill for a regime that grew out of a rural guerrilla insurgency, and some warn that the fate of the former Nationalist regime may befall the Communists. This seems like a plausible historical observation until one recalls that the two conditions that pulled rural discontent together—a revolutionary guerrilla insurgency and a massive invasion by a foreign army—are notably absent today.

Other observers link this wave of protest to rising levels of inequality in China—certainly to levels not seen since the late 1940s—and some now refer to China as one of the most unequal societies in the world. It is true that overall measures of inequality in China have risen since the late 1970s, when national Gini indices of inequality were around .32—roughly the same as those in Taiwan at that time. These indices rose rapidly to the mid-40 range by the late 1990s and remain at this level today. It is not true, however, that these levels are unusually high—Latin America has long had much higher levels of income inequality (Brazil and Colombia are both at .58) and many African nations have much higher Gini measures than this. Recent data suggest that income inequality in China peaked in the late 1990s and has moderated slightly since then. In any case, inequality per se is not directly connected to political dissatisfaction—recent surveys in China indicate that citizens judge current levels of inequality far less harshly than citizens in countries like Poland, where there is far more equal income distribution.

In sum, these commonly cited portents of looming political instability are not what they are sometimes claimed to be. They are symptoms of economic conflicts in a vastly transformed society, in the context of a regime that is more stable and enjoys greater popular support than was the case during the first decade of reform. Political change in China is likely to remain a protracted affair, driven forward by forces that are fundamentally different from those that toppled so many economically stagnant and illegitimate Communist regimes some two decades ago—and that briefly threatened the Chinese regime in 1989. By whatever standard, the Chinese body politic at sixty is healthier than it was at age forty.

9.

农业、进口与外交:
中国党的领导与群众意愿互动关系的三项个案研究
AGRICULTURE, IMPORTS, AND DIPLOMACY: THREE CASE STUDIES ON THE INTERACTION BETWEEN CHINESE PARTY RULE AND POPULAR WILL

牛大勇 NIU DAYONG

Abstract

Despite the theoretical requirement that the Chinese Communist Party (CCP) must make all decisions according to the will of the people, in its actual policy-making practices the CCP has always selected a particular type of "popular will" according to its own ideological needs. This chapter examines the interaction between party rule and popular will in three cases. 1) In the early 1950s, two tendencies coexisted among Chinese peasants: either for or against agricultural collectivization. During the critical debates between Mao Zedong and Liu Shaoqi, Mao and his local supporters subdued popular will to retain private household production. 2) When it was difficult to negotiate a consensus, the top-level party leadership often settled disputes according to its own interpretation of the "popular will." An example is the decision to import foreign production equipment during the Cultural Revolution. 3) In terms of diplomatic interactions, the popular will in other countries can also influence CCP decision-making processes. During the 1956 political unrest in Poland, the CCP seemed to rely more on information provided by trusted journalists than on its own ambassadors, because it was assumed that journalists had more access to information about the "popular will" than the embassy personnel, who were subject to Soviet propaganda. In the end, the CCP concluded that the Polish Communist Party was distancing itself from the people and thus losing popular support.

农业、进口与外交:
中国党的领导与群众意愿互动关系的三项个案研究

中国人口众多,幅员辽阔,各地区的情况差别很大。地区之间、甚至同一地区内的情况也很不同。另外,中共也是世界上唯一的从农村割据状态直接走上大国执政地位、并走向世界政治舞台的政党。所以,面对各地民众在同一个问题上实际存在的种种不同意愿,中共决策者必须做出判断和取舍。就传统和理论而言,中共强调政策的制定,必须走群众路线,"从群众中来,到群众中去"。但在实践中,决策者必须根据自己主观上的意识形态,特别是对"社会主义"的理解,在诸多不同的民众意愿中,选择自认为正确的那一种"群众意愿"来制订政策。

以下分别就三个事例,来分析中共领导与群众意愿之间的互动模式。

一. 农民的不同意愿在党内各级领导层中引起的不同政策选择

中共是靠长期的农民战争取得国家政权的。农民的生产组织形式,是中共执政后长期面临的重大问题。党内高层,意见分歧,政策变化,峰回路转。

最初的抉择是在1950年。中共刚刚通过土地改革取得广大农民的支持,打败了占绝对优势的国民党军队,取得政权。农民刚刚分到了自己的土地,在两三年的耕作之后就开始出现了贫富分化。在内战中较早地实行了土地改革的华北和东北"老解放区"的农村中,出现了让共产党人感到困惑的问题:

1. 出现土地买卖。
2. "新富农"和"中农"增加,"贫农"减少,贫富差别拉大。
3. 部分党员、干部发家致富,甚至成为剥削他人劳动的"新富农"。
4. 原有的农民互助组织开始瓦解,劳动力强的农户和干部退出去"单干"了。[1]

于是,东北地区领导人采取措施限制单干。山西省委要把农民进一步"组织起来"。[2]

1951年4月17日，中共山西省委向中央提出报告：《把老区互助组织提高一步》。指出农民的自发力量"不是向着我们所要求的现代化和集体化的方向发展，而是向着富农的方向发展，这就是互助组发生涣散现象的最根本原因"。山西省委认为："对于私有基础，不应该是巩固的方针，而应当是逐步地动摇它，削弱它，直至否定它"。所以农民如果退出互助组，不许带走原来被征集的公积金。[3] 山西省的长治地委根据"全区互助组代表会议"讨论的结果，决定试办土地入股的农业生产合作社。[4]

中共华北局政策研究室调查组到长治进行实地调查，提出了不同意见。山西省委支持长治地委。华北局的领导却支持调查组，并根据华北五省中除山西以外的其他省委代表的意见，质疑："山西全省参加互助的农户达55%，是否过高"？ "即便如此，也还有近一半农户未组织起来"。批评："逐步动摇、削弱私有基础直至否定私有基础，是和党的新民主主义时期的政策及共同纲领的精神不相符合的，因而是错误的"。[5]

中央领导人刘少奇面对各级组织反映来的不同"民意"，表态支持"单干"，主张目前应"确保私有"，继续让农村两极分化，待国家工业化达到一定程度后，再实行农业集体化。他批评：目前想用互助组和合作社的办法去阻止农民的自发势力和阶级分化，"这是一种错误的、危险的、空想的农业社会主义思想"。[6]

毛泽东则看中了"组织起来"的民意，质问刘少奇和华北局领导：为什么不能动摇私有？能保护之，就不能动摇之？西方资本主义可以在尚未采用蒸汽机的时候，就依靠手工业工场的方式形成新生产力，我们为什么不能直接过渡到社会主义？还要经过什么？毛泽东的这番批评，把刘少奇和华北局领导"说服了"。[7]

1951年9月下旬，中共中央召开全国第一次农业互助合作会议。毛泽东特意请熟悉农村情况的"农民作家"赵树理对会议的决议草案提意见。赵以家乡的哥哥嫂子等亲戚为实例，说明现在农民没有互助合作的积极性，只有个体生产的积极性。中共中央最后下达的《关于农业生产互助合作的决议（草案）》，采取了折中路线，指出农民既有个体经济的积极性，又有劳动互助的积极性。但强调："必须提倡'组织起来'"，"发展农民劳动互助的积极性"。"其发展前途就是农业集体化或社会主义化"。[8]

以后，中国农业的"集体化"和"个体化"，成为中共党内和广大农民中最有歧义的重大政策问题，争论不休，几起几落。许多"集体化"的积极拥护者，先后变成"个体化"的推行者。从

1978年开始，中国的改革以家庭承包的方式，突破了集体化体制，带动了中国的市场化改革，但分歧至今仍然存在。

这一事例所表现的中国"民意"与"决策"的互动模式是：

1950年代初，农民中确实存在着对发展道路的不同意愿。面对各种不同甚至相反的"民意"，参与政策制订的中共各级领导只能有所取舍。毛泽东、中共山西省委、长治地委、东北局的政策，代表了一部分农民要"组织起来"走集体化道路的意愿。刘少奇、中共华北局和另一些省委，却代表着另一部分农民要保持私有制和个体生产的意愿。

各级党组织和领导人，在选择不同的"民意"加以支持时，实际上是从各自不同的意识形态理念出发的。毛泽东等人是出于对苏式"社会主义"的追求，刘少奇等人是对"新民主主义"的维护。

但"民意"会随着实践的发展而变化。毛泽东当时之所以能够否定刘少奇等人的主张，在决策中取胜，无论是靠道理来"说服"的，还是靠权力来"压服"的，终归是用一种意识形态来抗拒农民的自发倾向，结果遭到了农民大众长期的"消极反抗"。他去世不到两年，农民就根据长期反复的亲身实践，认定个体生产的优越性。而党的各级领导，也只能改变政策以顺应民意，符合国情。

二. 进口成套工业设备的决策与反对派

"民意"上达"天听"的另一个重要渠道，是毛泽东有意地从身边工作人员那里了解社会情况。1971年8、9月间毛泽东在那次历史性的"南巡"中，一个附带的结果是听到一个服务员说，她排了两小时的队，"千辛万苦"地买到一条涤纶裤子。[9]

毛泽东对百姓穿衣如此困难感到惊讶，回北京处理过"林彪事件"后，对周恩来、李先念等谈起这件事，问我们能不能生产一点化学纤维？让老百姓买一件化纤衣服，不要千辛万苦，百辛百苦行不行？周恩来说我们没有这个技术，还不能生产。毛泽东又问：能不能买（国外设备）？周恩来说：当然可以。便马上布置各主要工业部门通盘研究了急需引进的项目，提交了一个进口成套化纤、化肥生产设备的方案。后来投入的资金扩大为43亿美元，最后又增加为51.8亿美元，引进的品种从化纤和化肥技术设备，扩大到1.7米轧钢机等钢铁项目、石油化工生产设备、大型发电站、综合采煤机组等等共26个大项目。这是继五十年代从苏联引进设备以来，第二次大规模地从国外引进成套技术设备。[10]

这次国外技术设备的大引进，是在"文化大革命"背景下做出的决策。当时全国正在大力批判"洋奴哲学"、"爬行主义"。尽管毛泽东支持引进，但从中央到民间都有所抵制。

上海在王洪文的领导下，提出要自己搞一套与国外同样先进的30万吨合成氨工厂，抢在外国设备进口之前投入生产。为此调动了全国的化工制造力量，要求国家保证支持，要什么给什么。结果10年后，技术难题还没有完全解决，只能勉强投入生产。江青听说有一套进口的大化肥设备建在大庆附近的卧里屯，在1975年秋天的一次政治局会议上，当着邓小平的面大发脾气(lost her temper)，要追究是谁决定的？认为这是有意"丢大庆的脸"，"丢中国人的脸"，是反对"自力更生"，要求下令拆掉。[11]

周恩来还准备引进一套60万千瓦的核电站，但遭到中国核技术部门领导和专家们的反对。周恩来生前未能实现这个计划。1981年法国总统访华，向中国提出非常优越的援建条件：中国从法国引进一对共180万千瓦的核电机组，价格为20亿美元；由法国给中国每年7.25％的低息贷款，以后物价上涨，核电站价格不变，由法国从总统特别费中补贴。建设7年可以投产，使用15年还完贷款。当时技术专利权属于美国，但1983年即归法国所有。法国答应到期后就转让给中国。[12]

这项引进的条件如此优惠，双方谈判已接近达成协议。但是中国的核技术部门的领导和专家们强烈主张自力更生，说我们的原子弹都可以上天，核电站为什么不能自己造？他们提出自己建设30万千瓦的核电站，预言三年就可以建成。于是中央一时难以决策进口核电站。结果自己在秦山建设了10多年，关键技术还是没有完全解决。最后赵紫阳总理毅然决定批准广东和香港合资，从法国引进大亚湾核电站。但是价格已经从20亿美元上升到40亿美元。[13]

这些事例展示了中共"决策"与"民意"互动中的一些特点：

处于集权结构顶端的最高领导人，往往可以在中央集体意见不一致的情况下，直接根据自己理解的民意，做出决策。他实际上是凌驾于"党"和"民众"之上的"第三角色"。而且，他未必不能比"党"更能体察纷纭的"民意"中那种代表正确方向的意见。

这种"第三角色"往往能够超越党和民众一时信奉的主流意识形态，做出不合"正统思潮"的决策。而这种决策反会遭到党内其他领导和民众的抵制。

三. 对外关系中的体察"民意"与选择决策

中共领导层在对外关系中也注意了解"对象国"的群众意愿，慎重权衡。这种权衡有时在很大程度上会影响中共的决策。以1956年的"波兰事件"为例：

据中国外交部的有关档案记载，从1956年夏季到10月下旬，中共中央至少通过三个渠道了解波兰的政治动态：大使馆，新华社记者，使馆武官处(主要负责军事方面的动态)。[14]

中国驻波兰使馆这一时期给中共中央提交的报告，几乎都是根据驻波兰的苏联大使、东欧国家大使和波兰执政党官员提供的信息，说当地事件的性质是"反苏"、"反共"。也有当地的中国留学生反映的情况。[15]

只有新华社驻波兰记者谢文清，10月20日电请外交部转报新华社（外交部同时抄报给中央各领导）：波兰执政党内部分为三派，主张改革和民主化的两派已经合作，在党内是绝大多数，"且得到全国工人、学生、青年和知识分子的拥护"。"十九日晚全波各大工厂和一些大学都集会表示坚决拥护党中央的大多数，要求坚决贯彻民主化，要求同苏联友好，但不能妨碍国家主权和自己建设社会主义的道路。十九日晚记者曾目击了华沙工业大学的集会有二千多人"。"工人和学生代表在会上强调我们坚决忠实于社会主义和波苏友好，但我们有我们走向社会主义的道路，友谊应该是平等的，不妨碍主权的友谊，反对外国干涉内政，群众强烈要求哥穆尔卡参加党的领导"。[16]

10月20日，中国使馆又报称：波兰党中央全会上"出现了两条路线的严重斗争"，"党内右派分子纠合犹太人以及一些狭隘民族主义者正在有组织有计划地开展一个反苏运动"。"目的在于使右派完全统治中央，把波兰拖向右转。在国家政治生活中已可看出许多右倾的真实情况，例如：在政治方面反苏活动和资产阶级民主化的倾向没有制止；在经济方面强调波兰有困难应多开展与资本主义国家的经济联系"；"各方面表现的这种右倾的资产阶级思想，现已发展到高峰"。报告还说：据苏大使表示，"为了防止意外事变，军队方面已作了一些准备"。"依目前情况看，发生流血事件并非完全不可能"。[17]至21日，中国使馆做出判断并以"特特急电"报告中共中央："波党右派"已经"篡夺了党的领导"；"波兰显然要走资本主义道路"。[18]

又是谢文清，10月22日电请外交部转新华社（立即被外交部抄报给中央各领导）："我个人看法是，今天不存在波兰脱离社会主义而投向资本主义的问题，也不存在资本主义在波兰复辟的问题。但按波兰党大多数制定的路线（可说是得到全国大多数拥护的路线），波兰在政治生活、经济管理和部分领域内起很大的变化，即政治上将更加民主（目前已产生一些极端民主的倾向）；经济上将改革机构，给工人更多管理和计划的权利；对私人经济和富农等已作出了让步，但波兰人认为是改变目前经济局面所需的"。"可是波兰仍然是社会主义国家，政治上仍然是无产阶级专政，经济上社会主义成分仍然是压倒性的优势，外交上仍然以波、苏联盟为基本原则。一句话，波兰试图根据自己的情况来制定自己走向社会主义的道路"。"据记者耳闻目击，波兰很多人提出的口号是民主化，各国人民都有自己走向社会主义的道路，波兰也有它自己的道路。同苏联友好合作，但要独立解决自己的事情"。"我个人认为，苏共代表团的到达，华沙的调集军队之举是不够明智的，引起人民强烈的不满。在华沙到处可听到这种不满的言论"。[19]

中国驻波使馆转发此电时特意加了按语："这篇报道只代表谢文清同志个人的意见，和使馆的看法有基本的差别"。[20]

国内领导层在反复比较了对波兰情况的不同反映后，开始担心中国大使馆脱离了驻在国的"民意"，偏听偏信"官方信息"。外交部23日特意致电王炳南大使："对波兰情况望客观地蒐集材料，及时报告国内。对情况的分析亦需客观、全面，不要人云亦云。在同波兰及其他兄弟国家使节接触中，应多听少说，不要轻易表示态度，更不宜对波兰政治情势轻下结论"。[21]

中共中央领导层最终肯定了谢文清的意见，批评了使馆的意见。10月25日新华总社请驻波大使馆转告谢文清：

"你十月二十二日发来的对波兰局势的看法的内部材料，甚好。你的估计基本上是正确的，得到了中央同志的好评"。[22]

同日外交部给驻波大使馆覆电："应该说使馆对波兰局势的看法是不正确的。使馆同谢文清同志的意见分歧中，谢的意见是正确的。请将此意见告诉谢，并请你们对波兰局势进行客观、全面的研究"。[23]

关于中共中央领导层对波兰事件的政策背景，沈志华先生已有专文探讨，本文不再赘述。[24]但需要补充的是，中共中央对波兰事件性质的判断，应该是在10月23日至24日间确定的。尽管外交部23日已经去电告诫驻波兰大使要"客观"、"全面"地蒐集材料和分析情况，但23、24日驻波兰使馆的来电仍用"右派"、"左派"

等概念表达自己的政治倾向性，从25日开始的来电才比较"客观"了一些。[25]

这一事例显示了中共中央对外"决策"与"民意"互动模式的一些特点：

毛泽东等领导人在了解外国民意和政情的信息渠道中，似乎对驻外记者的信任有时超过了对驻外大使的信任，因为他们认为记者更"深入群众"，更体察民意，更客观地反映情况。而大使和使馆官员，则太偏重于同苏联东欧的官方接触。中共领导人1956年对苏联东欧"兄弟国家"的看法，是认为它们的"党群关系"有问题：党脱离了群众，甚至违反了群众利益。这也是中共中央上述决策过程的一个背景。

而且广而言之，中共中央领导人那些年代中对国外信息的了解，在相当大程度上是依靠新华社国际部每日编发的《参考资料》(俗称"大参考")，里面都是外国媒体和中国驻外记者的时事报道。新华社随收、随译、随报，一天编发三大本，在中央领导层内部呈阅。[26]

但驻外记者的报告，又往往是通过中国大使馆转报国内的，重要电讯往往由外交部同步直接抄报给中央主要领导人。当记者意见和使馆意见有重大分歧时，如波兰那样的情况，使馆和外交部仍能把这种不同的意见如实转报，以供中央抉择，这也是难能可贵的。在"波兰危机"中，中国外交部和驻波兰大使馆能够这样做，和当时主持外交部常务工作的张闻天副部长重视调查研究、注意发扬民主的外交理念和工作作风有密切关系，和王炳南大使的民主作风也有关系。[27]从这里也可以看出："制度"和"人为"是相互作用，不可偏废的。

ENDNOTES

1. 史敬棠等编，《中国农业合作化运动史料》，下册(北京：生活、读书、新知三联书店，1959)，第235–253页。

2. 薄一波，《若干重大决策与事件的回顾》，上卷(北京：中共中央党校出版社，1991)，第195–196页。

3. 中共山西省委，《把老区互助组织提高一步》，1951年4月17日，中华人民共和国国家农业委员会办公厅编，《农业集体化重要文件汇编（1949–1957年）》，上册(北京：中共中央党校出版社，1981)，第35–36页。

4. 《若干重大决策与事件的回顾》，上卷，第186页。

5. 华北局，《华北局复山西省委<把老区互助合作提高一步>》，1951年5月4日，《农业集体化重要文件汇编（1949–1957年）》，上册，第34页。

6.《刘少奇同志山西省委<把老区互助合作提高一步>的批语》，1951年7月3日，《农业集体化重要文件汇编（1949–1957年）》，上册，第33页。《中国农业合作史资料》，1986年试刊，第35页。

7.《若干重大决策与事件的回顾》，上卷，第191页。《中国农业合作史资料》，1990年，第6期，第17页。

8.《中共中央关于农业生产互助合作的决议（草案）》，1951年12月，《农业集体化重要文件汇编（1949–1957年）》，上册，第37–44页。

9. 顾明口述，牛大勇采访整理，《历尽艰辛创四化》，程华编，《周恩来和他的秘书们》（北京：中国广播电视出版社，1992），第22页。《李先念传（1909–1992年）》下册，同书编写组（北京：中央文献出版社，2009），第763–764页。

10. 陈锦华，《国事忆述》，（北京：中共党史出版社，2005），第8-19页。逄先知、金冲及主编，《毛泽东传（1949–1976）》，下册（北京：中央文献出版社，2003），第1622页。

11.《历尽艰辛创四化》，《周恩来和他的秘书们》，第23页。

12.《历尽艰辛创四化》，《周恩来和他的秘书们》，第24页。

13.《历尽艰辛创四化》，《周恩来和他的秘书们》，第24–25页。张胜，《从战争中走来—两代军人的对话》（北京：中国青年出版社，2008），第422–426页。

14.《总参情报部致姜代武官成186号电》，1956年11月20日，档案号：109-00762-02，中华人民共和国外交部档案馆。

15.《王炳南致外交部午360号电》，1956年7月5日，档案号：109-00761-04《驻波使馆致外交部酉810号电》，1956年10月19日，档案号：109-00762-03；《驻波使馆致外交部酉841号电》，1956年10月20日，档案号：109-00762-03；《王炳南致外交部并报中央酉843号电》，1956年10月21日；《王炳南致外交部并中央酉876号电》，1956年10月22日，档案号：109-00761-06；俱存中华人民共和国外交部档案馆。

16.《谢文清致外交部转新华社酉827号电》，1956年10月20日，档案号：109-00762-03，中华人民共和国外交部档案馆。

17.《王炳南致外交部并报中央酉840号电》，1956年10月20日，档案号：109-00762-03，中华人民共和国外交部档案馆。

18.《王炳南致外交部并报中央酉859号电》，1956年10月21日，档案号：109-00762-03，中华人民共和国外交部档案馆。

19.《谢文清致外交部转新华社酉879号电》，1956年10月22日，档案号：109-00762-03，中华人民共和国外交部档案馆。

20. 同上。

21.《外交部致王大使酉297号电》，1959年10月23日，档案号：109-00762-02，中华人民共和国外交部档案馆。

22《新华总社致驻波大使馆转谢文清酉2014电（外交部发）》，1959年10月25日，档案号：109-00762-02，中华人民共和国外交部档案馆。

23.《外交部致王大使酉340号电》，1956年10月25日，档案号：109-00762-02，中华人民共和国外交部档案馆。

24. 沈志华，《一九五六年十月危机：中国的角色和影响》，柯伟林、牛大勇主编，《中国与世界的互动：国际化、内化与外化》（郑州：河南人民出版社，2007），第335–346页。

25.《驻波使馆致外交部并中央酉934号电》，1056年10月23日，档案号：109-00762-03；《王炳南致外交部并中央酉1044号电》，1956年10月24日，档案号：109-00762-03；《驻波使馆致外交部并中央酉1043号电》，1056年10月24日，档案号：109-00762-03；《王炳南致外交部并中央酉1045号电》，1956年10月24日，档案号：109-00762-03；《驻波使馆致外交部酉1059号电》，1056年10月25日，档案号：109-00762-03；俱存中华人民共和国外交部档案馆。

26.《李慎之谈话记录》，1995年9月20日于黄山，牛大勇记录并收存。

27. 何方口述、邢小群整理，《在外交部工作的日子》，《温故》之七(南宁：广西师范大学出版社, 2006)，第75-78、80-84、87-92、109-112、117-119页。

10.
URBAN RESIDENTIAL DISTRICT MAKING IN CHINA

PETER G. ROWE

In 1949, the vast majority of China's population lived in rural circumstances or in relatively small towns. There were relatively few sizable cities. By 1978, with the onset of the Deng Xiaoping era and China's historic opening up to the outside world the situation had changed somewhat, although only around 17 percent of the nation's population lived in urban areas, according to official estimates. By 2005, however, and at an accelerating rate, an additional 350 million or so people found themselves living in urban circumstances across a proliferation of urban centers, with heavy concentrations in the coastal region and to a lesser extent toward the central region. Today, according to an official calculus, there are around 656 cities and some 19,000 designated towns in China, with the propor-tion of urban dwellers up around 45 percent and probably on the way to 65 percent, or more, of the total population by mid-century.[1]

Within the cities there have also been other dramatic changes. Population density, though still relatively high by international standards, has declined overall in most places. Across the built areas of the top twenty cities by size, for instance, this decline was often due to the unwinding of appallingly overcrowded conditions, generally now approaching a density of some 10,000 people per square kilometer—a broad target for China's city urbanization.[2] Residential space standards have risen appreciably, with most new construction at an average of 20 to 25 square meters per person of built space. The rise in the height of residential environments, especially in larger cities, has also increased, along with signifi-cant upward extensions of commercial buildings. Shanghai, for example, currently boasts over 3,000 high-rise structures. Furthermore, the functionality of many cities has expanded to accommodate a burgeoning tertiary sector. This is particu-larly apparent under Beijing's 1993 master plan, for instance, with the creation of a new central business district on the eastern side of the city's east-west axis along Chang'an Avenue and with a smaller financial district to the west. Cities have also expanded outward, horizontally, in most if not all cases, with Beijing, again, more than doubling in area between 1984 and early into the new millennium.[3] And, to choose yet another dimension, the provision of public open space in cities has increased, often dramatically, responding to local demands for more recreational and leisure-time amenities.

Also of note, the physical form of China's urbanization is by no means uniform or singular in shape and appearance, ranging across a plethora of environments. For example, many historic areas are now more frequently under preservation and conservation.[4] Dense and bustling inner-city commercial areas also abound, often along recently pedestrianized thoroughfares like Shanghai's Nanjing Road or Beijing's Wangfujing and Xidan areas. Special administrative districts covering upscale commercial and mixed-use developments have also been created, often in side-by-side spatial relationships with previously well-established areas, with Lujiazui—the emerging financial district of Shanghai—a prime example.[5] More broadly, special economic zones have been established, bringing urbanization to some rural areas, like Shenzhen, just to the north of Hong Kong's New Territories. Many dilapidated inner-city neighborhoods have been given a new lease on life, often through conservation efforts as in the *lilong* environments of Luwan in Shanghai. Satellite town developments around major cities continue to occur, as they did during the early Maoist era, in an effort to rationalize the spread of urbanization and to provide sites for particular activities. Less-regulated development, however, on the periphery and in the hinterlands close to many major cities has also encroached on otherwise productive agricultural land, in some cases surrounding what now have become "urban villages." This phenomenon, along with counterpart township-village enterprises elsewhere, made use of surplus rural labor to produce a quasi-industrialization of the countryside that accounted for as much as 30 percent of the national gross domestic product in the late 1980s.[6] Today this contribution is much less but it has given China, particularly in Guangdong and Jiangsu provinces, the spatial and socio-economic characteristics of the so-called *desakota* regions.[7]

Nevertheless, since 1949 if not before, the bulk of China's city-scale urbanization has occurred through a succession of urban-district making activities and projects. Here the terms "urban district," or "built-up territories," to avoid confusion with Chinese political administrative terminology, refer to the meso-scale development that takes place between the macro-scale of overall city plans and the micro-scale considerations of specific buildings and building complexes. Typically involved are large residential components—structures also often referred to as "estates"—usually built at once, but also including other residentially-related uses, especially in the category of community services, and extending to sites of employment and, sometimes, complete subcenters of urban activity. To take an example somewhat at random, the Jinyang New District in the southern city of Guiyang, currently in the process of building out, accommodates large residential tracts, internally or adjacently served by community and commercial functions, together with nearby offices and other employment opportunities, as well as recreational and open-space activities. Parenthetically, such meso-scale development is not novel. Although with some differences, it is analogous to practices elsewhere in the world and at other times. Here, examples may range from the Cerda grid of Barcelona forming the *Ensanche*, *Eixample*, or extension of the old city, dating from the mid-nineteenth century. The *quartière* of Rome falls into much the same category, as do the sub-developments with a gridwork of streets and blocks in Los Angeles, or the residential estates accompanying new town development in places like Singapore.

In China, at the level primarily of residential development, this meso-scale urban-district making process yields results that can be readily characterized by a number of features. First, they are relatively large block configurations, often on the order of ten to twenty hectares in area. Second, these configurations provide a cellular pattern to urban development, with varying degrees of self-containment and urban-architectural specialization into different uses. Third, the large block configurations are also circumscribed by a coarse-grained deployment of roads and other elements of public infrastructure, essentially around their perimeters. Fourth, there is considerable uniformity in the architectural typology of housing, usually in the form of *zeilenbau* arrangements of parallel apartment blocks, facing in a southerly direction and taking advantage of passive solar heating and cooling. This was not always the case. During the mid-1950s there was considerable architectural debate between the benefits of perimeter-block configurations creating quadrangular enclosures of community open space and parallel-block arrangements with relatively narrow community spaces and passages in between. The resolution of building standards in favor of the parallel-block arrangements largely stemmed from spatial efficiencies and lower-cost climatic performance at a time when China was bereft of building resources, especially for "welfare" items like housing, outside of the pursuit of the production of the primary means of production, like industry, to use the parlance of the time. Finally, at least over certain periods, there was a fairly high degree of conformity between urban or residential districts and underlying models of social organization. Moreover, in this and other regards, the evolution of these meso-scale configurations since 1949, with some interruption, followed a reasonably consistent trajectory.

To begin with, there was the *danwei*, or work-unit, a configuration substantially influenced by similar Soviet arrangements and dating back by some accounts to experiments during the Republican era.[8] In principle and in practice, the *danwei* were highly focused on specific means of production. They usually took the form of either large-scale developments with separate residential compounds adjacent to production plants and administrative structures, or smaller-scale operations combining work places, services, and residences in a single compound. In addition, they could be located on the periphery of established urban areas or within existing urban areas. Beyond programs of accommodation and use, one of the urban-architectural aims was often to symbolize and reproduce the order of the socialist state and to promote a socialist collectivized lifestyle. One prime example is the massive No. 1 Automobile Manufacturing Complex in Changchun, built during the early 1950s. In this as well as in other cases, these urban-architectural aims were manifested by axial spatial arrangements of buildings; open spaces and access ways; a certain monumentality in building massing and centralization along axes; and expressions of a socialist realist style of presentation, along with quasi-traditional Sinic features like prominent roofs and supporting awnings. Schematically, the spatial structure of the *danwei* took the form of a nested spatial hierarchy of units, working upward from the "residential cluster"—sometimes colloquially referred to as "four dishes and one soup" because of the arrangement of four housing blocks centered around an element of community services like a day-care center—toward the more fundamental units, or building block, of the *xiaoqu*—small district—roughly corresponding in scale and form to the Soviet *microrayon*, with some 10,000 to 12,000 inhabitants. Further combinations of this unit with others of similar kinds, although with some local variations in function, resulted in larger and productively diversified urban ensembles. Provision of community services, including kindergartens, schools, health facilities, and the like, as well as administrative and production facilities, was also scaled-up at various levels of the underlying spatial hierarchy. One result, although primarily for residential use, is Caoyang New Village on the then western edge of Shanghai which expanded roughly between 1951 and the 1980s to accommodate around 100,000 inhabitants—a virtual city within the city—corresponding roughly to the Soviet *Gorodskorayon.*[9]

Skipping forward in time over the suspension of much architectural activity and practically all urban planning during the Peoples Commune era and the depths of the Cultural Revolution, by the 1980s and into the reform era, "work-unit society" was on the wane. Residential district development, however, continued to draw upon the housing typology, spatial arrangement, and inclusion of community services from the earlier era. *Danyuanlou*—big yard, parallel-block arrangements—continued to proliferate. Projects on the order of 50 hectares plus, like the Weifang Housing Estate in the Pudong District of Shanghai, housing some 10,000 residents, were not unusual. Indeed, well into the 1990s and onward, residential districts or estates continued to be built within large-block configurations with ancillary levels of mixed use, broad and coarse-grained road networks, and at a considerable scale. Comparisons among upscale developments in, say, Pudong, "starter housing" on the outskirts of Beijing under the 1998 Economic and Suitable Housing Program targeted at low-to-middle income households, and *anju* or comfortable housing, dating from 1995 and similarly targeted, all reveal many basic similarities. Nevertheless, coinciding with these relatively spatially consistent developments, the model of social organization officially shifted to the idea of the *shequ*—social district or collective—promulgated by the Ministry of Civil Affairs.[10] Basically, this involves a jurisdiction under an enlarged residential committee aimed at taking up the slack from the *danwei* system with regard to community service provision and solidarity. At present, however, it is often applied in a spatially amorphous manner and appears to muster inconsistent adherence from place to place.

Throughout much of this trajectory and certainly under current circumstances, urban residential district making has adhered to central government guidelines and largely top-down master-planning and building-regulatory exercises, applicable across the board. Tracing through some of the technical aspects of this process, city master plans are prepared on a regular basis—nominally from five to ten years—for approval by the State Council. Within these master plans, district-level layouts are drawn up according to ministerial guidelines provided by the Ministry of Housing and Urban-Rural Development, formally the Ministry of Construction. These guidelines specify, among other things, percentages and relationships of land use, ground cover characteristics, road layout requirements, amounts of service provision, and so on. Detailed control plans, as they are called, are then prepared for each block within a district or sub-district, designating allowable site coverage, floor area ratios, building heights, building setbacks, amounts of green-space provision, and parking requirements. Essentially, these specifications are similar to what is sometimes referred to as "form zoning" in the West. Building regulations are also harmonized with these master-planning and detailed control planning efforts, depicting further relationships among building heights, building volumes, widths, spacing, and setbacks, among other requirements.[11] Looking across examples of these regulations from a number of major cities there appears to be not much variation across current codes and working through all the technical specifications, the outcomes, as one might expect, are largely a case of "what's specified is what results."

Despite an inherent uniformity, or perhaps because of it, one can also observe that the general layout, spatiality, and, indeed, ambience of the generic Chinese residential district or estate are distinctive, if not entirely unique. It is at once enclave-like, surrounded and relatively isolated in a pedestrian sense by wide roads, relatively dense in occupation, typologically relatively invariant, well provided with open space, and reasonably serviced locally, at least with prescribed, if not demanded, community services and facilities. Comparison with the metrics of basic-block configurations in other places further accentuates this distinctiveness. Referring to the examples of meso-scale development noted earlier, the Barcelona *Ensanche* block is 113 meters by 113 meters and separated by road widths averaging 20 to 30 meters. New York's Manhattan grid has a building block of 244 meters by 61 meters, separated by 18 meters plus street widths and 30 meter plus avenue widths, and there is a roughly similar configuration in Los Angeles, with blocks of some 213 meters by 73 meters and street and road right of way widths on the order of 16 to 40 meters. Repetitive blocks in Shanghai's Pudong District are on the order of 400 meters by 300 meters, with little internal street circulation, and surrounded by roads typically on the order of 30 to 50 meters in width. Bundang in South Korea, to cite another example near the top end of the scale, has a block structure that is even larger, at around 550 meters by 330 meters. Looking across these examples, road density per block is much the same, although differently distributed among the examples, down to New York's fine-grained network. The building volume density per block for Shanghai, assuming mainly mid-rise construction, is in the middle of the range of the examples, whereas its open-space density is high. In design approach, the Chinese case certainly exhibits sustained adherence to modernist urban-architectural traits. Here one can refer to the relatively complete separation of vehicular and pedestrian traffic, deployment of assumed layout efficiencies of what are sometimes termed "slabs in a park," and separation and articulation of separate functions. In sum, a pervasive technological temperament seems to have been at work around detailed programmatic and spatial issues. Nevertheless, inherited aspects from much earlier imperial eras are also lurking. Qing-era Beijing, for instance, was no stranger to wide spatial parentheses deep within the city, as exhibited by the 1750 Qianlong map. Nor was Qing-era Beijing stranger to enclave-like and gated communities, like the Bannermen districts, with similar and relatively muted variation among building typologies.

At this juncture, questions may be asked regarding the suitability or fittedness of China's spatial recipe or physical template for urban residential construction in contemporary and emerging circumstances. Of particular importance, as anywhere else, is the longer-run sustainability of such developments when viewed against the backdrop of changing and more varied socio-economic circumstances, as well as pressing needs for higher degrees of environmental mediation. Until now, most of the emphasis has been placed on relatively basic provision of dwellings, ancillary activities, and infrastructural access, with a rising modicum of commodiousness and amenities. On par, what has been produced and is being produced presents a mixed bag of both problems requiring better resolution and opportunities for higher quality and more sustainable development.

To be sure, rising residential space standards, improving architectural qualities, and the often leafy, lane-like, introverted, and serene ambience of many contemporary residential enclaves—at least when present—make for pleasant, livable, neighborly, and community-oriented environments. However, along the edges of these enclaves, the predominance of a coarse-grained roadway network, with little circulation in between and with an increasing reliance on automobile transportation, leads to traffic congestion—severe in many cases—and associated environmental and social costs. Pedestrian or bicycle circulation is often impeded by the lack of intermediate public rights of way, shifting the balance away from appropriate levels of seclusion and security to levels bordering on isolation and spatial fragmentation. However, typical perimeter road rights way on the order of 50 to 60 meters or more in width, with wide spacing between cross streets, provide leeway for installing preferential mass transit, as occurred with Kunming's bus rapid transit system provided with the assistance of the Swiss government. Also, in Kunming, among other cities, a program of interstitial linear path and parkway connections is being tested and pursued to retrofit improved open-space amenities and access into the broad expanses of earlier *danwei* and other residential estates.

Unfortunately, rote carpet-like deployment of large modules of urban accommodation—the template again—within master plans can frequently run afoul of local environmental considerations regarding land cover, water conservation, and scenic as well as historic values. In instances like Wuhan, which is famous for its riverine, lake, and remarkable topographic underlying environment, *tabula rasa* fleshing out of an otherwise sensible master plan, without careful consideration at the meso- and micro-levels of urbanization can have significant cumulative negative impacts. In fact, this has occurred in the past, although the city's stance has altered appreciably in recent times, particularly when confronted with scenic and environmental stewardship of the exquisite East Lake environment. Again, however, at a local level the sheer size and aerial coverage of many emerging residential estates do offer leeway for water harvesting and for rainfall run-off control. Some recent applications, particularly in higher-end developments by the likes of Vanke, present useful examples, although much more could be done, even as retrofitting operations to existing estates. Among the highest resource and environmental priorities confronting China are water conservation and improvement of water quality in all respects.

In comparison with finer-grained networks of blocks and streets, like those referred to earlier, the typical Chinese broad and coarse-grained structure appears to be awkwardly positioned with regard to dynamic processes of local-level despecialization of use and other physical changes that flow over urban environments, so to speak, allowing cities to restructure themselves and often become more suitable and better places within the framework of existing urban fabrics. Indeed, this is often a pitfall of an otherwise over-determined, or particularly specialized, modernist approach to settlement layout. By contrast, the successive and continuing transformations of the Manhattan grid, to use but one other example, have been facilitated, if anything, by its underlying grid structure, originating from the early nineteenth century. On par, current Chinese practice is relatively inflexible in both building type and overall layout, impeding potential despecialization and functional diversification, but without incurring substantial and costly modification. Recent policy orientation toward improving the diversity of urban environments, in addition to ongoing efforts toward compact urbanization appear to recognize this potential planning defect.[12] Further, returning to environmental concerns, empirical studies show that either low or very high levels of diversification across characteristics of employment and use within districts lead to higher levels of inter-district travel and with automobile use to high levels of atmospheric emissions, *ceterus paribus*.

Finally, on the administrative side and somewhat independent of geometries and other considerations of physical layout, fragmentation of authority compared perhaps to earlier times, plus a lack of well-directed and coordinated incentives, has left many urban residential districts underserviced and out of affordable and logistical reach of the target populations. One case in point is the Hui Long Guan and Tian Tong Yuan area near the outskirts of Beijing. In fact, many broad swaths of new peripheral development in China are lagging in essential as well as discretionary services, along with mis-matches with transport and infrastructure provision, not to mention more local employment opportunities. Although the template of large-block development described here is meant to resolve these issues and may eventually do so, the outright scale and considerably more than incremental unfolding of development can present a significant interim impediment to well-rounded and adaptable urban settlements.

In summary, then, under the rubric of urban residential district making, a distinctive pattern of settlement has emerged in China. Moving forward in time, it seems to be less synchronous with emerging urban dynamics that have become far more numerous and complex than in former times. There also appears to be more slippage with officially preferred models of social organization for many of the same reasons of differentiation and complexity on the broader socio-economic front. In order to progress in pursuit of the laudable twin goals of continued compactness and increased diversification—along with a host of ameliorative environmental practices—it seems to be time to give serious reconsideration to current official practice in urban residential district making, especially to the all-important aspects of technical guidelines, regulatory criteria, controls, and enforcement. Moreover, as indicated here, this is by no means an insurmountable task, but one that will require a shift in emphasis away from macro considerations of master planning, where China has performed rather well, to more refined and inclusive meso-scale and micro-scale reformulations.

ENDNOTES

1. Based on a study of urban formation and projected urban development in China conducted at the Harvard Graduate School of Design and supported by the East-West Cultural Foundation of Singapore. Data are from a variety of sources drawn from the Chinese National Bureau of Statistics and Ministry of Public Security.

2. The population density of China's top twenty cities by size across nonagricultural population and built areas in 2005 was 11,088 people per square kilometer, well down from 16,608 people per square kilometer in 1985.

3. As documented in Beijingshi guihua guanliju (Beijing Municipal Institute of City Planning and Design), *Beijing maixiang ershiyi shiji* (Beijing Striding Forward to the 21st Century) (Beijing, 1992); Beijingshi renmin zhengfu (Municipality of Beijing), *Beijingshi zongti guihua 1991–2010 nian* (Master Plan of Beijing, 1991–2010) (Beijing, 1996), as ratified by the State Council in 1993; and Wu Liangyong, ed., *Jing Jin diqu chengxiang kongjian fazhan guihua yanjiu er qi baogao* (The Second Report on the Rural and Urban Spatial Development Planning Study for the Capital Region [Beijing, Tianjin, and Hebei]) (Beijing: Qinghua daxue chubanshe, 2006).

4. For instance, Beijingshi guihua guanliju (Beijing Municipal City Planning Department), *Beijing jiucheng 25 pian lishi wenhua baohu qu baohu guihua fang'an* (Conservation Planning of 25 Historic Areas in Beijing) (Beijing, 2002), as well as a more recent yet comparable plan for Shanghai.

5. Fully formed under the Shanghai-Pudong New Administrative District in 1993, following a variety of Pudong New Area planning exercises dating from 1987.

6. See Yasheng Huang, *Capitalism with Chinese Characteristics: Entrepreneurship and the State* (New York: Cambridge University Press, 2008), for an insightful and well-documented account.

7. Godfrey Linge, ed., *China's New Spatial Economy: Heading Towards 2020* (New York: Oxford University Press, 1997).

8. As described variously in E.M. Bjorklund, "The Danwei: Socio-Spatial Characteristics of Work Units in China's Urban Society," *Economic Geography*, 62, no. 1: 19–29; Duanfang Lu, *Remaking Chinese Urban Form: Modernity, Scarcity and Space, 1949–2005* (New York:

Routledge, 2006); and Lü Junhua, Peter G. Rowe, and Zhang Jie, eds., *Modern Urban Housing in China: 1840–2000* (Munich: Prestel, 2001).

9. R.A. French and F.E. Ian Hamilton, eds., *The Socialist City: Spatial Structure and Urban Policy* (New York: Wiley, 1979) and R. Antony French, *Plans, Pragmatism and People: The Legacy of Soviet Planning for Today's Cities* (London: UCL Press, 1995).

10. Minzheng bu (Ministry of Civil Affairs), *Minzheng bu guanyu zai quanguo tuijin chengshi shequ jianshe de yijian* (Ministry of Civil Affairs Views on Promoting Urban Shequ Building Throughout the Nation) (Beijing, 2002).

11. Post-1978 regulations began with the *1980 nian "Chengshi guihua ding e zhibiao de zanxing guiding"* (Temporary Regulations on Urban Planning Standards of 1980). These were replaced by the State Council issuance of the *1984 nian "Chengshi guihua tiaoli"* (Urban Planning Regulations of 1984) and the *1986 nian "Chengshi guihua fa"* (Urban Planning Act of 1986) that was ratified for cities in 1989 and subsequently revised into its latest form as *2007 nian "Chengxiang guihua fa"* (Urban-Rural Planning Act of 2007). Relevant meso- and micro-level regulations and guidelines can be found in the Jianshe bu (Ministry of Construction), *"Chengshi juzhuqu guihua sheji guifan"* (Urban Residential District Planning and Design Regulations), issued in 1993 with subsequent modifications. Also of note is Jianshe bu (Ministry of Construction), *2005 nian suofabu de "Zhuzhai jianzhu guifan"* (2005 Codes for the Design of Civil Buildings) and various city *Jianzhu gongcheng guihua guanli jishu guiding* (Urban Planning Bureau Building and Technical Management Regulations), most recently dating from about 2006.

12. Qiu Baoxing [Vice Minister for the Ministry of Housing and Urban-Rural Development], *Harmony and Innovation: Problems, Dangers and Solutions in Dealing with Rapid Urbanization in China* (Milano: L'arca 2007).

11.
"TURNING RUBBISH INTO SOMETHING USEFUL": CRIME AND PUNISHMENT IN MAO'S CHINA

KLAUS MÜHLHAHN

Building on experiments made in the base areas during the revolution, after 1949 the Chinese Communist Party (CCP) introduced a new nationwide system of criminal justice for the People's Republic of China (PRC). It is quite difficult to draw its contours as a unitary system, since the criminal justice apparatus was repeatedly reshuffled and reshaped in the wake of political changes and internal party disputes. Also, criminal justice under Mao's version of socialism was hardly an independent administrative system but was integrated into a network of social control and political mobilization. Enmeshed in larger bureaucratic circuits, the institutional boundaries of criminal justice were blurred. Criminal justice agencies pursued goals far beyond crime control or conflict resolution per se. At the same time, informal institutions that actually were not part of the legal system took on functions that previously fell under the authority of the judiciary, such as criminal investigation, adjudication, and sentencing. In short, the criminal justice system in the PRC was for a long time very much in flux, and it became mixed up with many other government agencies and political organizations.

The Chinese criminal justice system in the period from 1949 to 1979 was marked by an approach that saw law and the management of justice mainly as instruments of class struggle, political mobilization, and social transformation.[1] Either formally or informally, in court or out of court, China's socialist state regarded the criminal justice system as a powerful tool for social engineering and for the inculcation of values and norms. Criminal justice was supposed to become a dynamic force for social transformation, propelling China forward to the attainment of communism. It would help unleash the governing powers of the socialist state and would safeguard and enforce initiatives and campaigns devised by the central party. Party leadership regarding day-to-day operations and the formulation of guiding principles was therefore always strictly enforced.

This chapter intends to draw the contours of the criminal justice system and its role in society during the years of Mao Zedong's rule. It starts with a description of the theoretical discourse behind the Communist leadership's approach to law and justice. This legal discourse provided the leadership not only with a justification for its violent persecution of certain groups of the population. It also constructed target populations and created legal categorizations that turned social or political differences into hierarchies of legal privileges. The legal discourse produced epistemological claims that were powerful political ones. Criminal justice in the PRC consisted of two main features. The first component, which is discussed in the second section of this chapter, was the deployment of revolutionary tribunals, organized by local party cells with the support of local state agencies. The other was the use of labor camps for meting out punishments. This is examined in the third section of the chapter. The conclusion puts forward a simple argument: I will argue that state violence inflicted through the criminal justice apparatus had an enormous effect on life in China in the 1950s and 1960s. But this has been either ignored or downplayed in most scholarship, so the question of mass violence under Chinese socialism is still awaiting comprehensive and critical reassessment.

Law as a Weapon

Behind the state violence that regularly rippled though China in the 1950s was a particular politico-legal discourse, which defined the target populations, dehumanized and depersonalized these groups, and justified the use of violence against them. The leadership of the CCP viewed the state and the law as tools of class struggle, not as independent values. As such, state law could never pertain to values or rights existing independently of society. Also in the CCP's view, law was not tied to ideas of justice (or fairness); rather, it was seen as a weapon for dealing with the enemies of socialism. In the words of Mao Zedong: "The state apparatus, including the army, the police and the courts, is the instrument by which one class oppresses another. It is an instrument for the oppression of antagonistic classes."[2] Mao therefore advocated the use of law and legal institutions to suppress all opposition to the regime. The party rejected the idea of equality before the law. Rather, since law was regarded as the continuation of class struggle and as a tool for dealing with enemies, a fundamental distinction needed always to be made between "us" or "the people" and "them," i.e. "enemies of the people." The people were entitled to participate in public affairs, but the so-called "enemies of the people" or "counter-revolutionaries" were subject to the "democratic dictatorship" of the people. In Mao's texts as well as in later official and legal documents, it remained ambiguous who was an enemy or counter-revolutionary. Over time, criteria such as "backward political attitude," "historical questions," or "class background" were introduced that nonetheless were always porous and flexible, depending on the time and the context. Although designated enemies initially tended to be outside of the party, such as Guomindang (KMT) leftovers and other oppositional forces, by the mid-1950s the targeting focused on groups and individuals within work-units or party cells. Over the course of the 1950s, vagueness in defining the "enemies" increased rather than decreased, resulting also in increasing breadth of targeting. "Democratic dictatorship" meant that enemies or counter-revolutionaries had to be dealt with strictly and severely. They were to be treated differently and more violently than offenders who came from the ranks of the people. The enemies either had to be executed or forced to remold themselves through hard labor to become "new persons" (*xin ren*). Mao described the latter process as "turning rubbish into something useful."[3]

In general guidelines and statements of a more theoretical nature, the party focused on forced re-education. But at the same time, the use of violence was never revoked. Depending on the circumstances, counter-revolutionaries needed to be killed because, in the words of Mao, they "were deeply hated by the masses and owed the masses heavy blood-debts."[4] The use of violence was thus justified by popular resentment and the concept of "blood-debts" (*xue zhai*). The latter expression appears frequently in Mao's speeches and writing. The term "blood-debt" was used to argue that popular indignation compelled the party to seek retribution and retaliation when dealing with its worst enemies. Mao also made it clear that counter-revolutionaries would continue to exist in China, so campaigns would be necessary in the future as well. The socialist state had to be vigilant and could not afford to renounce the use of violence: "We cannot promulgate [a policy] of no executions at all; we still cannot abolish the death penalty. Suppose there is a counter-revolutionary who has killed people or blown up a factory, what would you say, should that person be executed or not? Certainly such a person must be executed."[5]

Revolutionary justice in Mao's thinking entailed the principle that "to right a wrong it is necessary to exceed the proper limits."[6] Justice would come through heavy-handed responses, through open and violent retaliation. The punishments had to be such that they could be understood as symbolic expressions of public indignation over previous heinous crimes. In general, if applied with skill, public spectacles of retribution were a powerful tool. They could be used to suppress and eliminate opponents. At the same time, when staged as public theater, the drama of retributive justice could serve as a vehicle to rally popular sentiment behind the party's course and could direct indignation toward the targeted opponents. Mao made no effort to hide his notion that this should take the form of terror. Terror was not only acceptable as a necessary evil, but in fact indispensable for the revolutionary project.

At the center of this discourse, then, was a binarism that introduced into the legal system a systematic friend-enemy distinction.[7] The division between friend and enemy framed law in China in a basic sense, so that the entire administration of law operated almost entirely on the basis of this binary divide.[8] The crucial question, however, was how to determine who is an enemy. In retrospect, the trajectory over the course of the 1950s was toward greater vagueness and increasing breadth of targeting. The guidelines that the party established were ambiguous at best, and they became even more so over the course of the 1950s. Class-based categories were promoted next to more blurred categories of someone with "historical questions" or a "backward political attitude." Class and family background, political views and activities, past records, and contacts with capitalists were all examined by the state to determine whether a subject belonged to the people or to the enemies.

Over time a scaled genre of law was created that produced and counted on gradations of rights. Multiple criteria were established for inclusion and for sliding scales of basic rights. This required constant judicial reassessments of who was outside and who was within the people and frequent redrawings of the categories of subject and citizen, fostering elaborate nomenclatures that distinguished between Rightists, counterrevolutionaries, landlords, intellectuals, and the bourgeoisie. In the end, complex scales of differentiation and affiliation were produced that, although fundamentally based on a binary distinction, often exceeded clear divisions. There was constant uncertainty about who actually belonged to the category of the enemy and who could really feel safe as a member of the people.

Political and legal matters became over-determined and over-written by the perceived need to police and guard the binary distinction between friend and foe. This allowed the state and its agencies to declare provisional impositions of states of emergencies and temporarily to suspend "the right to have rights" for certain groups, as Hannah Arendt once put it. The socialist Chinese state operated as a state of exception that vigilantly produced exceptions to its principles and exceptions to its laws. Carl Schmitt has defined absolute sovereign power not as the monopoly to sanction or to rule, but as the right to decide when and for whom laws are suspended and when and for whom they are not.

Overall, these discourses and practices of exclusion and exception allowed the state to enlist its own citizens to fight against the enemies within, to police themselves, and to protect the socialist order. The socialist project was designed to defend society against its enemies within. The question of loyalty or betrayal began to override concerns of transparence, accountability, and justice, opening the way for violent excesses that were conducted and permitted by the state. The

discourse of struggle produced disenfranchisements, persecutions, and intern-
ments; it ultimately also justified the liquidation of those deemed uncorrectable
or dangerous to socialism. Hence the notion that socialism must be defended
condoned a moral right to annihilate those outside.

People's Tribunals and Revolutionary Justice

In the 1950s the most important lever of the new government for wielding
state power against enemies was the so-called people's tribunal. Tribunals existed
alongside the formal people's courts, but they were ad hoc in nature and lasted
only during the duration of a given campaign.[9] The introduction of the tribunals
first took place in the context of the 1950 Land Reform movement. The tribunals
operated under a set of regulations that was made public on July 20, 1950, as the
Organic Regulations of the People's Tribunals.[10] The tribunals were formed by
people's governments at the provincial level or above and they were dissolved
upon completion of their tasks. Their main task was "the employment of judicial
procedure for the punishment of local despots, bandits, special agents, counter-
revolutionaries, and criminals who violate the laws and orders pertaining
to agrarian reform. . . ."[11] The tribunals were allowed to make arrests, detain sus-
pects, and pass sentences extending from imprisonment to the death penalty.[12]
The members of the tribunals mostly came from the local party organizations.
Thereafter, many were appointed to the regular courts on the grounds that they
had received judicial training through their work on the tribunals.

People's tribunals used "mass line" devices, such as mass trials or accusation
meetings, in order to dispense justice. In particular, three formats were widely
used by the tribunals: "accusation meetings" (*kongsu hui*), "big meetings to
announce the sentence" (*xuanpan dahui*), and "mass trials" (*gongshen*).[13] Each
of these could involve up to tens of thousands of people. They were organized
in ways that would best mobilize the population and educate it through negative
example and the deterrent of public punishment. Bypassing the formal court system, "people's tribunals," in cooperation with public security organs and party
organizations, often carried out massive purges. Between 1950 and 1953, in the
context of the nationwide campaigns and movements, several social groups were
singled out and isolated from the rest of society: landlords (the Land Reform
movement, 1950–52), counter-revolutionaries (the Campaign to Suppress Counter-
revolutionaries, 1950–51), corrupt bureaucrats (the Three-Anti Campaign:
anti-corruption, anti-waste, and anti-bureaucratism, 1952), capitalists and private
entrepreneurs (the Five-Anti Campaign, 1952: anti-bribery, anti-tax evasion,
anti-fraud, anti-theft of state property, anti-leakage of state economic secrets),
and the educational sector and intellectuals more generally (the Thought Reform

Campaign, 1951–52). Although these campaigns differed in scope and intensity, they all saw the deployment of tribunals as the main vehicles to deal with the target groups. Campaigns were also carried out in the latter half of the 1950s. The *Sufan* campaign ("Cleaning out the Counter-Revolutionaries") was launched in 1955, followed by and partly overlapping with the Anti-Rightist movement in 1957–58 and the "little leap" in 1960. These smaller campaigns were mainly conducted in factories, residential units, and government agencies.

The following example demonstrates the course of an "accusation meeting" held during the "Campaign to Suppress Counter-Revolutionaries" (*zhenfan yundong*). The Beijing Municipal People's Government held a huge public meeting for the accusation of counter-revolutionaries on May 20, 1951. Addressing the aroused crowd, Luo Ruiqing, minister of public security, suggested that some 220 criminals of the 500 or so accused persons be sentenced to death. His speech was followed by a speech by Mayor Peng Zhen, who wrapped up the process by saying:

> People's Representatives! Comrades! We have all heard the report given by Minister Luo and the accusations of the aggrieved parties. What shall we do to these vicious and truculent despots, bandits, traitors, and special service agents? What shall we do to this pack of wild animals? ["Shoot them to death!" the people at the meeting shouted.] Right, they should be shot. If they were not to be shot, there would be no justice.... We shall exterminate all these despots, bandits, traitors, and special service agents. We shall shoot as many of them as can be found. [Loud applause and loud shouts of slogans: "We support the people's government! We support Mayor Peng."] The other day, the Public Security Bureau transferred the results of its investigation to the Municipal Consultation Committee for discussion. Today those results were further discussed by all of you. You have expressed your unanimous opinion on that matter. After the meeting, we shall hand over the cases to the Military Court of the Municipal Military Control Committee to be convicted. Tomorrow, conviction; the day after tomorrow, execution. [Loud applause and loud shouts.]
>
> The present accused only represent a part of the counter-revolutionaries. There is still a group being kept in jail. Moreover, there are not a few who are concealing themselves in Peking. All the people of the municipality should rise and cooperate with the public security organs to liquidate and exterminate them [loud applause].[14]

Carefully arranged and organized as they were, mass trials and accusatory meetings were staged, meticulously prearranged shows that followed clear patterns. Dramatic devices such as staging, props, working scripts, agitators, and dramatic peaks were used to make the mass trials more efficient in engaging the emotions of the audience, stirring up resentment against the targeted groups, and mobilizing the audience into support for the regime. Those who served as material witnesses were not only exhaustively instructed or trained as to what to say and when, they were also equally carefully chosen for the degree to which they would be suited to attract the sympathies of the audience. Therefore, the organizers preferred to involve as witnesses and accusers the very old, the very young, or women, all of whom would testify in front of the masses and speak about their grievances. The close and direct participation of the masses in this process was also carefully rehearsed. The masses would not only watch the events, like the one described above; instead, the main purpose was to engage them and stimulate active participation. They would be "stirred up" (*fadong qunzhong*) whereby they were invited to play a vicarious role in the policy imposed by the state, thus collectively reaffirming popular state legitimacy.

The numerous trials and campaigns drew in people from all sectors of society, mobilizing the rank and file of cadres and rallying them behind government-sponsored objectives.[15] As in most villages, mass trials and accusation meetings were held in most urban areas. Through the organization of such events, the government deliberately tried to rally popular support behind the regime, extend the coercive formal and informal instruments of the revolutionary state, and vertically integrate and enhance the rule of the bureaucracy.[16] By conducting mass campaigns in the early 1950s, the government's goal was to end potential opposition, pacify the country, and win compliance and support from the populace. Significant personal and financial resources were set aside for these high-priority campaigns of the regime.

In the course of the movements in the early 1950s, according to official statistics an estimated 4 to 5 million arrests were made by the police, the army, or party organs without any real involvement of the regular courts.[17] Hundreds of thousands of "class enemies" or "enemies of the people" were sentenced to death and executed. After mass trials, the death penalty was carried out immediately or on the next day.[18] Most executions were public. The public display of excessive violence had a profound impact on society; it showed unequivocally what "class struggle" ultimately entailed. Many more suspected enemies were sentenced to imprisonment by irregular ad-hoc courts, the army, or the police.[19] Opponents and real or suspected enemies were subjected to a regime of violence and terror. The Chinese Communist Party proved to be ready to employ violence and terror against its own nationals, and, if deemed necessary, to substantially alter or pass over key provisions of the fragile socialist law and regulations at any time of its own choosing.

However, the scope of the arrests and executions and the willingness of local cadres to participate in the movement seemed to have taken the leadership by surprise. During the longer movements like the Land Reform movement and the

Campaign to Suppress Counter-Revolutionaries, as more blood was spilled on the execution grounds, urgent appeals by the central leadership to local units to exercise restraint increased.[20] The movements were apparently used by many local actors (cadres and militia) to settle old scores with neighbors and to decide long-term local conflicts.

It was incumbent on the central state to win over the leading local and municipal cadres upon whom it relied to implement its directives. Campaigns, mass trials, and people's tribunals played a very important role in the imposition and enforcement of the norms set by the central government. By bypassing the formal justice system, they provided the central state with a forceful set of ideological incentives and means of coercion to elicit compliance and responsiveness from low-level cadres and officials as well as from the broad population. Although the judicial system continued to serve as the organizational core of the sanctioning process, the mass trials and mass campaigns functioned as flexible and informal mechanisms for the effective, direct, and rapid transmission of socio-political norms and the mustering of broad popular support for these norms and their enforcement.

Displacement and Labor Reform

Tribunals, work and residential committees, and public security organs were very successful in carrying out the campaigns in the 1950s and 1960s. Millions of Chinese were rounded up during the campaigns. As we have seen above, some faced immediate execution, but most were deported to remote regions for forced labor. Only a few months after the founding of the PRC, the prisons were already severely overcrowded. Soon the regime was confronted with the challenge of how to handle the huge number of people labeled as enemies and suspected of being hostile to the socialist cause. The answer was to build up an extensive labor camp system.

In May 1951 a foundation for the labor camp system was established. For the first time, the Third National Conference on Public Security held at that time systematically discussed treatment of prisoners and what to do with those arrested.[21] Illustrating its importance, many important members of the leadership attended the conference. Among others, Liu Shaoqi gave a keynote speech, Peng Zhen delivered comments, and Mao Zedong personally revised the final resolution of the conference.[22]

In his address, Liu Shaoqi pointed out the significance of the problem. He told the conference that a solution to accommodate the large number of prisoners was urgently needed. Ways had to be found for the prisoners to be guarded, organized, reformed, and, if necessary, punished.[23] He proposed that instead of the Ministry of Justice, the Ministry of Public Security should be charged with running the prisons. Furthermore, Liu suggested organizing the camps in such a way that the prisoners would be given incentives to comply with the rules and to engage earnestly in labor. Those who worked would be rewarded: "If one works well, give him a little reward or give him a little pay. Give him small things like cigarettes, meat, or soap in order to heighten his activity." Liu also referred to the benefits of prison labor for the national economy: "If we handle this matter well, it has many benefits. This is a work force numbering XXX people [deleted in the text], as much as the whole workforce of a Bulgaria, [this workforce] does not need insurance or wages; it can do a lot of work and can build great things. In the Soviet Union, prisoners were used to build several canals. If we do this well, there are economic and political benefits. Because we didn't kill them, we can let them work and possibly they will at some time in the future turn into good people [hao ren]."[24]

The May 15, 1951, resolution was a crucial document that determined the basic organization of the work through labor system (laogai).[25] The most important issue discussed was supervision of the prison sector. The conference approved that in the future the Ministry of Public Security instead of the Ministry of Justice would oversee the entire prison sector. The resolution also contained detailed regulations that mapped out the internal structure of the laogai.[26] Convicts sentenced to five years or more would be organized into detachments (dadui) that were administered by laogai organs at the provincial level. Major production and construction projects, which were drafted in accordance with the need for national reconstruction, in the future would be assigned to laogai detachments. In organizational terms, the laogai detachments (laogai dadui) were tantamount to large labor camps; they formed the backbone of the laogai system.[27] Convicts sentenced to more than one year but less than five years were to be sent to smaller prisons or detention centers administered by special districts or counties. They would remain in the vicinity of their homes and be under the control of the local authorities. Convicts sentenced to prison terms of less than one year would work under surveillance (guanzhi) and remain in their units and homes. Apart from labor and production, it was stressed that the camps would organize educational measures in order to re-educate the criminals. Education in the laogai would entail political, ideological, and cultural education as well as hygienic education. Good performance in regard to thought reform and labor was to be rewarded with privileges up to parole, whereas insurgent behavior was to be punished, the most severe punishment being an extension of the prison term.

Finally, the resolution called for the creation of a special administration in charge of the labor camps. The public security organs were called upon to open special bureaus for the administration of the *laogai* and prison facilities. The provinces and large cities were to assign twenty to thirty officials to the *laogai* bureaus, the districts, five to ten, and the counties, two to three. The regulations concerning the administrative structure are quite remarkable, in particular when compared with those in the Soviet Union. The Chinese leadership obviously did not want to create a separate, central administration for the *laogai*, which was the system in place in the Soviet Union. Large *laogai* divisions or *laogai* camps came to be governed by the provincial public security bureaus and not by any central agency in Beijing. Whereas a central agency for the corrective labor camps in Moscow (the Gulag) was in charge of all camps,[28] the Public Security Ministry in Beijing did not have direct control over *laogai* institutions. Apart from a few inter-provincial infrastructure projects, the "eleventh department" (*shiyi ju*) of the ministry had limited tasks: it mainly drafted rules, regulations, and handbooks for use in the camps. The day-to-day operations of the camps were supervised by the provincial public security bureaus.[29]

Beginning in May 1951, the establishment of the *laogai* system began on a large scale. In order to coordinate *laogai* policy, the central government organized joint administrative committees staffed by different departments, such as public security, finance, water works, public construction, heavy industry, and railways at various branches and levels of the administration. The committees were to implement concrete steps for setting up the *laogai* institutions. An important issue that was discussed at committee meetings was related to the contributions of the *laogai* to the national economy. From the very beginning there was general agreement among the leadership that the *laogai* institutions should take over important economic functions within the project of national reconstruction. The central government viewed the deployment of *laogai* in water control works (Yellow River, Huai River), canal construction, and railway construction as particularly appropriate. The party also urged local authorities to find ways to quickly transfer large numbers of prisoners to the newly founded *laogai* institutions so that the *laogai* detachments would have sufficient workers and could commence operations without further delay. A few months later, at the September 1951 Fourth National Congress on Public Security, the question of imprisonment was discussed in detail.[30] In his report, Minister Luo Ruiqing stressed the task of reforming counter-revolutionaries. Labor and politics, punishment and education had to be combined in the processes of the *laogai*. Despite Luo's emphasis on re-education, the final resolution of the congress primarily focused on the organization of labor in the camps. It is thus obvious that from the very outset, there was tension over whether to place priority on labor or on re-education within the *laogai* system. Despite a lip-service commitment to re-education, prison labor and prison production in the early 1950s appear to have been most important for the leadership.

The initiatives from the central government soon produced tangible results. By June 1952, 62 percent of all inmates were engaged in labor. Prison labor quickly became an essential and indispensable economic force. At large construction sites, the deployment of prison labor made it possible for the government to slash the civilian workforce by about 80,000 workers. Apart from the use of *laogai* in the infrastructure projects that were coordinated and managed by Beijing, many provincial *laogai* facilities were agricultural farms. By 1952, there was a total of 640 *laogai* farms, fifty-six of which were larger camps holding more than one thousand prisoners. On a slightly smaller scale, there were also mining operations and kilns: 217 *laogai* units were involved in the industrial sector and 160 of these were operations that had more than one hundred prisoners; twenty-nine had more than 500 prisoners.[31] At the time, the government was also operating at least 857 stationary *laogai* camps. This number does not include the mobile camps used for the construction of railways and canals.

The implementation of the First Five-Year Plan, which formally covered the years 1953 to 1957, provided an opportunity to fully utilize prison labor for the task of national construction on a countrywide scale. The goal was to make maximum economic use of the *laogai* system. By 1954, the number of *laogai* facilities had grown exponentially; the central government could count a total of 4,671 *laogai* units. Many of these were relatively small units, run by county governments or local cadres. More than 83 percent of all prisoners were now engaged in forced labor: 40 percent of the *laogai* inmates were working on agricultural farms, 34 percent in industrial operations such as mining and heavy industry, and 20 percent in canal and railway construction sites.

The founding phase of the *laogai* was consummated by promulgation of the "Statute on Reform through Labor in the Chinese People's Republic" on August 26, 1954. The text of the statute was presumably drafted with the help of Soviet advisers. Its language suggests that the drafters were primarily interested in technical issues and organizational questions.[32] Only the first two articles of the statute deal with questions of a more principal nature. Article 1 articulates the purpose of the *laogai*: to "punish counter-revolutionaries and other criminal offenders and re-educate them into new persons through labor."[33] As Article 2 makes clear, all *laogai* institutions were regarded as "one of the instruments of the people's democratic dictatorship." This explanation of *laogai* as an instrument of the people's democratic dictatorship is a significant statement. In his 1949 speech, Mao explained democratic dictatorship as the rule of the people (that is, an alliance of workers and peasants) over the counter-revolutionary classes.[34] To exercise dictatorship over internal enemies is, as he continued to say at that time, a prerequisite for securing the victory of the revolution. It follows that the *laogai* were regarded as the state's main instrument for dealing with socialist China's assumed or real enemies. The democratic dictatorship of the people was a weapon to deal with the enemy so as to ensure that the people's government would not be overthrown. At stake was not justice or legal punishment, but victory of the revolution. This emphasis on dictatorship and class struggle as established in Article 2 carries an open connotation of being at war and thus vindicates the use of violence. As Minister Luo Ruiqing explained, this strategy was an "effective way to eradicate counter-revolutionary activities and all criminal offenses."[35]

Perhaps the most controversial paragraph in the statute was Article 62.[36] This article ruled that after completing their prison terms, those prisoners wishing to remain in the camps, or who had no residential registration and no prospect of finding work, or who were living in sparsely populated areas where their settlement was possible, should continue to be employed by the labor camps. In short, the paragraph said that under certain conditions, the prisoners had to remain in the camps even after serving their sentences. Most prisoners lost their residential registrations once they were sentenced, most inmates no longer had a home or work. Although the article was vague, it provided the basis for the so-called job placement system (*jiu ye*) for prisoners who had completed their terms. Released convicts were placed in jobs and residential units in or near the labor camps where they had just completed their prison terms.[37] Their official designation was "job placement personnel" (*jiuye renyuan*), but colloquially they were called "free convicts" (*ziyou fan*). In fact, most prisoners who were officially released after completion of their terms were still retained in the camps as free convicts for an indefinite period of time.[38] This was one of the main features of the *laogai* before 1978: only a very few inmates were ever able to return to their homes and resume their civilian lives. The number of "free convicts" grew continuously and, in some institutions, the job placement personnel even formed a majority. Although the job placement system formally existed alongside the *laogai* system, it has to be seen as an extension of the *laogai*. It is evident that political, economic, and security considerations led the authorities to adopt the general policy of "keeping more, releasing less" (*duoliu, shaofang*).[39] This policy was tantamount to deporting groups of the civilian population that were considered to be enemies. It also prioritized the general economic demands of the system over specific demands for reform and re-education. The *laogai* had a constantly growing workforce at its disposal; at the same time, it made sure that the counter-revolutionaries and other enemies would never again represent a threat to socialist China. This points to another remarkable inconsistency within official *laogai* theory. The entire *laogai* was officially praised for being able to reform and re-educate offenders, yet only a very few of these offenders were ever accepted as having been fully reformed.

The rapid and often uncoordinated establishment of *laogai* institutions in the early 1950s created a scattered and unprofitable system.[40] After 1955 the central government decided to rein in and encourage the provincial authorities to merge the existing smaller *laogai* camps and units. Nearly all the institutions that were created after 1955 were huge camp operations, with a capacity to hold tens of thousands of prisoners. In 1955, the number of *laogai* units, which previously had hovered around 4,600, was significantly reduced to 2,700. Two years later, in 1957, the Eleventh Bureau of the Public Security Ministry reported another slash of 700 facilities, bringing the total number down to about 2,000; 1,323 of these were industrial enterprises, 619 were agricultural farms, and 71 were engaged in infrastructure projects.[41] As can be seen from these numbers, within a few years the center of gravity clearly shifted away from agriculture to industry.

During the 1955–58 period, the labor camp system became an ever more important economic asset. It was quite bluntly stated that prisoners had the duty to produce "material riches" in exchange for the forgiveness of the collective.[42] Party and government stressed that offenders under socialism had an obligation to contribute to national construction. Although prison labor theoretically was regarded as a means of re-education, above all the leadership valued it as a significant economic resource that the state could not afford to waste. The benefits of forced labor were multifold: by gradually turning the camps into self-sufficient farms and factories, the central government could reduce its expenditures on the camps and prisons. At the same time, the *laogai* labor force became almost indispensable to the sustained implementation and consummation of large-scale ambitious construction projects that were regarded as symbolic hallmarks demonstrating the achievements of a socialist society. Forced labor took over important functions for huge infrastructure projects; it was systematically used as a replacement for work that civilian workers considered to be too dangerous or too hard. The cultivation of wastelands, the basic construction work for railways and canals, and the digging of shafts and galleries for mines were regularly assigned to the *laogai* workforce. Only after the most strenuous and most hazardous preparatory work was completed would the government bring in the vanguard of Chinese communism—the workers.

The total number of prisoners at the end of the 1950s is unknown. The 4 million prisoners in the early 1950s mentioned in official statements by leading CCP members seems credible. By the end of the 1950s official statements repeatedly mention the existence of 2,000 camps. Some of these camps held 20,000, 30,000, or even 40,000 prisoners, others only several thousand. Assuming an average of 10,000 prisoners per camp, it seems plausible to estimate that China had at least about 20 million prisoners in labor camps around 1960.[43] But this is just the tip of the iceberg. Only prisoners sentenced to more than five years were sent to *laogai* camps. Prisoners with shorter terms were placed under surveillance or sent to prisons, detention centers, and labor re-education camps (for terms from one to three years) (*laojiao*). These institutions are not included in the number of camps mentioned above. The number of short-term prisoners (sentenced in a simple procedure by the police rather than by the courts or tribunals) is presumably higher than the number of convicts sent to the *laogai* camps.

Despite a continuous enlargement of the labor camp system, the government faced daunting difficulties in accommodating and feeding the millions of prisoners. The situation was exacerbated by the unwillingness of the public security organs to make expenditures for the camps. On the contrary, the central authorities demanded profitable operations and budget surpluses. Prisoners not only had to build the barracks and fences that would hold them, they also had to work long hours (12–14 hours a day) to achieve ambitious production goals. Food rations were set in relation to work quotas. Prisoners who failed to achieve daily work quotas received less food. These factors gave way to inhumane and miserable conditions in the camps. Exhaustion, hunger, diseases, and unsanitary living conditions caused rampant diseases among prisoners and drastically shortened life expectancies. Death rates were staggeringly high. It has been estimated that the death rates in the camps rose to 10 percent annually during the years from 1959 to 1962. The total number of deaths during these four years was probably around 6 million people.[44] Two million prisoners died during the period from 1949 to 1952 that also witnessed elevated death rates, and 2 million may have died in the calmer period from 1953 to 1958. Altogether at least 10 million victims must have died in the PRC camps and prisons in the course of the 1950s and early 1960s as the result of execution, starvation, abuse, or disease. This number does not include the unknown millions who were executed or killed outside the camps, for instance, during the various campaigns. These numbers may be inaccurate, but we cannot ignore the fact that such estimates clearly point to mass violence and mass killings occurring in China in the 1950s.

Conclusion

The issue of the interaction between law and society in the early years of the PRC has not yet been widely researched. Such interactions underscore not the rise and fall of socialism, but the active and continual process of socialism's making and unmaking. Such research allows us to unpack the black box of Chinese socialism in the 1950s and 1960s. From this perspective, we can see the making of socialism as a policy of dislocation and as complex processes of appropriation, power, and displacement.

The labor camp was the epitome of these intractable developments. The labor camp regime, although seeming to pursue a specific goal, imposed forced labor and programs for re-education in China. But release from the camps was uncertain and depended on the will of the local staff. Since they were rarely given specific sentences, none of the prisoners could know the length of their terms of imprisonment. Moreover, the camps became sites of uncontrolled violence, deprivation, and horrendous mass death. For Giorgio Agamben, when writing about internment and concentration camps in general, the lawlessness of the camps indicates a "state of emergency" or a "state of exception." "In the camp," Agamben writes, "the state of exception, which was essentially a temporary suspension of the rule of law on the basis of a factual state of danger, is now given a permanent spatial arrangement, which as such nevertheless remains outside the normal order."[45] In this space outside of society, all rights, civilized standards, norms, and morals were permanently rescinded. Those interned were stripped of all their attributes and were, according to Agamben, reduced to their "bare lives." With this operation, the Communist state established a space of exception in which it no longer faced limits set by law or public opinion.

Law and politics in socialist China in the 1950s and 1960s were fundamentally based on a series of exceptions and emergencies that also formed the basis for a pervasive spread of violence and terror. However, the trajectory of this violence changed over time. The open and public use of violence in the early 1950s in the course of the mass campaigns and public trials was from 1953 onward superseded by a less public but spatial system that deported, exploited, and exhausted the "enemies of the people" in camps primarily in remote regions. Together these measures and technologies pushed state power in directions not seen in the periods before the revolution. In its continuing assault on the structure of feudal-capitalist authority, the revolutionary leadership was able to score an enormous success. The prerevolutionary social structure dwindled and most opponents and dissidents to the initiatives of party policy were eliminated within the first few years.

For maintaining control and security, the Communist state was fundamentally contingent on the unchecked use of legal suspensions, postponements, and deferrals. As a state of deferral, the emerging legal and political systems managed and produced their own exceptions, which can be easily called scales of legal differentiation, gradations of entitlements, suspension of rights, declarations of emergency in the name of a political campaign, and spaces of exception. Through such deferrals and suspensions the socialist order created new categories of subjects that needed to be relocated to be productive and exploitable, dispossessed to be in line with the new order, disciplined to be independent, re-educated to be human, stripped of the old cultural bearings to be citizens, and coerced to be free. Uncertain standards of jurisdiction and ad-hoc exemptions from law were the defining principles of this system. The PRC operated as a state of exception that vigilantly produced exceptions to its own principles and exceptions to its own laws. We can see this polity as a producer of excepted groups of the population, excepted spaces, and eventually the party's own exception from domestic laws.

ENDNOTES

1. This approach to law, of course, is common to all socialist countries. All socialist countries accepted the Marxist conception of the law and the state as instruments of coercion in the hands of the bourgeoisie and postulated the creation of popular, informal tribunals to administer revolutionary justice.

2. Mao Tse-tung, *Selected Works* (Beijing: Foreign Languages Press, 1967), 4: 445ff.

3. Mao, Zedong, "On the Ten Major Relationships," April 25, 1956, in Michael Y.M. Kau and John K. Leung, eds., *The Writings of Mao Zedong, 1949–1976* (Armonk, NY: M.E. Sharpe, 1992), 2: 57.

4. Ibid., p. 57.

5. Ibid., p. 57.

6. Mao Tse-tung, *Selected Works*, 1: 26–27.

7. See Michael Dutton, *Policing Chinese Politics: A History* (Durham, NC: Duke University Press, 2005), pp. 3ff.

8. Ibid., p. 4.

9. There were several types of campaigns, distinguished by their reach into society and the target groups; see Julia Strauss, "Morality, Coercion and State Building by Campaign in the Early PRC: Regime Consolidation and After, 1949–1956," *The China Quarterly*, no. 188 (December 2006): 891–912. In the following, I focus mainly on two types of campaigns: the great mass campaigns, or *qunzhong yundong*, that took place from 1950 to 1953 and the frequent, more limited campaigns implemented through the bureaucracy that targeted restricted social or occupational groups. Both campaign types deployed tribunals. The tribunals can be traced back to the period of revolutionary struggle when they played a significant role in fighting the enemies of the CCP; see Klaus Mühlhahn, *Criminal Justice in China: A History* (Cambridge, MA: Harvard University Press, 2009).

10. Leng Shao-chuan, *Justice in Communist China* (Dobbs Ferry, NY: Oceana, 1967), pp. 35–39.

11. Ibid., p. 36.

12. Sentences exceeding a five-year term of imprisonment required ratification by the provincial government.

13. Amnesty International, *Political Imprisonment in the People's Republic of China* (London: 1978), p. 56.

14. Quote from Henry Wei, *Courts and Police in Communist China to 1952* (Lackland Air Force Base, TX: Human Resources Research Institute, Research Memorandum no. 44, 1955), p. 38. The source is a report in *Renmin zhoubao* (Beijing), June 3, 1951.

15. As Julia Strauss argues with respect to the mass campaigns, an important audience was the "regional and local layers of the revolutionary state." See Julia C. Strauss, "Paternalist Terror: The Campaign to Suppress Counterrevolutionaries and Regime Consolidation in the People's Republic of China, 1950–1953," *Comparative Studies in Society and History*, 44, no. 1 (January 2002): 80–105, at 85.

16. Ibid., p. 97; Yang Kuisong, "Reconsidering the Campaign to Suppress Counter-revolutionaries," *The China Quarterly*, no. 193 (March 2008): 102–121.

17. See Dutton, *Policing Chinese Politics*, p. 167.

18. An example of a mass trial and a mass execution of about 50 landlords during the Land Reform movement is described in Gregory Ruf, *Cadres and Kin: Making a Socialist Village in West China, 1921–1991* (Stanford, CA: Stanford University Press, 1998), pp. 86–87.

19. A total of 800,000 executed counterrevolutionaries is often mentioned in official documents. In 1957 Mao Zedong explained that during the campaign to eliminate counter-revolutionaries between 1950 and 1953 about 700,000 people were killed. During the period from 1954 to 1957, an additional 70,000 people were executed as counterrevolutionaries. Mao admitted that mistakes had been made and innocent people had been killed; see Roderick MacFarquhar, et al., eds., *The Secret Speeches of Chairman Mao: From the Hundred Flowers to the Great Leap Forward* (Cambridge, MA: Council on East Asian Studies, Harvard University, 1989), p. 142. Yang Kuisong, "Reconsidering the Campaign to Suppress Counterrevolutionaries," pp. 120–121, concludes that the actual number of executions was much larger than the officially reported number of 712,000.

20. In spring 1951 Mao Zedong wrote several comments on the "Movement to Suppress and Liquidate Counterrevolutionaries." See Mao Zedong, *The Writings of Mao Zedong*, 1: 176, 180, 181, 189–90, 202. He expressed increasing uneasiness that the movement might get out of control. On May 8, 1951 (Ibid., 1: 189) he argued that only perpetrators who had committed the most severe crimes (murder, rape) should be executed immediately, all others should receive a two-year delay. A few weeks later, on June 15, 1951 (Ibid., 1: 202), he argued that the earlier policy should not be mistaken to be too lenient. In any case, Mao's frequent comments demonstrate the difficulties to control the movement.

21. See Yang Xian'guang, ed., *Laogai faxue cidian* (Juristic Dictionary on Labor Reform) (Chengdu: Sichuan cishu chubanshe, 1989), p. 25.

22. Yang Diansheng and Zhang Jinsang, eds., *Zhongguo tese jianyu zhidu yanjiu* (Studies on the Prison System with Chinese Characteristics) (Beijing: Falü chubanshe, 1999), p. 30.

23. See Cai Yanshu and Lu Junhao, *Laodong gaizao gongzuo gailun* (Concise History of Reform through Labor Work) (Guangdong: Guangdong gaodeng jiaoyu chubanshe, 1988), p. 9. Part of this speech is reprinted in Wang Gengxin, *Mao Zedong laodong gaizao sixiang yanjiu* (Mao Zedong's Thoughts on Labor Reform) (Beijing: Shehui kexue wenxian

chubanshe, 1993), pp. 163–64. In his speech Liu Shaoqi mentioned the total number of prisoners, but in the reprint this information is omitted.

24. See Liu Shaoqi, "Zai disanci quanguo huiyishang de jianghua" (Address to the Third National Conference on Public Security), May 11, 1951, in Wang Gengxin, *Mao Zedong laodong gaizao sixiang yanjiu*, pp. 163–64. Bulgaria had a population of 7.2 million people in 1950. At that time its total workforce was around 4 million people; see Eleanor Wenkart Smollett, "Life Cycle and Career Cycle in Socialist Bulgaria," *Culture*, 9, no. 2 (1989): 61–76. This gives credibility to the estimate of at least 4 million prisoners in 1951 before the establishment of the labor camp system.

25. "Disanci quanguo gong'an huiyi jueyi" (Resolution of the Third National Conference of Public Security), May 15, 1951, in Wang Gengxin, *Mao Zedong laodong gaizao sixiang yanjiu*, p. 162.

26. See Sun Xiaoli, *Zhongguo laodong gaizao zhidu de lilun yu shijian: Lishi yu xianshi* (The Theory and Practice of the Chinese Work through Labor System: History and Reality) (Beijing: Zhengfa daxue chubanshe, 1994), p. 22.

27. See Jean-Luc Domenach, *Chine, l'archipel oublié* (Paris: Fayard, 1992), p. 104.

28. Anne Applebaum, *Gulag: A History* (New York: Doubleday, 2003), pp. 60–72.

29. See Domenach, *Chine, l'archipel oublié*, pp. 146–47.

30. See Yang Xian'guang, *Laogai faxue cidian*, p. 24.

31. Unless otherwise noted, the numbers are all from Sun Xiaoli, *Zhongguo laodong gaizao zhidu*, p. 23. Harry Hongda Wu (*Laogai: The Chinese Gulag* [Boulder, CO: Westview Press, 1992], p. 60) gives similar numbers for the camps. However, his numbers for inmates are much higher.

32. This point is also made by Domenach, *Chine, l'archipel oublié*, pp. 110–12.

33. An English translation is available in Albert P. Blaustein, ed., *Fundamental Legal Documents of Communist China* (South Hackensack, NJ: F.B. Rothman, 1962), pp. 215–21.

34. See Mao Zedong, *Selected Works*, 4: 420.

35. Gong'anbu, ed., *Luo Ruiqing lun gong'an gongzuo 1949–1959* (Luo Ruiqing on Public Security Work 1949–1959) (Beijing: Qunzhong chubanshe, 1994), p. 233.

36. It seems that Article 62 was controversial within the leadership as well. Luo Ruiqing spent much time discussing the article in his general introduction to the statute. See Gong'anbu, ed., *Luo Ruiqing lun gong'an gongzuo*, p. 23.

37. The article was elaborated on in the "Temporary Disciplinary Methods for Releasing and Job Placement of Labor Reform Prisoners Who Have Completed Their Terms," September. 7, 1954; see Wu, *Laogai*, pp. 13–14 and 108–10; Domenach, *Chine, l'archipel oublié*, pp. 115–16.

38. Only the following group were released: convicts who had served terms of under two years, old and infirm prisoners, CCP cadres and their children, and those whose families were living in the countryside. See Wu, *Laogai*, p. 111.

39. See Ibid.

40. See Domenach, *Chine, l'archipel oublié*, pp. 104–9.

41. See Sun Xiaoli, *Zhongguo laodong gaizao zhidu*, p. 25.

42. See Yang Diansheng and Zhang Jinsang, *Zhongguo tese jianyu zhidu yanjiu*, p. 31.

43. From several witness reports we know, however, of some camps holding up to 40,000 prisoners. For examples, see Mühlhahn, *Criminal Justice in China*, pp. 244–50.

44. See Domenach, *Chine, l'archipel oublié*, pp. 58, 215, 248.

45. Giorgio Agamben, *Homo Sacer: Sovereign Power and Bare Life* (Stanford, CA: Stanford University Press, 1998), p. 169.

WEALTH AND WELL-BEING

12.
A FINE BALANCE:
CHINESE ENTREPRENEURS AND ENTREPRENEURSHIP IN HISTORICAL PERSPECTIVE

ELISABETH KÖLL

In recent years, Chinese entrepreneurs have made headlines in domestic and international media with the impressive success of their businesses that resulted in spectacular gains in personal wealth. Every year the list of Chinese U.S. dollar billionaires grows longer and more substantial by global comparison. At the same time, we also encounter the phenomenon of an increasing number of "businessmen behind bars," famous entrepreneurs arrested or charged with corrupt business practices, bribery, lack of regulatory compliance, and so forth. One of the more recent examples is the indictment and arrest of Huang Guangyu, the CEO of the electronics retail chain Gome, who, as of December 2008, was the wealthiest person in China with a fortune of $6.3 billion. At the end of 2008 he was charged with share price manipulation and bribery of government officials in exchange for the right to list a company on the Hong Kong Stock Exchange in 2004. Huang Guangyu and his wife Du Juan have since been imprisoned by Chinese authorities, their fortune has shrunk, and the company is in serious financial trouble.[1]

Considering that private enterprise in China was virtually abolished in 1956 and private entrepreneurship began its revival only in the wake of the economic reforms of the 1980s and 1990s, the spectacular rise of individual entrepreneurs, their financial success, and the return of descendants from old Chinese business families to the center stage of China's economy in about two decades is truly stunning. The Chinese Communist Party (CCP) allowed private entrepreneurs to become party members in 2001, and a web of complex networks links the political agenda of the government at various administrative and institutional levels with the interests of entrepreneurs and their businesses.[2] The scope and entrenchment of these networks sometimes come to light during the demise of larger-than-life entrepreneurial figures, underscoring the complex, multi-layered relationship between entrepreneurs and government. Understanding the relationship between business and government in China has been and still is crucial to understanding the development of the Chinese political economy, especially in the twentieth and twenty-first centuries. This chapter will provide the broader historical context to the questions of when, how, and why entrepreneurs lose government patronage, and what this might tell us about the political, economic, and cultural contexts of doing business in China, past and present.[3]

The trajectory of private entrepreneurship and the fate of entrepreneurs in China have to be understood against the background of the country's long history of vibrant commercial activities under state supervision. After the suppression of private business during the first thirty years of socialism in the PRC, the transition to market-oriented reforms after 1978 leaves us with the question of the extent to which characteristics from the pre-1949 period continue to shape private entrepreneurial activities in China. Economies around the world, notably in the United States, have had their fair share of entrepreneurs with criminal and corrupt motivations in recent months, yet their demise was primarily brought on by circumstances connected to the global financial crisis. No doubt, the global financial crisis has seriously impacted the fortunes of Chinese businessmen too, but the role of the government in exposing previously tolerated business practices and its refusal to grant bailouts to previously favored entrepreneurs point to the still vulnerable position of entrepreneurs and private entrepreneurship in China.

From the perspective of a business historian, the twentieth century, and in particular the past sixty years of the PRC, provides an amazing canvas to study the emergence, cooption, destruction, and revival of Chinese entrepreneurship and entrepreneurs. The comeback of entrepreneurs and private business in the wake of the economic reforms should not be a surprise to anyone. However, in contrast to the overly optimistic predictions of Chinese entrepreneurs as emerging independent agents of long-term change, I argue that the relationship between government and business today evokes some interesting parallels with institutional structures and socio-political patterns of the pre-1949 period. Whereas private entrepreneurship has made its comeback with China's market reforms, government influence/control over entrepreneurs and their businesses is actually growing, not weakening, particularly in the wake of the global financial crisis.

Entrepreneurs in Late Imperial China

The traditional social order propagated and supported by the Chinese imperial government over centuries is often portrayed as the reason for China's ambivalent position toward entrepreneurs and entrepreneurial activities. In imperial China, i.e., before 1911, power and prestige in Chinese society could be obtained through academic success by passing the multi-tiered government exams and entering the imperial bureaucracy, rather than by showing entrepreneurial talent or economic success. According to the narrow Confucian interpretation which placed merchants at the bottom of the social hierarchy, merchants' activities were considered motivated purely by self-interest and the desire to make profits, at the cost of the people and their livelihood.[4]

Most important, however, for an understanding of the interaction between government and business is the fact that the market as a concept in China's political economy did not exist independent of the state.[5] Although the imperial government exerted control over commerce through strict regulations, including trade monopolies, taxation policies, and close monitoring within urban communities, it refused to promote and regulate private business enterprises and financial organizations.[6] Historians have identified the so-called "brokerage concept of administration," i.e., the use of agents and intermediaries by the imperial state, as a system for interaction between government and the commercial sector.[7] However, rather than portraying the brokerage system as a predatory and purely extractive method by the state to raise funds, we should evaluate the system, at least until the mid-nineteenth century, primarily as a device to regulate the market rather than to raise funds for the state. Unfortunately, the military and financial crises of the late nineteenth century, such as the Taiping rebellion or the Boxer uprising, increasingly turned the system into a fund-raising tool until it became almost exclusively a tax-farming tool by the 1930s.[8]

There is absolutely no doubt that imperial China generated vast numbers of entrepreneurial businessmen running successful commercial enterprises that served the domestic market as well as overseas and border trading networks. Founded on and structured along the lines of lineage and family organization, Chinese enterprises operated with complex managerial hierarchies and perpetuity principles and flourished in locations with good infrastructure, be it coastal, canal- or river-based, and in the late nineteenth century from the security of the treaty ports. However, in the same way as the concept of a market independent of the state did not exist in imperial China, merchants and their commercial enterprises did not exist outside of government control through regulations, trade monopolies, and taxation policies.[9] Yet, the imperial government refused to promote and regulate private business enterprises. Despite the anti-commercial stance and the social disadvantages experienced by the merchant class in imperial China, we know of many very wealthy entrepreneurs from the communities of the Yangzhou salt merchants, the Shanxi long-distance traders, and the maritime merchants in Guangzhou. Large-scale commercial entrepreneurial activities tended to concentrate among businessmen who developed strong identities as groups with specific regional or professional identities, such as the Shanxi bankers or the Huizhou merchants. Family and lineage ties strengthened by land and lineage organization enabled these merchant families engaged in long-distance trade to cope with the insecurities and fluctuations of the market and to enhance their social and political capital.[10] Although these merchant entrepreneurs tried to keep a low profile—not always successfully—in dealing strategically with the state, patronage of the state remained a crucial requirement for doing business in China, particularly for large-scale ventures.[11]

It is true that without institutions for financial transactions sanctioned by the Chinese state, without property rights guaranteed by the state and absent a commercial law code until 1904, and without social clout against the bureaucratic elite, merchants were always in a vulnerable position, prone to official extortion and arbitrary regulations. However, in the Chinese context the institutional void and constant tension between government and private business led to the creation and perfection of informal institutions and networks which became the core factors enabling the impressive economic growth in imperial China. In short, rather than interpreting the lack of commercial legislation and property rights guaranteed by the state as by nature shortcomings of the Chinese economy, we should bear in mind that a sophisticated system of written land contracts and informal associations for dispute resolution and mediation kept Chinese business institutions and entrepreneurs flourishing over centuries.[12]

The last decades of the nineteenth century saw increasing efforts by the imperial state to insert itself into the Chinese economy as an entrepreneur by sponsoring modest projects in the industrial sector. All early industrial enterprises, from textile mills to steamship companies and cement factories, had to be founded as businesses under imperial patronage, even if the majority of the financial investments came from private sources. The resulting enterprise form was called *guandu shangban* (government-sponsored, merchant-managed), implying patronage, conferral of a monopoly, and sometimes a financial investment by an influential provincial government official combined with heavy private financial investment from the merchant promoter who also was in charge of day-to-day operations.[13]

If the monopoly broke down or the official patron lost his position, there was an immediate negative impact on the merchant promoters. As a result, when by the end of the nineteenth century the imperial government suffered from financial difficulties and officials withdrew their financial support and patronage, many of the *guandu shangban* enterprises were handed over to businessmen who originally came from the ranks of the imperial bureaucracy but were then turning themselves into savvy entrepreneurs. One of the most famous examples, Sheng Xuanhuai, managed the China Merchants' Steam Navigation Company which had started as a *guandu shangban* operation under the patronage of the provincial governor-general Zhang Zhidong. When Zhang Zhidong lost his position in disgrace due to the outcome of the Sino-Japanese war of 1895, Sheng Xuanhuai used this power vacuum to gain control over the company and turn it into a private enterprise.[14] Almost every single entrepreneur involved in the state-to-private transformation of these enterprises—Sheng Xuanhuai, Zhang Jian, and Zhou Xuexi to name just a few—were bureaucrats-turned-entrepreneurs with copious experience and contacts in the Chinese imperial administration. Although these officials-turned-entrepreneurs used some of their networks to get their enterprises off the ground, once these businesses became private, their success depended on their financial and managerial skills running large-scale business operations.[15]

The Entrepreneur's Dilemma in the Republican Period

Entrepreneurs in the Republican period benefited from an evolving commercial law, modern financial system, and increasing professionalization in terms of management and production. For the first time, individual Chinese entrepreneurs became famous for their achievements as individual business leaders. In particular, the commercial center of Shanghai produced a large number of industrialists, including Rong Zongjin, the Cotton King, Liu Hongsheng, the Match King, and Wu Yunchu, the MSG King, all of whom became prominent public, and sometimes notorious, figures. Of course, this is not to suggest that informal organizations based on personal or provincial ties among businessmen became irrelevant. For example, entrepreneurs from Zhejiang province dominated the majority of Shanghai's native banks, cotton cloth and yarn mills, and customs brokers, and the Zhejiang group also represented the overwhelming majority of members in the Shanghai General Chamber of Commerce in the early 1920s.[16]

Despite new commercial legislation and improved representation of business interests via chambers of commerce and industry-specific associations, the tensions between business and government interests, compounded by a politically volatile state, continued throughout the Republican period. As Parks Coble has shown, the Shanghai capitalists did not develop into an autonomous political force during the 1920s and 1930s; instead, the Nationalist (Guomindang) government was obsessed "with the problem of political control and was unwilling to allow any class or social group to develop independent power," including the capitalist class.[17]

In response to Chiang Kai-shek's rise to power in 1927, the Shanghai business community and its leaders had to carefully rearrange their political alliances. For example, Liu Hongsheng, the Match King of Shanghai, enjoyed privileges from both sides, the Nationalists and Sun Chuanfang, the regional warlord in control of the lower Yangzi area before Chiang Kai-shek's successful military campaign. When the Shanghai business community began to put its support behind the new Nationalist regime, Liu Hongsheng and entrepreneurs like Yu Qiaqing did not hesitate to renounce their alliance with the Shanghai General Chamber of Commerce, which had previously represented their interests but had a pro-warlord orientation. Instead, Liu and other pro-Nationalist businessmen set up the Shanghai Commercial Federation, which became an informal fund-raising institution for Chiang Kai-shek, to which Liu and other entrepreneurs felt compelled to contribute.[18]

Entrepreneurs walked a fine line to maintain a working relationship with the Nationalists who did not shy away from coercive measures to raise funds from the business community. For example, after he established his new government in Nanjing in May 1927, Chiang Kai-shek ordered the arrest of Rong Zongjing, Shanghai's biggest industrialist in the cotton-spinning business. The reason for this extraordinary step was Chiang Kai-shek's desire to squeeze funds out of prominent bankers and businessmen to support his own political agenda, and to that end Shanghai capitalists from all sectors of the city's economy were forced to purchase bonds issued by the Nationalist Government.[19] At the time, Rong Zongjing headed the Association of Chinese Cotton Mill Owners that had been ordered to pay 0.5 million yuan, but Rong refused to advance the full amount. Although the association came up with the money just before Rong's scheduled arrest, Chiang Kai-shek then justified the warrant with trumped-up political charges. Only intense lobbying efforts through Rong Zongjing's local networks led to the cancellation of his arrest order, and this gesture came with the price of having to buy a large number of government bonds.[20]

The Japanese annexation of Manchuria, the attacks on Shanghai in 1931 and 1932, and the state of impending crisis after 1935 compelled the Nationalist Government to develop and centralize state-owned ordnance and heavy industries.[21] Although war and occupation fostered stronger participation by the Chinese state as entrepreneur in the economy, the fate of Chinese private businessmen became increasingly difficult. Once the Japanese invasion of China began in 1937, Chinese private businessmen had to interact with national political factions as well as with the occupation forces and the physical impact of war. Most entrepreneurs were unable to flee the Japanese advance and move their firms into unoccupied areas in the interior; many lost their enterprises due to war damage or eventually saw them expropriated by the Japanese military authorities.[22] Those entrepreneurs who collaborated with the Japanese or the Wang Jingwei puppet regime lost their lives labeled as traitors after the end of the war. To this end, some business families like the Zhang family controlling the Dasheng textile conglomerate intentionally kept a low profile during the occupation period and handed over their companies' management to managers from outside their networks. This strategic decision allowed them to resume management after 1945 with untainted legitimacy.[23]

The beginning of the Chinese civil war pitched Communists versus Nationalists and exposed entrepreneurs and their families to the question of which side they were on. The Communist advance in the Chinese civil war forced every Chinese entrepreneur to make a life-altering decision: to stay and try to run the business under a socialist government or to leave the country, with or without the business assets. As research by Sherman Cochran has shown, many business families were divided among generations in their political aspirations and sought to devise strategies that would minimize the political and financial risks for their businesses.[24] Some entrepreneurs like Liu Hongsheng supported the Communist cause. After 1949 he began to reunite his family, ordering his sons to return to Shanghai from their abodes in the United States, Taiwan, and Hong Kong. Other entrepreneurs decided on the opposite strategy, like major branches of Rong Zongjing's family that moved during the late 1940s from the mainland to Hong Kong, Taiwan, Southeast Asia, Australia, and the United States. The exodus of these Chinese business families turned into a renewed wave of overseas Chinese entrepreneurship, with a major impact on the development of the destination economies, such as the textile industry in Hong Kong and so forth.[25]

The Undoing of Chinese Entrepreneurship after 1949

In contrast to the Soviet Union, the Chinese government did not replace its entrepreneurs with party cadres immediately after the 1949 revolution.[26] Yet the fate of entrepreneurs staying in mainland China after October 1, 1949 was uncertain, to say the least. Many business families had already been broken apart, and their enterprises had suffered from war damage and the economic chaos of hyperinflation and shortage of raw materials. The new government of the PRC adopted a slow approach to ownership transformation by not immediately expropriating the country's "national capitalists," careful not to alienate right away the entrepreneurial elite who had stayed behind. The term "national capitalists" expressed the party's approval of capitalists, in contrast to the so-called bureaucratic capitalists who had been members of the elite bourgeoisie during the Nationalist period; 2,858 of the latter's firms were socialized right away in 1949. This form of "controlled" capitalism under the direction of the CCP still tolerated small and medium-size private businesses by industrialists and merchants, whereas the new socialist government took charge of the overwhelming majority of the country's heavy industry, power production, railway and transportation systems, as well as banking and trade.[27]

In order to secure the cooperation of prominent entrepreneurs, the government often offered them supervisory positions in the expropriation process of their own companies and other political offices. For example, Zhang Jingli, the nephew of cotton textile industrialist Zhang Jian, supervised the first factory reforms in the Dasheng spinning mills in 1950. As a first step toward transferring ownership to the state, in 1951 the Dasheng business enterprise was restructured into a cooperative under Zhang's supervision. Zhang Jingli became a representative of the CCP and the government, with the explicit mandate to convince other private industrial entrepreneurs of the benefits of nationalization. The Dasheng mills became a state-owned enterprise in 1953.[28]

Some entrepreneurs like Liu Hongsheng genuinely believed in a potential convergence of capitalism and communism during the early 1950s. Entrepreneurs received dividends from the government on the capital investment in the industrial and commercial companies that they once had owned, or received interest on nonredeemable government bonds as compensation. However, these pensions/bonds could not be passed on as inheritance. Patriotism heavily influenced the attitude of those private entrepreneurs who had chosen to stay on the mainland, especially in response to the Korean War. For example, Liu Hongsheng was frightened by the initial success of the Americans in the war and feared an atomic bomb attack on Shanghai. When the Chinese army crossed into North Korea in December 1950, patriotic pride turned him into an active financial donor to and enthusiastic supporter of the war effort in particular and the national political agenda in general.[29]

However, political pressure on private businessmen began to emerge, first with the Three-Anti Campaign (*sanfan*) which, as a mass campaign in 1951, targeted corruption, waste, and obstructionist bureaucracy in offices and enterprises around the country. This campaign allowed the government to gain control over labor and to mobilize workers for an attack on their bosses.[30] This pressure was compounded by the fact that in the first months of 1952 entrepreneurs all over China became targets of the Five-Anti Campaign (*wufan*) against bribery, tax evasion, theft of state assets, cheating on government contracts, and stealing of state economic information. Chinese industrialists and businessmen were denounced by workers, fellow capitalists, and even their own family members. This well-orchestrated campaign, parallel to the rural campaign against landlords, exposed private entrepreneurs in the cities to tremendous psychological pressures and humiliation. For example, in February 1952, 3,000 public meetings were held in Shanghai alone.[31] In addition, businessmen had to open their factories and account books to inspection teams; some were subjected to enormous fines and in many cases were forced to "confess their crimes."[32]

The era of "National Capitalism" came to an end by 1953 when the percentage of private firms in industry, wholesale, and retail trade had declined drastically and whole sectors like transportation came under state ownership.[33] The socialist reconstruction phase of China's economy continued with any still-existing private industrial and commercial firms being reorganized as "joint state-private enterprises" before they were fully nationalized in 1956. By then the private sector of the urban economy ceased to exist, and what little remained of private enterprise was limited to self-employed handicraft workers, petty shopkeepers, and peddlers. According to the PRC's official interpretation, China's socialist revolution in the ownership of production was completed in 1956 and heralded as a great victory for the future industrialization and mechanization of agriculture.[34] With the arrival of the Great Leap Forward and mass collectivization of the rural and urban economies, private property and private entrepreneurship in China lost all their legitimacy.

The scope of the forced decline in private entrepreneurship was drastic: of roughly 8.4 million private businesses in China in 1953, only 160,000 remained at the end of 1956.[35] Although the failure of the Great Leap Forward saw a brief return of a modest level of individual small businesses, the arrival of the Cultural Revolution in 1966 put the final dictum on any still existing private entrepreneurship by labeling it the "rat-tail of capitalism."[36] In line with this political classification, capitalist entrepreneurs (who had already suffered during the Anti-Rightist movement of 1957) suffered once again during the horrendous purges of the Cultural Revolution, which brought enormous personal hardships and humiliation to members of the country's former entrepreneurial elite. Like so many other politically vulnerable groups, the descendants of entrepreneurs such as Zhang Jian, Rong Zongjing, and Liu Hongsheng were now labeled members of the bourgeois, exploitative capitalist class, and they were treated as counter-revolutionaries and enemies of the Chinese state.

The Revival of Entrepreneurship during the Post-1978 and Post-1989 Reforms

Following the end of the Cultural Revolution and Mao's death in 1976, the reforms of 1978 under the leadership of Deng Xiaoping brought a slow and careful opening of the country toward the West. Deng Xiaoping became the "second liberator" of China who recognized the importance of bringing China back into the international economy and again giving private economic initiative a role in its political economy. The revival of the responsibility system, meaning the customary practice of contracting land from the collective or the contracting of specific labor tasks, at the beginning of the rural reforms in the early 1980s served as the initial motor for private business activities, which went hand in hand with the abolition of the people's communes.[37] The reintroduction of private business institutions in terms of ownership and control first appeared in the countryside in the form of Township-Village Enterprises (TVEs), which became the motors for the economic growth of the 1980s.[38]

The slow reintroduction of market principles and new enterprise forms necessitated the revival of the entrepreneurial talent that had been forced into hibernation during the past three decades. The first wave of emerging entrepreneurs in the wake of the 1980s reforms consisted of a wide range of people from within Chinese society, including farmers, returnees from the countryside, and, in particular, women, who took the first steps as private entrepreneurs.[39] By the late 1980s, more and more experts with professional knowledge in engineering and technology—those who had been under severe attack during the Cultural Revolution—entered the private sector and quickly reestablished China's reputation for successful entrepreneurship.

In the spirit of reform and making amends for serious mistreatment in the past, the government also brought descendants of former prominent business families back into the fold of its new agenda. For example, Zhang Jian's grandson, Zhang Xuwu, was appointed vice mayor of Nantong in 1981, vice governor of Jiangsu province in 1983, and vice chairman of the All China Federation of Industry and Commerce in 1993. Another example of the government's use of former business elites is the political rehabilitation of the Rong family. Without restoring the family's former property or financial assets, the government made use of Rong Yiren's business expertise and overseas family connections to benefit economic modernization and national development. Under Deng Xiaoping's directive "to be boldly creative," Rong Yiren founded the China International and Trust Corporation (CITIC) as a state-owned investment company in 1979.[40] Following what looks like a reversed model of the *guandu shangban* enterprises discussed earlier, this time the government provided all the financial investment and the former private entrepreneurs contributed their reputation, capital, and personal networks inside and outside of China. As a reward and symbolic expression of continuing economic reform, the government appointed Rong Yiren to the office of state vice president in 1993, China's highest-ranking official without party membership. When *Forbes* magazine listed Rong Yiren as the richest businessman in China, with a fortune of about US$1.9 billion in CITIC shares in 2000, the nephew of Rong Zongjing, the Cotton King of Republican China, had truly reached the status of a "Red Capitalist."[41]

China's Entrepreneurs in the Twenty-First Century

Different stages of the post-1978 economic reforms generated different expectations for entrepreneurial success in China. Whereas the *"wanyuan hu"* (households with savings of 10,000 yuan) were the success story of the early 1980s, the more aggressively market-oriented economic reforms of the 1990s led to the creation of multi-millionaires and even billionaires. In recent years, the annual listing of China's richest businessmen seems to provide a convenient "wanted list" for government investigations of entrepreneurs for tax evasion or corruption.[42]

Although many of these entrepreneurs flaunt a luxurious lifestyle of conspicuous consumption, the government does not start the investigation just because they are "too rich"; instead, investigations and lawsuits against selected entrepreneurs often serve political ends in factional power struggles within the party at various administrative levels. For example, Shanghai's real estate tycoon Zhou Zhengyi was sentenced to sixteen years in prison on charges of bribery, forging tax receipts, and embezzlement in 2007.[43] However, an important part of the story is the fact that Chen Liangyu, Shanghai's party secretary and a Politburo member, was deeply embroiled in a major real estate scandal connected to Zhou Zhengyi; after losing a power struggle with the leaders in Beijing, Chen was ousted from the city government.[44] The same political angle applies to the arrest of Yang Bin, a Chinese businessman with Dutch citizenship with the sobriquet "the tulip king," who had planned an ambitious 544-acre Dutch village development in Liaoning province. Yang was sentenced to eighteen years in prison in 2003 for defrauding shareholders in Euro-Asia Holdings, a Hong Kong-listed company.[45] To some extent the indictment reflected the Chinese government's wish to demonstrate a serious effort to promote better corporate governance in Chinese firms, especially in light of demands from U.S. and European regulators and investors. However, purely political motives played a more significant role: Yang Bin had inserted himself actively into government affairs in Liaoning province and had tried to establish a free trade zone at China's border with North Korea.[46] Overstepping the line of political engagement accorded to entrepreneurs by the government, Yang was pulled back by the official investigation and lost his financial assets as well as his personal reputation.

Although Yang Bin and Zhou Zhengyi can be considered true start-up entrepreneurs without family pedigree, even entrepreneurs from prominent business families have to be prepared that the Chinese government might withdraw its patronage once the interests of government and entrepreneurs are no longer aligned. For example, Larry Yung, Rong Yiren's son, became chairman of CITIC's arm in Hong Kong, CITIC Pacific Ltd., with the blessing of the PRC government, enabling him to amass a large fortune and high-society lifestyle in Hong Kong. In October 2008, Larry Yung lost US\$1.6 billion for CITIC Pacific due to currency speculation.[47] In a spectacular move, he used his political connections to save the company by persuading CITIC Pacific's state-owned parent company in Beijing, the CITIC group, to cover the losses in exchange for convertible bonds. As a result, the Chinese government de facto bailed out CITIC Pacific in Hong Kong. When the company continued to incur spectacular losses due to bad currency bets, leading to a record-low share price and temporary suspension of trading in CITIC Pacific shares on the Hong Kong Stock Exchange on April 3, 2009, the Beijing government withdrew its patronage and refused another bailout by the state-owned parent company.[48] The government's decision resulted in Larry Yung's resignation from his position as chairman of the board and reorganization of the company's top management. Since the losses of CITIC Pacific as an established Hong Kong company had triggered massive complaints from investors and regulators in Hong Kong, it seems plausible that the Chinese government might have used this opportunity also to lift investor confidence in Chinese companies and Hong Kong's regulatory system during the gloom of the global financial crisis.

The Government-Business Relationship in China: A Fine Balance

Private entrepreneurship was an important factor in the success of China's economic reforms in the 1980s and 1990s, even if we have to take into consideration the enormous complexity and ambiguity of the definition of "private" with regard to ownership and control in Chinese enterprises.[49] Since the takeoff of the market reforms, a flood of biographies of Chinese entrepreneurs has filled the shelves of commercial bookstores, next to popular biographies of Bill Gates and Warren Buffet. In the spirit of the government's reform agenda and approval of private entrepreneurship and wealth accumulation, these hagiographies praise famous entrepreneurs of the early twentieth century, such as Rong Desheng, Zhang Jian, and Wu Yunchu, as "Shanghai Tycoons" and "China's Industrial Magnates" and promote the concepts of a historically conditioned, indigenous Chinese capitalism and entrepreneurship.[50]

Looking at the relationship between government and entrepreneurs from a historical perspective, the similarities surviving the past sixty years are baffling, especially given the trauma of certain periods in PRC history. In the late nineteenth and early twentieth centuries, the Chinese imperial state sponsored the emergence of industrial entrepreneurship under government patronage which, over time and inadvertently, resulted in privatization. As many aspects of management, ownership, and control were not directly addressed by the government, they had to be negotiated by the new managers and owners. During the Republican period, entrepreneurs were forced to cooperate with different political factions and regimes, sometimes under extremely hostile socio-economic conditions. During the first thirty years of the PRC, entrepreneurs slowly lost all their power to negotiate and cooperate with the government as private entrepreneurship was no longer aligned with the party's radical political agenda. The economic reforms and programmatic state capitalism during the second thirty years of the PRC revived private entrepreneurship, with the government setting clear political, economic, and social parameters for individual entrepreneurs and their businesses. Based on these developments, it seems appropriate to argue that the continuity of Chinese entrepreneurship and enterprise forms is not conditioned by culture or Confucianism but by the persistence of the imperial state followed by one-party governments.

When entrepreneurs were officially admitted as members of the Chinese Communist Party in 2001, their cooption presented a novelty in terms of the party's ideological program. However, we should view this measure as a reinforcement of the patronage system. In this context, it is not surprising that Chinese entrepreneurs do not consider party membership as an obstacle and have embraced this opportunity to join the political establishment. However, joining the party is not an absolute insurance against government intervention because as soon as an entrepreneur's business interests are no longer fully aligned with those of the government or challenge the government's authority in any way, political sponsorship is withdrawn. In particular, self-made businessmen without strong political pedigrees and networks may be easy targets for official intervention, as we have seen in the cases of Zhou Zhengyi and Yang Bin.

However, in its efforts to publicly denounce corruption and conspicuous consumption while promoting a more "harmonious society," the government has to be careful how it handles the investigation and punishment of private entrepreneurs, especially when corruption among government officials still presents a huge problem. It is interesting to note that in contrast to the 1990s, public opinion in 2009 concerning arrested multi-millionaires like Huang Guangyu has shifted from scorn for individual corruption to empathy with wealthy entrepreneurs as a group who are targeted by the government. Chinese blog comments like "Brother Hu [China's President Hu Jintao] said money is tight right now, so Little Huang [Gome's Huang Guangyu] must quickly share some" express a general dissatisfaction with the balance of money and political power in China.[51]

The nexus between politics and business in China remains an important ingredient to business success for domestic and foreign enterprises alike. Apart from the question of their future business success, one wonders how Chinese entrepreneurs will carve out their position in relation to the government and the party in the twenty-first century. By the late nineteenth century, the lines between the merchant and gentry classes had become fluid, and the process of China's transformation into a nation-state had been accompanied by a fundamental change in the social status of merchants. In the early twentieth century merchants began assuming new roles as civic leaders in city governance and took on political and social leadership beyond their business interests in organizations like the chambers of commerce.[52] Of course, private entrepreneurs in China were not a homogeneous social group and represented different political opinions. But as Lloyd Eastman states for the 1930s, the entrepreneurs' progress and Westernization in commercial hubs like Shanghai came at the price of their isolation from rural China and the pressing economic and social problems in the countryside.[53]

Perhaps we can draw a parallel here between Chinese entrepreneurs past and present. Today the spectacular wealth and elevated status of many prominent entrepreneurs in urban China are increasingly contrasted in the Chinese media with the poverty and underdevelopment of rural areas in the interior and western regions. It seems that, following the example of their predecessors in the early twentieth century, Chinese entrepreneurs are beginning to pay more attention to philanthropic activities, be it raising funds for victims of the Sichuan earthquake or setting up private foundations.[54] Needless to say, all these philanthropic activities proceed under supervision of the state, representing aligned interests in support of the government's agenda to create a "harmonious society."

In a special report on global entrepreneurship in March 2009, *The Economist* optimistically announced that "as for China's red capitalists, however much they are held back by the party, they in turn are forcing the party to change."[55] This wishful interpretation of entrepreneurs as agents of political change in China seems to persist, especially in the Western media, even though research has amply demonstrated that Chinese entrepreneurs as a diverse group pursue diverse political strategies and are not yet intent on challenging the state by demanding an autonomous position.[56] Quite to the contrary, "they seek to be embedded in the state, and the state in turn has created the institutional means for linking itself with private business interests."[57] However, in the future private entrepreneurs might benefit from recalibrating their status in Chinese society. Their support of social and environmental causes within the parameters set by the government's patronage will benefit society as well as enhance their identity and reputation in the public realm. Last but not least, pursuing philanthropy and greater engagement with society will also aid Chinese private entrepreneurs in their long-term goal of transforming themselves into global business leaders with broader social responsibilities.

ENDNOTES

1. *Financial Times*, "The Vanishing Billionaire," November 29, 2008; Yu Ning and Wang Shanshan, "Gome Hatches Plan to Raise HK$3 Billion," *Caijing*, June 16, 2009, at http://english.caijing.com.cn/2009-06-16/110185157.html (accessed January 1, 2010).

2. Bruce J. Dickson, *Red Capitalists in China: The Party, Private Entrepreneurs, and Prospects for Political Change* (Cambridge: Cambridge University Press, 2003).

3. Due to space constraints, I am not discussing the issue of state entrepreneurship in China.

4. See Lloyd E. Eastman, *Family, Fields, and Ancestors: Constancy and Change in China's Social and Economic History, 1550–1949* (Oxford: Oxford University Press, 1988), pp. 164–65.

5. David Faure, *China and Capitalism: A History of Business Enterprise in Modern China* (Hong Kong: Hong Kong University Press, 2006), pp. 14–15.

6. See, for example, Madeleine Zelin, *The Merchants of Zigong: Industrial Entrepreneurship in Early Modern China* (New York: Columbia University Press, 2005).

7. Eastman, *Family, Fields, and Ancestors*, pp. 130–31; Susan Mann, *Local Merchants and the Chinese Bureaucracy, 1750–1950* (Stanford, CA: Stanford University Press, 1987).

8. Eastman, *Family, Fields, and Ancestors*, pp. 130–31; see also Prasenjit Duara, *Culture, Power, and the State: Rural North China, 1900–1942* (Stanford, CA: Stanford University Press, 1988).

9. R. Bin Wong, *China Transformed: Historical Change and the Limits of European Experience* (Ithaca, NY: Cornell University Press, 1997).

10. Mann, *Local Merchants and the Chinese Bureaucracy*, p. 23.

11. Faure, *China and Capitalism*, pp. 93–94.

12. Ibid.; see also Wong, *China Transformed*.

13. Albert Feuerwerker, "Three Kuan-tu Shang-pan Enterprises," in Albert Feuerwerker, *Studies in the Economic History of Late Imperial China: Handicraft, Modern Industry, and the State* (Ann Arbor: Center for Chinese Studies, University of Michigan, 1995), p. 221.

14. Ibid., pp. 240–41.

15. Elisabeth Köll, *From Cotton Mill to Business Empire: The Emergence of Regional Enterprises in Modern China* (Cambridge, MA: Asia Center, Harvard University, 2003).

16. Parks M. Coble, Jr., *The Shanghai Capitalists and the Nationalist Government, 1927–1937*, 2nd ed. (Cambridge, MA: Council on East Asian Studies, Harvard University, 1986), p. 24.

17. Ibid., p. 11.

18. Kai Yiu Chan, *Business Expansion and Structural Change in Pre-War China: Liu Hongsheng and His Enterprises, 1920–1937* (Hong Kong: Hong Kong University Press, 2006), p. 104.

19. Coble, *The Shanghai Capitalists and the Nationalist Government*, pp. 34–35.

20. Sherman Cochran, *Encountering Chinese Networks: Western, Japanese, and Chinese Corporations in China, 1880–1937* (Berkeley: University of California Press, 2000), pp. 138–39.

21. Morris L. Bian, *The Making of the State Enterprise System in Modern China: The Dynamics of Institutional Change* (Cambridge, MA: Harvard University Press, 2005).

22. Parks M. Coble, *Chinese Capitalists in Japan's New Order: The Occupied Lower Yangzi, 1937–1945* (Berkeley: University of California Press, 2003).

23. Köll, *From Cotton Mill to Business Empire*, pp. 274–77.

24. Sherman Cochran, "Capitalists Choosing Communist China: The Liu Family of Shanghai, 1948-56," in Jeremy Brown and Paul G. Pickowicz, eds., *Dilemmas of Victory: The Early Years of the People's Republic of China* (Cambridge, MA: Harvard University Press, 2007), pp. 359–85.

25. Wong Siu-Lun, *Emigrant Entrepreneurs: Shanghai Industrialists in Hong Kong* (Hong Kong: Oxford University Press, 1988).

26. Willy Kraus, *Private Business in China: Revival Between Ideology and Pragmatism* (Honolulu: University of Hawai'i Press, 1991), p. 50.

27. Ibid., pp. 50–51.

28. Köll, *From Cotton Mill to Business Empire*, p. 277.

29. Cochran, "Capitalists Choosing Communist China," pp. 378–79.

30. Jonathan Spence, *The Search for Modern China*, 2nd ed. (New York: W.W. Norton, 1999), pp. 509–11.

31. Ibid., p. 511.

32. Ibid., pp. 511–12.

33. Kraus, *Private Business in China*, p. 54.

34. Ibid., p. 57.

35. Ibid., p. 59.

36. Ibid., p. 59.

37. Faure, *China and Capitalism*, pp. 66–88.

38. Jean C. Oi and Andrew G. Walder, eds., *Property Rights and Economic Reform in China* (Stanford, CA: Stanford University Press, 1999).

39. By the end of 1986, two-thirds of the 12 million individually licensed entrepreneurs in China were women. See Kraus, *Private Business in China*, pp. 61–62.

40. "Obituary: Rong Yiren," *The Times*, November 1, 2005.

41. *Taipei Times*, October 28, 2005.

42. See the annual listing in the *Hurun Report*, a Web page for Chinese business leaders, at http://www.hurun.net/listen162.aspx (accessed October 23, 2009).

43. Vivian Wai-yin Kwok, "Shanghai's 'First Tycoon' Sentenced to 16 Years," *Forbes*, January 12, 2007, at http://www.forbes.com/2007/12/01/zhou-zhengyi-sentencing-face-cx_vk_1130autofacescan01.html (accessed February 1, 2010).

44. "Scandal in Shanghai," *The Economist*, 368, no. 8337 (August 16, 2003); "China Property Tycoon Gets 16 Years for Graft," November 30, 2007, at http://www.reuters.com/article/newsMaps/idUSPEK35133320071130 (accessed January 1, 2010).

45. "Chinese Success Story Has Twist," *USA Today*, October 15, 2002; "China's 'Orchid King' Gets 18 Years," BBC News, July 14, 2003.

46. Michael Schumann, "The Hermit Kingdom's Bizarre SAR," *Time*, September 30, 2002.

47. "Citic Pacific Chairman Steps Down Amid Investigation," *New York Times*, April 9, 2009; "Citic Pacific's Crisis: More Real Than Rumor," *Caijing*, April 17, 2009, at http://english.caijing.com.cn/2009-04-17/110147678_1.html (accessed March 22, 2010).

48. "Larry Yung to Leave Citic Pacific," *Caijing*, April 8, 2009, at http://english.caijing.com.cn/2009-04-08/110134793.html (accessed March 22, 2010); "CITIC Pacific Chief Quits Amid Currency Probe," April 9, 2009, at http://www.chinadaily.com.cn/china/2009-04/09/content_7660213.htm (accessed January 1, 2010).

49. See the various enterprise examples and institutional arrangements in the volume edited by Oi and Walder, *Property Rights and Economic Reform in China*.

50. On this topic, see Tim Wright, "'The Spiritual Heritage of Chinese Capitalism': Recent Trends in the Historiography of Chinese Enterprise Management," in Jonathan Unger, ed., *Using the Past to Serve the Present: Historiography and Politics in Contemporary China* (Armonk, NY: M.E. Sharpe, 1993), pp. 203–38.

51. See, for example, the Chinese blog postings on ChinaSmack regarding "China's Richest Man and Gome Founder Arrested," November 26, 2008, at http://www.chinasmack.com/stories/china-richest-man-gome-founder-arrested/ (accessed April 15, 2009).

52. Eastman, *Family, Fields, and Ancestors*, pp. 195–96.

53. Ibid., p. 197.

54. "Uncharitable Questions Greet Tycoon's Giveaway," *Financial Times*, October 28, 2009.

55. "The More the Merrier: India and China Are Creating Millions of Entrepreneurs," *The Economist*, 390, no. 8622 (March 14, 2009): 14.

56. See Kellee S. Tsai, *Capitalism without Democracy: The Private Sector in Contemporary China* (Ithaca, NY: Cornell University Press, 2007), see especially ch. 5.

57. Dickson, *Red Capitalists in China*, pp. 84–85.

13.
TURNING AROUND STATE-OWNED ENTERPRISES UNDER CHINA'S POLITICAL BUSINESS MODEL

JEAN OI

The relative ease with which China managed to turn around the rural economy caused some to dub China's reforms as "reform without losers." Reforming China's state-owned enterprises (SOEs) has been a much greater challenge. Tinkering with the system around the edges, trying to change the system by "growing out of the plan," was impossible. To reform the SOEs would challenge the core of China's state socialist system. To increase firm efficiency, cut costs, and make firms internationally competitive China needed to reduce its industrial workforce and end the implicit social contract with the workers who had given their work lives to the state. Ultimately this meant breaking the "iron rice bowl" that guaranteed life-time employment in China's socialist system. Some have argued that to fully reform SOEs China needed to take an even more radical step and move from public to private ownership. Although there was economic merit to these goals, there was a huge political risk for the regime. Would these moves undermine the legitimacy of the CCP and allow it to continue to claim that it was socialist?

For much of the 1980s and into the 1990s, China refused to tackle these difficult issues head-on. Instead, it treaded carefully, trying to achieve economic goals where it could but always letting politics decide how far and how fast the reform would progress. By necessity, China's one-party authoritarian system adopted a political business model whereby growth and development were constrained by politics. Firms were encouraged to increase efficiency and profits, but firms could not simply lay off workers to improve the bottom line. When layoffs were finally implemented, firms had to provide for these workers, either by finding them new jobs or by offering them acceptable severance packages. There was a bankruptcy law but few dared to implement it because no one wanted to close firms and leave workers unemployed. For a long time, firms could not privatize, even when there were private buyers for the SOEs; when they finally were sold, the new owners had to commit to retain all of the firms' workers. The state was constrained by fear of workers' reactions and the potential threat to political stability. Political stability was the watchword. Local officials knew that demonstrations could negate all other accomplishments in their annual performance evaluations. The resulting half-way reform measures necessitated by China's political business model and the problems that developed in China's SOEs are well known. In the mid-1990s the SOEs were doing so poorly that net profits were less than 0.6 percent of GDP.

Many wondered whether reform would ever be possible under China's state socialist system. Critics inside and outside of China have lamented the slowness of SOE reform as either the outcome of a lack of understanding of what is necessary for economic development or a lack of will and/or the rampant corruption in the one-party state. Would the leadership summon the will to take the bitter medicine and thoroughly reform its SOEs? How far could the market reforms go with the state still in control of major industries? Studies abound on the problems that arose in the course of attempting to reform. When layoffs occurred, there were protests by laid-off workers as well as by pensioners who did not get their due after factory resources dried up due to the state's hardening of budget constraints. We have vivid reports of the plight and dislocation of the unemployed and the hardships that families endured as husbands and wives were laid off.

Yet, over the last number of years a surprising turnaround has occurred among China's SOEs, necessitating an update to our picture of China's SOEs. As unlikely as it may have seemed in the late 1990s, China's SOE reform, although slow, by mid-2006 had achieved overall success. The difficult period of layoffs ended by the early 2000s. The bulk of the SOEs had shed their surplus workers either through regular retirement, early retirement, or layoffs. This change is reflected in the indicators of SOE economic performance, which show dramatic economic improvement. The *People's Daily* (March 2, 2009) reports that profits of centrally run SOEs rose from 240.55 billion yuan in 2002 to 996.85 billion yuan in 2007, up an average of 150 billion yuan per year. One should note that the success of China's SOE reforms has been recognized and acknowledged by Western economists.

Reports by the State-owned Assets Supervision and Administration Commission (SASAC), the organization established in the early 2000s to oversee China's SOEs, detail these successes. In 2007 the SASAC reported that profits had reached 4.2 percent of GDP, whereas taxes paid by all SOEs in China registered 1.77 trillion yuan, equal to 34.5 percent of the total national fiscal revenue. Moreover, from 2004 to 2006, SASAC reported that for those firms that are categorized as centrally controlled SOEs the revenue from core businesses increased

78.8 percent, with an average growth rate of 21.4 percent. Total profits increased 40 percent, with an average annual growth rate of 33.8 percent. Moreover, taxes paid increased 96.5 percent, with an average annual growth rate of 25.2 percent. The dramatic growth of China's SOEs also allowed China to boast in 2008 that twenty-six of its state-owned or state-controlled firms had made the *Fortune 500*—fifteen more than in 2002. However, the economic crisis has since taken a toll—profits were down in 2008. On March 2, 2009, the *People's Daily* acknowledged that profits for centrally directed SOEs in 2008 were down 30 percent because of "natural disasters and economic-crisis and policy-induced losses." The 2008 snowstorms and the Sichuan earthquake resulted in a loss of 130 billion yuan. Although there have been setbacks, clearly the SOEs that exist in China today are not Chairman Mao's SOEs. How was this turnaround achieved? How can we explain continued state ownership and/or control along with such dramatic rises in profitability? Below let us briefly outline how China managed to achieve reform in a sector that many had long given up hope could be changed.

Politically Pragmatic Restructuring

China's political business model, although costly and hamstrung in the 1980s and 1990s, allowed the central state and its agents at the local levels to remain key political actors, who could craft strategies adaptable to a wide variety of political and economic constraints. The need to heed to dual constraints, especially political constraints, meant that the overall thrust of the reforms was necessarily slow and often only half-hearted, especially compared to those in the former Soviet Union and Eastern Europe. It was precisely the slowness and half-way measures that caused many to lament the hopelessness of SOE reform. However, in retrospect, this strategy permitted the state to control the speed and the form of restructuring, thus allowing China to meet both its political and economic goals with a minimum of political instability and social dislocation, albeit taking a much longer time to achieve restructuring. China's political business model was politically pragmatic restructuring. It eschewed rapid privatization and endured slow and costly transitional measures, but ultimately allowed tremendous change to take place.

Moreover, the flexibility and variation were necessary because the process of restructuring was decentralized to the city and county level across China. Unlike during the Mao period, there was no cutting with one big knife, requiring uniformity in the institution of the reforms. The central authorities gave a green light to reform, but provided no blueprint for exactly how each firm should be reformed. Nor did the central government provide any resources to the localities to pay the costs of reform—that remained the responsibility of the local levels. But this also was the problem. The localities were often too poor to have the resources to reform—they lacked funds to pay severance or to resettle those workers adversely affected by restructuring. Consequently, the form and speed of restructuring varied according to the political and economic constraints in each locality.

Although one finds tremendous variation in the speed of restructuring and in the methods used by the different localities to buy off workers, one does detect certain patterns that reflect the overall need to delay laying off workers for as long as possible. Instead of rapid privatization, as occurred in Russia or Eastern Europe, the majority of Chinese firms initially were restructured into shareholding cooperatives, allowing the workers to become shareholders. This was done in the hope that the workers would have more incentives to work harder, but it also provided a convenient and immediate source of credit for the firms, especially the poorly performing firms. Privatization was consciously delayed. Moreover, when privatization was finally allowed to occur, the policy only applied to small- and medium-sized firms. The policy was to "grasp the large and let go of the small." There were preconditions to allowing firms to be sold, including small firms. Before an actual sale, the new owners had to agree either to provide acceptable severance packages or to retain all the workers for an agreed amount of time.

Large SOEs did not privatize but they were corporatized, which means that their assets were assessed and their shares were denominated. Some of the shares then were sold to the workers and managers of the firm, but the state often held the controlling shares. In some cases, a former state-owned enterprise could hive off a portion of its assets, the best portion, as a spin-off to form a new, financially attractive entity that would then be listed on the stock market, while the parent firm would remain a state-owned entity. The parent firm would be allowed a much longer time horizon to reform. These various strategies resulted in a complex property rights mix within a single enterprise group.

This double-pronged strategy permitted variation and flexibility to pursue the dual agenda of improving economic efficiency and maintaining political stability. In some cases, a locality would form a corporate group (*jituan*) that would consist of all the enterprises in one sector. The idea was that the stronger, better-performing firms would help turn around the weaker firms. Again, the hope was to save as many firms as possible and keep workers employed for as long as possible. When the big state-owned firms were ready to take the big step and privatize, the process again reflected a decision to create as little dislocation as possible. For a big steel firm with thousands of workers, only a portion of the firm would undergo radical change—not all of the company would undergo reform at the same rate or at the same time. Much like what has happened to GM in the United States, the best assets of a big state firm were spun off to form a new company, often with the hope that the new company would be listed on the stock exchange. But unlike GM, what can be considered the parent company still remained a state-owned enterprise. It is also expected to reform, but it is given a much longer time frame to become profitable. It tries to adopt new measures to increase profitability while it still continues to carry the burden of its former debts—the least productive workers and many of the non-economic costs that characterized China's SOEs, i.e., the work-unit (*danwei*) system that included the funding of schools, hospitals, and other public goods that in the United States are the responsibility of local governments. However, the parent company could benefit from the spinoff as it also held shares in the new firm. China's reform of its SOEs was a phased, state-controlled restructuring that had to serve many different agendas simultaneously.

Explaining the Economic Turnaround

So what has changed? How is it that China's SOEs have been so successful in the last few years? First, the number of firms that are considered SOEs has been greatly reduced. The "letting go of the small" (*fangxiao*) policy succeeded in privatizing a vast number of small- and medium-sized firms. This resulted in a dramatic culling of the SOEs. In the mid-1990s there were 120,000 SOEs; by 2004 there were only 31,750. Obviously, one reason for these greatly improved statistics is that the state got rid of many of its poorest performers. Thus, part of the success reflected in the statistics cited earlier is due to the privatization story.

The watershed year was 1997. Prompted by the Asian financial crisis and the desire to join the WTO, the Fifteenth Communist Party Congress gave a green light for more radical and rapid restructuring. Workers were laid off in large numbers. Bankruptcy became more frequent and firms were closed down. Corporatization and/or privatization increased. Survey data show that the distribution of shareholding also shifted from relatively equal shareholding between managers and workers to more manager buyouts or managers holding much larger stakes in their companies. The data also show that privatization no longer was hampered by the requirement that buyers of their former state-owned firms retain all the former workers.

Whereas privatization explains part of this change, the role of privatization should not be overstated. The first half of China's restructuring strategy—"grasp the large" (*zhuada*)—is essential to understanding the dramatic turnaround of the SOEs. Some have interpreted "grasp the large" to mean that the state takes more control of its large firms. Although that is part of what has been happening, as I will discuss below, "to grasp the large" also encompasses giving preferential treatment to key firms. This strategy reflects the state's decision to focus its energies and resources on strategic sectors, such as energy and telecommunications. The goal of the focus on strategic sectors is to create national champions that can compete internationally. These selected strategic firms have preferential access to resources and they are able to cancel their former debts through a debt equity swap option. Only the large SOEs were allowed to take the radical step of spinning off the best assets from the parent to become a new firm that would be attractive for listing on the domestic or international stock markets.

Aside from their preferential treatment, all SOEs are now able to become more profitable because they are finally able to unburden themselves of the requirement that they pay non-productive costs, such as for schools and hospitals that used to be part and parcel of each work-unit. In many ways, large SOEs during the Mao period were a small society, able and expected to provide a large range of resources and services. The work-unit system was a central part of the iron rice bowl on which workers depended and on which they were made dependent. Unloading these expenses, especially the schools and hospitals, has not come easily as local governments have struggled to operate with their own hard budget constraints. For some SOEs this has occurred only recently as the upper levels of government have intervened to convince local governments to take on the extra costs of what in the United States would be considered public goods and services.

The improved performance of China's remaining SOEs is also due to organizational changes, performance incentives, and more stringent financial oversight. The central state created the SASAC to oversee the most important SOEs—those categorized as central-level SOEs—that currently number less than 150. These firms have been told to streamline and shed their auxiliary businesses to focus on their core businesses. To ensure better management, the SASAC has given managers benchmarks to meet and has toughened incentives, linking pay to performance and position. To get a better grip on firm financials and to ensure that a maximum amount of taxes are paid, SOEs have been forced to centralize their accounting, ending the system whereby a large firm with different branches might have hundreds of different bank accounts. Moreover, starting in 2008 SOEs were required to turn over between 5 and 10 percent of their profits to the state.

Finally, one of the most dramatic changes, and one that might reflect that a new day has come for the SOEs, is the spending of resources on product development—possibly signaling the sustainability of the improved SOE performance. Until the mid-1990s, R&D spending in China was modest, at best. However, according to a recent UNCTAD report, from 1996 to 2000 science and technology expenditures more than doubled. The share of GDP devoted to R&D increased from 0.6 percent to 1 percent. Since 2000 expenditures devoted to R&D have increased even more rapidly. In 2003 such expenditures were 1.13 percent of GDP; by 2007 they were almost 1.5 percent of GDP, putting China ahead of many OECD countries in terms of R&D spending. Again, the resources are focused— more than 70 percent of China's R&D is in the industrial sector and in SOEs or state-controlled enterprises.

Problems and Implications

One should not think that China's SOEs are completely out of the woods. The reforms are by no means complete and problems remain. Some SOEs are still plagued by a surplus of labor. There is also the rampant corruption and the massive inefficiencies that are widely reported in the press and in academic studies.

Moreover, the political constraints that necessitated the political business model have not completely disappeared. In fact, there are signs that they may have become stronger, or at least experienced something of a revival as restructuring accelerated after 1997. The New Left critics have charged that the reforms have gone too far—down the wrong track on an evil road. In summer 2007 a group of seventeen retired senior cadres wrote an open letter to Hu Jintao complaining about the reform. There has been a political backlash due to cadres in some SOEs becoming millionaires overnight through MBOs. Such criticisms led the state to stop, or at least to limit, the MBOs. Most recently, there have been caps on CEO compensation.

It is beyond the scope of this chapter to fully address the reasons for the turnaround in key SOEs and the problems that remain in terms of China's SOE reform. My purpose is to highlight the surprising economic turnaround—a turnaround one might easily miss given the poor performance of state-owned firms only a few years ago. This is a new day for China's SOEs. I do this to underscore the larger theoretical point that emerges from the case of China's state-owned enterprise reform. The recent economic success and turnaround amid continued heavy state involvement and ownership force us to reconsider the major causes of China's earlier poor performance. Is state ownership necessarily a hindrance to profitability and international competitiveness? Although there are many differences, one cannot help but note that the massive problems in the U.S. auto sector suggest that private ownership in a market economy can cause burdens that are in some ways similar to the burdens of China's pre-reform SOEs. What has occurred in both China and the United States should lead us to re-think institutions—in this case, the role and meaning of state ownership. We should not assume that state ownership today is the same as it was during the Mao period or even during the 1980s or the 1990s. We need to understand the operation of state ownership in China today. How is it different from that during the Mao period? The names and forms may be familiar, but how do these institutions actually function in China's new political economy?

14.
HEALTH, SUBJECTIVITY, AND MORAL CHANGE IN CHINA

ARTHUR KLEINMAN

To fully appreciate the immense transformation in China that has occurred in the past sixty years, it is essential to begin with what might be called ground zero in the terms of health, medicine, psychiatry, and moral life. Think back to the late 1940s in China—health conditions were not only abysmal, but shockingly (and despairingly) so. Infant mortality rates, to the best we can assess them, may have stood as high as half of all infants dying within the first year of life. Epidemic diseases were rampant: cholera, plague, tuberculosis, and syphilis. The war with Japan and the subsequent civil war had contributed to the deaths of tens of millions of Chinese and uprooted as many as 200 million. Moreover, there was no functioning health care system. The inequality between rich and poor, urban and rural was vast—China was still the "sick man" of Asia. And psychological and moral conditions were equally devastating. There was profound demoralization, fear, and uncertainty. The everyday moral conditions of life were grim, with widespread infanticide, substance abuse, sexual abuse, and other forms of violence. What was at stake for most people was simply survival, and although the Chinese valuing of endurance was laudable, when pushed to their limits, individuals, families, and communities did whatever it took to survive. This is understandable, but it creates the worst of moral conditions.

The record of communism is filled with dreadful policies and dangerous conditions, such as the Great Leap famine and the Cultural Revolution; yet, surely China in the early twenty-first century represents a vastly different health, psychological, and moral reality. And although much still needs to be improved, such as rebuilding a functional rural health care system and reforming the health care financing system and social security in urban settings, the situation for ordinary Chinese men and women is incomparably improved from that of the past. Hence, this perspective offers a balance to the more critical reviews that result from the continuing political oppression and the absence of democratic reform. This chapter takes a brief look at the history of the Chinese medical system since 1949 and considers the current state of health care and mental-health problems against the backdrop of the ethical and moral shifts in Chinese society toward individualism, materialism, and the quest for meaning that have accompanied the economic boom of the previous decades.

The Era of Radical Collectivization (1949–78)

The situation in 1949 was terrible, shaped by chaos and destruction. The early period of communism restored order and controlled infectious epidemics through the organization of society by providing health services, basic public health interventions, and food security. In its first thirty years, the People's Republic of China (PRC) achieved remarkable gains in health; life expectancy increased from 40 to 70 years.[1] Prostitutes were rehabilitated and trained for legal occupations. Traffic in women and drugs ended. Vaccinations, control of water and sewage, improved nutrition, more adequate housing and clothing—all of these measures stopped the cascade of disease mortality.

Beginning in 1965, Chairman Mao focused specifically on the poor health of rural peasants, decentralizing the medical system and establishing the "barefoot doctor system" in the late 1960s. The model was based on the commune system, which consolidated and collectivized the rural population into organized units that integrated work, family life, and community service. These organizational units were then used for the delivery of health services, most notably through the use of the barefoot doctors. They were trained in basic primary health care, the administration of vaccines, and in triaging patients in further need of medical assistance to the appropriate facility. This model for training lay persons in the delivery of basic primary care services became highly publicized and influential, and eventually it became a model utilized throughout the developing world.[2]

During this period of intensive focus on the development of the rural health care system, medical services were funded through the commune-level Cooperative Medical System, into which members contributed annual fees to pay for pharmaceuticals and coverage for health catastrophes. The government owned all hospitals, imposed strict pricing regulations, and paid hospital physicians according to a fixed salary system.[3] By 1978, there were approximately 1.8 million barefoot doctors and 4.2 million health aides and midwives.[4] In fact, in 1978 Chinese health authorities claimed that smallpox, cholera, plague, and venereal disease had all been eradicated.[5] In addition to the effective network of barefoot doctors, important public health advances were made in the control of infectious disease vectors and sanitation based on what had become a highly centralized public health system.[6] As the commune system began to decline in the late 1970s and land was divided up for privatized cultivation, marking the incipient move toward decentralization and economic reform, so too began the decline of the rural health care system.[7]

The Era of Economic Reforms (1978–Present)

In 1978, we see the beginning of China's growth toward becoming an economic superpower. However, economic success did not lead to unfettered improvements in health for China's population as a whole; instead the past thirty years have been marked by increasing disparities in health and wealth. There are improved health indices and a better life for most, but these gains have not been distributed evenly across Chinese society. For example, the wealthy cities of Beijing and Shanghai raised life expectancy by over four years between 1981 and 2000, but the poor province of Gansu had a rise in life expectancy of only 1.4 years.[8] Moreover, some data under-represent the health disparities between poor and wealthier regions. For example, figures reported in China show that mortality of children under 5 years of age dropped approximately 23 percent in urban areas and 47 percent in rural regions between 1996 and 2004. Yet, when wealthy rural areas are removed, the figure for the remaining poor rural areas decreases to as little as 16 percent.[9] These figures starkly illustrate the impact of the unequal distribution of access to health services and point to the decreasing public expenditures on health, particularly rural public health projects.

China's once-impressive system of rural health care has been allowed to deteriorate, and access to clean drinking water, sanitation, and primary health care services is far more limited in the poor rural areas in comparison to the cities. Tang et al. report that between the years 2000 and 2004, the death rates of children under 5 years of age in wealthy cities was 10 per 1,000, compared to 64 per 1,000 in poor rural regions.[10] Further, they note a trend toward an increased chronic-disease burden among adults,[11] which places the double burden on the rural poor of higher rates of infectious disease and malnutrition in children and higher rates of untreated chronic diseases, and therefore more serious sequalae in rural adults than for their wealthier urban counterparts. Thus, in many respects, the Maoist legacy of rural citizens being conceptualized and treated as second-class members of society remains,[12] particularly as much of the wealth created in the economic boom has been consolidated in urban centers.

Between 1978 and 1999, the central government's contribution to total national health care spending dropped from 32 to 15 percent, and the ability of the central government to reallocate health resources from wealthy to poorer provinces diminished accordingly.[13] Prior to the beginning of the economic reforms in 1978, more than 90 percent of the rural population was covered by the Cooperative Medical Scheme, whereas government and job-based insurance plans covered all but about 14 percent of the urban population through the mid-1980s.[14] Following the dismantling of the commune system, its attendant rural health system deteriorated rapidly and China's population distribution became increasingly urban, with a total population of 1.4 billion, fewer than 782 million of whom were rural residents.[15] (And if rural residents in county towns and migrants to cities are counted as urban, as I believe they should be, then China may be considered mostly urban at this time.) By the early 2000s, only 10 percent of the rural population had health care coverage, and nearly 50 percent of the urban population had no insurance.[16]

One of the main reasons for urban migration has been to seek proximity to health care facilities and wage-labor jobs that enable paying for health services. With the shift in population to urban centers, migrant workers from rural areas seeking new economic opportunities in cities are most at risk for poor health outcomes, and utilization of health services has declined in recent years. For example, due to poor living conditions and lack of access to prenatal care, maternal mortality rates for rural-to-urban migrant women are significantly higher than rates for permanent urban residents.[17]

During a period of immense economic growth, the accessibility and availability of health care for significant segments of the Chinese population actually decreased. Mental and social health indicators show the story of a downside to economic growth—rising rates of depression, suicide, substance abuse, and violence. And the rise of the AIDS epidemic and the reemergence of an epidemic of sexually transmitted diseases, such as gonorrhea and syphilis, illustrate an underside to social change.

Public Health Outcomes Today

Beginning in the early 1980s and continuing today, health care facilities have been decentralized and have moved to fee-for-service payment structures. The government has maintained tight control of routine services in public hospitals and clinics. Drugs and procedures provide a large part of the revenue because of government price regulation of hospital per-diem and clinic registration fees.[18] The result has been over-charging and overuse of drugs, testing, surgeries, and technologies of all kinds. This has created over-consumption; in urban China, greatly increased health care costs and, in rural China, bankruptcies owing to serious health conditions. In fact, from 48 to over 60 percent of health care expenses are paid out of pocket in China[19] and this has had disastrous effects for low-income and middle-class families faced with significant health concerns. Indeed, the chief cause of bankruptcy in rural China is a health catastrophe or serious chronic illness.

When the health system was decentralized, local governments were given the right to collect fees for some public health services, such as restaurant health certifications, and many local health agencies have since focused on these income-generating activities at the expense of public health education efforts.[20] Barefoot doctors, no longer employed by the government, have gone into (unregulated) private practice in droves, earning a living largely from the sale of pharmaceuticals and expensive services.[21] Private clinics and hospitals have emerged that are viewed as superior to public institutions, and corruption among doctors, who have a financial incentive to prescribe expensive drugs and procedures, has been a growing problem, with serious social and ethical consequences in addition to the more readily apparent economic results.

Ethical Consequences of Commercializing Health Care and Poorly Regulated Public Health

Not unlike the situation in the United States, but quite different from the situation in China under collectivism, the era of economic reform has intensified conflicts of interest among physicians and medical institutions. These conflicts reflect the reality that medicine has become a for-profit enterprise and a big business. This is easily seen in the over-prescribing of tests and pharmaceuticals and the over-utilization of high-tech procedures, such as MRIs, that increase the revenue for medical facilities. The emergence of under-the-table payments to care providers is similar to the situation in other sectors of the Chinese economy. These payments directly challenge the professionalization of medicine that has occurred rapidly over the last two decades. The outcome of these changes is poor care, increased distrust, and a lowering of the social status of health care workers. A 2002 household survey indicates that more than 80 percent of the respondents felt that the current free-market system of income distribution in China was unfair, and the same survey found satisfaction with the cost and quality of the health system hovering at or below 50 percent.[22]

Medical ethics has been slow to develop in China, and it has largely developed as a foreign import from the United States, with institutional review boards (IRBs), informed consent, and other procedures the same as those existing in the United States. The late development of medical ethics relates in part to the failure to build a Chinese, or Asian, equivalent to the Nuremburg Code of Ethics that led to multiple ethical advances in the West. Again, this is attributable in part to an inadequate ethical and legal response to Japanese wartime medical atrocities in China. Historical responsibility lies with the United States, Japan, and China, but the absence of the Chinese equivalent of the doctors trial at Nuremburg has led to an absence of an organically evolving, indigenous code of medical ethics.

Parallel to this is the failure of the Chinese legal system to protect the rights of patients. The absence of robust ethical training programs, a medical malpractice system, advanced forensic psychiatry, and the almost-complete inattention to conflicts of interest among hospitals and the pharmaceutical industry have contributed to a vacuum of medical regulations and an absence of consciousness-raising among physicians.

The medical ethics that does exist in China is treated as a foreign implant without real grounding in Chinese society. The Chinese Medical Association goes through the motions of ethical review boards, continuing education programs, and professional ethical standards, but these seem to be a very superficial covering, obfuscating troubling unregulated practices. This can be seen in a number of sectors, from the harvesting of prisoner organs for transplants to the development of largely unregulated, for-profit centers that use untested and unauthorized treatments for Parkinsonism and other neuro-degenerative diseases and advanced cancers. The failure to regulate the safety of drugs is another important issue. All of this takes place in an atmosphere of encouraging medical tourism but without adequate ethical or legal oversight. Although the worst of the abuses in family planning, such as coerced late-term abortions, seem to have been substantially reduced, the public health atmosphere is still one in which ethical and legal limits can be easily breached due to real or perceived threats, such as the national mobilization to control severe acute respiratory syndrome (SARS) and the more recent efforts to contain influenza.[23] I do not mean to overlook the large variety of efforts to advance professionalism and regulation in China, but to emphasize the long way these efforts have yet to go.

Recent Developments in Mental Health

Chinese rates of depression were almost unmeasurably low in the 1970s, but in the 1980s and 1990s, they were somewhat higher, although still low in comparison to the United States.[24] New epidemiology research indicates that rates of mental illness are still higher than previously estimated, which most likely is due to an advance in measurement as well as an increase in the actual rates of disease. Research in China suggests that adverse social changes—including economic losses, high health care costs, weakened family ties, and urban migration—can lead to expected increases in suicide rates, in part due to rising rates of untreated depressive disorders and in part due to increasing pressures on rural women.[25]

Most recently, there has been an increase in depression, suicide, anxiety disorders, and substance abuse associated with the economic boom of the past decade. These increased rates appear to relate to several factors. First, market socialism has increased mental illness for some segments of the population; for example, rural women left behind by men seeking wage labor in cities. Second, China's new middle class has become involved with increased risk-taking, such as experimenting with alcohol, drugs, sexuality, and lifestyle. A twentyfold increase in alcohol-related problems is reported between 1982 and 1998.[26] In particular, the increasingly marginalized Chinese minorities have begun to show the same mental-illness profile as indigenous populations worldwide—high rates of alcohol, drugs, violence, and related conditions.[27] It is still too early to determine the effects of the economic downturn. International data show that increased joblessness leads to increased mental-health problems,[28] so this is what we would expect in China as well.

The Chinese health system is ill-equipped to handle increased numbers of patients with mental-health conditions. There is only one psychiatric bed per 10,000 population and less than one mental-health professional per 100,000. Even given these low service-availability ratios, an estimated 30 percent of inpatient psychiatric hospital beds remained empty as of 2002 because the patients and their families could not afford treatment.[29] Demand for outpatient psychiatric services in urban areas does appear to be on the rise, with the increased popularity of mental-health hotlines and pharmaceuticals among those who can afford them.[30] Traditionally, families preferred to care for mentally ill relatives in the home, out of a sense of filial or familial duty as well as a mechanism for concealment and saving of face. Now, home care may be more the result of economic necessity than a sense of familial loyalty, as familial loyalty has eroded during the economic boom's emphasis on individual achievement and acquisition. Still, the vast majority of Chinese patients with mental-health problems receive neither psychiatric diagnosis nor treatment.

Moral Change

In his classic study of the core values of Chinese society, the great Chinese anthropologist Xiaotong Fei articulated rural values, based on peasant life: reverence for ancestors, prioritizing family ties, deep respect and privileging of the elderly, and the greater importance of interpersonal relationships than the individual self.[31] With the transformation of modern China into an increasingly urban population (especially when counting rural towns as urban) has come the development of an urban youth culture, middle-class lifestyle, and exposure to global culture through travel, the Internet, and material goods. Chinese society is now very different from the one outlined by Fei—hypermaterialist, overly pragmatic, hyperindividualistic, and cynical about values, notably communism, which in turn has further undermined traditional values.

Yunxiang Yan (forthcoming)[32] points to the earliest moves toward a market economy in the late 1970s and early 1980s as the beginnings of an important moral shift in China. After the harvest of 1978, in one village experiment the peasant families could keep whatever they produced beyond their quotas, which was meant to encourage hard work and innovation in cultivation techniques. Not too long thereafter, this practice spread to other villages and then, in 1984, leaders of state-owned enterprises were given more decision-making and management power.[33] From that time onward, China has progressed on a steady path of economic reform toward dominance of the globalized market economy. Along with this transition have come significant shifts in the way Chinese individuals perceive themselves and their relationship to the state. During the era of radical Maoism, individuals owed their lives to the state and the Chinese Communist Party. Conversely, the perception during the era of economic reform increasingly has become that the state owes the individual a good life. Part of that good life includes an emphasis on the material goods now attainable by the growing middle class and individual self-expression.

As highlighted during the 2008 Beijing Olympics, China seems to value a new kind of nationalism that emphasizes its ability to compete and dominate in the increasingly globalized market economy. Along with the ability of its athletes, China demonstrated its power both to produce and to consume—from the impressive facilities and ceremonies engineered for the event to the enjoyment of the festivities by masses of middle-class Chinese citizens. The emergence of a middle class and the shift away from staunch collectivist values increasingly have led to materialism and hyperindividualism. Not only at the level of the global economy, competition has become a central part of Chinese life—individuals compete for jobs, slots in higher education, and the achievement (and display) of wealth. In the past two decades as contacts with other cultures have grown dramatically, markers of status, such as style of dress, car, and so forth, have become increasingly salient and divisive within Chinese society. The rural poor have been left behind economically and socially as wealth has accumulated in urban centers. Collectivist ideals and social structures have deteriorated as individuals began to strive for self-advancement, achievement, and material gain. At both a societal and individual level, this has limited the capacity for empathy, compassion, and commitment to social security and public programming.

Early research shows that the subjectivity (or personhood) of the Chinese was deeply embedded in family and social relationships, to the extent that people were unwilling and unable to express feelings in psychological terms to the extent that people were unwilling and unable to express feelings in psychological terms, and instead used somatic complaints to express psychological troubles.[34] Expressions of self were subdued during the time when radical collectivization emphasized socio-centric presentations of self. In the past decade and a half of increased prosperity and lifestyle change, younger Chinese have become more open with self-expression, demonstrating new subjectivity and greater individuality.[35]

Current youth culture places its primary emphasis on conjugal relations and close friendships and is much more materialistic and pragmatic than previous generations. This is accompanied by a new emphasis on sexuality, with a complete return to prostitution and the widespread use of sex in marketing. Prostitution is once again openly practiced on the streets, in hotels, and through Internet chat sites.[36] In addition, mores have shifted so that premarital sex is the norm and same-sex relationships are prevalent and open. Everett Zhang goes further to build a compelling case linking the sexualization of contemporary Chinese society to the one-child-per-family policy initiated in the late 1970s, which (incidentally) supported the decoupling of sexual pleasure from reproduction.[37] This has had a crucial impact on both the stability of relationships and the traditional family structure.

The popular culture that is corrosive to traditional values is intensified by the widespread sense that government leaders no longer believe in communism nor do they value traditional Confucianism. There is less emphasis on respect for the aged. The elderly are often divested of their power and position in the family, replaced by their economically productive children.[38] The one-child policy has had the effect of placing filial responsibility to care for aging parents on the shoulders of a lone child. The one-child policy was widely (and justly) criticized for inciting female sex-selective abortions and infanticide. However, this may now be having a reverse effect for the valuation of solitary female children, as daughters seem to be continuing to fulfill the traditional filial responsibilities to aging parents more often than solitary sons.[39]

Cynicism surrounding the current state of the Communist Party is fueled by the perception that party leaders are not committed to Communist ideals and also by widespread corruption throughout the Chinese economy, a widening gap of income inequality, and the aforementioned dearth of affordable health care. As the oft-repeated joke goes—"What is communism? The longest road to capitalism." This highlights the dissatisfaction and disillusionment with the value system that has undergirded PRC social and economic policies for the past sixty years. This vacuum in values has led to an intensification of interest in religion, manifested particularly in the revival of Buddhism, Confucianism, and Chinese Christianity.[40] There are now a large number of cults, based on tenets ranging from martial arts to esoteric folk religions. Generally, religious practice is not heavily regulated by the party; however, the Falun Gong was suppressed after it became a political threat and some concerns have arisen over the reenergized religious practice by over 100 million Muslims due to fears of separatist groups, particularly among the Uyghur community near the border with Turkmenistan.

All of these trends indicate a change in value orientation, giving rise to two value problems. First, values have been lost and delegitimized. Second, the new set of values that have emerged—individualism and materialism—do not fit well with socialist ideology or collectivist traditions. However, there is also an optimistic trend toward a broader commitment to humanitarian goals and a societal response to human tragedy, as seen in the aftermath of the Sichuan earthquake through individual volunteerism and truly independent NGOs coupled with the government's rescue and recovery efforts. It is unclear what the long-term moral and ethical consequences of this conflict between contemporary economic and social norms and traditional values will be.

In this era of economic challenge, there is the realization that Chinese leaders cannot politically afford to have a major downturn in prosperity or in the individual prospects currently available to the Chinese population, as this would only further delegitimize their authority. Evidence of protests over corruption and legal protection in rural areas should be seen in two ways: as a sign of serious discontent but the moral protest as a good sign for both society and individuals. First, a society that has opened up to public criticism represents a moral climate in which citizens can stand up for their ethical and moral commitments without fear of sanction or retribution. China has moved only part way toward this goal because there is still police suppression of public protests and dissidents. Second, the opportunity to participate in protests is good for individuals in that it encourages taking an active part in shaping society and enables self-expression. On the negative side, although the middle class receives positive returns from the more open society, the inequalities facing the rural poor have not been adequately addressed. Remarkably, little work has been done about the deep popular resentment over the long term following the disasters of the Great Leap, Cultural Revolution, and the Tiananmen massacre. Many China experts treat these events as though their long-term effect on memory is absent. Moral protest regarding current conditions could lead to protests against the long historical abuses of the rural population. One of the big questions for the future is whether the changing moral climate will encourage expression of the deep discontent that has been diluted, deferred, and obscured by the economic prosperity.

I have explored the implications of ignoring the impacts of some of the tragic events of China's past on the psyches of individual citizens in my book.[41] Through a case study of a man whom I call Yan Zhongshu, a Chinese physician, one of the many Chinese professionals and intellectuals I have interviewed over the past decades, we can begin to see the distrust that was sown among colleagues during the era of radical communism. Yan has maintained feelings of rage toward colleagues who denounced him for minor violations of party policies as well as feelings of guilt surrounding how his own (in)actions resulted in negative outcomes for others. Even after the Maoist-era hospital system under which he worked was dismantled, Yan continued to feel isolated, as though he could not trust others or himself, and he experienced resentment and frustration over the lack of justice for the abuses that he had lived through. The openness of self-expression that is practiced by younger generations of Chinese today and that is increasingly tolerated by the government contrasts sharply with the experience of Dr. Yan who could not adequately convey his bitter feelings of betrayal, regret, criticism, and protest. The wounds experienced by Yan, and no doubt by millions of others, have yet to be satisfactorily examined and repaired on a societal level. The great question is whether one day there will be a bill sent by the Chinese people to the government that demands symbolic and practical repayment of this moral debt.

Conclusion

There are two parallel stories being woven into the fabric of Chinese society today, and it is unclear which will become the dominant narrative of our era. The government has opened many more options for self-determination and expression. On the downside, however, there is a nascent epidemic of social and mental-health problems that is indicative of a challenging moral era. Rather than a return to doctrinaire communism to regain control over public health, the medical system, and social ills, we are far more likely to continue to see a reliance on the possibilities of globalization. The Chinese government, in response to weakening health indicators and increased public concern over the current economic crisis, announced in August 2008 the "Healthy China by 2020" initiative, which promises a rapid return to universal health coverage.[42] It seems, then, that a new balance must be reached between the collectivist values that allowed for the rapid improvements in the overall health of the Chinese population and the individualist, free-market values and practices that launched China to global economic prominence.

On the psychological side, Chinese people today, especially but not only the youth, are far more expressive of both troubling affects and much more positive ones. There is a counseling and psychotherapy "boom" that no one could have predicted a decade ago. And in urban areas certain globally significant terms like "depression" are widely understood and employed by Chinese men and women to describe dysphorias that are no longer accepted as requiring endurance, but rather are seen as general health problems that are appropriate objects of health care. The serious stigma of common mental disorders like depression and anxiety is lessening. Women now complain openly of the negative effects of patriarchy and demand greater equality in everyday life. Urban youth culture has prioritized positive emotions like happiness as part of the middle-class lifestyle, marking a huge psychological shift from the past.

The religious and moral changes I have described speak to a widening quest for meaning in life that is a response to heightened individualism, globalized lifestyles, the development of a civic culture, and the growth of cynicism and materialism. This change potentially has far-reaching significance of a political kind on the demands ordinary Chinese make on their society and the willingness of the Chinese leadership to envision a different kind of citizen with a different set of needs, desires, and capacities. Anthropological and psychiatric studies suggest that in the future these moral, emotional, and religious issues may tell us more about where China is headed than the more established political and economic indices for studying China. Will they also fuel movements of moral resistance and protest that reshape the political landscape of China? After six decades of China studies fostered by the Fairbank Center, the time may have arrived for anthropological, psychiatric, and public health research to reformulate the object of enquiry in China studies around social experience, subjectivity, and on-the-ground value issues that have remade China in our times.

ENDNOTES

1. Shenglan Tang, et al., "Tackling the Challenges to Health Equity in China," *Lancet*, 372, no. 9648 (October 2008): 1493–1501.

2. Everett Yuehong Zhang, "Introduction: China, Incomplete Governmentality," in Everett Yuehong Zhang, Arthur Kleinman, and Weiming Tu, eds., *Governance of Life in Chinese Moral Experience* (New York: Routledge, 2010).

3. David Blumenthal and William Hsiao, "Privatization and Its Discontents: The Evolving Chinese Health Care System," *New England Journal of Medicine*, 353, no. 11 (September 15, 2005): 1165–70.

4. Everett M. Rogers, "Barefoot Doctors," in Committee on Scholarly Communications with the PRC, *Rural Health in the People's Republic of China* (Washington, DC: U.S. Department of Health and Human Services, 1980).

5. Kurt W. Deuschle, "Common Disease Patterns," in Committee on Scholarly Communications with the PRC, *Rural Health in the People's Republic of China.*

6. Blumenthal and Hsiao, "Privatization and Its Discontents."

7. Zhang, "Introduction: China, Incomplete Governmentality."

8. Tang, et al., "Tackling the Challenges to Health Equity in China."

9. Ibid.

10. Ibid.

11. Ibid.

12. Zhang, "Introduction: China, Incomplete Governmentality."

13. Blumenthal and Hsiao, "Privatization and Its Discontents."

14. Tang, et al., "Tackling the Challenges to Health Equity in China."

15. Blumenthal and Hsiao, "Privatization and Its Discontents"; National Bureau of Statistics, *China Statistical Yearbook, 2003* (Beijing: China Statistical Press, 2003).

16. Tang, et al., "Tackling the Challenges to Health Equity in China."

17. Ibid.

18. Blumenthal and Hsiao, "Privatization and Its Discontents."

19. Tang, et al., "Tackling the Challenges to Health Equity in China."

20. Blumenthal and Hsiao, "Privatization and Its Discontents."

21. Ibid.

22. Tang, et al., "Tackling the Challenges to Health Equity in China."

23. Arthur Kleinman and James L. Watson, eds., *SARS in China: Prelude to a Pandemic?* (Stanford, CA: Stanford University Press, 2006); Arthur M. Kleinman, et al., "Introduction: Avian and Pandemic Influenza, A Biosocial Approach," *Journal of Infectious Diseases*, 197, no. 1 Supplement (February 2008): S1–S3.

24. Doris F. Chang and Arthur Kleinman, "Growing Pains: Mental Health Care in a Developing China," *Yale-China Health Studies Journal*, no. 1 (2002): 85–98.

25. Michael R. Phillips, Huaqing Liu, and Yanping Zhang, "Suicide and Social Change in China," *Culture, Medicine, Psychiatry*, 23, no. 1 (March 1999): 25–50; Fei Wu, "Elegy for Luck: Suicide in a County in North China," Ph.D. dissertation, Department of Anthropology, Harvard University, 2005.

26. Wei Hao, et al., "Alcohol Consumption and Alcohol-related Problems: Chinese Experience from Six Area Samples, 1994," *Addiction*, 94, no. 10 (October 1999): 1467–76.

27. Alex Cohen, "The Mental Health of Indigenous Peoples: An International Overview" (Geneva: Department of Mental Health, World Health Organization, 1999), at http://whqlibdoc.who.int/hq/1999/WHO_MNH_NAM_99.1.pdf (accessed February 5, 2010).

28. Vikram Patel and Arthur Kleinman, "Poverty and Common Mental Disorders in Developing Countries," *Bulletin of the World Health Organization*, 81, no. 8 (2003): 609–15.

29. Chang and Kleinman, "Growing Pains: Mental Health Care in a Developing China."

30. Ibid.

31. Gary Hamilton and Wang Zheng, *From the Soil, The Foundations of Chinese Society: A Translation of Fei Xiaotong's* Xiangtu Zhongguo (Berkeley: University of California Press, 1992).

32. Yunxiang Yan, "Introduction: Remaking the Moral Person in Contemporary China," in Arthur Kleinman, et al., eds., *Deep China: What Psychiatry and Anthropology Teach Us About Chinese Society*, forthcoming.

33. Ibid.

34. Arthur Kleinman, *Social Origins of Distress and Disease: Depression, Neurasthenia, and Pain in Modern China* (New Haven, CT: Yale University Press, 1986).

35. Yunxiang Yan, "The Changing Moral Landscape," in Arthur Kleinman, et al., eds., *Deep China*, forthcoming.

36. Everett Yuehong Zhang, "Thirty Years of Change: Sexuality in China," in Arthur Kleinman, et al., eds., *Deep China*, forthcoming.

37. Ibid.

38. Yunxiang Yan, *Private Life under Socialism: Love, Intimacy, and Family Change in a Chinese Village 1949–1999* (Stanford, CA: Stanford University Press, 2003).

39. Lihong Shi, "Embracing a Singleton Daughter: Transforming Reproductive Choice in Rural Northeast China," *Anthropology News*, 50, no. 3 (2009): 15–16.

40. Meir Shahar and Robert P. Weller, eds., *Unruly Gods: Divinity and Society in China* (Honolulu: University of Hawai'i Press, 1996).

41. Arthur Kleinman, *What Really Matters: Living a Moral Life Amidst Uncertainty and Danger* (New York: Oxford University Press, 2006).

42. Andy Coghlan, "World's Largest Health System Rejects Free Market," *New Scientist*, October 20, 2008, at http://www.newscientist.com/article/dn14986-worlds-largest-health-system-rejects-free-market.html (accessed June 29, 2009).

15.
HEALTH CARE REFORMS IN CHINA:
SLOGAN OR SOLUTION?

BARRY R. BLOOM AND YUANLI LIU

There are three things one wants from a health system: provision of disease prevention interventions, access to quality health care, and health security. Despite the recent extraordinary economic gains in China, for many years the health system has met none of these goals. The premise of any health system is that illness can befall anyone and we are all at risk. Thus, it should inevitably be a shared responsibility of everyone to protect those who fall ill in any society. It was the slogan of the revolution "to serve the people" that inspired millions of Chinese to follow Chairman Mao in establishing the People's Republic of China in 1949. However, in the realm of health, the people of China have not been well served during the past thirty some years.

The health care problem of China is complex and deep-seated. But simply stated, in less than twenty years, following the demise of the barefoot doctors during the early phase of the revolution, China's health care system was transformed from one that provided very basic preventive and health care services to most people to one in which vast numbers of people cannot afford basic care and families are driven into poverty.[1]

The least efficient and most expensive way for anyone in any country to pay for health services is out-of-pocket. Out-of-pocket spending in China rose from 20 percent in 1978 to 60 percent in 2002. As demand for health services increased, costs of providing health services increased, and there was no system for coverage of the costs. They clearly needed to be covered somehow, and the result is that providers in China are paid simply on a fee-for-service basis. Consequently, this has resulted in an enormous amount of unnecessary prescribing and testing, opportunities for corruption, and fragmentation of health services.[2] Out-of-pocket payments have soared more than tenfold since 1990. Today, for example, the average cost of a single hospital admission is almost equivalent to China's annual per capita income, and is more than twice the average annual income of the lowest two deciles of the population.[3]

A more equitable and probably more efficient means of providing health services is through some sort of insurance, which is based on pooling risks of large numbers of people to provide care for those who are ill and security for those who are healthy.[4] However, in China only 55 percent of the urban population and 21 percent of the rural population had any health insurance before the inception of the recent health care reforms.

It is not surprising, then, that in 2003 14 percent of urban and 16 percent of rural households incurred catastrophic medical spending. Further, when they were ill, 15 percent of urban residents and 22 percent of rural residents had to forgo needed medical care because they could not pay.[5] Recognition of the urgency to solve these problems was further heightened by the SARS crisis, which helped reveal fundamental deficiencies of China's public health and health care systems.[6]

On April 6, 2009, the Chinese government formally unveiled its health care reform plan. The major goal of the plan is to provide basic insurance coverage for at least 90 percent of the population by 2011 and to establish universal access to health care by 2020.[7] In this chapter, we will first describe the major contents of China's new health care reform program. Then we will analyze some major issues confronting the process of successfully implementing the program.

The New Health Care Reform Program

Responding to the public's mounting demand for policy actions to reform China's broken health care system, as part of President Hu Jintao's "Harmonious Society Program" the State Council Health Care Reform Leading Group, involving fourteen ministries, was established in September 2006.

In an extraordinary gesture, on October 14, 2008 the Chinese government published a draft of its Health Care Reform Plan to solicit comments from the public. By absorbing input from ten think-tanks and integrating experiences both from China and abroad, the new guidelines provide for a reasonable distribution of health care resources and address the core issues of equity and accessibility.

The draft guidelines were made available for public comment for a full month, and more than 30,000 responses were received. "Too difficult to see a doctor, too expensive to see a doctor!" was one of the top issues that emerged from the responses and Chinese opinion polls. Inviting people to participate in the development of public policies is unprecedented in China. As a result of the public input, 190 revisions were made and a specific action plan for tangible targets was developed, which received strong public support. Thus, the public consultation process was not merely a public relations strategy and instead did have some tangible impact on the final policy document.[8]

In the plan released in April 2009, the government committed US$125 billion in new funding over the next three years (about 35 percent from the central government) to the health sector to finance reform. As of the present, there has not been a great deal of specificity about the allocations of the funds being committed.

The plan has lofty goals and, as summarized by Minister of Health Chen Zhu,[9] calls for:

1. A universal health insurance system to be established by 2010, which will provide every citizen access to basic health care services which will be "affordable, convenient, safe and effective." Wide medical insurance coverage will be provided for more than 90 percent of the Chinese people. This initiative will include basic medical insurance for urban employees and for residents of cities (elderly people without previous employment, university students, children, and migrant workers without stable labor contracts and their relatives), the new rural cooperative Medicare scheme for farmers, and a Medicaid system for urban and rural poor people. Benefit packages will vary and be determined by local governments, but must include two key provisions—catastrophic illness must be covered and enrollment must be voluntary (We presume the latter was included in recognition of the widespread distrust of the use of tax revenue by local governments).

2. A national essential drug system to be established to meet the basic need for treatment and prevention of diseases and to ensure safety, quality, and supply. All drugs on the list will be subject to a high reimbursement rate by the distinct medical insurance systems.

3. The medical care and public health service system will be improved at the grassroots level. In rural areas, emphasis will be on infrastructure and human-resource development of the three-tier network, namely at the county, town, and village levels. In urban areas, community health centers will be strengthened. Whether the poor quality of many community health centers can be upgraded to inspire trust is a question that remains to be answered.

4. There will be a major promotion of basic public health services. This objective will be realized through: a) establishment of health archives or databases for all citizens; b) provision of screening for major diseases for elderly people, women, and children; c) management of chronic non-communicable diseases; and d) health education. Furthermore, major public health projects are to be launched, including an expanded program of immunization for fifteen vaccine-preventable diseases for children younger than 15 years (e.g., against the hepatitis B virus which is responsible for the high prevalence of liver cancer in adults), prevention and control of major infectious diseases (HIV/AIDS and tuberculosis) and "geo-chemical endemic diseases," presumably deriving from environmental pollution, and hospital deliveries for all pregnant women.

Table 1:   Major Policy Interventions in China's Health Care Reform Plan.

Objective	Major Proposed Policies
Increasing financial access	• Expanding insurance coverage through premium subsidies • Controlling drug pricing, establishing an essential medicine policy
Increasing efficiency	• Strengthening public health, health education • Gradually separating prescribing and dispensing • Encouraging vertical integration • Gradually carrying out provider payment reforms
Increasing physical access	• Strengthening the rural infrastructure • Establishing a network of community-based health centers • Encouraging development of the private sector
Enhancing safety and quality	• Modernizing the medical information system • Strengthening medical education • Strengthening professional ethics

5. The final aim of the action plan is to launch a pilot reform of public hospitals. This project includes substantial increases in public investment, restructuring of hospital management systems, and regulation or limitations on excessive commercialization.

These are laudable goals, which are summarized in Table 1. Clearly, it is enormously exhilarating to see such a multifaceted and comprehensive reform plan. One can ask for early indicators of success in practice. One early test case should be its impact on tobacco-related illness. Tobacco is the largest preventable cause of death and disease in China and the world. It is estimated that it will needlessly kill 100 million Chinese by 2015.[10] Cigarette consumption in China, exceeding 2,000 billion in 2006, is increasing. Since taxes on tobacco represent the second largest tax stream to the government, it is appropriate to ask whether any policies relating to tobacco control will actually change.

Implementing the Reforms: Major Issues
Financing and Administration

Estimates suggest that the government will increase its investment (both central and local) in health to 1–1.5 percent of GDP, or about CNY850 billion (about US$124 billion) in the coming three years, doubling the average annual governmental expenditure in 2008. (By comparison, the United States spends about 17 percent of its GDP on health, estimated to be about $2.4 trillion.) There are two appropriate and critical questions that must be asked: Will these funds be spent wisely, increasing the duration and quality of life of the people, or will they largely be wasted? And who will act on behalf of the people to be sure that they are appropriately served?

Two approaches[11] are being debated that may be described simply as government provision of health care, or a regulated market approach. Each has certain problems. It would appear obvious that, with so many resources being made available, the Ministry of Health would wish to be in control of the provision of health services. But the history of health care in China is that both the central and local governments have failed to ensure quality. There is equal evidence that in the past the government, as the purchaser of services, specifically, in the case of the Ministry of Labor and Social Security, has been inefficient. A third model ought to be seriously considered, which would be a specialized non-governmental agency model, such as the Primary Care Trust that has been effectively implemented in the UK.

Can the Government Build the Necessary Trust?

Despite increasing costs, the government's health budget accounts for less than 10 percent of the actual costs of public hospitals. China's fee-for-service payment system exacerbates the escalation of costs: doctors have strong financial incentives to overprescribe because they rely on service revenue and drug sales for their income. In some village health clinics, up to 90 percent of payments for the provider derive from the sale of medicines, not care. Moreover, in view of the variable level of professional ethics, there is a widespread belief that health care providers put their financial interests ahead of their patients' medical needs. Mistrust is the major reason for the worsening relationship between patients and doctors.

Throughout China's history, its people have most often been passive recipients of bad policies, rather than active participants in the policy processes. Of course, health care democracy might turn out to be merely another political public relations ploy, and public opinion might not really matter in the end. But giving the people a chance to be heard at least helps enhance the probability of preventing the government from making huge mistakes; or, if there are mistakes, as there inevitably must be in a program of this scale, enabling mechanisms for them to be promptly corrected. To a large extent, this will be dependent on how transparent the programs are at the national and local levels, and how responsive the programs are to implementing feedback.

Will the New Reform Package Work?

China's current experiment in health care democracy could fail. Public expectations may be too high for any program realistically to meet. Interest groups may be too diverse and self-interested to enable a proper balance of power. Frustrated by all of this, the government might decide to suspend its attempts to include the public in policy making. But, if the process is perceived to be informative and inclusive, eliciting new and better ideas; if the process recognizes the role of the people as "co-providers" of health, not just recipients, and can help prepare the masses and obtain their support for implementing the new policies; and if the process can help increase the people's trust in the government and thus strengthen the government's legitimacy and effectiveness in governance by establishing a new image of transparency; the experiment might have powerful externalities and spillover effects beyond the health sector.

In this peculiarly complex and vital realm of health, it is possible that the great gate of democracy has been opened a bit, which, when allowed to open further, might just be difficult to close again. We, and the world, will watch with great anticipation.

ENDNOTES

1. Yuanli Liu, et al., "Transformation of China's Rural Health Care Financing," *Social Science and Medicine*, 41, no. 8 (October 1995): 1085–93.

2. David Blumenthal and William Hsiao, "Privatization and Its Discontents: The Evolving Chinese Health Care System," *New England Journal of Medicine*, 353, no. 11 (September 15, 2005): 1165–70.

3. Shanlian Hu, et al., "Reform of How Health Care Is Paid for in China: Challenges and Opportunities," *Lancet*, 372, no. 9652 (November 22–28, 2008): 1846–53.

4. Winnie Yip and William C. Hsiao, "The Chinese Health Care System at a Crossroads," *Health Affairs*, 27, no. 2 (March-April 2008): 460–68.

5. Liu, et al., "Transformation of China's Rural Health Care Financing," 1085–93.

6. Yuanli Liu, "China's Public Health-care System: Facing the Challenges," *Bulletin of the World Health Organization*, 82, no. 7 (July 2004): 532–38.

7. Central Committee of the Chinese Communist Party and the State Council, "Guanyu shenhua yigai yijian" (Suggestions on Deepening Health System Reforms), March 17, 2009, at http://news.sina.com.cn/c/2009-04-06/165217556355.shtml (accessed October 16, 2009).

8. Yuanli Liu, "Reforming China's Healthcare: For the People, By the People?" *Lancet* 373, no. 9660 (January 24–30, 2009): 281–83.

9. Zhu Chen, "Launch of the Health-care Reform Plan in China," *Lancet*, 373, no. 9672 (April 18–24, 2009): 1322–24.

10. Gonghuan Yang, et al., "Emergence of Chronic Non-communicable Diseases in China," *Lancet*, 372, no. 9650 (November 8–14, 2008): 1697–1705.

11. Yip and Hsiao, "The Chinese Health Care System at a Crossroads," 460–68.

16.

RUSHING TOWARD SOCIALISM:
THE TRANSFORMATION AND DEATH OF PRIVATE BUSINESS ENTERPRISES IN SHANGHAI, 1949–1956

冯筱才 FENG XIAOCAI

The year 1955 stands out as a significant turning point in the history of Communist rule in mainland China. In that year, Mao Zedong abruptly ended the "New Democracy" policies that had allowed for an uneasy coexistence of some pre-1949 economic and social organizations with the institutions of the new regime. During the course of a few brief months in late 1955 and early 1956, the transition to socialism struck the country like a violent storm. Under the instigation of the highest authorities, a campaign of "socialist transformation" (*shehuizhuyi gaizao*) speedily engulfed mainland China. Private business disappeared, seemingly overnight, and would not reemerge until Deng Xiaoping's rise to power. From the perspective of the early twenty-first century when private business is again responsible for a significant portion of China's economic output, one cannot help but wonder: Given the significance of private enterprise in the periods before 1955 and after 1979, what motivated the Communist government to promote such a hasty policy of socialist transformation? The official verdict on this era has always maintained the essential correctness of this policy, even as it has acknowledged that the demands of the socialist transformation campaign were too high, the work of implementing the campaign was too careless and too fast, and the campaign's benchmarks were applied in an overly uniform manner. The question remains, however, why did so many people respond to an extreme policy that broke with all previous practices? What were the attitudes of the people who participated in this campaign? What were the attitudes of the private business owners who were the object of this attempted transformation? What caused them to petition with such eagerness and zest to transform their businesses into state-private joint management?

Despite the steady growth of historical scholarship on the 1950s, there are still only a handful of specialized scholarly studies that focus on the socialist transformation of capitalist enterprises. Historian Chen Yongfa has likened this process to "euthanasia": the Chinese Communist Party (CCP) initiated various political campaigns to attack the reputation, moral legitimacy, and unity of the business community, while also using financial, material, and market assistance to increase the dependence of private business on the state. Thus, when the CCP issued its call for an all-out socialist transformation in 1955, the overwhelming majority of private business owners responded enthusiastically and "voluntarily accepted transformation."[1] In contrast to Chen Yongfa, Gui Yong's scholarship depicts business owners confronting a situation in which they had no alternative, and argues that acceptance of the socialist transformation was a rational choice on the part of the private business owners.[2] Yang Kuisong's work provides a third view, emphasizing the profound impact of the 1951–52 Three-Anti and Five-Anti Campaigns on the mindsets of the capitalist classes.[3]

In their depictions of this period, these three scholars emphasize the post-1949 experiences of private businesspeople and use them to explain the logic behind what official accounts term the "voluntary acceptance of socialist trans-formation." These scholars emphasize background factors that highlight the historical context of the socialist transformation campaign, but they do not explore the way in which contingent factors affected the campaign's development and implementation. The approach in this chapter, by contrast, focuses attention on the details of the campaign itself, thus demonstrating both the campaign's internal logic and the way in which this logic was disrupted by events. This, in turn, suggests a new path for writing the history of the political campaigns that dominated the first decades of the People's Republic.

Plans for the establishment of state-private joint management firms (*gongsi heying qiye*) had their origins in the first days of the new Communist government and were supposed to be carefully implemented. By 1955, however, these careful plans were abandoned and the government turned to a model of sudden, radical transformation. The sequence of this change deserves close scrutiny. During the various phases of the campaign, different types of private businesses had differ-ing reactions, and different businesspeople understood their interests differently at different moments. Even within a single group of business owners, there were differing ideas, actions, and choices about this issue. Thus, scholars must base their judgments on a careful analysis of the historical record.

Generally, people place an extremely high value on their private property. Thus, is it reasonable to assume that business owners will rush to support the idea of state-private joint management as soon as their firms encounter trouble? When the supply of raw materials and marketplace are controlled by others, will business owners proactively apply to become state-private joint management

firms? In my opinion, it is not obvious that either of these preconditions is sufficient in its own right to account for the massive transition to joint management
that occurred after 1955. We cannot take the words of official theorists or politicians, written long after the fact, to be an accurate reflection of the attitudes of
businesspeople caught in the midst of the socialist transformation campaign.
Instead, we need to immerse ourselves in the actual historical context to see what
really transpired.

The Five-Anti Campaign and Early State-Private Joint Management Enterprises, 1952

The 1952 Five-Anti Campaign engulfed the entire business community and left
a deep impression on private business owners. The campaign can be seen as a
line dividing Shanghai's earliest state-private joint management companies from
later ones; those formed during this period were very different from those formed
earlier or later.

State-private partnerships had antecedents in the CCP's wartime base areas.
After the May 1949 takeover of Shanghai, the new government, in addition to
taking control of industries belonging to the municipal government, moved to
place enterprises in which the departed Nationalist Government had held significant stakes under military supervision. These formed Shanghai's first group of
state-private joint management firms; by late 1949, a total of fifteen such firms
was operating in the city.[4] In January 1951, plans promulgated by the State Council
in Beijing sparked the reorganization of other partially state-owned companies
into joint management firms. In July of that year, the government reported that
486 Shanghai firms were under joint management, most of which were classified
as expropriated Nationalist assets. Among these, 10 percent or less of the stock of
76 percent of these enterprises was owned by the government, and 30 percent or
more of the stock of 121 firms was owned by the government.[5]

A handful of other businesses were reorganized as joint management firms
during this period as well. Some had financial or managerial links to the party
that dated back to before the revolution. The Construction Bank, founded with
party funds by Gong Yinbing and Fan Xudong during the war against Japan, is
an example of such a firm. Though originally located in Chongqing, it moved its
headquarters to Shanghai in 1946. In April 1950, after experiencing operational
difficulties, the bank successfully applied for reorganization as a joint management firm. Similarly, the Guan Leming Pen Factory and the Shanghai China
Standard Pencil Factory became state-private partnerships on the basis of early
CCP investments.[6]

Additionally, the local authorities also appear to have targeted investment at several firms that had good reputations or were involved in defense-related production in order to bring these firms under joint management. By 1951, these included the Shanghai Huatong Electronics Factory, the Zhonghua Shipyard Machinery Company, the Xinguang Undergarments Weaving and Dyeing Factory, the Guangzhong Weaving and Dyeing Factory, the Yuantong Bleaching and Dyeing Company, and the Xinfeng Printing and Dyeing Company. Beyond these types of firms, however, the local authorities at this time maintained a cautious attitude about the expansion of joint management to new businesses. They maintained strict requirements for such firms and the agencies responsible for managing partnerships had yet to develop systematic and detailed plans.[7]

The 1952 Five-Anti Campaign shook the foundations of the Chinese private business world. After the campaign began in February, in Shanghai many businesspeople killed themselves and others sought to save their lives by falsely confessing to hoarding "amounts of illegal cash." This resulted in over 10 trillion yuan in compensation extracted from the Shanghai business community.[8] After the Five-Anti Campaign, Shanghai's tax revenues declined, labor-management relations deteriorated, and owners were no longer able to control their own businesses. Under such dire conditions, some owners considered simply donating their shops or factories to the government, but most of them were refused. Other businesspeople hoped to use the joint management model to alleviate their difficulties. The government, faced with the political and fiscal implications of a wave of firms simultaneously converting to joint management status, undoubtedly felt that it could not then take on such a burden.[9] Various agencies within the government, however, seemed to hold differing opinions about how to proceed; many within the city and regional governments generally supported the creation of joint management firms, whereas the city's fiscal commission, viewing the issue from the perspective of public finance, thought that each firm should be considered on a case-by-case basis.[10]

Although there were differing ideas within the government about the advisability of state-private joint management firms, overall there was a nationwide increase in the number of conversions to this form of organization by the first half of 1953, when 91 enterprises were either preparing for, or had just received, permission for such a conversion.[11] These conversions, however, were not all prompted by the fines levied during the Five-Anti Campaign. According to a March 1953 Bank of Communications statistical analysis of 695 joint management firms, financial penalties directly prompted the creation of only 6 percent of this total, or about 40 firms.[12] The negative effects of the Five-Anti Campaign, however, led the highest CCP leaders to reassess their policies toward businesspeople. In

November 1952, the party center ordered that the localities readjust their policies. Emphasizing the positive aspects of private capital, this clearly signaled that if mass unemployment resulted from the blind implementation of joint management, then the national government would not help. The Shanghai city government announced that it would give "a little leeway" to private enterprises, and proposed, among other reforms, to equalize the tax rates between state and private enterprises, in the hopes of encouraging business owners to stay in business.

Joint Management in Shanghai after the 1953 "General Line for the Transitional Period"

In the wake of the Five-Anti Campaign, the moderate faction within the CCP implemented relatively relaxed policies toward businesspeople. Mao Zedong, however, had a very different idea about how to handle the continued existence of private enterprises. In May 1953, on the basis of an investigative report by Li Weihan of the party's United Front Department, Mao proposed a ten- to fifteen-year transitional period leading to the "completion" of socialism in China. During this period, the country would become industrialized, whereas agriculture, handicraft industries, and capitalist enterprises would all undergo socialist transformation. On October 1, 1953 the Xinhua News Service formally announced this policy as the "General Line for the Transitional Period."

In order to prod the business community into action, the authorities decided to call an October 23 meeting of the All-China Business Federation in order to publicize the campaign. Li Weihan, in his remarks at the meeting, declared that the general line's "transitional period" had begun with the establishment of the People's Republic in 1949. He told the attendees that the "the socialist component will take the leading role"[13] in state-private joint management enterprises. This indicated that the nature of state-private joint management had shifted from what was once a system of business management to an agent of political transformation. After the conclusion of the meeting, propaganda activities for the "general line" commenced in Shanghai. Businesspeople felt "enormous pressures" as they had to contemplate the future of their firms.

Trial Sites

In December 1953, the Shanghai Party Committee, on the basis of surveys and discussion meetings, announced that the Datong Ironworks and thirteen other factories would become test sites for implementation of state-private joint management. According to Gu Mu, vice secretary of the municipal party committee, the capitalist owners of these fourteen factories were basically all willing to participate.[14] Recent archival discoveries, however, tell a different story about these factories.

According to a report from the Shanghai Department of Private Industry, five of these fourteen test-site factories had been previously classified as "enemy or collaborator property," so the government already owned an average of 40.51 percent of their collective shares. This was "naturally occurring state-private joint management" and did not require much work on the part of the government. Of the other factories, one was already deeply in debt to the government and two others were slowly going bankrupt. The remaining six factories in the test group might have required persuasion and mobilization before accepting joint management and their owners might have harbored thoughts of resistance, as in the case of the Zhengtai Rubber Factory.[15]

At this early stage, many owners still did not understand how the CCP's policy of state-private joint management would actually work, and many made unfounded assumptions. For instance, some believed that even after the government's share of stock in the company exceeded 50 percent, managerial responsibility would still be apportioned according to the ratio of stock ownership. These businesspeople did not recognize the true nature of the policy—that "joint management" ultimately would lead to their total loss of control over their firms. It is worth noting, however, that in order to ensure that there would be no excessively negative reactions at any of the test factories, the authorities deliberately took a hands-off approach. This was especially the case in terms of personnel and salaries, which were generally left untouched. This naturally allowed the owners who were mobilized into these partnerships to remain optimistic.[16]

The initiation of this trial project in fourteen factories and Gu Mu's report to the business community had an impact: several leading members of the Shanghai business community applied for joint state-private status and others made inquiries, but only one-third of the applications were approved.[17] In order to create model institutions worthy of emulation and in order to demonstrate the benefits of joint management, the authorities, perhaps through their supportive policies for these test factories, used a form of "unfair competition" to force private enterprises to choose to take the path of joint management.

Planned Expansion

In January 1954, the CCP's Central Finance and Economics Committee in Beijing held a planning meeting on the expansion of joint management enterprises. At the meeting, various ministries, party committees, and local governments reported a total of 1,295 enterprises slated for conversion to state-private joint management. The Central Finance and Economics Committee demanded that each locality complete a survey of the enterprises that they were preparing for conversion, thus reducing the number to 651. Joint management conversion had entered a stage of planned expansion.

On February 27, 1954, the Shanghai Party Committee set up an industrial production committee to manage the task of transforming private industrial enterprises into joint management firms. Under this committee, offices for heavy industry, light industry, and textile industry were established. Within each office, a small group was to be responsible for drawing up lists of the firms. The principles for selecting the firms, according to publicity materials, were "national need and owner willingness" (guojia xuyao, zifang ziyuan).[18] In practice, however, private firms were first selected by the authorities and only then did mobilization activities directed at the owners begin. If a firm was selected but refused the joint management arrangements, then there could be negative consequences, including being labeled a "resister." By early March, the new plan for expansion was fully established; 205 firms, to be separated into three groups, were to become joint management firms. In this phase of the campaign, the government sought developed firms that would have a significant political influence after the transformation, such as the Anda Textile Factory, the Zhanghua Woolens Factory, the Xinmin Machinery Factory, the Yongda Textile Factory, the Xinyi Medicine Factory, the Jinxing Pen Factory, and others.

In order to prepare the plan for the new joint enterprises, the authorities sent cadres down into the factories. Beginning in March 1954, cadres were sent to the first trial group of thirty-three factories. Later, a second trial group of 270 factories was targeted; a total of 1,400 people, organized into 300 work groups, took control of these private firms.[19] After these cadres were sent to the factories, they joined forces with the grassroots-level party groups and unions, and together they intensified mobilization of the owners. Under this situation, the number of businesspeople applying for joint management status slowly increased, although they were applying for a series of complex reasons. Some held political positions within the government and were relatively clear about CCP policies, so they hoped to sign up early in the process in order to maintain their own statuses. Others sought to use the application process as a form of exploration. And, of course, some merely wished to "rid themselves of a burden."

On March 27, 1954, the Shanghai Industrial Production Committee formally announced a list of sixty firms that would take part in the first full round of joint management conversion. Many of the firms in this group had well-known brand names, factory equipment in good condition, large profits, and relatively small ratios of state-owned stock.[20] The local authorities believed that grassroots mass mobilization at these firms had been carried out with relative success. Additionally, many of the owners in this group, such as Liu Hongsheng, Liu Jingji, and Hu Juewen, were prominent businesspeople who were associated with national United Front efforts. Twelve of the other owners in this group were members of city-level United Front groups and the other district groups. The firms themselves belonged to industries targeted by the government.[21] The second wave, announced five months later, however, was weaker in all of these categories. The 106 firms in this group were relatively small, few were owned by members of the city-level United Front, and the level of owner cooperation was not nearly as high as that in the first group. Although they could not openly refuse, passive resistance was common.[22]

Industry-Wide Joint Management

In the latter half of 1954, private industrial firms across the country encountered enormous difficulties. To a great extent, these difficulties, including those caused by the insertion of state power into other aspects of the economic process, such as ordering, the supply of raw materials, and quality supervision, were due to intensified government control over the profits of private enterprises. In Shanghai, the initiation of the state-private joint management plan also reduced the interest of owners to manage their businesses. As factory conditions became more difficult, tax collection declined, the government was increasingly forced to intervene in management, and the owners' attitudes became even more negative and disengaged, all in an ever-worsening spiral. Consequently, the authorities encountered great difficulties in trying to select firms from the companies still in private hands that met the qualifications for conversion to joint management. Under these conditions, joint management had to be pushed down a different path. The policy that developed is known as "using the large to carry along the small." It focused on transforming entire industries all at once, rather than merely individual firms, and then adjusting the internal resources within that industry to mitigate any negative consequences.

A number of the firms converted to joint management in 1954 were taken over directly by central government agencies, leaving the localities unable to benefit from their revenue but still responsible for providing services for them. These firms were among the best in their respective fields and, after reorganizing as joint management firms, received extra considerations in the procurement process; the localities, however, did not have the resources to provide similar assistance to the small and medium enterprises that had not undergone conversion, and the latter's difficult economic positions adversely affected local finances and tax collection. Thus, although the localities had helped the central government reach its political target for establishing joint management firms, economic conflicts between the center and the localities became increasingly open. In December 1954, during a Beijing planning meeting for the expansion of joint management industry, the original proposal was to bring joint management to 2,508 additional firms nationwide by 1955 and to a total of 15,000 firms by 1957. During the meeting, however, cadres from many localities complained that unless the economic difficulties of private enterprise were first alleviated, the planning and administration of the joint management system would be very difficult.[23] In order to resolve this dilemma, the meeting proposed the adoption of a dual plan of joint management conversions targeted at individual firms and of reforms directed at entire industries as a means of continuing to carry out the plan for joint management.

Shanghai, too, began to modify its policies and prepared to select several products and industries for conversion to joint management, to be implemented simultaneously as a series of reductions, mergers, and restructurings. Such policies were compulsory rather than voluntary. The government adopted harsh measures to deal with any resistance. At the end of March 1955, the Shanghai city authorities announced Shanghai's plan for the expansion of the joint management model that year, proposing that the cotton, wool, and jute spinning industries, along with five other industries, undergo industry-wide reorganization into joint management firms, whereas shipyards, steel rolling, machinery, and thirteen other industries would be subject to either firm-based or product-specific reorganization. This was different from the earlier push for individual firms to accept joint management; this industry-wide collective conversion to joint management required the help of the business community. Therefore, the Shanghai Business Federation established three state-private joint management working groups, one each for textiles, light industry, and heavy industry. These groups called together members from the respective trade associations as well as the owners of private business to join mobilization meetings.

This kind of industry-wide mobilization was more difficult than previous efforts to mobilize individual firms. By July 1955, after four or five months of mobilization efforts, the Shanghai government approved 102 heavy industrial firms for joint management. In August, conversion of an additional 168 enterprises was announced. These 270 firms included enterprises from twenty-two different industries.[24] Among these were Rong Yiren's Shenxin Textile Group and Guo Dihuo's Yong'an Textile Group.

Under this trend of group, and even industry-wide, transition to joint management, active opposition was rare, but passive resistance was not uncommon. For example, when the Shanghai cotton textile industry implemented joint management, rumor-mongering, "reactionary slogans," and incidents of vandalism were recorded in over twenty factories.[25] Such behavior may not have been universal, but it reflected a hidden psychology of resistance to these policies occurring behind the scenes. Such opposition was sometimes expressed explosively. For example, according to an internal government report, after Rong Yiren's firm was converted to joint management, Rong was extremely displeased with the methods for organizing property and apportioning shares set by the same-trade association; in the end, Rong was forced to relent only after a private conversation with Zhang Chengzong, chief of the East China Textile Management Office. From the perspective of business owners, joint management had already become a political task.

Shanghai during the High Tide of Joint Management Conversion, 1955

In May 1955, as the Shanghai government worked to gradually implement its campaign for joint management, Mao Zedong voiced his displeasure with the pace of China's socialist transformation. He condemned Deng Zihui's relatively moderate policies for agricultural cooperatives in the countryside, deriding them as a "right opportunist line" taken by "women with bound feet trying to walk." He then personally initiated a feverish push for the complete collectivization of the countryside. In the cities, he abandoned the party center's original plan for measured conversion of private enterprises and promoted a program of complete transformation of all private enterprises into state-private joint management firms. The pace of the campaign accelerated rapidly. The Shanghai government energetically embraced this turn of events. Under pressure to produce political results, on the surface the drive for the total implementation of joint management was successful, but by this time the joint management project had already completely departed from any economic rationale and had become a kind of irrational political campaign.

Initial Reactions of the Shanghai Business Community

On October 11, 1955, at the closing session of Sixth Plenum of the Seventh Party Central Committee, Mao announced that his goal was the "extinction" of capitalism and the capitalist class in China.[26] This was an obvious hint to the cadres who had assembled for the meeting. As the meeting concluded, officials from all over the country began to take an active hand in developing plans for this "extinction" and for the related task of socialist transformation of urban private enterprises. Mao held two meetings with members of the business community and urged them to "take hold of their own destinies" by being receptive to the coming transformation; he also promised to make occupational and political accommodations for them.[27]

Between November 16 and 24, the Politburo of the Central Committee held a work meeting on the transformation of capitalist business for representatives from the provincial, municipal, and autonomous region party committees. The meeting passed a draft resolution that proposed completing the major work of implementing joint management in all industries by the end of 1957. On November 21, the All-China Business Federation published a "letter to the business community," urging support for this new policy. The lead editorial in the *People's Daily* likewise called on capitalists to end their exploitative ways.[28] Those businesspeople who had been marked as "capitalists" or as members of the "bourgeoisie" naturally hoped to use this campaign for joint management to remove those damaging political labels.

Of course, under these serious circumstances, the reactions of prominent businesspeople were not necessarily identical. Some business leaders with close connections to the authorities were not particularly worried because they had early access to information and many of them held positions in the political system. Representatives from some large industries were interested in the issue of specialized firms and hoped to become cadres in those companies after implementation of industry-wide joint management. However, some owners who had depended on the power of capital and connections within an industry for their positions feared that they could not keep up with the CCP's plans for change; they worried that without a special technical skill they would have a hard time earning a living. But no matter what, most businesspeople undoubtedly understood that the situation had reached a point whereby no one wanted to be labeled as "harming the transformation" (*pohuai gaizao*), which would indicate the end of their political lives. They understood clearly that once they were not able to survive politically, they would lose everything economically.

Deployment and Expansion of Industry-Wide Joint Management in Shanghai

The "high tide of socialism" that Mao called for was supposed to be implemented in an orderly, planned manner.[29] Under political pressure, however, local governments successively began to announce all-out mobilization. Up until January 10, 1956, the Shanghai government was able to maintain a relatively orderly process amidst this growing frenzy.

In order to reach the goal of "being understood at all levels and following through with all classes," the Shanghai Party Committee held three meetings, beginning in mid-November, 1955, to pass the message from the city's highest cadres to district- and county-level cadres, and then down to bureau-level cadres and branch secretaries at privately owned factories. The authorities devoted a month to this work, in the hopes that this would allow everyone in the party to "understand," to unify thought, and to build a broader movement based on this foundation. At the same time, the city party committee held an expanded meeting to discuss the transformation of capitalist enterprises and invited leaders from the various same-trade associations and representatives of private enterprises to attend as observers, with the goal of persuading them to comply with the government's programs. The third meeting of Shanghai's First People's Congress also focused on the "transformation of capitalist enterprises." Shanghai Mayor Chen Yi pointed to incidents of "doubt," "resistance," and "trouble-making" on the part of the business community and reminded them not to attempt resistance to transformation. Vice mayor and Shanghai Business Federation leader Sheng Pihua told the participants that they must remorselessly expose those who "harbored thoughts of sabotaging socialist transformation" and ensure that such people would be "punished according to the law."[30] As a result, political pressures on business owners increased.

After the mobilization meeting, on December 28, 1955 the Shanghai Party Committee established a small working group to have complete control over the campaign. The policy of the Shanghai Party Committee was to make full use of the business federation, the same-trade associations, and other popular organizations in order to initiate a movement for the complete transition to joint management from inside the business community itself. Approximately 20,000 activists across Shanghai were involved in the campaign.[31]

By December 8, as a result of these layers of mobilization, 78 individual industrial firms, 11 whole industries, and portions of 20 other industries, as well as 104 individual commercial firms, 28 entire commercial sectors, and portions of 21 other commercial sectors had applied for joint management status.[32] But by January 10, 1956, actual implementation of this status was not particularly rapid, indicating that the attitude in Shanghai was still relatively conservative. Many of the applications for industry-wide transformation were not immediately approved; this was a natural outgrowth of the size of Shanghai's private business community and the great fiscal pressures the state would face after conversion. The Shanghai authorities hoped to complete the process of conversion to industry-wide joint management for most firms within two years in a measured process of mobilization, industry-specific application, careful approval processes, and careful accountings of property and capital. Only then would a formal transition to the status of joint management occur.

The Sudden Arrival of the High Tide of Business Conversions, 1956

On New Year's Day, 1956, the *People's Daily* published an editorial in favor of an "all-out struggle to complete the five-year plan early and to exceed its targets," inspiring local leaders to compete with one another to reach these goals. On January 10, Beijing Mayor Peng Zhen declared that his city was the first in China to complete the process of transformation of private industry and had already entered socialism. This announcement threw the Shanghai government into confusion, and its original plan for a relatively orderly transition process was utterly smashed. In the wake of Beijing's announcement, Tianjin, Xi'an, and Chongqing all announced that they had completed the conversion process as well. Shanghai was faced with increased pressure to finish this task quickly.[33]

On January 13–14, the Shanghai authorities held a meeting for representatives from the business community and demanded that they come to terms with the new situation by switching the campaign into high gear. Rong Yiren called for all to "strive to implement joint management across the city within a week," and some cadres expressed their "displeasure" at the heretofore conservative stance of the government. At the end of the meeting, the "unanimous" consensus was to complete the task of transformation within seven days.[34] On January 15, the Shanghai Business Federation held a meeting of "provisional representatives of the Shanghai business community" at the Tianchan Theater. The meeting decided that all industries throughout the city should complete their application work for transition to joint management by January 20. The push for this came from the same-trade associations and the district-level business federations, among others. The method was to task the district governments to assist all business owners to complete the application procedures. The district business federations established reception offices, staffed by members of the local party committee, ready to answer questions, or to accept applications from the business owners around the clock. In order to create the right spirit, the same-trade associations and the district business federations also organized an all-out publicity effort, creating groups to manage street demonstrations and other festive activities.

Time was very short. Shanghai's approximately 100,000 private firms needed to complete their applications within only a few days, so many of the local and industry-specific work groups resorted to procedures that did not accord with normal government policy. The Shanghai Business Federation later admitted that "a minority of cadres [involved in the process] were interested in taking credit for the accomplishments of others."[35] In order to vie for glory, some industry-specific joint management work groups "improperly applied political labels" to business owners, resorted to "compulsory orders," or used dishonest methods to meet their numerical targets. Many work groups forced factory, store, and business owners to increase their investments at the time of transition to joint management or demanded that owners pay back-wages or back-taxes before being allowed to complete this mandatory process.

Various points of view existed among the plethora of small business owners, which included mobilized enterprises as small as one-person handicraft businesses. Their understanding of, and reaction to, the campaign was naturally different from that of the cadres and activists who had planned it. Whereas cadres and activists placed emphasis on the struggle for political positions, these small business owners were more interested in guarantees of economic survival. Of course, the orientation of this emphasis was tightly linked to the particular conditions of each firm.

Transition to joint management in one firm or industry affected others connected to it. The reconstitution of a client or a supplier as a state-private joint management firm, or the cooperativization of a rural supplier, could sever preexisting lines of production, supplies, and sales. This had a snowball effect, causing firms that initially had not been interested in joint management to apply for such a status. Many of the medium and small shops and factories in Shanghai had been tied into larger chains of marketplace relationships; they were not self-contained producers, but were engaged in a piece of a larger production process. Thus, transformation in one part of the chain immediately influenced the other parts. From the perspective of many businesspeople, this was one of the major reasons for participating in the joint management movement.

The main targets during the campaign's high tide in Shanghai were small and medium factories, small commercial shops, and peddlers; the earlier stages of the campaign had already brought the most important large and medium-sized enterprises under the joint management system. Some of the newly targeted businesses had been categorized as "poor households." For them, participating in the joint management campaign meant work and livelihood guarantees. Many of these small business owners and craftspeople, however, found it difficult to complete the application forms. They lacked an understanding of the joint management policies. Some did not even understand the meaning of "state-private joint management."[36] As the entire city slipped into a frenzy, no one wished to be left out of the new socialist system and risk becoming a social outcast. Thus, even some private hospitals, private schools, and foreign churches raced to join the new system.[37] The medium and small business owners who, willingly or not, entered into joint management arrangements during the high tide of the campaign did not necessarily receive the "iron rice bowl" that they had expected; instead, they were labeled "bourgeois businesspeople" and suffered political discrimination.

On the basis of the work of tens of thousands of cadres, the Shanghai government was able to declare on January 20, 1956, that it had completed the transformation of private enterprises into joint management firms and, consequently, had "entered socialism." Supposedly, during this process, 106,274 businesses in 242 industries, as well as 24,000 handicraft firms and over 60,000 people were cooperativized.[38] The transformation of such a large number of firms within such a short period of time during this campaign was obviously not a normal phenomenon. The implementation of joint management in all industries, from the perspective of many business owners and artisans, was the result of "mass compulsion." This kind of coercion was enacted in the name of the same-trade associations and the business federations, placing the businesspeople in a position in which they found it difficult to resist, thus creating a false impression of "voluntary agreement."

Conclusion

The all-out campaign for state-private joint management, much like the collectivization campaign in the countryside, was essentially an economically irrational political movement that contravened basic human nature. These campaigns resulted in the speedy CCP nationalization of the economy and the elimination of all privately owned means of production, but they also reduced economic efficiency, wasted resources, and affected government finances. Before Deng Xiaoping's reforms, the authorities were unable to solve these basic problems, either through political campaigns or through temporary economic stimuli. Although the government proclaimed that this new economic system was built on "voluntary joint management," after a careful study of the historical evidence, a more complex picture emerges. Most joint management enterprises did not represent equal exchanges of value, but rather were improper thefts of private wealth by a variety of extraordinary channels. During this process, overt and covert resistance by businesspeople were always present, as were deceptive promises and naked uses of administrative compulsion, including sometimes violent coercion. When faced with an irresistible political campaign, political and economic survival became the people's highest priority.

During different phases of the campaign, "state-private joint management" was a policy aimed at different parts of the business community by different parts of the government; various members of the business community also had different understandings of the policy. In the first years of CCP rule in Shanghai, the policy generally meant absorption of the former regime's "bureaucratic capitalist" enterprises; the authorities very rarely proactively invested capital into private industry. During the Three-Anti and Five-Anti Campaigns in 1951–52, "joint management" was expanded to include the property of businesspeople who could not afford to pay the fines that they had been assessed. Afterward, once the "general line for the transitional period" was announced in 1953, the government implemented joint management for selected large- and medium-scale enterprises in order to enhance the power of the state-run economy. This included the conversion both of firms that were prospering and firms that were struggling. The former were not willing to submit to joint management, but did so under political pressure; the latter included owners who, under economic pressures, hoped to rid themselves of their companies.

The so-called "high tide" of 1955–56 was actually nothing more than a platform for mid-level cadres to compete in an irrational political numbers game. For activists involved in the implementation of the campaign, "joint management" was a method for improving one's political position. The main targets of this "high tide" were small and medium business owners, including handicraft workers, freelancers, and others. Many of these had already been labeled "capitalists," and thus they saw participation in the campaign as a chance to reshape their political statuses. From the perspective of small business owners with uncertain incomes or handicrafts people in difficult economic circumstances, "joint management" was perhaps seen as an opportunity to ensure economic survival. Workers in many factories, or employees at many shops, likely had the same hopes. From the perspective of the CCP, initially "state-private joint management" was a means to extract more fiscal and economic benefits from the private sector. Later, it became a method for officials at all levels to demonstrate their "political correctness" and a weapon to compete for advantage in political struggles. In sum, calculations about "political survival" and "economic survival" ran throughout the entire campaign for joint management.

In the midst of this struggle for survival, calls for the "general line of the transitional period" and the even more idealistic "socialist transformation of capitalist enterprise" were a kind of instrumental discourse. There was a huge gap between the actual initiation and development of joint management on the one hand and these discursive images on the other. In fact, the abstract and idealistic notion of "transforming the bourgeois class" could not be realized. The grassroots-level cadres and workers who participated in the campaign were not interested in this kind of transformation; instead, they were fighting for their own political and economic benefits. For this reason, after state-private joint management was implemented nationwide, not only were the "bourgeoisie" not eliminated, "bourgeois thinking" became even more widely spread throughout society during the reorganization of resources. Thus, the seeds for a future political campaign—one that would take "Down with the capitalist roaders!" as its slogan—were sown.

ENDNOTES

This essay was translated from the original Chinese by Joshua Hill.

1. Chen Yongfa, *Zhongguo gongchan geming qishinian* (Seventy Years of the Chinese Communist Revolution) (Taibei: Lianjing chuban shiye gongsi, 1998), pp. 622–57; Chen Yongfa, "Zhonggong jianguo chuqi de gongshang shuishou: Yi Tianjin he Shanghai wei zhongxin" (Business Tax Collection during the Early Period of Communist Rule: A Study of Tianjin and Shanghai), *Zhongyang yanjiuyuan jindaishi yanjiusuo jikan*, no. 48 (June 2005), pp. 183–84.

2. Gui Yong, *Siyou chanquan de shehui jichu: Chengshi qiye chanquan de zhengzhi chonggou, 1949–1956* (The Social Basis of Private Property Rights: The Political Reconstruction of Urban Enterprise Property Rights, 1949–1956) (Shanghai: Lixin kuaiji chubanshe, 2006), pp. 23–30.

3. Yang Kuisong, "Jianguo qianhou Zhongguo gongchandang dui ziben jieji zhengce de yanbian" (The Evolution of CCP Policy Toward the Capitalist Class Before and After 1949), *Lishi yanjiu*, no. 2 (2006): 25.

4. *Zhongguo zibenzhuyi gongshangye de shehuizhuyi gaizao, Shanghai juan* (The Socialist Transformation of Chinese Capitalist Businesses, Shanghai Series) (Beijing: Zhonggong dangshi chubanshe, 1993), pp. 1460–61.

5. "Shanghai shi gongsi heying qiye qingkuang he wenti" (The Situation and Issues Surrounding Shanghai's Joint State-Private Enterprises), *Gongshang qingkuang tongbao*, no. 15 (July 5, 1951), pp. 3–4.

6. *Zhongguo zibenzhuyi gongshangye de shehuizhuyi gaizao, Shanghai juan*, pp. 1005, 1102, and 1476.

7. "Shanghai gong-si heying qiye zhong de gong-si guanxi wenti" (The Problems of the Relationship Between State and Private in Shanghai's State-Private Joint Management Enterprises), *Gongshang qingkuang tongbao*, no. 16 (August 1, 1951): 12.

8. Rashid Malik, *Chinese Entrepreneurs in the Economic Development of China* (London: Praeger, 1997), pp. 29–34; Yang Kuisong, "Shanghai 'wufan' yundong zhi jingguo" (Shanghai's Experiences during the Five-Anti Campaign), *Shehui kexue*, no. 4 (2006): 10–14.

9. Hong Jun, "Bu yao shuai 'baofu'" (Don't Hand Off Your 'Burdens'), *Shanghai gongshang*, 3, no. 12 (May 5, 1952): 18–19; "Zhou zongli yu ruogan zibenjia daibiao renwu tanhua jiyao" (Extracts from Premier Zhou's Conversation with Several Capitalist Representatives), *Gongshang xingzheng tongbao*, no. 1 (January 5, 1953): 2.

10. "Zuijin Shanghai jingji qingkuang de fenxi he Shanghai caiwei de yijian" (Analysis of Shanghai's Economic Conditions and the Views of the Shanghai Financial Committee), *Neibu cankao*, no. 254 (November 14, 1952): 162–66.

11. "1953 nian shang ban nian siying gongshangye de jiben qingkuang" (The Basic Condition of Private Enterprises During the First Half of 1953), *Gongshang xingzheng tongbao*, no. 13 (August 20, 1953): 3.

12. "Gong-si heying qiye de jiben qingkuang jiqi zuoyong" (The Basic Conditions and Actions of State-Private Joint Management Enterprises), *Gongshang xingzheng tongbao*, no. 18 (December 5, 1953): 2.

13. *Tongzhan zhengce wenjian huibian* (Collected United Front Policy Documents) (N.p.: Zhonggong zhongyang tongyi zhanxian gongzuobu, 1958), December 1953, vol.1 p. 383.

14. "Ge quwei gongye buzhang huiyi jilu" (Minutes of a Meeting of District Department Industry Heads), April 1, 1954, in the Shanghai Municipal Archives (hereafter SMA), record group A38-2-199.

15. "Qing gongye 5 ge dianxing chan gong-si heying gongzuo zonghe baogao" (General Report on Five Typical Models of State-Private Joint Management Firms in Light Industry), March 1954, SMA, record group A36-1-11, p. 48.

16. "Guanyu 14 ge heying gongchan heying qianhou chanzhang biandong qingkuang" (Changes among Factory Managers in Fourteen State-Private Joint Management Firms after Conversion), March 8, 1954, SMA, record group A36-1-11, p. 104.

17. *Zhongguo zibenzhuyi gongshangye de shehuizhuyi gaizao, Shanghai juan*, pp. 276–77.

18. "Di 1 pi heying chang gongzuo zongjie baogao, cao'an" (Final Report of the First Group of Joint Management Factories, Draft Version), 1954, SMA, record group A36-1-11, pp. 1–2.

19. "Zhonggong Shanghaishiwei gongye shengchan weiyuanhui baogao" (Report of the Committee for Industrial Production of the CCP Shanghai Committee), June 25, 1954, SMA, record group A38-2-15, p. 38.

20. "Gongye buzhang, juzhang lianxi huiyishang heying chang de tigang" (Outline of the Speeches by the Department and Office Heads of the City Department of Industry Concerning Joint Management), SMA, record group A38-2-199, p. 1.

21. "Di 1 pi heying chang gongzuo zongjie baogao, cao'an," p. 1.

22. "Di 2 pi heying chang de ruogan qingkuang he jinhou gongzuo de jidian yijian" (A Few Observations on the Condition of the Second Wave of Joint Management Factories and Several Thoughts on Future Work), SMA, record group A38-2-199, pp. 2–3.

23. *Tongzhan zhengce wenjian huibian*, vol. 1 p. 455.

24. "Ben shi you 100 duo ge siyingchan bei pizhun gong-si heying" (Over 100 Shanghai Firms Approved for Joint Management), *Wenhuibao*, August 19, 1955, p. 2.

25. *Neibu cankao*, no. 199 (September 3, 1955): 13–14.

26. *Mao Zedong xuanji* (Selected Works of Mao Zedong) (Beijing: Renmin chubanshe, 1977), vol. 5, p. 198.

27. *Mao Zedong wenji* (Collection of Mao Zedong's Writings) (Beijing: Renmin chubanshe, 1999), vol. 6, pp. 488–503.

28. *Renmin ribao*, November 22, 1955, p. 1.

29. "Zai zibenzhuyi gongshangye shehuizhuyi gaizao wenti zuotan huishang de jianghua" (Remarks at the Meeting on Problems of Socialist Reconstruction of Capitalist Enterprises), *Mao Zedong wenji*, vol. 6, pp. 493–503.

30. "Shanghaishi di 1 jie renmin daibiao dahui di 3 ci huiyi huikan" (Collection of Articles on the Third Meeting of Shanghai's First People's Congress) (Shanghai: Shanghaishi di 1 jie renmin daibiao dahui di 3 ci huiyi mishuchu, n.d.), pp. 24 and 111.

31. *Zhongguo zibenzhuyi gongshangye de shehuizhuyi gaizao, Shanghai juan*, pp. 492–93.

32. Ibid., pp. 544–46.

33. "Shanghai yao jia kuai!" (Shanghai Needs to Speed Up!), *Xinmin wanbao*, January 12, 1956, p. 1.

34. *Zhongguo zibenzhuyi gongshangye de shehuizhuyi gaizao, Shanghai juan*, p. 589.

35. *Quanshi shenqing heying gongzuo jianxun* (Brief Report on the City-wide Applications for Joint Management), no. 13 (January 20, 1956), SMA, record group C48-2-1595, p. 132.

36. One woman, who owned a rickshaw taxi in Shanghai's Changshu district, thought that state-private joint management meant "donating the means of production to the nation." "Quan shi gong-si heying qingkuang fanying, 7 hao" (Reactions to State-Private Partnerships Across Shanghai), no. 7, January 20, 1950, SMA, record group C47-2-365, p. 33.

37. Ibid., p. 32.

38. *Zhongguo zibenzhuyi gongshangye de shehuizhuyi gaizao, Shanghai juan*, pp. 680–81.

17.
SHORT-TERM STIMULI AND THE PROSPECTS FOR LONG-TERM GROWTH IN CHINA

DWIGHT H. PERKINS

Beginning in the latter half of 2008, the Chinese government, in response to the global economic crisis then unfolding, first announced and then implemented one of the largest stimulus packages of any of the major economies in the world. The object was to keep Chinese Gross Domestic Product (GDP) growth rates from falling and possibly even sliding into negative territory. By the first quarter of 2009, the Chinese GDP growth rate had already fallen to 6.1 percent on an annualized basis, down from the heady 9 to 10 percent growth rates of recent years. By international standards 6.1 percent was an enviable performance given that the GDP growth rates of most of the world's major economies had by then slid into negative territory. The stated objective of the Chinese government, however, was to maintain a GDP growth rate of 8 percent per year, a rate thought necessary to produce enough jobs to prevent unemployment from rising to an unacceptable level.

The most common question asked about the Chinese stimulus package is whether it will be able to meet the stated target of the government in 2009 and, if the global recession continues, in 2010. A question of equal or perhaps greater importance, however, is whether the short-term measures needed to keep growth up in 2009 and 2010 will also contribute to China's ability to maintain a high growth rate over the longer term of the next one to two decades. Alternatively, will efforts to maintain high growth in 2009 and 2010 by any means available create conditions that will undermine the prospects for sustained rapid growth in the future?

The analysis in this chapter will begin with a discussion of what it will take to maintain a high rate of GDP growth in China over the longer term of the next one to two decades. We will then turn to an analysis of the Chinese short-term stimulus package to see if the measures undertaken within that short-term framework will enhance or inhibit the conditions needed for long-term high growth rates. As will become apparent in the discussion that follows, the answers to the latter question depend on what the stimulus package is able to accomplish. Will the package lead to an increase in sustainable levels of household consumption that are now at extraordinarily low levels, or will the package instead, among other things, lead to the creation of capacity in industries where there is already overcapacity and inefficient construction of infrastructure?

The Sources of Long-Term Rapid Growth

The starting point for analyzing the prospects for future rapid growth in China begins from an understanding of what has made possible China's extraordinarily high growth rate over the past three decades since the economic reform period began in 1978. We will explore that understanding from both the supply side and then more briefly from the demand side. Because of space limitations, these issues will only be analyzed at a macro level. The micro reforms that made possible the macro performance will be mentioned only in passing and at a very general level.

Data on the sources of growth from the supply side are presented in Table 1 that is taken from a study I conducted with Thomas Rawski. This kind of source of growth analysis divides the explanation for growth into the rate of growth of the physical capital stock, the rate of growth of the employed labor force, and increases in the quality of that labor force generated by rises in the level of education (the increase in human capital). The part of growth not explained by increases in these inputs measures the growth in productivity of these inputs. The technical term is "total factor productivity" (TFP) because what is measured in Table 1 is the productivity of all of the inputs together.

The central question in analyses of this type is whether growth is primarily explained by the increase in inputs, particularly capital, or whether it is explained by the increase in the productivity of these inputs. How one answers this question has a profound impact on what policies a country pursues in its efforts to achieve a high growth rate. As the data in Table 1 indicate, China achieved a high rate of total factor productivity growth in the 1950s largely due to rapid recovery from the long years of war and instability, but after 1957 and through 1978 China's GDP growth slowed markedly to only 3.9 percent per year. That growth was explained almost entirely by China's high rate of investment and resulting rapid accumulation of capital (73.7 percent of the growth was explained by capital). Productivity was actually negative throughout these two decades. There was a high rate of investment but it was used inefficiently.

The change in this pattern after 1978 was dramatic. From 1978 through 2005 China's growth rate averaged 9.5 percent a year according to official statistics and its TFP accounted for 40.1 percent of that growth. The actual contribution of

Table 1:   Average Annual Growth of GDP, Fixed Capital, Labor, and TFP, with Contributions to TFP Growth, 1952–2005 (percent).

| | | Average Growth of Inputs | | | | Percentage Shares of GDP Growth Attributable to | | |
| | | | Labor Input | | | | | |
Period	GDP	Fixed Capital K	Raw Labor L	Education Enhanced H	Average TFP Growth	Fixed Capital K	Education Enhanced Labor H	TFP
1952–2005	7.0	7.7	1.9	2.6	2.1	47.7	21.4	30.9
1952–1978	4.4	5.8	1.9	2.5	0.5	56.3	32.7	11.0
1952–1957	6.5	1.9	1.2	1.7	4.7	12.7	14.9	72.4
1957–1978	3.9	6.7	2.0	2.7	−0.5	73.7	39.7	−13.4
1957–1965	2.4	5.2	1.5	2.1	−1.0	93.1	49.5	−42.6
1965–1978	4.9	7.7	2.4	3.1	−0.2	67.7	36.7	−4.4
1978–2005	9.5	9.6	1.9	2.7	3.8	43.7	16.2	40.1
1978–1985	9.7	9.2	3.4	4.5	3.2	40.6	26.6	32.8
1985–1990	7.7	6.9	2.5	2.9	3.1	38.8	21.5	39.7
1990–1995	11.7	9.1	1.4	1.9	6.7	33.3	9.5	57.3
1995–2000	8.6	10.5	0.9	1.6	3.2	52.7	10.5	36.8
2000–2005	9.5	12.6	1.0	1.8	3.1	57.1	10.6	32.3

Source: Dwight H. Perkins and Thomas G. Rawski, "Forecasting China's Economic Growth to 2025," in Loren Brandt and Thomas G. Rawski, eds., *China's Great Economic Transformation* (Cambridge: Cambridge University Press, 2008), pp. 829–86.

productivity growth was even higher because the jump in productivity led to a spurt in growth and in the productivity of investment that made possible much of the increase in the growth of the capital stock. Put differently, the rate of investment as a share of GDP changed little before and after 1978 but the increase in GDP made possible by the rise in TFP meant that a given rate of investment produced a much larger increase in capital than would have been the case if TFP were negative, as it was in the 1957–78 period. Thus, the post-1978 story is primarily one of economic reforms leading to a major rise in productivity. It is not primarily a story about rising rates of savings and investment.

This rise in TFP was caused by a long series of economic reforms that ultimately transformed China's economy from a Soviet-style centrally planned command economy where market forces played only a small role into an economy where market forces played the primary role in economic decision making. During the first phase of the reform, from 1978 to 1984, the most important reforms were the opening up to foreign trade and the dismantling of the commune system in favor of a return to household-based agriculture. The next phase, beginning in late 1984, involved making industrial inputs readily available to all at market prices, while retaining state-set input prices for certain favored state-owned enterprises. The surprise result was a boom in what came to be called township and village enterprises, enterprises that were collectively owned by local people and local governments but that behaved much like private enterprises.

China had formally abandoned its policy of prohibiting foreign direct investment (FDI) early on in the reform period, but it was not until the 1990s that the supporting laws and institutions for FDI were in place and foreign direct investment took off, rising to over US$50 billion and continuing up from there to lead to another jump in productivity growth as the example of the efficient foreign firms together with the competition they provided put pressure on all Chinese enterprises to do better. Then, in the late 1990s, China changed its negotiating position regarding the terms it would accept in order to join the World Trade Organization (WTO). Basically China simply accepted the terms offered by the United States and the European Union that called for China to eliminate most of its government interventions in the market with respect to industry and many services. Joining the WTO, and the resultant removal of protective barriers on imports, was then used by the Chinese government to put great pressure on the state-owned enterprises to reform. Among other results of this pressure, the bloated payrolls of many of the state-owned enterprises were greatly reduced as over 20 million surplus workers in these enterprises were dismissed.

Each of these major reform efforts helped sustain the high growth rate of TFP throughout the three decades leading up to 2009. Many of these reforms, however, were one-shot affairs that led to a jump in productivity for a few years but thereafter to a slowdown in productivity growth. In agriculture, for example, there was an enormous jump in productivity as farmers moved from farming collectively to farming on a household basis, but thereafter further gains in productivity were much more difficult to achieve. Similarly, the boom in township and village enterprises filled many niches ignored by the central planners and the state-owned enterprises and that too led to a spurt in productivity, but this dynamic role for township and village enterprises came to an end by the late 1990s. It is also likely that the boom in FDI had a larger impact on productivity during the high FDI growth period of the 1990s than it did later when the FDI growth rate slowed and the differences narrowed between the best practices of the FDI firms and those of domestic Chinese enterprises.

The reason why the one-shot impact on productivity of many of the early reforms is important is because continued high productivity growth is essential if high GDP growth rates are going to continue into the future. The nature of the challenge can be seen from the data in Table 2. The central question asked in

Table 2:   Productivity Consequences of Input Projections and 6 or 9 Percent Growth to 2025.

	Annual Average Growth of Inputs %					Annual Growth of GDP (%)			
			Labor Input				Attributable to		
	GDP Growth	Fixed Capital	Raw Labor	Education Enhanced Labor	Average TFP Growth	Fixed Capital	Education Enhanced Labor	TFP Growth	TFP Share of GDP Growth
Period	%	K	L	H	%	K	H	Growth	%
Version 1									
2005–2015	9.0	9.8	0.7	2.0	3.6	4.2	1.1	3.6	40.4
2015–2025	9.0	8.2	−0.3	1.0	4.9	3.5	0.6	4.9	54.4
2005–2025	9.0	9.0	0.2	1.5	4.3	3.9	0.8	4.3	47.4
1978–2025	9.3	9.4	1.2	2.2	4.0	4.0	1.2	4.0	43.1
1952–2025	7.5	8.1	1.4	2.3	2.7	3.5	1.3	2.7	36.3
Version 2									
2005–2015	9.0	9.0	0.7	2.0	4.0	3.9	1.1	4.0	44.5
2015–2025	9.0	6.6	−0.3	1.0	5.6	2.8	0.6	5.6	62.4
2005–2025	9.0	7.8	0.2	1.5	4.8	3.3	0.8	4.8	53.4
1978–2025	9.3	8.8	1.2	2.2	4.2	3.8	1.2	4.2	45.6
1952–2025	7.5	7.7	1.4	2.3	2.9	3.3	1.3	2.9	38.3
Version 3									
2005–2015	6.0	8.1	0.7	2.0	1.4	3.5	1.1	1.4	23.1
2015–2025	6.0	5.6	−0.3	1.0	3.0	2.4	0.6	3.0	50.7
2005–2025	6.0	6.8	0.2	1.5	2.2	2.9	0.8	2.2	37.0
1978–2025	8.0	8.4	1.2	2.2	3.1	3.6	1.2	3.1	39.1
1952–2025	6.7	7.5	1.4	2.3	2.2	3.2	1.3	2.2	32.4
Version 4									
2005–2015	6.0	7.3	0.7	2.0	1.7	3.1	1.1	1.7	28.7
2015–2025	6.0	4.0	−0.3	1.0	3.7	1.7	0.6	3.7	61.7
2005–2025	6.0	5.7	0.2	1.5	2.7	2.4	0.8	2.7	45.4
1978–2025	8.0	7.9	1.2	2.2	3.3	3.4	1.2	3.3	41.8
1952–2025	6.7	7.1	1.4	2.3	2.3	3.1	1.3	2.3	34.5

Memo item: average TFP growth 1978–2005: 3.8 percent (Table 1)

Notes: Versions 1 and 2 assume 9 percent GDP growth; Versions 3 and 4 assume 6 percent growth. The ratio of fixed capital formation to GDP declines linearly from the 2005 figure of 42.3 percent to a terminal 2005 level of 35 percent (Versions 1 and 3) or 25 percent (Versions 2 and 4).

Source: Dwight H. Perkins and Thomas G. Rawski, eds., "Forecasting China's Economic Growth to 2025," in Loren Brandt and Thomas G. Rawski, eds., *China's Great Transformation* (Cambridge: Cambridge University Press, 2008), pp. 829–86.

constructing this table is what would the growth in TFP have to be for China to achieve a 9 percent GDP growth rate over the next one to two decades, as contrasted to what TFP would have to be to achieve a 6 percent growth rate. Those interested in the underlying assumptions involved in constructing these tables are referred to the published chapter by Thomas Rawski and me. Here we present the table to make one simple point. For China to achieve a 9 percent growth rate over the next one to two decades beginning from 2006, the country would have to achieve sustained TFP growth of from 3.6 to 4.0 percent for the first decade ending in 2015 and 4.9 to 5.6 percent in the second decade ending in 2025. Given that TFP growth was 3.8 percent during the first three decades of reform when, as suggested above, China got big TFP boosts from simply dismantling the Soviet-type system and replacing it with a market system, achieving another decade of this level of TFP growth will be difficult at best. This conclusion was initially reached prior to the global economic recession of 2008–9 and that recession makes TFP growth rates of the magnitude required even more of a challenge. The TFP growth rates needed to sustain 9 percent growth in the second decade (2015–25) appear to be highly unlikely. A GDP growth rate of 6 percent a year, in contrast, requires TFP growth rates that are not unusually high. Such a growth rate would require continued reform of China's economic system but should be achievable by a government that continues to be dedicated to making the market system work better. We will explore how the current global recession and the Chinese stimulus package might alter this conclusion later in this chapter.

There is one further piece of information that indicates that China's GDP growth rate is likely to slow down from the levels of the past three decades even if major continued reform efforts keep total factor productivity growing at a fairly rapid rate. As the data in Figure 1 indicate, no country continues to grow at 9 and 10 percent per year indefinitely. The highest-income countries seldom grow much faster than 3 percent a year on a sustained basis, and even middle-income countries run into barriers that lead to marked declines in their GDP growth rates. For all but a few special cases, these growth rates decline sharply when a country reaches a per capita income of between US$10,000 and US$16,000 (in purchasing power dollars). This chapter is not the place to explain in detail why this occurs, but it is probably to a large degree due to the fact that countries at this level of per capita income can no longer simply rely on modest adaptations of the experience of other economies that have gone ahead, what is referred to by Alexander Gerschenkron as the "advantages of backwardness." There are also certain structural changes that promote high growth (the migration of labor from low productivity agriculture to higher productivity urban jobs, for example) that come to an end at this level of income.

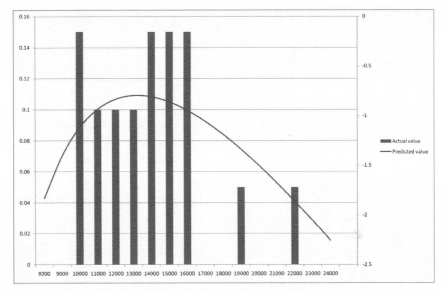

Figure 1:   Per Capita Income at Which GDP Growth Decelerated
Note: This is a sample of 20 sustained decelerations with some countries represented by two different episodes of deceleration in this table.
Source: Barry Eichengreen, Dwight Perkins, and Kwanho Shin, *The Growth of the Korean Economy* (forthcoming).

The most often quoted figure for China's per capita income in 2008 in purchasing power parity terms is US$3,000, but most analysts of the Chinese economy, at least those outside China, believe the true figure is probably higher—perhaps US$4,500 or even a bit higher. At a per capita growth rate of 8 percent a year, more or less what China achieved over the past three decades, China's per capita GDP would double in nine years and increase fourfold in eighteen years, which would give China a per capita GDP of US$18,000 in 2026. Put differently, if China's experience mirrors that of other successful economies, China's per capita GDP growth rate will fall below 8 percent a year well before 2026 and that would be the case even if there was no global recession. If China's GDP growth rate slows to say 6 percent per capita (7 percent overall), it will take the country twenty-four years to increase GDP per capita fourfold. As already pointed out, however, that rate of growth assumes that China will continue to achieve substantial rates of growth of TFP over that entire time period.

The Demand Side Problem: Both Long- and Short-Term

Solving the supply side of the growth problem is part of the challenge, although in most developing countries it is the more difficult part. However, in China there is also a major challenge on the demand side. Someone must be willing to buy the items produced with capital and labor. In most advanced economies domestic consumers buy 70 percent or more of what is produced at home or imported (Table 3). Private investors buy much of the rest, with the government also purchasing goods for both consumption and investment. In China, in contrast, consumption makes up a much smaller share of total expenditure of GDP and that share has been falling steadily since the reform period began, as the data in Table 4 indicate. Furthermore, consumption by households has fallen from a low of 49.1 percent of GDP when the reforms began to a miniscule 36.6 percent in 2004–7 (Table 5). In formal accounting terms this gap in demand has been filled by a rising rate of investment (capital formation) and a rising surplus of exports over imports (Table 4).

Formal accounting calculations do not give a clear picture of just how dependent China has become on exports as a major source of demand for domestic products. Exports as a share of GDP have risen from 5.7 percent of GDP at the beginning of the reform period to 33 percent in 2008 (Table 6). This latter figure exaggerates the importance of exports as a source of demand for domestically produced Chinese goods because many of the components for these exports are imported rather than produced in China. Nevertheless, exports are a large

Table 3:   International Comparisons of the Structure of GDP.

	Household Consumption	Government Consumption	Capital Formation	External Balance
		(Year 2007 as % of GDP)		
United States	71	16	19	−6
Japan	57	18	23	1
South Korea	55	15	29	1
Malaysia	50	13	23	14
Thailand	57	10	30	4
Vietnam	67	6	35	−8
Indonesia	63	8	25	4

Table 4:   Consumption and Investment (as % of GDP).

	Consumption	Capital Formation	Net Exports
1978–1979	63.3	37.1	−0.4
1980–1989	65.0	34.2	−0.9
1990–1999	59.7	37.8	2.4
2000–2003	59.8	37.9	2.3
2004–2007	50.8	42.6	6.5

Table 5: China Consumption Breakdown (as % of GDP).

	Final Consumption	Household Consumption	Government Consumption
1978–1979	63.3	49.1	14.2
1980–1989	65.4	51.2	14.2
1990–1999	60.2	45.9	14.3
2000–2003	58.9	43.4	15.5
2004–2007	50.2	36.6	13.6

Table 6: Ratio of Exports to GDP (as % of GDP).

1978–1979	5.7
1980–1989	9.8
1990–1999	17.8
2000–2003	22.8
2004–2007	33.9
2008	33.0

share of demand for Chinese domestic products—how large requires detailed calculations well beyond the scope of this chapter, but work by Lawrence Lau and others estimates exports net of imported components at around half of gross exports, or around 15–17 percent of GDP.[1]

Filling the demand gap with high rates of investment together with exports has solved the problem of inadequate demand over the past decades, but there are reasons to believe that this will not succeed as a long-term solution. High rates of investment above 40 percent of GDP imply that much of this investment is producing investment goods used for further expansions in investment, a pattern that is common in Soviet-type economies where firms do what central planners tell them to do. This process keeps demand up but the price of state direction is usually low productivity and low quality of output, as was the case in China in the pre-reform period. In a market economy with independent firms that respond to market forces rather than to orders from the state, steadily rising rates of investment are likely to reach a point when investors become skeptical that there is a market out there for all of the increased capacity being created. When this occurs, they cut back on investment, the demand for investment goods falls, and the economy spirals down into a recession.

The problem with relying on rapid increases in exports to fill the demand gap is that resistance from the rest of the world to these rising exports will increase over time. China's gross exports in 2008 reached US$1,428.5 billion, a figure that is just short of twice the level of Japan's gross exports in that year. Over the past five years, Chinese exports have grown at a nominal rate of 26.7 percent per year. Even at less than half that rate of growth (13 percent per year), Chinese exports five years from now will have increased by more than another trillion U.S. dollars, or by more than the total trade of Japan. It is not likely that the rest of the world will willingly continue to absorb Chinese exports growing at this rate. As it turned out, in early 2009 Chinese exports fell by a substantial amount largely because of the global recession. Therefore, the global recession has brought home the fact that solving the Chinese demand gap problem with exports is not likely to be a viable long-term strategy. Japan discovered this same obstacle some years ago and has had to find other ways of filling the demand gap, not always with great success.

If high rates of investment and export growth are risky for China going forward once the global recession is over, what is the alternative? The simple answer is that China has to increase the role of household consumption from its current extraordinarily low levels. This would have been the case even if there had been no global recession, but the recession has underlined the importance of moving in this direction. How does one increase household consumption? There are really only two ways of doing so on a sustained basis. A country must either find ways to raise the growth rate of household income or reduce the rate of household savings.

Raising the growth rate of household income is mainly achieved when a high growth rate of GDP translates into a comparable or higher rate of real wage growth in the urban areas and a similarly high rate of growth in rural incomes from farming and related rural activities. But in China rural incomes have grown at a slower pace than GDP (6.7 percent per year in the seven years ending in 2007). Urban household real incomes have risen more rapidly (at 10.1 percent per year in real terms in the seven years ending in 2007), but that rate is slightly below the rate of growth of GDP (10.5 percent per year). The only sustainable way to raise real incomes and real wages in a market economy is to either raise the marginal product of urban labor or the output and prices of farm products. Both methods are largely, although not entirely, determined by market forces over the long run, not by actions by the government. If China's GDP returns to a high growth path, shortages of labor will appear and wages will rise more rapidly. In the global recession of 2009, however, unemployment is rising sharply among urban workers and so incomes are growing at a much slower pace.

Lowering the savings rates mainly can be achieved by eliminating where possible the need for savings. In China that means creating a better and more complete national health insurance system, particularly in the rural areas, and a more reliable and complete pension system for the elderly. The greater use of credit cards to purchase large consumer durables, together with more liberal bank mortgages for those buying homes, might also reduce the savings rate. These measures, however, are complex and take time to design and implement and thus cannot or should not be used to deal with a short-term lack of demand.

Therefore, over the long term, China's problem of low household consumption as a share of GDP will be solved by a combination of market forces that raise wages and incomes at a rate that is at least comparable to the rate of growth of GDP, together with government-led measures to provide national health and pension insurance.

The Short-Term Lack of Demand and the Stimulus Package

China's aggregate demand gap as of mid-2009 is an immediate problem, not a long- term one. The Chinese government has stated a goal of maintaining a real GDP growth rate of 8 percent a year in 2009, despite a drop in exports of roughly 20 percent in the first quarter of 2009. The question then becomes how to fill the gap in demand without compromising the long-term prospects for China's economic growth, prospects that require China to maintain a high rate of growth of total factor productivity.

GDP from the expenditure or demand side is made up of the following components:

$$Y = C + I + G + X - M$$

where Y is GDP, C is private consumption, I is non-government investment, G is government consumption and investment, X is exports, and M is imports. A stimulus package designed to eliminate the lack of sufficient demand must raise one or more of these components. We will take up each in turn.

As pointed out in the previous section, raising household consumption through rising incomes and lowered rates of savings is mainly a long-term endeavor. However, there are measures that can make some difference in the short run and China has been implementing these measures for reasons that go beyond the immediate problem of the global recession. Subsidies to the rural poor have been increased, the agricultural tax has been eliminated, and many education expenditures have been taken over by the government. These measures, and other related ones, do help maintain or increase household consumption in the rural areas and unemployment payments play a similar role in the urban areas. There are limits as to what can be done in this way, however, because subsidies that are too large become unsustainable.

The most common East Asian way of facing a recession has been to promote exports. China has made some efforts to keep exports from falling further, but, as made clear above, China cannot continue vigorously to promote its exports, even in the absence of a global recession. With the global recession, export promotion or import-restricting measures will be seen by the rest of the world as "beggar thy neighbor" policies and will elicit retaliation. Economic historians and many others have argued that beggar thy neighbor policies had much to do with why the Great Depression of the 1930s was so deep and so long. Such policies are also widely believed to have contributed to the tensions that led to World War II.

Raising non-governmental investment (I) is also difficult to achieve in the face of a global recession, but in one important respect China is not yet a complete market economy. State-owned enterprises, or shareholding enterprises where the state has majority control, still account for large shares of the nation's industrial and service sectors. Furthermore, management of these enterprises is largely chosen by the government and the Chinese Communist Party. The largest commercial banks are themselves state-owned, with similar management selection practices. Thus the government has a high degree of direct control over these banks and industrial enterprises and it has exercised that control during the current global crisis. In effect, the banks were ordered to increase lending to the industrial and other state enterprises to increase their investment despite the global recession. The response of the banks was immediate, with lending rising to over RMB 4 trillion in the first quarter of 2009, a nearly fourfold increase over the comparable period in 2008.

Initially much of this increase in lending involved many measures that did not provide any real additional demand-side stimulus. Banks in the first quarter, it is said, asked their regular clients to take bills that were then repaid right after the end of the month. Such measures are a way of meeting a monthly target without actually doing anything to increase real activity, a common phenomenon in any economy that relies on government-set targets. In other cases, it is said, state-owned enterprises agreed to take out longer-term loans when they had no need for them or plans to use them. Alternatively, instead of investing in increased capacity, they may have used the loans to buy shares on the stock exchanges, thus becoming partly responsible for the rise in stock prices in China in early 2009.

Of more significance for aggregate demand but also of greater danger for long-term growth is if China's state-owned enterprises have used the additional funds to invest in increased capacity where overcapacity already exists. This appears to have begun to occur in a number of heavy industry sectors ranging from chemicals to steel and non-ferrous metals. For example, by May 2009 China had a stockpile of 190 million tons of steel and hence little reason to expand capacity in that sector.[2] In a worst-case scenario, state-owned banks could be pressured to lend large amounts to state-owned industrial enterprises and the state-owned enterprises could be pressured to expand capacity well beyond demand. The net result would be state enterprises with large unsalable inventories and greatly reduced profitability and state banks with increasing numbers of non-performing loans. In effect, China would be moving back in the direction of the first era of reform in the 1980s when the state-owned banks accumulated large quantities of non-performing assets. The government is likely to pull back well before creating a situation like that in the 1980s, but even a partial move in the direction of overcapacity and non-performing loans will damage China's long-term growth prospects.

The most likely area for a large-scale short-term stimulus is direct government investment in infrastructure, financed through central and local government budgets, although the fiscal capacity of the local governments is limited and lately the local governments have also been resorting to bank loans in order to play their assigned role in the stimulus package. China used government infrastructure investment as a means to avoid a major economic slowdown during the Asian financial crisis of 1997–98. At that time, there were large unmet needs in the area of infrastructure. As a result, China was able to use the funds over the next decade to replace its wholly inadequate highway system with a modern limited-access multi-lane superhighway system that now covers all of the highly populated parts of the country. Starting much earlier, China also carried out a massive urban housing construction program that raised the average per capita size of living space in apartments from 3.6 square meters in 1978 to 27.1 square meters in 2006.[3] The railroad system, provincial airports, and many other parts of the infrastructure have also been upgraded and expanded.

The challenge going forward is to use government stimulus expenditures on infrastructure in ways that are equally productive. Doing so, however, will not be easy because the most obvious shortcomings in this area have already been dealt with. Simply building more high-speed highways and more provincial airports is not likely to produce high-return investments. China is not yet in the situation Japan finds itself, where stimulus packages are used to build "bridges to nowhere" and all kinds of other construction projects that no one really wants or is likely to use. Stimuli of this sort keep up demand for a time, but have no impact on the long-term productivity of the Japanese economy. In China, in contrast, there are still large infrastructure needs, but identifying these needs will be much more of a challenge in the future than it was in the past. For many construction companies, the simplest thing will be to do more of what they have been doing and that may not produce high-return investments. China certainly does not have a real need for more first-class airports in small cities with limited air traffic or for more high-speed highways where the current ones are underutilized.

One area where China does have a large and rising need is urban housing for the tens of millions of migrants who are now pouring into the cities. Government-built housing up to now largely has been for registered urban residents and the current stimulus package calls for more housing for poor registered urban residents. What is needed much more is housing for those migrants who are registered in the rural areas but have little desire to return to those areas. They now live in tents, in small rooms shared by many workers, and in other places unsuitable for families. The stimulus package used in this way would meet a real need and no doubt would contribute to long-term growth. In terms of the stimulus package, however, migrant housing of this sort is not "shovel ready" because government officials have been slow to acknowledge the need and to begin to design programs to meet that need.

The challenge for China's stimulus package is to use the funds expended in ways that promote growth and social welfare. The easiest path to follow in this regard is to do more of the same that has been done over the past decade. This latter path of least resistance, however, is likely to produce many low-return investments that will create problems for China's longer-term growth prospects. For China, using the investments of the stimulus package productively is more important than trying to maintain a GDP growth target of 8 percent during the coming year or two. The more appropriate goal is to maintain a growth rate of 8 percent over the next decade and that can only be achieved if the productivity of new investments remains high.

ENDNOTES

1. Major efforts have been made by a number of scholars to estimate the domestic value-added component of Chinese exports, both overall and with respect to specific products and trade with specific countries (mainly the United States). See Lawrence J. Lau, Web Appendix A: "The Domestic Value Added of Chinese Exports," July 2008, at http://docs .google.com/viewer?a = v&q = cache:e2YGsjIEY_AJ:www.cbo.gov/ftpdocs/95xx/doc9506/ AppendixA.pdf + lawrence + lau + domestic + value + added + of + chinese + exports&hl = en &gl = us&sig = AHIEtbSKCzmon5YyoeqRCEzBZs-EJg1cSw (accessed February 1, 2010).

2. For a brief discussion of this problem, see Editorial, "Redundant Industry," *China Daily*, May 18, 2009, p. 4.

3. State Statistical Bureau, comp., Zhongguo *tongji nianjian 1990* (China Statistical Yearbook 1990) (Beijing: China Statistics Press, 1990), p. 289; and National Bureau of Statistics, comp., *China Statistical Yearbook 2008* (Beijing: China Statistics Press, 2008), p. 315.

18.
MYTH OF THE SOCIAL VOLCANO:
POPULAR RESPONSES TO RISING INEQUALITY IN CHINA

MARTIN KING WHYTE

As many others in this volume have observed, the history of the People's Republic of China after sixty years can be divided into two quite different eras of almost equal length, the socialist era dominated by Mao Zedong and the market-reform era dominated by one of his former lieutenants, Deng Xiaoping. It is also worth noting that Mao's programs and policies did not outlive him for long and were largely repudiated starting in 1978, only two years after his death. Deng has had better luck thus far, with his reform program still going strong more than a dozen years after his death in 1997.

In this chapter I examine popular reactions to the inequality trends that have been unleashed by China's post-1978 market reforms. As I do so, I argue that these reactions are shaped in powerful ways by prior experiences in the socialist system in the roughly thirty years that preceded the launching of the market reforms. However, I also argue that much current analysis of how the socialist past influences citizens' views about present inequalities is oversimplified or dead wrong. The title of this chapter is drawn from my recent book with Stanford University Press, *Myth of the Social Volcano: Perceptions of Inequality and Distributive Injustice in Contemporary China*. That work in turn is based on a national survey of Chinese popular attitudes toward inequality patterns and trends that I directed in 2004. The results of this survey have led me to re-think not only our basic assumptions about inequality in China today, but also about patterns of inequality in the socialist era that preceded Deng's reforms. As the detailed results of the 2004 survey are available elsewhere,[1] in this chapter I mainly focus on the implications of the 2004 survey findings for our assessment of the two eras into which the PRC's history can be divided.

Conventional Views about China's Post-Socialist Transition

It has become common to view the transition from the socialist era to the market-reform era as entailing a clear shift of priorities as well as important tradeoffs.

Whereas in the Mao era both economic growth and the pursuit of social equality were emphasized, a common assessment is that the latter often took priority, particularly in Mao's later years, and sometimes with disastrous consequences. On the economic front the fairly robust growth of the 1950s gave way to the Great Leap Forward depression and famine of 1959–61, followed by a strong economic recovery that was then disrupted by the Cultural Revolution and then by the relative stagnation of the 1970s. Although on some fronts, such as rail construction, military hardware, and even bicycle production, there was considerable progress during the first thirty years, in general popular consumption levels at the time of Mao's death were in many respects no better (and in some realms, such as urban housing space per capita, clearly worse) than they were in the late 1950s.

In the conventional account, the balance sheet on Mao's pursuit of social equality is more positive. The revolution itself and then the socialist transformation launched in 1955 eliminated major inequalities based on property ownership, inherited wealth, and foreign capital, and produced a more equal society based on wages (for women as well as for men, and with work-points, a version of wages, for farmers). But that is not the end of the story. Mao became disenchanted with the remaining inequalities in the socialist society based on Soviet models that he had created, and he was determined to do better. Rejecting Soviet-style inequality patterns as "revisionist," Mao set out during the Cultural Revolution launched in 1966 to eliminate as many of Chinese socialism's material differentials and rewards as possible. To many observers China in the wake of the Cultural Revolution, with its unisex and uniform styles of dress and minimal differentiation in housing quality, material possessions, and lifestyles, as well as its radical experiments with status reversals (e.g., sending urban educated youths to the countryside, having teams of workers manage universities), seemed an unprecedentedly egalitarian social order.

However, the conventional wisdom on the Mao era is that this radical effort to attack social inequality and material rewards and differentials did major damage to China's other primary goal—economic development. In launching their reform program after 1978, Deng Xiaoping and his colleagues were determined to reverse the priorities. As reflected in Deng's famous 1983 phrase, "it is good for some people to get rich first," the reform program embodied an effort to revive differentials and incentives (and repudiate Maoist condemnation of the same) in order to stimulate economic growth. If Mao was obsessed with the pursuit of social equality, Deng and his colleagues have been equally obsessed with the pursuit of economic growth. The conventional view is that social equality has fallen by the wayside, at least until recently.[2]

The reform program launched in 1978 has been remarkably successful by most indicators, producing close to 10 percent annual growth sustained over three decades and dramatic improvements in general standards of living, possession of consumer goods, modernization of the urban landscape and transport system, and most other economic indicators. However, this success has been accompanied by at least one more worrisome trend: social inequality has increased sharply. The Gini coefficient that is conventionally used as a measure of national income distribution was estimated by the World Bank to be .29 in 1981, a relatively low level of income inequality.[3] By 2002 the Gini coefficient for China had increased to .45 (or even higher in some estimates), indicating that China had shifted from a relatively low to a moderately high level of income inequality.[4]

Much more is involved than simply increased income inequality. The entire system of distribution of centrally planned socialism has been replaced by market-oriented institutions, and in the process forms of wealth and privilege that the revolution set out to destroy have returned with a vengeance—for example, millionaire business tycoons, foreign capitalists exploiting Chinese workers, and gated and guarded private mansion compounds. The downsides of capitalism have also returned to China with a vengeance—unemployment, inflation, loss of health insurance, bankruptcy, and confiscations of housing and farmland in shady development deals. Many who planned their lives in the expectation that they would be honored for their contributions to the construction of socialism now find themselves unexpectedly out of work and facing bleak prospects for the future, even as they see some Chinese becoming millionaires or even billionaires.

In the conventional view it is assumed that most Chinese regret the loss of the security and social equality of the Mao era and are angry about the increases in inequality and distributive injustice that the market reforms have spawned. Since the legitimacy and authority of CCP rule are now seen as primarily resting on popular assessments of the economic situation (rather than, say, on faith in the CCP's leadership in pursuing socialism), it is widely assumed that popular anger about rising inequality has had the effect of cancelling out or at least undermining popular gratitude for increases in living standards.

One somewhat more fine-grained version of the conventional wisdom focuses on trends *within* the reform era. During the initial years of the reforms—say, from 1978 up until the mid-1990s—the economic benefits of the reforms were, according to this account, fairly widely shared, with no social groups suffering major losses, a pattern referred to in one influential study as "reform without losers."[5] In more recent years, in contrast, some Chinese have become fabulously wealthy, whereas the "smashing of the iron rice bowl" reforms of state-owned enterprises launched after 1994 and extra tax levies and land confiscations in the countryside have impoverished large numbers of Chinese citizens. Given these objective trends, it is widely assumed that feelings of anger about distributive injustice have been spreading, at least since the mid-1990s.

It is these perceptions of widespread and growing anger about current inequalities that are emphasized in what I call "the social volcano scenario," the contention that protest activity stimulated by such anger is mounting and could eventually explode into large-scale turbulence that would threaten CCP rule.[6] For example, one account of the findings reported in the 2006 "Blue Book" (an annual publication of the Chinese Academy of Social Sciences reporting on social trends) states, "The Gini coefficient, an indicator of income disparities, reached 0.53 last year, far higher than a dangerous level of 0.4."[7] A similar view was expressed in *The New York Times* in 2006 by correspondent Joseph Kahn, "Because many people believe that wealth flows from access to power more than it does from talent or risk-taking, the wealth gap has incited outrage and is viewed as at least partly responsible for tens of thousands of mass protests around the country in recent years."[8]

An additional element in the conventional view is the assumption that attitudes about inequalities today are correlated with current social status and whether particular individuals or groups have been winners or losers as a result of the reform-era changes. Those with high incomes and social status who have prospered in the reform era are assumed to view current inequality patterns as fair. In contrast, disadvantaged groups, such as unemployed workers, migrants, farmers, and residents of interior provinces, are assumed to be particularly angry about distributive injustice. If China is headed toward a social volcano, in this account it is likely to be reform-era losers who will be at the forefront of the eruption.

One sign of the influence of these assumptions is that the new leaders who took charge of the CCP after 2002 clearly accept the "social volcano scenario" as a dangerous possibility and thus have adopted vigorous policy measures to try to reduce the danger. Hu Jintao's slogans about China becoming a more "harmonious society" have been backed up by a number of important policy changes, particularly policies designed to combat rural poverty and disadvantages. For example, since 2002, agricultural taxes have been eliminated, rural school fees are being phased out, and a state-subsidized new village cooperative medical insurance program has been introduced to replace the Mao-era village cooperative medical insurance systems that collapsed early in the reform era. After decades of neglect of rural needs under both Mao and Deng, these new programs, and the increased state funding that they provide, indicate that the CCP leadership genuinely fears what a recent *Time* magazine article referred to as "the pitchfork anger of peasants."[9]

Challenging the Myth: Results of the 2004 China National Survey

About a decade ago my colleagues and I became interested in launching surveys in China to measure popular attitudes about inequality trends and distributive injustice issues.[10] We were struck by the fact that many detailed surveys were being conducted to measure objective inequality patterns and trends in China, but none to assess popular feelings about these trends, with many assuming that research on distributive injustice sentiments was too politically sensitive to be feasible in the PRC. In order to test whether it was feasible to conduct rigorous surveys on popular attitudes toward current inequalities, our team carried out a pilot survey in Beijing in 2000.[11] Based on the success of the Beijing pilot survey, we planned and carried out a national survey with the same focus in 2004. We wanted to use our surveys to assess the accuracy of various elements of the social volcano scenario.

The 2004 China survey on inequality and distributive injustice attitudes used spatial probability sampling methods to draw a sample that was representative of Chinese adults between the ages of 18 and 70, with a final sample size of 3,267 respondents and a response rate of about 75 percent.[12] The questionnaire used in the survey asked about many distinct inequality and distributive injustice issues. We also made use of the fact that comparative international surveys previously had been conducted on attitudes toward inequality issues. In particular, the International Social Justice Project (ISJP) had conducted several rounds of surveys on attitudes toward inequality in a number of East European post-socialist societies, as well as in several advanced capitalist societies, including the United States.[13] We translated and replicated many ISJP questions in our 2000 and 2004 surveys, a procedure that allowed us to examine how Chinese popular attitudes regarding current inequalities compare with the views of citizens in other societies, particularly in other post-socialist societies.

In the 2004 survey we found that respondents did have strong criticisms of certain features of the current inequalities. For example, 71.7 percent felt that national income gaps were too large, 55.8 percent said that it was unfair for individuals in official positions to receive special privileges, 76.8 percent responded that it was unfair to bar the children of migrants from attending urban public schools, and 50.1 percent claimed that officials do not care what ordinary people think (about social justice issues).

However, these responses were limited exceptions to a general pattern in which the average respondent expressed acceptance or approval rather than anger over current inequalities. For example, most respondents thought that differences in ability are an important factor explaining who is rich (69.5 percent) versus who is poor (61.3 percent), whereas the unfairness of the economic system was stressed by many fewer respondents—only 27 percent thought that such unfairness has a large influence on who is rich, and 21 percent stressed this explanation of who is poor. Only 29.5 percent of respondents favored redistribution from the rich to the poor, and only 33.8 percent advocated setting a maximum limit on individual incomes. On the other hand, 50.4 percent of respondents agreed that extra rewards are necessary to motivate people to work hard, 62.8 percent thought that people should be able to keep what they earn even if this leads to greater inequality, and 64.2 percent said it is fair if rich people use their incomes to obtain better schooling for their children. Along the same lines, by identical percentages of 61.1 percent our survey respondents agreed with statements that "hard work is always rewarded" and that "opportunities for someone like you to raise your standard of living are still great."

Even in realms where respondents expressed relatively critical attitudes, there is little sign of generalized feelings of distributive injustice. For example, even though 71.7 percent of our respondents viewed current national income inequality as excessive, it turns out that this is a relatively low figure in comparative terms. In the ISJP surveys, only Americans in 1991 were less likely to view national income gaps as too large (at 65.2 percent); in 1996 about 95 percent of respondents in both Hungary and Bulgaria thought that their national income gaps were too large. Furthermore, when we asked our China respondents their views on income gaps within their work-units and neighborhoods, many fewer viewed these local income gaps as excessive (39.6 percent and 31.8 percent, respectively). It is also important to point out that the features of the current inequalities that respondents objected to most strongly have their roots in the socialist era (such as special treatment of officials and discrimination against those who lack urban *hukou*), rather than being products of the market reforms.

A systematic comparison of the attitudes of Chinese respondents with their counterparts in the countries surveyed in the ISJP reinforces the view that most Chinese are substantially more approving rather than angry about current inequalities.[14] In general, Chinese attitudes toward various aspects of the current inequalities are either similar to other societies or more accepting or positive. Compared to post-socialist societies in Eastern Europe, Chinese attitudes in general are much more positive, and for some questions Chinese respondents expressed views about current inequalities that are even more positive than their counterparts in established and successful capitalist societies such as Japan and the United States. For example, many more Chinese respondents than those in any other ISJP country thought that lack of ability is an important reason why people in their society are poor, and many more agree with the proposition that hard work is always rewarded. It is also worth noting the surprising finding that the proportion of Chinese respondents agreeing with the statement that officials do not care what ordinary people think (50.1 percent) is substantially lower than the proportion in all ISJP comparison countries, whether post-socialist or established capitalist. Generally, two-thirds or more of the respondents in these (more democratic) countries expressed agreement with this statement, with roughly 75 percent of respondents in Japan, Bulgaria, and the former East Germany expressing agreement. In general, the high levels of approval by Chinese respondents of current, market-based inequalities provide the basis for my conclusion that the Chinese "social volcano" scenario is a myth.

One further pattern in our survey results merits comment before turning to the question of how to interpret these unexpected findings. In order to examine the assumption that anger is likely to be found particularly among disadvantaged groups who have lost out in China's market transition, we also wanted to find out in which social groups, and in which locales, were Chinese citizens most angry about current inequalities. Even if the most common survey responses involved acceptance of current inequalities, on every question perhaps 20–30 percent of respondents expressed more critical attitudes, and we wanted to find out where those more critical voices were concentrated.

In *Myth of the Social Volcano* I end up using more than a dozen distinct measures covering the complex conceptual terrain of inequality and distributive injustice attitudes, and it turns out that there are no particular social groups or geographic locations associated with more critical attitudes across this whole range of indicators. However, there are some at least relatively consistent patterns, and once again these turn out to contradict the conventional wisdom. On many although not all of these measures, rural people in general, and farmers in particular, express more accepting or positive views than others about current inequalities and show less enthusiasm for government redistribution, despite their low relative social status.[15] In contrast, urban people in general, and particularly the well-educated, and in some cases those with state enterprise ties, the middle-aged, those who are Han Chinese rather than minorities, and CCP members, tend to express somewhat more critical attitudes toward current inequalities and would like the government to engage in more redistribution.[16]

It should be noted that these Chinese results in general are very different from the patterns found in other societies. Elsewhere it is usually the case that individuals with high social status tend to accept current inequalities and oppose redistribution, whereas those who are disadvantaged are more critical and favor greater government efforts to redistribute from the rich to the poor.[17] Thus we are left with dual puzzles in interpreting the results of the 2004 China survey—why do average Chinese respondents have such favorable views about current inequalities, and why is it the relatively disadvantaged groups, and farmers in particular, who are the most favorable?

Reassessing China's Post-Socialist Transition

When we launched our surveys I assumed that in assessing the current social order, Chinese citizens would weigh in their minds two contrary trends—the positive consequences of raised average living standards versus the negative consequences of heightened inequality. That assumption was based on a view that the Mao era, whatever its excesses and faults, had one redeeming feature in the eyes of most citizens—extensive social equality. However, the 2004 survey results call into question these assumptions. Our findings indicate that most survey respondents view both increased growth and heightened inequality in a positive light. By implication, Chinese today view the patterns of inequality in the late Mao era negatively—as manifesting distributive injustice rather than distributive justice. In the following pages I explore the implications of this revised view by reassessing the nature of stratification patterns at the close of the Mao era.

What were the stratification patterns in China during the 1970s, and in what sense were these patterns just or unjust? Under closer inspection it turns out that the socialist order that existed at the time of Mao's death was not so egalitarian after all. In reexamining the social reality of the time, it is useful to consider levels of equality and inequality both within particular localities (work-units and communities) and across such localities.[18] It is also important to keep in mind the basic conceptual distinction between inequality and inequity. Inequality refers to an objective situation in which certain resources are unevenly distributed within a society or locality. In contrast, inequity refers to a subjective judgment that the actual pattern of distribution of resources differs from the ideal or preferred pattern. This distinction is important because it is a sense of inequity, not objective levels of inequality per se, that can provide the basis for discontent and even political challenges. If individuals think that existing differentials and income gaps are suitable or even necessary, such gaps will not generate anger. In fact, individuals may feel that too much equality constitutes an inequitable situation.

Viewed from this perspective, how does the socialist stratification system at the end of the Mao era stack up? Oversimplifying a complex reality, in general it was a system that emphasized and zealously pursued equality within local employment and residential units, but at the same time generally ignored, and in many instances even aggravated, inequalities across such units. Let us focus on this latter tendency first. Within urban areas we have a number of systematic accounts of the way in which the institutions of socialist distribution treated urban localities and work organizations quite differently in terms of the allocation of resources and the opportunities for individual members, depending on where the units were ranked in the stratified bureaucratic system.[19] Employees of collective enterprises generally fared worse than those working in state enterprises, and the latter differed both in terms of the strategic priority of their organizational system (*xitong*) and their size and bureaucratic rank (from central down to local) within that system. So how well an urban citizen lived and the opportunities he or she enjoyed depended as much, or even more, on where he or she was situated within the ranked hierarchies of Chinese socialism as on their human capital or individual diligence.

There were similarly large differences in incomes and other resources across sub-units of rural communes (production brigades and teams), across communes, and across rural regions and provinces, differences that official policy was not designed to limit or reduce. However, the most extreme status and resource cleavage within Chinese socialism was not found within the urban social landscape or within the countryside generally, but between city and countryside. We again have multiple accounts documenting both the size and the growing sharpness of the rural-urban gap during the Mao era.[20] Despite official propaganda slogans about shrinking the rural-urban gap and advocating that industry should serve agriculture, Mao and his colleagues introduced institutions and practices that consigned the great majority of Chinese citizens—the more than 80 percent who lived in the countryside prior to 1978—to a status that can only be considered "socialist serfdom," as they were effectively bound to the soil. Individuals born in rural areas (more specifically, those born to rural mothers, despite China's patrilineal tradition) inherited agricultural household registrations which, from 1960 onward, basically prevented them from migrating to any Chinese town or city. Official priorities stressed urban industrial development, and the government provided very little (and generally declining) funding for rural development. Furthermore, commune members were forbidden from engaging in any of a whole range of activities catering to urban needs (e.g., commerce, construction, domestic services, handicraft making, etc.) that their counterparts in earlier eras had undertaken to earn money. The effectively permanent relegation of rural residents to the bottom of the stratification hierarchy of socialist China is the most egregious instance of how inegalitarian and inequitable the stratification system became under Mao.[21]

To sum up the discussion to this point, in both rural and urban China, and particularly across the rural-urban divide, Chinese socialism consisted of bounded units (local communities and work organizations) whose resources and opportunities were bureaucratically controlled and decidedly unequal. Mao-era political discourse, particularly during the class struggle-obsessed Cultural Revolution decade, essentially ignored these non-social class status cleavages, and there was no systematic effort to enact redistribution to control or reverse the growing inequalities across such boundaries.[22] For the most part, individuals were either born into or bureaucratically assigned to their niches within this socialist stratification system, and they were expected to remain toiling where they were unless the state decided to transfer them elsewhere. So individuals had little ability to influence or change a basic determinant of their status and opportunities. It is hard to imagine a stratification system any more different from the one that existed in China before 1949, which was characterized by huge inequalities but virtually no caste-like barriers preventing individuals and families from competing to change their lives and better their standards of living (but, at the same time, providing minimal security against the possibility of failure and individual and familial impoverishment). The nature of Chinese socialism is replete with ironies—a rural revolution led by a son of the soil and proclaiming the goal of combating feudalism in order to create a more egalitarian society in reality ended up producing a social order with striking resemblances to feudalism, with the mass of China's rural residents consigned to serf-like status at the bottom of society.

Why did so many observers believe that Mao had successfully created an unusually egalitarian social order? That impression derives from the other side of the post-1955 (and even more so post-1966) stratification transformations that Chinese socialism produced—the assault on inequalities within localities and work organizations (even as inequalities across such boundaries were becoming entrenched and even enlarged). Within local bounded units, Mao-era campaigns and institutions did lead to a truncation of inequalities compared to the situation prior to the revolution (or today). Urban employees received fixed monthly wages that were maintained within relatively modest ranges (e.g., a factory manager making only about 2–3 times as much as an ordinary worker), with no chances after the Cultural Revolution to augment their incomes through bonuses, overtime, over-quota production efforts, or moonlighting. Many work-unit employees lived in work-unit-supplied (and subsidized) apartments that again differed only modestly in quality and space from those of their supervisors and subordinates, with all utilizing the same dining halls, medical clinics, and other collective facilities.

In the countryside, the collectivized agricultural organization of the communes, with work-point systems and preliminary grain distributions, helped to keep family consumption differences within any production team confined to relatively narrow ranges that were determined more by family composition (number of laborers compared to number of dependents) than by differences in human capital or agricultural effort or skill.[23] Members of the rural labor force were uniformly obligated to participate in collective field labor, particularly by growing grain to meet state procurement quotas. As noted earlier, they were forbidden from engaging in the tactics poor Chinese farmers had used for centuries to escape from poverty—growing specialized crops, making handicrafts to sell, starting a family business, specializing in rural or rural-to-urban commerce, and, most importantly, leaving to seek better opportunities elsewhere, particularly in the cities.[24] On top of these institutional practices designed to keep inequalities within localities and work organizations restricted to relatively narrow ranges, there was of course the general imposition of obligatory proletarian styles of dress, leisure activities, and lifestyles, particularly in the wake of the "destroy the four olds" stage of the Cultural Revolution in the fall of 1966. In the final decade of Mao's life, engaging in conspicuous consumption of any kind was decidedly dangerous politically.

To what extent was this imposition of relative equality within particular cells in China's socialist stratification order seen as desirable and just, even if the large and growing gaps across cells were largely ignored? In important respects even the relative equality achieved within local units is seen (today, at least) as unjust. An important feature of Mao's obsession with promoting equality in his later years is that this was entirely a matter of "leveling down," rather than affirmative action or other measures designed to achieve equality by "leveling up." In other words, the various measures taken during the late Mao era involved prohibiting the industrious, talented, entrepreneurial, and innovative, as well as those in superior positions, from seeking and enjoying extra material and other rewards compared to others in their local cells. But there was no corresponding effort to redistribute extra rewards to those who were particularly disadvantaged. In the 2004 survey only about one in three respondents approved of equality as a primary distribution principle or of setting a maximum limit on individual incomes. In contrast, about 62 percent of respondents approved of the government providing extra assistance to help those who are particularly disadvantaged (i.e., "leveling up"). More to the point perhaps is the fact that the Cultural Revolution-era policies regarding remuneration fundamentally contradicted what

Chinese citizens had earlier been taught was the correct (and therefore just) distribution principle of socialism: from each according to his abilities, and to each according to his contributions. Mao's critics in the Soviet Union had some reason for claiming that it was he rather than they who was revising and violating Marxist principles, and they denigrated the kind of social order Mao was trying to create as "barracks communism."[25]

So even where social equality was successfully pursued under Mao, within local units, the result was a social order which expected individuals to accept their assignments and fates and to labor to the best of their abilities without any concern about the remuneration and benefits they would receive, and without any ability to change their circumstances and to seek better opportunities and rewards for themselves and their families. The resulting stratification system was in direct contradiction not only with prior understandings of socialism (in Eastern Europe, but also in China prior to 1966), but also with centuries of Chinese tradition. In short, in multiple ways the stratification patterns of the late Mao era violated basic principles of social equity.

The nature of stratification patterns at the end of the Mao era also helps explain the unexpected finding that some disadvantaged groups, and farmers in particular, now have more positive attitudes toward current inequalities than their more advantaged fellow citizens. If you are a farmer who has been confined to something that is tantamount to socialist serfdom, in a sense you had nowhere to go but up in social status after 1978, and you are also likely to want to pursue such mobility through individual and family efforts, rather than by relying on state redistribution. In contrast, urban residents in general, and the well-educated and workers and others connected to state enterprises in particular, faced the possibility of reform-era gains but also of loss of the advantages and privileges that they had enjoyed in the socialist system. So it is not so surprising after all that somewhat more of China's urban than of her rural citizens today lament the demise of socialist distribution and wish that the state would do more to limit inequality and promote redistribution.

Conclusions

The results of the 2004 China national survey on attitudes toward inequality and distributive injustice indicate that most ordinary Chinese citizens see both the raised living standards and the more unequal society in which they now live in a favorable light. We find precious little evidence of nostalgia for the patterns of the late Mao era, at least in terms of inequality patterns. The average survey respondent approves of the market-based principles and competition that characterize China today and rejects distribution principles that require strict equality or do not allow the rich to keep their wealth or to spend it to buy better lives for their families. Our survey respondents are telling us that they regard the current patterns of inequality as more fair than those that existed at the close of the Mao era. As noted earlier, the fact that there is so little popular support for the view that current inequality patterns are mainly the product of unfair connections and dishonesty leads to my labeling of the "social volcano" scenario as mythical.[26]

However, we cannot be certain whether this rejection of the inequality patterns of the late Mao era reflects how people felt then, since there were no systematic surveys of Chinese popular attitudes conducted at that time. Could positive views about current inequalities be recent beliefs that Chinese citizens have come to accept as a result of being exposed to the incessant championing of market-based inequalities by China's official propaganda media? Since we have no empirical evidence that would allow us to answer this question, let me close by providing my own thoughts and speculations on this issue.

My sense is that whatever the level of popular acceptance and support of the distinctive stratification order during the late Mao era, it was sustained only with considerable difficulty and with much popular grumbling beneath the surface. I do not think the main difficulty was gaining acceptance of the sharp inequalities across locales and organizations, and between rural and urban China, even though these were the most important axes of inequality at the time. I say this because the evidence on distributive injustice attitudes in all societies, and thus I assume also in China both in the 1970s and today, is that individuals are particularly sensitive to how they are doing relative to reference groups that are near at hand (e.g., neighbors, workmates, and friends), and they are relatively less concerned about how they are doing compared with others who are farther away and only dimly perceived.[27]

However, I think it must have been difficult to gain popular acceptance of a social order in which nearby individuals who are better educated, who hold more responsible positions, who produce more than their colleagues, and who create innovations do not receive rewards and promotions within their local units and might in some instances even be subjected to special criticism and abuse. Furthermore, it could not have been very popular to see lazy or incompetent colleagues receive the same rewards as everyone else, while political sycophants sometimes enjoyed special praise and promotion opportunities.[28] Similarly, I think it must have been difficult to convince ordinary Chinese that it was fair to require them to remain content with their bureaucratically assigned lots and not to use whatever talents and ingenuity they might have to try to get ahead and provide better lives for their families. Again, these speculations are not based primarily on distinctive features of Chinese citizens and their historical tradition, but on research on social equity and distributive justice in societies around the world. In trying to minimize or even eliminate local inequalities, Mao was directly challenging fundamental and probably universal principles that value equity rather than equality, and I wonder how he could have thought that in the long run this challenge could succeed.

In sum, current inequalities by and large are accepted by the average Chinese citizen because they conform more closely to fundamental principles of equity and distributive justice than the inequality patterns Mao championed at the close of his life. This is not to say that the actual patterns of inequality in China today are a model of distributive justice, as there surely remain serious problems of corruption and distributive injustice—regarding the latter, particularly involving the remaining systemic discrimination against rural residents and migrants. Nor do I claim that Chinese citizens feel they live in a society that is just in all respects, as procedural injustices and abuses of power abound.[29] Rather, my conclusion is more limited. If we consider the two thirty-year periods into which PRC history is roughly divided, the first closed with a quixotic quest for social equality envisioned in a very unusual way, and in the midst of sharp inequalities that at the time were largely ignored. By repudiating Mao's quirky vision of social equality China's reformers during the past three decades have created, or in some respects have returned to, a social order that is in some ways more unequal. However, at the same time they have been able to release incredible energy and popular ingenuity from Chinese citizens because, whatever its faults, today's stratification order is seen as more just than the Maoist social order that preceded it.

ENDNOTES

1. The Stanford book appeared in 2010. Also in print are "The Social Contours of Distributive Injustice Feelings in Contemporary China" (with Chunping Han), in Deborah S. Davis and Wang Feng, eds., *Creating Wealth and Poverty in Postsocialist China* (Stanford, CA: Stanford University Press, 2009); "Zhongguo minzhong ruhe kandai dangqian de shehui bu pingdeng" (Views of Chinese Citizens on Current Inequalities), *Shehuixue yanjiu* (Sociological Research) (in Chinese), no. 1 (2009): 96–120; "What Do Chinese See as Fair and Unfair about Current Inequalities?" in Jean Oi, Scott Rozelle, and Xueguang Zhou, eds., *Growing Pains: Tensions and Opportunities in China's Transition* (Washington, DC: Brookings Institution Press, 2010); "How Angry Are Chinese Citizens about Current Inequalities? Evidence from a National Survey" (with Maocan Guo), in Chan Kwok-bun, et al., eds., *Social Stratification in Chinese Societies* (Leiden: Brill, 2009); and "Do Chinese

Citizens Want the Government to Do More to Promote Equality?" in Peter Hays Gries and Stanley Rosen, eds., *Chinese Politics: State, Society, and the Market* (New York: Routledge, 2010).

2. Starting with the "Develop the West" campaign launched by Jiang Zemin in 2000 and continuing with Hu Jintao's championing of a "harmonious society" since 2002, new policy initiatives and resources in recent times have been directed somewhat more in the direction of disadvantaged localities and social groups, as will be discussed later in this chapter.

3. *China 2020: Sharing Rising Incomes: Disparities in China* (Washington, DC: World Bank, 1997), p. 1. A Gini of 0 indicates total equality, whereas a Gini of 1.0 indicates total inequality. No reliable income distribution data are available for China for the 1970s or earlier.

4. The Gini = .45 figure is reported in Björn A. Gustaffson, Li Shi, and Terry Sicular, eds., *Inequality and Public Policy in China* (New York: Cambridge University Press, 2007). The United Nations Human Development Report for 2007/2008 (available online at http://hdr.undp.org/en/reports/global/hdr2007-2008/ (accessed February 8, 2010), gives a Gini of .469 for China at that time, compared to .408 for the United States, .249 for Japan, .368 for India, and .334 for Bangladesh. The same source gives Brazil's Gini index as .57 and South Africa's as .578.

5. See Lawrence Lau, Yingyi Qian, and Gérard Roland, "Reform without Losers: An Interpretation of China's Dual-Track Approach to Transition," *Journal of Political Economy*, 108, no. 1 (February 2000): 120–43. For a similar analysis, see Yasheng Huang, *Capitalism with Chinese Characteristics: Entrepreneurship and the State* (New York: Cambridge University Press, 2008). During the initial period of this first half of the reform era, up until about 1985, rural incomes increased faster than urban incomes, producing a decline in China's foremost social cleavage, the rural-urban income gap. Since then the rural-urban income gap has generally widened, from below 2:1 in 1985 to more than 3:1 in 2002. See the discussion in Gustaffson, Li, and Sicular, eds., *Inequality and Public Policy in China*.

6. Numerous scholarly and journalistic accounts of these trends offer various versions of the speculation or fear that increasing anger about distributive injustice might eventually feed growing protests and social volatility that could threaten CCP rule. The most explicit use of the "social volcano" metaphor I have found is in the writings of He Qinglian, an economic journalist and critic of distributive injustice who was forced into exile in 2001 as a result of her controversial writings. See Qinglian He, "A Volcanic Stability," *Journal of Democracy*, 14, no. 1 (January 2003): 66–72.

7. Josephine Ma, "Wealth Gap Fueling Instability, Studies Warn," *South China Morning Post*, December 22, 2005.

8. Joseph Kahn, "China Makes Commitment to Social Harmony," *The New York Times*, October 12, 2006.

9. Hannah Beech, "Seeds of Fury," *Time Asia*, 167, no. 11 (March 13, 2006).

10. Our research team includes Albert Park, Wang Feng, Jieming Chen, Pierre Landry, and Chunping Han, and our primary collaborators in the PRC have been Shen Mingming at the Research Center for Contemporary China of Peking University and his colleagues, Yang Ming and Yan Jie.

11. See the results reported in Martin Whyte and Chunping Han, "Popular Attitudes toward Distributive Injustice: Beijing and Warsaw Compared," *Journal of Chinese Political Science*, 13, no. 1 (April 2008): 29–51. The current chapter will not discuss the findings of the Beijing pilot survey, although they are broadly similar to the results of the 2004 China national survey.

12. Most prior sample surveys in China, including my own earlier work, used household registration (*hukou*) records as the basis for sampling. However, as people are increasingly moving around, household registration is more flawed, with migrants and people who move into new housing not included. Temporary registration that is supposed to catch migrants does not solve the problem, because perhaps as many as half of all migrants do not bother to register. Spatial probability sampling, in contrast, uses maps and population density estimates to select actual physical points, with probability proportional to population size. Then a member of each household within a set boundary surrounding each such point is selected to be interviewed, whether or not he/she is registered in that locality. See Pierre F. Landry and Mingming Shen, "Reaching Migrants in Survey Research: The Use of the Global Positioning System to Reduce Coverage Bias in China," *Political Analysis*, 13 (Winter 2005): 1–22.

13. The initial round of the ISJP surveys in 1991 involved selected Eastern European societies as well as the United States, the UK, West Germany, and Japan. A second round was conducted in selected Eastern European societies in 1996. See James R. Kluegel, David S. Mason, and Bernd Wegener, eds., *Social Justice and Political Change: Public Opinion in Capitalist and Post-Communist States* (New York: Walter de Gruyter, 1995); David S. Mason and James R. Kluegel, eds., *Marketing Democracy: Changing Opinion about Inequality and Politics in East Central Europe* (Lanham, MD: Rowman & Littlefield, 2000). Subsequently, in 2005 and 2006, the ISJP surveys were repeated in a smaller number of Eastern European societies.

14. For details, see my *Myth of the Social Volcano: Perceptions of Inequality and Distributive Injustice in Contemporary China* (Stanford, CA: Stanford University Press, 2010), ch. 4.

15. This general pattern is subjected to detailed examination in the doctoral thesis of project member Chunping Han. See Chunping Han, "Rural-Urban Cleavages in Perceptions of Inequality in Contemporary China," unpublished Ph.D. dissertation, Department of Sociology, Harvard University, 2009.

16. We examined a large number of other predictions about the social contours of distributive injustice attitudes; here we only focus on those that stand out across the multiple attitude scales that are focused on here. For example, we used several geographic measures to test predictions that respondents in inland and in "rust-belt" localities would display more critical attitudes than respondents in areas that have benefited more from the market reforms, but when controlling for the social backgrounds of the individual respondents, few of these geographic predictions were supported by the survey evidence.

17. See Jennifer L. Hochschild, *What's Fair? American Beliefs about Distributive Justice* (Cambridge, MA: Harvard University Press, 1981); James R. Kluegel and Eliot R. Smith, *Beliefs about Inequality: Americans' Views of What Is and What Ought to Be* (New York: Aldine de Gruyter, 1986). However, in many past studies in other societies, as in the 2004 China survey, the highly educated tend to have somewhat more critical attitudes toward

current inequalities, even though those who have high status by other criteria (e.g., income, occupational status, ethnic majority status) tend to have relatively positive views.

18. See the framework used in Wang Feng, *Boundaries and Categories: Rising Inequality in Post-Socialist Urban China* (Stanford, CA: Stanford University Press, 2008).

19. See, for example, Andrew G. Walder, "The Remaking of the Chinese Working Class, 1949–1981," *Modern China*, 10, no. 3 (July 1984): 3–48; Yanjie Bian, *Work and Inequality in Urban China* (Albany, NY: SUNY Press, 1994); Martin King Whyte and William L. Parish, *Urban Life in Contemporary China* (Chicago: University of Chicago Press, 1984). Cities were also bureaucratically ranked in ways that affected the resources and opportunities available to their citizens.

20. See, for example, Rhoads Murphey, *The Fading of the Maoist Vision: City and Country in China's Development* (New York: Methuen, 1980); Sulamith Heins Potter, "The Position of Peasants in Modern China's Social Order," *Modern China*, 9, no. 4 (October 1993): 465–99; Mark Selden, "City versus Countryside? The Social Consequences of Development Choices in China," in Selden, ed., *The Political Economy of Chinese Socialism* (Armonk, NY: M.E. Sharpe, 1988), ch. 6; Kam Wing Chan, *Cities with Invisible Walls: Reinterpreting Urbanization in Post-1949 China* (New York: Oxford University Press, 1994); Dorothy Solinger, *Contesting Citizenship in Urban China: Peasant Migrants, the State, and the Logic of the Market* (Berkeley: University of California Press, 1999); and Fei-Ling Wang, *Organizing through Division and Exclusion: China's Hukou System* (Stanford, CA: Stanford University Press, 2005).

21. For further discussion of the origins and ironies of the sharp rural-urban cleavage that is a legacy of Chinese socialism, see Martin K. Whyte, ed., *One Country, Two Societies: Rural-Urban Inequality in Contemporary China* (Cambridge, MA: Harvard University Press, 2010).

22. A further irony of this institutional system is that in 1956 and 1957, in the wake of the Hungarian uprising, Mao Zedong recognized the importance of managing such non-social class inequalities in Chinese society (in his articles, "On the Ten Major Relationships" in 1956 and "On the Correct Handling of Contradictions Among the People" in 1957). However, in later years Mao seems to have completely forgotten his earlier wisdom about the need to manage multiple stratification cleavages.

23. Preliminary grain distributions allowed families to receive grain to consume, even if in the year-end accounting after the final harvest they did not end up having accumulated enough work-points for their labor in the fields to pay for what they had already consumed. The existence of such "over-consuming households" (*chaozhi hu*) acted to equalize consumption levels across families and provided basic food security to labor-poor families, as long as the team had grain to distribute (an important qualification, given the mass famine in which at least 30 million excess deaths occurred in 1959–61). See the discussion in William L. Parish and Martin King Whyte, *Village and Family in Contemporary China* (Chicago: University of Chicago Press, 1974); Mark Selden, "Income Inequality and the State in Rural China," in Selden, ed., *The Political Economy of Chinese Socialism*, pp. 129–52. However, across teams within brigades and across brigades within a commune the income gaps could be larger—sometimes 3:1 or 4:1 or even higher—and there was no mechanism in place to redistribute from richer teams to poorer teams.

24. In most periods and places after the initial Great Leap high tide, rural families were allowed to grow crops on small private plots and to raise a pig or two. However, restrictions

were in place to prevent members of the rural labor force from diverting most of their energies from collective field labor to these private pursuits, and particularly to prevent them from making more than occasional visits to rural markets. (Marketing private-plot produce in the cities was strictly prohibited, unlike the practice in the Soviet Union and Eastern Europe.) In a similar vein, there was some encouragement of rural industry within the commune system, but only to produce things like cement and tools to meet local needs (rather than making items for sale in the cities, much less overseas), and workers were supposed to be paid with work-points, whose value was set to be comparable to the levels received for agricultural labor in order to prevent rural factory workers from becoming a privileged stratum. See American Rural Small-Scale Industry Delegation, *Rural Small-Scale Industry in the People's Republic of China* (Berkeley: University of California Press, 1977).

25. "Barracks communism" is a term coined by Karl Marx to denounce the kind of bureaucratically regimented and (in our terms) leveled-down social equality he saw being advocated by nineteenth-century "primitive socialists" such as Sergei Nechayev. One can assume that Deng Xiaoping also had come to see the "leveled-down" equality of Mao's socialism circa 1976 as highly inequitable. See my article, "Deng Xiaoping: The Social Reformer," *The China Quarterly*, no. 135 (September 1993): 515–55.

26. However, the 2004 survey cannot tell us in what direction Chinese popular attitudes on these issues are changing, and particularly whether the negative consequences within China due to the global financial meltdown that erupted in 2008 have undermined Chinese acceptance of current inequalities. Our research team carried out a five-year follow-up survey late in 2009 to determine how during the period since our original 2004 survey Chinese attitudes may have changed and why, with the results to be reported in future publications.

27. On these general points about influences on distributive injustice views, see the discussion in Hochschild, *What's Fair?*; Kluegel and Smith, *Beliefs about Inequality*.

28. Susan Shirk describes Mao's goal as replacing "meritocracy" with "virtuocracy" and insightfully describes the difficulties and contradictions that such a virtuocratic emphasis entails. See Susan L. Shirk, "The Decline of Virtuocracy in China," in James L. Watson, ed., *Class and Social Stratification in Post-Revolution China* (Cambridge: Cambridge University Press, 1984), ch. 4.

29. See the discussions of the procedural injustices faced by China's rural citizens in Thomas Bernstein and Xiaobo Lü, *Taxation without Representation in Contemporary Rural China* (Cambridge: Cambridge University Press, 2003); Kevin J. O'Brien and Lianjiang Li, *Rightful Resistance in Rural China* (Cambridge: Cambridge University Press, 2006).

CULTURE, BELIEF, PRACTICE

19.
THE MAKING OF A HERO:
LEI FENG AND SOME ISSUES OF HISTORIOGRAPHY

XIAOFEI TIAN

People's Liberation Army soldier Lei Feng (雷锋) (1940–62), who was famous for his loyalty to the party and Chairman Mao and for his selfless acts of helping others, became a cultural icon in the twentieth century in the People's Republic of China. Nearly half a century after his death, books, essays, and news articles about him are still being produced in print and Internet media; his name is ingrained in popular culture;[1] and his story was being made into a new TV drama in 2009, starring Tian Liang, a hot young actor and a former diver who had garnered a number of Olympic gold and silver medals. At the same time, questions about the authenticity of Lei Feng's diary and indeed about the genuineness of Lei Feng's existence itself continue to trouble the public consciousness. This chapter aims to examine the case of Lei Feng and, by doing so, raise two larger points: one is the continuity of the premodern cultural tradition in modern China, embodied in the many deep cultural concerns coming to surface in the Lei Feng phenomenon; the other is the limitations of modes of historiography that seek to base truth-claims on "hard evidence" but fail to take into consideration the complexities of forms of representation and self-representation.

Beddings, Cabbage, and Moral Capital

I shall begin with a quote:

> Today is Sunday. I did not go out. I washed five sets of bedding for the comrades of my squad; I patched up one quilt for comrade-in-arms Gao Kuiyun; I helped the Cooking Division wash over six hundred catties of cabbage. I also cleaned indoors and outdoors, and did some other chores .... In a word, today I have fulfilled the duty of a *qinwuyuan*; although I am a bit tired, I feel very happy. My comrades were all wondering who laundered their beddings so clean. Comrade Gao Kuiyun said in amazement: "Who replaced my worn quilt?..." Ha, he actually has no idea that it was I who did it. I feel it is the greatest glory to be a nameless hero. From now on [I] should do more of those routine, petty, and ordinary jobs, and say fewer pretty words.

This quote comes from the October 15, 1961, entry in the diary of Lei Feng, the most famous PLA soldier of the twentieth century.[2] Whether or not it was penned by a historical person named Lei Feng—and we will come back to this question—it always strikes me as an extraordinary piece of writing. There are a number of things worth noticing. There is, first of all, a theatrical show of surprise on the part of Lei Feng's fellow soldiers, who, according to Lei Feng, co-operatively expressed due amazement at the anonymous launderer and mender of their bedding. It certainly should not have been hard to figure out that it might be the person who stayed behind and the person who had been famously doing "anonymous good deeds." But Lei Feng's good comrades-in-arms were all playing their parts faithfully: they probably knew very well that this was exactly what Lei Feng wanted in return for laundering their bed sheets and sewing their quilts. It was not an unfair exchange. It does not matter whether or not they had really expressed surprise: what matters is that the narrative of doing good requires such an expression of surprise. It made the "anonymous hero" possible.

In this passage Lei Feng refers to himself as a *qinwuyuan* (勤务员), which I have left un-translated. It means an "odd-jobman," an "orderly" in the army context; but Lei Feng was no orderly at the time—in fact, he was the squad leader, *banzhang* (班长).[3] The self-reference evokes Mao Zedong's famous remark, which was echoed by Chairman Hu Jintao in 2008 when he was visiting the earthquake victims in Sichuan:

> All our cadres, no matter whether their offices are high or low, are all *qinwuyuan* of the people.[4]

> (我们的一切工作干部，不论职位高低，都是人民的勤务员.)

We should note that here only cadres can be *qinwuyuan*; the "common folk" are not fit for this lowly position because, paradoxically, their social status is not high enough. In other words, condescension marks and affirms power. We always say that with great power comes great responsibility, but the reverse is also true: when one takes on responsibility, one also takes on power. These two things are two sides of the same coin. In serving his fellow soldiers, Lei Feng is asserting his social authority by establishing moral superiority. He is, in a word, accumulating (*de* 德), both in the sense of "virtue and merit" and in the archaic sense of the word, which is power.

There is something intriguing about the nature of the work Lei Feng threw himself into as a *qinwuyuan*: washing, sewing, cooking, and cleaning. Yes, this is, traditionally, woman's work. A man goes out and comes home and finds his house in order and a cooked meal readied for him on the stove—if this "plot" sounds familiar, then it is because it is one of the common motifs in Chinese folktales in which a good-hearted young man, living alone, is rewarded by the Heavenly God who sends a fairy to help him out with the domestic chores while he is out working in the fields. The earliest of such tales appeared in early medieval times, but there are numerous later transformations.[5] The crucial element in such tales is the anonymity of the fairy—once her identity is discovered, she can no longer remain in the mortal world. There is also a distinct hierarchy in such stories: the fairy represents a higher order of beings; more importantly, she is sent down by the Heavenly God himself.

By delineating this familiar folk tale structure I am not suggesting that Lei Feng's diary entry is strewn with innuendos of some strange sexual dynamics amongst a group of young PLA solders, even though Lei Feng the historical person was very short—just about five feet tall—was sometimes bullied by his taller fellow soldiers, had played the role of a girl raped by Japanese soldiers in a school play, and was once dressed up as a girl during a festival celebration.[6] I bring up this common motif to call attention to the immense cultural resonance of the Lei Feng figure. This shows that the popularity of Lei Feng is not simply a product of Communist Party propaganda; rather, the story of Lei Feng represents some deep concerns of the culture. The party, after all, is not an abstract entity: it consists of people who have numerous connections with the Chinese cultural past, and the past persists in the present in permutations and transformations. This demonstrates precisely what Paul Cohen eloquently describes as "the tenacity of culture" in his chapter in this volume.

With this I come to the most striking element about the diary entry quoted above, and this is the numbers: 5 sets of bedding, 1 quilt, and 600 catties of cabbage. What do we make of this?

The answer lies not in Communist ideology, but once again in the cultural past: the system of merit accumulation, slowly developing from the early medieval period and reaching its apex of popularity in late imperial times. This system found a particular form: the ledger of merit and demerit, a form of literature (literature in its broad sense) that has been so brilliantly explored by Cynthia Brokaw in her work.[7] Ledgers are morality "how-to" books that list a series of good deeds to pursue and bad deeds to avoid. The most important feature of such ledgers is the quantification of the good and bad deeds, so that each good and bad deed is assigned numerical merit or demerit points. The other important characteristic is that a ledger usually includes a calendar for the user to record his daily score; a carefully maintained balance book will, at year's end, give an indication of one's fortune in the year ahead, for the gods will mete out rewards or punishments according to the merits and demerits a person has earned. Yet another noteworthy aspect of the system is the emphasis on doing good deeds in secret, *ji yinde* (积阴德).

It is easy to see how Lei Feng fits into all these traditional categories of the merit accumulation system. His diary should more accurately be called a ledger in which he records his daily tally: giving 1 catty of apples to the patients in a hospital on February 16, 1961; giving 10 yuan and 1 catty of biscuits to a comrade in need on December 30, 1961; spending 1 hour and 40 minutes to walk a mother of two home in the pouring rain on May 2, 1962; spending an entire Sunday morning to fill the potholes on the street, 1 hour maintaining the army truck, and 2 hours helping a local peasant plow his field on May 6, 1962.[8] There are numerous similar instances. It is interesting how Lei Feng always carefully records the exact amount of money or time he spends on others: this is Lei Feng's moral capital.

The merit accumulation system was directly translated from the flourishing commercial culture of late imperial China; and one of the new phenomena in the old structure of *bao* (报), retribution, in connection with the developing money economy, was capital. The essential thing about capital is its invisibility: you cannot always tell from the surface what a person has; and a person who has capital awaits the moment to invest it in a secure venture in hopes of getting returns. Contrary to what many people once believed—that Lei Feng was an "ordinary soldier" whose accidental death and the subsequent discovery of whose diary made his fame—Lei Feng already was a well-known media figure when he was alive. He won honors as a "Frugality Model" (*jieyue biaobing* [节约标兵]); he was also constantly invited to give speeches about his "miserable childhood in the old society" because he was an effective, infectious speaker.[9] His first media exposure occurred in November 1961, shortly after he became a member of the Communist Party (considered highly unusual for a relatively new soldier like Lei Feng, who had joined the army only ten months earlier). A news report about Lei Feng, with the title, "Chairman Mao's Good Soldier," was published on November 26, 1961, in no. 1309 of *Qianjin bao* (前进报), the newspaper of the Shenyang Military Region, with a photo of Lei Feng reading Chairman Mao's work. The same report was sent to the Xinhua News Agency, the Liberation Army newspaper (*Jiefangjun bao* [解放军报]), and other newspapers.[10] Lei Feng rapidly acquired social and political prestige during his brief life of twenty-two years, and his moral capital continued to earn him returns even after his death.

Just as the ledger system was originally principally associated with Buddhism and Daoism, there is also an unmistakably religious aspect to the Lei Feng figure. For Lei Feng, the ultimate reward was to see Chairman Mao face to face one day, and the diary entries record a number of dreams in which his wish is fulfilled.[11] This is, in fact, one of the classic modes of Buddhist meditative visualization: to see the Buddha with the mind's eye or in one's dream is considered an important means of obtaining ultimate enlightenment. Although the political vocabulary in Lei Feng's diary is contemporary and completely in line with the 1950s and 1960s socialist ideology, the cultural vocabulary in his diary is age-old and fully inscribed within Chinese tradition. Lei Feng did get what he wanted: his physical demise—a martyrdom, regardless of the mundane reason for his death—made his name known to Chairman Mao, the god who conferred socialist sainthood on Lei Feng by writing the famous inscription, "Learn from Comrade Lei Feng."

Snapshots, Posing, and Taking Pictures to Fill in Blanks (抓拍、摆拍与补拍)

The question is: Did Lei Feng really die? The answer to this question depends, of course, on whether you believe Lei Feng had ever been alive. Indeed, two questions have constantly come up regarding Lei Feng: one question is, Was Lei Feng for real? The other question is, Was Lei Feng real? Both are deceptively simple questions that elicit complex answers; the second question in particular touches on some of the essential issues of historiography.

One major approach to historiography is to gather evidence and make referential statements in the form of truth-claims based on that evidence. Dominick LaCapra terms this approach "a documentary or self-sufficient research model" which gives priority to research based on primary documents that enable one to derive authenticated facts about the past.[12] This research model is, however, necessarily complicated by the nature of the documents used as evidence. It is one thing to have a set of numbers and statistics in front of you as the object of observation, although even statistics are subject to human manipulation and interpretation; nevertheless, it is an entirely different thing to face such primary documents as diaries and photographs, both being complicated and problematic forms of self-representation.

Lei Feng left behind nine books of diaries and reading notes as well as more than three hundred photographs.[13] How could an "ordinary" PLA soldier like Lei Feng possibly have had so many pictures of himself, both black-and-white and colored, in an age when taking pictures was still considered a luxury? More importantly, how could there be so many pictures of Lei Feng doing his "anonymous good deeds"? When the latter question was posed by reporters from the Associated Press, it seems to have been particularly stinging, as it came from "the outside." As a result, several recent books about Lei Feng take pains to account for this odd phenomenon, and when they do, they unanimously cite the question from the Associated Press reporters.[14]

According to the explanations offered by these books, a professional army photographer reportedly followed Lei Feng around as much as he could so as to catch Lei Feng in the act of doing a good deed and snap a picture of it, *zhuapai* (抓拍), whenever possible. Sometimes, we are told, the photographer even relied on "informants" to achieve his purpose.[15] This information, if true, gives us a new perspective on Lei Feng: we might even say that it was the first socialist "reality show" in photographic stills. In a reality show people are recorded as "being themselves," but at the same time they are intensely aware that they are "being themselves." Does this make whatever they do real, or unreal, or hyper-real? Or should we redefine the real and the unreal?

A much more convincing, though no less troubling, explanation, given in the more recent publication *Lei Feng*, states that many of the "classic" pictures of Lei Feng doing good deeds or performing various tasks were designed and taken by professional army photographers as part of preparations for a traveling exhibit of Lei Feng's accomplishments within the People's Liberation Army.[16] Some of the occasions represented in these pictures are in fact exactly what the other books insist were spontaneously photographed "on the spot." Before we decry the fakeness of such an arrangement, however, we must consider a directive issued by the "leaders" of the Shenyang Military Region: "The photographs [taken of Lei Feng] must be real, and they must represent the good deeds that Lei Feng has actually done."[17] The photographer Zhang Jun thereupon drafted a "plan" based on Lei Feng's speeches, oral accounts, as well as his diary entries, and Ji Zeng, the junior photographer, implemented it. After citing Zhang Jun's plan, the authors of *Lei Feng: 1940–1962* make a fascinating observation:

> From this plan we may see the effect produced by Lei Feng's own writings on taking "documentary photos" of Lei Feng .... To take pictures of Lei Feng is but a technical link in the whole propaganda project. The materials written by Lei Feng unintentionally became a "script" for the picture-taking.[18]

In other words, what the photographers did was to "take pictures to fill in the blanks" (*bupai* 补拍), so that each worthy action by Lei Feng has an accompanying visual image to illustrate and document it, to show—and herein lies the irony of the situation—that it really happened. The pictures are based on "reality" and so cannot possibly be "fake." As the author of *Lei Feng's True Life* stresses defensively:

> Although there is a "time difference" for some of Lei Feng's "pictures taken on the spot," this is no stain on a white jade and this is certainly not staged by a director. Lei Feng was real and the events were real, therefore the pictures cannot but be real.[19]

Many of Lei Feng's photos were, however, nothing but carefully staged, so much so that the authors of *Lei Feng: 1940–1962* refer to him as "one of the people made to pose for pictures most often in Chinese history" (有史以来中国被摆拍最多的人物之一).[20] The famous image of Lei Feng lovingly and smilingly polishing the army truck is just such a staged photo. Normally Lei Feng drove a Russian GAZ truck; but the photographer switched it with a Jiefang ("Liberation") truck made in China, and adjusted the angle and lighting in such a way that the word *jiefang* occupies a prominent position in the picture frame.[21] The allegorical meaning is obvious. Nevertheless, if we believe the account given by photographer Zhang Jun, the photo was initially inspired by a poem entitled "When Putting on the Army Uniform" ("Chuanshang junzhuang de shihou" [穿上军装的时候]) written by Lei Feng in January 1960. In the poem, Lei Feng mentions polishing his truck so that it will be "as bright as a shining mirror."[22] The true "director" of Lei Feng's staged photos was none other than Lei Feng himself, who in many ways remained the central figure in the production of his images.

The most famous image of Lei Feng shows him wearing a fur-lined army hat with ear flaps, holding an automatic rifle, standing tall, and gazing into the distance. We learn that the hat did not belong to Lei Feng but was borrowed so that he would look better; the photographer chose his perspective carefully so that Lei Feng, who was rather short, might look tall and majestic.[23] The most interesting revision occurred posthumously. In 1977, when the Shanghai People's Fine Arts Press was publishing a Lei Feng album, a pine tree was added to the background to symbolize the tough revolutionary spirit of the PLA soldier. This tree, however, was identified by the villagers of Tieling (铁岭 in Liaoning), where Lei Feng's regiment was stationed in 1962, as one of the local pine trees. They even named it the "Lei Feng tree." It has subsequently become a pilgrimage site and has brought much fame as well as economic benefit (including a ¥60,000 donation from the People's Liberation Army to build a "Lei Feng Tree of Hope Elementary School") to the otherwise obscure little village. According to a newspaper article published in the *Liao Shen Evening News* (*Liao Shen wanbao* [辽沈晚报]), after it became known that the photo was altered and the pine tree in the photo was added, many upset villagers still adamantly maintained that *their* pine is the "real" one, although the villager in charge of the "Lei Feng Exhibition Room" at the local elementary school wisely said, "What we admire is the 'Lei Feng spirit'; we do not dispute the origins of the tree in the photo. . . ."[24]

The Making of a Hero

Much more so than photography, a diary is an intricate form of self-representation, as it negotiates the private and public, memory and objectivity, real happening and reconstructed experience. One of the recent biographies of Lei Feng, published in 2003, relates an interesting anecdote: the 16-year-old Lei Feng asked the editor of a Hu'nan county newspaper how to keep a diary and how to "write it well."[25] This anecdote seems to suggest that Lei Feng was quite aware of the artifice of the genre of a diary.

As noted above, Lei Feng successfully turned his diary into a ledger to record his good deeds in quantifiable terms, and he either actively showed his diary to others or left the diary in the open for it to be read by anyone who cared to.[26] Excerpts of Lei Feng's diary were first published in *Qianjin bao*, December 1, 1960. For Lei Feng, a diary was definitely not a private form, and indeed "privacy" must have been an alien concept to a Communist soldier for whom the "public" (*gong* 公) was the only valid category. Once again, Lei Feng's use of a diary bears an amazing resemblance to the use of a blog today: both ostensibly claim to be the record of one's personal sentiments and opinions that is available in the most public venue imaginable. The value of a publicized diary does not lie in the privacy of the form but in the form's *claim* of privacy.

Sometimes one cannot help wondering if Lei Feng, a young man with great political instincts, consciously or unconsciously used his diary to get what he wanted. In the diary entry for April 24, 1961, for instance, he recorded how some people thought he was already a corporal (*xiashi* 下士) instead of merely a "first-class private" (*shangdeng bing* 上等兵), and he emphasized, perhaps a little too eagerly, how he was too busy devoting himself to the party's great enterprise to care about such things as promotion and rank.[27] Shortly thereafter, however, he was promoted to vice squad leader, a military rank generally the equivalent of a corporal.

The publicized diary also affords Lei Feng a place to explain and defend himself. In the entry for September 10, 1961, he records a conversation with his superior who informed Lei Feng that his comrades had complained about his authoritarian management style. Although Lei Feng profusely praises his superior for his excellent advice and swears he will improve in his future work, he nevertheless gives a full account, in his own words, of the incident that led to such criticism and by doing so implicitly justifies his behavior. He also says: "Even if some complaints are not entirely accurate, I still welcome them."[28] In the entry for July 29, 1962, he records another instance of a "complaint" made by a certain comrade that he was carrying on a romantic affair with a "female comrade."[29] In this case there is nothing but vehement denial of the accusation, although Lei Feng also adds an interesting comment, "I have also thought to myself: I grew up from the nurturing of the party, and there is no need for me to worry about the issue of my marriage myself. . . ." If the "party" were to read his diary and pick up the hint, it certainly would not work to Lei Feng's disadvantage.

The artifice of Lei Feng's diary is also reflected in the fact that it has been much edited for publication. The public is never allowed to see the diary in its entirety, only in excerpts; within individual diary entries, there are often ellipses that indicate deletions, and these ellipses appear in the very first printing of *Lei Feng riji* in 1963. Subsequent reprints sometimes supply the deleted parts and sometimes drop other parts. Incidentally, indicating omissions by ellipses is evidence that Lei Feng's diary, although certainly having undergone a make-over, was not entirely fabricated; otherwise we would have to imagine that the initial fabricators of the diary were deliberately leaving blanks for the later editors to fill in.

Comparing the variations as well as the exclusions and inclusions in the different editions of Lei Feng's diary proves fascinating. The changes, effected to either refine Lei Feng's writing or to suit current circumstances of the day, reflect shifting ideological trends in different eras. In the preface to the edition published in November 1968, a time marking the height of the Cultural Revolution, the editors stress that the earliest 1963 edition was a "distorted" version of Lei Feng's diary, with many entries either deleted or pruned, and that this serves to show the evil intention of a "small group of capitalist roaders" led by Liu Shaoqi (刘少奇) (1898–1969), who had just been deprived of his title of president of the People's Republic of China in October 1968. The edition published in November 1968 claims to have restored the original look of the diary, with previously deleted entries or passages supplied and marked either with asterisks or in a different font. Two thing stand out: this edition contains more entries heartily praising the greatness of Mao Zedong and extolling the importance of Mao's works in Lei Feng's daily life; it also portrays Lei Feng not only as a good-hearted server of the people but also as a fierce fighter against "class enemies." For example, an added entry for February 15, 1960, records how several comrades made sarcastic comments on Lei Feng's petite size and how Lei Feng overcame his self-doubt by studying Chairman Mao's essay, "In Memory of Norman Bethune."[30] Another added entry for June 29, 1962, gives a detailed account of an incident in which Lei Feng noticed a "suspicious person" at his military base and reported him to the local police station, and that the person turned out to be a "counter-revolutionary."[31] The entry includes an uncharacteristic reconstruction of the dialogue between Lei Feng and the said person, as in a stage play, and is in fact the most "suspicious" of all entries in Lei Feng's diary in terms of authenticity.

The entry for April 29, 1961, contains an outline of a report Lei Feng was to give about his study of Chairman Mao's works. In the outline, Lei Feng lists a number of Chairman Mao's essays and how each essay helped him achieve some worthy deed. In the 1963 edition, Mao's essay entitled "An Analysis of China's

Various Social Classes" did not seem to motivate Lei Feng in any particular situation except for having "elevated [his] thought."[32] In the 1968 edition, however, the study of the above-mentioned essay inspired Lei Feng to "struggle against Chairman Zhu of the Workers' Union, who came from a 'rich peasant' family background." An editor's note indicates that Chairman Zhu was a bad guy who "slipped into the party" but was exposed by Lei Feng, and that Lei Feng "utterly defeated" Chairman Zhu at a public meeting.[33] The image of Lei Feng as a vigilant soldier battling the "bad elements" in society was very much in line with the Cultural Revolution atmosphere, but the same diary entry in the 1982 edition of the diary reverts back to the original edition, calling into question the authenticity of both of the earlier editions.

There are other editorial modifications that reveal the ups and downs in the Chinese political arena, such as the appearance and disappearance of the name of Mao's appointed successor, Lin Biao (林彪) (1907–71), who staged a failed coup and died in a plane crash in 1971.[34] Apart from alterations motivated by contemporary political needs, the various editions of Lei Feng's diary also show an interesting trajectory of how Lei Feng was first stripped of his human attributes and how he was later restored to humanity. Both manipulations of Lei Feng's image, however, serve to keep the legend of Lei Feng alive for social and political purposes. Not surprisingly, the de-emphasis and emphasis on Lei Feng's humanity always fall into the sphere of food and sex, what had been called "where the greatest human desires lie" by Confucius.[35] For instance, an innocent remark about Chairman Mao "dining with me and giving me many delicious dishes to eat" in the entry for February 22, 1961, in the original edition is deleted in the 1968 edition.[36] Written during a period of famine and economic depression by a 21-year-old soldier who must have been constantly hungry, the remark reveals a human Lei Feng who transformed his fantasy about Chairman Mao's fatherly and nurturing nature into a literal image of granting food and allaying hunger. In recent years much has been made of Lei Feng's several purported "girlfriends," but the most telling sign of the trend of "humanizing Lei Feng" since the 1980s is the inclusion in his diary of the hitherto excluded entry, cited earlier, on his denial of any romantic liaison with a certain "female comrade." Although it might appear counter-intuitive that the denial of romance indicates an attempt to humanize Lei Feng, it should be pointed out that any mention of romance, even in the form of negation, was considered a moral stain in a Communist hero in the earlier era.

To draw a conclusion from the above discussion about Lei Feng's diary: saying a diary is not fabricated is not tantamount to saying that it is not an artifact. Although speculation about the authenticity of Lei Feng's diary is not likely to ever be resolved, it also seems to have missed the point: the point is that not only Lei Feng's diary was a highly self-conscious production, but Lei Feng himself was a made hero. He was made by the state, the army, the press, but more importantly, he was self-made in every sense of the word, as he rose from an orphaned peasant boy to a national hero and finally to a cultural icon largely by the intensity of his will power and by his active engagement in the verbal and visual productions of his own image. Because Lei Feng was never "real," he cannot have been "unreal." In such a context, when we confront the diary much mediated by both writer and editor, as well as the doctored photographs of an apparently highly self-conscious subject, the question to put forward should not be, "Are they real?" but instead should be, "what does 'real' mean?"

Ultimately, we may want to use Lei Feng as an occasion to reflect on historiography: apart from figures, numbers, and statistics, we must also confront the complex human truths in the writing of history. If in the writing of history we stop at asking the question, "Was Lei Feng a real person, or was he the party's fabrication?" then we are not looking at a large part of the picture, that is, the structure of the Lei Feng narrative and the very real cultural, social, political, and ideological factors that constitute the structure. If we do not understand Lei Feng, but regard him as either a hypocritical careerist or a brain-washed fool, then we do not understand the age that made him.

ENDNOTES

1. A song composed by pop singer Xue Cun (雪村), "All Northeasterners Are Living Lei Fengs" (东北人都是活雷锋), was released in 1995 and acquired national fame, especially after it was combined with comical animation on the Internet six months later (and sparked nationwide enthusiasm for FLASH animation). A computer game named "Learn From Lei Feng Online" was designed in 2005.

2. *Lei Feng riji* (雷锋日记) (Beijing: Jiefangjun wenyishe, 1964; reprint), p. 57.

3. Lei Feng recorded in his diary that he was promoted to vice squad leader on May 14, 1961. *Lei Feng riji*, p. 42. He was promoted to squad leader in August of the same year. See Hua Qi (华琪), ed., *Lei Feng de zhenshi rensheng* (雷锋的真实人生) (The True Life of Lei Feng) (Beijing: Qunzhong chubanshe, 2003), p. 156.

4. Mao Zedong, "1945 nian de renwu" (1945年的任务) (The Tasks for 1945), first published in *Jiefang ribao* (解放日报) (Liberation Daily), December 16, 1944. Cited by Hu Jintao in *Renmin ribao* (人民日报) (People's Daily), June 1, 2008.

5. The best-known example is the story about the "snail girl" in the collection *Soushen hou ji* (搜神后记) (A Sequel to the *Record of Searching for the Divine*) attributed to Tao Yuanming (365?–427) (Tao Qian 372?–427) (Beijing: Zhonghua shuju, 1981), pp. 30–31. Translated in Karl S.Y. Kao, *Classical Chinese Tales of the Supernatural and the Fantastic:*

Selections from the Third to the Tenth Century (Bloomington: Indiana University Press, 1985), pp. 132–33.

6. Sun Jianhe (孙建和) and Yin Yunling (殷云岭), eds., *Lei Feng zhuan* (雷锋传) (A Biography of Lei Feng) (Beijing: Zhongguo qingnian chubanshe, 2003), pp. 150–52; 28–29; Hua Qi, ed., *Lei Feng de zhenshi rensheng*, p. 11. According to the latter source (p. 11), Lei Feng also played on a women's basketball team to "fill in the blank" as the team did not have enough women players.

7. See Cynthia J. Brokaw, *The Ledgers of Merit and Demerit: Social Change and Moral Order in Late Imperial China* (Princeton, NJ: Princeton University Press, 1991).

8. *Lei Feng riji*, pp. 27, 60, 79–80.

9. Sun and Yin Yunling, eds., *Lei Feng zhuan*, pp. 160–61, 191; Shi Yonggang (师永刚) and Lei Qiongxiong (雷琼雄), eds., *Lei Feng: 1940–1962* (Beijing: Sanlian, 2006), p. 120.

10. Shi Yonggang and Lei Qiongxiong, eds., *Lei Feng: 1940–1962*, p. 121.

11. See *Lei Feng riji* (1964 reprint), October 1959, p. 5; February 22, 1961, p. 29; July 1, 1961, p. 47.

12. Dominick LaCapra, *Writing History, Writing Trauma* (Baltimore: Johns Hopkins University Press, 2001), p. 1.

13. For the number of Lei Feng's notebooks, see the colophon to *Lei Feng riji*, p. 90; Hua Qi, ed., *Lei Feng de zhenshi rensheng*, p. 206. Two army photographers, Zhang Jun (张峻) and Ji Zeng (季增), took the most photographs of Lei Feng. Zhang Jun claimed to have taken 223 photographs of Lei Feng (many of which were taken on the same occasion). Ironically, in 2004, Zhang Jun and Ji Zeng were involved in a publicized dispute over the copyright of Lei Feng's photographs and had a falling out that was not very much in the "Lei Feng spirit." Yang Shiyang (杨时旸), "Bei 'xiugai' de Lei Feng" (被 '修改' 的雷锋) "The 'Revised' Lei Feng," in *Zhongguo xinwen zhoukan* (中国新闻周刊) (China News Weekly), no. 14 (2009): 78; Zhang Wan (张婉), "Tudi 'paohong' qinquan, shifu nutao Lei Feng zhaopian 'shuming quan'" (徒弟炮轰侵权，师父怒讨雷锋照片署名权) (Disciple Blasts Copyright Violation; Teacher Angrily Demands Signing Right to Lei Feng Pictures), March 3, 2004, *Dongbei xinwen wang* (东北新闻网) (Northeast News Web site), at http://liaoning.nen.com.cn/77972966595362816/20040302/1350447.shtml (accessed February 7, 2010).

14. See, for instance, Hua Qi, ed., *Lei Feng de zhenshi rensheng*, p. 148; Sun Jianhe and Yin Yunling, eds., *Lei Feng zhuan*, p. 267. Interestingly, although the former book places the Associated Press reporters' trip to the Lei Feng Museum in Fushun, Liaoning, in "the spring of 1990," the latter pinpoints the event as happening in August 1989, which, of course, is politically sensitive timing because of the student movement and the Tiananmen Square tragedy in the summer of 1989. Also see Shi Yonggang and Lei Qiongxiong, eds., *Lei Feng: 1940–1962*, p. 133.

15. Hua Qi, ed., *Lei Feng de zhenshi rensheng*, pp. 143–46; *Lei Feng zhuan*, pp. 225–32.

16. Shi Yonggang and Lei Qiongxiong, eds., *Lei Feng: 1940–1962*, p. 133.

17. Ibid., p. 133.

18. Ibid., p. 138.

19. Hua Qi, ed., *Lei Feng de zhenshi rensheng*, p. 149.

20. Shi Yonggang and Lei Qiongxiong, eds., *Lei Feng: 1940–1962*, p. 129.

21. Much mystery shrouds this photo, which is apparently only one of the many photos taken on the same occasion or occasions. It is unclear which photographer, Zhang Jun or Ji Zeng, took the photo or was the first person to come up with the idea of photographing Lei Feng polishing the Jiefang truck, as each seems to claim credit for himself. One thing is clear in the various, mutually conflicting accounts: the idea was so attractive that it was used twice, once in the winter of 1960 and once in the summer of 1961. The initial photo was entitled "Once a Suffering Child, Now a Good Soldier" ("Ku haizi, hao zhanshi" [苦孩子，好战士]) and was printed in *Jiefangjun huabao* (解放军画报) (People's Liberation Army Pictorial), no. 3 (1961). For different accounts of how the photo was taken, see "Lei Feng zhaopian beihou de gushi" (雷锋照片背后的故事) (Stories Behind the Lei Feng Photos), at http://www.southcn.com/news/community/dqsj/200203061288.htm (accessed February 8, 2010); "Lei Feng zhaopian beihou de gushi," *Zhongguo dang'an bao* (中国档案报), August 31, 2007; "Lei Feng zhaopian beihou de gushi," in Hua Qi, ed., *Lei Feng de zhenshi rensheng*, p. 146; and Sun Jianhe and Yin Yunling, eds., *Lei Feng zhuan*, p. 228.

22. Shi Yonggang and Lei Qiongxiong, eds., *Lei Feng: 1940–1942*, p. 140. For the poem, see *Lei Feng riji shiwen xuan: 1958 nian-1962 nian* (雷锋日记诗文选: 1958年–1962年) (A Selection of Poetic Prose in the Lei Feng Diary) (Beijing: Zhanshi chubanshe, 1982), p. 129.

23. See Sun Jianhe and Yin Yunling, eds., *Lei Feng zhuan*, p. 233. The photo was taken by Zhou Jun (周军).

24. "'Lei Feng shu' chengwei hongyang Lei Feng jingshen de yizuo fengbei" ("雷锋树"成为弘扬雷锋精神一座丰碑) (The 'Lei Feng Tree' Has Become a Monument for Promoting the Lei Feng Spirit), *Liao Shen wanbao*, March 5, 2009.

25. Sun Jianhe and Yin Yunling, eds., *Lei Feng zhuan*, p. 48.

26. Shi Yonggang and Lei Qiongxiong, eds., *Lei Feng: 1940–1962*, pp. 143, 154; Hua Qi, ed., *Lei Feng de zhenshi rensheng*, pp. 202–203.

27. *Lei Feng riji*, pp. 34–35.

28. Ibid., pp. 49–50.

29. *Lei Feng riji shiwen xuan*, pp. 87–88. *Lei Feng riji xuan* (雷锋日记选) (A Selection from the Lei Feng Diary) (Beijing: Jiefangjun wenyi chubanshe, 1989), pp. 62–63.

30. *Lei Feng riji* (1968), pp. 18–19. A comparison of this entry with that in the 1982 edition of *Lei Feng riji shiwen xuan* shows that the earlier version is more drawn-out and written in a more colloquial, cruder language. *Lei Feng riji shiwen xuan*, p. 15.

31. *Lei Feng riji* (1968), pp. 100–102.

32. *Lei Feng riji* (1964 reprint), p. 36.

33. *Lei Feng riji* (1968), p. 56.

34. Lin Biao's name appears in *Lei Feng riji* (1968), p. 49.

35. *Liji zhushu* (礼记注疏) (The Book of Rites with Annotations), in Ruan Yuan 阮元, comp., *Shisanjing zhushu* (十三经注疏) (The Thirteen Classics with Annotations) (Taipei: Yiwen yinshuguan, 1955), 22: 431.

36. *Lei Feng riji* (1964 reprint), p. 29; *Lei Feng riji* (1968), p. 47. The part about Chairman Mao feeding Lei Feng "delicious dishes" is replaced by an ellipsis.

20.
REDISCOVERY OF THE FRONTIER IN RECENT CHINESE HISTORY

XIAOYUAN LIU

Certain dates and geographical locations may assume special importance when they serve as coordinates for historians to interpret the trajectory of a historical development. The year 1949 and the place of China are such coordinates. Historians will continue to debate whether or not 1949 should be privileged as a landmark date in the study of modern Chinese history, but there is no question that significant events did take place in China in 1949. After the events in 1949, there was a sense of a new departure among Chinese. Indeed, in the thick of the Cold War, it was easy for contemporary historians to treat post-1949 Chinese history as a separate unit. Only recently have historians begun to reconsider the historical continuities between the periods separated by 1949. What I wish to discuss here is one such continuity, that is, the frontier history of modern China. The year 1949 is important to this history not because there was any clear-cut departure, but because it marked a series of new efforts to bring closure to a long historical process.

The Open Frontier of *Tianxia*

Unfortunately, the frontier theme is missing from recent Chinese history. In this sense, the state of existing historiography on twentieth-century China is similar to American historiography prior to the Turner thesis of 1898. This is not to say that historians have done nothing about the frontier history of China. Previous scholarship on China's ethnic frontiers, however, although capturing certain features of Chinese frontier history before and after 1949, does not provide an integral historical narrative and systematic analysis of the frontier as part of modern Chinese history. Especially disappointing is the lack of connection between this scholarship and mainstream modern China studies that tend to focus on developments within China proper or in the eastern half of China.

Actually, even more so than the United States, China has been a "frontier state." About seven decades ago, when discussing China's dynastic history Owen

Lattimore characterized China as a frontier state by identifying the constant rivalries for control between dynasties founded on or beyond the frontier and those within China.[1] By no means did the rivalries between the forces of Inner Asia and China cease in modern times. Since ancient times, China has had an "ethno-political frontier"—a stage for exchanges and segregation, control and resistance, acculturation and alienation, and war and peace between Chinese and non-Chinese regimes and peoples. Whereas America's "pioneer frontier" came to an end in 1890, China's ethno-political frontier has continued in China's many life cycles.

Before the twentieth century, a prominent feature of the Chinese frontier was its ongoing openness to contest. In capturing the nature of China as such a "frontier state," a poem of the Song dynasty states, "The Central Plain [China] and the *Yidi* ["barbarians"] rise and fall alternately."[2] Non-stop competition on the frontier rendered the territory of historical China as fluctuating as a seasonal lake, even though some of these "territorial seasons" lasted for centuries.

This is perhaps the reason why obsessive conceptions about the shape and size of dynastic territories were scarce in premodern Chinese history. Ancient Chinese used "*shanhe*" (mountains and rivers) to symbolize their homeland that was observable within their visual and mobile ranges. They also used the term "*jin'ou*" (golden goblet) to convey the idea of territorial intactness, which was abstractly expressed but not precisely defined. These conceptions were obviously territorial in contrast to *tianxia* (all under heaven) that was more cultural-ideological, even though the shattered *shanhe* and the imperfect *jin'ou* tended to coexist with a chaotic *tianxia*.

China has a long history of using maps. Yet, the antique political maps of China conveyed messages drastically different from those of modern maps. A preliminary survey of extant antique Chinese maps shows that although ancient Chinese occasionally depicted the territorial realm of their states by imaginary lines of vague significance, typical maps did not demarcate the areas of Chinese dynasties and their neighboring states by "national boundaries." The Great Wall was a frequent feature in ancient Chinese maps, but it often signified a cultural divide or a defensive device, not a state boundary.[3] In premodern China, confining the domain of the Chinese empire to a certain shape or to a certain size would have contradicted the *tianxia* ideology and misrepresented the political reality of China's constantly shifting frontiers. As a result, the ancient interstate politics of East Asia did not produce any precise map image of *shanhe*.

Demarcating Chinese territories with definite borderlines therefore is a modern phenomenon, or part of China's cartographic modernization. This development brought images of modern Chinese territory first in the shape of a begonia leaf and later in the shape of a rooster.[4] Although the influence of Western cartographic techniques and geographic knowledge played a key role, China's cartographic modernization primarily reflected a profound transformation of Chinese territoriality that began in the nineteenth century. This was a time of trial and tribulation in China's misguided encounters with Western challenges. It was, however, also a period during which imperial China tried to match the "national" game of the West. In the process, whereas Western colonial empires and Japan used wars and diplomacy to redefine the geopolitical limits of the Qing Empire, the Qing government, belatedly, attempted to exercise effective control over its former "hollow" frontiers. In one defeat after another, the Qing lost tributary overlordship over its Asian neighbors in the east and the south, such as Burma, Korea, Liuchiu, and Vietnam. In the meantime, its Inner Asian dependencies were internalized and became integral parts of China's imperial domain.[5]

This domain was accepted by Western countries. Throughout the nineteenth century, Western cartographers commonly included Manchuria, Mongolia, Xinjiang, and Tibet as part of the "Chinese Empire," but used lines to separate these territories from the area of "China." Thus it was in the West that the map image of China in the shape of a begonia leaf was first created, though such maps were meant to represent the political domain of the Qing Empire, not that of a Chinese nation-state.[6]

At the beginning of the twentieth century, China's frontier puzzle was finally solved, at least on paper. During the last decade of the Qing dynasty, maps published in China caught up with Western cartography and began to present the begonia-leaf image of China's territorial sovereignty.[7] In this image, China's Inner Asian frontiers were enclosed by fixed international boundaries and not separated from China proper by special borderlines. Such Chinese maps suggest that even before the Revolution of 1911, Chinese territoriality had already achieved certain "national" characteristics in accordance with the norms of modern-cum-Western nation-states.

Identity of the Chinese Nation

In the early twentieth century, the upsurge of nationalistic consciousness among Chinese, especially Chinese elites, was closely associated with the cartographic consequences of nationalized Chinese territoriality. For instance, China's territorial and sovereignty losses due to the Russo–Japanese War moved Qiu Jin to write indignantly: "How can we watch the color of the map being changed and tolerate our rivers and mountains being smashed into ashes!" Yet, ambiguity about modern Chinese territoriality continued. In his "patriotic lyrics" of 1903, Liang Qichao wrote: "Oh how great our *zhonghua*: the vastest country of the largest continent, and twenty-two provinces in one family." At the time, the twenty-two provinces included Xinjiang and the three provinces of Manchuria, but not Mongolia, Qinghai, or Tibet.[8]

Such ambiguity decisively disappeared when Sun Yat-sen, in his capacity as provisional president of the Republic of China, declared on New Year's Day of 1912: "People are the essence of the state. To combine the areas of the Han, Manchu, Mongols, Hui, and Tibetans into one state is to combine these races into one nation. This is national unification." Soon this notion was codified in the Republic's provisional constitution, which stipulated that the area of the Chinese Republic included the twenty-two provinces plus Inner and Outer Mongolia, Qinghai, and Tibet.[9] The inclusion of the Inner Asian borderlands within the territory of the Chinese Republic not only proclaimed a geographic extension but also a multi-ethnic configuration of a modern Chinese nation, or *Zhonghua minzu* in Chinese. Unlike *shanhe* that never coincided with *tianxia*, for the first time in Chinese history the Chinese state's claimed territorial domain was congruent with its geopolitical ideology.

Yet, before the Chinese state could substantiate a multi-ethnic composition, modern Chinese nationality was almost a nationalized version of Chinese ethnicity. The traditional ethno-politics of China did not end in the early twentieth century. It renewed itself and began to assume certain new characteristics. First, whereas ancient Chinese ethnicity was found mainly in Chinese-Inner Asian encounters, modern Chinese nationality emerged principally from confrontation with the West. It is therefore not surprising that in the continued contests over the frontiers, China's nationalist discourse was reluctant to give full agency to the people of the Inner Asian frontiers. Second, unlike ancient Chinese ethnicity that was exclusive to and yet coexistent with Inner Asian ethnicities, modern Chinese nationality was a centralizing and homogenizing force in its relations with the emerging Inner Asian nations. As history has shown, nationalism affected Chinese and Inner Asian people alike. As a result, a modern ethno-politics of China unfolded in the form of tense struggles between a centralizing Chinese nationalism and separatist Inner Asian nationalisms.

Third, although claiming centrality in the universal *tianxia* in the past, Chinese ethnicity stressed the cultural barriers between the Central Kingdom and the frontiers and beyond. Whether China was a unified empire or a divided stage for multi-state competition, the ethno-geographic divides between Chinese and non-Chinese shifted to reflect the actual power relationship between the two sides. In contrast, as Chinese ethnicity renewed itself in the form of Chinese nationality and the universal *tianxia* continued in its modern incarnation, the parochial *Zhonghua minzu* ideological pretension moved far ahead of geopolitical realities. Despite official proclamations, for instance Sun's announcement on the combination of the areas and people of the so-called five races into "one state" and "one nation," throughout the period of the Republic the Chinese authorities were unable to overcome the de facto separation of Tibet and Outer Mongolia from the Chinese state. Nor could they effectively deal with foreign intrigues and local autonomous movements in Inner Mongolia, Manchuria, and Xinjiang.[10]

These characteristics demonstrate that from the very beginning modern Chinese nationality suffered from certain congenital defects. These included hypersensitivity toward foreign interference compounded by anxiety over the loyalty of "internal" ethnic groups, a multi-ethnic composition based on Han centralism, and cartographic unification without actual territorial and inter-ethnic unity. All these relational tensions bedeviled the ethnic peripheries of the Chinese Republic, but all these "peripheral" matters were central to the very vitality of the newly forged Chinese Nation.

Communist Alternative?

In comparison to the Chinese Nationalists, the Chinese Communists were of a different pedigree, but only to a certain degree. They waged class struggle and appeared to be committed to an international cause. However, the trajectory of communism in China shows that the supra-national ideology served only as a remedy to cure China's "national" ills. In its formative years, the Chinese Communist Party (CCP) functioned as a branch of the Comintern. It followed Leninist principles regarding the "national question" and supported national self-determination by people on the Mongolian, Tibetan, and Xinjiang frontiers. Yet, Mao Zedong's search for a winning strategy indigenized the party, and the CCP's encounter with ethnic minorities during the Long March significantly modified its view of the revolutionary potential of the frontier people. Eventually, Japan's aggression against China nailed down the CCP's nationalistic persona.

During China's eight-year war against Japan, the war-forced CCP-KMT cooperation resulted in drastic changes in the CCP's ethno-political stance. For the CCP, Chinese nationalism was no longer a "trap" to avoid but a worthy banner with which to compete with the Nationalists. During the war years the CCP actually adopted the Nationalist Government's official definition of the Chinese Nation. Although the Communists would maintain a distinctive terminology, they no longer disagreed with the Nationalists on the fundamentals, such as the multi-ethnic composition and the territorial extension of the Chinese Nation.[11]

Now that the CCP was committed to the defense of the officially defined national territory of China, in one of his famed wartime writings Mao Zedong urged China's minority nationalities to earn the "right to self-government" by joining China's war of resistance against Japan.[12] Mao thereby not only substituted national "self-determination" (*zijue*) for "self-government" (*zizhi*), but also changed a "right" into a privilege. Squatting on the inter-ethnic fault lines of northwestern China and competing with the Japanese invaders for the allegiance of the people on the frontier, during the war years the CCP assessed the Inner Mongols and the Hui at close range. The assessment substantiated the party's conviction that these were "backward nationalities" incapable of carrying out spontaneous revolutions. Therefore, they would have to achieve "liberation" through the Chinese revolution.[13] In this way, the CCP incorporated the frontier peoples ideologically into its own revolutionary, yet nevertheless Han-centric, nationalism.

Thereafter, as far as China's ethnic frontiers were concerned, the only remaining squabble between the Communists and the Nationalists focused on the status of the minority groups within China. Whereas the Nationalists defined the ethnic minorities as member "branches" (*zongzhi*) of the Chinese Nation, the Communists insisted that they were member "nationalities" (*minzu*).[14] The policy implications of these conceptions were not about two fundamentally different approaches to deal with the ethnic frontiers but about the extent to which the "self-government" device should be applied.

Before it relocated to Taiwan in 1949, the Chinese Nationalist Government seriously considered granting Tibet and Outer Mongolia the status of a "high-degree of self-government" (*gaodu zizhi*), or political autonomy congruent with those peoples' living areas under Chinese sovereignty. The Nationalist regime contemplated this measure to lure Outer Mongolia and Tibet, the two "particular-ized" areas, back to China. In the meantime, such treatment was denied to other territorial ethnic groups like the Uygurs of Xinjiang and the Inner Mongols.[15] Although history does not allow a comparison between the "degrees" of the Communist and Nationalist brands of ethnic autonomy, it should be clear that territorial autonomy was a centralizing device available to the Nationalists as well as to the Communists.

In the case of the Chinese Communists, the device, called *"quyu zizhi"* (regional nationality autonomy), was first adopted as a pragmatic and reactive concession to the conditions on the Inner Mongolian frontier, an area vitally important to the CCP's struggle for power after World War II.[16] At the end of the war, the Inner Mongols surprised every observer of Chinese affairs by mounting a powerful separatist movement. In a large area bridging Inner Mongolia and Manchuria, the Eastern Mongolian Autonomous Movement became a formidable third force in the final round of the power struggle between the Chinese Nationalists and the Communists.[17] By insisting that the Inner Mongolian question was a

CCP-Soviet conspiracy that would disappear automatically when the Chinese Communist problem was resolved, the Nationalist Government unwittingly provided room for the CCP to maneuver with the Inner Mongols. Not yet in power either to grant or to deny the Inner Mongols' political aspirations in relation to the official Chinese state, on the one hand the CCP was sympathetic enough to secure the Inner Mongols' cooperation, but, on the other, suppressed Inner Mongol separatist trends.

Through a series of negotiations between 1945 and 1947 the CCP succeeded in cajoling the leaders of the Eastern Mongolian movement to abandon their idea of accession to Outer Mongolia and to settle with the formula of *quyu zizhi*. In May 1947, an Inner Mongolian Autonomous Government was launched as the CCP's ethnic ally against the Nationalists. However, the body was based on Inner Mongol, not CCP, principles. One principle was "unified autonomy" that provided a governing body to all Inner Mongols, and another was territorial autonomy that included all "original lands" of Inner Mongolia. It is conventional in the People's Republic to suggest that the state's regional autonomy system for minority nationalities began in Inner Mongolia in 1947. A more accurate account should be that in 1947 the Chinese Communists supported the Inner Mongols' claim to a "high degree of self-government" within the Republic of China, the same right that the Nationalist regime had promised the Tibetans and the Outer Mongols.[18]

All Under Heaven by the Party

By the time the People's Republic of China was established, the political prospects offered by Chinese communism to the ethnic frontiers differed little from those of the Chinese Nationalists. In other words, as far as the evolving relationship between the frontiers and China proper was concerned, the year 1949 marked neither a change of direction nor a change in frame of reference. Modernization of Chinese territoriality and nationalization of Chinese statehood continued. Nevertheless, if the ultimate goal of these processes was to close the traditionally open frontiers of China, the emergence of the PRC in 1949 reflected certain cumulative results.

Liu Bang, founder of the Han dynasty, bequeathed an oath to his successors: "One whose name is not Liu but claims the throne should be attacked by all under heaven."[19] Of course, the Han dynasty did not last forever, nor did the Liu family monopolize the royal titles in Chinese history. Nevertheless, Liu Bang's oath reflects a convention central to China's imperial system: "All under heaven" was equated with the royal household, or *jia tianxia*. Sun Yat-sen, the nemesis of the Chinese dynastic tradition, exalted the idea that "all under heaven is for all" (*tianxia weigong*). The most enduring legacy of his revolution, however, was the party-state (*dang guo*). Until 1949, Sun's Nationalist successors engaged both domestic and foreign enemies, just managing to hold the party-state together. In the process, conceptually they rendered the domain of the bygone Qing Empire "national." However, they were unsuccessful, as Benedict Anderson memorably puts it, in "stretching the short, tight, skin of the nation over the gigantic body of the empire" in any practical sense.[20] The incongruence between *shanhe* and *tianxia* thus lingered in the discrepancy between the political reality of the Republic of China and the official image of the Chinese Nation.[21]

Within two years after the CCP established the People's Republic of China, the Chinese Nation, with all its political and territorial connotations, superimposed itself on both China proper and the ethnic frontiers. Consequently, the CCP presided over not only a party-state but also a party-nation.[22] As indicated in the cases of Inner Mongolia, Xinjiang, and Tibet, as of 1949 the kinetic energy of these frontiers pointed in directions from, not toward, China. The amalgamation of these peoples and areas into the PRC would not have occurred without the party-directed nation building.

There are interesting historical coincidences. One of these is that while re-centralizing the frontier dependencies of the Qing Empire around Beijing, the CCP, like the Manchus in the seventeenth and eighteenth centuries, assigned the Mongols a prominent role. Whereas the Manchus relied on the Mongolian cavalries, the CCP promoted the political model of Inner Mongolia and applied *quyu zizhi* to all areas inhabited by compact communities of non-Han groups. This policy became official when it was included in the "Common Program of the Chinese People's Political Consultative Conference" passed on September 29, 1949. Although *quyu zizhi* led to a government effort to eventually identify fifty-five ethnic minorities throughout China as its recipients, the most important historical significance of the system is that it redefined the status of the Inner Asian frontiers within China.[23]

During the following years, CCP leaders, including Mao Zedong and Zhou Enlai, offered various explanations as to why the CCP decided not to follow the Leninist principle of national self-determination when arranging the ethno-political landscape of the PRC.[24] As committed as their Nationalist predecessors were to nationalizing the territories bequeathed by the Qing Empire, CCP leaders, informed by their Long March experience and by the ethno-political realities of Inner Mongolian, Xinjiang, and Tibetan separatism as of 1949, were keenly aware of how counterproductive the right to national self-determination could be to their goals. But the Inner Mongolian model of *quyu zizhi* could satisfy two basic requirements of Chinese sovereignty. Internationally, *quyu zizhi* indicated that the frontiers were *within* the boundaries of the Chinese state, and, domestically, *quyu zizhi* prescribed that governance of the frontiers was *under* the Chinese central authorities.[25]

Although devoid of the mutual consent that national self-determination would have provided, *quyu zizhi*, at least in 1949, appeared superior to the "province building" (*jian sheng*) approach of the late Qing and the Republican periods. It was able to partially appease frontier separatism and at the same time achieve political homogenization. In Inner Mongolia and Xinjiang, *quyu zizhi* appeared to roll back the provincial expansion that existed under the Qing and Nationalist regimes. In 1954, when Suiyuan province was abolished and its area was incorporated into the Inner Mongolian Autonomous Region, the *People's Daily* hailed the step as a "great event" that only could occur in people's China and a "monumental measure" that erased the "policies of national oppression and national assimilation" of the old regimes.[26]

Tibet was an entirely different story. In 1949, the Chinese provincial system skirted the issue of Tibet. As a result, CCP leaders had to use force on two occasions, once in 1950 and again in 1959, to deny Tibet any chance of independence. *Quyu zizhi* was not installed in Tibet until the sixteenth year of the PRC. By then leaders in Beijing were confident that they had completely suppressed the efforts by Tibetan elites to preserve the old status quo.[27]

Initially, the CCP leadership envisioned that *quyu zizhi* at various levels would be established in ten provinces. Eventually, however, the system was established in nineteen provinces covering 64.5 percent of China's territory.[28] At the end of 1956, the Xinhua News Agency reported that *quyu zizhi* had already been established in nearly all of the ethnic minority regions. This development led Ulanfu, then director of the National Minority Affairs Commission, to declare at the CCP's Eighth National Party Congress that "the party has victoriously solved the domestic nationality question."[29]

Ulanfu's 1956 announcement is comparable to the 1890 U.S. census statement. Whereas the latter marked the "end" of America's continuously expanding "pioneer frontiers," the former alleged the "close" of China's openly contested ethno-political frontiers. The similarity between these two kinds of frontiers is that both were vitally important in defining the geo-bodies of the two "nation-states" and in delimiting their domestic and international sovereignties. The difference is that the American frontiers would not reopen after 1890 whereas the Chinese frontiers would reopen or, more precisely, remain open after 1956.

Revolution for All Under Heaven

The acclaimed nationwide success of *quyu zizhi* in the mid-1950s was misleading on three counts. First, the "minorities" of the Inner Asian frontiers had always posed a "question" to the Chinese authorities that was vastly different from that posed by those long existing or newly identified ethnic minorities residing inside the Chinese provinces. The question would not disappear simply because a new form of administration was installed. Second, since *quyu zizhi* was by origin a centralizing device in lieu of national self-determination, its so-called success indicated Beijing's achievement in overcoming frontier separatism but not consensual acceptance by all parties involved of the legitimacy of one another's ethno-political stance.[30] Finally, because revolution was the ultimate legitimizing rationale of Chinese Communist politics, *quyu zizhi* was merely a step in Beijing's program for revolutionizing the frontiers. Ethno-political contention on the frontiers actually intensified as Mao Zedong's "continuous revolution" wreaked havoc in China.

As of 1949, while Mongolian, Uygur, and Kazakh partisans began their own revolutions in Inner Mongolia and Xinjiang, the traditional status quo persisted in Tibet. Such socio-political differences among these frontiers paled in comparison to their commonality in the perception of the CCP that required that all frontier societies, progressive or conservative, must be "liberated" as part of the Chinese Nation. After 1949, as members of the same "great family," all ethnic groups in the PRC were to "enter the stage of socialism." Socialist revolution was thus declared the new foundation for the unity of the multi-ethnic Chinese Nation.[31]

In 1949, poised to lead the second largest state of the "socialist camp," the CCP was ready to exert revolutionary leadership in the East Asian sphere that previously had been dominated by China's dynastic empire. As Liu Shaoqi stated shortly after the PRC was established: "From the beginning, the October Revolution of the Soviet Union was not a revolution confined to the realm of a nation, but an international and worldwide revolution. Similarly, the great people's revolution against imperialism and feudalism in China directly continues the October Revolution."[32] Such rhetoric explicated a conviction among CCP leaders that as part of the world revolution, the PRC's incorporation of the ethnic frontiers and projection into East Asia were seamlessly connected.

Despite such an internationalist conviction, the direct and lasting effects of the Chinese Communist revolution were confined to the realm of the officially defined Chinese Nation. As far as the ethnic frontiers were concerned, the Maoist revolution, unfolding in its "New Democracy," "Socialist Transition," and Cultural Revolution phases, became the very drive for fleshing out the authority of Beijing. The CCP's approach of using a theoretically supranational revolution to enforce national goals perhaps can explain both Beijing's initial success in the frontiers and the new inter-ethnic tensions as the PRC aged. Not until very late did the CCP leadership realize that although the Chinese revolution was powerful enough to rein in the alienated frontier peoples, it turned out to be a frail rope to pull the Chinese Nation out of the quagmire of inter-ethnic conflicts.

In the formative years of the PRC, having secured the rooster image of the state's territorial domain, Beijing pursued rather moderate policies toward the frontiers for the sake of establishing credibility with the frontier peoples. "Democratic reforms," a program intended for the "backward" frontier societies to catch up with China proper, were introduced to the frontiers as a voluntary process and the former ruling elites were allowed to stay on in various places.[33] The luster of "socialist construction" in China proper initially appeared seductive to the frontier elites. Following the supporters of Inner Mongolian autonomy who joined hands with the CCP in the late 1940s, in the mid-1950s the leading group of the former "Eastern Turkestan Republic" of Xinjiang collectively joined the CCP. For a while, even the young Dalai Lama proclaimed his conversion to socialism and sought to become a CCP member.[34]

Yet, politics in Mao's China was antagonistic by nature. The initial inter-ethnic entente cordiale did not last because it anticipated a moment when Maoist-style class struggle could be fully implemented in the frontiers regardless of their ethnic particularities. To the leaders of the newly founded PRC, the differences between means and goals were murky when it came to asserting their "central authority" in every inch of the land and spreading the Chinese revolution to every corner of the country. Any political compromise or socio-economic expediency in the frontiers could only be temporary for it meant the incompleteness of Beijing's domestic sovereignty and the lack of thoroughness of the CCP revolution.

As the Anti-Rightist Campaign and the Great Leap Forward movement engulfed China, the political frenzy rapidly erased the remaining differences between the ethnic frontiers and the Chinese provinces in the east. In late 1957 and early 1958, CCP officials at the provincial and central levels launched attacks against "local nationalism." The label incriminated activities and words seeking greater autonomous rights or allegedly having anti-CCP and anti-Han undertones. The CCP leadership identified Xinjiang, Inner Mongolia, and the Guangxi Zhuang Autonomous Region as such troubled areas.[35] Tibet was not included because at the time it still lagged behind the other frontier regions in terms of political homogenization with the rest of China. In the meantime, in the Tibetan areas of western Sichuan, southern Gansu, and Qinghai, armed resistance against the "democratic reforms" broke out between late 1955 and 1958. The People's Liberation Army carried out "rebellion suppression" operations in these provinces, which were followed by a spillover effect in Tibet proper.[36] The already delicate political balance in Tibet soon collapsed, and in March 1959 armed conflict in Lhasa decisively ended Beijing's gradualist approach in Tibet.

According to the constantly victorious logic of Maoist politics, the frontier antagonisms in the late 1950s meant nothing but the progress of the Chinese revolution. Entering the 1960s, socialism had made such enormous strides in the PRC that it no longer entertained the inconvenience of the "national question." In 1964, an authoritative article in the *People's Daily* cited Mao: "The national question and the class question are related, and in essence the national question *is* the class question."[37]

Under this new creed, thousands of "local nationalists" in regions like Xinjiang and Inner Mongolia were relegated to the category of "people's enemies" and persecuted accordingly.[38] These cases turned out to be the clouds before the storm. No longer restrained by concerns about the "national" particularities of the frontiers, Maoist "class struggle" could now sweep every ethnic frontier of China. During the "Great Proletarian Cultural Revolution," political homogenization pushed forward ruthlessly and reached a peak. It is revealing that in those years Inner Mongolian herdsmen in the grassland changed their daily greeting from the Mongolian *sainu* (how are you?) to an awkward mimicry of the prevalent Chinese phrase at the time, *Mao zhuxi wanshou wujiang* (wish chairman Mao boundless longevity).[39]

Although Inner Mongolian autonomy in the late 1940s laid the foundation for the multi-ethnic structure of the PRC, the Cultural Revolution in Inner Mongolia demonstrated how far the CCP had traveled along the path of "forced assimilation."[40] Whereas in Xinjiang and Tibet, the chaotic Cultural Revolution created opportunities for ethnic opposition groups to organize or even rebel from the bottom, in Inner Mongolia the "rebellion" was started at the top by Beijing. As Mao brought the Chinese revolution to its so-called "cultural" phase, Ulanfu, the highest-positioned non-Han CCP official and the first administrator of the *quyu zizhi* system, was targeted. He was the first provincial leader deposed by the Cultural Revolution. Significantly, one of Ulanfu's "crimes" was his re-issuance in the 1960s of a 1935 statement by the CCP. Originally issued under Mao's name, the statement treated the Inner Mongols as a "nation" and asserted that "the nation is the most revered and all nations are equal." During the Cultural Revolution, the Inner Mongolian Autonomous Region was dismembered and the Inner Mongols suffered the largest mass persecution of that period.[41]

In examining the government's "anti-splittist struggle" in Xinjiang between 1950 and 1995, Chinese author Ma Dazheng notes an unexplained phenomenon: during the entire 1970s not a single "splittist case," meaning an ethnic separatist incident, took place in Xinjiang. The Cultural Revolution caused bloodshed in Tibet in the 1960s, but the 1970s were relatively quiet. In Inner Mongolia, inter-ethnic tensions also began to relax in the 1970s after Beijing decided that the

Cultural Revolution leadership in the region had gone too far in persecuting alleged members of the "New Inner Mongolian People's Revolutionary Party" (*Xin Neirendang*).[42]

The relative tranquility of the frontiers in the 1970s is not surprising. This was a decade, according to Mao, of "great order from great chaos." After Mao and the other cultural revolutionaries had mobilized and caused societal violence to enforce their will, all voices of dissent were silenced.

Socialist Frontiers with Chinese Characteristics

"China's nationality policy emerged from the debris of conflict between class and ethnicity," Uradyn Bulag states deftly.[43] By the end of the Cultural Revolution, the Maoist "class struggles," which were mainly political persecutions through arbitrary labeling, had already driven ethnicity off the PRC's political stage. In the chronicles of the CCP's "nationality work" published in the PRC in recent years, the period of the Cultural Revolution receives minimal or no coverage. Such a historical blackout shows how thoroughly the Cultural Revolution obscured the issue of ethnicity.[44] In the post-Mao era, Beijing's reorientation indicated that Maoist "class struggle" had exhausted the credibility of Marxist doctrine both in China proper and on the frontiers. Yet, when China's reforms began gingerly in a manner of "wading across the river by feeling for the stones," as far as the ethnic frontiers were concerned, leaders in Beijing seemed convinced that the river ahead was overly treacherous and there were few stones for them to step on.

As the CCP was re-legitimizing the "party-state" via the economic reforms, a "new era" was proclaimed for the "party nation." The "new era" meant rehabilitation of those practices proved effective in the early 1950s, focusing in particular on *quyu jizhi*. The "rights to autonomy" for the ethnic minorities were codified in the early 1980s; the original area of the Inner Mongolian Autonomous Region was restored; and the united front approach in "nationality work" was re-emphasized.[45] However, these measures were more of a restoration than a reform.

Before Hu Yaobang was deposed, for a brief period of time the CCP leadership showed a degree of audacity. A set of experimental policies was implemented that treated Tibet as a special ethno-political zone, echoing from afar the special economic zones (SEZs) along China's southeast coast. In encouraging new policies in Tibet, the CCP leadership dismissed "unnecessary worries about deviation from the socialist path, weakening of the party leadership, expansion of religious influence, and the possibility of large rebellions." Although not intended for the other ethnic frontiers, the Tibetan experiment in the 1980s contained two potentially powerful ideas of general significance. One was the salient emphasis on the uniqueness of a particular ethnic frontier in contrast to the homogenizing trend since 1949, and the other was explicit sensitivity to international criticism, in contrast to the defiance of the Mao era against the outside world.[46]

Whereas the economic SEZs eventually led to a complete transformation of the PRC, the ethno-political SEZ did not proceed very far. In a discussion about the conditions in Tibet in the late 1980s, Deng Xiaoping indicated that the essence of the Tibetan problem was the "low level of material and cultural life" of the Tibetan people.[47] Thus, having shifted gears from revolution to economic development in the post-Mao era, Beijing opted to maintain the direction of homogenization between China proper and the frontiers.

At the onset of the reform era, Deng Xiaoping established *xiaokang*, or a "relatively comfortable life," as the initial goal of China's economic reforms. In the meantime, he appeared to be satisfied with China's ethno-political conditions, stating that China "does not have large ethnic conflicts." This may be dubbed as *xiaozhi*, or a "relatively stable order."[48] These criteria were pragmatic for a country that was still recovering from the catastrophic Cultural Revolution. They are insignificant today, however, as China is headed toward becoming a leading global power. Until the recent global financial crisis, the PRC awed the rest of the world with its sustained double-digit growth rate. Yet, thirty years after the beginning of the reform era, the PRC is yet to achieve an index of stability in the ethnic frontiers comparable to its economic feats. The *quyu zizhi* plus economic modernization formula has not been able to end inter-ethnic conflicts in the frontier regions. Researchers in China have found that during the past few decades, "political disturbances," "counterrevolutionary armed rebellions," and "terrorist activities" in Xinjiang have been as frequent as they were in the 1950s and 1960s. In the meantime, the "leaping development" (*kuayue shi fazhan*) in Tibet promoted by Beijing has not been able to remove the issue of Tibet from the front pages of Chinese and Western newspapers.[49]

Thus, Owen Lattimore's characterization of China as a "frontier state" remains valid in the twenty-first century. During China's long imperial history, the frontiers were shifting zones that reflected the balance of power between the Inner Asian powers and the Chinese or non-Chinese dynasties based in China proper. As early as the mid-nineteenth century, the modern transformation of Chinese territoriality resulted in an internalization of China's Inner Asian frontiers. Yet, within the legal boundaries of the newly forged Chinese nation-state, the old frontier contests continued in new forms. A common theme runs through the late Qing, Republic, and People's Republic periods, that is, confrontation between the centralizing and homogenizing drive of the ruling center and the separatist and particularistic aspirations of the ethnic frontiers. As of today, the frame of the nation-state has managed to confine the ethnic frontiers within the PRC, but a shared ethos is yet to be found to coordinate the kinetic energies of China proper and the frontiers. The status quo can be described as "socialist frontiers with Chinese characteristics." Inspired by Deng Xiaoping's subterfuge—"socialism with Chinese characteristics" —the phrase is nevertheless more honest in its suggestion that although the ethnic frontiers and China proper have been homogenized under a supra-ethnic ideology, homogenization remains Chinese in nature. To those who still harbor a desire to permanently close China's frontiers, it may be comforting to realize that it took nearly 120 years for the United States to end its frontier, twice as long as the PRC experience we are discussing today.

ENDNOTES

1. Owen Lattimore, *Inner Asian Frontiers of China* (Boston: Beacon Press, 1940), p. 409.

2. Li Gang, a poem of indignation written after reading the March 6 edict on the emperor's abdication and announcement to the troops, expressing concerns about the crisis of the royal family, pity for the suffering of the people, sorrow about rejected advice, and outrage against those crafty sycophants who undermined the state, in Wang Qixing and Zhang Hong, eds., *Zhongguo lidai aiguo shici jingpin* (The Best Patriotic Poems from the Chinese Dynasties) (Wuhan: Wuhan daxue chubanshe, 1994), p. 93.

3. "Hua yi tu" (Map of the Chinese and Barbarian Areas [Southern Song, 1136]); "Gujin hua yi quyu zongyao tu" (Comprehensive Map of the Chinese and Barbarian Regions in Ancient and Current Times [Southern Song, 1185]); "Tang Yixing shanhe fenye tu" (Tang Yixing's Map of the Divide Between Mountains and Rivers [Southern Song, year unknown]); "Yudi zongtu" (Comprehensive Map of the Territorial Domain [Ming, year unknown]); and "Da Ming hunyi tu" (Map of the Unified Great Ming [Ming, 1389]). These can be found in the online collection of the Department of Geography, Hong Kong Baptist University, at http://geog.hkbu.edu.hk/geog1150/chinese (accessed September 20, 2010).

4. Begonia leaves, of course, come in many different shapes. The image of Chinese territory is likened to the more rounded and star-shaped leaves. Although the image of Chinese territory minus Outer Mongolia has been likened to the profile of a rooster in the PRC, interestingly it is likened to that of an "old hen" in Taiwan. An example of the latter can be found in a recent middle-school text on Chinese geography. Wang Wen-lung, "Taiwan zhongxue dili jiaokeshu de zuguo xiangxiang [1949-1999]" (An Imaginary Motherland in a Taiwanese Middle School Geography Textbook [1949-1999]), *Guoshiguan xueshu jikan* (Scholarly Journal of the Academia Historica), no. 17 (September 2008): 201–46.

5. For relevant nineteenth-century international treaties concerning Chinese boundaries, see Chu Dexin and Liang De, eds., *Zhongwai yuezhang huiyao* (Principal Chinese-Foreign Treaties and Agreements) (Harbin: Heilongjiang renmin chubanshe, 1991).

6. Such examples include maps of Asia in *The London Atlas of Universal Geography* (London: J. Arrowsmith, 1832), *Colton's Atlas Of The World, Illustrating Physical And Political Geography* (New York: J.H. Colton and Co., 1856), *Allgemeiner Hand-Atlas der Erde und des Himmels nach den besten astronomischen Bestimmungen, neuesten Entdeckungen und kritischen Untersuchungen entworfen* (Weimar: Geographisches Institut in Weimar, 1856), *Lettres Popular Atlas* (London: Letts, Son & Co. Limited, 1883), and *The Times Atlas* (London: Cassell & Co., 1895). These can be found in the David Rumsey Map Collection, at http://www.davidrumsey.com (accessed September 20, 2010).

7. Two modern maps of the Qing Empire from *Da Qing diguo quantu* (Complete Atlas of the Great Qing Empire) (Shanghai: Shangwu yishuguan, 1905) and *Huangchao zhisheng ditu* (Provincial Maps of the Imperial Dynasty) (Wuchang: Yaxin dixuehui, 1903) can be found in *China in Ancient and Modern Maps* (London: Philip Wilson, 1998), pp. 261, 267. But one has to go to the Chinese originals to see the complete images. According to Zou Zhenhuan, *Wan Qing xifang dilixue zai Zhongguo* (Western Geography in Late Qing China) (Shanghai: Shanghai guji chubanshe, 2000), pp. 324–30, Chinese cartographer Zou Daijun's *Zhongwai yudi quantu* (Complete Atlas of China and Foreign Countries), published in 1903, had the greatest influence on the new Chinese cartography of the early twentieth century.

8. Qiu Jin, "Huanghai zhou zhong Riren suoju bing jian Ri E zhanzheng ditu" (Requested a Poem by a Japanese and Saw a Map of the Russo-Japanese War Aboard a Ship in the Yellow Sea), in Wang Qixing and Zhang Hong, eds., *Zhongguo lidai aiguo shici jingpin*, p. 317; Liang Qichao, "Aiguo ge si zhang" (Four Patriotic Lyrics), in ibid., p. 312; Gu Jiegang and Shi Nianhai, *Zhongguo jiangyu yange shi* (A History of China's Changing Territories) (Beijing: Shangwu yinshuguan, 1999 [1938]), pp. 203–7.

9. "Linshi dazongtong Sun Wen xuanyanshu, 1912 nian 1 yue 1 ri" (Provisional President Sun Wen's [Yat-sen] Proclamation, January 1, 1912), in Zhang Yuxin and Zhang Shuangzhi, eds., *Minguo Zangshi shiliao huibian* (Collection of Historical Materials on the Tibetan Affairs of the Republic of China) (Beijing: Xueyuan chubanshe, 2005), 1: 31; "Zhonghua minguo linshi yuefa, 1912 nian 3 yue 11 ri gongbu" (Provisional Constitution of the Republic of China, issued on March 11, 1912), in ibid., 1: 42.

10. For frontier ethno-politics in the Republican era, see Linda Benson, *The Ili Rebellion: The Moslem Challenge to Chinese Authority in Xinjiang, 1944–1949* (Armonk, NY: M.E. Sharpe, 1990); Andrew D.W. Forbes, *Warlords and Muslims in Chinese Central Asia: A Political History of Republican Sinkiang 1911–1949* (New York: Cambridge University Press, 1986); David D. Wang, *Under the Soviet Shadow: The Yining Incident* (Hong Kong: The Chinese University Press, 1999); Melvyn C. Goldstein, *A History of Modern Tibet, 1913–1951: The Demise of the Lamaist State* (Berkeley: University of California Press, 1989); Lin Hsiao-ting, *Tibet and Nationalist China's Frontier: Intrigues and Ethnopolitics, 1928–49* (Vancouver: University of British Columbia Press, 2006); Christopher P. Atwood, *Young Mongols and Vigilantes in Inner Mongolia's Interregnum Decades, 1911–1931* (Leiden: E.J. Brill, 2002); Baabar, *Twentieth Century Mongolia* (Cambridge: The White Horse Press, 1999); Xiaoyuan Liu, *Reins of Liberation: An Entangled History of Mongolian Autonomy, Chinese Territoriality, and Great Power Hegemony, 1911–1950* (Stanford and Washington DC: Stanford University Press and Woodrow Wilson Center Press, 2006).

11. "Zhongyang guanyu fandi douzheng zhong women gongzuo de cuowu yu quedian de jueyi," December 2, 1931 (CCP Center's Resolution on the Party's Mistakes and

Shortcomings in the Anti-imperialist Struggle), in Zhongyang dang'an guan (Central Archives), ed., *Zhonggong zhongyang wenjian xuanji* (Selection of Central Committee Documents) (Beijing: Zhonggong zhongyang dangxiao chubanshe, 1991–92), 7: 532; "Zhongyang guanyu muqian zhengzhi xingshi yu dangde renwu jueyi," December 25, 1935 (Resolution of the Central Committee on the Current Political Situation and the Party's Tasks), in ibid., 10: 609–17; Liu Shaoqi, "Guanyu guoqu baiqu gongzuo gei zhongyang de yifeng xin," March 4, 1937 (Letter to the Central Committee on Past Work in the White [KMT] Regions), in ibid., 11: 801–18; Mao Zedong, "Lun xin jieduan," October 12–14, 1938 (On the New Phase), in ibid., 11: 557–662; "Guomindang yu minzuzhuyi" (The KMT and Nationalism), *Jiefang ribao* (Liberation Daily), editorial, September 18, 1943, in ibid., 14: 566–76; Mao Zedong, "Zhongguo geming he Zhongguo gongchandang," 1939 (The Chinese Revolution and the Chinese Communist Party), in Zhonggong zhongyang tongzhanbu, ed., *Minzu wenti wenxian huibian: Yi jiu er yi. qi—yi jiu si jiu jiu* (Collected Documents on the Nationality Question: July 1921–September 1949) (Beijing: Zhonggong zhongyang dangxiao chubanshe, 1991) (hereafter, *MWWH*), pp. 625–32; Dong Biwu, "Gongchanzhuyi yu sanminzhuyi (zhaiyao)," June 14, 1937 (Communism and the Three People's Principles), in ibid., pp. 538–41; Zhou Enlai, "Lun Zhongguo faxisizhuyi xin zhuanzhizhuyi (zhaiyao)," August 16, 1943 (On China's Fascism—New Authoritarianism [excerpts]), in ibid., pp. 723–27.

12. Mao Zedong, "Lun xin jieduan."

13. CCP Northwestern Working Committee, "Zhonggong zhongyang xibei gongzuo weiyuanhui guanyu hui huizu wenti de tigang," April 1940 (Outline on the Question of the Hui Nationality), *MWWH*, pp. 648–56; "Zhonggong zhongyang xibei gongzuo weiyuanhui guanyu kangzhan zhong Menggu minzu wenti tigang" (CCP Northwestern Working Committee on the "Outline on the Question of the Mongolian Nationality During the War of Resistance), July 1940, in ibid., pp. 657–67.

14. For the CCP-KMT debate during the war years about the nationality status of China's ethnic groups, see Chiang Kai-shek, *China's Destiny* (New York: Macmillan Company, 1947) and Chen Boda, "Ping 'Zhongguo zhi mingyun' (zhaiyao)," July 21, 1943 (On China's Destiny [excerpts]), pp. 945–49. In Chiang's book, ethnic groups, having been incorporated into historical China, are defined as large or small clan branches (*zongzhi*) of the Chinese Nation.

15. Wu Zhongxin's memo to Chiang Kai-shek, "Huifu lunxian Mengqi ji zhanhou Meng Zang zhengzhi sheshi fang'an" (Plan for Recovering the Lost Mongolian Banners and for the Postwar Political Establishment in Mongolia and Tibet), August 27, 1944, Zongtongfu dang'an (Archives of the Presidential Palace) (hereafter ZD), 055/1631; Wu Zhongxin and Luo Jiangjia to Chiang Kai-shek, May 26, 1945, ZD, 055/0501; *Xian zongtong Jianggong sixiang yanlun zongji* (General Collection of Late President Chiang's Thoughts and Words) (Taipei: Guomindang dangshi weiyuanhui, 1984), 21: 170–75; Wang Chonghui, "Duiyu Xinjiang wenti zhi buchong yijian" (Supplementary Comments on the Xinjiang Question), September 1, 1941, in Jiang zhongzheng zongtong dang'an: Geming wenxian (Kangzhan shiqi) (Archives of President Chiang Kai-shek: Revolutionary Documents [of the Period of the War of Resistance]), 3: 53–54; "Neizhangbu minzhengsi chaosong taolun Maisiwude deng jianyi qingyu Xinjiang gaodu zizhi yi an zhi huiyi jilu" (Civil Affairs Desk of the Interior Ministry Transmits the Minutes of the Meeting Discussing the Suggestion by Masud

and Others to Grant a High Degree of Autonomy to Xinjiang), October 22, 1945, in Ministry of Foreign Affairs of the Republic of China, comp., *Waijaobu dang'an congshu; Jiewu lei, disan ce: Xinjiang juan (1)* (Series of Foreign Ministry Archives; Border Affairs, Book Three: Volume on Xinjiang [1]) (Taipei: Waijiaobu, 2001), p. 366; Secretariat of the Executive Yuan to the Ministry of Foreign Affairs, "Guomin zhengfu jiaoxia Xinjiang sheng Wu zhuxi dui gaisheng zhi zhengzhi yijian an" (Chairman Wu on Xinjiang Province's Opinion about Provincial Politics, Circulated by the Nationalist Government), April 8, 1946, in ibid., p. 368. A little-known yet highly interesting case is that of the KMT government's negotiations with Kanjud, a tribal state of Kashmir, between 1947 and 1948 to convert the state into an autonomous region of the ROC. See the documents in *Waijaobu dang'an congshu; Jiewu lei, disan ce: Xinjiang juan, de er ce,* pp. 27–30, 102–3.

16. Apart from Tibet, a separatist "Eastern Turkestan Republic" existed in Xinjiang between 1944 and 1949. However, because CCP influence did not reach these areas until 1949 and 1950, conditions in Tibet and Xinjiang did not have a direct impact on CCP deliberations of the *quyu zizhi* formula in the postwar years.

17. "Meimeng yunniang zizhi jiqi huodong qingxing" (Facts of the Inner Mongolian Autonomous Movement), June 3, 1947, Zongtongfu dang'an (Archives of the Presidential Palace), 055/1657; Zhang Ce, "Guanyu dong Menggu diqu (Xing'an) de gongzuo qingkuang he jingyan," August 15, 1946 (The Conditions and Experiences of the Work in the Eastern Mongolian Region [Xing'an]), *MWWH,* pp. 1315–21.

18. This discussion is based on Xiaoyuan Liu, *Reins of Liberation.* pp. 115–280.

19. Sima Qian, *Shiji: Lu Taihou benji* (Records of the Grand Historian: Lu Taihou Imperial Biography).

20. Benedict Anderson, *Imagined Community* (London: Verso, 1991), p. 86.

21. Anderson, *Imagined Community,* pp. 84–85, notes that in the nineteenth century Germany acquired a dual capacity combining "universal-imperial" and "particular-national," and that the pursuit of the former resulted in the accentuation of the latter. The Republic of China in the first half of the twentieth century represented a reverse case: its outright search for a nation-state pointed to an implicit reclamation of China's imperial legacies.

22. "Party-nation," or *dangzu,* cannot be found in either the KMT's or the CCP's official discourse. Although both upheld *Zhonghua minzu,* literally "Chinese citizens' nation," as the inclusive and collective identity of all ethnic groups within China, the KMT came close to admitting the statist connotation of the conception by sometimes using "citizens' nation" and "state-nation," or *guozu,* interchangeably. Since the "state" was a party-state, a "state-nation" by nature would be a "party-nation." For such examples, see Wu Zhongxin to Jiang Jieshi, August 27, 1944, and appendix, "Huifu lunxian Mengqi ji zhanhou Meng Zang zhengzhi sheshi fang'an," 055/1631, Archives of the Presidential Palace, Taipei; Wu Zhongxin and Luo Liangjian to Jiang Jieshi, May 26, 1945, in ibid., 055/0501.

23. "Zhongguo renmin zhengxie shanghuiyi gongtong gangling" (Common Program of the Chinese People's Political Consultative Conference), September 29, 1949, in Central Office of Documentary Research, comp., *Jianguo yilai zhongyao wenxian xuanbian* (Selected Important Documents Issued Since the Founding of the State) (Beijing: Zhongyang wenxian chubanshe, 1992), 1: 1–14; Wang Jianmin, et al., *Zhongguo minzuxue shi* (History of Ethnology in China) (Kunming: Yunnan jiaoyu chubanshe, 1998), 2: 106–29.

24. "Zhonggong zhongyang guanyu shaoshu minzu 'zijuequan' wenti gei ye qianwei de zhishi," October 5, 1949 (CCP Center's Directive to the Second Field Army on the

Question of Minority Nationalities' Right to Self-Determination), in Central Office of Documentary Research, comp., *Jianguo yilai zhongyao wenxian xuanbian*, 1: 24; "Zhou Enlai zai zhongyang minwei juban de Zangzu ganbu yanjiuban shang de baogao" (Zhou Enlai's Report at the Tibetan Cadre Study Group Held by the Central Nationality Commission), April 27, 1950, in Office on the Party History of the Tibetan Autonomous Region, comp., *Zhou Enlai yu Xizang* (Zhou Enlai and Tibet) (Beijing: Zhongguo zangxue chubanshe, 1998), p. 112; Zhou Enlai, "Minzu quyu zizhi youli yu minzu tuanjie he gongtong jinbu" (Regional Nationality Autonomy Is Beneficial to National Unity and Common Progress), March 25, 1957, in ibid., pp. 155–64; Zhou Enlai, "Guanyu woguo minzu zhengce de jige wenti" (A Few Questions about the Nationality Policies of Our Country), August 4, 1957, in ibid., pp. 165–87; "Mao Zedong zai Chengdu huiyishang de jianghua" (Mao Zedong's Talks at the Chengdu Conference), March 10, 1958, cited in Luo Guangwu, ed., *Xin Zhongguo minzu gongzuo dashi gailan, 1949–1999* (Survey of Important Events in the Nationality Work of the New China, 1949–1999) (Beijing: Huawen chubanshe, 2001), pp. 295–296; Li Weihan, "Guanyu minzu gongzuo zhong de jige wenti," September 1961 (A Few Questions in Nationality Work), in *Li Weihan xuanji* (Selected Works of Li Weihan) (Beijing: Renmin chubanshe, 1987), pp. 366–72.

25. On August 8, 1952, the People's Central Government adopted the "Zhonghua renmin gongheguo minzu quyu zizhi zhizhi gangyao" (Basic Measures of the People's Republic of China for Implementing Regional Nationality Autonomy), prominently stipulating that the autonomous regions were the PRC's inalienable territories and their "local" status. See Luo Guangwu, ed., *Xin Zhongguo minzu gongzuo dashi gailan, 1949–1999*, pp. 79–82.

26. "Zhongguo lishishang jiejue minzu wenti de zhongyao cuoshi" (Monumental Measure in Chinese History for Solving the Nationality Question), *Renmin ribao* (People's Daily), editorial, February 28, 1954, p. 1.

27. In October 1950, the People's Liberation Army decisively defeated the Tibetan army in the battle of Chamdo. In May 1951, the now-famous "17-point agreement" was concluded between representatives of Beijing and Lhasa, which included the right of Tibet to implement *quyu zizhi* in the future. The Tibetan Autonomous Region was established in September 1965, ten years after a preparatory committee was established under the Dalai Lama and six years after the Dalai Lama was exiled due to the failed Lhasa uprising of 1959.

28. Mao Zedong, "Guanyu quyu zizhi wenti de piyu," September 16, 1950 (Comments on the Issue of Regional Autonomy), in Mao Zedong, *Jianguo yilai Mao Zedong wengao* (Mao Zedong's Manuscripts Since the Founding of the State) (Beijing: Zhongyang wenxian chubanshe, 1987), 1: 518; Xiao Gen, *Zhongguo shaoshu minzu xingzheng zhidu* (China's Administrative System for the Minority Nationalities) (Kunming: Yunnan daxue chubanshe, 1999), pp. 474–75.

29. Luo Guangwu, ed., *Xin Zhongguo minzu gongzuo dashi gailan, 1949–1999*, pp. 222–23; Ulanfu, "Dang shengli di jiejuele guonei minzu wenti," September 19, 1956 (The Party Has Victoriously Solved the Domestic Nationality Question), in *Wulanfu wenxuan* (Selected Writings of Ulanfu) (Beijing: Zhongyang wenxian chubanshe, 1999), 1: 408–18.

30. Between 1945 and 1947 Ulanfu played a key role in channeling the autonomous movements of Inner Mongolia into the CCP orbit. When recalling the experience years later,

the only positive significance he was willing to attribute to the Eastern Mongolian Autonomous Movement was that it had allowed the CCP to negotiate with a unified movement, not many divided groups, in Inner Mongolia. See Liu Jieyu, "Neimenggu zizhi yundong de biyou zhilu" (The Necessary Path of the Inner Mongolian Autonomous Movement), in *Neimenggu wenshi ziliao; Di wushi ji* (Literary and Historical Materials on Inner Mongolia, Volume 50) (Hohhot: Neimengu zhengxie wenshi shudian, 1997), pp. 216–35.

31. Zhou Enlai, "Guanyu woguo minzu zhengce de jige wenti," pp. 165–87; Ulanfu, "Qingdao minzu gongzuo zuotanhui zongjie" (August 5, 1957) (Conclusion of the Qingdao Forum on Nationality Work), Ulanfu, *Wulanfu wenxuan* (Selected Writings of Ulanfu) (Beijing: Zhongyang wenxian chubanshe, 1999), 1: 474–83.

32. Liu Shaoqi, "Zai jinian shiyue geming sanshier zhounian dahuishang de jiangyan," November 7, 1949 (Speech at the Assembly to Commemorate the 32nd Anniversary of the October Revolution), in Liu Shaoqi, *Jianguo yilai Liu Shaoqi wengao* (Liu Shaoqi's Manuscripts since the Founding of the State) (Beijing: Zhongyang wenxian chubanshe, 1998), 1: 113–19; Liu Shaoqi, "Zai Yazhou Aozhou gongzuo huiyishang de kaimushi," November 16, 1949 (Opening Address at the Conference of Asian-Oceanic Labor Unions), in ibid., 1: 130–39.

33. Deng Xiaoping, "Guanyu Xi'nan shaoshu minzu wenti," July 21, 1950 (On the Minority Nationalities Question in the Southwest), in Office of Documentary Research of the CCP Central Committee and the CCP Committee of the Tibetan Autonomous Region, comp., *Xizang gongzuo wenxian xuanbian* (Selected Documents on Tibetan Work) (Beijing: Zhongyang wenxian chubanshe, 2005) (hereafter, *XGWX*), pp. 22–29.

34. Luo Guangwu, ed., *Xin Zhongguo minzu gongzuo dashi gailan, 1949–1999*, pp. 4–5; Melvyn Goldstein, *A History of Modern Tibet, Volume 2: The Calm before the Storm, 1951–1955* (Berkeley: University of California Press, 2007), pp. 491–520.

35. Luo Guangwu, ed., *Xin Zhongguo minzu gongzuo dashi gailan, 1949–1999*, pp. 274–75, 279–82, 288–90.

36. Sichuan Provincial Committee on Compiling the Local Annals, comp., *Sichuan sheng zhi: Junshi zhi* (Annals of Sichuan Province: Volume on Military Affairs) (Chengdu: Sichuan renmin chubanshe, 1999), pp. 294–319; Qinghai Provincial Committee on Compiling the Local Annals, comp., *Qinghai sheng zhi: Junshi zhi* (Annals of Qinghai Province: Volume on Military Affairs) (Xining: Qinghai renmin chubanshe, 2001), pp. 513–32; Gansu Provincial Committee on Compiling the Local Annals, comp., *Gansu sheng zhi: Junshi zhi* (Annals of Gansu Province: Volume on Military Affairs) (Lanzhou: Gansu renmin chubanshe, 2001), pp. 804–7.

37. Luo Guangwu, ed., *Xin Zhongguo minzu gongzuo dashi gailan, 1949–1999*, pp. 274–75, 284–85, 288–92, 388–91.

38. Hao Weimin, *Neimenggu zizhiqu shi* (A History of the Inner Mongolian Autonomous Region) (Hohhot: Neimenggu daxue chubanshe, 1991), pp. 163, 369; Deng Liqun, et al., ch. eds., *Dangdai Zhongguo de Xinjiang* (Xinjiang in Contemporary China) (Beijing: Dangdai Zhongguo chubanshe, 1991), p. 244.

39. This is based on the experiences of the author, who resided in Eastern Ujumuchin for six years from the late 1960s to the mid-1970s.

40. Ulanfu, "Minzu quyu zizhi de guanghui licheng," July 14, 1981 (The Glorious Path of Regional Minority Autonomy), *Wulanfu wenxuan*, 2: 377.

41. According to Li Sheng, *Zhongguo Xinjiang: Lishi yu xianzhuang* (Xinjiang of China: History and Current Situation) (Urumqi: Xinjiang renmin chubanshe, 2003), pp. 344–48, and Committee for Collecting Party History Materials of the Tibetan Autonomous Region, comp., *Zhonggong Xizang dangshi dashiji* (Important Events in CCP History in Tibet) (Lhasa: Xizang renmin chubanshe, 1995), pp. 187–89, between 1967 and 1970 a secret "Eastern Turkestan People's Revolutionary Party," with nearly 6,000 members, was active in Xinjiang, and armed rebellions took place in several locations in Tibet in 1969. For an insightful discussion of the Cultural Revolution in Tibet, see Melvyn C. Goldstein, Ben Jiao, and Tanzen Lhundrup, *On the Cultural Revolution in Tibet: The Nyemo Incident of 1969* (Berkeley: University of California Press, 2009). Tumen and Zhu Dongli's, *Kang Sheng yu "Nei Ren Dang" yuan'an* (Kang Sheng and the Wronged Case of the "Inner Mongolian People's Revolutionary Party") (Beijing: Zhonggong zhongyang dangxiao chubanshe, 1995) reflects China's mainstream interpretation of the Cultural Revolution events in Inner Mongolia. It should be balanced with Gao Shuhua and Cheng Tiejun, *Neimeng wenge fenglei: Yiwei zaofanpai lingxiu de koushu shi* (The Storm of the Cultural Revolution in Inner Mongolia: An Oral History by a Rebel Leader) (Carle Place, NY: Mirror Books, 2007). The 1935 CCP statement can be found in *MWWH*, pp. 322–24.

42. Ma Dazheng, *Guojia liyi gaoyu yiqie: Xinjiang wending wenti de guancha yu sikao* (State Interest Is Superior to Everything Else: Observations and Deliberations on the Question of Stability in Xinjiang) (Urumqi: Xinjiang renmin chubanshe, 2003), p. 44. One of the bloodiest conflicts in Tibet in the 1960s was the so-called Nyemo incident of 1969. The introduction to Goldstein, Jiao, and Lhundrup, *On the Cultural Revolution in Tibet*, summarizes the ongoing debate among researchers about the nature of the incident. Before leaving Eastern Ujumuchin in 1974, the author witnessed the wholesale exoneration of Inner Mongolian herdsmen for their alleged involvement with the so-called "Neirendang."

43. Uradyn Bulag, *The Mongols at China's Edge: History and the Politics of National Unity* (Lanham, MD: Rowman and Littlefield, 2002), p. 132.

44. Examples of such annals are Editorial Board of *Dangdai Zhongguo de Minzu Gongzuo* (Nationality Work of Contemporary China), comp., *Dangdai Zhongguo minzu gongzuo dashiji, 1949–1988* (Chronicle of Important Events in the Nationality Work of Contemporary China, 1949–1988) (Beijing: Minzu chubanshe, 1990), pp. 201–38; Luo Guangwu, ed., *Xin Zhongguo minzu gongzuo dashi kailan, 1949–1999*, pp. 415–16.

45. Luo Guangwu, ed., *Xin Zhongguo minzu gongzuo dashi gailan, 1949–1999*, pp. 481, 579–582; "Xin shiqi dangde minzu gongzuo yu zongjiao zhengce—Zhaizi zhonggong zhongyang pizhuan de quanguo tongzhan gongzuo huiyi wenjian 'Xin de lishi shiqi tongyi zhanxian de fangzhen renwu,'" September 13, 1979 (The Party's Nationality Work and Religious Policy in the New Era—Excerpts from 'The Orientation and Tasks of the United Front in the New Historical Period,' a Document of the National United Front Conference Circulated by the CCP Central Committee), in State Nationalities Commission and Central Documentation Research Institute, eds., *Xin shiqi minzu gongzuo wenxian xuanbian* (Selected Documents on Nationalities Work during the New Period) (Beijing: Zhongyang wenxian chubanshe, 1990), pp. 18–20; "Zhongyang shujichu taolun Neimenggu zizhiqu gongzuo de jiyao," July 16, 1981 (Summary of the Discussion by the Secretariat of the CCP Central Committee of the Work in the Inner Mongolian Autonomous Region), in ibid., pp. 150–153; Hu Yaobang, "Xin shiqi de minzu guanxi he tongyi zhanxian," September

1, 1982 (Inter-Nationality Relations and the United Front in the New Era), in ibid., pp. 175–76; and "Zhonghua renmin gongheguo minzu quyu zizhifa," May 31, 1984 (Law for Regional Nationality Autonomy of the People's Republic of China), in ibid., pp. 235–50.

46. "Zhonggong zhongyang guanyu yinfa 'Xizang gongzuo zuotanhui jiyao' de tongzhi," April 1, 1984 (Notice of the CCP Central Committee on Circulation of the "Summary of the Symposium on Tibetan Work"), *XGWX*, pp. 358–69. For a detailed survey of Beijing's policy toward Tibet and the Dalai Lama in the post-Mao era, see Tashi Rabgey and Tseten Wangchuk Sharlho, *Sino-Tibetan Dialogue in the Post-Mao Era: Lessons and Prospects* (Washington, DC: East-West Center, 2004).

47. Deng Xiaoping, "Cujin ge minzu gongtong fanrong," June 15, 1979–September 15, 1990 (Promote the Common Prosperity of All Nationalities), *XGWX*, pp. 298–99; Jiang Zemin, "Zai minzu gongzuo huiyi ji Guowuyuan di sanci quanguo minzu tuanjie jinbu biaozhang dahuishang de jianghua," September 29, 1999 (Speech at the Central Nationality Work Conference and the State Council Conference on Commending National Unity and Progress), in ibid., pp. 525–32; Deng Xiaoping, "Guanjian yao shi Xizang renmin tigao wuzhi wenhua shenghuo shuiping," October 16, 1987 (The Key Is to Enhance the Level of the Tibetan People's Material and Cultural Life), in ibid., p. 399. "Socialist nationality relations" was included in the 1982 PRC constitution.

48. Deng Xiaoping, "Cujin ge minzu gongtong fanrong."

49. Ma Dazheng, *Guojia liyi gaoyu yiqie*, pp. 30–136; Li Sheng, *Zhongguo Xinjiang: Lishi yu xianzhuang*, pp. 330–77; Jiang Zemin, "Cujin Xizang shixian kuayue zhi fazhan he chang zhi jiu'an," June 25, 2001 (Promote the Realization of Leaping Development and Lasting Order and Stability in Tibet), *XGWX*, pp. 547–60; Hu Jintao, "Zhuazhu youli shiji tuidong Xizang kuayue shi fazhan," March 5, 2002 (Seize the Favorable Moment and Promote Leaping Development in Tibet), in ibid., pp. 612–16.

21.
THE ROLE OF CHINA'S PUBLIC INTELLECTUALS IN THE PEOPLE'S REPUBLIC OF CHINA

MERLE GOLDMAN

The differentiation that a number of political scientists make between totalitarian and authoritarian regimes is particularly relevant to an evaluation of the role of intellectuals in the People's Republic of China.[1] Under its first leader, Mao Zedong, who ruled from 1949 until his death in 1976, China was governed by a totalitarian system, in which Mao and the party not only dominated the country's political and economic life, but also controlled the intellectual, artistic, and personal lives of its subjects through party institutions and intensifying political campaigns against dissident intellectuals.

During the period of Mao's successor and former Long March comrade, Deng Xiaoping, who was China's paramount leader from 1978 until his death in 1997, China moved from a totalitarian to an authoritarian regime. The party still dominated the political system and, except for the elections at the village level, determined the political hierarchy. At the same time, however, as China moved to a market economy, controls over the economic, social, cultural, intellectual, artistic, and personal lives of the people were loosened. Coupled with China's opening to the outside world, these changes allowed a degree of freedom in the lives of China's populace. Though an authoritarian one-party state, the relaxation of controls over most areas of people's lives unleashed a proliferation of ideas, activities, and artistic endeavors outside of party control. These changes made possible the appearance of public intellectuals in the People's Republic during the post-Mao era.

Public intellectuals are not unique to Western civilization. They have played a major role throughout Chinese history. China's pre-modern intellectuals, the Confucian literati, not only ran government bureaucracies, they were also regarded as the conscience of the society. They were generalists who publicly discussed and dealt with political, ideological, economic, and social issues, organized philanthropic efforts, and supervised education. Most importantly, some Confucian literati regarded it as their responsibility to criticize officials and even the emperor when their ideas and behaviors diverged from the Confucian ideals of morality and fairness. The literati's commitment to improving the human condition led them to assume responsibilities comparable to those of public intellectuals in the modern West.

Public intellectuals also helped to bring about the end of China's dynastic system during the 1898 Hundred Days of Reform during the late Qing dynasty and they also paved the way for the 1911 revolution, which was led by the public intellectual Sun Yat-sen. Even though the Guomindang government of Chiang Kai-shek (1928–49) attempted to stifle criticism and dissent, it was too weak to silence intellectuals, who publicly criticized the repressive Guomindang officials and policies and advocated political reforms. With the exception of brief periods, such as during the Hundred Flowers campaign from 1956 to June 1957, under the totalitarian leadership of Mao Zedong China's public intellectuals remained basically silenced and unable to play their traditional role. Of course, one major difference between the West and China during the dynastic, Guomindang, Mao Zedong, and post-Mao eras is that there never were any laws in China to protect public intellectuals when what they said displeased the leaders, who could then silence them with relative impunity.

Mao Zedong's Totalitarian Rule (1949–76)

Even before the Chinese Communist Party established the People's Republic of China in 1949, there was already evidence that Mao Zedong would not tolerate any dissent or public criticism of his policies. In the early 1940s, in the party's revolutionary base area of Yan'an, Mao launched a campaign against a group of writers who were committed to the humanitarian aspirations of Marxism and who believed they were being true to basic Marxist ideals when they publicly called for equality, democracy, and intellectual freedom.

As intellectuals in the past had criticized the government in the name of Confucian ideals, these writers criticized the party on the basis of Marxist principles. Several of them published their critiques in the party's official newspaper at the time, the *Jiefang ribao* (Liberation Daily), expressing their disillusionment to find that life in the revolutionary base area did not measure up to their expected ideals of an equal, just, and free society.[2] They explicitly criticized the bureaucratism, corruption, and inequalities in the party. In response, in spring of 1942 Mao issued his famous Yan'an "Talks on Literature and Art," in which he served notice that henceforth literature and the arts, i.e., all aspects of intellectual activity, would be dictated by party policy.[3] At the same time, he launched a rectification campaign against those writers and intellectuals who opposed his policies. Thus, even before the establishment of the People's Republic, Mao had made it clear that any intellectuals whose views deviated from party policy would be publicly attacked and purged.

During the early years of the People's Republic, party policy toward intellectuals oscillated between stifling intellectual discourse and debate and encouraging the creativity that was needed to modernize. Thus, the party approach was contradictory. On the one hand, the party indoctrinated intellectuals with the principles of Marxism-Leninism; on the other hand, it tried to stimulate intellectuals to work productively and creatively in their respective disciplines. These conflicting goals produced a cyclical policy toward intellectuals, in which periods of repression were followed by (briefer) periods of relative relaxation. Each cycle was determined by internal political and economic factors as well as by international events.[4]

From 1949 until early 1951, the party briefly relaxed controls over intellectuals as it sought to consolidate its rule over all of China and to gain the support of China's intellectuals and professionals. But in late 1951 it began an effort to reorient Chinese intellectuals away from the West and toward its major ally at the time, the Soviet Union, by denouncing liberal values and spreading the principles of Marxism-Leninism. In 1954, the party attacked the ideas of the well-known Western-oriented scholar Hu Shi, who in the early decades of the twentieth century had introduced John Dewey's theory of pragmatism into China. In 1955, the party launched an ideological campaign against the writer Hu Feng and his disciples, who had rebelled against being forced to write in Soviet-style socialist realism and to conform to party dictates. The Hu Feng campaign established a model for future campaigns, as the scope was broadened beyond a small group of literary intellectuals to a nationwide campaign encompassing nearly all intellectuals and professionals, who were ordered to abandon any non-Marxist-Leninist ideas.

By the end of 1955, a large segment of China's intellectuals had been silenced because of the unprecedented ferocity of the Hu Feng campaign. The campaign's crusading zeal even alienated some of China's scientists whose help was needed to modernize the economy. Confronted with a passive and disgruntled intellectual community but in urgent need of its services, in 1956 and the first half of 1957 Mao launched the Hundred Flowers Campaign, relaxing controls and providing a degree of intellectual freedom.[5] Intellectuals were urged to engage in independent thinking, wide-ranging discourse, and critical thought. Mao encouraged direct criticism, discussions of political issues, and the airing of grievances. Moreover, he called on intellectuals to criticize the leadership and to point out how it had misused its power.

In response, intellectuals began to question Marxism-Leninism and to call for political and cultural reforms. They not only criticized Mao's "Talks on Literature and Art," but they also called for intellectual autonomy and demanded that the earlier campaigns against writers who had been publicly criticized, such as Hu Feng, be reopened. In spring 1957, as the Hundred Flowers Campaign spread beyond the intellectuals to the population at large, which also began to voice demands for more freedom, the party suddenly reversed its tolerance and relaxation of controls. In June 1957, it launched the Anti-Rightist movement, with sweeping attacks on those who had publicly criticized party policies and party officials. Those who had expressed such criticisms, as well as their families and colleagues, were labeled "Rightists," were forced to make public confessions, and were dismissed from their positions. By late 1957, the cycle had come full circle and had returned to the ideological rigidity and persecution of intellectuals that had prevailed prior to the Hundred Flowers Campaign.

With the subsequent launch of the Great Leap Forward in 1958–59, the gap between the party and intellectuals was widened still farther as Mao sought to rapidly transform China into a Communist society ahead of the Soviet Union. In this effort, intellectuals were dispatched to factories and villages to remold their thinking through manual labor and to bring culture to the masses. Virtually all intellectual work was stopped. Even the highly prized scientists were told to learn from the achievements of Chinese peasants and workers. The failure of the Great Leap Forward, causing the deaths of at least thirty million Chinese due to food shortages and economic chaos in the countryside, created disillusionment with Mao's policies, not only among intellectuals and technocrats, but also among Mao's party colleagues.[6] As Mao withdrew from policy making in the early 1960s, a brief period of intellectual relaxation ensued, during which intellectuals published essays in the traditional *zawen* style of short critical essays and used traditional Chinese opera to subtly criticize Mao's policies. Several of these criticisms were even produced under party auspices.

In response, in 1966 Mao launched the Cultural Revolution against all those whom he believed were conspiring against him. During the following ten years, most intellectuals, together with their families and colleagues, were ostracized, persecuted, or driven to suicide in the most severe intellectual suppression in modern Chinese history.[7] The only exception was a small number of politically radical intellectuals associated with the Gang of Four who acted as Mao's spokespersons. Educational institutions were closed down and intellectual and cultural endeavors were stifled. Even China's scientists, who were supposed to lead China's economic modernization, were cut off from the outside world and persecuted. By the time of Mao's death in September 1976, China's intellectual community had been decimated and its educational institutions were non-functioning.

Restricted Freedoms in China's Post-Mao Authoritarian State

Although the People's Republic after Mao's death in 1976 still remained under the political control of the Chinese Communist Party, when Mao's Long March comrade Deng Xiaoping became the paramount leader in the late 1970s, China could no longer be called a totalitarian state. It remained under the political control of the Communist Party, but Deng's policies of moving China to a market economy and opening China to the outside world allowed a degree of personal, intellectual, and artistic freedom. In 1987 Deng purged Hu Yaobang, whom he had appointed as head of the party in the early 1980s and in spring 1989, he purged Zhao Ziyang, who had replaced Hu as the head of the party, because they had each advocated political reforms.[8] Moreover, Zhao had refused to go along with Deng's order to use the military to crack down on the demonstrators in Tiananmen Square on June 4. Nevertheless, after a brief pause, China's intellectual and cultural life resumed and was relatively open and engaged with the outside world.

As China's third generation of leaders came to power in the aftermath of the June 4, 1989 violent crackdown, led by former Shanghai mayor Jiang Zemin (1989–2002), and the fourth generation of party leaders, headed by Hu Jintao and his associates, who assumed power in 2002, the leadership sought to re-centralize political authority and re-strengthen the party's capacity to deal with the increasing inequalities and rampant corruption unleashed by China's move to a market economy. Nevertheless, despite a re-tightening of party power over academic and cultural institutions after June 4, a degree of pluralistic discourse and openness to foreign ideas continued to exist in China's universities, artistic circles, academic journals, and think-tanks, particularly in the sciences.[9] The post-1989 leaderships of Jiang Zemin and then Hu Jintao, however, also detained, put under surveillance, or expelled from the academic establishment those intellectuals who dared to openly express their dissent and criticize party policies.

Nevertheless, although there were still no laws to protect political and civil rights, most of the intellectuals whom Mao had earlier persecuted were rehabilitated in the 1980s and most found positions in the political and intellectual establishments. Yet, when some of them began to call for reform of the Leninist party-state, they were once again purged. It had been expected that when China's fourth generation of leaders who were better educated than previous generations and came primarily from the Communist Youth League, a supposedly less doctrinaire organization, came to power in 2002 with Hu Jintao, the opening up of public space for political discourse would expand, while still remaining circumscribed within certain limits. That, however, has not been the case. In fact, there was a contraction of public space for political discourse beginning in the late 1990s.

The Hu Jintao leadership cracked down on a number of people who used the new communications technologies and the Internet to discuss political issues.[10] Scores of cyber-dissidents were imprisoned as a warning to others as to how far they can go in discussing political reforms. Public intellectuals who spoke out and published essays on controversial issues were briefly detained. In 2004, for example, the military doctor, Jiang Yanyong, who had treated victims during June 4 and was the first to counter the party's assertion in 2003 that the SARS epidemic had been brought under control, was detained and then put under surveillance for calling on the party to change its designation of the 1989 Tiananmen Square demonstrations from a "counterrevolutionary" movement to a "patriotic" movement.

Along with the suppression of a number of well-known public intellectuals and limitations on public discourse, the Hu Jintao government tightened controls over the media. Reports on the growing protests against corruption, abusive officials, property confiscations, and peasant and worker demonstrations were banned from the media.[11] Journalism professor Jiao Guobiao, who had criticized the party's repressive control of the media, was no longer allowed to teach at Peking University. Another public intellectual, Wang Yi, a law lecturer at Chengdu University who had called for a system of checks and balances, was also barred from teaching. The journal *Zhanlüe yu guanli* (Strategy and Management), a former outlet for intellectuals of a liberal persuasion, was closed down in 2004.

Although the Ministry of Public Security announced that 87,000 protests had taken place in 2005,[12] journalists were ordered not to report on the myriad of protests spreading across the country. When China was struck by a devastating earthquake in Sichuan province in 2008, initially the media and civic groups were allowed to report freely on the disaster, but when the parents of the children who had been buried in their classrooms began to point out that the quake had led to the collapse of so many schools due to shoddy construction and official corruption, the openness in the media was quickly curtailed.

Nevertheless, despite the crackdown on public intellectuals and media and the Internet censorship, unlike during the Mao period when millions were harshly persecuted for the acts of a small number, in the post-Mao period persecution for public dissent does not reach far beyond the accused and their immediate associates. Moreover, though they may lose their jobs in academia and the media or may be briefly detained, they are able to find jobs and other outlets for their views in China's expanding market economy.

Thus, public intellectuals are not completely silenced. Some still try to function as citizens, either on their own or with others, and they continue to express their political views in unofficial publications, and increasingly in organized petitions and protests. Although their writings may be officially banned, they have found ways to distribute their views on street corners, through private publications, or over the Internet by means of connections to outside servers. In addition, for the first time in the People's Republic, despite continuing repression of dissent, a number of lawyers are willing to defend those accused of political crimes and journalists report on the party's repressive policies in some media outlets, such as the *Nanfang zhoumo* (Southern Weekend), based in Guangdong.

There are also major differences between the actions of public intellectuals in the 1980s and their activities in the early twenty-first century. Public intellectuals in the former period, imbued with a different political consciousness, used very different political strategies. A number of prominent public intellectuals in the 1980s, such as journalist Liu Binyan or poet Ai Qing who called themselves "Marxist humanists," focused on pointing out how party policies differed from the ideals of Marxist doctrine.[13] But because of the increasing bankruptcy of Marxism-Leninism as a governing philosophy by the end of the twentieth century, most public intellectuals in the first decade of the twenty-first century moved away from a focus on ideology and instead emphasized the establishment of new institutions in order to achieve political reforms. In addition, whereas prior to the 1989 Tiananmen demonstrations public intellectuals considered themselves an elite and they did not join with other social classes in political activities, beginning with the Tiananmen Square demonstrations in spring 1989 a small number of intellectuals started to join with workers and several rising entrepreneurs to organize groups and petition drives to bring pressure on the government for political reform. Journalists wrote about these events and lawyers defended the leaders of these movements when they were arrested.

A Qualitative Intellectual Change

Therefore, in the first decade of the twenty-first century, despite the continuing repression, there was a qualitative change in the thinking and actions of China's public intellectuals: they increasingly became independent political actors who were willing to join with other social groups in political action.

China's growing interactions with the outside world, particularly with the West, also promoted a more liberalizing intellectual environment within China. In 1997, China signed the UN Covenant on Economic, Social, and Cultural Rights and in October 1998, China signed the UN Covenant on Civil and Political Rights. Although the former was ratified by China's rubber-stamp National People's Congress, the latter has yet to be ratified. Nevertheless, China's signature on these documents, coupled with the easing of political controls, were part of an effort to create goodwill abroad, particularly with the United States and other Western countries. In addition, thousands of Chinese students and scholars traveled abroad for study at American and West European universities. China's expanded engagement with the international community paralleled the relaxation of ideological controls at home.

One hundred years after China's 1898 Hundred Day Reforms that led to the beginning of political change and ultimately to the fall of the dynastic system in 1911, the year 1998 ushered in broad-ranging public discourse on political reforms. And like the Hundred Day reformers in 1898, the major proponents of political reforms in the late twentieth and early twenty-first centuries were establishment intellectuals—academics, writers, journalists, lawyers, and ex-officials—who were not at the center of power. They worked in think-tanks, universities, newspapers, and law offices, or they were already retired, but they managed to promote their ideas about political reform in books, scholarly journals, at academic meetings, and through other channels in the public arena. At times they even joined with those outside the establishment to call for political change.

Advocates of political reform in the late twentieth and early twenty-first centuries represented a broad ideological spectrum, from the older generation of Marxist humanists, who still couched their calls for political reform in Marxist language, to younger intellectuals from the party's think-tanks, such as the Chinese Academy of Social Sciences, China's premier center for social science research, or in the universities. Members of the younger generation cited a broad range of Western liberal thinkers from Adam Smith to Karl Popper to support their arguments.

Although none of the establishment intellectuals publicly proposed a multiparty system or direct elections of the political leadership by universal suffrage, a small number advocated the establishment of other institutions associated with liberal democracy: some emphasized the rule of law; others stressed freedom of expression and association; and still others called for more competitive elections. Some were concerned with inner-party democracy; others with grassroots democracy. And a few urged the establishment of an elected parliamentary system. Virtually all advocates of reform, however, called for a political system based on some form of checks and balances.[14] What they had in common was their shared emphasis on the need for reform of the political system in order to deal with the rampant corruption and accelerating economic and social inequalities that accompanied China's economic reforms.

Those expressing liberal political views in the early twenty-first century differed from the Marxist humanists of the 1980s in that they were relatively more independent of political patronage and they were seeking more intellectual autonomy, due in no small part to China's growing market economy and its increased openness to the outside world.

Another new phenomenon in the People's Republic in the early twenty-first century is that Chinese citizens from all walks of life were urging their government to live up to the principles to which it has expressed verbal or written approval. For example, on December 10, 2008, on the 60th anniversary of the Universal Declaration of Human Rights, about 300 people launched the Charter '08 movement, which presented a blueprint for fundamental legal and political reform to achieve a democratic political system. Patterned on Vaclav Havel's Charter '77 movement in the former Czechoslovakia, Charter '08 criticized the government for failing to implement the human rights provisions in the UN Covenant and the 2004 amendments to the Chinese constitution that include the phrase to "respect and protect human rights." In calling for democratic institutions of checks and balances, Charter '08 pointed out: "Unfortunately, most of China's political progress has extended no further than the paper on which it is written." The political reality, it stated, "is that China has many laws but no rule of law; it has a constitution but no constitutional government."

Demands for political reform were made periodically by intellectuals and students in post-Mao China. The most well-known effort of course is the 1989 demonstrations of students and intellectuals throughout the country. What makes Charter '08 qualitatively different from past protests is that it was a political movement that crossed class lines.[15] Past demonstrations were usually carried out by specific classes focusing on specific economic issues, such as peasant protests against the confiscation of their land by local officials or workers' protests against the non-payment of their salaries. During the 1989 demonstrations, students initially linked arms to keep the workers and other urbanites from joining the protests, knowing that what the party feared most was an alliance between intellectuals and workers. When other social classes forced their participation in the protests in late May 1989 and the movement spread to other cities, paramount party leader Deng Xiaoping, seeing a threat to party rule, ordered the violent military suppression on June 4.

What makes the Charter '08 unprecedented in China is that although initially it was signed by over 300 intellectuals, as it circulated on the Internet and elsewhere, ordinary Chinese citizens from all walks of life—entrepreneurs, professionals, local officials, workers, farmers, housewives, and street venders—also signed their names. Unprecedented as well was the participation of lawyers who were willing to defend those accused of political crimes. Despite the arrest of one of its originators, the writer Liu Xiaobo, and the party's denunciation of the Charter, before the party completely shut down the Charter's Web site in mid-January 2009, over eight-thousand people from all walks of life had signed the document on the Internet. The conviction of Liu Xiaobo on Christmas day 2009 for subversion and his sentence of eleven years brought an abrupt end to this movement.

The Charter '08 episode reveals that intellectuals were not alone in expressing dissatisfaction with the authoritarian party-state. Farmers, workers, and small entrepreneurs, who are the supposed beneficiaries of the Chinese political model, were also at the forefront of the protests. Their broad participation in the Charter '08 movement may be attributed to the deteriorating economic conditions in late 2008 due to the closure of some export industries because of slackening demand for Chinese consumer goods in the West and the unprecedented difficulties college graduates faced in finding employment. As a result, there was a questioning of the political system that based its legitimacy on the Chinese Communist Party's ability to deliver economic growth. Nevertheless, despite the crackdown and the conviction of Liu Xiaobo, Charter '08 represents a multi-class movement for political change that is likely to continue in the future.

Unlike during the Mao era when any dissent was brutally suppressed, in the post-Mao era, and especially during the early years of the twenty-first century, along with periodic repression, China's intellectuals experienced intellectual pluralism, engaged in vigorous debates, and sought international intellectual engagement. At the same time, some intellectuals joined with other classes and groups to call for political reforms. Thus, although China's movement from a totalitarian to an authoritarian polity did not protect public intellectuals in China from reprisals or detention, it made it possible for a small number of intellectuals periodically to speak out publicly on political issues and to have an impact beyond their immediate intellectual circles. Intellectuals had more freedom than during the Mao Zedong era, but they still did not have the wide-ranging freedom of intellectual discourse and the political impact that they had in the early decades of the twentieth century.

ENDNOTES

1. Gabriel Almond, et al., *Comparative Politics Today: A World View*, 7th ed. (New York: Longman, 2000); and Juan J. Linz, *Totalitarian and Authoritarian Regimes* (Boulder, CO: Lynne Rienner, 2000).

2. Gregor Benton and Alan Hunter, eds., *Wild Lily, Prairie Fire: China's Road to Democracy, Yan'an to Tian'anmen, 1942–1989* (Princeton, NJ: Princeton University Press, 1995).

3. Bonnie S. McDougall, *Mao Zedong's "Talks at the Yan'an Conference on Literature and Art": A Translation of the 1943 Text with Commentary* (Ann Arbor: Center for Chinese Studies, University of Michigan, 1980).

4. Merle Goldman, *Literary Dissent in Communist China* (Cambridge, MA: Harvard University Press, 1967).

5. Roderick MacFarquhar, ed., *The Hundred Flowers* (London: Stevens, 1960).

6. Jasper Becker, *Hungry Ghosts: Mao's Secret Famine* (New York: Henry Holt, 1998); Roderick MacFarquhar, *The Origins of the Cultural Revolution: The Coming of the Cataclysm, 1961–1966* (New York: Columbia University Press, 1997).

7. Roderick MacFarquhar and Michael Schoenhals, *Mao's Last Revolution* (Cambridge, MA: Belknap Press of Harvard University Press, 2006).

8. Merle Goldman, *Sowing the Seeds of Democracy in China: Political Reform in the Deng Xiaoping Era* (Cambridge, MA: Harvard University Press, 1994); Zhao Ziyang, "Advance Along the Road of Socialism with Chinese Characteristics," Political Report to the Thirteenth Party Congress, October 1987, *Beijing Review*, 30, no. 45 (November 9–15, 1987): i–xxvii.

9. Merle Goldman, *From Comrade to Citizen: The Struggle for Political Rights in China* (Cambridge, MA: Harvard University Press, 2005); Joseph Fewsmith, *China Since Tiananmen: From Deng Xiaoping to Hu Jintao*, 2nd ed. (New York: Cambridge University Press, 2008).

10. Philip P. Pan, *Out of Mao's Shadow: The Struggle for the Soul of a New China* (New York: Simon and Schuster, 2008).

11. Ching Kwan Lee, *Against the Law: Labor Protests in China's Rustbelt and Sunbelt* (Berkeley: University of California Press, 2007); Kevin J. O'Brien and Lianjiang Li, *Rightful Resistance in Rural China* (New York: Cambridge University Press, 2006).

12. *BBC Monitoring, Asia Pacific-Political*, January 20, 2006.

13. Goldman, *Sowing the Seeds of Democracy*; Goldman, *From Comrade to Citizen*.

14. Qiu Shi, ed., *Jiefang wenxuan, 1978–1998* (Liberation Literature, 1978-1998) (Beijing: Jingji ribao chubanshe, 1998); Su Shaozhi, *Zhongguo dalu zhengzhi tizhi gaige yanjiu* (Research on Mainland China's Reform of the Political System) (Taipei: Zhongguo wenhua daxue chubanshe, 2001); Zhao Ziyang, *Prisoner of the State: The Secret Journal of Zhao Ziyang*, translated and edited by Bao Pu, Renee Chiang, and Adi Ignatius (New York: Simon and Schuster, 2009).

15. *BBC Monitoring, Asia Pacific-Political*, December 11, 2008; Ariana Eunjung Cha, "In China, a Grass-Roots Rebellion; Rights Manifesto Slowly Gains Ground Despite Government Efforts to Quash It," *Washington Post*, January 29, 2009, p. A01.

22.

THE END OF INTELLECTUALS:
SIXTY YEARS OF SERVICE, SUBVERSION, AND SELLING IN CHINA

TIMOTHY CHEEK

The People's Republic of China (PRC) placed intellectuals at the center of its political life, as guardians of the all-important "politics" (or guiding ideology) of the nation, as well as the indispensable contributors to modernization and development, but at the same time as a potent threat to that politics and development. Under Mao, *zhishi fenzi*, or "knowledge elements," as intellectuals were called, were given the highest role in teaching the nation, yet they were created as a problematic, indeed, as a despised, political class in socialist society. The relationship has been tortured and treacherous, but it has been central to the history of the PRC, at least until recently.

"The End of Intellectuals" can serve as a summary description of this long and complex relationship between China's educated classes and their state and society. The first impression on hearing "the end of intellectuals" is, of course, the demise of intellectual freedom. However, we will see that a reverse reading also applies: the fulfillment of the ultimate goals of China's politically oriented educated elites of the twentieth century. Finally, by the early 2000s many have come to see the social status of the *zhishi fenzi* so changed as to declare the status (*shenfen*) of the intellectuals that we knew under Mao no longer exists: the era of the socialist *zhishi fenzi* has ended with the alienation of critical intellectuals from the party-state and their submission to the professions and market forces.

Thus, "the end of intellectuals" invokes the end of intellectual liberty in Yan'an and nationwide with the establishment of the socialist state in the PRC in 1949; it also names the attractions of service to the Chinese Communist Party (CCP) as the most promising avenue for the expression of the ends of intellectual service—that noble vocation to transform and strengthen China through the mental tools intellectuals wield—and it suggests the end of an intellectual identity in the current era of neo-liberal globalization under a continuing authoritarian party-state. It suggests a chronology of abandoning intellectual liberties in the

1940s and 1950s since such liberties failed to contribute to a workable polity and of believing the message of the United Front that service to the new regime could provide the opportunity to realize long-frustrated goals of cultural and scientific service to China in the 1950s and 1960s and again in the 1980s, combined with the negation of that promise in the Anti-Rightist movement and the Cultural Revolution, and finally of the losses as well as gains of China's brave new world of economic liberalization and political authoritarianism since the 1990s.

Although this is a satisfactory plot line, it is of course insufficient to capture the diversity of individual experience. Hence, the subtitle, "Sixty Years of Service, Subversion, and Selling." Where "the end of intellectuals" speaks to the *institutions* or structural relationship between China's educated citizens and the state and their local society, the subtitle speaks to the *activities* or agency of intellectuals. Among service, subversion, and selling we shall see there is no diachronic progression, though one could argue that service dominated in the 1950s and 1960s, subversion (from the left or the right) in 1956–76, and selling in the post-Mao period. These activities name a synchronic overlap: most intellectuals were doing some amount of each, all of the time. And again, whereas the three terms cannot do justice to the range and diversity of intellectual agency in the PRC, nonetheless, service, subversion, and selling as non-mutually exclusive activities remind us to resist seeing Chinese intellectuals as heroes or villains and to try to account for the full range of their activities when assessing the significance or meaning of intellectuals in the PRC.

Telling the story of China's intellectuals in this way stands in some tension with the topic of this section of the book, "Destruction and Renewal of Cultural and Educational Elites." Whereas the abuses of the Mao period are very real, I am not sure that intellectuals were so much destroyed then as they were treated badly; equally, I am not as sanguine as some about the renewal of intellectual life under neo-liberal economics and authoritarian political rule today. The interesting work being done in China today sees the socialist period as more than a negation of the promise of intellectual flowering in the previous Republican period.[1] The findings are not so uniform or as satisfying as the "up from the ashes" story line, but they reveal continuities as well as contradictions over the decades and identify powerfully living habits and practices in today's China that derive from the Mao period.

What has intellectual life been like over the past sixty years? We can scan the decades of intellectual life in the PRC by focusing on *ideological moments* as a way to capture change over time, as well as the continuity of service, subversion, and selling across a diverse range of intellectuals. Ideological moments are the intellectuals' experiences in historical context—created from inherited problems and tools, the facts of geography and economy, and contingent events—that shape the questions of the day. In intellectual history we often define "communities of discourse"—and we could say "publics"—by the questions they share. Republicans and Democrats in the United States are in the same community of political discourse since they share the same questions—how to govern America through the current constitution—and they only differ in terms of their answers. Looking to "the questions of the day" will help us walk through the sixty years of the PRC (and the decades of pre-PRC history in the 1930s and 1940s) in a way that helps us make sense of the experiences of China's intellectuals.

Ideological moments are a useful focus because ideology is the main work of those intellectuals in which outside scholars and journalists have most been interested, and indeed, with which the PRC party-state has had the most trouble. Ideological moments are defined by those shared questions that organize public behavior. Within those broader social-political orientations, different social groups have different concerns and interests that, nonetheless, get translated into those shared broader questions. Although I will focus on examples of intellectuals who engaged the public, which for most of the time meant the party-state, we need to keep in mind the minor keys or contrary responses of a variety of intellectuals. For example, in the 1980s not everyone was a Fang Lizhi (the famous dissident astrophysicist), any more than a Hu Qiaomu or a Zhou Yang (conservative and reformist party propaganda leaders respectively). Throughout these ideological periods of the PRC individuals carried on, albeit deeply affected by what was happening, but beyond that, there were consistently some intellectuals who resisted the norms of the day, who challenged the dominant project, and who were fundamentally dissident to the system. At a minimum, we should note two streams of Chinese thought that fit this contrarian bill in the PRC: advocates of Western political liberalism and post-May Fourth Confucians. Although the first group was harshly attacked in the 1950s and 1960s (and are covered in Merle Goldman's chapter), the second group was broadly ignored.[2] Yet, both have come back with renewed strength in the intellectual life of the PRC during the past twenty years, so much so that they offer an increasing challenge to the dominant party discourse of socialism (which strikes many as silly in the face of China's obvious move to capitalist economics) and patriotism.

The sweep of intellectual life in the PRC takes us through at least a half dozen ideological moments. The first, defined by "Revolution," came together most effectively in the North China base areas of the CCP in the 1940s, most figuratively in Yan'an. For intellectuals of the 1940s the CCP's rural revolution promised an opportunity to participate meaningfully in serving China. In the context of World War II and then the Civil War, there was fateful challenge in the air. The second ideological moment we can call Renewal, during the first years of CCP urban administration and national rule in the late 1940s and up through 1956. Here the challenge for intellectuals was discipline in order to contribute to making *Xin Zhongguo* (New China) into the verb phrase it can be: "Renewing China." There was hope in the air. Our third moment: "Daring." The giddy self-confidence of the Hundred Flowers Campaign and Great Leap Forward in 1958, the tough purges of the Anti-Rightist movement before and Socialist Education movement after, and the thrilling violence of the Cultural Revolution up to 1969. "Dare to Speak! Dare to Build! Dare to Rebel!" Most intellectuals succumbed to such euphoria at some time during this period. The fourth ideological moment is, of course, the morning after this Red Bash. It is defined by "Defending," defending oneself from political and personal attack, from the vagaries of the next political campaign, and from the primal doubts raised by the bitter contrast between rhetoric and lived experience. Most intellectuals between 1969 and 1976 focused on surviving and serving the master most likely to provide security. The fifth ideological moment, "Reviving," in the post-Mao era of the 1970s and 1980s up through 1989, began by reviving lost cadres, stalled moderate party programs, and then earlier ideological resources in Marxism, such as "alienation theory," and finally reviving some imagined sense of Chinese democracy, or at least popular agency around the demonstrations in Tiananmen Square in 1989. The challenge taken up by intellectuals during this period was to renew the system. Finally, our present moment, since the early 1990s, is characterized by promise and distraction under the forces of globalization. Call this ideological moment "Selling." Everybody has to find what it is that they have to sell because the market model has taken the ideological, as well as the political and economic, realm by storm. The market is the real party line today, in China as in Western societies.[3] Chinese intellectuals sell what they have in order to find a footing now that they have been released from active party repression. But they are still only free within the bird cage of the propaganda system of the ruling CCP. The party leadership also has to sell its line, eager to find political legitimacy for an unelected authoritarian state in this brave new world.[4] And, across the range of social classes, people struggle to find what they can sell, so they can get what they need—legitimacy for the leaders, both national and local, meaning and identity for the middle classes in the absence of faith in the party, and food and security for the poor. The challenge for intellectuals in our current ideological moment is to find their public role now that they have been disestablished from the party-state.[5] They can choose to return to government service, or become a professional, or sell their talents on the market as experts, business resources, or media content providers.

Of course, what intellectuals are we talking about? The ones who get into trouble by entering the public sphere on political topics. These people are important because for most of the life of the PRC the party-state thought they were important, important enough to entice, train, corral, and discipline. We should keep in mind the much larger group of ordinary intellectuals—educated people in the technical, teaching, and service industries who did not engage in such public debates over policy or social issues. Indeed, it is well to remember that in one way the PRC created intellectuals, *zhishi fenzi*, at least as a legible social category or status. That category was viewed with deep ambivalence by the party—needed but not trusted. Eddy U's recent research on such ordinary intellectuals in Shanghai in the early years of the PRC goes so far as to describe intellectuals as a sort of "despised class."[6] Here we are talking about high-level intellectuals with advanced training who were active in prominent positions and public affairs of the CCP and PRC establishment doing "thought work."

Let us turn now to these ideological moments in action, through the lives of several intellectuals. I propose to focus on only three moments: Revolution during the 1940s, Daring in the 1957–69 decade, and Selling since the 1990s. Of course, the ideological moments I am skipping over, Renewal in the 1950s and Defending in the 1969–76 period, blend in with the first two moments to some degree. Reviving in the late 1970s and 1980s began the transition to Selling. These moments blended into each other and were not neatly divided. To give a sense of continuity over these ideological moments, as after all, most intellectuals lived through more than one, I propose to follow in sketch form the public intellectual work of four examples, two from the senior ranks of the CCP and two who served as PRC academics in Beijing. They are: Deng Tuo (1912–66), founding editor of the *People's Daily*, Yue Daiyun (1931–), a literary scholar who has spent most of her career at Peking University, Wang Ruoshui (1926–2002), junior editor to Deng Tuo but more famous for his writings on humanism in the 1980s, and Qin Hui (1953–) a professor of history at Qinghua University and a noted public intellectual. Even this range cannot do justice to the diversity of Chinese intellectuals, but it can trace the changing ideological worlds in which they have all had to work.

Revolution

In his "Yan'an Talks" in 1942, Mao Zedong called on Chinese intellectuals to become part of a cultural army: "since this kind of army is indispensible in achieving unity among ourselves and winning victory over the enemy." This cultural army, Mao went on, is to lead the cultural front of the revolution "to ensure that literature and art become a component part of the whole revolutionary machinery, so they can act as a powerful weapon in uniting and educating the people while attacking and annihilating the enemy. . . ."[7] This is the defining mandate of the first ideological moment in the 1940s and very early 1950s: Revolution.

Such an invitation to intellectuals to become a meaningful, active, effective part of the military, political, and social revolution led by the CCP came at a price; the price was intellectual autonomy, because, like soldiers, the writers and artists in Mao's cultural army, they would be expected to obey orders. Still, the offer contained a siren call attractive to intellectuals steeped in Neo-Confucian ethics and/or May Fourth activism—to educate and lead the people toward a noble goal. This was compelling to many of the displaced university students in that dusty, northwest market town of Yan'an in the middle of the anti-Japanese war and continued to attract thousands from all backgrounds over the next decade.[8] Of course, it was not attractive to all intellectuals. From the start, Ding Ling and other writers and artists had already responded to Mao's call to participate in his new rectification movement of 1942 with independent left-wing criticisms and suggestions that in turn provoked Mao's "Yan'an Talks" to pull them back into line. Wang Shiwei is best known among this independent-minded group of leftists for articulating the artist's vision of pure revolution against the worldly revolution of the politician.[9] Wang and his colleagues lost that battle. Independent public criticism was not to be tolerated in the revolution. That is why it is hard to follow the lives of such fundamental dissidents in the PRC over the next decades—they disappeared or were killed, jailed, or silenced in one way or another. Their story is the counter-narrative to the CCP's teleology and tragically is the one constant theme in the story of intellectuals in the PRC: "if you don't want to play our game, you're out; if you harass our game, you're in deep trouble." This was true for Wang Shiwei in 1942, and is true for Charter '08 advocates such as Liu Xiaobo in 2009.[10] They are testimony to the Dark Side of the Force in this revolutionary project.

Deng Tuo

In the 1940s Deng Tuo worked as a Communist propaganda chief in the hills of Shanxi and Hebei. Editor of the *Jin-Cha-Ji Daily*, soon to be editor of Mao's first *Selected Works* (in 1944), Deng Tuo, a man in his mid-30s, believed in Mao's revolution and was pleased to serve in Mao's cultural army. The edition of the *Selected Works of Mao Zedong* that he edited included the "Yan'an Talks," but unlike Ding Ling and Wang Shiwei, Deng Tuo expressed no concerns about the rigors of party loyalty. In fact, he wrote classical-style poetry with CCP generals and leaders. Today, Deng Tuo is not remembered as a hack or toady; so submitting to this revolutionary discipline was not experienced as being contrary to the goals of an intellectual's life for many like Deng Tuo who staffed the growing cultural army of the CCP. Indeed, Deng Tuo saw it as a noble vocation—to revive China.[11]

Yue Daiyun

In the 1940s Yue Daiyun, a school girl in the embattled Southwest, found in the CCP a salvation she felt she would never otherwise have found—especially with the corrupt Guomindang government she had watched plunder her hometown in Guizhou province during the anti-Japanese war. She struggled to study and to take the 1948 university exams in Chongqing, Sichuan. She passed and was admitted to Peking University (Beida). With help from American missionaries and distant relatives, she managed to get to Beijing. Too young to participate significantly in the revolution, she nevertheless appreciated it and joined student radicals at Beida in the CCP underground.[12] The CCP was her hope and her pathway to success.

Wang Ruoshui

Slightly older than Yue, Wang Ruoshui was active in the CCP in the 1940s and joined the staff of the *People's Daily* as a junior editor in 1950. Both Wang and Yue felt they were riding the crest of a wonderful historical wave propelling both themselves and China into a new era. Wang too had studied at Beida, leaving just as Yue arrived in 1948. Wang then traveled to the nearby CCP base areas and became active in CCP journalism.[13] He was in the theoretical department—studying and applying Marxism-Leninism-Mao Zedong Thought. For this young intellectual such theory, and the party that implemented it, promised to end the corruption and poverty of the Guomindang government.

Qin Hui

Qin Hui was born in southwest China at the end of this ideological moment in 1953. He grew up in the ages of Renewal and Daring and came of age in the grueling time of Defending, as a sent-down youth in the later Cultural Revolution.[14] His parents were schoolteachers in Nanning, the capital of the southwestern province of Guangxi, where he grew up. The Cultural Revolution hit town just as he graduated from primary school.

Daring

Beginning in 1957 Mao Zedong challenged everyone to dare. In the Hundred Flowers he began his talk on "The Correct Handling of Contradictions Among the

People" daring intellectuals to step up and speak up in a new rectification campaign to purify the CCP so it would not continue the mistakes of the East European communist parties. He stressed his old Yan'an line of "unity-criticism-unity" and his methods of persuasion on ideological questions. In another mood, in 1958, Mao called on intellectuals to join the workers, peasants, and soldiers to create a Great Leap Forward, not only in production but also in communal life.[15] In 1966 Chairman Mao did not call on intellectuals, but rather on young students, quite simply telling them: "It is right to rebel."[16] That each of these daring adventures ended in disaster did not dampen the enthusiasm of many intellectuals, though time and repetition took their toll. What is amazing in retrospect is that so many people we have come to respect fell for it.

Yue Daiyun ignored the warnings of her elders (who had seen the Dark Side of the Yan'an Force) and dared to speak up on her university party committee, only to be struck down as a Rightist. She had stayed on at Beida, became an instructor, married a noted scholar (Tang Yijie), and in the 1950s lived the charmed life of the new revolutionary elite. It all came to an end with her participation in the Hundred Flowers Campaign and Anti-Rightist movement. Not a dissident, Yue supported the early purges of the Anti-Rightist movement, only to be struck down herself for some modest literary activities during the previous Hundred Flowers opening. A loyal party member, Yue accepted that "in curing cancer, some healthy cells must be cut out." She would spend the next several years as a Rightist, a political pariah, nearly starving to death in a distant village (to which she had been sent for labor reform) during the Great Leap. She survived, returned to Beida, and carried on, chastened but still loyal to the party. During the Cultural Revolution she was attacked again and sent to labor in the countryside, only to return in the 1970s when her husband Tang Yijie served the radical elite (later known at the Gang of Four) as a way for their family to survive. From Daring, Yue Daiyun experienced suffering and compromise.

Deng Tuo, seasoned revolutionary intellectual and party cadre that he was, succumbed to the hot-headedness of 1958–59 and supported the Great Leap in several essays; this he lived to regret, as only a few years later he was assigned to do field research on the results of the Great Leap in Huairou district of Beijing. In the early 1960s Deng Tuo was daring, but not in the way Mao desired. He dared to criticize the Great Leap, albeit through metaphor in popular essays in the *Beijing Evening News* and more directly in restricted party publications. His purpose was to correct and reform the party that he served. However, Mao Zedong no longer trusted that party and Deng Tuo became one of Mao's first victims, and the first to die in 1966 during the Cultural Revolution. The daring of others marked the death of this loyal Communist.

Wang Ruoshui prospered during the beginnings of this period. He loyally criticized "bourgeois" intellectuals such as Hu Shi and Hu Feng and supported party policies. He was sent to the countryside to learn from the peasants in the late 1950s, but returned in good form—he dared to criticize the establishment leaders of the CCP Central Party School (and became involved in the purge of Yang Xianzhen in 1964). This work put Wang on the "leftist" side of the party divide as the Cultural Revolution began. His 1963 essay, "The Philosophy of the Table," caught Mao's eye and, as a result, he became trusted for his work in Marxist theory, epistemology, and attacks on liberal thought. Wang's problem in the Cultural Revolution was that he was on the side of the perpetrators. Although not guilty of the notorious excesses of the decade, this affiliation would continue to haunt him during the post-Mao period.

Qin Hui managed to survive. He wasn't daring at all. As a very young Red Guard during the Cultural Revolution, Qin was in one of the "dissident" groups that did not favor violent tactics. In 1969, he was sent to a poor mountain village near the Yunnan border, where he worked as a farmer for nine years. He studied, avoided trouble, and managed to pass the famous "*lao sanjie*" exams at the end of the Cultural Revolution (the first university exams in a decade), and in 1978 he was accepted at Lanzhou University in the northwestern province of Gansu. The lesson of daring that Qin Hui took from the Cultural Revolution was the utter failure of such "glorious" mass movements to serve the needs of China's poor rural majority.

The results of Daring were disastrous, both individually and collectively. During the time of Defending in the 1970s and Reviving after 1976 these and other intellectuals tried to make sense and move on. Deng Tuo was dead, but finally received posthumous rehabilitation in 1979 and the treasured afterlife of an intellectual—re-publication of his works. Yue Daiyun encountered difficulties, as the service of her husband to the forces of the Gang of Four landed them both in trouble in the immediate post-Mao period. But they endured and settled down to an academic life that included a number of visits to the West, including Berkeley and Harvard. Wang Ruoshui emerged as a nationally prominent advocate of Marxist humanism—which would become one of the big political debates in China of the 1980s—and was ultimately purged for these efforts, though he was exiled to Harvard rather than to a mountaintop. Qin Hui emerged as an academic, becoming a professor at Shaanxi Normal University. Those who survived still hoped to bring out the best in what the party could offer while avoiding any repetition of its sorry mistakes. They all admired the student demonstrators in Tiananmen Square in 1989, worried about the public disorder (knowing the party would likely respond with force), and grieved at the violence. They had hoped the post-Cultural Revolution party would reform, but it seemed that reform would be painfully slow. They, like Western observers, had no idea how much things would change by the 1990s.

Selling

In 1992 Deng Xiaoping declared: Shenzhen is good! The market and global engagement exemplified by that bold "special economic zone" next to Hong Kong was in China to stay. Mao had been dead some fifteen years and the charismatic authority of the Helmsman, the party, and formal ideology in general had taken a beating from the combined results of over thirty years of political campaigns and bloody reversals in line and policy. The popular demonstrations in Tiananmen Square in 1989, followed by their brutal suppression, and other demonstrations across China added a grim and sour tone to public pronouncements. Deng Xiaoping cunningly claimed for the CCP what he could: the only government able to keep order and provide the conditions for a more open, vibrant, and economically flourishing environment.[17] The call in the post-Tiananmen ideological moment was then, as it is today, to sell whatever you have because cumulatively it will contribute to some more distant, vague version of Mao's revolution. Stay out of trouble (that is, politics) and you can do pretty much what you want.

The party's call to sell provided a relief and an opportunity to improve for most intellectuals. The formal ideological requirements are minimal—patriotism, a polite word about the government and socialism, and avoidance of unpleasant attacks on specific leaders or current policy goals. One does not even have to claim to be a Marxist or to use party vocabulary. This all sounds great and I don't think any of my friends in China particularly hanker to live in any of the previous moments of the PRC. However, everyone knows the limits: free political expression is not allowed if it upsets party leaders. The most recent example is Charter '08 (see the chapter by Merle Goldman).

More fundamental for China's intellectuals has been the ongoing social change that these new freedoms have occasioned. In short, the moral and professional autonomy of intellectuals has been restored, but at the price of their political relevance. Today it is easier than before to publish a critical article on Marxism but there is no longer a national intellectual public sphere that will read it to match the *Guangming Daily* of the 1980s. When Wang Ruoshui published on alienation theory in *Guangming Daily*, it was to the thrill of intellectuals across China, all of whom read that official newspaper because there were few others. In the 1980s, one had to get past the likes of Hu Qiaomu and similar party censors, but if you did, you reached a national audience. Today, there no Hu Qiaomu, but also no Wang Ruoshui with a national audience—unless you are on the Chinese version of *American Idol*.

Also today, there is no Deng Tuo. Although rehabilitated posthumously and the subject of a healthy reminiscence literature in the 1980s as one of the noble martyrs of the Cultural Revolution, few intellectuals take any interest in this tragic figure. More significantly, there is no longer a social role like his available to Chinese intellectuals. In fact, it is considered laughable to be simultaneously a respected high-level intellectual and a high-level party cadre. Wang Ruoshui, who passed away in 2002, continued his outspoken criticism of party excesses, often from the United States or Europe. But he did so not as a member of the party establishment.

Yue Daiyun is still at work, and since the 1990s has divided her academic time teaching and researching on comparative literature between Beijing and North America.[18] She is the president of the Comparative Literature Institute of China and the All China Women's Federation (*Fulian*) has publicized her 2008 memoir of sixty years at Beida.[19]

Qin Hui came of age in this ideological moment, beginning his publishing career in the late 1980s, and becoming radicalized by the 1989 Tiananmen demonstrations, and has become one of the best known public intellectuals in China today. He is of the left-leaning liberal persuasion and has focused much of his research on the rural China he came to know as a sent-down youth in the 1970s. He is a relentless advocate of social justice and a critic of government oppression of the farming population. Although Qin Hui attends international conferences on both historical and intellectual topics, he focuses his time and energy on his academic and public Chinese audiences. Unlike Yue Daiyun who writes in English as well as Chinese, the texts we have from Qin Hui in English are translations. He is now an example of an academic public intellectual, appearing in broader circulation intellectual journals like *Dushu* (Reading), as well as a number of his own books published over the past ten years.[20] Qin Hui's research and writings deal with critical issues of governance, rural justice, and the inequities of reform China. But they are academic in tone and audience, not privileged pronouncements of a high official, such as those by Deng Tuo, nor do they appear in nationally read outlets, like Wang Ruoshui's essays of the 1980s.

Three Masters: The Party, the Professions, and the Public

Today the intellectual world of China has become fragmented. One can see this as a pluralization of opportunities and voices, or as Balkanization of the public sphere. The most important change in recent years for China's intellectuals has been the *disestablishment* of China's intellectuals from the party-state and the increasing professionalization of intellectual work.[21] The CCP's withdrawal from its totalitarian goals to control all of society as it did under Mao while embracing "market socialism" has ended the intellectuals' role as public officials: the party will simply no longer pay the bill. The end of their role as direct propagandists for the party has given intellectuals much greater professional autonomy (and for some a much higher income), but the price of today's relative autonomy for China's intellectuals has come at a loss of public influence and the birth of self-doubt and questioning.[22] At the same time, we have seen the *disaggregation of intellectuals* in China—no longer will a Fang Lizhi or a Wang Ruoshui (heroes of the reform in the 1980s) stand for all China's intellectuals. We now regularly see a range of intellectual roles—creative writers, artists, journalists, academics, scientists, technical government or business advisers. And these intellectuals palpably do not agree with one another. Indeed, intellectual feuding, most famously between "liberal" and "new-left" intellectuals, is common and public. This has paralleled the *disaggregation of the establishment*. The state, that is the party-state under the CCP, is still very much with us. Just ask any Chinese academic. Nonetheless, the authority of the state is more than matched on a day-to-day level by the requirements of professions (universities, institutes, and the media and legal professions) and the financial inducements of commercial publishing and business consulting.[23] China's intellectuals now have three masters: the party, the professions, and the commercial public.

As in the Republican period (1911–49) when the educated elite decidedly lost their role as a local elite, intellectuals in contemporary China are cut off from local, and particularly rural, society. This has resulted in one of the profound social problems in China during the twentieth century, from the local bullies and evil gentry (*tuhao lieshen*) of the Republican times to the rapacious local cadres and labor bosses of the PRC today. The educated elite have been siphoned away from rural China and much of local society in urban areas as well. This alienation from local societies, combined with the political disestablishment of intellectuals, sets the key question for intellectuals in China today: How does one get intellectual talent and social capital back into rural communities without making them landlord gentry (per late imperial China) or forcing them to be state propagandists or prisoners (per Maoist China)? Clearly, market forces are not doing the job. The market, under the continuing rule of the CCP, is pushing China's educated elites to become urban professionals and academics.

The Chinese state is stronger and more robust today than it has been in some two decades. That the spiraling problems of employment, environmental sustainability, corruption, and similar social issues profoundly challenge the state does not lessen its successes in building state capacity, particularly its ability to repress those groups or individuals it views as threats to its survival and the continued privileges of the current political elite associated with the CCP.[24] This renewed strength is reflected in the resurgence of party media control. Not only has the infamous Central Propaganda Department (*zhongxuanbu*) been revitalized, but also CCP control mechanisms are in place from the Politburo to the locality. The State Leadership Group on Information, now headed by Premier Wen Jiabao, is what Zhao Yuezhi calls the "information cabinet" of the government.[25] Parallel to this is another central oversight group, evocatively called the Central Guidance Commission on Building Spiritual Civilization (*Zhongyang jingshen wenming jianshe zhidao weiyuanyhui*), led by Politburo propaganda chief Li Changchun. The General Administration of Press and Publications (GAPP) monitors the publishing industry, as do a host of ministries (including the Ministry of Culture and the Ministry of Education), and offices in the party, state, and military (e.g., the General Political Department of the PLA). As David Shambaugh has shown, these organs of the propaganda and education system (*xuanjiao xitong*) are alive and well in China today, and, indeed, "the Party has been very adept at utilizing commercialization to enhance and strengthen the propaganda apparatus."[26] This system works, Zhao and Shambaugh agree, more by soft power or, in Zhao's words "domination," rather than through total control; it operates by a localized and dispersed responsibility system that encourages producers and editors to internalize party norms and to self-censor.

Beyond the resilient party-state, the two main forces with which China's public intellectuals have to deal today are commercialization and professionalization—fundamental changes in their conditions of employment. The commercialization of literary production resulted in the demise of serious literature and the rise of a range of popular media.[27] The impact of the professionalization over the past twenty years is clear as more top intellectuals find their social niche in China's keypoint universities and academies of social science (both central and in the regions) with strong certification in terms of international norms of academia.[28] This professionalization has a distinct global, or Western, character. The norms are derived from Euro-American institutions and practices, as embraced widely around the world and also by China's government and major universities.[29] Yet, as we have seen, the return of the professions, and particularly academic disciplines and the relative autonomy of universities in post-Mao China, has not created full intellectual or professional freedom: there are still political controls that the CCP can and does enforce.[30] Furthermore, there are other ways for educated Chinese today to do well in life and to have an impact on society—as entrepreneurs, as politicians, and as creative writers and artists (and the relationship between, say, a novelist and an intellectual in China is as contested as it is in various Western societies).[31] Thus, there is no longer a dominant model of intellectual praxis that has wide currency; the intellectual field, like the public arena, in China has exploded.

Public Intellectuals with Chinese Characteristics

If political parties are illegal, the professions demanding narrow specialization, and the mass media awash with commercial distractions, what are China's intellectuals doing today? A major activity of China's academic intellectuals-turned-public intellectuals is finding ways to use the existing system to meet, rather than to confront, their interests. They use existing structures—from the state-controlled publishers and loopholes in the PRC's legal regime to what appears to be a commercial Internet blog and business association—as legal ways to form public associations to promote public interest issues. This "amphibious organizing" often escapes the attention of researchers, since the whole point is to avoid attention in the first place. Two examples will give a flavor of intellectual activity in these amphibious realms.[32] The first is non-official book publishing, described in Chinese as *minjian chuban*. One Shanghai bookshop owner, through just such amphibious organizing, has been publishing academic and ideological books for the past six years on topics that would not likely appear from the major presses.[33] First of all, legally, he is not a publisher, but rather a "consultant," so his editorial work is subject to the Enterprise Law rather than the depredations of the GAPP or Propaganda Department. Second, he secures a manuscript, edits it, and arranges for its printing, while he buys the all-important ISBN number from a minor or cash-strapped legal publisher who is not too fussy. Our entrepreneur publishes his book, and the press has a title that sells. (Guangxi Normal College Press is a notable example of a cooperating press.) Both make money, money the party-state used to provide but no longer does. There are some two hundred such small private "publishers" across China, each publishing from a dozen to a hundred books annually. In truth, most of the titles our Shanghai entrepreneur publishes are cookbooks, novels, and pop books (such as a translation of *The Da Vinci Code*), but this supports a small line of serious books on social and cultural criticism. Although all legally published books are subject to censorship, small regional presses in poor provinces are often less scrutinized than the major presses. This is a small doorway to *de facto* press liberalization. In our second example, environmental issues and commercial services serve as similar amphibious vehicles for legal organizing on public issues. A prominent example is the Alxa League (*A-la-shan lianmeng*), which is an environmental group running a busy blog site, which includes commercial coordination for member companies nationwide, as well as a communication portal and even a dating service.[34] The private publishers, among others, use this as one avenue to organize and communicate information about their independent publishing work.

China's intellectuals, and not just academic intellectuals-turned-public intellectuals, have not created a vigorous political public sphere. As we have seen, they have not been especially inclined to stake out an independent—or isolated—sphere separate from the media controlled by the party-state. It is simply too dangerous even to try. The party-state is repressive and protective of its ultimate monopoly on political expression. Most recently, it has set out to crush Charter '08. The case of Falun Gong is another example: state repression of this rogue *qigong* club had much more to do with its organizational strength and the 1999 demonstration of the group's ability to put on a huge demonstration without prior awareness by the CCP's vigorous public security apparatus than it did with the content of the group's beliefs.[35] At present, it seems that China's intellectuals have found sufficient leverage through using the system—as in the case of our clever Shanghai publisher, or via NGOs based in universities (that avoid scrutiny of the Ministry of Civil Affairs), or through established channels— and they are less inclined to risk all for a better system of publicity.[36]

Chinese intellectuals over the sixty years of the PRC have left an enduring record of agency, of a refusal to give up. As individuals and as a social group, they have believed, tried, failed, made mistakes, suffered terribly, but they have picked up and continued. Denied open political parties and a free press, they continue to work the system in which they find themselves to fulfill a public role. The august and terrible social place of the *intellectual* under Mao—the despised political class and the privileged political adviser—may have ended, but not the effort of China's educated citizens to achieve the moral ends of an intellectual.

ENDNOTES

1. Guobin Yang, *The Power of the Internet in China: Citizen Activism Online* (New York: Columbia University Press, 2009); Xu Jilin, ed., *20 shiji Zhongguo zhishi fenzi shi lun* (Essays on the History of China's Twentieth-Century Intellectuals) (Beijing: Xinxing chubanshe, 2005).

2. Merle Goldman chronicles the first group in *China's Intellectuals: Advise and Dissent* (Cambridge, MA: Harvard University Press, 1981) and *From Comrade to Citizen: The Struggle for Political Rights in China* (Cambridge, MA: Harvard University Press, 2005); on new Confucianism, see John Makeham, ed., *New Confucianism: A Critical Examination* (New York: Palgrave Macmillan, 2003).

3. A thesis nicely put forward by Yuezhi Zhao, *Media, Market and Democracy in China: Between the Party Line and the Bottom Line* (Urbana: University of Illinois Press, 1998).

4. Anne-Marie Brady, *Marketing Dictatorship: Propaganda and Thought Work in Contemporary China* (Lanham, MD: Rowman & Littlefield, 2008); David L. Shambaugh, *China's Communist Party: Atrophy and Adaptation* (Washington, DC: Woodrow Wilson Center Press and Berkeley: University of California Press, 2008).

5. This search for a public purpose has defined intellectual discussions in China for the past decade. See Wang Hui, *China's New Order: Society, Politics, and Economy in Transition* (Cambridge, MA: Harvard University Press, 2003); Xu Jilin, *Huigui gonggong kongjian* (Back to the Public Space) (Nanjing: Jiangsu renmin chubanshe, 2006); Goldman, *From Comrade to Citizen*; Gloria Davies, *Worrying About China* (Cambridge, MA: Harvard University Press, 2007).

6. Eddy U, *Disorganizing China: Counter-Bureaucracy and the Decline of Socialism* (Stanford, CA: Stanford University Press, 2007).

7. Bonnie S. McDougall, *Mao Zedong's "Talks at the Yan'an Conference on Literature and Art": A Translation of the 1943 Text with Commentary* (Ann Arbor: Center for Chinese Studies, University of Michigan, 1980); full text in Stuart R. Schram, ed., *Mao's Road to Power*, vol. 7 (Armonk, NY: M.E. Sharpe, 2010); and selections in Timothy Cheek, *Mao Zedong and China's Revolutions: A Brief History with Documents* (Boston: Bedford Books, 2002), pp. 112–17.

8. David Holm, *Art and Ideology in Revolutionary China* (Oxford: Clarendon Press, 1991); David E. Apter and Tony Saich, *Revolutionary Discourse in Mao's Republic* (Cambridge, MA: Harvard University Press, 1994).

9. See Wang Shiwei, "Politicians, Artists," in Dai Qing, *Wang Shiwei and "Wild Lilies": Rectification and Purges in the Chinese Communist Party, 1942–1944* (Armonk, NY: M.E. Sharpe, 1994), pp. 90–93.

10. Again, see Goldman, *China's Intellectuals* and *From Comrade to Citizen*; on Charter '08 see Perry Link's translation of the now famous democratic petition with commentary, in "China's Charter 08," *The New York Review of Books*, 56, no. 1 (January 15, 2009).

11. Details in Timothy Cheek, *Propaganda and Culture in Mao's China: Deng Tuo and the Intelligentsia* (Oxford: Clarendon Press, 1997).

12. Details of Yue Daiyun's life from Yue Daiyun and Carolyn Wakeman, *To the Storm: The Odyssey of a Revolutionary Chinese Woman* (Berkeley: University of California Press, 1985).

13. The best work in English on Wang Ruoshui is by David A. Kelly, "The Emergence of Humanism: Wang Ruoshui and the Critique of Socialist Alienation," in Merle Goldman, with Timothy Cheek and Carol Lee Hamrin, eds., *China's Intellectuals and the State: In Search of a New Relationship* (Cambridge, MA: Council on East Asian Studies, Harvard University, 1987), pp. 159–82, and Kelly's introduction and bibliographic note to his translations of Wang's writings on humanism, alienation, and philosophy, in *Chinese Studies in Philosophy*, 16, no. 3 (Spring 1985).

14. Qin Hui gives an account of his life in "Dividing the Big Family Assets," originally published in *New Left Review*, no. 20 (March-April 2003) and included in the anthology, Chaohua Wang, ed., *One China, Many Paths* (New York: Verso, 2003), pp. 128–59; David Kelly provides further information in his introduction to his translations of Qin Hui's essays, "The Mystery of the Chinese Economy, Part 1," *The Chinese Economy*, 38, no. 4 (July–August 2005): 3–11.

15. For Mao's unexpurgated announcements in 1957 and 1958, see the texts translated in Roderick MacFarquhar, Timothy Cheek, and Eugene Wu, eds., *The Secret Speeches of Chairman Mao: From the Hundred Flowers to the Great Leap Forward* (Cambridge, MA: Council on East Asian Studies, Harvard University, 1989), esp. pp. 131 ff. and pp. 397 ff.

16. An excellent collection of documents, including Mao's call to rebel, is Michael Schoenhals, ed., *China's Cultural Revolution, 1966–1969: Not a Dinner Party* (Armonk, NY: M.E. Sharpe, 1996).

17. See special coverage in *Renmin ribao* (People's Daily), March 31, 1992, and "Zai Wuchang Shenzhen Zhuhai Shanghai dengdi de tanhua yaodian" January 18–February 21, 1992 (Excerpts from Talks Given in Wuchang, Shenzhen, Zhuhai, and Shanghai), in *Deng Xiaoping wenxuan* (Selected Works of Deng Xiaoping), 3: 370–84, all covered in Joseph Fewsmith, *China Since Tiananmen: From Deng Xiaoping to Hu Jintao* (New York: Cambridge University Press, 2008).

18. See, for example, her English-language study in the edited volume published in China, Cheng Aimin and Lixin Yang, eds., *Comparative Literature in the Cross-Cultural Context* (Nanjing: Yilin Press, 2003).

19. The memoir is entitled *Siyuan, shatan, weiminghu: 60 nian Beida shengya (1948–2008)* (Beijing: Beijing daxue chubanshe, 2008); see the March 29, 2009, English announcement at: http://www.womenofchina.cn/Profiles/Writers/209939.jsp (accessed October 16, 2009).

20. A recent selection of translated articles from Qin Hui, with an introduction by David Kelly, appears in "The Mystery of the Chinese Economy," *The Chinese Economy*, 38, no. 4 (July-August 2005) and 38, no. 5 (September-October 2005).

21. Timothy Cheek, "The New Chinese Intellectual: Globalized, Disoriented, Reoriented," in Lionel M. Jensen and Timothy B. Weston, eds., *China's Transformations: The Stories Beyond the Headlines* (Lanham, MD: Rowman & Littlefield, 2007), pp. 265–84.

22. There is a huge literature in China on this disestablishment and self-doubt and many key articles have been brought together in large collections, such as the three-volume Luo Gang and Ni Wenjian, eds., *90 niandai sixiang wenxuan* (Selections of Thinking from the 90s) (Nanning: Guangxi renmin chubanshe, 2000). A good set of English translations of these debates is found in Xudong Zhang, ed., *Whither China? Intellectual Politics in Contemporary China* (Durham, NC: Duke University Press, 2001).

23. An equally broad range of studies in English covers intellectual developments since the 1990s. Particularly useful are Zhidong Hao, *Intellectuals at a Crossroads: The Changing Politics of China's Knowledge Workers* (Albany: State University of New York Press, 2003); Fewsmith, *China Since Tiananmen*; Goldman, *From Comrade to Citizen*; Geremie Barmé, "The Revolution of Resistance," in Elizabeth J. Perry and Mark Selden, eds., *Chinese Society: Change, Conflict and Resistance*, 2nd ed. (London: RoutledgeCurzon, 2003); and Xudong Zhang's introduction, "The Making of the Post-Tiananmen Intellectual Field," in Zhang, ed., *Whither China?*, pp. 1–75.

24. Dali L. Yang, *Remaking the Chinese Leviathan: Market Transition and the Politics of Governance in China* (Stanford, CA: Stanford University Press, 2004); Shambaugh, *China's Communist Party*.

25. Yuezhi Zhao, *Communication in China: Political Economy, and Conflict* (Lanham, MD: Rowman & Littlefield, 2008), ch. 2, and David Shambaugh's detailed accounting, "China's Propaganda System: Institutions, Processes and Efficacy," *The China Journal*, no. 57 (January 2007): 25–58.

26. Shambaugh, "China's Propaganda System," p. 27.

27. See the essays in Perry and Selden, eds., *Chinese Society*, and, especially, Shuyu Kong, *Consuming Literature: Best Sellers and the Commercialization of Literary Production in Contemporary China* (Stanford, CA: Stanford University Press, 2005).

28. An excellent study of professionalization among Chinese intellectuals is Hao's *Intellectuals at a Crossroads*, esp. pp. 205–60. Hao provides a strong empirical base for his analysis of Chinese intellectuals in terms of critical, professional (bourgeoisified), and organic social roles.

29. A classic statement of the definition of professionalization as specialized and institutionalized education, formation of professional associations, and a defined ethical code is given in Howard M. Vollmer and Donald M. Mills, eds., *Professionalization* (Englewood Cliffs, NJ: Prentice Hall, 1966). On the Chinese experience during the Republican period, see Xiaoqun Xu, *Chinese Professionals and the Republican State: The Rise of Professional Associations in Shanghai, 1912–1937* (New York: Cambridge University Press, 2001).

30. Goldman, *From Comrade to Citizen.*

31. Xiuwu R. Liu provides a nice case study in *Jumping into the Sea: From Academics to Entrepreneurs in South China* (Lanham, MD: Rowman & Littlefield, 2001).

32. The concept of "amphibious organizations" in the PRC is introduced in Xueliang Ding, *The Decline of Communism in China: Legitimacy Crisis, 1977–1989* (NY: Cambridge University Press, 1994), esp. p. 32.

33. This information comes from my interview with the bookshop owner and independent publisher, July 2006. Given that his goal is to avoid attention, it seems unhelpful to identify this company at this point.

34. See www.alsyz.com and www.alsm.unzt.com (accessed August 26, 2009) for "Alxa Outdoor" and the Alxa League blog site. On the link with independent publishers, see the interview in ftn. 33.

35. David Ownby, *Falun Gong and the Future of China* (New York: Oxford University Press, 2008).

36. This is the conclusion, as well, in Wenfang Tang. *Public Opinion and Political Change in China* (Stanford, CA: Stanford University Press, 2005).

23.
THE POLITICS OF NATIONAL CELEBRATIONS IN CHINA

CHANG-TAI HUNG

In the sixty years since the founding of the People's Republic of China (PRC), few things have struck people more forcefully about Chinese Communism than its theatrical nature: huge parades, mass rallies, grand celebrations of historical events, and public commemorations of dead heroes. Anthropologists have used the term "theatrical state" to describe these government-run spectacles, linking them with the study of power and considering them central to the political system. Two prime examples of such spectacles are the national parades in the early decades of the PRC and the 2008 Beijing Olympics.

At a press conference before the opening of the Beijing Games, President Hu Jintao warned against "politicizing the Olympics,"[1] yet the 2008 Summer Olympics turned out to be the most politically charged international sports event in recent decades, supporting George Orwell's famous saying that "serious sport has nothing to do with fair play. . . . [I]t is war minus the shooting." For the Chinese government, the main purpose of the games was unmistakably to announce China's ascent to world-power status with surging wealth and growing confidence. To that end, nothing was more striking and effective than putting on a spectacular show.

Ever since the establishment of the PRC, the Chinese Communist Party (CCP) has been noted for using mammoth celebrations to promote its political goals. Although the National Day (October 1) and May Day (May 1) parades have distinctively different purposes than the Beijing Olympic Games—the former featured annual domestic rituals of the early PRC whereas the latter was a unique international sports event—all these activities reveal a close relationship between politics and propaganda, and an all-pervasive control system mounted by the authoritarian state.

National Day and May Day Parades in the 1950s and 1960s

In the first half of the twentieth century Soviet leaders used parades and spectacles, such as the anniversary of the October Revolution in Red Square, to propagate socialist programs and display the nation's growing power. These were often conceived as military marches, demonstrating painstaking planning and precision.[2] The Chinese Communists followed suit, but with an even greater degree of control and a tighter organizational network.

Mao Zedong was a master in conducting mass movements. However, the mass movements required space to accommodate the assemblage of large numbers of participants and cheering crowds. Like his Soviet counterparts who used Red Square as a parade ground, Mao preferred clearly delineated spaces where the performances could be carefully staged and the crowds easily controlled. An obvious choice to exhibit the CCP's authority was Beijing's Tiananmen Square, the center of the capital and a sacred space in front of Tiananmen Gate dating back to the Ming and Qing dynasties. In order to hold massive parades, the CCP expanded the square by tearing down centuries-old city walls and demolishing countless houses. By 1959, in time to celebrate the tenth anniversary of the founding of the PRC in October, the square was a vast 44 hectares.

The first parade in Tiananmen Square took place at the founding ceremony of the People's Republic on October 1, 1949, which began immediately after Mao's declaration of the establishment of the new regime. An opening military march was followed by what is commonly called a "people's parade," with thousands of exuberant civilians passing through Tiananmen Gate to salute China's new leaders. For Mao and senior party leaders, these soon-to-be biannual rituals in the heart of the capital were the best channel to announce the party's bold dreams of building a new socialist country.[3]

Although these parades were often billed as the people's celebration of the government's achievements, the party exercised tight control over every facet of their planning. As a Leninist party, the CCP viewed tight organization and complete control as essential in staging a successful show. In 1951 the Beijing municipal government established committees to plan the celebrations.[4] Peng Zhen, the mayor of Beijing and a member of the Politburo, was put in charge of these committees. However, the entire operation was overseen by the most senior party leaders and the party's central organizations. Although the planning was directly supervised by the Ministry of Culture, the ultimate authority rested in the powerful Propaganda Department of the CCP Central Committee. The control was overwhelming, as every single slogan used in the parades had to be approved by this department, as it made clear in a 1955 directive: "No single unit is allowed to come up with its own slogans."[5]

The total number of participants in the parades ranged from 300,000 to 450,000, with an additional 100,000 assembled in Tiananmen Square forming artistic patterns and cheering the marchers. The 1959 parade was the largest, with half a million participants.[6] The marchers generally formed nine columns, each containing 110 people lined up side by side. The two elements of the parade—the military and the civilian—lasted three to four hours, with the civilian part occupying three-quarters of the time. Parades normally started at 10:00 in the morning, and ended before 2:00 in the afternoon.[7] The sheer number of marchers made a spectacular sight, which was precisely what the organizers had in mind. The processions, Peng Zhen instructed the participants, had to be continuous and uninterrupted, like "waves upon waves."[8] The entire parade had to display the "heroic spirit of the [Chinese people's] hard and bitter struggle."[9]

The themes of each parade varied, but they generally reflected the political and economic realities at the time. In 1951 the dominant themes were the "Resist America, Aid Korea" campaign and support for the Chinese Volunteer Army in the Korean battlefields, both reflecting a strong anti-American sentiment. In 1955 the theme revolved around the First Five-Year Plan. In 1959 the theme shifted to an emphasis on the Great Leap Forward and the People's Communes.[10]

The biannual parades were never overtly nationalistic. The May Day parade, for example, visually promoted internationalism, with paraders carrying the portraits of Marx and Engels ahead of the portrait of Mao.[11] Nevertheless, a nationalistic undertone was at the core of each parade. The nation's foremost political and economic issues always occupied center stage, and special attention was given to the unity of the different nationalities. Indigenous colors were particularly evident, as the artistic paraders featured signature Chinese touches such as *yangge* (rural dances), waist drums, and lotus dances, which were popular since the Yan'an days and evoked memories of the immediate revolutionary past.[12] Mao sent a clear directive: the national parades must "center on us [China]" (*yi wo wei zhu*).[13]

During these celebrations, the masses were supposed to be active participants, but in reality the entire procession was carefully organized and tightly controlled from above, with participants merely comprising a passive audience herded into a controlled space to sing and dance party tunes. Simply put, the national parades were a dramatic CCP ritual in praise of itself, a self-portrait of the party as it wanted to be seen.

The 2008 Beijing Olympic Games

If national parades signaled the birth of the PRC and the gradual rise of China as a great socialist state, the 2008 Beijing Olympics marked an even more important milestone in the history of the CCP—the emergence of China as a world superpower. Although the official slogan of the Beijing Games was "One World, One Dream," in reality the CCP used this greatest global sporting festivity as an international platform to enhance national pride and buttress rule at home. The games were hailed by the official newspaper, the *Renmin ribao* (People's Daily), as "the historic fusion of a great nation and a great sports event."[14]

Ordinary Chinese, understandably, were proud that their country hosted the games. Their exhilaration was clearly epitomized in a front-page article in the *Renmin ribao* on August 9, a day after the opening ceremony: "Tonight we finally realized the hundred-year dream of the Olympics."[15] Many hoped that the games would herald China's return to center stage of the world, and the Middle Kingdom would once again revel in the global spotlight.

Like the earlier National Day parades, a critical feature of the Beijing Olympics was its powerful organization committees. Because of the high profile of the Olympic Games, the key persons in charge were senior party officials. For instance, Liu Qi, the president of the Beijing Olympic Organizing Committee, was a former mayor of Beijing and a member of the CCP Politburo. But the man who oversaw the games in their entirety was Xi Jinping, vice president of the PRC. These high-level arrangements attested to the importance the party placed on this international event.

Similar to the reconstruction of Beijing in the late 1950s, the capital had undergone an extensive facelift since 2001, the year when China won its bid to host the 2008 games. In preparation for the games, the municipal government undertook an aggressive remodeling of the capital, employing hundreds of thousands of workers and turning the city into a dusty construction site. The government devised plans to clean up foul air, relocate factories with noxious emissions, and regulate traffic to lessen congestion. In just a few years, the city had built a huge airport terminal, added roughly 140 kilometers of rail lines and subways, and planted 22 million trees.[16] New spectacular sports venues were erected, most notably the ethereal Water Cube aquatics center and the new National Stadium, known as the Bird's Nest, which quickly assumed iconic status. Hosting the Beijing Games cost China about $50 billion, the most money ever spent to stage the Olympic Games.[17] The massive transformation of Beijing, however, came with enormous human costs and cultural losses, including a huge displacement of residents and the obliteration of many centuries-old neighborhoods. Before the grand spectacle of the games' opening day, petitioners were curtailed and Web sites were blocked by the government. Along the lines of the Soviets' actions during the 1980 Moscow Games,[18] Beijing harnessed journalists and put dissidents under close surveillance.

But inevitably the Olympics put Beijing in the spotlight of international scrutiny, exposing the country's pressing labor problems, human rights abuses, and ill-treatment of dissidents. The games thus reflected the government's paradoxical mix of pride and paranoia, a contrast between an increasingly confident nation proud of its economic achievements and a nervous Communist Party facing an ongoing crisis of legitimacy. These contradictions were fully evident in some of the most noticeable symbols and rituals during the games, namely, the torch relay, the opening ceremony, military overtones, and the myriad forms of tight control imposed by the authorities. For a little more than two weeks in August 2008, Beijing became the focus of the world's joy, praise, and condemnation.

The Torch Relay

The Olympic torch is perhaps the most recognizable symbol of the Olympic festivities, and it is the torch relay that inextricably linked Chinese politics and sports. In fact, the entire route of the torch relay from Greece to Beijing from March 24 to August 8, covering an unprecedented 137,000 kilometers in 129 days, was dubbed a "journey of harmony." This description is clearly an affirmation of the policy of a "harmonious society" that has been actively promoted by Hu Jintao in recent years.[19] But the relay turned out to be anything but "harmonious." Angry protests against China's human rights violations and its crackdown on Tibetan demonstrators in Tibet in March 2008 erupted when the flame passed through stops in London, Paris, and San Francisco, causing embarrassment and anguish for the Beijing government.

But as soon as the Olympic flame reached the Chinese mainland at Sanya, Hainan province, in early May, the relay immediately turned into a jubilant nationwide political parade. To generate maximum impact, the Organizing Committee early on set up an official torch relay Web site to update the progression of the flame.[20] Security personnel were dispatched to keep the necessary routes free of less-disciplined, overenthusiastic crowds or unanticipated incidents. Replete with musical performers, the routes were decorated with Chinese national flags and lined with well-wishers, many wearing red headbands and with red flags painted on their cheeks. The runners were carefully selected and included the usual illustrious pedigree of leaders and heroes: high local party officials, veteran Red Army soldiers, model laborers, famed scientists, and, in many cases, local entrepreneurs who had a proven record of making sizable monetary contributions to their communities. A large number of specially trained torch protectors—described by officials as "volunteers"—separated into pairs to flank and protect each runner.[21]

During the Olympic flame's domestic journey, at least five discernable patterns demonstrate the CCP's exploitation of the event to serve its political ends. First, in addition to key provincial capitals, the torch made its way through the legendary former Communist revolutionary bases, including Jinggangshan and Ruijin in Jiangxi, the first rural bases of the CCP in the 1930s, and Yan'an in Shaanxi, the Red Capital during the War of Resistance against Japan. Second, also included on the route were key cities along the celebrated Long March, such as Zunyi in Guizhou province, where in 1935 Mao secured the supreme position in the leadership of the party. Third, Mao's and Deng Xiaoping's birthplaces—Shaoshan in Hunan and Guang'an in Sichuan, respectively—were chosen as stops in tribute to the two paramount Communist leaders during two different eras: one who during the nation's critical founding days brought China out of obscurity to become a formidable global power, and the other who launched a series of market reforms to turn the country into an economic giant. Such heavy emphasis on the history and leaders of the CCP rendered the torch relay a form of re-education of the masses regarding party history. It also underlined the familiar practice whereby the party sought to reaffirm the CCP's legitimacy through a retelling of the victory of the Communist revolution. In many ways, the routes that the CCP had carefully chosen may be viewed as "the CCP-in-motion," as it retraced part of the legendary Long March of the mid-1930s. This repeated official production of historical remembrance is part of the continuing institutionalization of party memory. The task of maintaining the party's supremacy proved all the more urgent in light of the recent massive labor unrest and domestic ethnic tensions. The Olympic Games thus provided a golden opportunity for political education.

Fourth, on May 8, the organizers took the Olympic flame to the summit of Mount Everest (called Mount Qomolangma by the Chinese). The climb to the mountaintop was intended to show more than a remarkable triumph over difficult physical conditions; for a short time at least, China, symbolically and literally, was on top of the world. More importantly, perhaps, Chinese media underscored that most members of the relay team were Tibetans—in fact a young Tibetan woman, Cirenwangmu, had been selected to actually place the torch at the summit, thus showing there was national harmony and unity and reaffirming the CCP's long-advertised policy of equality among the different ethnic minorities. Finally, when the Olympic flame reached Sichuan, where in May 2008 a devastating earthquake had killed thousands of people, the torch relay was transformed into a "journey of solace and hope."[22] Heroic rescuers during the earthquake were recruited to be torchbearers, and in many places the relay allowed an opportunity to raise funds for the victims. This simply repeated the government's common practice of turning a disaster into a display of national unity.

During the domestic torch run, the stop in Yan'an is especially telling in terms of understanding the CCP's exploitation of political and traditional symbols. The day began on the morning of July 2, at Date Garden (Zao Yuan), the former site of the CCP Central Secretariat. The activities commenced with the frail Liu Tianyou, a 93-year-old female, formerly a Red Army soldier and a veteran of the Long March, raising the torch high with both hands, as dozens of popular *yangge* dancers and waist-drummers cheered her on with great fanfare. The Olympic flame then passed through the residences of the five famous former members of the CCP Central Secretariat—namely, Mao Zedong (chairman), Zhu De, Liu Shaoqi, Zhou Enlai, and Ren Bishi. These historic locations were chosen as a clear tribute to the old revolutionary leaders. The flame then made its way to the Yan'an Cadres School, next to Victory Square, and then crossed the Yangjialing Bridge to Yan'an News Memorial Hall on Qingliang Hill, the former site of the party newspaper *Jiefang ribao* (Liberation Daily) and the New China News Agency. The next destination, after crossing the Yan River Bridge, was Pagoda Hill, another landmark of this earlier revolutionary site.[23]

The torch was then brought by car, traveling 127 kilometers south from Yan'an to Huangling county, where, according to legend, the Yellow Emperor, the great ancestor of the Han Chinese, is buried. In recent years a grand memorial hall, temples, and pavilions had been constructed by local officials with the endorsement of the central government to honor China's legendary forebear. The political symbolism of the Yan'an torch relay reached its apogee when the last torchbearer, a noted local philanthropist and newly elected member of the Chinese People's Consultative Conference, was given the honor of lighting the flame, at noon, in the cauldron in front of the memorial hall. The event was intended "to comfort [the soul] of our ancestor, the Yellow Emperor," described local officials.[24]

The torch relay from Yan'an to Huangling formed a historic bridge connecting Yan'an, the modern Communist revolutionary site, to the ancient burial ground of the Yellow Emperor. Politically, it also linked the current Communist government with the reign of the legendary founder, casting Beijing's leaders as the true heirs of the ancient sage and ruler. Nothing is more powerful and nationalistic than inventing a claim to legitimacy.

The Opening Ceremony

The opening ceremony on the night of August 8 was truly an extraordinary moment in China's modern history. A giant five-starred red flag was carried into the stadium by fifty-six children dressed in distinctive ethnic costumes representing China's fifty-six official ethnic groups. Simultaneously, a 9-year-old girl, Lin Miaoke, dressed in red, performed a charming rendition of the famous song "Ode to the Motherland." The organizers' principal goal was to use selected themes to tell the world how China had journeyed through history, culminating in its current moment of emerging as a world superpower. With thousands of drummers announcing the opening of the games, multitudes of costumed men dressed as students of Confucius chanted "friends have come from afar, how happy we are" to welcome the guests from different parts of the world to China's capital. A gigantic digital scroll was unfurled on the stadium floor to chronicle the distinct cultural symbols of China (tea and porcelain). Dancers used their bodies as ink brushes to create the word "harmony." China's four major inventions—paper, gunpowder, printing, and the compass—were exhibited with grace and high technology. The massive fireworks display added sound and excitement to the show.

The four-hour ceremony was a visual extravaganza chronicling Chinese history, music, art, and dance at their very best. Every detail was tightly choreographed and involved more than 14,000 performers, many said to have rehearsed for thirteen months.[25] In an interview with the New China News Agency, famed filmmaker Zhang Yimou, the ceremony's director, described the opening ceremony as "an avant-garde exploration."[26] Zhang's imaginative spectacle seemed to win wide acclaim for its breathless scale (thousands of performers moving in synchronized precision) and overwhelming numbers (drummers and endearing children). The spectacle inspired pride and patriotism among hometown folks and amazed television audiences worldwide with its enchanting artistry. Ironically, however, despite its harmonious tones and charming gestures, the show was also a festival of patriotism and, more troubling, a spectacle of control. It can be read as tightly organized pageantry staged by an authoritarian party in the latticework shell of the National Stadium, where the audience watched in a restricted, rigidly prescribed setting. The strong nationalistic appeals were clearly evident in the raising of the national flag and the singing of "Ode to the Motherland."

Composed in 1950 in the style of a march, "Ode to the Motherland" is a quintessential paean to the founding of the People's Republic. The song opens with the euphoria of national liberation: "The five-starred red flag is fluttering in the wind; the song of victory is loud and clear." It recounts the past misfortunes of the Chinese people, but in the end gleefully welcomes the day of liberation. And it proudly announces: "The heroic [Chinese] people have now stood up," a line echoing Mao's famous declaration in 1949. But the song also sends a strong warning to China's adversaries: "We love peace and we love our country. But those who dare to invade us will be annihilated!" When first released, "Ode to the Motherland" became an instant hit in China. In September 1951, shortly before the third anniversary of the founding of the PRC, the Ministry of Culture officially adopted it as one of the two "primary songs" to be sung at the National Day celebration, the other being "All the People in the World Are of the Same Mind." It was published in the *Renmin ribao* to be disseminated to a wide audience.[27]

Superficially the "Ode to the Motherland" sung at the opening ceremony was different from its earlier incarnations. In the hands of Olympics music director Chen Qigang, the song had a less political, softer, slower, and more lyrical delivery. Many of the original revolutionary phrases were removed, including "the heroic people" and "our leader Mao Zedong." That it was sung by a pig-tailed, smiling little girl also conveyed an impression of innocence and intimacy intended to engender a visceral sense of joy among the audience.

Clearly the decision was not to air an overtly nationalistic sentiment. It seemed wise that a party song would downplay its patriotic tone at a major international sports gathering such as the Olympics. Nevertheless, the political subtext continued to dominate. From the beginning, the national flag remained a powerful symbol. Certainly the reference to the four smaller stars—the peasants, the workers, the petty and national bourgeoisie—seemed outdated, but the biggest star—the Chinese Communist Party—retained its unchallenged hold on China. Therefore, the revised "Ode to the Motherland" remained an exemplary party song to enhance native pride and underscore national unity in line with current official policies. The song's images of the Yellow River and the Yangzi River never fail to remind Chinese that the great land in which they reside now enjoys unprecedented prosperity. And the repetition of the line "from now on we are marching toward wealth and power" signals the dawning of yet another promising era under CCP rule.

Songs, of course, appeal primarily to feelings rather than intellect, but in order to be effective their timing and setting are vital. "Ode to the Motherland" was sung to coincide with the entrance of the national flag into the National Stadium. Singing it in the newly constructed grand stadium to predominantly hometown crowds generated instant patriotism. Emotions ran even higher when it became clear that billions of TV viewers worldwide were watching. The singing part of the festivities reached its peak when, as soon as the song ended, the children handed the flag to eight People's Liberation Army (PLA) soldiers, who, in high goose-step, marched to the flagpole to raise the banner high in the stadium, a reminder of the glory of the party, the force ultimately in control of the games and the country.

In an interview with state-controlled Radio Beijing shortly after the opening ceremony, Chen Qigang admitted that the smiling Lin Miaoke actually lip-synched the song to the voice of another girl, Yang Peiyi. After watching a final rehearsal, Chen revealed, a senior Communist Party official had deemed 7-year-old Yang, chubby-cheeked and with crooked teeth, not presentable enough to impart the best image of Chinese youth to the world. Thus she was immediately replaced by the more acceptable face of Lin. "It was for the national interest," Chen told Radio

Beijing. "The child on camera should be flawless in appearance, internal feelings, and expression."[28] The involvement of a senior party leader in the decision to replace one girl's face for another's spoke volumes about the political significance the party placed on this crucial ceremony. It also lay bare the fact that the games were an exercise of tight control imposed from above. In an interview, Zhang Yimou admitted: "[In the preparation for the games,] we were subjected to the highest level of review—the highest since the founding of the nation. Fundamentally it was screened by the Party Central Committee. . . . I have never seen an artistic show undergo so many stages, and so high a level of [government] review."[29]

Military Overtones

From the beginning the opening ceremony was infused with a strong military presence, both inside and outside the Bird's Nest. It thus conveyed an image that was in sharp contrast to the idea of harmony the government was emphatically preaching. The capital was under tight security as the games drew near. A military director of the Olympics Security Command Center admitted that the PLA had "deployed seventy-four jets and forty-eight helicopters, and ringed the Olympic stadium with surface-to-air missiles as well as equipment designed to thwart a biological or chemical attack."[30] The government had installed about 300,000 cameras in Beijing during a seven-year program called the Grand Beijing Safeguard Sphere.[31] And an estimated 100,000 security forces and police were positioned throughout the capital.[32] The government also recruited "thousands of Beijing taxi drivers and hundreds of thousands of neighborhood busybodies to keep an eye on foreigners and its own citizens," reported one American journalist.[33] The all-pervasive presence of military and security forces was apparent in Beijing, creating a state of controlled tension and signaling the government's willingness and readiness to use any means, including the military, to ensure that the events proceeded smoothly.

Inside the National Stadium, thousands of costumed men from the PLA performed with great precision and gusto. When 2,008 soldiers, a number chosen to represent the current Olympics in China, pounding out in unison a hypnotic beat on traditional *fou* drums to announce the opening of the games, the thunderous display of masculine military power had a mesmerizing effect. The soldiers' participation clearly reinforced the idea of orderliness and discipline. All spectacles are invented, but the painstakingly constructed illusion of unity and uniformity by the military performers infused the 2008 Olympics spectacle with even greater symbolic meaning.

Sports and the military, of course, are often intertwined in the development of societies, but this entanglement is especially evident in Communist states, where, according to James Riordan, "the role of the military in sport has been particularly heightened by centralised control over sport."[34] In her study of Russian rituals, Christel Lane argues that parades and state ceremonies in the Soviet Union were often organized as military shows.[35] The participation of soldiers in the past Olympic Games was also common. In the opening ceremony of the 1980 Moscow Games, for instance, thousands of Soviet Red Army soldiers formed the so-called "artistic background" in the Lenin Stadium by carrying myriad colored boards to fashion an impressive kaleidoscope of patterns to impress the audience.[36] Moscow was also under tight military control at the time, with an estimated two hundred thousand troops and militia men deployed during the opening ceremony. The Soviet capital was infused with a "strange air of tension," observed a British journalist.[37]

The military presence at the Beijing Games, however, did not seem to surprise anyone. Surely the government had legitimate security concerns, especially with the threat of terrorist attacks. Moreover, the Tibet riots in March of that year, when 22 people were killed, continued to be a major concern for Chinese officials. Later, three attacks against security forces by suspected Muslim separatists in Xinjiang further worried the government. Just before the opening of the Games, sixteen police officers had been killed in the Xinjiang region. Hence, the heavy involvement of soldiers, paramilitary security forces, and police appeared to be natural. As one policeman publicly announced in Beijing's *Renmin gong'an bao* (China Police Daily), "Keeping the Olympic Games safe is like every people's policeman winning a gold medal."[38]

China is unique, however, for its history and degree of military involvement. It is now widely known that sports are closely associated with both nationalism and the dignity of a nation, but China particularly felt the pain of humiliation, for it had long been ridiculed as the "Sick Man of East Asia." This, argues Xu Guoqi, prompted "the Chinese [to] have long identified sports with a warlike spirit, and in so doing [to] have equated sports with aggressive nationalism."[39] The *Guangming ribao* (Enlightenment Daily) argued that with today's great advancements, China had already removed the hat of the "Sick Man of East Asia" and had become "a great sports nation."[40]

Chinese media reported that more than 14,000 performers participated in the opening ceremony, and among them almost two-thirds were members of the PLA and paramilitary police.[41] This overwhelming number of military participants made the games unique, conjuring up an image of awe and might. The Chinese organizers surely believed that national grandeur had to be colorfully displayed and symbolically demonstrated, and the best way to do this was through spectacular shows performed by professional, highly trained, and extremely disciplined soldiers. It is significant that China's 639 athletes, the largest contingent among all participating nations, were called "China's Army" (*Zhongguo juntuan*) by the official media, another reminder of the strange mix of sports and military metaphors in the games.[42]

Zhang Yimou spoke with pride about the precision of the performances in the opening ceremony. He admitted that their presentation was a variation of "the group exercises" commonly used in China,[43] inspired perhaps by the earlier national parades. He also acknowledged that he had learned about these performances directly from China's neighbor, North Korea, whose gymnasts were synchronized in every detail and performed with clockwork precision. "The North Koreans' performances were in remarkable unison. This kind of exactness and unity brings one a sense of beauty," the director said. "We are number two in the world, and North Korea is number one. This is a level that many foreigners cannot achieve. . . . I feel that no country in the world can do this except North Korea."[44]

For Zhang, the use of numerous performers, a "military tactics of massive crowds" (*renhai zhanshu*) as he called it, was necessary in a gargantuan stadium like the Bird's Nest.[45] The director might be right, but the involvement of massive numbers of people, most of them PLA soldiers, in staging choreographed precision moves did not necessarily convey uninhibited elation. Instead, it communicated an uneasy feeling of regimentation and a fearful sense of being controlled, precisely the opposite of the genuine smiles and laughter the Olympic Games were intended to promote. On a popular Chinese blog site, a Chinese journalist and blogger based in Sichuan province wrote scathingly about the spectacle, saying that, "[it was] a sea of humans without an ounce of humanity."[46]

Many were surprised that Zhang, a former chronicler of the hard life of Chinese society in his films *Judou* and *To Live*—a man whom the government had banned for accepting a prize at the Cannes Film Festival in 1994—had turned into a court artist, earning him the top honor as the artistic adviser to the Beijing Olympics. Critics accused him of pandering to Beijing's propaganda plot of championing prosperity and harmony, and they dubbed him "a kind of Chinese Leni Riefenstahl."[47] Zhang dismissed the criticism by contending that the Olympics were "a once in a lifetime opportunity that any Chinese would be foolish to pass up."[48] Zhang Yimou's conversion to a loyalist director was probably prompted by his patriotic yearnings, but it also indicated the party's increasing sophistication in luring the country's top talents into its system by showering them with fame and rewards.

Tentacles of Control

The party's order that the girl singing the patriotic song during the opening ceremony had to be "flawless" led to an embarrassing admission of lip-synching, but this was just one of many admissions that fakery had been used in order to present the nation's best image to the world. Chinese officials also admitted that digital enhancement had been used to perfect the so-called live TV pictures of the twenty-nine giant "footprints." These had been created by fireworks in recognition of the twenty-ninth Beijing Olympiad at the beginning of the opening ceremony.[49]

The ceremony was further marred by the revelation that the fifty-six children who carried a national flag into the stadium, each wearing a costume representing one of China's official ethnic groups, were all members of the Han majority. The government's obvious intent was to display the country's multiethnic diversity and to promote national unity, a goal that was all the more urgent at a time of rising ethnic riots in Tibet and Xinjiang. But such manipulation in a closed sports arena seemed to produce just the opposite effect; as one ethnic minority member commented: "They all looked like Han Chinese. It was clear to everyone at the start. But I suppose they thought there was too much risk that even a child could make an unacceptable gesture."[50]

The digital trickery and lip-synching underscore a deeper and more troubling problem: the Chinese government, in doing everything possible to control policies, information, and images during the world's greatest sports festivity, revealed its extreme paranoia. During the games, Tiananmen Square was sealed off for fear that it would become a magnet for demonstrations. Under pressure from the International Olympic Committee, Beijing had set up three parks as protest zones during the games to accommodate citizens who wished to voice complaints against the government. The application procedure was simple; a citizen merely had to fill out a petition form at a local police station. At the conclusion of the Olympics, officials reported that they had received seventy-seven applications from 149 people, yet not a single demonstration had actually taken place. Chinese officials came forward to say that the government was pleased to see that all seventy-seven protest applications were "resolved" through "dialogue and communication." "Chinese culture always emphasizes the concept of harmony," they remarked.[51] But this official explanation hid the cruel reality that the petitioners had been harassed. In fact, many who dared to apply were either detained or sentenced to political re-education. According to human-rights groups, two Chinese women, including a nearly blind 77-year-old, did step forward to protest against local authorities for forcibly evicting them from their homes. But as soon as they submitted their applications, they were detained and interrogated by police for ten hours and eventually ordered to serve a year of "reeducation through labor."[52]

This was a clear breach of the promises Chinese organizers had made that there would be more openness and more respect for human rights, which had helped China win its bid to host the 2008 games in the first place.[53] Many believed that the designated protest zones were merely a government ploy to quell recurring criticisms of China's lack of free expression and, worse still, to ferret out potential troublemakers.[54]

Conclusion

National celebrations and state parades are a complex political text, but the Chinese Communist Party was, and remains, a master practitioner of using these rousing spectacles as a propaganda tool to affirm its power and broadcast its policies. Whereas the National Day and May Day parades displayed distinctive nationalistic colors, the Beijing Games embraced a larger goal of China's global vision and determination to become a world power.

State spectacles and nationalism obviously have been linked in China since 1949 to create a particularly important element in the formation of a modern Chinese identity. The nationalistic element was associated, of course, with the image of China as a "victim," dating back to the Qing dynasty's defeats and humiliation by the West in the mid-nineteenth century. This victim mentality, coupled with national shame, ran deep among the Chinese. Restoring China's sovereignty and pride have been the primary goals of many reformers and revolutionaries since the late Qing.

Inevitably, because of their association with physical strength and competition, sports came to be identified with both national pride and state power.[55] For many Chinese at home and abroad, the Beijing Games represented a long-awaited moment for the final restoration of China's "face" and due recognition of its well-deserved place on the world stage.

The CCP initially exploited this nationalistic sentiment skillfully but then moved well beyond the painful memory of victimization. During the opening ceremony of the Beijing Games, for instance, the carrying of the national flag by basketball star Yao Ming, flanked by a 9-year-old survivor of the devastating Sichuan May earthquake, conveyed a new, powerful message—even at a time of great joy the Chinese people did not forget their disaster-stricken brethren, and the nation was united in combating natural calamities. At the same time, the invitation to Taiwan's political leaders, including Lien Chan of the Nationalist Party and James Soong of the People First Party, which was given prominent coverage in major Chinese media, addressed another issue of utmost importance: there is only one China, and eventually Taiwan will be united with the motherland.[56]

Chinese national celebrations in the form of state parades and international sports festivities are filled with contradictions, revealing a nation still troubled by conflicts between pride and victimization, exhilarating joy in China's ascent to the status of a world power and profound paranoia that drove the organizers to control every detail of the festivities. The belief that the economic reforms initiated by Deng Xiaoping will see a loosening of the party's grip on power is highly debatable. The bottom line for the party is its continuing hold on power. The 2008 Olympic Games will be remembered as an international sports festival conducted by a regime obsessed with control. The lavish games can be read as a collective celebration in the service of the state, while also revealing a party uneasy about its own legitimacy.

ENDNOTES

1. *Renmin ribao* (People's Daily; *RMRB*), August 2, 2008, p. 1.

2. Christel Lane, *The Rites of Rulers: Ritual in Industrial Society: The Soviet Case* (Cambridge: Cambridge University Press, 1981), p. 224.

3. Chang-tai Hung, "Mao's Parades: State Spectacles in China in the 1950s," *The China Quarterly*, no. 190 (June 2007): 411–431.

4. Beijing Municipal Archives (BMA), 99-1-1; 99-1-3.

5. BMA, 99-1-47.

6. BMA, 99-1-196.

7. BMA, 99-1-94.

8. BMA, 99-1-78.

9. BMA, 99-1-226.

10. BMA, 99-1-1; BMA, 99-1-61; BMA, 99-1-196.

11. BMA, 99-1-3.

12. BMA, 99-1-2.

13. Zhongguo renmin zhengzhi xieshang huiyi Beijingshi weiyuanhui wenshi ziliao weiyuanhui, ed., *Zhuangyan de qingdian* (Solemn Festivities) (Beijing: Beijing chubanshe, 1996), p. 47.

14. *RMRB*, August 8, 2008, p. 3.

15. *RMRB*, August 9, 2008, p. 1.

16. *Time*, August 11, 2008, p. 3.

17. *The Times* (London), August 18, 2008, p. 45.

18. Alfred Erich Senn, *Power, Politics, and the Olympic Games* (Champaign, IL: Human Kinetics, 1999), p. 183.

19. See http://torchrelay.beijing2008.cn/en/image/ (accessed January 28, 2009).

20. See http://torchrelay.beijing2008.cn/ (accessed September 6, 2008).

21. See http://www.china.com.cn/policy/txt/2008-04/18/content_14974161.htm (accessed April 18, 2008).

22. See http://torchrelay.beijing2008.cn/en/journey/guangan/news/n214500920.shtml (accessed September 6, 2008).

23. See http://www.yanan.gov.cn/n16/n1059/n1825/n8923/n8985/107943.html (accessed February 18, 2009).

24. Ibid.

25. *The Times* (London), August 9, 2008, p. 3.

26. *Guangzhou ribao* (Guangzhou Daily; *GZRB*), August 9, 2008, p. 8.

27. *RMRB*, September 15, 1951, p. 3.

28. *Los Angeles Times*, August 13, 2008, p. A15.

29. *Nanfang zhoumo* (Southern Weekend), August 14, 2008, p. 4.

30. *Los Angeles Times*, August 2, 2008, p. A6.

31. *Los Angeles Times*, August 7, 2008, p. A5.

32. *International Herald Tribune*, August 9–10, 2008, p. 16.

33. *Los Angeles Times*, August 7, 2008, p. A5.

34. James Riordan, *Sport in Soviet Society: Development of Sport and Physical Education in Russia and the USSR* (Cambridge: Cambridge University Press, 1977), p. 288.

35. Lane, *The Rites of Rulers*, p. 224.

36. Christopher Booker, *The Games War: A Moscow Journal* (London: Faber and Faber, 1981), p. 77.

37. Ibid., p. 82.

38. *Renmin gong'an bao* (China Police Daily), August 9, 2008, p. 7.

39. Xu Guoqi, *Olympic Dreams: China and Sports, 1895–2008* (Cambridge, MA: Harvard University Press, 2008), pp. 60–61.

40. *Guangming ribao* (*GMRB*), July 29, 2008, p. 1.

41. *Nanfang zhoumo*, August 14, 2008, p. 6; *The Globe and Mail*, August 12, 2008, p. A10.

42. *GMRB*, August 18, 2008, p. 1.

43. *GZRB*, August 8, 2008, p. 8.

44. *Nanfang zhoumo*, August 14, 2008, pp. 5–6.

45. Ibid., p. 3.

46. Quoted in *The Globe and Mail*, August 12, 2008, p. A10.

47. *New York Times*, August 8, 2008, p. A8.

48. Ibid.

49. *The Times* (London), August 13, 2008, p. 18.

50. *The Times* (London), August 16, 2008, p. 4.

51. *The Globe and Mail*, August 21, 2008, p. A9.

52. Ibid.

53. Minky Worden, et al., *China's Great Leap: The Beijing Games and Olympian Human Rights Challenges* (New York: Seven Stories Press, 2008), p. 26.

54. *The Globe and Mail*, August 21, 2008, p. A9.

55. Andrew D. Morris, *Marrow of the Nation: A History of Sport and Physical Culture in Republican China* (Berkeley: University of California Press, 2004), pp. 77–140.

56. *RMRB*, August 9, 2008, p. 4.

THE PRC'S FUTURE IN LIGHT OF ITS PAST

24.
MING FEVER:
THE PAST IN THE PRESENT IN THE PEOPLE'S REPUBLIC OF CHINA AT SIXTY

MICHAEL SZONYI[1]

Browsing the main Xinhua bookstore in Beijing in 2007, I was struck that among all the books on how to succeed in business or prepare for the TOEFL, the best-seller with the most prominent display was a work of history. The book was the first volume of a series called *Those Happenings of the Ming Dynasty* (*Mingchao naxie shi*), and over the next few months, I often noticed people, young and old, on airplanes and long-distance buses, in university cafeterias and on park benches, engrossed in the series. I was also struck by how often history was a topic of conversation, both among my friends and with the villagers whom I interview for my research. Evening plans for interviews sometimes had to be scheduled around the nightly television broadcast of a miniseries about the founding emperor of the Ming, the Hongwu emperor Zhu Yuanzhang. Everyone was talking about the previous night's episode. China had caught "Ming fever" (*Ming re*).

Since its founding, the People's Republic of China has had a complex and fraught relationship with its own history. Mao Zedong was a voracious reader of history, but also initiated political campaigns, such as the Anti Four Old movement, that sought to destroy the past in order to make a blank slate on which to build a utopian future. In China as elsewhere historical narratives have played an important role in the construction of Chinese national identity and in the legitimization of national policies. Paul Cohen shows in his chapter that stories about the

1. An earlier version of this chapter appeared in the e-journal *China Heritage Quarterly*, no. 21 (March 2010), at www.chinaheritagequarterly.org (accessed September 1, 2010). I am grateful to Macabe Keliher, Sarah Schneewind, Wei Yang, Ray Lum, Wang Xiaoxuan, and Geremie Barmé for their suggestions and comments. Full references for this chapter are available at http://isites.harvard.edu/k30925 (accessed February 10, 2010).

past have long been used for political purposes, in the PRC as well as its predecessors. The current Ming fever suggests that the past is still very much a part of life in present-day China. In this chapter, I use the Ming fever as a way of exploring the uses and power of history in the People's Republic. I am not interested in the accuracy of any particular historical narrative or representation; rather, I focus on how and why such narratives are seen as relevant to present-day concerns.

I do not wish to over state the significance of the contemporary interest in history in general or the Ming (1368–1644) in particular. Stories about history are obviously of less importance to ordinary people today than some of the issues discussed in other chapters—economic worries, political instability, and social turmoil—and for most people, interest in the distant past probably pales in comparison with national pride over more recent accomplishments. But the Ming fever is nonetheless a social phenomenon worthy of our attention, one that can tell us something important about the PRC today and perhaps tomorrow. In the body of this chapter, I will argue that many people today are fascinated by the Ming because they see in the dynasty both a parallel with their own world and the origins of some key elements of their own world. The Ming today stands as evidence that an economically vibrant, globally engaged China can be true to the perceived spirit of Chinese civilization. But the fate of the Ming can serve as a warning about the pressing problems facing China today, such as official corruption and elite profligacy. The Ming can also serve as an analogy to reflect on sensitive issues in contemporary China, specifically the idea of a multi-ethnic nation. History is used in China today both to legitimize the present and as a safe tool by which to criticize aspects of a present in which open discussion of politically sensitive themes remains constrained. Popular understandings of history can thus serve as a window into how Chinese people think about themselves, their society, and their prospects.

Chronology of the Ming Fever

The first stirrings of what would come to be called the Ming fever appeared in 2005, the six hundredth anniversary of the voyages of Zheng He, the eunuch who led a series of massive official naval missions throughout Southeast Asia, as far as the Middle East and perhaps the west coast of Africa. The anniversary inspired a host of commemorations, culminating in the State Council declaring July 11 to be "China National Maritime Day." There were conferences and exhibitions, historical reconstructions, and a high-budget television drama about the exploits of the fifteenth-century traveler.

In the next year, several other television miniseries aired to great acclaim, including "The Great Ming Dynasty in 1566: The Jiajing Emperor and Hai Rui," a retelling of the famous story of a dynasty under threat and of the minister whose loyalty and honesty were his undoing. Popular interest in the Ming dynasty took several other forms as well. In 2007, the distinguished Renmin (People's) University historian Mao Peiqi gave a well-received series of seventeen lectures about the Ming on the television program "Lecture Room" (*Baijia jiangtan*). The show has been a sleeper hit for CCTV since it first aired in 2001. Almost cancelled due to low initial ratings, it later became one of the most popular shows on television, creating several academic media stars such as Yu Dan.

There has also been a publishing boom of popular works on the Ming, including biographies of emperors and leading ministers, fictionalized accounts of the fall of the dynasty, and several collections of lectures by prominent scholars. Of the more than 15,000 books on history published in the PRC in 2006, the largest number reportedly dealt with the Ming. Ray Huang's *1587: A Year of No Significance*, first published in Chinese in 1982, has been re-issued in a new and expensive commemorative edition. A Chinese translation of Gavin Menzies' *1421: The Year China Discovered America* appeared in 2005. Though Menzies claims that Zheng He's fleets went as far as Australia and California have been almost universally dismissed by professional historians both in China and the West, the book aroused considerable popular interest.

Popular interest in the Ming has been most evident on the Internet. Here the central figure is Shi Yue, a young official in China's Customs Service, who is better known by his Internet pseudonym, Bright Moon of Yesteryear (Dangnian mingyue). The name is a reference to continuities over time; though everything changes, the moon is as bright as it was long ago. In March 2006, Dangnian began to post tales of the Ming dynasty on the popular BBS site Tianya, under the subject line "Those Happenings of the Ming." The posts apparently were very popular, generating huge numbers of hits and a considerable uproar. Netizens divided into two camps. Dangnian's admirers called themselves "Ming fans" (*Mingfan*). His opponents, accusing Dangnian of artificially pumping up his numbers or disagreeing with his historical views, launched attacks on the BBS. Some posted graphic pictures of traffic accident victims in the comments' section, hoping to dissuade readers. Some launched screen-flooding or spamming to interfere with the operations of the Web site. Accusations of "Internet terrorism" flew back and forth. There were calls for the Tianya moderators to step down.

Recognizing the interest, publishers quickly bought the rights to Dangnian's work. The first volume—the one that I saw at the Xinhua bookstore—appeared by late 2006 to great acclaim. As one effusive reviewer put it, Dangnian's book was written with "the patience of a Swiss watchmaker, the attention to detail of a German engineer, the romanticism of a French vintner, and the humor of an American movie star." Six more volumes have appeared since, with total sales reportedly reaching two million, a remarkable figure given that the content of the earlier books can easily be downloaded for free. Dangnian is now said to be the bestselling author of history in decades and has undergone a remarkable transformation from a retiring and sometimes awkward blogger to a polished celebrity. His stage adaptation of the King Lear story, titled "Ming," premiered at the National Theater in October 2008.

At some point, all of this interest was given the label "Ming fever." The phenomenon having been labeled, it became necessary to analyze it, and stories about the Ming fever began to appear in the media in 2007, with headlines such as, "Why Is the Ming So Hot?" "How Did the Ming Dynasty Become a Tasty Snack?" My own favorite appeared in the journal *Contemporary Nursing*: "A Psychological Interpretation of the Ming History Fever." It truly seemed, as a popular catchphrase ran, that "this year is the Year of Ming" (*jinnian shi Mingnian*). (The term "Year of Ming" can also be read "Next Year," so the phrase is a pun that also means "This Year Is Next Year.") By mid-2009, the marketers had taken over the idea, and copies of *Those Happenings of the Ming Dynasty* were being sold with a sticker that read, "Re-heat the 2008 Ming fever."

Why the Ming Fever? Parallels and Origins

The Ming is not the only historical period about which there has been a surge of popular interest in the last few years. There is the National Studies (*guoxue*) fever that centers on contemporary interpretations of classical texts. Related to it is the Yu Dan fever, named for the charismatic young scholar whose popularized interpretations of Confucius were launched on the very same television show as Mao Peiqi's talks on the Ming, CCTV's "Lecture Room." There has been a high Qing fever and a late Qing fever. There has also been a fever for world history, most evident in the 2006 CCTV documentary "The Rise of the Great Nations" (*daguo jueqi*), which implicitly compares China today to the great empires of the past. What is it that makes some historical periods "feverish"? What is the character of these fevers? More broadly, what explains these waves of general interest in history and historical topics in contemporary China?

The recent fevers have all been multi-media phenomena, taking shape in books; on the Internet; on electronic bulletin boards; sometimes also as computer games; and on television in the form of televised lectures and historical miniseries. As Matthias Niedenführ has noted, since the 1980s television miniseries or historical soap operas have effectively created nationwide events by virtue of their simultaneous daily broadcasts. These events encourage the citizenry to reflect on and talk about national history.

In all of these media, the content of the new history shifts away from the explanatory frameworks that dominated historical writing in the early years of the People's Republic. Class struggle and historical materialism are no longer the key driving forces of history. Instead, there is a new focus on the role of the individual in making history. Earlier black-and-white caricatures of historical actors are being rejected in favor of new efforts to recognize their complexity. This means reassessing their historical significance. The effort to show more nuanced personalities extends even to more sensitive recent history, such as the sympathetic portrayal of a Japanese soldier in "City of Life and Death," a recent film about the Nanjing massacre. A second focus has been to trace the development of modernity in China.

Clearly, the fevers are tied to the market and to the commodification of history. Without a certain critical mass of middle-class consumers of history who purchase books and DVDs, use the Internet, and watch ads, there would be no historical fever. The influence of market considerations is most evident in big-budget television miniseries. In publishing, the popularity of Dangnian's work quickly spawned a host of imitators, and within a year of *Happenings of the Ming Dynasty* appearing on bookstore shelves it was joined by *Happenings of the Han Dynasty*, *Happenings of the Tang Dynasty*, and so on. Several of the recent Ming books are written by academic historians who are seeking a broader market.

In some cases, there is a direct link between the fever and the state. One example is the production of the miniseries, "The Great Ming Dynasty in 1566." It seems that in 2003 Wu Guanzheng, at the time a Politburo Standing Committee member and secretary of the Central Commission for Discipline Inspection, the body within the Chinese Communist Party charged with maintaining internal party discipline, was on an inspection tour of Hainan province when he decided to visit the home of Hai Rui, a famously virtuous Ming official. He asked senior provincial officials why they were not doing a better job of propagandizing Hai Rui as a symbol of anti-corruption. Production of the miniseries began not long thereafter, with Hainan party leaders giving strong backing and a unit of the Commission for Discipline Inspection named as co-producer. (This is of course not the first time Hai Rui's history has been politically manipulated. It was a play about Hai Rui, interpreted as an allegorical critique of Mao Zedong, that launched the first salvoes of the Cultural Revolution.)

The role of the Internet means that the capacity of both the government and the media to control the field of interpretation of history is limited. All of the historical fevers have generated considerable public debate. These debates, often highly impassioned, are played out in private conversations, in the press, and above all on the Internet. They can be broadly divided into three issues. First, there are debates about form and genre, about the validity of different types of historical representation. For example, there has been much discussion about how to situate *Happenings of the Ming Dynasty* in the traditional schema of official versus non-standard histories (*yeshi*), and of history versus historical fiction. Second, there are debates about the actual historical judgments themselves. For example, as part of the late Qing fever, some nineteenth-century figures who were formerly portrayed as reactionaries, such as Li Hongzhang or the Empress Dowager, have been reassessed and in some cases even re-labeled in some works as progressives. Not everyone agrees with these more positive assessments. The sympathetic portrayal of the Japanese soldier in "City of Life and Death," though he is only a fictional character, led to death threats against the film's director. Third, there are debates about the possible parallels between historical events and contemporary China.

What is it about the Ming that makes it interesting to people in China today? People's University historian Mao Peiqi frames the argument in terms of market forces of supply and demand. A high Qing fever had begun almost a decade earlier, and by 2006, he writes, "aesthetic exhaustion" had set in, and people were hungry for something fresh. Surrounded by obvious signs of Ming greatness in the form of relics like the Forbidden City and the Great Wall, Mao Peiqi continues, the general public, the consumers of history, turned their interest to the dynasty that produced such monuments.

Mao's explanation is only a partial one. The Ming fever also arises from a widespread sense that there are real and significant connections between the Ming and the present. These connections fall into two types. First, there is a sense of parallelism, that there are many similarities between the Ming and the People's Republic. Second, there is a sense that one can trace the origins of much that is important in the present day back to the Ming. These connections can serve as resources for operating in the present and for debating and projecting particular images of the present and future, and this potential has much to do with the Ming fever.

The parallelism begins at a high level of generality, with the overall contours of the dynasty. According to the standard narrative taught today in Chinese schools, the rise of the Ming is the story of a strong, authoritarian founder, Zhu Yuanzhang, with an overarching social vision. After a period of terrible social turmoil and suffering, by sheer force of will the founding emperor expels foreign invaders, restores order, and sets about implementing his vision. But frustrated by his inability to realize his vision, to turn people and institutions to his will, he lashes out, causing further suffering. In the end, much of his vision dies with him. The narrative of the dynastic founder had already become "public property" by the late Ming, as historian Sarah Schneewind points out in her introduction to a recent collection of essays on the political uses of Zhu Yuanzhang. Since then, his image has frequently been used to comment on, legitimize, or criticize other historical figures. One twentieth-century example is the biography of Zhu Yuanzhang written by the great Ming historian Wu Han in the 1940s, which was widely interpreted as a veiled critique of Chiang Kai-shek. Today, many people in China see a connection between Zhu Yuanzhang and Mao Zedong. The parallels between the two are invoked often in my own conversations. "Zhu Yuanzhang was very brutal. But he had to do what he did, or he could never have become emperor. He was just like Mao Zedong," one elderly villager told me in early 2009. (Here I should point out that there is a fundamental flaw in the "experimental design" of this project. I am a historian of the Ming, and many of my interviews with rural people involve questions about the Ming. So of course people talk to me a lot about the Ming because that is what I ask them about.)

The possible parallels between Zhu Yuanzhang and Mao Zedong have long been obvious. Anita Andrew and John Rapp have written a book on this very subject. But the parallelism that strikes readers of *Those Happenings of the Ming Dynasty* and viewers of "The Great Ming Dynasty in 1566" today goes beyond the similarities between the two regime founders. Until the 1980s, the standard narrative of the Ming after Zhu Yuanzhang was that the dynasty grew backward, inward-looking, and corrupt. Today that view is changing. Readers of Ming history now learn that out of the fourteenth-century Ming founding grew the prosperous, vibrant, and mobile society of the sixteenth century, with its colorful urban life, diverse intellectual currents, and relatively fluid gender relations. This picture of a society growing by dint of its people's creativity, entrepreneurialism, and diligence, "out of the plan" established by the dynastic founder, resonates with the self-image of many people in China today. In other words, the standard narrative of the Ming, the version which is taught in schools today, follows an arc in which many people of the PRC today see their own story.

Interestingly, academic history in China has had much to do with this popular re-evaluation of Ming history. Mao Zedong proposed long ago that China's "feudal society" contained embryonic "sprouts" (*mengya*) of capitalism prior to the arrival of Western imperialism. PRC historians of the Mao era sought to identify and analyze these sprouts and explain why they failed to develop into mature capitalism, in keeping with the Marxist expectations of universal patterns of progress. These efforts led to the discovery of the high level of commercial development in rural China in the late Ming and Qing and to studies of urbanization and urban culture. Professional historians have been interested in these topics since the 1970s; through the media they now reach a mass audience of consumers of history.

Besides a general sense of the parallels between the arc of Ming history and recent developments in the PRC, there are also more specific and more explicitly normative parallels. By explicitly normative parallels, I mean ways in which actors in the PRC today compare aspects of the contemporary situation with the Ming case in order to present a particular vision of the present. A recent example comes from the celebration of the sixtieth anniversary of the founding of the People's Liberation Army Navy (PLAN), held in April 2009 in Qingdao. Xinhua reportage compared the current situation with the Ming voyages. "During seven voyages by Zheng He (1371–1433), China's own Christopher Columbus–like navigator, what was then the largest flotilla in the world neither imposed a colonial treaty nor claimed a piece of soil." Comparisons between the current naval buildup and the Ming voyages are intended to convey a long history of peaceful intentions toward the outside world, in contrast to the baleful history of European and American imperialism.

These new narratives of the Ming challenge another stereotype of the Ming as a dynasty that turned inward, rejecting contact with the outside world. The emphasis on the Zheng He voyages, comparisons with which have also been used in support of the "Going Out" (*zou chuqu*) policy proposed by Jiang Zemin in the 1990s, is only part of the story. There has also been growing interest, again supported by less well-known academic history, to show that the end of the Zheng He voyages did not mean the closure of the country. On the contrary, private trade between southeast China and Southeast Asia continued to flourish and helped to drive the newly discovered general prosperity of the mid-Ming.

This in turn challenges the old notion of the Ming as fundamentally backwards and stagnant. In the new narrative, the question becomes why the Ming did not go on to develop a full-blown overseas empire. Mao Peiqi's answer is that "the real failure" of the Ming was that the state never fully supported these private commercial endeavors in the way that European countries would do in the coming centuries. His explanation for this failure is "uneven regional development" and the fact that "political authority" fell into the hands of people from these less economically developed regions, and later the Manchus. It would be difficult not to read this argument as a commentary on contemporary China and a call for continued reform, even at the cost of uneven economic development. Thus the Ming fever also serves as a way of talking about China's relations with the larger world in the past, and therefore also in the present and future. Criticisms of insular and closed-minded groups who would turn back the clock on policies of global engagement for economic development and modernization have obvious resonance in today's China.

These parallels rest on a sense that historical patterns recur, that we can look to the past for instructive parallels to the present, and that time is cyclical. A second set of connections between the present and the Ming involves a search for origins, and therefore rests on a different notion of time as linear. In this line of thinking, the Ming represents a critical historical convergence of the traditional Chinese order and the beginnings of modernity. As one avid historical blogger sums up the new story of the Ming, "Ming China's political system was inherited from the Han and Tang dynasties, and its thought was open-minded. In his attitudes and policies toward the outside world, the emperor, the supreme political authority, not only was not the representative of conservative factions but could be called the vanguard of opposition to conservatism. The economy and popular spirit attained a high level of development; philosophy and thought were extremely lively. Society was fundamentally different from what had come before. [Ming China] was the main beneficiary of economic globalization and the economic center of the world. It produced the world's leading anti-authoritarian philosophers." Though there have been other times of relative openness to the world in Chinese history, such as during the Tang, the late Ming commercial development and the new currents of thought that are tied to it are now seen by many historians and non-historians as the origins of an indigenous Chinese modernity. As one newspaper reporter commented in 2007, "the intellectual enlightenment in the scholarly world, of which Huang Zongxi, Gu Yanwu, and Wang Fuzhi are representative figures, contained within it the origins of China's modernization." In light of current efforts to re-evaluate traditional Chinese culture and construct a distinctively Chinese form of modernity, the Ming is widely seen as offering evidence that Chinese culture contains the potential for modernity even without European imperialism and influence.

Prasenjit Duara has recently coined the term "hegemonic modernity" to convey the idea that modernity has been constructed and institutionalized as an ideology or worldview that has become hegemonic or dominant over other ideologies. But the hegemony of modernity does not exclude the possibility that it can take multiple forms. The concept of an indigenous Chinese modernity with its roots in the Ming allows Chinese people today to challenge the hegemony of Western-style modernity without challenging the hegemony of modernity in general. This has important implications for thinking about China's place in the world today. If China since the Ming has been following its own path to modernity, a path from which China may have been diverted due to the negative influence of Western imperialism but which it never completely lost, a path to which China has now returned by recognizing the value of its own traditions, then China's current modernity should be judged on its own terms and not held to falsely universalized standards of Western modernity.

Tensions and Contradictions

The search in the Ming for parallels with or origins of contemporary China leads down some problematic paths. Efforts to make connections between past and present generate tensions or contradictions in how the past, and its relations with the present, are comprehended. By tensions I do not mean concerns about the accuracy of a given historical interpretation (though specific interpretations do generate endless debates on the Internet). Rather, my interest is in the logics by which a given historical interpretation does the work it is desired to do in the present. Any specific use of history disrupts or undermines other uses. It may be that these tensions also have something to do with the appeal of the Ming today. Perhaps the history of the Ming dynasty can serve as a venue for reflecting on contemporary issues precisely because one can use the Ming to make such a wide variety of arguments.

The ultimate contradiction in the use of the Ming as an analogy with the present is that the Ming dynasty eventually fell. As William Kirby noted in his introductory comments to the Fairbank Center's "PRC at 60 Conference," "if the PRC can be the Ming to the Yuan, it can also be the Ming to someone else's Qing." If people in the PRC today see themselves as following a narrative that follows a similar arc to the transition from early to mid-Ming, the late Ming then becomes a harbinger of future dangers. The purpose of the analogy then becomes to break from the arc. This use of history as both a model of the present and a warning for the future is of course not new. The notion that one can learn from the past and thereby avoid repeating its mistakes runs through Chinese historiography. One sees it in the title of the great eleventh-century historical compendium *Comprehensive Mirror for Aid in Governance* (*Zizhi tongjian*). It is not even a new use of the Ming. In the 1930s, a previous outbreak of Ming fever tried to use historical analogy to rouse anti-Japanese resistance. This episode focused on the late Ming, especially its political failure to respond to the Manchu threat on its borders, and celebrated those late Ming heroes who sacrificed themselves in defense of the nation. Today there is no obvious immediate comparable threat on China's borders. Nor is there much danger of palace eunuchs hijacking national politics, another factor to which late Ming weakness is typically ascribed. But some of the other causes of the Ming collapse: official corruption, elite disunity, public and private profligacy, and a decline of public morals are, as other chapters in this volume show, very much concerns of the present day. Part of the appeal of the Ming today surely is that it provides a forum for comment on the problems of the present. Wu Guanzheng was of course thinking of the Ming in this way when he called for propaganda work on Hai Rui.

A second tension in current accounts of the Ming relates to the dynasty that succeeded it—the Qing. Here the Ming fever intersects with two concurrent but distinct Qing fevers—a high Qing fever that celebrates the prosperity of the late seventeenth and eighteenth centuries, the reigns of emperors Kangxi, Yongzheng, and Qianlong, and a late Qing fever that explores the dramatic changes of the nineteenth century and the efforts of statesmen and ordinary people to respond to the challenges of Western imperialism and internal crisis. Both of these fevers contain within them their own contradictions that make it difficult for people to find in them either the origins of modern China or parallels with China's rise today. The logic of the high Qing fever is troubled by the decline that followed so closely upon this reign. If this was such a splendid age, what explains the disasters of the next century? If China's finest statesmen could do nothing to stop foreign imperialism, what does this say about the potential for modernity inherent in Chinese culture? It is hard to make a case for a distinctive Chinese modernity with indigenous origins by looking at a period when Western imperialism seemed to be the dominant historical force. The two fevers also share a common element that limits their effectiveness as historical analogy: the fact of Manchu rule.

When the history of the Ming was deployed in the 1930s to rouse patriotic sentiments against the Japanese threat, the foreign origin of the Manchus was central to the effectiveness of the parallel. The Han Chinese Ming was to the Manchu invaders (and later the Qing) as the Republic of China was to the Japanese. But in the PRC official perspective, the Qing is celebrated as the multi-ethnic imperial predecessor of today's multi-ethnic harmonious society. So within officially sanctioned versions of history, the analogy of anti-Manchu resistance can no longer play the same mobilizing role it once did. But the rising influence of nationalism in contemporary China, both nationalism contrived and manipulated by the state and nationalism bubbling up from below, means a growing contradiction between the two views of the Qing—as a great Chinese empire and as a foreign empire ruled by foreign invaders. This contradiction came to a head in late 2008, when the Qing scholar Yan Chongnian, who sees the significance of the Qing as a merging and exchange between the different ethnicities that make up the Chinese people, was assaulted at a Shanghai book signing. His assailant, it subsequently was revealed, had been offended by Yan's efforts to whitewash what he saw as the reality of the Qing entry into China—a foreign invasion. On the Internet, Yan was "outed" as an ethnic Manchu. One can read the event as expressing a tension between authoritative narratives of the Qing—authoritative in the sense of being linked to political authority—and popular nationalist understandings. (The importance of the Qing in expanding the boundaries of its empire to those of China today tends to be forgotten by its critics, at least its Han nationalist critics.) Popular nationalist interpretations of history tend to be more favorable to the Ming, the last imperial dynasty whose ruling house was Han Chinese. As one scholar put it, "The Qing had the additional element of ethnicity, of a foreign ethnic group ruling. If you want to use the past to look at the present, today there is no such factor. . . . If we get rid of this factor, what we're left with is the Ming." Or in the words of an anonymous commentator on an article about the Ming fever, "Only with the revival of true Han culture can there be a revival of China." In today's China, the politics of historical representation embodies a tension between a larger but multi-ethnic Qing empire and a smaller but Han Ming empire. Both as a mirror of the present and as an important historical moment in the making of modern China, representations of the Ming are in uneasy tension with representations of the Qing. This uneasiness relates in turn to contesting visions of the Chinese nation, past, present, and future. Interest in the Ming or the Qing reflects very different positions on the question of what is China's most important legacy from the past, and therefore very different positions on the character of China today.

Conclusions

Paul Cohen has written that to live on as myth, an event or a person must embody themes or characteristics that are pertinent to later times. To put this another way, certain eras or issues are more likely to generate fevers, to become "feverish," precisely because of their perceived relevance to the present. The current Ming fever, I have suggested, arose because many people perceived the Ming as relevant or useful as a set of analogies to the present, as a source for important dimensions of the present, and therefore as a resource for reflecting on the present. This is, I admit, a speculative argument. But it is one that many of those involved in the Ming fever would accept. As the young author Dangnian has put it, "People who read (kan) history do so in order to look at (kan) themselves. Historical fevers are a refraction of the confusion and puzzlement of people who live in a time of transition." Another popular blogger compares the Ming fever to the passion for history in Taiwan several decades ago. "Perhaps such historical fevers [are a response to] a general anxiety in times of transformation."

Like so many other domains of life in the PRC today, popular interest in history is shaped by—but not fully determined by—the two great forces of state and market. Despite the power of the state to impose an authoritative vision and of the market to impose a commodified vision, many of the most interesting aspects of popular history lie in the interstices of the two. History retains a striking capacity to serve as a venue for commenting on the present and the future, and therefore as a site of competition for the power to speak. In other words, my argument here is that we should look at the presentation of history in China today because to some degree history is a venue for politics. Part of the reason the Ming is feverish has to do with the way it can simultaneously serve to legitimize certain aspects of the current order while still leaving scope for criticism of other aspects. Perhaps the Ming is feverish in the sense of generating such heated passions precisely because of the limits that are still placed on serious open discussion of political and social issues in China today. If this hypothesis is correct, then the historical fevers in China today may be another manifestation of the same forces that drive the more overtly political expressions of dissent and protest explored in other chapters in this volume.

Though much of the attention to the sixtieth anniversary of the People's Republic rightly focuses on China's future, many Chinese people are also thinking about the past. The past remains both a mirror for reflecting on the present and a resource for constructing the future. This is probably truer than ever in this year of historical anniversaries, some of which are being officially commemorated and others suppressed, but all of which are contested. Historical fevers inhabit an ambiguous space between cyclical and linear time, between a China of recurring patterns and a China moving forward into its own distinctive modernity. Popular narratives about the past embody ambiguities and unresolved tensions. This is not only because of the inadequacies of the historical evidence or the challenges of representation, but because of the ambiguities and tensions that surround China's current situation and future course. In their influential 1995 account of the historical profession in the United States, *Telling the Truth About History*, Joyce Appleby, Lynn Hunt, and Margaret Jacob note the power of historians to "fashion the nation's collective self-understanding." They do not mean that historians are simply the servants of political power. Rather, "the political imperatives embedded in the uses of national histories are complicated by the dispersal of authority in a democracy." Whether China today is a democracy, as the regime claims, or a system of resilient authoritarianism, as other contributors to this volume call it, or something else again, the political imperatives embedded in the uses of national history surely also apply to the PRC at sixty.

25.
THE TENACITY OF CULTURE:
OLD STORIES IN THE NEW CHINA

PAUL A. COHEN

Most historians have long since moved beyond the old view that for China to become a "modern society" it must turn its back completely on the values, behavior patterns, and cultural traits that characterized Chinese life for centuries. But there is still a sense, certainly among the general run of people and perhaps among some scholars as well, that while conspicuous pockets of China's old culture persist—one thinks of such things as acupuncture, tai chi, Chinese temple rituals and festivals, and so on—these things are not to be compared in importance to, say, the industrial revolution the country has undergone in recent decades or its growing military power or the many ways in which Chinese today engage the world, politically, economically, and culturally. This view is perhaps especially prevalent among non-Chinese, who have much easier access to the modern features of today's China than to older cultural patterns that persist and still exert a strong influence but are less available to the senses.

I want to challenge this view in my contribution to this volume by calling attention to a manifestation of Chinese culture that, although immensely important, is largely sealed off from the eyes of foreigners—and may often, for an entirely different set of reasons, also be given insufficient weight by the Chinese themselves. I refer to the great variety of old stories, some of them distinctly secular, others deeply embedded in the religious beliefs and practices of the country, that have continued to play a vital part in the modernizing China of the twentieth and twenty-first centuries. Such stories have long been apparent, at least to scholars, in places like Taiwan and Hong Kong; they have been less well recognized in the PRC.

In a recent book I focus on one such story, that of King Goujian of the southeastern state of Yue in the latter part of the Eastern Zhou dynasty, exploring the ways in which this story—and its linked proverb *woxin changdan* ("to sleep on brushwood and taste gall")—was adapted by Chinese throughout the twentieth century. This is the saga of a young king who, after suffering a humiliating defeat at the hands of his main rival, the larger and more powerful neighboring state of Wu, spent three years as a prisoner/slave in Wu. After eventually convincing the Wu king of his loyalty and trustworthiness, he was permitted to return to Yue, where for twenty years, determined to avenge the earlier disgrace, he patiently built up the state's population and military and economic strength. Finally, after getting the go-ahead from his top ministers, Goujian led his armies in a series of attacks against his rival, which ended in the death of the Wu king, the destruction of the state of Wu, and the eradication of the original humiliation.

The humiliation/revenge core of the story of King Goujian was hugely influential during the 1920s and 1930s when China, under the leadership of Chiang Kai-shek (who identified strongly with Goujian), came under mounting pressure from Japan and there was widespread popular sentiment in favor of resisting Japanese aggression. The theme of a small weak state, through hard work and determination, taking on a larger, more powerful state had strong appeal for Chinese in post-1949 Taiwan, where the foundational policy of the Chiang Kai-shek government was epitomized in the slogan *fangong fuguo*, "launch a counterattack and recover the country." In the PRC during the early 1960s, when the mainland faced a profound crisis owing to rapidly deteriorating relations with the Soviet Union and the catastrophic famine resulting from the Great Leap Forward, a hundred or so different operas dealing with the Goujian story were performed all over China, stressing such themes as "self-reliance" (*zili gengsheng*) and "going all out to build up the country" (*fafen tuqiang*) that the Communist leadership was pushing hard at the time. And in the "reform and opening" era that emerged after Mao Zedong's death, the story's influence continued unabated: it served in the 1980s as a thinly veiled critique of Maoist despotism (in the ancient saga, after his triumph over Wu, Goujian, prefiguring the behavior of Mao during the Cultural Revolution, turned against the loyal ministers who had contributed to his success); and in the rapidly privatizing and commercializing China of the 1990s and 2000s, it supplied a model for individual Chinese to follow when they encountered obstacles in their efforts to succeed in life.[1]

A historical story of much more recent vintage, one that played a particularly important part in the run-up to the Cultural Revolution, is that of the intrepid Ming dynasty official Hai Rui (1513-87), who in late 1565 had submitted a memorial that was scathingly critical of the Jiajing emperor's personal conduct and disastrous neglect of public business over a twenty-year span. This action resulted in the brave official's dismissal from office, imprisonment, and near death due to torture. In the years immediately following Mao's controversial dismissal of Defense Minister Peng Dehuai, in retaliation for the latter's serious criticism of the Great Leap Forward at the Lushan Conference of August 1959, the Hai Rui story became the subject of a number of dramas. The best known of these is *Hai Rui Dismissed from Office* (*Hai Rui ba guan*), an opera by the historian and deputy mayor of Beijing Wu Han, which was first performed in 1961. The opera, although well received at the time, was severely criticized in November 1965 by Yao Wenyuan (later to become a member of the infamous Gang of Four) in an article that has often been regarded as the opening salvo of the Cultural Revolution. In December 1965, Mao himself, in a speech in Hangzhou, although praising Yao's article, added: "Its defect is that it did not hit the crux of the matter. The crux of *Hai Rui Dismissed from Office* was the question of dismissal from office. The Jiajing emperor dismissed Hai Rui from office. In 1959 we dismissed Peng Dehuai from office. And Peng Dehuai is Hai Rui too." Although there is some question as to whether Wu Han's opera in its origins had been intended to serve as a criticism of Mao, it was not long after the chairman's Hangzhou talk that the writer was thrown into prison, where he died in 1969.[2]

The impact of the Hai Rui story was greatest among Chinese intellectuals. Far more sweeping in its influence in post-1949 China was the ancient Daoist fable of "The Foolish Old Man Who Removed the Mountains" ("Yu gong yi shan"), the point of which is that, with sufficient resolve, any goal can be achieved, no matter how great the difficulty. This tale, which was also familiar to Chinese school children in Taiwan, is well known for having been promoted by Mao during the Cultural Revolution to encourage the Chinese people to tear down the twin "mountains" of feudalism and imperialism. It was one of the "Three Essays" that everyone was supposed to memorize, and it became so deeply ingrained in Chinese culture—a "root metaphor" in Jerome Bruner's sense[3]—that a passing reference to it was all that was necessary to make one's point, without having to tell the whole story. Thus, Ji Chaozhu, who spent much of his youth in the United States and was for years Mao's top English-language interpreter, concludes his recent memoir with the following expression of hope in reference to Chinese-American mutual understanding: "Like the Foolish Old Man, I have confidence that the descendants of my descendants will keep at it, shovelful by shovelful, until the mountains have been removed and we live in a harmonious world."[4]

Old cultural stories have also played an important part in the lives of PRC Chinese on a more intimate and personal level. Some readers may recall an article by Jianying Zha that appeared in *The New Yorker* several years ago. It was about her half-brother Zha Jianguo, an imprisoned democracy activist, who as a boy went to a boarding school and came home only on Sundays. I quote from the article: "Divorce was uncommon in China at the time, and no doubt it cast a shadow on Jianguo's childhood. My mother recalls that, when Jianguo slept in the house, she sometimes heard him sobbing under his quilt. In letters written from prison, he described those weekends as 'visiting someone else's home' and said that he 'felt like a Lin Daiyu'—referring to the tragic heroine in the Chinese classic *The Dream of the Red Chamber* who, orphaned at a young age, has to live in her uncle's house and compete for love and attention." The article continues, noting that Jianguo's own mother says that he was "ambitious from a very young age. When she first told him the story of Yue Fei, a legendary general of the Song dynasty who was betrayed and died tragically, Jianguo looked up at her with tears in his eyes, and said, 'But I'm still too young to be a Yue Fei!'"[5]

As can be gathered from this quotation, fictional and historical stories (not to mention historical stories that have been heavily fictionalized, like that of Goujian) have equal standing in the Chinese cultural repertoire. Such narratives, although often disseminated orally—typical vehicles were opera, the professional story-teller, intrafamilial transmission, and in twentieth-century radio, film, and television—were firmly embedded in China's written literary traditions. They had circulated sometimes for centuries, were known throughout the land, and as often as not supplied cognitive models that Chinese, individually or collectively, could readily relate to and measure their own thoughts and actions against. But there were other kinds of stories as well. One such kind, very different in nature, consisted of the tales that circulated in times of extreme fear and anxiety, such as external threat, disease, drought, and famine. These stories—rumors and other forms of "improvised news"[6] that passed rapidly from mouth to mouth—emanated largely from Chinese oral tradition; they tended to be local or regional in scope, although they could extend beyond this; they frequently targeted specific scapegoats; and rather than being stories that simply existed in people's heads, they often called for—and resulted in—collective action.[7]

Such stories, embodying what Barend ter Haar has termed the "demonological paradigm," have been deeply rooted in Chinese religious culture for centuries and remain so to this day.[8] Their focus is the constant danger to human beings posed by all sorts of demons (*gui, yao, mo*). Even ordinary people might be labeled demonic, "for instance old single women or ugly people who were regarded as human transformations of the ferocious child-eating Granny Tiger (*laohu waipo*)"—the subject of a folk legend that, in one form or another, circulated (and probably still circulates) through much of China. "Small children crying at night were warned to be quiet or else Granny Tiger would come and devour them."[9] The pervasiveness of such demons is hard to overstate. "Literally at every corner of the street and on every bridge," according to ter Haar, "demons [were] waiting to snatch someone away." In the words of the early Western student of Chinese popular religion, J. J. M. de Groot, humanity, "enslaved to the intense belief in the perilous omnipresence of spectres, is engaged every day in a restless defensive and offensive war against those beings"; to protect itself in this war required a wide range of ritual strategies and techniques.[10]

Demons posed a threat not only to individuals but also to society as a whole. Many of the rituals performed during the New Year Festival (the first two weeks of the new lunar year) and the Ghost Festival (the middle of the seventh lunar month) were geared toward the expulsion of demons. To counter the whole range of evil and harmful influences, it was also common in many parts of China to appeal for the aid of "heavenly armies," "celestial generals" (shenjiang), and "spirit soldiers" (shenbing). Not infrequently in such instances, certain demons, such as the popular Three Kingdoms military hero Guan Yu (another historical and fictional figure whose story is known to all in post-1949 China), were recruited to lead the fight against the rest of the demonic population.[11]

Narratives centering on demonic forces sometimes had an important impact on actual historical events. Thus, at the turn of the twentieth century, the Boxers thought of themselves as spirit (or heavenly) soldiers called upon by the gods to kill all Westerners, who were regularly referred to as demons from across the sea (yanggui). The Western demons were held directly accountable for the severe drought plaguing northern China at the time. Numerous rumors circulated among the Chinese population concerning the demonic practices of the Christians, which, the Boxers believed, had to be combated by fire, magic rituals, and other traditional exorcist methods.[12]

Most interesting for the purposes of the present volume, demonic stories also had a significant place in the political realm in post-1949 China. Steve Smith's study of rumors that were rife in the early 1960s in Jilin, Shanghai, and elsewhere is studded with interesting insights, which can only be hinted at here. In 1959–61 China had suffered possibly the worst famine in human history in terms of absolute numbers of deaths. The country began to recover in 1962 and, interestingly, it was then, rather than at the height of the famine, that an epidemic of what the state called "superstitious rumors" broke out.[13] The rumors, Smith argues, were a reflection of acute uncertainty about the future—an uncertainty doubtless compounded by the threat of war with Taiwan (where Chiang Kai-shek in 1962 was loudly announcing plans to invade the eastern coastal provinces). One of the rumors circulating at the time focused on talking toads; the toads forecast that old people would die but that they might survive if, within a certain time period, they ate a toad or consumed steamed or baked toads made of flour. The most obvious message of the rumors was that the young should take care of the old, very possibly reflecting, in Smith's view, "a determination on the part of the elderly . . . to bolster their entitlement to food" after a period when millions of Chinese (including substantial numbers of old people) had died of starvation.[14]

The other rumor that was rampant in the early 1960s—involving sightings of chinless ghosts—also, it is clear, related back to the famine, when huge numbers of people had died "bad deaths," thereby becoming hungry ghosts who could wreak serious harm on the living. The problem was nationwide. Erik Mueggler, in a vivid account of what one of his informants in Yongren county, Yunnan, described as "the age of wild ghosts," writes: "*All* those who had died of hunger in the famine became wild ghosts. None had been properly admitted to the underworld; none had been given stores of grain and herds of goats to sustain them in death." As a result, according to the same informant, years later the wild ghosts still wandered the fields and paths, waylaying their descendants and demanding gifts of grain and meat: "They are always starving, always greedy. These days, we perform exorcism after exorcism, far more than ever before. But few are successful for long; the ghosts keep coming back, and their descendants keep falling ill."[15]

Smith articulates a broader understanding of what was going on in the minds of ordinary Chinese at this time: "For millions of peasants and workers, . . . the debate as to whether the famine was a natural or man-made cataclysm missed the point; they were convinced that it was the neglect—or active proscription—of rituals designed to energize relations between the spirit and human worlds that was the root cause of the disaster. . . . In the countryside, the belief that catastrophe had struck because the regime was inhibiting rituals of propitiation and exorcism was particularly entrenched."[16]

Smith's talking toads and chinless ghosts refer to demonic stories that the government tried to suppress. It is, however, an indication of the traction such stories had in Chinese culture that, in other instances, the government itself sought to exploit them in the political campaigns it launched after 1949. These campaigns, again and again, pointed to dangerous apocalyptic threats (whether posed by counterrevolutionaries and spies or insects, mice, rats, and starlings) and the need to combat such threats with violent actions. During the Cultural Revolution the demonological paradigm was explicitly appropriated by China's Communist rulers. Political enemies were designated as "evil demons" (*yaogui*) and "tigers" (in their role as demonic animals), and, echoing the part taken by young people in the Boxer movement, a heavenly army of Red Guards was now assigned the role of carrying out the exorcism of the nation.[17] A major propagandistic part was also taken, ter Haar suggests, by the "model operas" (*yangbanxi*), which (heavily influenced by Beijing Opera tradition) "portray[ed] political enemies as demon-like adversaries against whom the use of violence was fully justified."[18]

Although "there has been some scholarly resistance," Donald Sutton observes, "to the application of cultural interpretations to the People's Republic . . . , even to the idea that culture matters at all," he argues compellingly that the struggle movements launched by the state during the Mao years "had to seem persuasive in terms of Chinese culture."[19] Evidence in support of this position is abundant. During the Cultural Revolution, the influence of traditional demonology was seen in the widespread use of the expression "ox demons and snake spirits" (*niugui sheshen*) to dehumanize people and of ox pens to punish and imprison political enemies. Ox demons and snake spirits were evil spirits disguised as human beings; once exposed, however, they were widely believed to lose their evil powers. This was the basis for Mao's earlier use of these labels (during the Anti-Rightist movement of 1957–58) to unmask those intellectuals who, although pretending to be loyal to the party, actually (in his view) attacked it through their speeches and writings.[20] Traditionally, the ox demon was one of the assistants of the City God, a supernatural analogue to the local magistrate in the human realm. In the Cultural Revolution political transgressors were paraded through the streets and subjected to mock trials in which they were exposed to verbal abuse and physical violence, judicial practices closely associated with the worship of the City God in the past.[21] It seems clear that (as ter Haar, echoing Sutton, puts it) "the extreme violence of political campaigns during the post-1949 period," above all during the Cultural Revolution, "was not something exclusively introduced from the top downward, but also produced from the local level upward following a well-established cultural logic."[22]

Xiaofei Tian, in her stunning deconstruction of the Lei Feng phenomenon in the 1960s (included elsewhere in this volume), identifies a parallel logic, which, although having nothing to do with the demonic, confirms the abiding importance of China's older story culture. The Lei Feng saga, Tian contends, was indeed a product of Communist propaganda, but major themes in it resonate with similar themes embedded in age-old Chinese fairy and folk tales, and this both facilitated and reinforced Lei Feng's popularity.

Despite the influence of important aspects of Chinese religious culture on political rhetoric and behavior during the Cultural Revolution, the infrastructure of popular religion in its more visible manifestations suffered harsh suppression during these years. Thousands of temples were destroyed or converted into schools, granaries, or other secular uses. Buddhist monks and nuns and Daoist priests were forcibly returned to lay life. And although the situation varied from one region to another, in many parts of the country the yearly cycle of temple-based religious functions suffered severe disruption. With the end of the Mao era in the late 1970s, however, there was a substantial reversal of government religious policy, and in the course of the 1980s and 1990s all over China a vibrant popular religion, centered on newly built temples and temple-centered rituals and celebrations, reemerged, to the point that the scale of such observances today is enormous, involving between a quarter and a half of the Chinese population (in Robert Weller's very rough estimate).[23]

Temple-based activities, especially the story-tellers and opera troupes engaged to liven the annual celebrations of a temple god's birthday, reintroduced familiar historical and mythological stories, many of which had circulated in one form or another for centuries and were well known even to illiterate Chinese. Stories were also deeply embedded in the religious beliefs and rites that were now being revived. Among the specific rituals that experienced a sharp rise in popularity in northern Shaanxi, for example, was one that directly addresses the demonic fears discussed earlier. According to northern Shaanxi folk belief, before reaching the age of 12 (sui) small children are susceptible to all kinds of dangers, especially to those relating to "life-course obstacles" (guan or guansha). "In the past," Adam Chau reports, "only those children who were very vulnerable to soul loss and other serious illnesses needed to go through the ritual called 'passing the obstacle' [guoguan] or 'exterminating the obstacle-demon' [po guansha]. But today many parents feel the need to let their children go through the ritual, which is conducted at temple festivals annually for a small fee. . . . At age twelve a child passes the last obstacle, at which point the parents present a white rooster to the deity as [a] token of gratitude for his or her protection."[24]

Let me conclude with a few general observations. First, it is clear that, as China has moved along its modernizing course during the twentieth and early twenty-first centuries, a lively and tenacious popular culture, often centering on widely circulated, sometimes centuries-old stories, has remained firmly in place. These stories may be broken down into a range of different types. In the present chapter, I have dealt with two broad examples, one focusing on prototypical individuals (often, though not necessarily, embodying positive traits), with whom people may choose to identify (or, in the case of negative models, disidentify) in their collective or personal lives; the other centering on dangers, threats, and other sources of fear or anxiety, against which people are urged to take measures for self-protection. Other common types of narratives, not dealt with here or dealt with only in passing, might include children's stories, folklore, fairy tales, legal case histories, dream interpretations, and narratives pertaining to illness and health. The boundaries separating different categories of stories were often extremely fluid. There was an intimate connection, for example, between theories of dream interpretation and Chinese folklore.[25]

Second, some of the stories I have discussed here have been influential mainly among less well-educated rural folk, others among better-educated urban dwellers who scoff at the "superstitious" beliefs of their country cousins. Still others (as disseminated typically via opera and, more recently, television dramatizations) have jumped class and sectoral lines, reaching people throughout the population. These last are of special interest. "In the Ming and Qing dynasties," Barbara Ward tells us, "the overwhelming majority of opera performances took place in public . . . , in front of unrestricted audiences as mixed as and very much larger than those of sixteenth-century England." During this time, she adds, for the great mass of the population, festival operas, in particular, "were the most significant source of information about the believed-in historical past, the values and manners of the elite, attitudes and relationships between and among people of different status, and ideas of good . . . and evil."[26] Through much of the twentieth century, opera continued to function in this cross-class manner, often being called upon to take part in Chinese political life (as we have seen in the case of the Goujian operas of the early 1960s and the model operas during the Cultural Revolution). By the end of the century, although regular viewing of live opera had declined, the audience for televised historical dramas, which occupied an important place in television programming overall, had become immense, penetrating rural areas and embracing individuals with little or no formal education. This remarkable development, in terms of story dissemination, is nowhere better exemplified than by the fact that in 2006–7 alone, the Goujian story was the subject of no fewer than three major multi-part television productions, each featuring a star male actor in the role of Goujian.[27]

Third, the meanings of the stories, far from being frozen in time, have tended to evolve in response to changing historical situations. The story of King Goujian signified different things depending on what was going on at any given moment. "The Foolish Old Man Who Removed the Mountains" was applied to the challenges presented in the construction (during the late 1960s and early 1970s) of the Zengwenxi Reservoir in southern Taiwan,[28] whereas on the mainland, as we have seen, it was used during the Cultural Revolution to promote the elimination of the two "mountains" of feudalism and imperialism and, more recently, in Ji Chaozhu's memoir, as a metaphor for the long and difficult—but ultimately hopeful—process of improving Sino-American mutual understanding. Yue Fei, who in earlier times was admired for his loyalty to the Song dynasty, in the twentieth century was transformed into an icon of *Chinese* patriotism.[29] The strong exorcist dimension of the mass campaigns of post-1949 China, in particular the Cultural Revolution, shared the same dynamic as earlier scares, consisting of the identification of an "inner demon" now stigmatized in contemporary political class language and its violent expulsion.[30] And Adam Chau conjectures that, in northern Shaanxi during the reform era, the great popularity of the ritual for exterminating the "obstacle-demon" may reflect the highly restrictive birth control policy adopted early in the Deng Xiaoping era, "which has made each child a lot more precious than before."[31] What all of these examples suggest is that, much as in earlier periods of Chinese history, older cultural stories have endured, but rather than enduring unchanged, they have been continually modified in response to new circumstances.[32]

Finally, I want to pose a historian's question: How do we assess the importance of cultural phenomena that, although clearly continuing to enjoy widespread influence in post-1949 China, are far less available to the senses and may or may not relate in significant ways to the more readily accessible changes, such as rapid economic growth and increased military strength, that have captured everyone's attention in China's recent history? Clearly, there is a strong historical bias in favor of the importance of economic wealth and military power, but in seeking to understand a society—what makes its inhabitants tick—it may be no less vital to probe its less visible, harder-to-get-at aspects. The shared stories I have focused on supply essential data about the interior of the Chinese world. They form an undercurrent of intellectual/psychic meaning that flows beneath the surface of conventionally recounted history. But Westerners certainly—and perhaps Chinese as well—if we are to gain a deeper and fuller understanding of China, need to do a much better job of mapping these stories and illuminating how they fit into the larger picture of Chinese life.

ENDNOTES

1. Paul A. Cohen, *Speaking to History: The Story of King Goujian in Twentieth-Century China* (Berkeley: University of California Press, 2009).

2. My summary of the Wu Han/Hai Rui affair, in *Speaking to History*, pp. 169–71, is based mainly on Roderick MacFarquhar, *The Origins of the Chinese Cultural Revolution, 2: The Great Leap Forward, 1958–1960* (New York: Columbia University Press, 1983), pp. 207–212, and Tom Fisher, "'The Play's the Thing': Wu Han and Hai Rui Revisited," in Jonathan Unger, ed., *Using the Past to Serve the Present: Historiography and Politics in Contemporary China* (Armonk, NY: M. E. Sharpe, 1993), pp. 9–45. The quotation from Mao's Hangzhou speech is in Stuart Schram, ed., *Chairman Mao Talks to the People: Talks and Letters, 1956–1971* (New York: Pantheon, 1974), p. 237.

3. Jerome Bruner, *Making Stories: Law, Literature, Life* (Cambridge, MA: Harvard University Press, 2002), pp. 7, 34–35, 60.

4. Ji Chaozhu, *The Man on Mao's Right: From Harvard Yard to Tiananmen Square, My Life Inside China's Foreign Ministry* (New York: Random House, 2008), p. 333. The original

source of the Foolish Old Man fable is the Daoist text *Liezi*. In the ROC, see "Yu gong yi shan," in Guoli bianyi guan (National Institute for Compilation and Translation), comp., *Guomin xiaoxue guoyu* (National Primary School Chinese) (Taipei, 1974), 4 (lesson 23): 65–66; "Yu gong yi shan," in Guoli bianyi guan (National Institute for Compilation and Translation), comp., *Guomin zhongxue guowenke jiaokeshu* (National Middle School Chinese Textbook) (Taipei, 1974), 3 (lesson 15): 67–70. An early instance of Mao's application of the story is in his concluding speech at the Seventh National Congress of the Communist Party of China, delivered on June 11, 1945. See his "The Foolish Old Man Who Removed the Mountains," in *Selected Works of Mao Tse-tung* (Beijing: Foreign Languages Press, 1965), 3: 321–24. For later references, see "Carry Out the Cultural Revolution Thoroughly and Transform the Educational System Completely," *Peking Review*, 9, no. 26 (June 24, 1966): 15–17; Liang Heng and Judith Shapiro, *Son of the Revolution* (New York: Vintage Books, 1984), pp. 78, 175.

5. Jianying Zha, "Enemy of the State: The Complicated Life of an Idealist," *The New Yorker*, 83, no. 9 (April 23, 2007): 48–49.

6. Tamotsu Shibutani, *Improvised News: A Sociological Study of Rumor* (Indianapolis, IN: Bobbs-Merrill, 1966), as cited in S. A. Smith, "Talking Toads and Chinless Ghosts: The Politics of 'Superstitious' Rumors in the People's Republic of China, 1961–1965," *American Historical Review*, 111, no. 2 (April 2006): 408.

7. These are key themes in an important recent book by Barend J. ter Haar, *Telling Stories: Witchcraft and Scapegoating in Chinese History* (Leiden: Brill, 2006).

8. Barend J. ter Haar, "China's Inner Demons: The Political Impact of the Demonological Paradigm," in Woei Lien Chong, ed., *China's Great Proletarian Cultural Revolution: Master Narratives and Post-Mao Counternarratives* (Lanham, MD: Rowman & Littlefield, 2002), pp. 27–68; on the "profoundly demonological" character of popular religious culture, see also Smith, "Talking Toads and Chinless Ghosts," p. 416 and passim.

9. ter Haar, "China's Inner Demons," p. 29; ter Haar has a much fuller account of the Granny Tiger story in *Telling Stories*, pp. 52–78.

10. ter Haar, "China's Inner Demons," p. 32; J. J. M. de Groot, *The Religious System of China*, 6 vols. (Leiden: Brill, 1910), 6: 931–932.

11. ter Haar, "China's Inner Demons," pp. 32–33; Paul A. Cohen, *History in Three Keys: The Boxers as Event, Experience, and Myth* (New York: Columbia University Press, 1997), p. 108. On the thin and ambiguous line often separating the demonic from the counter-demonic, see Stephan Feuchtwang, *Popular Religion in China: The Imperial Metaphor* (Richmond, Surrey: Curzon, 2001), pp. 47, 55. On the story of Guan Yu, see Moss Roberts, trans., *Three Kingdoms: A Historical Novel* (Berkeley: University of California Press, 1991).

12. Cohen, *History in Three Keys*, especially chs. 2–4; also Paul A. Cohen, "Boxers, Christians, and the Gods: The Boxer Conflict of 1900 as a Religious War," in Cohen, *China Unbound: Evolving Perspectives on the Chinese Past* (London: RoutledgeCurzon, 2003), pp. 112–18.

13. Smith has also studied another instance of "superstitious rumors": the stories attending the quests for holy water that were rampant in many parts of China during the 1950s and early 1960s. There was a popular health dimension to these quests, since the ingestion of holy water was believed to have an exorcistic function vis-à-vis the demons that caused illness. In the general uncertainty that characterized the years immediately

following the advent of Communist rule, the author writes, "the stories that accompanied the discovery of holy water served to remind people that the power of the gods was still at work in the world, still a resource that could be accessed in order to deal with their tribulations." Steve A. Smith, "Local Cadres Confront the Supernatural: The Politics of Holy Water (*Shenshui*) in the PRC, 1949–1966," *The China Quarterly*, no. 188 (December 2006): 999–1022 (quotation on p. 1020).

14. Smith, "Talking Toads and Chinless Ghosts," p. 414.

15. Erik Mueggler, "Spectral Chains: Remembering the Great Leap Forward Famine in a Yi Community," in Ching Kwan Lee and Guobin Yang, eds., *Re-envisioning the Chinese Revolution: The Politics and Poetics of Collective Memories in Reform China* (Washington, DC: Woodrow Wilson Center Press and Stanford, CA: Stanford University Press, 2007), pp. 64–65.

16. Smith, "Talking Toads and Chinless Ghosts," passim (quotation on pp. 411–12).

17. The parallels drawn in Cultural Revolution propaganda between the Red Guards and the Boxers (in particular the Boxers' female counterparts, the Red Lanterns) are discussed in Cohen, *History in Three Keys*, pp. 262–70.

18. ter Haar, "China's Inner Demons," pp. 52–60 (especially pp. 56–57).

19. Donald S. Sutton, "Consuming Counterrevolution: The Ritual and Culture of Cannibalism in Wuxuan, Guangxi, China, May to July 1968," *Comparative Studies in Society and History*, 37, no. 1 (January 1995): 144.

20. For an informative discussion of the early origins of *niugui sheshen* and its subsequent usage during the Mao years, see Xing Lu, *Rhetoric of the Chinese Cultural Revolution: The Impact on Chinese Thought, Culture, and Communication* (Columbia: University of South Carolina Press, 2004), p. 59.

21. Sutton, "Consuming Counterrevolution," pp. 144–45; "In the unseen world," A. R. Zito writes, "the City God occupied the same place held by the chief official of the city in this world." See her "City Gods, Filiality, and Hegemony in Late Imperial China," *Modern China*, 13, no. 3 (July 1987): 334.

22. ter Haar, "China's Inner Demons," p. 58.

23. Robert Weller, "Religious Growth and Regulation: Reconfiguring State and Society in China," paper presented at "The People's Republic at 60: An International Assessment, Fairbank Center, Harvard University, May 1–3, 2009. Numerous examples of the astonishing revival of popular religion in the post-Mao era have been studied. Adam Chau's work on northern Shaanxi is touched on in the text. For rural China in general, with a particular focus on the township of Longchuan in Sichuan, see Ole Bruun, "The *Fengshui* Resurgence in China: Conflicting Cosmologies Between State and Peasantry," *The China Journal*, no. 36 (July 1996): 47–65, especially p. 50. For southern Fujian, see Tan Chee-Beng, "Chinese Religious Expressions in Post-Mao Yongchun, Fujian," in Tan Chee-Beng, ed., *Southern Fujian: Reproduction of Traditions in Post-Mao China* (Hong Kong: The Chinese University of Hong Kong Press, 2006), pp. 98–99 and passim, and Kuah-Pearce Khun Eng, "The Worship of Qingshui Zushi and Religious Revivalism in South China," in ibid., pp. 121–44.

24. Adam Yuet Chau, "Popular Religion in Shaanbei, North-Central China," *Journal of Chinese Religions*, no. 31 (2003): 59–60.

25. Fang Jing Pei and Juwen Zhang, *The Interpretation of Dreams in Chinese Culture* (Trumbull, CT: Weatherhill, 2000).

26. Barbara E. Ward, "Regional Operas and Their Audiences: Evidence from Hong Kong," in David Johnson, Andrew J. Nathan, and Evelyn S. Rawski, eds., *Popular Culture in Late Imperial China* (Berkeley: University of California Press, 1985), pp. 172, 186–87.

27. Cohen, *Speaking to History*, p. 221.

28. "Zengwenxi shuiku" (The Zengwenxi Reservoir), in *Guomin xiaoxue guoyu*, 12 (lesson 6): 17–19.

29. Cohen, *Speaking to History*, pp. 40–42; Sun Jiang and Huang Donglan, "Yue Fei xushu, gonggong jiyi yu guozu rentong" (Narratives of Yue Fei, Public Memory, and National Identity), *Ershiyi shiji*, no. 86 (December 2004): 88–100.

30. ter Haar, *Telling Stories*, p. 347.

31. Chau, "Popular Religion in Shaanbei, North-Central China," p. 60.

32. Essentially the same point is made with respect to southern Fujian by Tan Chee-Beng: "Traditions are reproduced according to changing circumstances rather than transmitted in an unchanged manner." "Chinese Religious Expressions in Post-Mao Yongchun, Fujian," p. 114. Helen Siu, in an early reform-era study of the social meaning of funeral and wedding rituals in Guangdong, notes that the younger generations were often ignorant of the stories underlying the rituals; although her conclusion—that "the resurgence of these rituals in their transformed state represents cultural fragments recycled under new circumstances"—sounds similar to Tan's, she places much greater emphasis on the new-ness—the discontinuity—of these "reconstitutions of tradition." See her "Recycling Rituals: Politics and Popular Culture in Contemporary Rural China," in Perry Link, Richard Madsen, and Paul G. Pickowicz, eds., *Unofficial China: Popular Culture and Thought in the People's Republic* (Boulder, CO: Westview Press, 1989), pp. 121–137 (quotations on p. 134).

26.

NATIONAL MINDS AND IMPERIAL FRONTIERS:
INNER ASIA AND CHINA IN THE NEW CENTURY

MARK C. ELLIOTT

It was in mid-spring 2008 that the stories first began to circulate about the so-called "Fuwa Curse," or *Fuwa zainan lun* (福娃灾难论). The Fuwa (福娃), it will be remembered, were the five cute "good fortune doll" mascots, at one point nicknamed in English "Friendlies," devised to help promote the Beijing Olympics. First introduced in 2005, four of the Fuwa were drawn as animals, the fifth being a flame. Each was associated with a color, one of the Olympic rings, and an element of nature. Beibei (贝贝), the sturgeon, was blue and stood for water; Jingjing (晶晶), the panda, was black and represented the forest, or wood; Huanhuan (欢欢), the red flame, corresponded to the Olympic torch, i.e., fire; Yingying (迎迎), the antelope, was yellow, symbolizing earth; and Nini (妮妮), the swallow, was green and stood for the sky. Read together, their names (贝-晶-欢-迎-妮) spelled out the happy, homophonic phrase *Beijing huanying ni* (北京欢迎你): "Beijing welcomes you."[1]

As 2008 unfolded, however, the Five Friendlies of the Olympics became the Five Dolls of the Apocalypse. After the devastating May earthquake in Sichuan, bloggers in China decided that the Fuwa were responsible for the disasters that had come in succession in the first half of the year: freak snowstorms in the south during the New Year that left millions stranded were said to have set the stage for disaster, beginning as they did on January 25—the notion being that the digits for the date (1/25) added up to eight, as did the digits of the date of the Sichuan quake (5/12)—thereby perversely portending a year of bad luck rather than the good luck supposedly brought by the number 8. The March riots that erupted in Tibet and in Tibetan areas of Gansu, Sichuan, and Qinghai were retrospectively linked to Yingying, the prancing yellow Fuwa with little horns who represented the endangered Tibetan antelope (*Zang lingyang* 藏羚羊). For a terrible train collision that took place in Shandong on April 28, Nini, the green swallow, took the fall. The kite depicted with Nini provided a connection to the town of Weifang (潍坊), located very close to the site of the accident, which is famous as a center of kite culture in China and the home of a major international kite festival.[2] Huanhuan was easily associated with the stormy progress of the Olympic flame as it made its way around the world in late March and April, greeted at every stop by protests over the government's handling of the Tibet problem. The earthquake itself, which occurred on May 12 with its epicenter at Wenchuan, was tied, naturally enough, to Jingjing the panda, since pandas make their home in Sichuan. With four of the five elements accounted for, bloggers in May predicted that a water-related disaster was sure to follow. As if on cue, in the second week of June torrential rains caused massive floods across much of the southern half of the country. The Fuwa Curse was complete.[3]

The official line was strongly to discredit the "Fuwa Curse," which the government dismissed as superstition, and to explain that there were rational, scientific explanations for each disaster. But for many people, such a series of misfortunes in what was supposed to be China's year of glory was too much of a coincidence. For them, some more proximate agent had to be found, and the "Friendlies" furnished a handy and persuasive framework for making sense of all the bad luck. Some said that the creators of the Fuwa (led by Beijing artist Han Meilin 韩美林) had wantonly reassigned geomantic values to the different mascots, and this had resulted in imbalances generating unrest and instability in the earth, land, water, and sky, and, as in Tibet, among the people themselves. As one Netizen wrote, "Inadvertently, or by fate, the five Fuwa have been designed to be ill omens that contravene Yin and Yang, the Five Elements, and the Eight Trigrams."[4] In other words, the crises visited upon the country were the direct consequence of a failure by the country's leaders to properly regulate the national order.

Arguably, it was the harmony of that order, and not the Olympic spirit of "Stronger, Faster, Higher," that lay at the core of what the Fuwa were really meant to represent, before they were overtaken by events. For the purposes of this chapter, the most important of these events were the violent riots in March 2008, in which it is estimated that scores of Tibetans and Han Chinese lost their lives and countless more suffered serious injuries and arrest. These led, as already mentioned, to large-scale protests and demonstrations that ended up clouding the triumphant tour of the Olympic flame around the world. The unrest quickly invested Yingying, the antelope, with a very different kind of significance, turning him from an icon of health and environmental concern into a grotesque symbol of heavy-handed rule and failed policies, making a mockery of the originally intended message.

China's leaders may well have regretted politicizing the Fuwa as they did, especially with respect to Tibet, but they could hardly blame the connection between Yingying and the western frontier on the overactive imaginations of Chinese bloggers. In fact, it was there explicitly on the official Beijing Olympics Web site:

> Yingying is a Tibetan antelope, alert, frisky, and fleet of foot. From China's vast Western lands he comes to spread wishes for health and beauty to the world. As a Tibetan antelope, a protected species unique to the Qinghai-Tibetan plateau, Yingying is the manifestation of a Green Olympics. The designs on his head incorporate the decorative style of the western regions of the Tibetan plateau and Xinjiang. Nimble and agile as a track star, he represents the yellow ring in the five Olympic rings.
>
> 迎迎是一只机敏灵活、驰骋如飞的藏羚羊，他来自中国辽阔的西部大地，将健康美好的祝福传向世界。迎迎是青藏高原特有的保护动物藏羚羊，是绿色奥运的展现。迎迎的头部纹饰融入了青藏高原和新疆等西部地区的装饰风格。他身手敏捷，是田径好手，他也代表奥林匹克五环中黄色的一环。[5]

Yingying's role, then, as avatar for Tibet and Xinjiang, was planned from the beginning. The authorities meant to use him as a reminder of the inseparability of these places from the rest of China and of the importance of these frontier regions to the nation. To further underscore this point, the Olympic Organizing Committee made sure that the Olympic flame passed through the western parts of the country, including not only cities such as Lhasa, Urumqi, and Kashgar, but also the top of Mt. Everest (in Tibetan, Chomolungma).

The scale of the protests in March 2008 surprised many people, but the grievances that gave rise to them were familiar enough, given the prominence around the world that the controversies surrounding Chinese rule in Tibet have gained in the last several decades. Further unrest in Xinjiang, another part of Yingying's domain, erupted during the Olympics themselves, when an attack on a police station in Kashgar in August 2008 resulted in the death of several policemen. The details of this event still remain unclear (two men were convicted and executed for the crime in May 2009), but the incident nonetheless did much to raise awareness of the plight of the Uyghur people, who, like the Tibetans, find themselves the objects of discrimination by ordinary Han Chinese and find their culture coming under ever-greater pressure from the Han-dominated party-state. The violent uprising that took place in Urumqi in July 2009, resulting in at least 200 deaths and thousands of arrests, further underscored the explosive tensions that simmer just below the surface of the state's ideal of ethnic harmony.

Although, as with Yingying, the PRC government typically chooses to present an optimistic picture to domestic and foreign audiences willing to listen, the widely held perception—namely, that central rule in the western third of the country is problematic—is in fact shared by knowledgeable officials and scholars in the PRC. Recent evidence suggests that at least some Chinese policy makers are coming to acknowledge that the challenges faced by Beijing's authority on the western frontier are not, as the usual formula has had it, simply the result of external actors "meddling in China's domestic affairs" or of a "small group of splittists" raising trouble. They concede, if obliquely, that the difficulties inherent in governing regions where the population is so far removed from the center, culturally as well as geographically, are not unique to the Chinese situation and bear similarities to challenges encountered by other states elsewhere.[6]

To the extent that the deterioration in Han-Tibetan and Han-Uighur relations is seen as the manifestation in China of a marked increase in ethnic tensions around the world since 1989, this would appear to be yet another aspect of post-Cold War globalization, a darker counterpoint to the mostly positive messages surrounding China's new economic power and increasing technological sophistication. Certainly it is true that the problems the PRC government faces in its Inner Asian border areas are made more complicated by the changes in the last several decades, not least the Internet, and one would not wish to deny the existence of shared elements between ethnic problems in Xinjiang and ethnic problems in other parts of the world, including the United States. But these relationships and problems are of far greater vintage than 1989, or even 1949, and carry another dimension that is in fact particular to the Chinese case.

A longer perspective suggests that the challenges faced by the Chinese government in Tibet and Xinjiang are not really so new. Managing the Inner Asian frontier was a major preoccupation of every imperial state since the Qin unification in the third century BCE and even before, during the Warring States period. The biggest headaches, from the point of view of the Chinese, were always to the north and west, and the inability of Chinese rulers to meet rising powers on the steppe resulted in the downfall of more than one dynasty. The last such case was of course the Ming, which fell to the Manchu-led armies of the rival Qing state in 1644. The Qing, itself of northern origin, brought this pattern to an end, with the Manchus' 1755–59 conquest of western Mongolia and eastern Turkestan that eliminated the age-old threat from the north, at least until the Japanese invasions of the 1930s. Manchu rulers, such as Kangxi, Yongzheng, and Qianlong, managed to restore the "grand unity" (*da yitong* 大一统) of the empire in their successful pursuit of expansion and conquest, bringing not only Manchuria and China proper, but also Mongolia, Xinjiang, Taiwan, and Tibet within the borders of their realm.

From a historian's point of view, however, the assumption that the realm created by the Qing would necessarily survive the dynasty's fall is false. In 1912 there was no knowing which parts of the Manchu empire the emerging Chinese state would inherit. After all, China has been through many periods of disunity, some a few decades in duration and some a few centuries, and has been reconstituted in many guises, each time shaped by the particular historical context. Indeed, a fundamental challenge confronted by various modern leaders, from Sun Yat-sen and Chiang Kai-shek to Mao Zedong and Hu Jintao, has been to transform the Qing empire into a Chinese nation-state, to consolidate central control, and to make it all look "natural."[7] Here the historic achievement of the PRC has been the restoration of the old imperial borders (with the notable exception of Mongolia), which was accomplished in part through military force and in part through political control and the promise of economic and social reform. Although at first glance it would seem that the PRC has succeeded where preceding governments had failed—indeed, as shown below, there are many points of commonality between the Qing and Communist systems of rule for Inner Asia—the lingering problems surrounding the integration of the territories and peoples of Inner Asia encourage us to take a closer look.

It has often been noted that the foundations of the modern Chinese state were laid down during the years of Manchu rule.[8] With respect to the government of Inner Asia, it is not hard to discover a number of similarities between the Qing regime and the PRC order. Qing policy toward the Inner Asian frontier was a patchwork of special arrangements that reflected the particular conditions under which each region was brought into the empire. In southern Manchuria, the civil administration put in place to govern Han subjects was overlaid by a military administration headed by garrison commanders who oversaw all aspects of government; until late in the Qing, there were no Chinese officials there. The military governor, always a Manchu bannerman, also supervised the management of tribute relations with tribal peoples living in the far north. In Mongolia, too, there was a bannerman appointed at Urga, but his role was limited; the Qing court gave Mongolian nobles a wide berth in exchange for their loyalty, and these jasag-princes exercised considerable economic and judicial power. Dzungaria, after the conquest of 1758, also became a zone of military administration, with extensive garrisons of the Eight Banners and a limited number of civil officials; the oases of Kashgaria were governed through local headmen, whose activities were monitored by light garrison forces stationed at a few major cities. As for Tibet, a number of different arrangements were tried at various points, but after 1750 Manchu rule there was represented by two banner officials and a small garrison of troops from Sichuan; in the main, Qing suzerainty depended on the special relationship between the emperor and the Dalai Lama. As a rule, Qing officials never intervened in local administration.

What we find, then, is a crazy-quilt of ad-hoc compromises that proved over time to be effective. The diversity of this system, the lack of consistency across regions, and the fact that it differed so utterly from the administrative system used in the interior provinces, seems not to have bothered anyone very much until the very last years of the dynasty. Instead, the Qing put an emphasis on adapting to local conditions, on taking advantage of existing local systems of authority and ruling through them, and on keeping its ambitions modest (e.g., the queue was never imposed in Xinjiang or Tibet). It also tried to limit Han migration to Inner Asia.

What do we see in Chinese Inner Asia today? For one thing, it is constituted differently: Manchuria is smaller and completely integrated with the rest of China, much of Qing-era Mongolia is gone, part of an independent Mongolian state, and Xinjiang is a little smaller than it was under the Manchus. On the surface, there is far more regularity and comparability across the administrative horizon than there was during the Qing, and unquestionably there is a far greater presence of the center even in remote regions. Yet we can also see that, like the Qing, the PRC has gone to great lengths to accommodate the special needs of the frontier in its administrative structures and to an extent in its permissiveness toward the variety of local cultural, legal, and economic life. Thus we find that, as in the Qing period, Tibet, Mongolia, Ningxia, and Xinjiang, along with significant portions of Qinghai, Gansu, and Sichuan, are all assigned a special place in the make-up of the state—as autonomous regions, counties, or prefectures. (In fact, in the PRC, 64 percent of the national territory is classified as part of a non-Han autonomous administration.) Officials of the state and party, who are overwhelmingly Han, have long recognized the need to work with, or act through, members of local ethnic groups and to cooperate with religious figures.[9] The PRC has even claimed the same right as the Qing to approve the choice of major Buddhist incarnations —a bizarre and awkward role for the government to play when it is led by an officially atheist organization. So we see some of the same characteristics that appeared in the Qing: high adaptability and recognition of the importance of local sources of authority.

For all these similarities, the Qing empire, based as it was as much on an Inner Asian as on a Chinese political model, provided an imperfect—not to say highly problematic—foundation for twentieth-century Chinese political leaders to build upon.[10] This has resulted in numerous ironies and contradictions in the constitution of the state, such as the persistent involvement of the party in the spiritual affairs of the Gelugpa Buddhist hierarchy, which are like uncooked lumps in the baking of the Chinese "nation-cake."[11] On the one hand, the exigencies of a new nationalism at the turn of the twentieth century prompted the declaration of a belief in the separate fate of the Han people, constructed as distinct from the Manchus, and in their right to govern themselves and their own lands. On the other hand, geopolitical realities hindered most (but not all) nationalists from pursuing this proclamation through to its logical conclusion: a declaration of independence of Han territories from the lands of the non-Han. This, of course, would have meant the loss of over half of the territory that had belonged to the Qing and to which the new republic wished to lay claim, a cost most viewed as unacceptable. Thus, the predicament of Han revolutionary intellectuals was that they were the spiritual heirs of the nativist Ming but the political heirs of the cosmopolitan Qing. No wonder the effort to rebuild the Chinese republic on the imperial model was not very successful at first and that by the 1930s the Nationalist Government exercised no meaningful control over Manchuria, Mongolia, Xinjiang, Taiwan, or Tibet.

To escape this predicament, countless thinkers, polemicists, politicians, and scholars set about to redefine who the "Chinese" were. Some (such as Zhang Binglin) argued that this group was limited to the Han and that the non-Han should be cut off from a new Chinese state; others insisted that China should not be narrowly limited to the Han, but should encompass all of the former subjects of the Qing, up to and including the late-reviled Manchus. The consensus that eventually emerged across the political spectrum leaned toward the latter solution: for practical purposes, "the Chinese"—to be known as *Zhonghua minzu* 中华民族—were de facto all the people within the borders claimed by the central government, which by and large coincided with the extent of the Qing territory.[12] Elaborate justifications of this decision were produced to assert its "scientific" accuracy, and hence its legitimacy and the legitimacy of the state itself, none more famous than that later provided by the anthropologist Fei Xiaotong (费孝通).[13]

With this stumbling block removed, and serious military and political rivals vanquished after the victory of the CCP in 1949, it was possible in short order for the party to take in hand the chaotic situation on China's Inner Asian frontiers. Needless to say, there was no plebiscite held as to whether those living in the frontier territories dominated by non-Han groups were interested in joining the new Chinese republic; the decision was imposed, backed up ultimately by force or threat of force. And so, with the exception of Mongolia and Taiwan, these frontier lands, together with the provinces of China proper (in Chinese, *neidi* 内地), became what we today call, usually without reflecting on it very much, "China."

Yet it is difficult—difficult for a historian, at least—to accept that this some-how represents the East Asian equivalent of a Fukuyama-like "end of history."

However successful the effort has been to naturalize the present "geo-body" of the Chinese state, and however persuasive may be its claim to sovereignty over the former Qing territories (in most cases, the principle of *uti posseditis*, widely recognized in international law, would seem to apply), today's leaders in Beijing must be aware that history is not on their side. They are doubtless familiar with the Republican government's limited success at converting the Qing empire into a Chinese nation, and they must know that no state of the same geographic scale as the present-day People's Republic ever managed to last very long under Chinese-led (that is, Han-led) rule.[14] PRC leaders must also bear in mind the ultimate failure of the USSR in turning the multi-ethnic Russian empire into a viable multi-ethnic state.[15] For all these reasons, the evident fragility of the party's hold on the loyalties of the majority of Tibetans and Uyghurs (and of many Mongols as well) is of particular concern to Beijing.

Given the stakes involved, it is worth asking whether, in spite of the absence of the age-old nomadic military threat, two thousand years of history have ceased to matter when it comes to the relationship between sedentary China and its continental frontier. Of course, the Chinese state today is much more centralized than it was under the Qing, but the expectations held of the state are quite different as well. The PRC represents a very different kind of political formation: in principle, it is a nation-state—a "unified polyethnic nation-state" (*tongyi de duominzu guojia* 统一的多民族国家), to be precise—and not an empire. Empires are fine with being uneven, asymmetrical, and hierarchical, but nation-states are supposed to be regular, symmetrical, and smooth. Additionally, the demands on the modern state to tell a consistent story are far greater than they were on the pre-modern state. If there was slippage between different conceptions of "China" and "the Chinese" in Qing-style grand unity, no one was much bothered by it. But because modernity presupposes precision, transparency, and finite boundaries, twentieth-century states have found much less room to maneuver between ideologies of sovereignty and twenty-first-century states have even less. As a consequence, the notion of unity in China today is understood much more literally than it was during the Qing.

On top of this, with the abandonment of orthodox Communist ideology and the implementation of economic reform after 1989, there is the fact that neither the Chinese government nor the party can appeal to Marxism-Leninism-Mao Zedong Thought for a set of valid and universal claims that offer political legitimacy. In place of communism, the state and party alike have had to look elsewhere, particularly to a chauvinist brand of nationalism, to shore up their position. Nationalism was always an important ideological tool of the CCP, to be sure, but for the last twenty years it has been asked to do even more work than before. All the more difficult, then, for the party to tolerate threats to national unity, whether from inside or outside, real or imagined: any perceived injury may potentially threaten the general political stability of the regime.

It is for this reason, I would argue, that PRC sovereignty over its Inner Asian frontier has become ever more essential to the continued legitimacy of the party. The Qing did not need to be quite so obsessed with this idea; it had Heaven on its side and Confucian virtue, not to mention Manjusri and the mandate of the Mongol khans. The PRC does not have this luxury, and symbols such as Yingying the antelope are clearly not up to the task. How the PRC will solve the chronic problems facing Chinese rule in Inner Asia is one of the major unresolved questions for the next sixty years.

ENDNOTES

1. This explanation of the significance of the Fuwa is taken from the Chinese-language Web site of the Beijing Olympic Committee, at http://www.beijing2008.cn/spirit/symbols/mascots/n214067075.shtml (accessed August 19, 2009). The English-language site offers the following explanation: "Designed to express the playful qualities of five little children who form an intimate circle of friends, Fuwa also embody the natural characteristics of four of China's most popular animals—the Fish, the Panda, the Tibetan Antelope, the Swallow—and the Olympic Flame." See http://en.beijing2008.cn/spirit/beijing2008/graphic/n214068254.shtml (accessed August 19, 2009). Earlier descriptions in English refer to the Fuwa as "Friendlies." See, for instance, http://www.chinese-tools.com/beijing2008/fuwa.html (accessed December 22, 2009).

2. See the organizers' Web site, at http://www.weifangkite.com/index.asp (accessed December 22, 2009).

3. Reports of the "Fuwa Curse" may be found at http://news.sohu.com/20080605/n257287297.shtml, http://hi.baidu.com/st1678/blog/item/f65b08a4e099b7f29052eeb6.html, and http://www.kanzhongguo.com/news/247310.html (all accessed December 22, 2009). Some sources refer to a story in the June 17, 2008, edition of the *Wall Street Journal*, but no such story appeared until July 23. Rumors spread quickly via Internet chat-rooms and blogs (e.g., http://q.sohu.com/forum/7/topic/2433643, http://t-tfamily.super-forum.net/forum-f46/topic-t667.htm, and http://0668.cc/blog/hello/index.php?cmd = showentry &eid = 2115 (all accessed December 22, 2009), though many sites were scrubbed in June 2008 to remove any references.

4. "这样一来五个"福娃"就被无意（或天意）中设计成了一个反阴阳五行八卦的凶煞大阵," May 30, 2008, at http://secretchina.com/news/247310.html (accessed December 22, 2009).

5. I have translated from the Chinese-language page of the Beijing Olympics Web site, found at http://www.beijing2008.cn/spirit/symbols/mascots/n214067075.shtml (accessed January 26, 2010). The official English page, available at http://en.beijing2008.cn/spirit/

beijing2008/graphic/n214068254.shtml (accessed January 26, 2010), reads as follows: "Like all antelopes, Yingying is fast and agile and can swiftly cover great stretches of land as he races across the earth. A symbol of the vastness of China's landscape, the antelope carries the blessing of health, the strength of body that comes from harmony with nature. Yingying's flying pose captures the essence of a species unique to the Qinghai-Tibet Plateau, one of the first animals put under protection in China. The selection of the Tibetan Antelope reflects Beijing's commitment to a Green Olympics. His head ornament incorporates several decorative styles from the Qinghai-Tibet and Sinkiang cultures and the ethnic design traditions of Western China. Strong in track and field events, Yingying is a quick-witted and agile boy who represents the yellow Olympic ring."

6. This is the thrust of a recent news release by Xinhua, extensively quoting the American anthropologist Dru Gladney's comments relativizing the situations in Tibet and Xinjiang: "'Everybody recognizes that the problem is shared by the whole world,' such as the 2005 riots in France and Basque separatism in Spain, said Gladney. 'Language, religion played a role while the Internet and global communications make it (the ethnic problem) more complicated,' he noted. 'All modern nations in the era of globalization face tremendous challenges from migration, economic imbalance, and ethnic unrest,' said the scholar" (Yang Qingchuan, "Separatism Bad for China, the World: US Scholar," Xinhua News Agency, August 12, 2009), at http://callcenterinfo.tmcnet.com/news/2009/08/12/4319454.htm (accessed January 26, 2010). At question here is not Gladney's actual position, but that the Chinese mainstream media have found it expedient to place China's ethnic problems on a comparable footing with ethnic problems in other parts of the world, as well as its tacit admission that such problems do in fact exist.

7. The idea common to much nationalistic thinking, that nations are somehow endowed with natural features (populations, territories, boundaries, etc.), is analyzed in much of the literature on nationalism; a good starting point is Benedict Anderson, *Imagined Communities: Reflections on the Origin and Spread of Nationalism*, rev. ed. (New York: Verso, 1991). A useful exploration of this notion with respect to modern China may be found in Uradyn Bulag, "Naturalizing National Unity: Political Romance and the Chinese Nation," in Bulag, *The Mongols at China's Edge: History and the Politics of National Unity* (Lanham, MD: Rowman & Littlefield, 2002), ch. 3. See also the discussion in James Leibold, *Reconfiguring Chinese Nationalism: How the Qing Frontier and Its Indigenes Became Chinese* (New York: Palgrave/Macmillan, 2007).

8. The classic statement of this point is perhaps Ping-ti Ho, "The Significance of the Ch'ing Period in Chinese History," *Journal of Asian Studies*, 26, no. 2 (February 1967): 189–95. For an expanded, alternative interpretation, see also Evelyn Rawski, "Reenvisioning the Qing: The Significance of the Qing Period in Chinese History," *Journal of Asian Studies*, 55, no. 4 (November 1996): 829–50. Another recent evaluation is Joseph Esherick, "How the Qing Became China," in Joseph W. Esherick, Hasan Kayali, and Eric Van Young, eds., *Empire to Nation: Historical Perspectives on the Making of the Modern World* (Lanham, MD: Rowman & Littlefield, 2006), pp. 229–59.

9. The story of the party's long and troublesome relationship with the non-Han, especially in Mongolia, and the many awkward ideological and political accommodations it engendered, is well told in Xiaoyuan Liu, *Frontier Passages: Ethnopolitics and the Rise of Chinese Communism, 1921–1945* (Washington, DC: Woodrow Wilson Center Press and Stanford, CA: Stanford University Press, 2004).

10. See the essay by the present author, "La Chine moderne: Les mandchous et la défi-nition de la nation," *Annales: Histoire, Sciences Sociales*, 61, no. 6 (November–December 2006): 1447–77.

11. I borrow this metaphor from James Leibold, "Whose Peoples' Games?" December 3, 2008, at http://www.thechinabeat.org/?p = 299 (accessed August 26, 2009).

12. Different aspects of this process of redefinition are discussed extensively in Prasenjit Duara, *Rescuing History from the Nation: Questioning Narratives of Modern China* (Chicago: University of Chicago Press, 1995), John Fitzgerald, *Awakening China: Politics, Culture, and Class in the Nationalist Revolution* (Stanford, CA: Stanford University Press, 1996), and Leibold, *Reconfiguring Chinese Nationalism*; see also Thomas Mullaney, *Coming to Terms with the Nation* (Berkeley: University of California Press, 2010).

13. Fei Xiaotong, *Zhonghua minzu duoyuan de yiti geju* (中华民族多元一体格局) (The Pattern of Diversity in Unity of the Chinese Nation) (Beijing: Zhongyang minzu xueyuan chubanshe, 1989).

14. Though of lasting historical significance, direct Han and Tang rule over parts of Inner/Central Asia each lasted only about a century. The Ming exercised no effective control over Mongolia, Tibet, or the area of modern Xinjiang.

15. See David Shambaugh, "The Chinese Discourse on Communist Party-States," in Shambaugh, *China's Communist Party: Atrophy and Adaptation* (Washington, DC: Woodrow Wilson Center Press and Berkeley: University of California Press, 2008), pp. 41–86.

CONCLUDING COMMENTS

SUSANNE WEIGELIN-SCHWIEDRZIK

At the beginning of this conference, the question was asked whether or not the PRC at sixty had reached the stage of being at ease. I would answer this question in the following manner: The PRC at sixty might not be at ease with itself, but it is at ease with China. What might sound good to everybody outside of China, is, as a matter of fact, no good news for the PRC and the CCP. I will try to illustrate why this is so.

Let us first take a quick look at the structure of the Chinese economy. During this conference we spent quite some time discussing the implications of the mixed economy that has been developing in China since the decision of the CCP Central Committee on reform and opening in 1978. What looks like an important step forward in the right direction is to some extent an important step backward in the right direction. As we know, the idea that a mixed economy was the best answer to China's problems was first articulated by Sun Yat-sen, later translated into a development strategy by Guomindang technocrats in the late 1920s, and finally translated into Marxist vocabulary and put into practice under the name of new democracy by Mao Zedong and the CCP during the 1940s and 1950s. Additionally, many elements of the reform and opening policy of the CCP were first tried out in Taiwan, even if politicians and academics from the mainland usually refuse to admit this.

I know, of course, that there is a substantial difference between articulating an idea and implementing it, and in this respect the CCP and the government in Beijing have indeed shown quite some dynamism during the last thirty years. However, if I say that the PRC at sixty is at ease with China, I am implying that we have been watching the CCP moving from its claim to find new solutions for China which differ from what the Guomindang suggested to policies that remind us a lot of the Republican era.

If we look at the political side of the question, we will come to a similar conclusion. William Kirby writes in his preface to *The Realm of Freedom in China* that the idea of the party-state that the CCP is still upholding is an idea that was generated after the Revolution of 1911 and implemented by both the Guomindang and the CCP. Since that time, no remarkable progress has been made in inventing a political system for China which would be able both to preserve the unity of the country and reflect not only the regional but also the social diversity of a modernizing society. Much in contrast to what the rhetoric of the new China suggests, the Communist takeover in 1949 did not install a new political system but rather the Communists inherited their political system from the Guomindang and staffed it mostly with new people.

The one-party dictatorship so many people around the world regard as lacking sustainability has shown an astonishing persistence in China: not only over the years but despite war, turmoil, and revolution. This, too, is what I mean when I say the PRC at sixty is at ease with China. And if we look at the way the CCP leadership is designing the future of the country by consciously drawing on Chinese tradition, there is even more reason to believe that the CCP regime is normalizing itself by integrating the revolution into the continuity of history. Elizabeth Perry's analysis of the Chinese polity in terms of the Mandate of Heaven and popular support in the form of *minben* also follows this direction. This implies that one myth which, if I remember correctly, was not mentioned at the beginning of this conference, the myth that the Communist Party of China would create a new China different from whatever had existed before, can no longer be upheld.

Simultaneously, the idea that whatever we do not like in China is Communist also can no longer be upheld. Even if this is politically incorrect, the logic of my argument implies that much of what we are observing in China today is less Communist than Chinese! Roderick MacFarquhar spoke about the claim for particularity as a result of traumatization. I strongly agree with him that the claim of the Chinese intellectual elite for particularity was a reaction—learned from the Japanese—to China's loss of its position as the center of the world, or *tianxia*. Up until today, the Communist Party claims that China's modernization has Chinese characteristics, that China's market economy has Chinese characteristics, and that Chinese socialism is a Chinese form of socialism. This claim for particularity allows China to define the terms under which it is compared to other countries of the world. However, the argument has also been often used to disengage from the world, to isolate China from the world, and to deny access to the world. Traumatization as the basis of particularism has more to it than just the idea that we are different from others, an idea, by the way, that most people regard as the basis for their respective identities.

Being at ease with China provides the Chinese ruling elite with a special form of legitimacy that helps us understand why China thus far has not fallen into pieces and why resistance against one-party rule seems to be quite weak. However, being at ease with China is not everything the CCP needs to achieve so as to be less nervous than it has been lately about its legitimacy. The founding myths William Kirby talked about in his opening remarks include more than preserving the particularity of China. They also include the idea that China no matter how poor it might be in material terms can prove its moral superiority to the West. The idea that moral superiority can outweigh material inferiority is actually one of the reasons why the very slow pace of poverty reduction during the Maoist period was accepted by many people in China. Even today, some people in China believe that earthquakes and bad weather are signs of heaven punishing people for being unable to control their desires. But moral superiority in terms of what the CCP thinks goes beyond these traditional ideas. It can only be proven by establishing a society based on the idea of equity and equality. As we heard from Shen Zhihua, the CCP took its legitimacy for granted when it took over power in 1949 because it had fought a protracted armed struggle against the Guomindang and had turned out to be the obvious winner on the battlefield. However, the CCP also knew and still knows that people expect the party to take care of their livelihoods in a way in which everyone is able to participate and profit from the growing collective wealth. Interestingly enough, the CCP has never been able to live up to its promises and people's expectations with regard to this aspect of its founding myth. This is most clearly shown by looking at the persistent urban-rural divide and all its consequences. The peasants who supposedly helped the party come to power were the first to fall victim to the CCP's inability and unwillingness to establish the kind of egalitarian society that they had been promised. With the takeover of the cities, the CCP realistically saw the need to win over the urban population and bestow the cities with a myriad of privileges. To achieve this goal, it sent many unemployed or otherwise difficult to handle people to the countryside—albeit not as radically as during the Pol Pot years later in Cambodia—and thus made life for peasants difficult because in most parts of China they did not have enough land. Collectivization, which began soon thereafter, was not only a means to make agriculture more efficient, it was also, and maybe even primarily, a means to force the peasants into a regime which eventually would compel them to feed the people in the cities before feeding themselves. The unfortunate outcome of this policy was, as we all know, the great famine with at least 30 million deaths.

The fact that the revolutionary youth were sent to the countryside to learn from the peasants is nothing but a bad joke. When I managed to be sent to the countryside by Peking University in 1976 I felt for the first time in my life something that I am still doing research on today: the enormous distance between the countryside and the state, a distance that takes many shapes and that we regarded as impossible in Maoist times: Only 35 km away from Beijing, the peasants did not speak in the language of the *Renmin ribao*. They simply refused to participate in the party discourse and showed us their lack of interest in everything the party wanted them to be interested in. As we know today, their revolutionary enthusiasm, if it ever existed, had vanished already during the days of the Great Leap Forward and the great famine. Today, many Chinese intellectuals as well as the party leadership know that the party has betrayed the peasants. The CCP openly admitted in its Document No. 1 of 2004 that the peasants had been exploited, and offered as an excuse for their betrayal that the urban-rural divide was necessary to provide momentum for industrialization. However, not everyone sees the peasants as victims. Some, including historians such as Gao Wangling and Jiang Yihua as well as the writer Mo Yan, see the peasants as the only force capable of resisting the Communist Party. Once the peasants realized that confidence in the party was to their detriment, they started resisting the terms of the contract that the party had tried to impose on them. The risk of encountering bad weather seemed less dangerous to them than being forced to accept the system of the People's Communes, public dining halls, and other forms of so-called communism in the countryside. In the course of this resistance they gradually regained the kind of autonomy that traditionally had always shaped their way of life. Document No. 1 of 2004 states that it is now time for the cities to support the countryside and for the industrialized sector to support agriculture. This shows that the party leadership is more fearful of the many uprisings in the countryside than most of us would believe.

Despite the fact that, at least to some analysts, the peasants are conscious of their being betrayed, they have not attempted to overthrow the Communist regime. As a matter of fact, during Maoist rule, they were the only segment of society that was not tied into the regime; rather, they were left outside of it. This outside position makes it possible for the state and the party to continue exploiting rural resources for the purpose of power consolidation and industrialization. However, this outside position also explains why the peasants can resist and to a certain degree change the terms of their contract with the state. But, realistically speaking, whatever the peasants did, it never affected the whole of the political system. Because of this, the party knows that there will be no problems caused by introducing local elections to the countryside.

During the Maoist era the urbanites were all in a more or less privileged position and therefore part and parcel of the new regime. But since 1978 the state has retreated from controlling and subsidizing every aspect of Chinese urban life. The growing diversification of the urban population is a new source of possible destabilization, especially as we see that the more educated urban population uses the

CCP's claim of guaranteeing social justice to criticize the obvious lack of equity and equality. The PRC regime is unlike any other suppressive regime. It is not only an authoritarian regime, but it is also a revolutionary regime. It is a regime with a revolutionary history and an ideology that can be used against the regime as it diverts from its founding myths. So far the CCP's ability to claim particularity and its inability to live up to its promises of social equity and equality have out-balanced each other. However, there is reason to believe that with China's plan for a so-called peaceful rise to world power status, this equation will have to be recalculated.

Looking at the two sides of the coin, I come to the conclusion that in some aspects—and not the least important ones—China at the beginning of the twenty-first century is pretty much where it was at the beginning of the twentieth century. Despite a century of revolution and although the CCP has claimed to create a new China, the new China we hoped for does not yet exist. So what does this mean for our understanding of the future of China?

First of all, it means that we are confronted with a political and economic system in China that is persistent beyond recognition. To say this does not mean that this system is stable in the common sense of the word. On the contrary, it is a system that is both persistent and in constant crises, some of which are man-made and induced by the leadership, others of which are the consequences of natural disasters or international developments. We cannot overlook the fact that from the perspective of the twentieth century China has undergone enormous change. The China of the 1920s and 1930s is surely not the China of the 1960s and 1970s. The people who lived through all this can tell us unending stories about the insecurity and uncertainty in the midst of all this change. But I can assure you, for at least some of those who survived this turmoil, what we observe today amounts to a déjà-vu experience. In fact, the China of the early twenty-first century resembles the China of the 1920s and 1930s. This means that in trying to understand where China is heading we have to be very careful not to be trapped by misinterpreting short-term change for fundamental change.

Second, we have to learn that this political system is going through multiple legitimacy crises and that its ability to overcome these crises is astonishingly well developed. However the PRC disposes of most of those mechanisms of conflict resolution that we cherish in the democratic systems in which most of us live. This also means, at least to me, that the political elite believe in the long *durée* of this system and even though they are trained to cope with constant crises, they are always afraid of defeat of the system. When comparing the CCP's form of conflict resolution in 1989 to that of countries in Eastern Europe, we discussed that a one-party system has only two options. It either works or fails. As it must oppress any kind of alternative, the party must run the show. This is what some of us addressed when we referred to the Chinese ruling elite being under enormous pressure. The pressure stems from being conscious of the lack of legitimacy of the system and of the necessity of having to renew this legitimacy on a day-to-day basis. The CCP as the organization of the ruling elite in China is a learning institution because it sticks to its claim of monopolizing power. As it cannot allow an alternative political force to exist within the Chinese polity, it is under constant pressure to learn. Consequently, the Chinese political elite are well trained to survive any kind of crisis, much more than those people who are running countries with democratic systems. To make this clear, with what I just said I am not implying that I think the Chinese way of conflict resolution is good. I am only saying that it is astonishingly efficient.

Third, and perhaps most importantly, we have to admit that if my analysis is correct, we will have to abandon the modernization paradigm and give up the idea that sooner or later China will catch up with us and its society and polity will work in the same way as we think a modern society and polity should work. We make our lives comfortable as long as we think that China is lagging behind. Instead, however, we should get used to the fact that China is competing with "us" for what the future should be like. Of course, it is much easier to think that we are still powerful enough to define what the world should be like because this way of thinking makes anticipating the future so easy. However, this conference has made one thing as clear as it can be. Anticipating the future for China is nearly futile. And one of the reasons why we feel anticipating the future for China is so difficult is that our epistemological instruments are inadequate. I think we know this and yet we have not yet found an alternative to this way of looking at China. We are still prisoners of the modernization paradigm, not the least of which because most Chinese intellectuals are prisoners of this paradigm as well. We will need a new paradigm to actually come to grips with China's past, present, and future because, let's face it, China might not be changing itself, but it certainly is changing the world.